Lecture Notes in Computer Science 15899

Founding Editors

Gerhard Goos
Juris Hartmanis

AF173102

The series Lecture Notes in Computer Science (LNCS), including its subseries Lecture Notes in Artificial Intelligence (LNAI) and Lecture Notes in Bioinformatics (LNBI), has established itself as a medium for the publication of new developments in computer science and information technology research, teaching, and education.

LNCS enjoys close cooperation with the computer science R & D community, the series counts many renowned academics among its volume editors and paper authors, and collaborates with prestigious societies. Its mission is to serve this international community by providing an invaluable service, mainly focused on the publication of conference and workshop proceedings and postproceedings. LNCS commenced publication in 1973.

Osvaldo Gervasi · Beniamino Murgante ·
Chiara Garau · Yeliz Karaca ·
Maria Noelia Faginas Lago · Francesco Scorza ·
Ana Cristina Braga
Editors

Computational Science and Its Applications – ICCSA 2025 Workshops

Istanbul, Turkey, June 30 – July 3, 2025
Proceedings, Part XIV

 Springer

Editors
Osvaldo Gervasi ⓘ
University of Perugia
Perugia, Italy

Beniamino Murgante ⓘ
University of Basilicata
Potenza, Italy

Chiara Garau ⓘ
University of Cagliari
Cagliari, Italy

Yeliz Karaca ⓘ
University of Massachusetts
Worcester, MA, USA

Maria Noelia Faginas Lago ⓘ
University of Perugia
Perugia, Italy

Francesco Scorza ⓘ
University of Basilicata
Potenza, Italy

Ana Cristina Braga ⓘ
University of Minho
Braga, Portugal

ISSN 0302-9743   ISSN 1611-3349 (electronic)
Lecture Notes in Computer Science
ISBN 978-3-031-97662-9   ISBN 978-3-031-97663-6 (eBook)
https://doi.org/10.1007/978-3-031-97663-6

Preface

The compiled 14 volumes (LNCS volumes 15886–15899) consist of the peer-reviewed papers from the 68 Workshops of the 2025 International Conference on Computational Science and Its Applications (ICCSA 2025), which was held between June 30 – July 3, 2025 in Istanbul (Türkiye). The peer-reviewed papers of the main conference tracks are published in a separate set made up of three volumes (LNCS 15648–15650).

The conference was held in a hybrid form, with the large majority of participants in presence, hosted by Galatasaray University, Istanbul, Türkiye. We enabled virtual participation for those who did not attend the event in person due to logistical, political and economic problems, by adopting a technological infrastructure via open-source software (jitsi + riot) and a commercial Cloud infrastructure.

With the 2025 edition, ICCSA celebrated its 25th anniversary, a quarter of a century as a memorable moment that is harmoniously aligned with Istanbul, an extraordinary city located at the crossroads and acting as a bridge connecting Asia and Europe, representing different cultures, beliefs as well as lifestyles, which highlights its intercultural fabric.

ICCSA 2025 marked another fruitful and thought-provoking academic event in the International Conferences on Computational Science and Its Applications (ICCSA) conference series, previously held in Hanoi, Vietnam (2024), Athens, Greece (2023), Málaga, Spain (2022), Cagliari, Italy (hybrid with a few participants in presence in 2021 and completely online in 2020), whilst earlier editions took place in Saint Petersburg, Russia (2019), Melbourne, Australia (2018), Trieste, Italy (2017), Beijing, China (2016), Banff, Canada (2015), Guimaraes, Portugal (2014), Ho Chi Minh City, Vietnam (2013), Salvador, Brazil (2012), Santander, Spain (2011), Fukuoka, Japan (2010), Suwon, South Korea (2009), Perugia, Italy (2008), Kuala Lumpur, Malaysia (2007), Glasgow, UK (2006), Singapore (2005), Assisi, Italy (2004), Montreal, Canada (2003), and (as ICCS) Amsterdam, the Netherlands (2002) and San Francisco, USA (2001).

Computational Science constitutes the main pillar of most present research, industrial and commercial applications, and plays a unique role in exploiting ICT innovative technologies, and the ICCSA conference series has, accordingly, provided ample opportunities to researchers and industry practitioners to discuss new ideas, to share complex problems and their solutions, and to shape new trends in Computational Science. As the conference mirrors society from a scientific point of view, this year's undoubtedly dominant theme was large language models, machine learning and Artificial Intelligence (AI) and their applications in the most diverse technological, economic and industrial fields, amongst the others.

The ICCSA 2025 conference was structured in six general tracks covering the fields of computational science and its applications: Computational Methods, Algorithms and Scientific Applications – High Performance Computing and Networks – Geometric Modeling, Graphics and Visualization – Advanced and Emerging Applications – Information Systems and Technologies – Urban and Regional Planning. In addition, the conference consisted of 68 workshops, focusing on topical issues of utmost importance to science, technology and society: from new computational approaches for earth science, to mathematical methods for image processing, new statistical and optimization methods, several Artificial Intelligence approaches, sustainability issues, smart cities and related technologies, to name some.

In the Workshops' proceedings, we accepted 362 full papers, 37 short papers and 2 Ph.D. Showcase papers from total of 1043 submissions (Acceptance rate 38.4%). In the Main Conference Proceedings, we accepted 71 full papers, 6 short papers and 1 Ph.D. Showcase paper from 269 submissions to the General Tracks of the Conference (with an acceptance rate of 29.9%). We would like to convey our sincere appreciation to the workshops' chairs and co-chairs and program committee members for their diligent work, commitment and dedication.

The success and consistent maintenance of the ICCSA conference series in general, and of ICCSA 2025 in particular, rely upon the support of many people: authors, presenters, participants, keynote speakers, workshop chairs, session chairs, organizing committee members, student volunteers, Program Committee members, Advisory Committee members, International Liaison chairs, reviewers and other individuals in various roles. Thus, we take this opportunity to wholehartedly thank each and everyone.

We additionally wish to thank publisher Springer for their agreement to publish the proceedings, besides sponsoring part of the best papers awards and for their kind assistance and cooperation during the editing process.

We would cordially like to invite you to refer to the ICCSA website https://iccsa.org, where you can find the relevant details regarding this academic endeavor and event of ours.

June 2025

Osvaldo Gervasi
Yeliz Karaca
Beniamino Murgante
Chiara Garau

A Welcome Message from the Organizers

The International Conference on Computational Science and Its Applications (ICCSA) reflects a culmination of meticulous and dedicated efforts and academic endeavors toward the progress of science and technology.

One of the most noteworthy aspects of ICCSA is its fostering of a collective spirit, bringing together a plethora of participants from all over the world. Correspondingly, this merging power manifests itself in the 25th anniversary of ICCSA, which is a quarter of a century, in Istanbul, Türkiye, which connects and acts as a bridge between two continents, namely Asia and Europe. This unique location in the world hosts the 25th year of ICCSA at Galatasaray University, located on Çırağan Avenue by Istanbul's Bosphorus, which is an established international university bestowed with a distinctive past of teaching tradition, research and education exceeding five centuries.

Istanbul, having served as the capital city of four empires, namely the Roman Empire (330–395), the Byzantine Empire (395–1204 and 1261–1453), the Latin Empire (1204–1261) and the Ottoman Empire (1453–1922), is an exceptional city of the Republic of Türkiye founded by Mustafa Kemal Atatürk.

Situated at a strategic location along the historic Silk Road, Istanbul is at the core of extending rail networks which span across Europe and West Asia along with the only sea route between the Black Sea and the Mediterranean.

The cultural, historical and economic pulses of the country are evident in Istanbul whose rooted origins have embraced varying beliefs, lifestyles and populace, which highlights the city's mosaic quality with blended fabric in a constant harmonious flow. This has enabled cultures to grow and be nurtured, which is profoundly rooted in its urban culture.

Computational Science constitutes the main pillar of most present research, industrial and commercial activities besides manifesting a unique role in exploiting and addressing innovative Information and Communication Technologies. Thus, the 25-year-old ICCSA conference series provides remarkable opportunities to get acquainted with leading researchers, scientists, scholars, practitioners and many more while exchanging innovative ideas and initiating new partnerships, associations and bonds.

With the hosting of Galatasaray University, I would personally and on behalf of the Local Organizing Committee, with the members Emre Alptekin, Gülfem Işıklar Alptekin, Cengiz Kahraman, Abdullah Çağrı Tolga and Ayberk Zeytin, like to convey our sincere gratitude and thanks to everyone who exerted their efforts in and contributed to the realization of ICCSA 2025. With these notes and remarks, welcome to Istanbul!

Cordially yours,

On behalf of the Local Organizing Committee.

June 2025   Yeliz Karaca

Organization

Honorary General Chairs

Bernady O. Apduhan   Kyushu Sangyo University, Japan
Kenneth C. J. Tan   Sardina Systems, UK

General Chairs

Yeliz Karaca   University of Massachusetts, USA
Osvaldo Gervasi   University of Perugia, Italy
David Taniar   Monash University, Australia

Program Committee Chairs

Beniamino Murgante   University of Basilicata, Italy
Chiara Garau   University of Cagliari, Italy
Ana Maria A. C. Rocha   University of Minho, Portugal
A. Çağrı Tolga   Galatasaray University, Turkey

International Advisory Committee

Jemal Abawajy   Deakin University, Australia
Dharma P. Agarwal   University of Cincinnati, USA
Rajkumar Buyya   Melbourne University, Australia
Claudia Bauzer Medeiros   University of Campinas, Brazil
Manfred M. Fisher   Vienna University of Economics and Business, Austria
Pierre Frankhauser   University of Franche-Comté/CNRS, France
Marina L. Gavrilova   University of Calgary, Canada
Sumi Helal   University of Florida, USA & Lancaster University, UK
Bin Jiang   University of Gävle, Sweden
Yee Leung   Chinese University of Hong Kong, China

International Liaison Chairs

Ivan Blečić	University of Cagliari, Italy
Giuseppe Borruso	University of Trieste, Italy
Elise De Donker	Western Michigan University, USA
Maria Noelia Faginas Lago	University of Perugia, Italy
Maria Irene Falcão	University of Minho, Portugal
Robert C. H. Hsu	Chung Hua University, Taiwan
Yeliz Karaca	University of Massachusetts Chan Medical School, USA
Tae-Hoon Kim	Zhejiang University of Science and Technology, China
Vladimir Korkhov	Saint Petersburg University, Russia
Takashi Naka	Kyushu Sangyo University, Japan
Rafael D. C. Santos	National Institute for Space Research, Brazil
Maribel Yasmina Santos	University of Minho, Portugal
Anastasia Stratigea	National Technical University of Athens, Greece

Workshop and Session Organizing Chairs

Beniamino Murgante	University of Basilicata, Italy
Chiara Garau	University of Cagliari, Italy

Award Chair

Wenny Rahayu	La Trobe University, Australia

Publicity Committee Chairs

Elmer Dadios	De La Salle University, Philippines
Nataliia Kulabukhova	Saint Petersburg University, Russia
Daisuke Takahashi	Tsukuba University, Japan
Shangwang Wang	Beijing University of Posts and Telecommunications, China

Local Organizing Committee Chairs

Emre Alptekin	Galatasaray University, Turkey
Gülfem Işıklar Alptekin	Galatasaray University, Turkey
Cengiz Kahraman	İstanbul Technical University, Turkey
A. Çağrı Tolga	Galatasaray University, Turkey
Ayberk Zeytin	Galatasaray University, Turkey

Technology Chair

Damiano Perri	University of Perugia, Italy

Program Committee

Vera Afreixo	University of Aveiro, Portugal
Vladimir Alarcon	Northern Gulf Institute, USA
Filipe Alvelos	University of Minho, Portugal
Debora Anelli	Polytechnic University of Bari, Italy
Hartmut Asche	Hasso-Plattner-Institut für Digital Engineering Ggmbh, Germany
Nizamettin Aydın	İstanbul Technical University, Turkey
Ginevra Balletto	University of Cagliari, Italy
Nadia Balucani	University of Perugia, Italy
Socrates Basbas	Aristotle University of Thessaloniki, Greece
David Berti	ART SpA, Italy
Michela Bertolotto	University College Dublin, Ireland
Sandro Bimonte	CEMAGREF, TSCF, France
Ana Cristina Braga	University of Minho, Portugal
Tiziana Campisi	Kore University of Enna, Italy
Yves Caniou	Université Claude Bernard Lyon 1, France
Alessandra Capolupo	Polytechnic University of Bari, Italy
José A. Cardoso e Cunha	Universidade Nova de Lisboa, Portugal
Rui Cardoso	University of Beira Interior, Portugal
Leocadio G. Casado	University of Almería, Spain
Mete Celik	Erciyes University, Turkey
Maria Cerreta	University of Naples Federico II, Italy
Ta Quang Chieu	Thuyloi University, Vietnam
Rachel Chien-Sing Lee	Sunway University, Malaysia
Birol Ciloglugil	Ege University, Turkey
Mauro Coni	University of Cagliari, Italy

Florbela Maria da Cruz Domingues Correia	Polytechnic Institute of Viana do Castelo, Portugal
Alessandro Costantini	INFN, Italy
Roberto De Lotto	University of Pavia, Italy
Luiza De Macedo Mourelle	State University of Rio De Janeiro, Brazil
Marcelo De Paiva Guimaraes	Federal University of Sao Paulo, Brazil
Frank Devai	London South Bank University, UK
Joana Matos Dias	University of Coimbra, Portugal
Aziz Dursun	Virginia Tech University, USA
Laila El Ghandour	Heriot-Watt University, UK
Rafida M. Elobaid	Canadian University Dubai, United Arab Emirates
Maria Irene Falcao	University of Minho, Portugal
Florbela P. Fernandes	Polytechnic Institute of Bragança, Portugal
Paula Odete Fernandes	Polytechnic Institute of Bragança, Portugal
Adelaide de Fátima Baptista Valente Freitas	University of Aveiro, Portugal
Valentina Franzoni	University of Perugia, Italy
Andreas Fricke	University of Potsdam, Germany
Raffaele Garrisi	Centro Operativo per la Sicurezza Cibernetica, Italy
Ivan Gerace	University of Perugia, Italy
Maria Giaoutzi	National Technical University of Athens, Greece
Salvatore Giuffrida	University of Catania, Italy
Teresa Guarda	Universidad Estatal Peninsula de Santa Elena, Ecuador
Sevin Gümgüm	Izmir University of Economics, Turkey
Malgorzata Hanzl	Technical University of Lodz, Poland
Maulana Adhinugraha Kiki	Telkom University, Indonesia
Clement Ho Cheung Leung	Chinese University of Hong Kong, China
Andrea Lombardi	University of Perugia, Italy
Marcos Mandado Alonso	University of Vigo, Spain
Ernesto Marcheggiani	Katholieke Universiteit Leuven, Belgium
Antonino Marvuglia	Luxembourg Institute of Science and Technology, Luxembourg
Michele Mastroianni	University of Salerno, Italy
Hideo Matsufuru	High Energy Accelerator Research Organization, Japan
Fernando Miranda	Universidade do Minho, Portugal
Giuseppe Modica	University of Reggio Calabria, Italy
Majaz Moonis	University of Massachusetts, USA
Nadia Nedjah	State University of Rio de Janeiro, Brazil
Paolo Nesi	University of Florence, Italy

Workshops

Workshop on Advancements in Applied Machine-Learning and Data Analytics (AAMDA 2025)

Workshop Organizers

Alessandro Costantini	INFN, Italy
Daniele Cesini	INFN, Italy
Elisabetta Ronchieri	INFN, Italy
Barbara Martelli	INFN, Italy

Workshop Program Committee Members

Alessandro Costantini	Istituto Nazionale di Fisica Nucleare (INFN), Italy
Daniele Cesini	Istituto Nazionale di Fisica Nucleare (INFN), Italy
Elisabetta Ronchieri	Istituto Nazionale di Fisica Nucleare (INFN), Italy
Barbara Martelli	Istituto Nazionale di Fisica Nucleare (INFN), Italy
Luca Dell'Agnello	Istituto Nazionale di Fisica Nucleare (INFN), Italy

Advanced and Innovative Web Apps 2025 (AIWA 2025)

Workshop Organizers

Damiano Perri	University of Perugia, Italy
Osvaldo Gervasi	University of Perugia, Italy
Stelios Kouzeleas	International Hellenic University, Greece
Sergio Tasso	University of Perugia, Italy

Workshop Program Committee Members

David Berti	ART SpA, Italy
JungYoon Kim	Gachon University, South Korea
TaiHoon Kim	Zhejiang University of Science and Technology, China

Advanced Processes of Mathematics and Computing Models in Complex Data-Intensive Computational Systems (AMCM 2025)

Workshop Organizers

Yeliz Karaca	University of Massachusetts Chan Medical School and Massachusetts Institute of Technology, USA
Dumitru Baleanu	Lebanese American University, Lebanon
Osvaldo Gervasi	University of Perugia, Italy
Yudong Zhang	University of Leicester, UK
Majaz Moonis	University of Massachusetts Chan Medical School and Massachusetts Institute of Technology, USA

Workshop Program Committee Members

TaeHoon Kim	Zhejiang University of Science and Technology, China
Martin Bohner	Missouri University of Science and Technology, USA
Shuihua Wang	University of Leicester, UK
Khan Muhammad	Sungkyunkwan University, South Korea
Mahmoud Abdel-Aty	Sohag University, Egypt
Aziz Dursun	Virginia Polytechnic Institute and State University, USA
Kemal Güven Gülen	Namık Kemal University, Turkey
Akif Akgül	Hitit Üniversitesi, Turkey

Advanced Numerical Approaches for Assessment and Design of No-Tension Masonry Structures (ANAMS 2025)

Workshop Organizers

Antonino Iannuzzo	Universitá degli studi del Sannio, Italy
Carlo Olivieri	Universitá Telematica Pegaso, Italy
Andrea Montanino	CIMNE, Spain
Elham Mousavian	University of Edinburgh, UK

Workshop Program Committee Members

Pietro Meriggi	Roma Tre University, Italy
Francesca Perelli	University of Naples Federico II, Italy
Marialuigia Sangirardi	University of Oxford, UK
Sam Cocking	University of Cambridge, UK

Matteo Salvalaggio	University of Minho, Portugal
Vittorio Paris	University of Bergamo, Italy
Luigi Sibille	Norwegian University of Science and Technology, Norway
Natalia Pingaro	Politecnico di Milano, Italy
Martina Buzzetti	Politecnico di Milano, Italy
Generoso Vaiano	Pegaso Telematic University, Italy
Alessandra Capolupo	Politecnico di Bari, Italy
Amal Gerges	Università degli Studi di Cagliari, Italy
Fabian Orozco	National Autonomous University of Mexico, Mexico
Nathanael Savalle	Polytech Clermont and Université Clermont Auvergne, France
Luca Umberto Argiento	University of Naples Federico II, Italy
Bartolomeo Pantó	Durham University, UK

Unveiling the Synergies Between Air Quality and Climate PlAnning (AQCliPA 2025)

Workshop Organizers

Angela Pilogallo	University of L'Aquila, Italy
Luigi Santopietro	University of Basilicata, Italy
Filomena Pietrapertosa	IMAA CNR, Italy
Monica Salvia	IMAA CNR, Italy
Carlo Trozzi	IMAA CNR, Italy
Valeria Scapini	Central University of Chile, Chile

Workshop Program Committee Members

Lucia Saganeiti	IMAA-CNR, Italy
Lorena Fiorini	University of L'Aquila, Italy
Antonio Mazza	IMAA-CNR, Italy
Gabriele Nolè	IMAA-CNR, Italy
Carmen Guida	University of Naples "Federico II", Italy
Floriana Zucaro	University of Naples "Federico II", Italy
Sabrina Lai	University of Cagliari, Italy
Chiara Garau	University of Cagliari, Italy

Advancements in Spatial assessment of Socio-Ecological SystemS (ASSESS 2025)

Workshop Organizers

Daniele Cannatella	TU Delft, The Netherlands
Giuliano Poli	University of Naples Federico II, Italy
Eugenio Muccio	TU Delft, The Netherlands
Claudiu Forgaci	TU Delft, The Netherlands

Workshop Program Committee Members

Daniele Cannatella	TU Delft, The Netherlands
Giuliano Poli	University of Naples Federico II, Italy
Eugenio Muccio	University of Naples Federico II, Italy
Claudiu Forgaci	TU Delft, The Netherlands
Maria Cerreta	University of Naples Federico II, Italy
Maria Somma	University of Naples Federico II, Italy
Laura Di Tommaso	University of Naples Federico II, Italy
Sabrina Sacco	Politecnico di Milano, Italy
Piero Zizzania	University of Naples Federico II, Italy
Gaia Daldanise	CNR IRISS, Italy
Benedetta Grieco	University of Naples Federico II, Italy
Giuseppe Ciciriello	University of Naples Federico II, Italy
Marta Dell'Ovo	Politecnico di Milano, Italy
Francesco Piras	University of Cagliari, Italy
Diana Rolando	Politecnico di Torino, Italy
Stefano Cuntò	University of Naples Federico II, Italy
Ludovica La Rocca	University of Naples Federico II, Italy

Blockchain and Distributed Ledgers: Technologies and Applications (BDLTA 2025)

Workshop Organizers

Vladimir Korkhov	Saint Petersburg State University, Russia
Elena Stankova	Saint Petersburg State University, Russia
Nataliia Kulabukhova	Saint Petersburg State University, Russia

Workshop Program Committee Members

Adam Belloum	University of Amsterdam, the Netherlands
Dmitrii Vasiunin	Deutsche Telekom Cloud Services E.P.E., Greece
Serob Balyan	Osensus Arm LLC, Armenia
Suren Abrahamyan	Osensus Arm LLC, Armenia
Ashot Sergey Gevorkyan	NAS of Armenia, Armenia

Michal Hnatic	Univerzita Pavla Jozefa Šafárika v Košiciach, Slovakia
Michail Panteleyev	Saint Petersburg Electrotecnical University, Russia
Martin Vala	Univerzita Pavla Jozefa Šafárika v Košiciach, Slovakia
Nodir Zaynalov	Tashkent University of Information Technologies named after Muhammad al Khwarizmi, Uzbekistan
Michail Panteleyev	Saint Petersburg Electrotecnical University, Russia
Alexander Degtyarev	Saint Petersburg University, Russia
Alexander Bogdanov	St. Petersburg State University, Russia

Bio and Neuro Inspired Computing and Applications (BIONCA 2025)

Workshop Organizers

| Nadia Nedjah | State University of Rio de Janeiro, Brazil |
| Luiza de Macedo Mourelle | State University of Rio de Janeiro, Brazil |

Workshop Program Committee Members

Nadia Nedjha	State University of Rio de Janeiro, Brazil
Luiza de Macedo Mourelle	State University of Rio de Janeiro, Brazil
Luigi Maciel Ribeiro	State University of Rio de Janeiro, Brazil
Joelmir Ramos	Federal University of Rio de Janeiro, Brazil
Rogério Moraes	Brazilian Navy, Brazil
Marcos Santana Farias	Institute of Nuclear Energy, Brazil
Luneque Silva Jr.	Federal University of ABC, Brazil
Alan Oliveira	University of Lisboa, Portugal
Brij Bhooshan Gupta	Asia University, Taiwan

Computational and Applied Mathematics (CAM 2025)

Workshop Organizers

| Maria Irene Falcão | University of Minho, Portugal |
| Fernando Miranda | University of Minho, Portugal |

Workshop Program Committee Members

Fernando Miranda	University of Minho, Portugal
Graça Tomaz	Polytechnic of Guarda, Portugal
Helmuth Malonek	University of Aveiro, Portugal

Isabel Cacao	University of Aveiro, Portugal
João Morais	Autonomous Technological Institute of Mexico, Mexico
Lidia Aceto	University of Eastern Piedmont, Italy
Luís Ferrás	University of Porto, Portugal
M. Irene Falcão	University of Minho, Portugal
Patrícia Beites	University of Beira Interior, Portugal
Paulo Amorim	FGV EMAp, Brazil
Regina de Almeida	University of Trás-os-Montes e Alto Douro, Portugal
Ricardo Severino	University of Minho, Portugal

Computational and Applied Statistics (CAS 2025)

Workshop Organizer

| Ana Cristina Braga | ALGORITMI Research Centre, LASI, University of Minho, Portugal |

Workshop Program Committee Members

Adelaide Freitas	University of Aveiro, Portugal
Andreas Futschik	Johannes Kepler University Linz, Austria
Ana Cristina Braga	University of Minho, Portugal
Ângela Silva	University of Minho, Portugal
Arminda Manuela Gonçalves	University of Minho, Portugal
Carina Silva	Polytechnic Intitute of Lisbon, Portugal
Elisete Correia	University of Trás-os-Montes e Alto Douro, Portugal
Frank Westad	Norwegian University of Science and Technology, Norway
Isabel Natario	New University of Lisbon, Portugal
Irene Oliveira	University of Trás-os-Montes e Alto Douro, Portugal
Ivan Rodriguez Conde	University of Vigo, Spain
Joaquim Gonçalves	Instituto Politécnico do Cávado e do Ave, Portugal
Lino Costa	University of Minho, Portugal
Marco Reis	University of Coimbra, Portugal
Maria Filipa Mourão	Polytechnic Institute of Viana do Castelo, Portugal
Maria João Polidoro	Polytechnic Institute of Porto, Portugal
Martin Perez Perez	University of Vigo, Spain
Michal Abrahamowicz	McGill University, Canada
Vera Afreixo	University of Aveiro, Portugal

Werner G. Müller	Johannes Kepler University Linz, Austria
Bruna Silva Ramos	University Lusiada de Famalicão, Portugal
Inês Sousa	University of Minho, Portugal
Luís Miguel Rocha Matos	University of Minho, Portugal
Manuel Carlos Figueiredo	University of Minho, Portugal

Cyber Intelligence and Applications (CIA 2025)

Workshop Organizer

Gianni D'Angelo	University of Salerno, Italy

Workshop Program Committee Members

Gianni D'Angelo	University of Salerno, Italy
Francesco Palmieri	University of Salerno, Italy
Massimo Ficco	University of Salerno, Italy
Arcangelo Castiglione	University of Salerno, Italy

Computational Methods for Business Analytics (CMBA 2025)

Workshop Organizers

Cláudio Alves	Universidade do Minho, Portugal
Telmo Pinto	Universidade do Minho, Portugal

Workshop Program Committee Members

Abdulrahim Shamayleh	American University of Sharjah, United Arab Emirates
Ana Rocha	University of Minho, Portugal
Angelo Sifaleras	University of Macedonia, Greece
Cristóvão Silva	University of Coimbra, Portugal
José Valério de Carvalho	University of Minho, Portugal
Miguel Vieira	Universidade Lusófona, Portugal
Rita Macedo	Université de Lille, France
Ana Moura	Universidade de Aveiro, Portugal
Cristina Lopes	ISCAP, Portugal
Eliana Costa e Silva	Instituto Politécnico do Porto, Portugal

Computational Methods, Statistics and Industrial Mathematics (CMSIM 2025)

Workshop Organizers

Maria Filomena Teodoro	IST ID, Instituto Superior Técnico, Portugal
Marina Alexandra Pedro Andrade	ISCTE – Lisbon University Institute, Portugal
Paula Simões	University of Lisbon, Portugal
Teresa A. Oliveira	IST ID, Instituto Superior Técnico, Portugal

Workshop Program Committee Members

Amilcar Oliveira	Universidade Aberta and Universidade de Lisboa, Portugal
Victor Lobo	Escola Naval and NOVA IMS Almada, Portugal
António Pacheco	IST Universidade de Lisboa, Portugal
Eliana Costa	Escola Superior de Tecnologia e Gestão IPPorto, Portugal
Aldina Correia	Escola Superior de Tecnologia e Gestão IPPorto, Portugal
Fernando Carapau	University of Évora, Portugal
Ricardo Moura	Portuguese Naval Academy, Portugal
Ana Borges	Escola Superior de Tecnologia e Gestão IPPorto, Portugal
Cristina Lopes	ISCAP IPPorto, Portugal
Fernanda Costa	University of Minho, Portugal
Cabrita Carlos	IPBeja, Portugal
Maria Luísa Morgado	University of Trás os Montes e Alto Douro and University of Lisboa, Portugal
Rosário Ramos	Universidade Aberta, Portugal
Sofia Rézio	Iscal, Instituto Politécnico de Lisboa, Portugal
Matteo Sacchet	University of Turin, Italy
Marina Marchisio Conte	University of Turin, Italy
António Seijas-Macias	University of Coruña, Spain
Luís F. A. Teodoro	University of Glasgow, UK and University of Oslo, Norway
Christos Kitsos	University of West Attica, Greece
M. Filomena Teodoro	Universidade de Lisboa, Portugal
Marina A. P. Andrade	Instituto Universitário de Lisboa, Portugal
Paula Simões	Military Academy and Universidade Nova de Lisboa, Portugal
Teresa Oliveira	Universidade Aberta and Universidade de Lisboa, Portugal

Computational Optimization and Applications (COA 2025)

Workshop Organizers

Ana Rocha	ALGORITMI Research Centre, LASI, University of Minho, Portugal, Portugal
Humberto Rocha	ALGORITMI Research Centre, LASI, University of Minho, Portugal, Portugal

Workshop Program Committee Members

Florbela Fernandes	Polytechnic Institute of Bragança, Portugal
Clara Vaz	Polytechnic Institute of Bragança, Portugal
Ana Pereira	Polytechnic Institute of Bragança, Portugal
Filipe Alvelos	University of Minho, Portugal
Joana Dias	University of Coimbra, Portugal
Eligius M. T. Hendrix	University of Málaga, Spain
Emerson José de Paiva	Federal University of Itajubá, Brazil
Ana Paula Teixeira	University of Trás-os-Montes and Alto Douro, Portugal
Lino Costa	Universidade do Minho, Portugal

Coastal Cities Versus Inland Areas. Hypotheses for Sustainable Regeneration Through Ecosystem Services of 'Hooking' and Rehabilitation of Brownfield Sites (CoastalCities_VS_InlandAreas 2025)

Workshop Organizers

Celestina Fazia	Università di Enna Kore, Italy
Angrilli Massimo	University of Chieti-Pescara, Italy
Valentina Ciuffreda	University of Chieti-Pescara, Italy
Maurizio Oddo	Università di Enna Kore, Italy
Marcello Sestito	Università di Enna Kore, Italy
Clara Stella Vicari Aversa	University of Reggio Calabria, Italy

Workshop Program Committee Members

Alessandro Camiz	Università d'Annunzio, Italy
Thowayeb Hassan	King Faisal University, Saudi Arabia
Alessandro Barracco	Università Kore di Enna, Italy
Mario Morrica	University of Urbino, Italy
Mariana Ratiu	University of Oradea, Romania
Alanda Akamana	Mohammed VI Polytechnic University, Morocco
Kaoutare Amini Alaoui	Mohammed VI Polytechnic University, Morocco

Computational Astrochemistry 2025 (CompAstro 2025)

Workshop Organizers

Marzio Rosi	University of Perugia, Italy
Daniela Ascenzi	University of Trento, Italy
Nadia Balucani	University of Perugia, Italy
Stefano Falcinelli	University of Perugia, Italy

Workshop Program Committee Members

Dario Campisi	Università degli Studi di Perugia, Italy
Giacomo Giorgi	Università degli Studi di Perugia, Italy
Andrea Giustini	Università degli Studi di Perugia, Italy
Luca Mancini	Università degli Studi di Perugia, Italy
Albert Rimola	Universitat Autònoma de Barcelona, Spain
Gianmarco Vanuzzo	Università degli Studi di Perugia, Italy
Dimitrios Skouteris	Master-Tec, Italy
Piero Ugliengo	Università degli Studi di Torino, Italy
Franco Vecchiocattivi	Università degli Sudi di Perugia, Italy
Giacomo Pannacci	Università degli Studi di Perugia, Italy
Costanza Borghesi	Università degli Studi di Perugia, Italy
Marco Parriani	Università degli Studi di Perugia, Italy
Marta Loletti	Università degli Studi di Perugia, Italy
Fernando Pirani	Università degli Studi di Perugia, Italy
Andrea Lombardi	Università degli Studi di Perugia, Italy
Noelia Faginas Lago	Università degli Studi di Perugia, Italy
Paolo Tosi	Università di Trento, Italy
Cecilia Coletti	Università degli Studi Chieti-Pescara, Italy
Nazzareno Re	Università degli Studi Chieti-Pescara, Italy
Linda Podio	Osservatorio Astrofisico di Arcetri INAF, Italy
Claudio Codella	Osservatorio Astrofisico di Arcetri INAF, Italy
Gabriella Di Genova	Università degli Studi di Perugia, Italy

Computational Methods for Porous Geomaterials (CompPor 2025)

Workshop Organizers

Vadim Lisitsa	IPGG SB RAS, Russia
Evgeniy Romenski	IPGG SB RAS, Russia

Workshop Program Committee Members

Vadim Lisitsa	Institute of Petroleum Geology and Geophysics SB RAS, Russia
Evgeniy Romenski	Sobolev Institute of Mathematics SB RAS, Russia
Vladimir Cheverda	Sobolev Institute of Mathematics SB RAS, Russia
Tatyana Khachkova	IPGG SB RAS, Russia
Dmitry Prokhorov	IPGG SB RAS, Russia
Mikhail Novikov	Sobolev Institute of Mathematics SB RAS, Russia
Sergey Solovyev	Sobolev Institute of Mathematics SB RAS, Russia
Kirill Gadylshin	LLC RNBashNIPIneft, Russia
Olga Stoyanovskaya	Lavrentev Institute of Hydrodynamics SB RAS, Russia
Yerlan Amanbek	Nazarbaev University, Kazakstan

Workshop on Computational Science and HPC (CSHPC 2025)

Workshop Organizers

Elise de Doncker	Western Michigan University, USA
Hideo Matsufuru	High Energy Accelerator Research Organization, Japan

Workshop Program Committee Members

Elise de Doncker	Western Michigan University, USA
Hideo Matsufuru	High Energy Accelerator Research Organization (KEK), Japan
Fukuko Yuasa	KEK, Japan
Issaku Kanamori	RIKEN, Japan
Hiroshi Daisaka	Hitotsubashi University, Japan
Norikazu Yamada	KEK, Japan
Naohito Nakasato	University of Aizu, Japan
Robert Makin	Western Michigan University, USA

Cities, Technologies and Planning 2025 (CTP 2025)

Workshop Organizers

Giuseppe Borruso	University of Trieste, Italy
Beniamino Murgante	University of Basilicata, Italy
Malgorzata Hanzl	Lodz University of Technology, Poland
Anastasia Stratigea	National Technical University of Athens, Greece
Ljiljana Zivkovic	Republic Geodetic Authority, Serbia
Ginevra Balletto	University of Trieste, Italy

Workshop Program Committee Members

Giuseppe Borruso	University of Trieste, Italy
Beniamino Murgante	University of Basilicata, Italy
Malgorzata Hanzl	Lodz University of Technology, Poland
Anastasia Stratigea	National Technical University of Athens, Greece
Ljiljiana Zivkovic	Republic Geodetic Authority of Serbia, Serbia
Ginevra Balletto	University of Cagliari, Italy
Silvia Battino	University of Sassari, Italy
Mara Ladu	University of Cagliari, Italy
Maria del Mar Munoz Leonisio	University of Cádiz, Spain
Ahinoa Amaro Garcia	University of Las Palmas of Gran Canaria, Spain
Maria Attard	University of Malta, Malta
Enrico D'agostini	World Maritime University, Sweden
Francesca Krasna	University of Trieste, Italy
Brisol Garcia Garcia	Polytechnic University of Quintana Roo, Mexico
Tu Anh Trinh	UEH University, Vietnam
Giovanni Mauro	Università degli Studi della Campania, Italy
Maria Ronza	University of Naples Federico II, Italy
Massimiliano Bencardino	University of Salerno, Italy
Tomasz Bradecki	Silesian University of Technology, Poland
Dorota Kamrowska-Załuska	Gdańsk University of Technology, Poland
Iwona Jażdżewska	University of Lodz, Poland
Yiota Theodora	National Technical University of Athens, Greece
Apostolos Lagarias	University of Thessaly, Greece
George Tsilimigkas	University of the Aegean, Greece
Akrivi Leka	National Technical University of Athens, Greece
Maria Panagiotopoulou	National Technical University of Athens, Greece
Andrea Gallo	Ca' Foscari University of Venice, Italy
Francesca Sinatra	University of Trieste, Italy

Digital Transition: Effects on Housing Mobility, Market, Land Governance (DIGITRANS 2025)

Workshop Organizers

Fabrizio Battisti	University of Florence, Italy
Fabiana Forte	University of Campania, Italy
Orazio Campo	Sapienza University of Rome, Italy
Alessio Pino	Kore University of Enna, Italy
Carlo Pisano	University of Florence, Italy
Mariolina Grasso	Kore University of Enna, Italy

Workshop Program Committee Members

Fabrizio Battisti	University of Florence, Italy
Fabiana Forte	Università della Campania Luigi Vanvitelli, Italy
Orazio Campo	University of Rome "La Sapienza", Italy
Alessio Pino	Kore University of Enna, Italy
Carlo Pisano	University of Florence, Italy
Mariolina Grasso	Università Kore di Enna, Italy

Evaluating Inner Areas Potentials (EIAP 2025)

Workshop Organizers

Diana Rolando	Politecnico di Torino, Italy
Alice Barreca	Politecnico di Torino, Italy
Manuela Rebaudengo	Politecnico di Torino, Italy
Giorgia Malavasi	Politecnico di Torino, Italy

Workshop Program Committee Members

John Accordino	Virginia Commonwealth University, USA
Francesco Bruzzone	Università Iuav di Venezia, Italy
Maria Cerreta	Università degli Studi di Napoli Federico II, Italy
Maddalena Chimisso	Università degli Studi del Molise, Italy
Chiara Chioni	Università degli Studi di Trento, Italy
Annalisa Contato	Università degli Studi di Palermo, Italy
Cristina Coscia	Politecnico di Torino, Italy
Marta Dell'Ovo	Politecnico di Milano, Italy
Benedetta Di Leo	Università Politecnica delle Marche, Italy
Sara Favargiotti	Università degli Studi di Trento, Italy
Maddalena Ferretti	Università Politecnica delle Marche, Italy
Salvo Giuffrida	Università degli Studi di Palermo, Italy
Barbara Lino	Università degli Studi di Palermo, Italy
Umberto Mecca	Politecnico di Torino, Italy
Beatrice Mecca	Politecnico di Torino, Italy
Giuliano Poli	Università degli Studi di Napoli Federico II, Italy
Marco Rossitti	Politecnico di Milano, Italy
Alexandra Stankulova	Politecnico di Torino, Italy
Elena Todella	Politecnico di Torino, Italy
Asja Aulisio	Politecnico di Torino, Italy
Giulia Datola	Politecnico di Milano, Italy

Francesco Calabrò	Università degli Studi Mediterranea di Reggio Calabria, Italy
Valeria Saiu	Università degli Studi di Cagliari, Italy
Maria Rosa Trovato	Università di Catania, Italy

Econometric and Multidimensional Evaluation in Urban Environment (EMEUE 2025)

Workshop Organizers

Maria Cerreta	University of Naples Federico II, Italy
Carmelo Maria Torre	Polytechnic University of Bari, Italy
Pierluigi Morano	Polytechnic University of Bari, Italy
Simona Panaro	University of Naples Federico II, Italy
Felicia Di Liddo	University of Naples Federico II, Italy
Debora Anelli	University of Naples Federico II, Italy

Workshop Program Committee Members

Carmelo Maria Torre	Polytechnic University of Bari, Italy
Maria Cerreta	University of Naples Federico II, Italy
Pierluigi Morano	Polytechnic University of Bari, Italy
Francesco Tajani	Sapienza University of Rome, Italy
Simona Panaro	University of Naples Federico II, Italy
Felicia di Liddo	Polytechnic University of Bari, Italy
Debora Anelli	Sapienza University of Rome, Italy
Giuliano Poli	University of Naples Federico II, Italy
Maria Somma	University of Naples Federico II, Italy
Simona Panaro	University of Campania Luigi Vanvitelli, Italy
Laura Di Tommaso	University of Naples Federico II, Italy
Caterina Loffredo	University of Naples Federico II, Italy
Ludovica La Rocca	University of Naples Federico II, Italy
Sabrina Sacco	Politecnico di Milano, Italy
Piero Zizzania	University of Naples Federico II, Italy
Gaia Daldanise	CNR IRISS, Italy
Benedetta Grieco	University of Naples Federico II, Italy
Giuseppe Ciciriello	University of Naples Federico II, Italy
Marta Dell'Ovo	Politecnico di Milano, Italy
Daniele Cannatella	TU Delft University, The Netherlands
Eugenio Muccio	University of Naples Federico II, Italy
Sveva Ventre	University of Naples Federico II, Italy

Governance of Energy Transition: Environmental, Landscape, Social and Spatial Planning (ENERGY_PLANNING 2025)

Workshop Organizers

Mara Ladu	University of Cagliari, Italy
Ginevra Balletto	University of Cagliari, Italy
Emilio Ghiani	University of Cagliari, Italy
Alessandra Marra	University of Salerno, Italy
Roberto De Lotto	University of Pavia, Italy
Balázs Kulcsár	Chalmers University of Technology, Sweden

Workshop Program Committee Members

Riccardo Trevisan	University of Cagliari, Italy
Marco Naseddu	University of Cagliari, Italy
Giuseppe Borruso	University of Trieste, Italy
Andrea Gallo	University of Trieste, Italy
Francesca Sinatra	University of Trieste, Italy
Maria Attard	University of Malta, Malta
Tu Anh Trinh	UEH University Ho Chi Minh City, Vietnam
Marcello Tadini	University of Eastern Piedmont, Italy
Luigi Mundula	University for Foreigners of Perugia, Italy
Silvia Battino	University of Sassari, Italy
Maria del Mar Munoz Leonisio	University of Cádiz, Spain
Anna Richiedei	University of Brescia, Italy
Michele Pezzagno	University of Brescia, Italy
Federico Mertellozzo	University of Firenze, Italy
Marco Mazzarino	IUAV University Venice, Italy

Ecosystem Services in Spatial Planning for Climate Neutral Urban and Rural Areas (ESSP 2025)

Workshop Organizers

Sabrina Lai	University of Cagliari, Italy
Francesco Scorza	University of Basilicata, Italy
Corrado Zoppi	University of Cagliari, Italy
Beniamino Murgante	University of Basilicata, Italy
Carmela Gargiulo	University of Naples Federico II, Italy
Floriana Zucaro	University of Naples Federico II, Italy

Workshop Program Committee Members

Alfonso Annunziata	University of Basilicata, Italy
Ginevra Balletto	University of Cagliari, Italy
Ivan Blečić	University of Cagliari, Italy
Giuseppe Borruso	University of Trieste, Italy
Barbara Caselli	University of Parma, Italy
Maria Cerreta	University of Naples Federico II, Italy
Chiara Garau	University of Cagliari, Italy
Carmen Guida	University of Naples Federico II, Italy
Federica Isola	University of Cagliari, Italy
Francesca Leccis	University of Cagliari, Italy
Federica Leone	University of Cagliari, Italy
Silvia Rossetti	University of Parma, Italy
Luigi Santopietro	University of Basilicata, Italy
Carmelo Torre	Polytechnic of Bari, Italy

The 15th International Workshop on Future Information System Technologies and Applications (FiSTA 2025)

Workshop Organizers

Bernady O. Apduhan	Kyushu Sangyo University, Japan
Rafael Santos	Brazilian National Institute for Space Research, Brazil

Workshop Program Committee Members

Agustinus Borgy Waluyo	Monash University, Australia
Andre Ricardo Abed Grégio	Federal University of Paraná, Brazil
Eric Pardede	La Trobe University, Australia
Kai Cheng	Kyushu Sangyo University, Japan
Ching-Hsien Hsu	Asia University, Taiwan
Fenghui Yao	Tennessee State University, USA
Yusuke Gotoh	Okayama University, Japan
Alvaro Fazenda	Federal University of São Paulo, Brazil
Kazuaki Tanaka	Kyushu Institute of Technology, Japan
Tengku Adil	MARA Technological University, Malaysia
Toshihiro Yamauchi	Okayama University, Japan
Yasuaki Sumida	Kyushu Sangyo University, Japan
Earl Ryan Aleluya	MSU-Iligan Institute of Technology, Philippines
Cherry Mae G. Villame	MSU-Iligan Institute of Technology, Philippines
Anton Louise De Ocampo	Batangas State University, Philippines
Krishnamoorthy Ranganthan	Chennai Institute of Technology, India

Flow Management in Urban Contexts (FMUC 2025)

Workshop Organizers

Alessio Pino	Kore University of Enna, Italy
Giovanna Acampa	Kore University of Enna, Italy

Workshop Program Committee Members

Giovanna Acampa	University of Florence, Italy
Alessio Pino	Kore University of Enna, Italy
Mariolina Grasso	Università Kore di Enna, Italy
Fabrizio Battisti	University of Florence, Italy
Fabrizio Finucci	Roma Tre University, Italy
Antonella G. Masanotti	Roma Tre University, Italy
Daniele Mazzoni	Roma Tre University, Italy

Geographical Analysis, Urban Modeling, Spatial Statistics 2025 (Geog-And-Mod 2025)

Workshop Organizers

Beniamino Murgante	University of Basilicata, Italy
Giuseppe Borruso	University of Trieste, Italy
Hartmut Asche	University of Potsdam, Germany
Rodrigo Tapia McClung	CentroGeo, Mexico
Andreas Fricke	University of Potsdam, Germany

Workshop Program Committee Members

Giuseppe Borruso	University of Trieste, Italy
Beniamino Murgante	University of Basilicata, Italy
Hartmut Asche	University of Potsdam, Germany
Rodrigo Tapia-McClung	Centro de Investigación en Ciencias de Información Geoespacial (CentroGeo), Mexico
Andreas Fricke	University of Potsdam, Germany
Malgorzata Hanzl	Lodz University of Technology, Poland
Anastasia Stratigea	National Technical University of Athens, Greece
Ljiljiana Zivkovic	Republic Geodetic Authority of Serbia, Serbia
Ginevra Balletto	University of Cagliari, Italy
Silvia Battino	University of Sassari, Italy
Mara Ladu	University of Cagliari, Italy
Maria del Mar Munoz Leonisio	University of Cádiz, Spain
Ahinoa Amaro Garcia	University of Las Palmas of Gran Canaria, Spain
Maria Attard	University of Malta, Malta

Enrico D'agostini	World Maritime University, Sweden
Francesca Krasna	University of Trieste, Italy
Brisol García García	Polytechnic University of Quintana Roo, Mexico
Tu Anh Trinh	UEH University, Vietnam
Giovanni Mauro	Università degli Studi della Campania, Italy
Maria Ronza	University of Naples Federico II, Italy
Massimiliano Bencardino	University of Salerno, Italy
Andrea Gallo	Ca' Foscari University of Venice, Italy
Francesca Sinatra	University of Trieste, Italy
Salvatore Dore	University of Trieste, Italy

Geogames for Sustainable Development (Geogames 2025)

Workshop Organizer

Alenka Poplin	Iowa State University, USA

Workshop Program Committee Members

Alenka Poplin	Iowa State University, USA
Bruno Amaral de Andrade	Portucalense University, Portugal
Brian Tomaszewski	Rochester Institute of Technology, USA
Deepak Marhatta	Tribhuvan University, Nepal
Alessandro Plaisant	University of Sassari, Italy
David Schwartz	Rochester Institute of Technology, USA
Silvia Rossetti	University of Parma, Italy
Floriana Zucaro	University of Naples Federico II, Italy
Alfonso Annunziata	University of Basilicata, Italy
Reza Askarizad	University of Cagliari, Italy
Chiara Garau	University of Cagliari, Italy
Tanja Congiu	University of Sassari, Italy

Geomatics for Resource Monitoring and Management (GRMM 2025)

Workshop Organizers

Alberico Sonnessa	Politecnico di Bari, Italy
Eufemia Tarantino	Politecnico di Bari, Italy
Alessandra Capolupo	Politecnico di Bari, Italy

Workshop Program Committee Members

Umberto Fratino	Politecnico di Bari, Italy
Valeria Monno	Politecnico di Bari, Italy

Antonino Maltese	Università degli studi di Palermo, Italy
Athos Agapiou	Cyprus University of Technology, Cyprus
Michele Mangiameli	Università di Catania, Italy
Angela Gorgoglione	Universidad de la República de Uruguay, Uruguay
Roberta Ravanelli	University of Liège, Belgium
Ester Scotto di Perta	Università degli studi di Napoli Federico II, Italy
Giacomo Caporusso	CNR, Italy
Andrea Montanino	International Centre for Numerical Methods in Engineering of Barcelona, Spain
Antonino Iannuzzo	Università degli studi del Sannio, Italy
Alessandro Pagano	Politecnico di Bari, Italy
Francesco Di Capua	Università degli Studi della Basilicata, Italy
Albertini Cinzia	CNR-IREA, Italy
Alessandra Saponieri	Università degli studi del Salento, Italy
PierFrancesco Recchi	Università degli studi di Napoli Federico II, Italy
Vincenzo Totaro	Politecnico di Bari, Italy
Stefania Santoro	CNR Water Research Institute, Italy
Francesco Bimbo	University of Foggia, Italy
Cristina Proietti	Istituto Nazionale di Geofisica e Vulcanologia, Italy
Carla Cavallo	University of Salerno, Italy
Gaetano Falcone	Università degli Studi di Napoli Federico II, Italy
Valeria Belloni	Sapienza University of Rome, Italy
Alessandra Mascitelli	University of Chieti-Pescara, Italy

HERitage and CLIMAte neutrality. Resilient approach for nature centered/based sustainable cities (HERCLIMA 2025)

Workshop Organizers

Celestina Fazia	Università di Enna Kore, Italy
Angrilli Massimo	University of Chieti-Pescara, Italy
Clara Stella Vicari Aversa	University of Reggio Calabria, Italy
Dorina Camelia Ilies	University of Oradea, Romania
Mariana Ratiu	University of Oradea, Romania

Workshop Program Committee Members

Alessandro Camiz	Università d'Annunzio, Italy
Mario Morrica	University of Urbino, Italy
Thowayeb Hassan	King Faisal University, Saudi Arabia
Alessandro Barracco	Università Kore di Enna, Italy
Kaoutare Amini Alaoui	Mohammed VI Polytechnic University (UM6P), Morocco

Mariana Ratiu	University of Oradea, Romania
Valentina Ciuffreda	Università Chieti-Pescara, Italy

International Workshop on Information and Knowledge in the Internet of Things (IKIT 2025)

Workshop Organizers

Teresa Guarda	Universidad Estatal Península de Santa Elena, Ecuador
Luis Enrique Chuquimarca Jimenez	Universidad Estatal Península de Santa Elena, Ecuador
Gustavo Gatica	Universidad Andrés Bello, Chile
Filipe Mota Pinto	Polytechnic Institute of Leiria, Portugal
Arnulfo Alanis	Instituto Tecnológico de Tijuana, Mexico
Luis Mazon	Universidad Estatal Península de Santa Elena, Spain

Workshop Program Committee Members

Arnulfo Alanis	Instituto Tecnológico de Tijuana, Mexico
Bruno Sousa	University of Coimbra, Portugal
Carlos Balsa	Instituto Politécnico de Bragança, Portugal
Filipe Mota Pinto	Instituto Politécnico de Leiria, Portugal
Gustavo Gatica	Universidad Andrés Bello, Chile
Isabel Lopes	Instituto Politécnico de Bragança, Portugal
José-María Díaz-Nafría	Universidad a Distancia, Spain
Maria Fernanda Augusto	BiTrum Research Group, Spain
Maria Isabel Ribeiro	Instituto Politécnico Bragança, Portugal
Modestos Stavrakis	University of the Aegean, Greece
Simone Belli	Universidad Complutense de Madrid, Spain
Walter Lopes Neto	Instituto Federal de Educação, Brazil

International Workshop on territorial Planning to integrate Risk prevention and urban Ontologies (IWPRO 2025)

Workshop Organizers

Beniamino Murgante	University of Basilicata, Italy
Roberto De Lotto	University of Pavia, Italy
Elisabetta Maria Venco	University of Pavia, Italy
Caterina Pietra	University of Pavia, Italy

Workshop Program Committee Members

Stefano Borgo	Consiglio Nazionale delle Ricerche ISTC, Italy
Valentina Costa	Università di Genova, Italy
Hamid Danesh Pajouh	Middle East Technical University, Turkey
Ilaria Delponte	Università di Genova, Italy
Lorena Fiorini	Università de L'Aquila, Italy
Veronica Gazzola	Politecnico di Milano, Italy
Ghazaleh Goodarzi	Islamic Azad University, Iran
Michele Grimaldi	Università degli Studi di Salerno, Italy
Alessandra Marra	Università degli Studi di Salerno, Italy
Naghmeh Mohammadpourlima	Åbo Akademi University, Finland
Francesca Pirlone	Università di Genova, Italy
Silvia Rossetti	Università di Parma, Italy
Bahareh Shahsavari	University of Minnesota, USA
Ilenia Spadaro	Università di Genova, Italy
Maria Rosaria Stufano Melone	Politecnico di Bari, Italy

Regional Connectivity, Spatial Accessibility and MaaS for Social Inclusion (MaaS 2025)

Workshop Organizers

Mara Ladu	University of Cagliari, Italy
Ginevra Balletto	University of Cagliari, Italy
Gianfranco Fancello	University of Cagliari, Italy
Tanja Congiu	University of Sassari, Italy
Patrizia Serra	University of Cagliari, Italy
Francesco Piras	University of Cagliari, Italy

Workshop Program Committee Members

Marco Naseddu	University of Cagliari, Italy
Italo Meloni	University of Cagliari, Italy
Giuseppe Borruso	University of Trieste, Italy
Andrea Gallo	University of Trieste, Italy
Francesca Sinatra	University of Trieste, Italy
Maria Attard	University of Malta, Malta
Tu Anh Trinh	UEH University, Vietnam
Marcello Tadini	University of Eastern Piedmont, Italy
Luigi Mundula	University for Foreigners of Perugia, Italy
Silvia Battino	University of Sassari, Italy
Brunella Brundu	University of Sassari, Italy
Veronica Camerada	University of Sassari, Italy

Maria del Mar Munoz Leonisio	University of Cádiz, Spain
Anna Richiedei	University of Brescia, Italy
Michele Pezzagno	University of Brescia, Italy
Marco Mazzarino	IUAV University Venice, Italy

The Development of Urban Mobility Management, Road Safety and Risk Assessment (MANTAIN 2025)

Workshop Organizers

Antonio Russo	Università degli Studi di Enna, Italy
Corrado Rindone	University of Reggio Calabria, Italy
Antonio Polimeni	University of Messina, Italy
Florin Rusca	Politehnica University of Bucharest, Romania
Grigorios Fountas	Aristotle University of Thessaloniki, Greece
Antonio Comi	University of Rome Tor Vergata, Italy

Workshop Program Committee Members

Massimo Di Gangi	University of Messina, Italy
Orlando Marco Belcore	University of Messina, Italy
Antonio Polimeni	University of Messina, Italy
Socrates Basbas	Aristotle University of Thessaloniki, Greece
Claudia Caballini	Polytechnic of Torino, Italy
Efstathios Bouhouras	Aristotle University of Thessaloniki, Greece
Stefano Ricci	Sapienza University of Rome, Italy
Marina Zanne	University of Lubljana, Slovenia
Kh Md Nahiduzzaman	Mohammed VI Polytechnic University, Morocco
Alexsandra Deluka Tibljaš	University of Rijeka, Croatia
Guilhermina Torrao	Aston University, UK

Multidimensional Evolutionary Evaluations for Transformative Approaches (MEETA 2025)

Workshop Organizers

Maria Cerreta	University of Naples Federico II, Italy
Giuliano Poli	University of Naples Federico II, Italy
Maria Somma	University of Naples Federico II, Italy
Gaia Daldanise	CNR IRISS, Italy
Ludovica La Rocca	University of Naples Federico II, Italy

Workshop Program Committee Members

Maria Cerreta	University of Naples Federico II, Italy
Giuliano Poli	University of Naples Federico II, Italy
Maria Somma	University of Naples Federico II, Italy
Laura Di Tommaso	University of Naples Federico II, Italy
Sabrina Sacco	Politecnico di Milano, Italy
Piero Zizzania	University of Naples Federico II, Italy
Gaia Daldanise	CNR IRISS, Italy
Benedetta Grieco	University of Naples Federico II, Italy
Giuseppe Ciciriello	University of Naples Federico II, Italy
Marta Dell'Ovo	Politecnico di Milano, Italy
Daniele Cannatella	TU Delft, The Netherlands
Eugenio Muccio	University of Naples Federico II, Italy
Francesco Piras	University of Cagliari, Italy
Diana Rolando	Politecnico di Torino, Italy
Sveva Ventre	University of Naples Federico II, Italy
Caterina Loffredo	University of Naples Federico II, Italy
Ludovica La Rocca	University of Naples Federico II, Italy
Simona Panaro	University of Campania Luigi Vanvitelli, Italy

Building Multi-dimensional Models for Assessing Complex Environmental Systems (MES 2025)

Workshop Organizers

Vanessa Assumma	University of Bologna, Italy
Caterina Caprioli	Politecnico di Torino, Italy
Giulia Datola	Politecnico di Milano, Italy
Federico Dell'Anna	University of Bologna, Italy
Marta Dell'Ovo	Politecnico di Milano, Italy
Marco Rossitti	Politecnico di Milano, Italy

Workshop Program Committee Members

Vanessa Assumma	Università di Bologna, Bologna
Caterina Caprioli	Politecnico di Torino, Italy
Giulia Datola	DAStU Politecnico di Milano, Italy
Federico Dell'Anna	Politecnico di Torino, Italy
Marta Dell'Ovo	Politecnico di Milano, Italy
Marco Rossitti	Politecnico di Milano, Italy
Francesca Torrieri	Politecnico di Milano, Italy
Mariarosaria Angrisano	Università Telematica Pegaso, Italy
Maksims Feofilovs	Riga Technical University, Latvia

Danny Caprini	Politecnico di Milano, Italy
Giulio Cavana	Politecnico di Torino, Italy
Sebastiano Barbieri	Politecnico di Torino, Italy
Marta Bottero	Politecnico di Torino, Italy
Francesco Cosentino	Politecnico di Milano, Italy
Silvia Ronchi	Politecnico di Milano, Italy
Chiara Mazzarella	TU Delft, Netherlands
Marco Volpatti	Politecnico di Torino, Italy
Chiara D'Alpaos	Università degli Studi di Padova, Italy
Alessandra Oppio	Politecnico di Milano, Italy
Alessia Crisopulli	Politecnico di Milano, Italy
Domenico D'Uva	Politecnico di Milano, Italy
Giorgia Malavasi	Politecnico di Torino, Italy
Rubina Canesi	Università degli Studi di Padova, Italy
Elena Todella	Politecnico di Torino, Italy
Beatrice Mecca	Politecnico di Torino, Italy
Giulia Marzani	University of Bologna, Italy
Isabella Giovanetti	University of Bologna, Italy
Lucia Petronio	University of Bologna, Italy
Franco Corti	University of Padova, Italy
Salvatore De Pascalis	Politecnico di Milano, Italy
Valeria Vitulano	Politecnico di Torino, Italy
Lorenzo Diana	Università degli studi di Napoli Federico II, Italy
Maksims Feofilovs	Riga Technical University, Latvia
Marco De Luca	Politecnico di Torino, Italy
Ilaria Cazzola	Politecnico di Torino, Italy
Andrea De Toni	Politecnico di Milano, Italy
Eugenio Muccio	University of Naples Federico II, Italy
Giuliano Poli	University of Naples Federico II, Italy
Francesco Sica	University "La Sapienza" of Rome, Italy
Elena Di Pirro	Università degli Studi del Molise, Italy
Riccardo Alba	Università di Torino, Italy
Irene Regaiolo	Università di Torino, Italy
Francesca Cochis	Università di Torino, Italy

Modelling Liveable Cities: Techniques, Methods, Challenges, and Perspectives Behind the 'X-Minute' City (MLC 2025)

Workshop Organizers

Federico Mara	University of Pisa, Italy
Valerio Cutini	University of Pisa, Italy
Alessandro Araldi	Université Côte d'Azur, France

Flávia Lopes   Chalmers University of Technology, Sweden
Giovanni Fusco   Université Côte d'Azur, France

Workshop Program Committee Members

Simone Rusci   University of Pisa, Italy
Lorena Fiorini   University of L'Aquila, Italy
Chiara Di Dato   University of L'Aquila, Italy
Francesco Zullo   University of L'Aquila, Italy
Alfonso Annunziata   University of Basilicata, Italy
Beniamino Murgante   University of Basilicata, Italy
Alessandro Araldi   Universitè Côte d'Azur, France
Chiara Garau   University of Cagliari, Italy
Giampiero Lombardini   Università di Genova, Italy
Flavia Lopes   Chalmers University of Technology, Sweden
Giovanni Fusco   Universitè Côte d'Azur, France

Mathematical Methods for Image Processing and Understanding 2025 (MMIPU 2025)

Workshop Organizers

Ivan Gerace   Università degli Studi di Perugia, Italy
Gianluca Vinti   Università degli Studi di Perugia, Italy
Arianna Travaglini   Università degli Studi della Basilicata, Italy

Workshop Program Committee Members

Ivan Gerace   University of Perugia, Italy
Gianluca Vinti   University of Perugia, Italy
Arianna Travaglini   University of Basilicata, Italy
Marco Baioletti   University of Perugia, Italy
Marco Donatelli   University of Insubria, Italy
Anna Tonazzini   C.N.R. Pisa, Italy
Muhammad Hanif   Ghulam Ishaq Khan Institute of Engineering
                                   Sciences and Technology, Pakistan
Francesco Marchetti   University of Padua, Italy
Wolfgang Erb   University of Padua, Italy
Danilo Costarelli   University of Perugia, Italy
Francesco Santini   University of Perugia, Italy
Valentina Giorgetti   University of Perugia, Italy

Mobility Opportunities Bridging Inequalities: Social Inclusion and Gender Equity Initiatives Strategies Against Fragmentation and Complexity of Mobility (MOBIL-EGI 2025)

Workshop Organizers

Tiziana Campisi	University of Enna Kore, Italy
Guilhermina Torrao	Aston University, UK
Socrates Basbas	Aristotle University of Thessaloniki, Greece
Tanja Congiu	University of Sassari, Italy
Stefanos Tsigdinos	National Technical University of Athens, Greece
Florin Nemtanu	Politehnica University of Bucharest, Romania

Workshop Program Committee Members

Massimo Di Gangi	University of Messina, Italy
Orlando Marco Belcore	University of Messina, Italy
Francesco Russo	Mediterranean University of Reggio Calabria, Italy
Alexandros Nikitas	University of Huddersfield, UK
Marilisa Nigro	Rome Tre University, Italy
Kh Md Nahiduzzaman	Mohammed VI Polytechnic University, Morocco
Efstathios Bouhouras	Aristotle University of Thessaloniki, Greece
Antonio Comi	University of Rome Tor Vergata, Italy
Edouard Ivanjko	University of Zagreb, Slovenia
Osvaldo Gervasi	University of Perugia, Italy
Beniamino Murgante	University of Basilicata, Italy
Chiara Garau	University of Cagliari, Italy

MOdels and indicators for assessing and measuring the urban settlement deVElopment in the view of NET ZERO by 2050 (MOVEto0 2025)

Workshop Organizers

Lorena Fiorini	University of L'Aquila, Italy
Lucia Saganeiti	CNR-IMAA, Italy
Angela Pilogallo	CNR-IMAA, Italy
Alessandro Marucci	University of L'Aquila, Italy
Francesco Zullo	University of L'Aquila, Italy

Workshop Program Committee Members

Ginevra Balletto	University of Cagliari, Italy
Giuseppe Borruso	University of Trieste, Italy
Chiara Garau	University of Cagliari, Italy

Beniamino Murgante	University of Basilicata, Italy
Giulia Desogus	University of Cagliari, Italy
Ljiljana Zivkovic	Republic Geodetic Authority, Serbia
Luigi Santopietro	University of Basilicata, Italy
Ilaria Delponte	University of Genoa, Italy
Carmen Guida	University of Naples Federico II, Italy
Chiara Di Dato	University of L'Aquila, Italy

5th Workshop on Privacy in the Cloud/Edge/IoT World (PCEIoT 2025)

Workshop Organizers

Lelio Campanile	Università degli Studi della Campania Luigi Vanvitelli, Italy
Mauro Iacono	Università degli Studi della Campania Luigi Vanvitelli, Italy
Michele Mastroianni	Università degli Studi di Foggia, Italy

Workshop Program Committee Members

Arcangelo Castiglione	Università degli Studi di Salerno, Italy
Maria Ganzha	Warsaw University of Technology, Poland
Daniel Grzonka	Cracow University of Technology, Poland
Antonio Iannuzzi	Università degli Studi Roma Tre, Italy
Armando Tacchella	Università degli Studi di Genova, Italy
Biagio Boi	University of Salerno, Italy
Marco De Santis	University of Salerno, Italy
Fiammetta Marulli	Università degli Studi della Campania "L. Vanvitelli", Italy
Christian Riccio	Università degli Studi della Campania "L. Vanvitelli", Italy
Luigi Piero Di Bonito	Università degli Studi di Napoli Federico II, Italy

Preserving Our Past: Spatial and Remote Sensing Technologies for Cultural Heritage in a Changing Climate (POP 2025)

Workshop Organizers

Maria Danese	CNR-ISPC, Italy
Nicola Masini	CNR-ISPC, Italy
Rosa Lasaponara	CNR-IMAA, Italy

Workshop Program Committee Members

Maria Danese	CNR-ISPC, Italy
Nicola Masini	CNR-ISPC, Italy
Rosa Lasaponara	CNR-IMAA, Italy
Dario Gioia	CNR-ISPC, Italy
Giuseppe Corrado	Università degli Studi della Basilicata, Italy
Canio Sabia	CNR-ISPC, Italy

Processes, methods and tools towards RESilient cities and cultural and historic sites prone to SOD and ROD disasters (RES 2025)

Workshop Organizers

Elena Cantatore	Polytechnic University of Bari, Italy
Dario Esposito	Polytechnic University of Bari, Italy
Alberico Sonnessa	Polytechnic University of Bari, Italy

Workshop Program Committee Members

Elena Cantatore	Politecnico di Bari, Italy
Dario Esposito	Politecnico di Bari, Italy
Alberico Sonnessa	Politecnico di Bari, Italy
Valeria Belloni	Sapienza University of Rome, Italy
Michela Ravanelli	Sapienza University of Rome, Italy
Silvano Dal Sasso	University of Basilicata, Italy
Francesco Chiaravalloti	CNR - IRPI, Italy
Roberta Ravanelli	University of Liège, Belgium
Alessandra Mascitelli	University of Chieti-Pescara, Italy
Francesco Di Capua	University of Basilicata, Italy
Gabriele Bernardini	Università Politecnica delle Marche, Italy
Vito Domenico Porcari	University of Basilicata, Italy
Carmen Rosa Fattore	University of Basilicata, Italy
Stefania Santoro	Water Research Institute, Italy

Scientific Computing Infrastructure (SCI 2025)

Workshop Organizers

Vladimir Korkhov	Saint Petersburg State University, Russia
Elena Stankova	Saint Petersburg State University, Russia
Nataliia Kulabukhova	Saint Petersburg State University, Russia

Workshop Program Committee Members

Adam Belloum	University of Amsterdam, the Netherlands
Dmitrii Vasiunin	Deutsche Telekom Cloud Services E.P.E., Greece
Serob Balyan	Osensus Arm LLC, Armenia
Suren Abrahamyan	Osensus Arm LLC, Armenia
Ashot Sergey Gevorkyan	NAS of Armenia, Armenia
Michal Hnatic	Univerzita Pavla Jozefa Šafárika v Košiciach, Slovakia
Michail Panteleyev	Saint Petersburg Electrotecnical University, Russia
Martin Vala	Univerzita Pavla Jozefa Šafárika v Košiciach, Slovakia
Nodir Zaynalov	Tashkent University of Information Technologies named after Muhammad al Khwarizmi, Uzbekistan
Michail Panteleyev	Saint Petersburg Electrotecnical University, Russia
Alexander Degtyarev	Saint Petersburg State University, Russia
Alexander Bogdanov	St. Petersburg University, Russia

Ports and Logistics of the Future - Smartness and Sustainability (SmartPorts 2025)

Workshop Organizers

Andrea Gallo	Università degli Studi di Trieste, Italy
Gianfranco Fancello	University of Cagliari, Italy
Giuseppe Borruso	Università degli Studi di Trieste, Italy
Enrico D'agostini	World Maritime University, Sweden
Silvia Battino	Università degli Studi di Sassari, Italy
Veronica Camerada	Università degli Studi di Sassari, Italy

Workshop Program Committee Members

Giuseppe Borruso	University of Trieste, Italy
Beniamino Murgante	University of Basilicata, Italy
Ginevra Balletto	University of Cagliari, Italy
Silvia Battino	University of Sassari, Italy
Mara Ladu	University of Cagliari, Italy
Maria del Mar Munoz Leonisio	University of Cádiz, Spain
Ahinoa Amaro Garcia	University of Las Palmas of Gran Canaria, Spain
Maria Attard	University of Malta, Malta
Enrico D'agostini	World Maritime University, Sweden
Francesca Krasna	University of Trieste, Italy

Tu Anh Trinh	UEH University - Ho Chi Minh City, Vietnam
Giovanni Mauro	Università degli Studi della Campania, Italy
Maria Ronza	University of Naples Federico II, Italy
Massimiliano Bencardino	University of Salerno, Italy
Andrea Gallo	Ca' Foscari University of Venice, Italy
Francesca Sinatra	University of Trieste, Italy
Salvatore Dore	University of Trieste, Italy
Veronica Camerada	University of Sassari, Italy
Brunella Brundu	University of Sassari, Italy
Gianfranco Fancello	University of Cagliari, Italy
Marcello Tadini	University of Eastern Piedmont, Italy
Marco Mazzarino	IUAV University Venice
José Ángel Hernández Luis	University of Las Palmas de Gran Canaria, Spain
Marco Naseddu	University of Cagliari, Italy
Maurizio Cociancich	Adriafer, Italy
Giovanni Longo	University of Trieste, Italy
Luca Toneatti	University of Trieste, Italy
Martina Sinatra	University of Cagliari, Italy
Enrico Vanino	University of Sheffield, UK
Patrizia Serra	University of Cagliari, Italy
Agostino Bruzzone	University of Genoa, Italy
Marco Petrelli	University of Roma 3, Italy

Smart Transport and Logistics - Smart Supply Chains (SmarTransLog 2025)

Workshop Organizers

Francesca Sinatra	University of Trieste, Italy
Maria del Mar Munoz	Universidad de Cádiz, Spain
Brunella Brundu	University of Sassari, Italy
Patrizia Serra	University of Cagliari, Italy
Salvatore Dore	University of Trieste, Italy
Marco Naseddu	University of Cagliari, Italy

Workshop Program Committee Members

Giuseppe Borruso	University of Trieste, Italy
Beniamino Murgante	University of Basilicata, Italy
Ginevra Balletto	University of Cagliari, Italy
Silvia Battino	University of Sassari, Italy
Mara Ladu	University of Cagliari, Italy
Maria del Mar Munoz Leonisio	University of Cádiz, Spain
Ahinoa Amaro Garcia	University of Las Palmas of Gran Canaria, Spain

Maria Attard	University of Malta, Malta
Enrico D'agostini	World Maritime University, Sweden
Francesca Krasna	University of Trieste, Italy
Tu Anh Trinh	UEH University, Vietnam
Giovanni Mauro	Università degli Studi della Campania, Italy
Maria Ronza	University of Naples Federico II, Italy
Massimiliano Bencardino	University of Salerno, Italy
Andrea Gallo	Ca' Foscari University of Venice, Italy
Francesca Sinatra	University of Trieste, Italy
Salvatore Dore	University of Trieste, Italy
Veronica Camerada	University of Sassari, Italy
Brunella Brundu	University of Sassari, Italy
Gianfranco Fancello	University of Cagliari, Italy
Marcello Tadini	University of Eastern Piedmont, Italy
Marco Mazzarino	IUAV University Venice
José Ángel Hernández Luis	University of Las Palmas de Gran Canaria, Spain
Marco Naseddu	University of Cagliari, Italy
Maurizio Cociancich	Adriafer, Italy
Giovanni Longo	University of Trieste, Italy
Luca Toneatti	University of Trieste, Italy
Martina Sinatra	University of Cagliari, Italy
Enrico Vanino	University of Sheffield, UK
Patrizia Serra	University of Cagliari, Italy
Agostino Bruzzone	University of Genoa, Italy
Marco Petrelli	University of Roma 3, Italy

Smart Tourism (SmartTourism 2025)

Workshop Organizers

Silvia Battino	University of Sassari, Italy
Francesca Krasna	University of Trieste, Italy
Ainhoa Amaro	University of Las Palmas de Gran Canaria, Spain
Maria del Mar Munoz	University of Cádiz, Spain
Brisol García García	Polytechnic University of Quintana Roo, Mexico
Marta Meleddu	University of Sassari, Italy

Workshop Program Committee Members

Giuseppe Borruso	University of Trieste, Italy
Beniamino Murgante	University of Basilicata, Italy
Gianfranco Fancello	University of Cagliari, Italy
Mara Ladu	University of Cagliari, Italy

Martina Sinatra	University of Cagliari, Italy
Salvatore Dore	University of Trieste, Italy
Marco Mazzarino	IUAV University Venice, Italy
Veronica Camerada	University of Sassari, Italy
Brunella Brundu	University of Sassari, Italy
Maria Attard	University of Malta, Malta
Ginevra Balletto	University of Cagliari, Italy
Giovanni Mauro	University degli Studi della Campania, Italy
Salvatore Lampreu	University of Sassari, Italy
Maria Ronza	University of Naples, Italy
Massimiliano Bencardino	University of Salerno, Italy

Sustainable evolution of long-Distance frEight and paSsenger Transport (SOLIDEST 2025)

Workshop Organizers

Francesco Russo	University of Reggio Calabria, Italy
Andreas Nikiforiadis	Democritus University of Thrace, Greece
Orlando Marco Belcore	University of Messina, Italy
Antonio Comi	University of Rome Tor Vergata, Italy
Tiziana Campisi	Kore University of Enna, Italy
Aura Rusca	Politehnica University of Bucharest, Romania

Workshop Program Committee Members

Massimo Di Gangi	University of Messina, Italy
Orlando Marco Belcore	University of Messina, Italy
Antonio Polimeni	University of Messina, Italy
Socrates Basbas	Aristotle University of Thessaloniki, Greece
Efstathios Bouhouras	Aristotle University of Thessaloniki, Greece
Marina Zanne	University of Lubljana, Slovenia
Marilisa Nigro	Rome Tre University, Italy
Edoardo Marcucci	Molde University College, Norway
Eugen Rosca	Polytechnic University of Bucharest, Romania
Kh Md Nahiduzzaman	Mohammed VI Polytechnic University, Morocco
Beniamino Murgante	University of Basilicata, Italy
Chiara Garau	University of Cagliari, Italy

Sustainability Performance Assessment: Models, Approaches, and Applications Toward Interdisciplinary and Integrated Solutions (SPA 2025)

Workshop Organizers

Francesco Scorza	University of Basilicata, Italy
Sabrina Lai	University of Cagliari, Italy
Francesco Rotondo	Università Politecnica delle Marche, Italy
Jolanta Dvarioniene	Kaunas University of Technology, Lithuania
Michele Campagna	University of Cagliari, Italy
Corrado Zoppi	University of Cagliari, Italy

Workshop Program Committee Members

Federico Amato	University of Lausanne, Switzerland
Ferdinando Di Carlo	University of Basilicata, Italy
Maddalena Floris	University of Cagliari, Italy
Federica Isola	University of Cagliari, Italy
Giuseppe Las Casas	University of Basilicata, Italy
Federica Leone	University of Cagliari, Italy
Giampiero Lombardini	University of Genoa, Italy
Federico Martellozzo	University of Florence, Italy
Alessandro Marucci	University of L'Aquila, Italy
Ana Clara Moura	Universidade Federal de Minas Gerais, Brazil
Beniamino Murgante	University of Basilicata, Italy
Silviu Nate	Lucian Blaga University of Sibiu, Romania
Anastasia Stratigea	National Technical University of Athens, Greece
Francesco Zullo	University of L'Aquila, Italy
Luigi Santopietro	University of Basilicata, Italy
Benedetto Manganelli	University of Basilicata, Italy

Specifics of Smart Cities Development in Europe (SPEED 2025)

Workshop Organizers

Chiara Garau	University of Cagliari, Italy
Katarína Vitálišová	Matej Bel University, Slovak Republic
Marco Fanfani	University of Florence, Italy
Anna Vaňová	Matej Bel University, Slovak Republic
Kamila Borsekova	Matej Bel University, Slovak Republic
Paola Zamperlin	University of Florence, Italy

Workshop Program Committee Members

Claudia Loggia	University of KwaZulu-Natal, South Africa
Francesca Maltinti	University of Cagliari, Italy
Alessandro Plaisant	University of Sassari, Italy
Alenka Poplin	Iowa State University, USA
Silvia Rossetti	University of Parma, Italy
Gerardo Carpentieri	University of Naples Federico II, Italy
Carmen Guida	University of Naples Federico II, Italy
Floriana Zucaro	University of Naples Federico II, Italy
Anastasia Stratigea	National Technical University of Athens, Greece
Yiota Theodora	National Technical University of Athens, Greece
Giovanna Concu	University of Cagliari, Italy
Paolo Nesi	University of Florence, Italy
Emanuele Bellini	University of Roma Tre, Italy
Mana Dastoum	Polytechnic University of Madrid, Spain
Barbara Caselli	University of Parma, Italy
Martina Carra	University of Brescia, Italy
Alfonso Annunziata	University of Basilicata, Italy
Elisabetta Venco	University of Pavia, Italy
Caterina Pietra	University of Pavia, Italy
Enrico Collini	University of Florence, Italy
Luciano Alessandro Ipsaro Palesi	University of Florence, Italy

Smart, Safe, and Healthy Cities (SSHC 2025)

Workshop Organizers

Chiara Garau	University of Cagliari, Italy
Gerardo Carpentieri	University of Naples Federico II, Italy
Carmen Guida	University of Naples Federico II, Italy
Tanja Congiu	University of Sassari, Italy
Martina Carra	University of Brescia, Italy
Alenka Poplin	Iowa State University, USA

Workshop Program Committee Members

Rosaria Battarra	Istituto di Studi sul Mediterraneo, Italy
Barbara Caselli	University of Parma, Italy
Francesca Maltinti	University of Cagliari, Italy
Romano Fistola	Università degli Studi di Napoli Federico II, Italy
Alessandro Plaisant	University of Sassari, Italy
Silvia Rossetti	University of Parma, Italy
Marco Fanfani	University of Florence, Italy
Reza Askarizad	University of Cagliari, Italy

Floriana Zucaro	University of Naples Federico II, Italy
Anastasia Stratigea	National Technical University of Athens, Greece
Yiota Theodora	National Technical University of Athens, Greece
Giovanna Concu	University of Cagliari, Italy
Francesco Zullo	University of L'Aquila, Italy
Paola Zamperlin	University of Florence, Italy
Vincenza Torrisi	University of Catania, Italy
Tiziana Campisi	University of Enna Kore, Italy
Katarína Vitálišová	Matej Bel University, Slovakia
Tazyeen Alam	University of Cagliari, Italy
Mana Dastoum	Polytechnic University of Madrid, Spain
Martina Carra	University of Brescia, Italy
Alfonso Annunziata	University of Basilicata, Italy
Elisabetta Venco	University of Pavia, Italy
Caterina Pietra	University of Pavia, Italy

Smart and Sustainable Island Communities (SSIC 2025)

Workshop Organizers

Chiara Garau	University of Cagliari, Italy
Anastasia Stratigea	National Technical University of Athens, Greece
Yiota Theodora	National Technical University of Athens, Greece
Giovanna Concu	University of Cagliari, Italy

Workshop Program Committee Members

Milena Metalkova-Markova	University of Portsmouth, UK
Tarek Teba	University of Portsmouth, UK
Alenka Poplin	Iowa State University, USA
Gerardo Carpentieri	University of Naples Federico II, Italy
Carmen Guida	University of Naples Federico II, Italy
Floriana Zucaro	University of Naples Federico II, Italy
Silvia Rossetti	University of Parma, Italy
Barbara Caselli	University of Parma, Italy
Martina Carra	University of Brescia, Italy
Alfonso Annunziata	University of Basilicata, Italy
Maria Panagiotopoulou	National Technical University of Athens, Greece
Apostolos Lagarias	University of Thessaly, Greece
Paola Zamperlin	University of Florence, Italy
Vincenza Torrisi	University of Catania, Italy
Giuseppina Vacca	University of Cagliari, Italy
Roberto Minunno	Curtin University, Australia
Marco Zucca	University of Cagliari, Italy

Elisabetta Venco	University of Pavia, Italy
Caterina Pietra	University of Pavia, Italy
Pietro Crespi	Politecnico di Milano, Italy

From STreet Experiments to Planned Solutions (STEPS 2025)

Workshop Organizers

Silvia Rossetti	Università degli Studi di Parma, Italy
Angela Ricciardello	Kore University of Enna, Italy
Francesco Pinna	Università degli Studi di Cagliari, Italy
Chiara Garau	Università degli Studi di Cagliari, Italy
Tiziana Campisi	Kore University of Enna, Italy
Vincenza Torrisi	University of Catania, Italy

Workshop Program Committee Members

Martina Carra	University of Brescia, Italy
Barbara Caselli	University of Parma, Italy
Tanja Congiu	University of Sassari, Italy
Gabriele D'Orso	University of Palermo, Italy
Matteo Ignaccolo	University of Catania, Italy
Md Kh Nahiduzzaman	Mohammed VI Polytechnic University, Morocco
Muhammad Ahmad Al-Rashid	University of Malaya, Malaysia
Alessandro Plaisant	University of Sassari, Italy
Marianna Ruggieri	University of Enna Kore, Italy
Michele Zazzi	University of Parma, Italy

Sustainable Tourism Evaluations: approaches, methods and indicators (STEva 2025)

Workshop Organizers

Mariolina Grasso	Università Kore di Enna, Italy
Fabrizio Finucci	Roma Tre University, Italy
Daniele Mazzoni	Roma Tre University, Italy
Antonella G. Masanotti	Roma Tre University, Italy
Giovanna Acampa	University of Florence, Italy

Workshop Program Committee Members

Giovanna Acampa	University of Florence, Italy
Fabrizio Finucci	Roma Tre University, Italy
Mariolina Grasso	"Kore" University of Enna, Italy

Alberto Marzo	Ministero della Cultura, Italy
Antonella G. Masanotti	Roma Tre University, Italy
Daniele Mazzoni	Roma Tre University, Italy
Rocco Murro	Sapienza University of Rome, Italy
Claudio Piferi	University of Florence, Italy
Alessio Pino	"Kore" University of Enna, Italy
Nicoletta Setola	University of Florence, Italy
Laura Calcagnini	Roma Tre University, Italy
Antonio Magarò	Roma Tre University, Italy
Janos Ghyerghyak	University of Pécs, Hungary
Ágnes Borsos	University of Pécs, Hungary
Fabrizio Battisti	University of Florence, Italy

Sustainable Development of Ports (SUSTAINABLEPORTS 2025)

Workshop Organizers

Tiziana Campisi	University of Enna KORE, Italy
Giuseppe Musolino	University of Reggio Calabria, Italy
Efstathios Bouhouras	Aristotle University of Thessaloniki, Greece
Elen Twrdy	University of Ljubljana, Slovenia
Elena Cocuzza	University of Catania, Italy
Aura Rusca	Politehnica University of Bucharest, Romania

Workshop Program Committee Members

Massimo Di Gangi	University of Messina, Italy
Orlando Marco Belcore	University of Messina, Italy
Antonio Polimeni	University of Messina, Italy
Claudia Caballini	Polytechnic of Torino, Italy
Gianfranco Fancello	University of Cagliari, Italy
Marina Zanne	University of Lubljana, Slovenia
Stefano Ricci	Sapienza University of Rome, Italy
Beniamino Murgante	University of Basilicata, Italy
Chiara Garau	University of Cagliari, Italy

Theoretical and Computational Chemistry and Its Applications (TCCMA 2025)

Workshop Organizers

Noelia Faginas Lago	Università di Perugia, Italy
Andrea Lombardi	Università di Perugia, Italy
Marcos Mandado Alonso	University of Vigo, Spain

Workshop Program Committee Members

Noelia Faginas-Lago	University of Perugia, Italy
Andrea Lombardi	University of Perugia, Italy
Marcos Mandado	University of Vigo, Spain
Angeles Peña	University of Vigo, Spain
Luca Mancini	Universiy of Perugia, Italy
Massimiliano Bartolomei	CSIC, Spain
Cecilia Coletti	University of Chieti-Pescara, Italy
Iñaki Tuñón	Universidad de Valencia, Spain
Albert Rimola Gilbert	Universitat Autònoma de Barcelona, Spain
Stefano Falcinelli	University of Perugia, Italy
Dario Campisi	University of Perugia, Italy
Ernesto García Para	University of the Basque Country, Spain
Giacomo Giorgi	University of Perugia, Italy
Tomás González Lezana	IFF CSIC, Spain
Enrique M. Cabaleiro Lago	Universidade de Santiago de Compostela, Spain
Aurora Costales	Universidad de Oviedo, Spain
Angel Martin	Universidad de Oviedo, Spain
Jose Manuel	University of Vigo, Spain
Annarita Laricchiuta	CNR ISTP Bari, Italy
Fernando Pirani	University of Perugia, Italy

Transport Infrastructures for Smart Cities (TISC 2025)

Workshop Organizers

Francesca Maltinti	University of Cagliari, Italy
Mauro Coni	University of Cagliari, Italy
Benedetto Barabino	University of Brescia, Italy
Nicoletta Rassu	University of Cagliari, Italy
James Rombi	University of Cagliari, Italy

Workshop Program Committee Members

Francesco Pinna	University of Cagliari, Italy
Chiara Garau	University of Cagliari, Italy
Mauro D'Apuzzo	University of Cassino, Italy
Roberto Minunno	Curtin University, Australia
Tiziana Campisi	University of Enna Kore, Italy
Roberto Ventura	University of Brescia, Italy
Alessandro Plaisant	University of Sassari, Italy
Massimo Di Francesco	University of Cagliari, Italy

| Vincenza Torrisi | University of Catania, Italy |
| Paola Zamperlin | University of Florence, Italy |

Transforming Urban Analytics: The Impact of Crowdsourced Mapping and Advanced AI Techniques on Future Cities (Tr-UrbAna 2025)

Workshop Organizers

Ayse Giz Gulnerman Gengec	Ankara Hacı Bayram Veli University, Turkey
Müslüm Hacar	Tildiz Technical University, Turkey
Himmet Karaman	Istanbul Technical University, Turkey

Workshop Program Committee Members

Beniamino Murgante	University of Basilicata, Italy
Abdulkadir Memduhoğlu	Harran University, Turkey
Zeynel Abidin Polat	İzmir Katip Çelebi University, Turkey
Güzide Miray Perihanoğlu	Van Yüzüncü Yıl University, Turkey
Tugba Memisoglu Baykal	Ankara Hacı Bayram Veli University, Turkey

From structural to TRAnsformative-change of City Environment: challenges and solutions and perspectives (TRACE 2025)

Workshop Organizers

Pierluigi Morano	Polytechnic University of Bari, Italy
Maria Rosaria Guarini	Sapienza University of Rome, Italy
Francesco Sica	Sapienza University of Rome, Italy
Francesco Tajani	Sapienza University of Rome, Italy
Marco Locurcio	Polytechnic University of Bari, Italy
Debora Anelli	Polytechnic University of Bari, Italy

Workshop Program Committee Members

Felicia di Liddo	Politecnico di Bari, Italia
Valeria Saiu	Università di Cagliari, Italia
Emma Sabatelli	Sapienza Università di Roma, Italia
Antonella Roma	Sapienza Università di Roma, Italia
Giuseppe Cerullo	Sapienza Università di Roma, Italia
Lucia della Spina	Università di Reggio Calabria, Italia
Alejandro Segura de la Cal	Politecnico di Madrid, Spain
Yilsy Nuñez	Politecnico di Madrid, Spain
Gabriella Maselli	Università di Salerno, Italy
Maria Rosa Trovato	Università di Catania, Italy

Manuela Rebaudengo	Politecnico di Torino, Italy
Pierfrancesco De Paola	Università di Napoli Federico II, Italy
Daniela Tavano	Università della Calabria, Italy
Maria Saez	University of Granada, Spain
Paola Amoruso	LUM "Giuseppe Degennaro" University, Italy

Temporary Real Estate management: Approaches and methods for Time-integrated impact assessments and evaluations (TREAT 2025)

Workshop Organizers

Chiara Mazzarella	TUDelft, The Netherlands
Hilde Remoy	TUDelft, The Netherlands
Maria Cerreta	University of Naples Federico II, Italy

Workshop Program Committee Members

Chiara Mazzarella	TU Delft, The Netherlands
Hilde Remoy	TU Delft, The Netherlands
Maria Cerreta	University of Naples Federico II, Italy
Maria Somma	University of Naples Federico II, Italy
Simona Panaro	University of Campania Luigi Vanvitelli, Italy
Laura Di Tommaso	University of Naples Federico II, Italy
Caterina Loffredo	University of Naples Federico II, Italy
Ludovica La Rocca	University of Naples Federico II, Italy
Sabrina Sacco	Politecnico di Milano, Italy
Piero Zizzania	University of Naples Federico II, Italy
Gaia Daldanise	CNR IRISS, Italy
Benedetta Grieco	University of Naples Federico II, Italy
Giuseppe Ciciriello	University of Naples Federico II, Italy
Marta Dell'Ovo	Politecnico di Milano, Italy
Daniele Cannatella	TU Delft, The Netherlands
Eugenio Muccio	University of Naples Federico II, Italy
Sveva Ventre	University of Naples Federico II, Italy

Supporting the Transition to Ecological Economy in Cities Regeneration: Circular Model Tools for Reusing Architecture and Infrastructures (TReE 2025)

Workshop Organizers

Mariarosaria Angrisano	Pegaso University, Italy
Giulio Cavana	Politecnico di Torino, Italy
Francesca Buglione	CNR-ISPC, Italy

| Antonia Gravagnuolo | CNR-ISPC, Italy |
| Piera Della Morte | Pegaso University, Italy |

Workshop Program Committee Members

Giulia Datola	Politecnico di Milano, Italy
Vanessa Assumma	University of Bologna, Italy
Marco Volpatti	Politecnico di Torino, Italy
Sebastiano Barbieri	Politecnico di Torino, Italy
Caterina Caprioli	Politecnico di Torino, Italy
Marta Dell'Ovo	Politecnico di Milano, Italy
Federico Dell'Anna	Politecnico di Torino, Italy
Elena Todella	Politecnico di Torino, Italy
Danny Casprini	Politecnico di Milano, Italy
Grazia Neglia	Università Telematica Pegaso, Italy
Francesca Nocca	Università degli Studi di Napoli Federico II, Italy
Giulio Cavana	Politecnico di Torino, Italy
Francesca Buglione	CNR-IPSC, Italy
Marco Rossitti	Politecnico di Milano, Italy
Jhon Escorcia	Politecnico di Torino, Italy
Beatrice Mecca	Politecnico di Torino, Italy
Sara Biancifiori	Politecnico di Torino, Italy

Urban Digital Twins and Data Spaces: Shaping the Future of Sustainable Cities (TwinAbleCities 2025)

Workshop Organizers

Dessislava Petrova Antonova	Sofia University, GATE Institute, Bulgaria
Beniamino Murgante	University of Basilicata, Italy
Senthil Rajendran	RMSI, Bahrain
Tiziana Campisi	Kore University of Enna, Italy
Mila Koeva	University of Twente, The Netherlands

Workshop Program Committee Members

Dessislava Petrova-Antonova	Sofia University, Bulgaria
Mila Koeva	The University of Twente, The Netherlands
Beniamino Murgante	University of Basilicata, Italy
Senthil Rajendran	RMSI, Bahrain
Tiziana Campisi	Kore University of Enna, Italy

Urban Regeneration: Innovative Tools and Evaluation Model (URITEM 2025)

Workshop Organizers

Fabrizio Battisti	University of Florence, Italy
Giovanna Acampa	University of Florence, Italy
Orazio Campo	Sapienza University of Rome, Italy
Melania Perdonò	University of Florence, Italy

Workshop Program Committee Members

Fabrizio Battisti	University of Florence, Italy
Giovanna Acampa	University of Florence, Italy
Orazio Campo	University of Rome "La Sapienza", Italy
Melania Perdonò	Università degli Studi di Firenze, Italy

Urban Space Accessibility and Mobilities (USAM 2025)

Workshop Organizers

Chiara Garau	DICAAR, University of Cagliari, Italy
Alessandro Plaisant	University of Sassari, Italy
Barbara Caselli	University of Parma, Italy
Mauro D'Apuzzo	University of Cassino and Southern Lazio, Italy
Gabriele D'Orso	University of Palermo, Italy
Matteo Ignaccolo	University of Catania, Italy

Workshop Program Committee Members

Mauro Coni	University of Cagliari, Italy
Martina Carra	University of Brescia, Italy
Tiziana Campisi	University of Enna Kore, Italy
Tanja Congiu	University of Sassari, Italy
Francesca Maltinti	University of Cagliari, Italy
Silvia Rossetti	University of Parma, Italy
Barbara Caselli	University of Parma, Italy
Angela Pilogallo	University of L'Aquila, Italy
Lorena Fiorini	University of L'Aquila, Italy
Reza Askarizad	University of Cagliari, Italy
Francesco Pinna	University of Cagliari, Italy
Aime Tsinda	University of Rwanda, Rwanda
Youssef El Ganadi	International University of Rabat, Morocco
Marco Migliore	University of Palermo, Italy
Alessio Salvatore	Italian National Research Council, Italy
Giuseppe Stecca	Italian National Research Council, Italy

Paola Zamperlin	University of Florence, Italy
Vincenza Torrisi	University of Catania, Italy
Gerardo Carpentieri	University of Naples Federico II, Italy
Carmen Guida	University of Naples Federico II, Italy
Floriana Zucaro	University of Naples Federico II, Italy
Alfonso Annunziata	University of Basilicata, Italy
Elisabetta Venco	University of Pavia, Italy
Caterina Pietra	University of Pavia, Italy
Tazyeen Alam	University of Cagliari, Italy
Valerio Cutini	University of Pisa, Italy

UX Mobility 2025: Placing User Experience at the Center of Urban Mobility: Methods and Frameworks (UXM 2025)

Workshop Organizers

Carmen Guida	Università degli Studi di Napoli Federico II, Italy
Gerardo Carpentieri	Università degli Studi di Napoli Federico II, Italy
Federico Messa	Systematica srl, Italy
Lamia Abdelfattah	Systematica srl, Italy

Workshop Program Committee Members

Rosaria Battarra	Istituto di Studi sul Mediterraneo CNR, Italy
Romano Fistola	Università degli Studi di Napoli Federico II, Italy
Lucia Saganeiti	IMAA-CNR, Italy

Virtual Reality and Augmented reality and applications (VRA 2025)

Workshop Organizers

Damiano Perri	University of Perugia, Italy
Osvaldo Gervasi	University of Perugia, Italy
Chau Ma Thi	University of Engineering and Technology, Vietnam National University, Hanoi, Vietnam
Paolo Nesi	University of Florence, Italy
Pierfrancesco Bellini	University of Florence, Italy

Workshop Program Committee Members

| David Berti | ART SpA, Italy |
| JungYoon Kim | Gachon University, South Korea |

TaiHoon Kim	Zhejiang University of Science and Technology, China
Marcelo de Paiva Guimares	Federal University of São Paulo, Brazil
Sergio Tasso	University of Perugia, Italy

Workshop on Advanced and Computational Methods for Earth Science Applications (WACM4ES 2025)

Workshop Organizers

Luca Piroddi	University of Cagliari, Italy
Patrizia Capizzi	University of Palermo, Italy
Marilena Cozzolino	University of Molise, Italy
Sebastiano D'Amico	University of Malta, Malta
Chiara Garau	University of Cagliari, Italy
Giuseppina Vacca	University of Cagliari, Italy

Workshop Program Committee Members

Andrea Angelini	CNR ISPC, Italy
Ilaria Barone	Università degli Studi di Padova, Italy
Patrizia Capizzi	University of Palermo, Italy
Luigi Capozzoli	CNR, Italy
Alberto Carletti	University of Cagliari, Italy
Emanuele Colica	University of Malta, Malta
Marilena Cozzolino	Università del Molise, Italy
Sebastiano D'Amico	University of Malta, Malta
Chiara Garau	University of Cagliari, Italy
Luciano Galone	University of Malta, Malta
Peter Iregbeyen	University of Malta, Malta
Mariano Lisi	Basilicata Aerospace Cluster CLAS, Italy
Raffaele Martorana	Università di Palermo, Italy
Paolo Mauriello	Università del Molise, Italy
Veronica Pazzi	University of Florence, Italy
Raffaele Persico	Università della Calabria, Italy
Luca Piroddi	University of Cagliari, Italy
Sina Saneiyan	Binghamton University, USA
Mercedes Solla	Universidade de Vigo, Spain
Deodato Tapete	ASI, Italy
Giuseppina Vacca	University of Cagliari, Italy
Enrica Vecchi	University of Cagliari, Italy

Sponsoring Organizations

ICCSA 2025 would not have been possible without the tremendous support of many organizations and institutions, for which all organizers and participants of ICCSA 2025 express their sincere gratitude:

Galatasaray University, Istanbul, Türkiye
(https://gsu.edu.tr/en)

African Mathematical Union
(https://www.africanmathunion.org/)

Springer Nature Switzerland AG, Switzerland
(https://www.springer.com)

The University of Massachusetts, USA
(https://www.umass.edu/)

University of Perugia, Italy
(https://www.unipg.it)

University of Basilicata, Italy
(http://www.unibas.it)

Monash University, Australia
(https://www.monash.edu/)

Kyushu Sangyo University, Japan
(https://www.kyusan-u.ac.jp/)

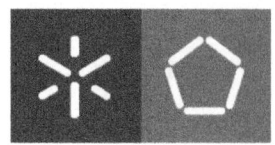

Universidade do Minho
Escola de Engenharia

University of Minho, Portugal
(https://www.uminho.pt/)
Venue
ICCSA 2025 took place in: **Galatasaray University, Istanbul, Türkiye**

Additional Reviewers

Reviewers
The review tasks for each workshop have been carried out by the workshop Organizers and the members of the workshop Program Committee.

Plenary Lectures

Sky Safe with GAI and Post-quantum Computing

Elizabeth Chang

Professor of Cyber Security and Head of Discipline, University of the Sunshine Coast, Australia

Abstract. Professor Chang's talk in this presentation has two distinct parts. To start, she will introduce the landscape of cybersecurity development, attacks, threats, and vulnerabilities, as well as state-of-the-art cyber protection, cyber defence, and cyber incident prevention. This is followed by a discussion of the impact of Generative AI (GAI) and quantum-safe cryptographic computing, highlighting the major issues and challenges in research, education, and training. In conclusion, she will present a vision for Sky Safe solutions, aiming to achieve cyber resilience that supports business and economic stability, enhances human capabilities, and promotes environmental sustainability.

Disaster Preparedness and Risk Profiling in the Digital Era from Earth Observation Lens

Jagannath Aryal

Department of Infrastructure Engineering, University of Melbourne, Australia

Abstract. Natural hazards which turn into disasters result in severe losses of lives, infrastructure, and property. Disasters such as earthquakes and landslides and their impacts on transportation safety, infrastructure resilience, and displacement of people to new places are challenges. To address such challenges, earth observation data and intelligent methods can provide potential solutions in developing decision support systems. This talk will present the state of the art in Earth observation for disaster resilience using intelligent methods. In the Earth observation space, digitalisation has revolutionised the way we map, monitor, and develop decision support systems. Global case study examples covering earthquake-induced landslides from the Himalayan region will cover the digital capabilities. The digital capabilities will embrace object recognition, interpretation, and their accurate and precise capture to integrate into digital models. The developed digital models from representative case studies can be leveraged in other jurisdictions in profiling risks to protect lives and infrastructure and creating disaster preparedness in the era of digital age and digital economy.

Intelligent Image Enhancement for Real-World Applications in Adverse Atmospheric Conditions

Khan Muhammad

Department of Global Convergence, Sungkyunkwan University, South Korea

Abstract. The adverse impacts of atmospheric conditions such as haze, fog, and low-light environments pose significant challenges for real-world applications reliant on computer vision, including autonomous driving, surveillance, and remote sensing. This keynote explores cutting-edge advancements in intelligent image enhancement, drawing insights from two pivotal studies. The first introduces HazeSpace2M, a comprehensive dataset and novel classification-guided dehazing framework that improves image clarity across diverse atmospheric conditions, addressing the gap between synthetic and real-world dehazing performance. The second focuses on LoLI-Street, a benchmark for low-light image enhancement tailored to urban environments, extending beyond enhancement to enable robust object detection and scene understanding. Taken together, these contributions demonstrate how integrating domain-specific datasets, advanced algorithms, and performance benchmarks can significantly elevate the reliability of computer vision systems under challenging weather and lighting conditions. Attendees will gain valuable insights into the methodologies, datasets, and practical applications driving innovation in this field, with implications for research and industry alike.

In Memory of Carmelo Torre

Unfortunately, Professor Carmelo Torre, one of the cornerstones of the ICCSA Conference, passed away last December, leaving everyone stunned and deeply saddened. His loss has created a profound void within our academic community. Carmelo was not only a respected scholar and dedicated contributor to the success and growth of ICCSA, but also a generous colleague, mentor, and friend to many. His intellectual rigor, warm personality, and unwavering commitment to advancing research will be remembered with great admiration. As we continue the work he helped shape, we honor his legacy and the indelible mark he left on all of us. Carmelo Torre graduated in engineering at the Polytechnic of Bari with a thesis on urban planning under Dino Borri's guidance. He began his research career by collaborating with Franco Selicato. During his PhD at the University of Naples Federico II under Luigi Fusco Girard, he specialized in real estate market analysis and multi-criteria evaluation methods. He explored the social impacts of urban transformations with his lifelong friend Maria Cerreta. His first ICCSA participation was in Perugia in 2008, in the session Geographical Analysis, Urban Modeling, Spatial Statistics. Instantly captivated by the conference, his charisma enabled him to involve various Italian scientific communities, including those in real estate and statistics. ICCSA became a yearly commitment for him, where he valued the high editorial quality of the proceedings and the dynamic post-presentation discussions and debates he passionately and expertly enriched. In 2012, alongside Maria Cerreta and Paola Perchinunno, he organized the workshop Econometrics and Multidimensional Evaluation in the Urban Environment (EMEUE), fostering dialogue on critical topics. His influence steadily grew, drawing numerous research groups to ICCSA and establishing real estate and assessment as one of the conference's leading fields. A pillar of ICCSA, he was involved across all facets of the event. Torre's contributions to academic discourse were marked by intellectual rigor and innovative thinking. His conference interventions consistently challenged conventional wisdom, offering insights transcending disciplinary boundaries. Beyond the conference, he passionately advocated for equity and social justice. His left-leaning ideology, though firm, earned respect from those with differing views, thanks to his sincerity and loyalty. He was creative, generous, and always willing to help, even at a personal cost. Despite battling illness, he maintained his characteristic optimism, warmth, cheerfulness, and commitment, supported by his partner, Caterina Rinaldo. His legacy lives on in his ideas, dedication, and unmatched generosity.

Contents – Part XIV

Mobility Opportunities Bridging Inequalities: Social Inclusion and Gender Equity Initiatives Strategies Against Fragmentation and complexity of Mobility (MOBIL-EGI 2025)

Future Scenarios and Equity Implications in Pedestrian Accessibility in Athens, Greece

Maria Eleni Samouri📧 and Stefanos Tsigdinos(✉)📧

School of Rural and Surveying Engineering, National Technical University of Athens, 15780 Athens, Greece
distlp@mail.ntua.gr

Abstract. The purpose of this study is to evaluate pedestrian accessibility in a suburban area in Athens Metropolitan Area (AMA) and to explore future scenarios for road space allocation schemes. To assess the existing conditions, the study followed a geospatial analysis approach that incorporated various criteria such as pavement width, quality of pavement, the existence of crosswalks, tactile paving, and the number of curb ramps. Afterwards, five further scenarios were developed through considering socioeconomic characteristics and the preliminary assessment of the current conditions. The new scenarios are the following: a) the active mode corridors in the approved Sustainable Urban Mobility Plan (SUMP) of the municipality, b) conventional interventions (ramps and crosswalks), c) land use-oriented based interventions (improvements around transit stations and basic amenities), d) social-oriented interventions in areas with high share of disadvantaged groups and e) enhanced social-equity strategy focusing on areas with low accessibility and high share of disadvantaged groups. Equity implications were examined through the lens of both the horizontal (Gini index) and the vertical approach (Bivariate Moran's I index). Applied to the municipality of Egaleo, a suburban area in the western part of the AMA, the Gini index demonstrated that the SUMP delivers the most equitable conditions. On the other hand, the Bivariate Moran's I index indicated that the enhanced social equity strategy is the most effective in promoting vertical equity. These intriguing outcomes, particularly helpful for policymakers, strongly note that if communities strive for social equity in pedestrian accessibility, they should emphasise socio-economic data in planning.

Keywords: accessibility · pedestrians · spatial analysis · equity · scenario planning

1 Introduction

Cities in Greece suffer from a serious lack of pedestrian accessibility. At the same time, proposed planning and design solutions, do not intrinsically consider the social characteristics of urban and suburban neighbourhoods. Poor walkability conditions can lead to social exclusion, limited access to essential services, and reduced quality of life [1]. This strongly highlights the need to assess pedestrian accessibility and to explore potential future takeaways for inclusive street spaces [2].

© The Author(s), under exclusive license to Springer Nature Switzerland AG 2026
O. Gervasi et al. (Eds.): ICCSA 2025 Workshops, LNCS 15899, pp. 3–19, 2026.
https://doi.org/10.1007/978-3-031-97663-6_1

Notably, the main characteristics of a just city in terms of transport planning, are equity and accessibility [3, 4]. More specifically, social exclusion refers to the inability to participate in a community's economic and social activities at a basic level, despite a willingness to do so, due to limited access to opportunities [5, 6]. In the same direction, Martens [7] defined "transport equity" as ensuring a minimum level of access for everyone. This notion reflects a sufficientarian perspective of equity. Conversely, the egalitarian perspective underscores the need for an equal distribution of resources and opportunities among all members of society [8]. Overall, transport equity includes policies, infrastructure, and services that play a crucial role in making transport systems more inclusive and tailored made to the needs of the users [9]. Delving more into that notion, we should that it can be further divided into two categories: horizontal equity and vertical equity related to socio-economic status and needs According to the utilitarian approach, horizontal equity refers to the greatest benefit for most individuals from policies. Vertical equity, according to the intuitionist approach, proposes a pluralistic perception of justice to address moral issues in real-world situations [10, 11].

Previous research has shown that active modes accessibility is significantly influenced by the type of infrastructure and policy solutions, brought forward by central or local stakeholders. Barmpas et al. [12] demonstrated that small Greek cities experience serious problems related to pedestrian accessibility. Remaining in Greece, Tsigdinos [13] explored the impact of future active corridors scenarios (based on different street classification schemes) on equity in a suburban municipality of Athens and found that radical solutions (well-integrated network) tend to provide more horizontal equity conditions. This portrays the ability of road space allocation to define the accessibility levels of active travellers. Likewise, Arellana et al. [14] who studied the case of two Colombians cities, underscore that the lack of prioritisation for pedestrian infrastructure creates barriers that discourage walking, potentially exacerbating social inequities, particularly in low-income areas. It is indeed very promising, while challenging, that countries in the Global South, e.g., Chile, experience high shares of walking as the predominant transport mode (especially for lower-middle-income groups), despite the ongoing investment in car infrastructure [15]. This discrepancy between persistence of walking, but low pedestrian accessibility conditions, calls for tailored made solutions which enhance pedestrian infrastructure and support more equitable, active transportation options. Looking also into other contexts, we may find that walking facilities and their impact on a fair level of pedestrian accessibility is often ignored, thus resulting in inequitable transport systems with severe spatial disparities [16, 17].

Therefore, it is demonstrated that pedestrian accessibility problems that might lead to social exclusion phenomena, are still present in urban areas, highlighting the urgent need for more human-centric and inclusive spatial planning schemes. In this demanding "landscape", this study aims to assess pedestrian accessibility in a suburban area of the Athens Metropolitan Area (AMA) and explore potential future road space allocation strategies. To evaluate the current conditions, a geospatial analysis was conducted, considering factors such as pavement width, pavement quality, the presence of crosswalks, tactile paving, and the number of curb ramps. Subsequently, five additional scenarios were developed, taking into account socioeconomic characteristics and an initial assessment of existing conditions. The novelty of this research lies in the development of a cohesive methodology for evaluating pedestrian accessibility through a complete equity lens (both horizontal and vertical aspect) that could be beneficial for policymakers. The structure of the paper is as follows. The second section presents the methods used in detail, the third section illustrates the results obtained, while the last section discusses the result with relevant literature as well as draws the conclusions of this study.

2 Methodology

This study was carried out in four main stages: First, the analysis of existing situation, then the scenario formulation, third, we calculated the accessibility index and finally we evaluated equity through different indices. Spatial data were used, and the analysis was done with Geographic Information System (GIS) software (QGIS and GeoDa) and statistical models (MS excel and R). The flowchart in Fig. 1 shows the process followed.

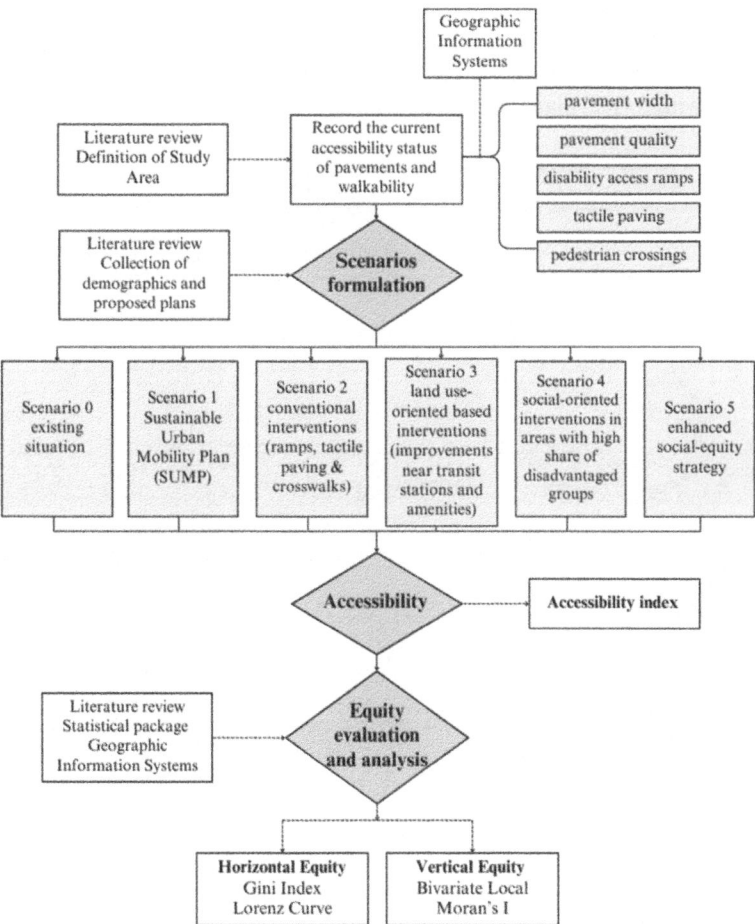

Fig. 1. Methodological framework (source: own elaboration).

2.1 Study Setting and Dataset

First and foremost, acknowledging pedestrian accessibility problems requires a challenging study area that shows context-based interest and will act as a proper study setting. Bearing this in mind, this research used the municipality of Egaleo as a study case.

This municipality is located within the AMA and it belongs to the western sector of the Athens' Regional Unit. Figure 2 shows the location of the study area within the AMA and the Attica Region. It's a rather sizable municipality (5.65 km^2), with diverse land uses like several commercial centres, metropolitan parks, two university campuses and three metro stations. Furthermore, the municipality has a great role to play for metropolitan Athens as well, as per the Regional of Attica, it is one of the most significant intermunicipal centre in the entire area. The municipality was selected because of its diverse land uses that embrace walking and due to its relatively fair connectivity with fixed route public transport (metro) compared to the rest of Athens. Afterall, pedestrians should have adequate access to public transport stations and stops [18]. Moreover, the municipality of Egaleo functions as a suitable case study, since it has an approved Sustainable Urban Mobility Plan (SUMP), thus making room for comparison with formal planning initiatives.

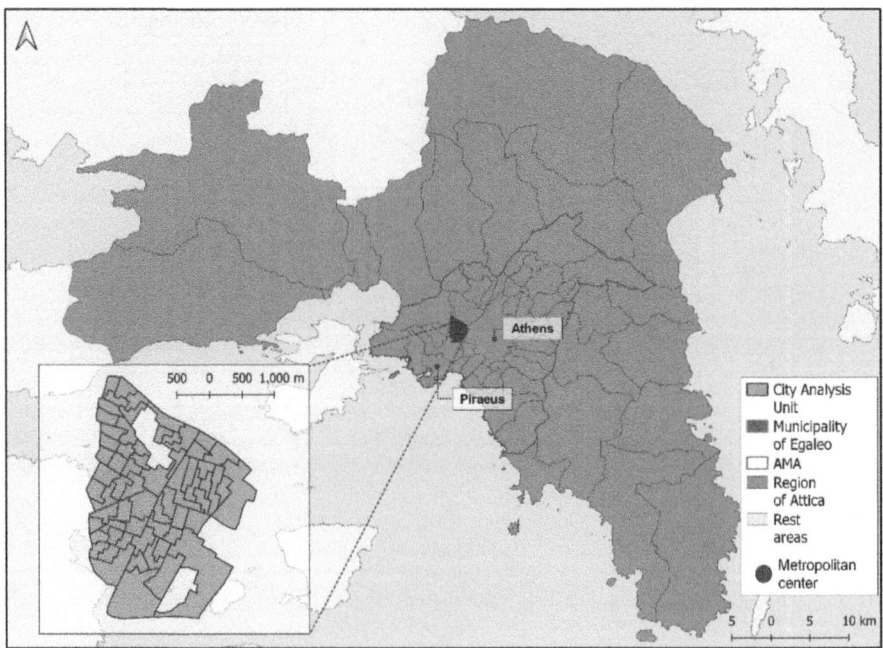

Fig. 2. Municipality of Egaleo in Athens Metropolitan Area (source: geodata.gov.gr, Panorama Greek census data and own elaboration).

Looking into the data, the Hellenic Statistical Authority (ELSTAT) provides socioeconomic data, at a city analysis unit level (CAUs) [19]. These CAUs are groups of building blocks with a population of approximately 900–1,000 individuals. Therefore, the research was conducted at the CAU level for the incorporation of this data. Notably, Egaleo consists of 63 CAUs. The obtained data referred to the socioeconomic characteristics of the residents. To facilitate the measurement of vertical equity, this study used the unemployment rate, the percentage of no-car households, and the percentage of citizens aged from 0 to 15 and over 65 according to the census of 2011 (recent data are not available yet). Figure 3 illustrates the distribution of these characteristics.

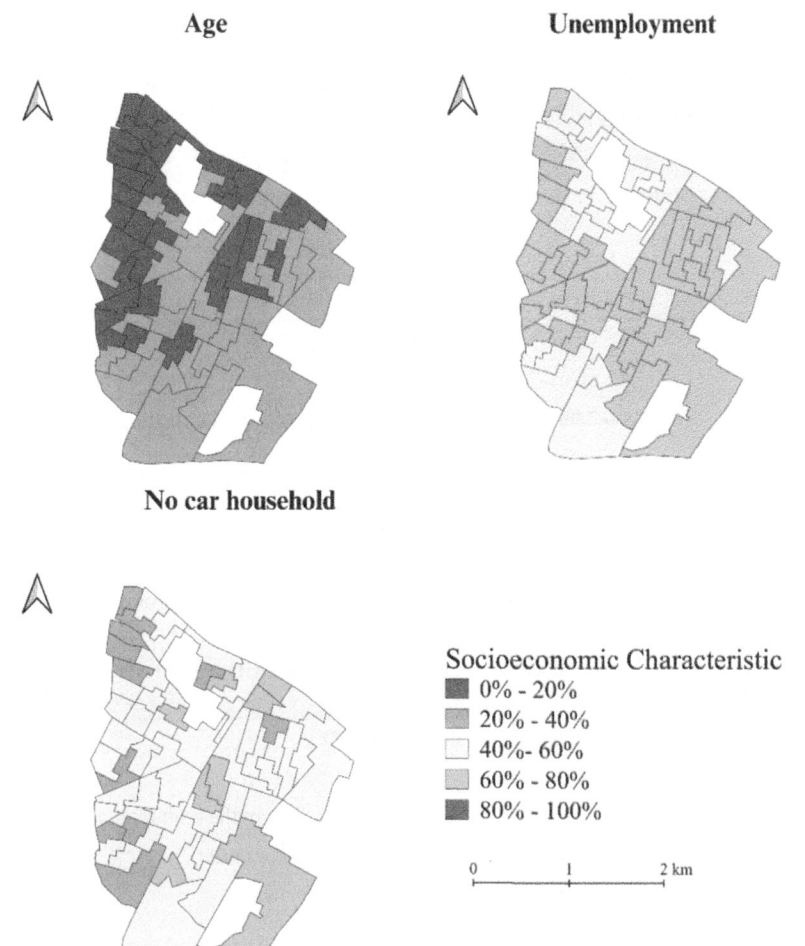

Fig. 3. Distribution of the socioeconomic characteristics in the municipality (source: own elaboration).

In particular, we observe that regarding the age factor, there are 30 CAUs where residents aged under 15 or over 65 make up to 10% of the population. Additionally, 33 CAUs exhibit a higher concentration of these age groups, reaching up to 20% of the population. Regarding the unemployment, 26 CAUs fall within the 20–30% category, while 37 CAUs belong to the 30–40% category. Lastly, in terms of households without personal car, 11 CAUs fall within the 10–20% range, 44 CAUs within 20–30%, and 8 CAUs within 30–40%.

2.2 Current Accessibility Status

An on-site survey was conducted regarding the pavement's factors, to assess the current accessibility status in the municipality. This was incorporated through the concept of "walkability index"[20] with the selection of specific subcategories, forming a checklist. The key elements included a) pavement width and b) quality, c) the presence and d) condition of tactile paving for the visually impaired, and e) the number of ramps and f) crossings. The following table (Table 1) marks the attributes and the thresholds.

Table 1. Pavement Attributes and Accessibility Thresholds

Attributes	Values (Threshold)
Pavement width	0.10 m–1.00 m
	1.10 m–1.50 m
	1.60 m–2.00 m
	>2.00 m
Pavement quality	Very low, without tiles, without cement, with numerous barriers, without curb
	Low, broken tiles, some barriers, no homogeneity of tiles or materials
	Moderate, acceptable condition of materials, not so many barriers
	Good, homogeneity of tiles, acceptable condition of materials, not so many barriers
	Very good, homogeneous material, without barriers and broken tiles
Number of curb ramps	Number of curb ramps (**over 2**)
Tactile paving	Absent
	Existent but with some differences from the requirement
	Existent and consistent with requirements
Number of crosswalks	Number of crosswalks (**over 2**)

Thresholds Justification

Regarding the pavement width, since the free pedestrian zone was recorded approximately, the threshold value was set at 1.50m, conforming to the Greek legislation standards [21]. When it comes to the pavement quality category, the chosen minimum threshold is 'moderate', as it corresponds to areas with acceptable conditions of materials, and only a few barriers. Concerning the rest of the attributes, at least two ramps and tactile paving that comply with the relevant regulations, are required to ensure accessibility for people with disabilities. Additionally, crossings at both ends of the pavement are necessary to establish continuous pedestrian routes.

The need and ability for mobility, within the vertical equity approach, is addressed through specific threshold elements, such as ramps and tactile paving. These features are designed to safeguard accessibility for individuals with varying mobility needs. Pavements are then evaluated based on how well these thresholds support the principles of vertical equity, ensuring that all individuals can access and navigate public spaces effectively. In this way, the design of pavements and urban infrastructure becomes a key factor in promoting equitable pedestrian mobility.

2.3 Socioeconomic Factors

As previously mentioned, vertical equity was examined for the unemployed, the households without a car, and citizens under 15 or over 65 years old. Lack of accessibility can cause the exclusion of the unemployed and equity in transport can be a crucial factor in attracting job opportunities [22]. Similarly, accessibility is an important factor for children under 15 years of age as pedestrian infrastructure can affect their independence and access to school, recreation, and social opportunities [23]. Regarding citizens over 65, pedestrian accessibility is considered as an important factor for their health status [24]. Last, households without cars are dependent on public transport and walking as without these modes, they have limited access to work, health, and services [25].

2.4 Accessibility Rate

Subsequently, the Accessibility Index (A) was developed as the primary means of measurement. This index is defined as follows (Eq. 1):

$$A = \frac{length\ of\ fair\ pavements}{total\ length\ of\ pavements}\% \qquad (1)$$

This simple indicator incorporates the evaluation of pavements relying on the aforementioned threshold levels. It represents an index focusing on accessibility for individuals with different mobility needs and abilities. Specifically, it evaluates pavements in an essence of a checklist where all thresholds simultaneously apply. This index is based on a similar index found in [13] that measured sufficiency through the ratio of active travel-oriented streets to the total length of streets in each neighbourhood.

2.5 Gini Index and Lorenz Curves

After measuring the accessibility index for each CAU in the study area, we used the Gini Index and the Lorenz Curves to address horizontal equity. A high value of Gini Index indicates that accessibility is unevenly distributed, with some areas receiving significantly better services than others. In contrast, low values of the index indicate a more balanced distribution of urban resources. In the present study, the application of the index was used to examine the distribution of fair pavements across the population of each CAU.

The analysis of the Gini Index in street space development contributes to the formulation of policies aimed at reducing inequalities, ensuring that accessibility is fair and more inclusive for the entire population. Therefore, as previously mentioned, it serves as a simple tool for evaluating horizontal equity of accessibility in the study area. The Gini index can be calculated using Eq. 2 [26]:

$$G = 1 - \sum_{k=1}^{n} (X_k - X_{k-1}) * (Y_k + Y_{k-1}) \tag{2}$$

X_k: is the cumulative proportion of the population in CAU k.

Y_k: is the cumulated proportion of the accessibility of CAU k.

2.6 Bivariate Local Moran's I

The Bivariate Local Moran's I is a very powerful statistical tool that explores the spatial patterns between two variables [27]. It serves as an assessment of vertical equity regarding the socioeconomic status and an evaluation of scenarios in the most burdensome CAUs. This is calculated through Eq. 3.

$$I_i = \frac{(x_i - \bar{x})}{\sum_{j=1}^{n}(y_i - \bar{y})^2/n} \times \sum_{j=1}^{n} W_{ij}(y_i - \bar{y}) \tag{3}$$

I_i is the Bivariate Local Moran's I statistic for CAU i.

x_i and y_i are the values of the two variables, e.g., accessibility and unemployment at CAU i.

x_i and y _i are the means of the two variables across all CAUs.

W_ij represents the spatial weights between CAU i and neighbours j (queen contiguity weights in this case).

n is the total number of CAUs.

This equation evaluates the relation between the values of two variables at a specific location i and their corresponding values in neighbouring locations, taking into account spatial weights (e.g., based on geographical boundaries). It determines whether there is a clustering of similar values (High-High or Low-Low), contrasting values (High-Low or Low-High), or no spatial association, with a 5% confidence level [28]. In this study, the Bivariate Moran's I is used to analyse the connection between proportional accessibility differences and key socioeconomic factors such as unemployment, age and no-car households.

2.7 Scenarios Formulation

The research progressed with the development of scenarios to analyse the problem, with the existing situation defined as Scenario 0 (S0). This scenario forms the basis for building the subsequent scenarios. Scenario 1 (S1) incorporated the green routes from the SUMP of the municipality. In these areas, pavement conditions were improved by assigning them their best possible values. The next scenario (S2) focused on conventional interventions, common measures that municipalities typically implement to enhance pavement accessibility. These included the installation of tactile paving for visually impaired pedestrians, the construction of ramps for people with disabilities, and the marking of pedestrian crossings. As conventional interventions we considered those that slightly improve the pedestrian accessibility index, while not claiming additional urban space like curb ramps and tactile paving [29].

For the following scenario 3 (S3), an assessment was conducted based on the social characteristics of the CAUs. The analysis identified the 90th quantile (i.e., the worst 10%) for each characteristic to pinpoint the most vulnerable areas, where pavement conditions were subsequently improved. Scenario 4 (S4) was designed to drastically improve pedestrian mobility around metro stations and key municipal services. A three-minute walking radius was defined, within which pavement conditions were substantially upgraded. Finally, the last scenario (S5) was developed based on the outcomes from S0. The CAUs identified as the most vulnerable, characterised by a high socio-economic burden and low accessibility, according to bivariate Local Moran's I analysis, underwent significant improvements.

The structure of the scenarios is designed to enhance a specific aspect of equity in each case. Scenarios that involve the universal implementation of measures (1, 2, and 4) without incorporating socio-economic factors into their policies focus on horizontal equity, as well as vertical equity in terms of mobility needs and capabilities. On the other hand, scenarios that introduce targeted interventions in CAUs with disadvantaged socio-economic indicators (3 and 5) aim to improve vertical equity in both its dimensions: mobility needs and capabilities, as well as socio-economic status.

3   Results

In this section, we present the results as derived from the implementation of the checklist method. Firstly, we demonstrate the existing pavement conditions (fair or poor) per segment. Next, the final outcomes of the accessibility rate will be presented. Afterwards, the evaluation of horizontal equity through the Gini index and the Lorenz curves will take place and finally, the vertical equity will be revealed by the Bivariate local Moran's I analysis via a detailed illustration of bivariate clusters (accessibility and socio-economic factor) as found in similar studies [27].

Initially, the above map (Fig. 4) illustrates the outcome of the pavement assessment based on their characteristics and the defined thresholds. Pavements that meet the thresholds are shown in blue, while those with the lowest performance are highlighted in red. Among the total pavements, only 8% successfully met the established thresholds. Subsequently, the Accessibility Index A was calculated per CAU across all scenarios. The figure below (Fig. 5) portrays the results for each scenario, categorised according to the index percentages.

It is clearly demonstrated that none of the scenarios can overcome completely today's troublesome condition. However, some scenarios achieve moderate to high values of pedestrian accessibility, signifying that solutions tailored to pedestrians and people with disabilities could promote change to spatial allocation practices. Focusing on each scenario separately, we may find that the existing situation (S0) is characterised by relatively low percentages of accessibility, with only CAUS out of 63 exceeding 20%. When it comes to S1, i.e., the SUMP proposals scenario, accessibility conditions are substantially better compared to S0 with 2 CAUs exceeding 60%, 7 CAUs found in the 40–60%

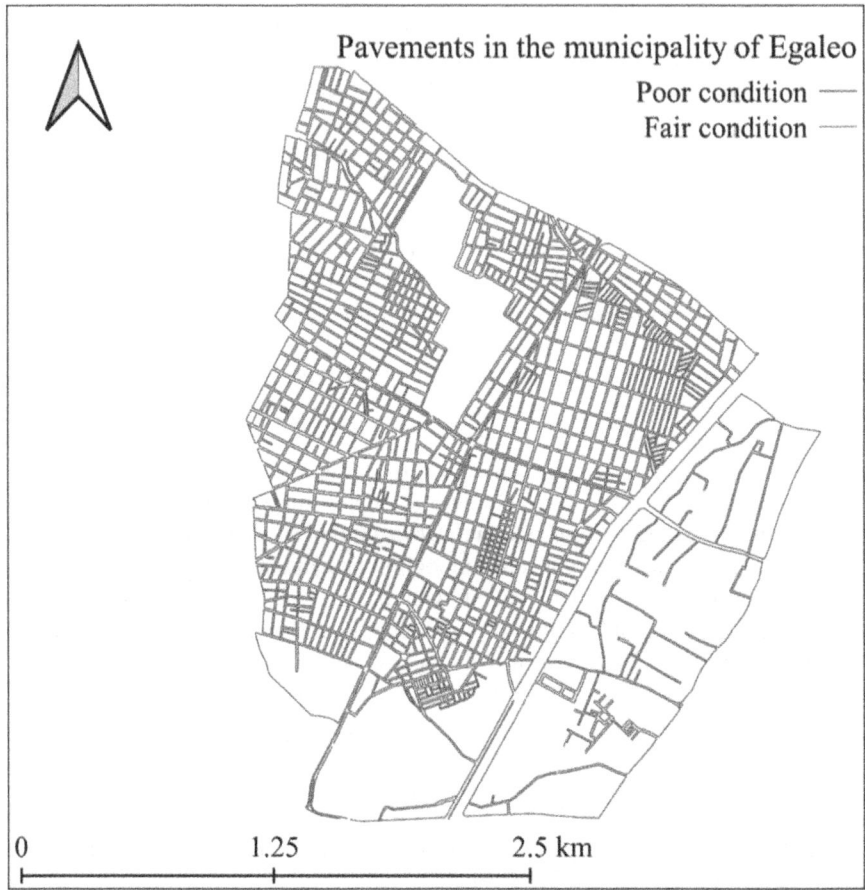

Fig. 4. Current pavement conditions in the municipality of Egaleo (source: own elaboration).

and 13 in 20–40% category. Moving on, the conventional interventions scenario (S2) did not manage to bring about sincere changes in pedestrian accessibility distribution. Only some minor changes are found and specifically, 4 CAUs fall now into the 40–60% category and 12 into the 20–40% category. At the next scenario (S3), conditions related to accessibility are clearly better than S0; nevertheless, values do not reach a high standard. In contrast, S4 articulating radical solutions around key land uses achieves high values of pedestrian accessibility, with even some CAUs (4) exceeding 80%. Finally, the social equity-based scenario leads to very meaningful changes towards better pedestrian accessibility with several CAUs falling into the 60–80% category.

Apart from pedestrian accessibility which is one key factor pinpointing the conditions in which people move around the study area, we shed light on the way this accessibility scores are distributed throughout the entire area. The initial assessment of equity, related with the horizontal aspect, was conducted using the Gini Index. The index examined the distribution of pedestrian accessibility based on the population of

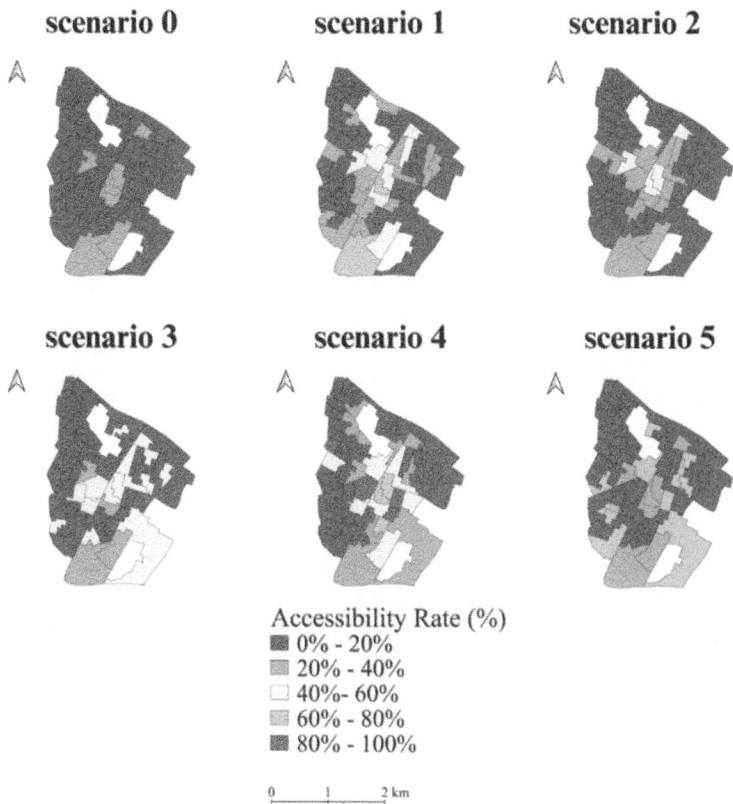

Fig. 5. Accessibility index CAUs. (source: own elaboration).

each CAU, unveiling that S1 achieves the most equitable conditions, whereas S5 leads to the most unbalanced distribution. These outcomes are distinctly displayed in the next Figure (Fig. 6), accompanied by the Lorenz curve of each scenario.

Next, the analysis of the vertical aspect of equity is conducted using the Bivariate Local Moran's I (Fig. 7). The results of the analysis are presented as separate visualisations with colour gradients, illustrating the correlation between the two variables-accessibility and socio-economic factors:

- High Accessibility-High Socioeconomic factor (HH) – Areas where both variables have high values, shown in red (desired).
- Low Accessibility -Low Socioeconomic factor (LL) – Areas where both variables have low values, shown in blue.
- High Accessibility -Low Socioeconomic factor (HL) – Areas with high accessibility and low social burden, shown in pink.
- Low Accessibility -High Socioeconomic factor (LH) – The opposite of HL, shown in light blue (troublesome).

The observation of the multiple separate visualisations unveils major differences between the socio-economic factors, but similarities within them. Desired clusters (HH)

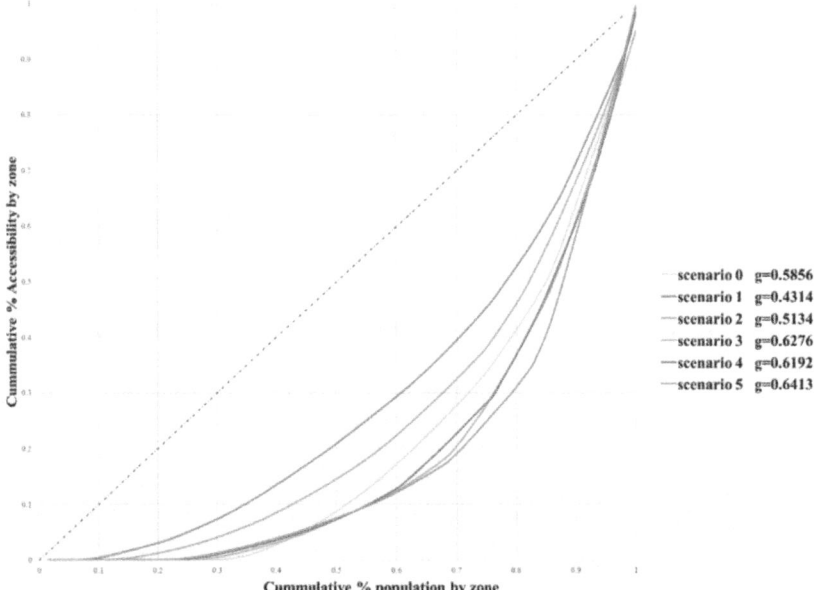

Fig. 6. Gini index and Lorenz curves per scenario (source: own elaboration).

are mainly found in the centre of Egaleo in case of cars and age, while in the southern part when referring to unemployment. On the other hand, troublesome clusters (HL) are encountered in the peripheral parts of the municipality in all scenarios. Notably, among the scenarios, we should stress that S5 leads to fairly different outcomes compared to the rest by achieving the lowest number of troublesome clusters.

4 Discussion

This paper explored one of the most important attributes in urban street space, pedestrian accessibility [20]. It not only examined the current situation, but also developed five new future pathways that might improve pedestrian accessibility levels in the study area. In other words, it comprises a study with contribution both for today and for tomorrow.

Looking into the findings, it should be noted that the existing condition of the study area is found to be inadequate for pedestrians and people with disabilities, regardless of their socio-economic characteristics. Tellingly, accessibility of Egaleo exhibits significant problems. As noted above, the multicriteria assessment of pavements through a comprehensive checklist, revealed their poor condition, with notable shortcomings in ramps, tactile paving for the visually impaired, and pedestrian crossings. Indicatively, 18 CAUs have zero accessible pavement length, while only 8% of the overall pavements are considered accessible in the study area. Through Fig. 4 we may understand more comprehensively the spatial distribution of this issue. Segments with fair pavements are mainly located within the central area of Egaleo or around metro stations and universities. These results are also encountered in other similar studies addressing pedestrian accessibility in urban areas [16, 17].

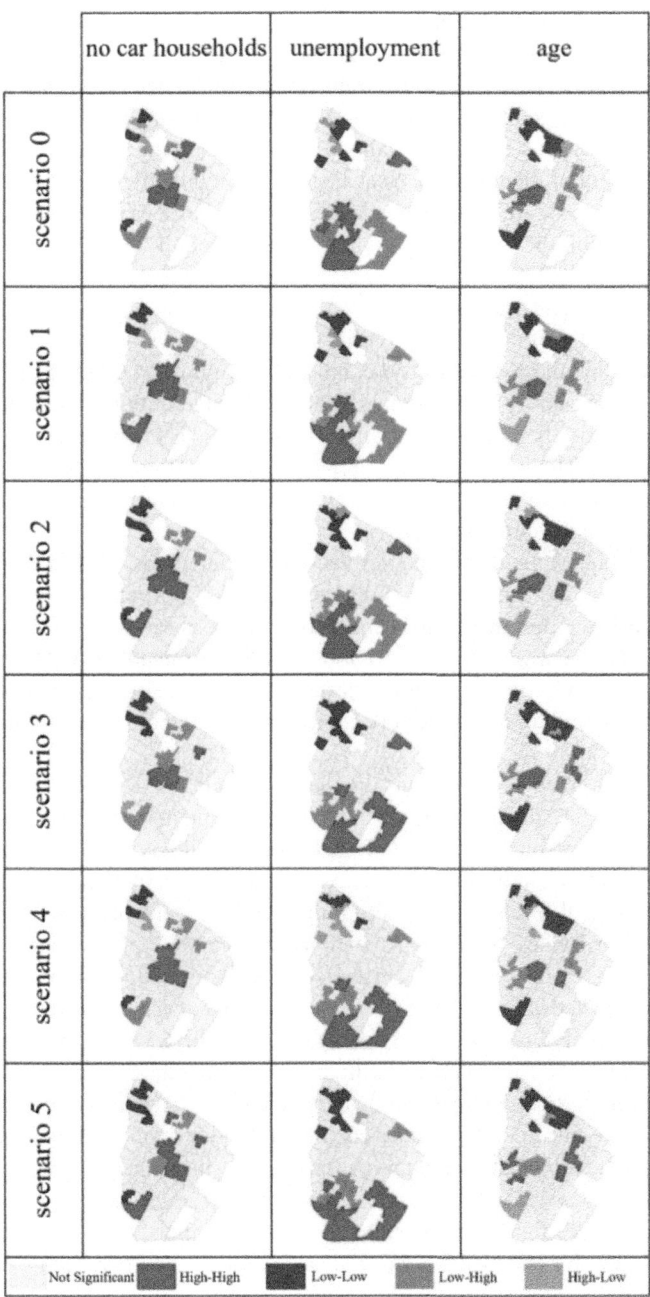

Fig. 7. Bivariate Local Moran's I results (source: own elaboration).

Continuing with equity, the analysis of the Gini index demonstrates that S1 (SUMP scenario) is the strategy that ensures the greatest horizontal equity in pedestrian accessibility. Radical strategies are also favourable to horizontal equity in other cases as well [13]. This outcome is quite expected, as the green corridors proposed by SUMP are evenly distributed across the municipality's territory. Delving more into the results of this index, we should mention that Scenarios 3 (90% quantile) and 5 (equity-based), which aim to improve CAUs with high socio-economic burdens (these two scenarios are very similar), exhibit the highest levels of horizontal inequity (though lower than other contexts like [17]).

Regarding the Bivariate Local Moran's I index that depicts the vertical aspect, the focus is on the category Low (accessibility) – High (socioeconomic factor), which is represented in light blue. Scenarios 0–4 exhibit an average of 14 CAUs with high vertical inequity, whereas Scenario 5, which includes targeted interventions based on the existing conditions (Scenario 0), reduces inequalities to 9 CAUs. This outcome is confirmed by relevant literature. Though not directly related with walking, but with cycling, Mora et al. [30] and Pritchard et al. [31] highlighted the potential negative effects of future scenarios appraising cycling on equity.

Focusing more explicitly on the vertical equity outcomes, it is identified that the interventions proposed by S1 have minimal impact on vertical equity, regardless of social characteristics, despite being the most equitable scenario in terms of the horizontal aspect. S2 involving conventional interventions, shows an increase in CAUs with vertical equity and a lower Gini index than the current state. This suggests that, despite their simplicity, such interventions positively contribute to equitable accessibility within the study area.

Following, targeted interventions in the most burdened areas based on socio-economic factors (S3), do not bring substantial improvements to the study area's overall condition, as revealed by the Bivariate Local Moran's I index. This indicates that "untargeted" interventions in disadvantaged areas does not constitute a solution at either a horizontal or vertical level. In S4, where improvements were suggested around points of interest within Egaleo (e.g., metro stations, universities, public services), vertical inequity increases compared to the current state, without distinct improvements. This outcome was expected, as points of interest are not evenly distributed throughout the area, failing to cover the entire population adequately. Finally, S5 which proposes targeted interventions relying on the data from the existing situation (S0), exhibits significant improvements in vertical equity, significantly reducing CAUs classified as LH. However, this outcome intriguingly contradicts the Gini index results (highest value among all scenarios) indicating that such interventions do not simultaneously ensure horizontal equity.

To define a pedestrian-friendly strategy for similar areas, this research proposes a combined solution for enhancing pedestrian accessibility incorporating:

- S1 (SUMP), which includes routes distributed across the study area to ensure accessibility for the entire population (horizontal equity)
- S5 (Equity-based), which includes targeted interventions in areas identified as troublesome in the analysis of the existing situation (vertical equity)

Neither of the two scenarios are sufficient on their own. Hence, a multidimensional approach to planning is essential, integrating both spatial and socio-economic dimensions to achieve "complete" equity, both horizontal and vertical, in urban transportation accessibility within the study area. This cohesive strategy might be very helpful, especially for areas with poor pedestrian infrastructure.

5 Conclusions

The present research shed light on pedestrian accessibility in a rather challenging context, unveiling insights for policy recommendations that could be beneficial to policymakers and planners. Exploring future pathways is surely critical for making cities and towns accessible and equitable. A key outcome of this study is that future solutions should be combinatorial and that equity cannot be achieved, without addressing socio-demographic characteristics properly. Apart from the insights delivered, this research contributes to the development of evaluation methods and tools related to the horizontal and vertical aspect of pedestrian accessibility, as reflected by pavements. It is very important that it looks both into today and into the future. Employing scenarios is also an asset of this study.

Notwithstanding, despite its useful contribution, this research has certainly several limitations. First and foremost, as recent data are not available yet, we utilised sociodemographic data referring to 2011 (as these were the only available); today's socio-economic realm might be very different. Moreover, another limitation is the absence of valid data related to people with disabilities in Athens. Obtaining such data would be very meaningful in calculating vertical equity. Additionally, the index developed in this study, was a rather simple (though understandable) index, mostly resembling a checklist exceeding some thresholds. Last, recording all these detailed data of pavements is truly a labour-intensive work; therefore, we believe that advanced techniques for mapping streets via image recognition, undoubtedly have a role to play.

As future steps, we recommend that new papers could implement this method into diverse areas and carry out comparative analysis to obtain more generalisable results. Apparently, the simplicity of our method facilitates its application to varying urban contexts (metropolitan areas, large or small cities and towns). The essential data for reproducing the pedestrian accessibility analysis are the (detailed) pavements' attributes, while regarding the equity evaluation one needs to know the sociodemographic characteristics of the study area. What is more, for going beyond the existing situation, new studies should place particular emphasis on well-structured and clear planning scenarios. Tellingly, more scenarios could be tested and more sociodemographic characteristics (minorities, gender, people with disabilities, etc.) could be integrated in the future. Finally, new research attempts could try to enrich the present index by integrating models and weights. For instance, methods like Analytical Hierarchy Process or Multicriteria decision analysis (REGIME, DELPHI, etc.) could be very useful towards that direction. Adding weights to the index is expected to advance the method demonstrated in this paper and enhance the reliability of the outcomes. Plus, this index could include more characteristics of infrastructure (streetscape design) and land uses.

References

1. Ma, L., Kent, J.L., Mulley, C.: Transport disadvantage, social exclusion, and subjective well-being: the role of the neighborhood environment—evidence from Sydney, Australia. J. Transp. Land Use **11**(1), 31–47 (2018)
2. Su, S., Pi, J., Xie, H., Cai, Z., Weng, M.: Community deprivation, walkability, and public health: highlighting the social inequalities in land use planning for health promotion. Land Use Policy **67**, 315–326 (2017)
3. Fainstein, S.S.: The just city. Int. J. Urban Sci. **18**(1), 1–18 (2013)
4. Curl, A.: The importance of understanding perceptions of accessibility when addressing transport equity: a case study in Greater Nottingham, UK. J. Transp. Land Use **11**(1), 1147–1162 (2018)
5. Titheridge, H., Achuthan, K., Mackett, R.L., Solomon, J.: Assessing the extent of transport social exclusion among the elderly. J. Transp. Land Use **2**(2), 31–48 (2009)
6. van Wee, B.: How suitable is CBA for the ex-ante evaluation of transport projects and policies? A discussion from the perspective of ethics. Transp. Policy **19**(1), 1–7 (2012)
7. Martens, K.: Transport Justice. Routledge (2016)
8. Van Wee, B., Geurs, K.: Discussing equity and social exclusion in accessibility evaluations. Eur. J. Transp. Infrastruct. Res. **11**(4), 350–367 (2011)
9. Vasconcellos, E.A.: Urban Transport Environment and Equity. Routledge (2014)
10. Caggiani, L., Camporeale, R., Binetti, M., Ottomanelli, M.: A road network design model considering horizontal and vertical equity: Evidences from an empirical study. Case Stud. Transp. Policy **5**, 392–399 (2017)
11. Pereira, R.H.M., Schwanen, T., Banister, D.: Distributive justice and equity in transportation. Transp. Rev. **37**(2), 170–191 (2017)
12. Barmpas, G., Georgiadis, G., Nikolaidou, A., Katkadigkas, R., Tsakiris, D.: Evaluating pedestrian environments: evidence from small cities in Greece. In: Nathanail, E.G., Adamos, G., Karakikes, I. (eds.) Advances in Mobility-as-a-Service Systems. CSUM 2020. Advances in Intelligent Systems and Computing, vol. 1278, pp. 595–605. Springer, Cham (2021)
13. Tsigdinos, S.: Examining the impact of different street classification scenarios on active transportation equity. Insights from Athens, Greece. J. Regional City Plann. **35**(1), 1–20 (2024)
14. Arellana, J., Alvarez, V., Oviedo, D., Guzman, L., A.: Walk this way: pedestrian accessibility and equity in Barranquilla and Soledad, Colombia. Res. Transp. Econ. **86**, 101024 (2021)
15. Herrmann-Lunecke, M.G., Mora, R., Sagaris, L.: Persistence of walking in Chile: lessons for urban sustainability. Transp. Rev. **40**(2), 135–159 (2020)
16. Khattak, M.M.H., Khan, M.A., Din, S.U., Khan, M.Z., Habib, M.F.: Examining equity of walking accessibility to green spaces: a case study of Islamabad. Ain Shams Eng. J. **14**(12), 102556 (2023)
17. Li, Z., Fan, Z., Song, Y., Chai, Y.: Assessing equity in park accessibility using a travel behavior-based G2SFCA method in Nanjing, China. J. Transp. Geogr. **96**, 103179 (2021)
18. Choi, Y., Guhathakurta, S.: Do people walk more in transit-accessible places? J. Transp. Land Use **13**(1), 343–365 (2020)
19. Hellenic Statistical Authority. Panoramaps2. https://panoramaps2.statistics.gr/. Accessed 27 Mar 2025
20. Bartzokas-Tsiompras, A., Bakogiannis, E., Nikitas, A.: Global microscale walkability ratings and rankings: a novel composite indicator for 59 European city centres. J. Transp. Geogr. **111**, 103645 (2023)
21. Ministry of Environment and Energy: National Plan for Accessibility with emphasis on Climate Change-Climate Crisis (2022)

22. Lucas, K.: Transport and social exclusion: where are we now? Transp. Policy **20**, 105–113 (2012)

23. Forsyth, A.: What is a walkable place? The walkability debate in urban design. Urban Design Int. **20**, 274–292 (2015)

24. Loo, B.P.Y., Lam, W.W.Y.: Geographic accessibility around health care facilities for elderly residents in Hong Kong: a microscale walkability assessment. Environ. Plann. B. Plann. Des. **39**(4), 629–646 (2012)

25. Lucas, K., Mattioli, G., Verlinghieri, E., Guzman, A.: Transport poverty and its adverse social consequences. Proc. Inst. Civ. Eng. – Transp. **169**, 353–365 (2016)

26. Brown, M.C.: Using gini-style indices to evaluate the spatial patterns of health practitioners: theoretical considerations and an application based on Alberta data. Soc Sci Med **38**(9), 1243–1256 (1994)

27. Shiode, N., Morita, M., Shiode, S., Okunuki, K.: Urban and rural geographies of aging: a local spatial correlation analysis of aging population measures. Urban Geogr. **35**(4), 608–628 (2014)

28. Zhang, Y., Liu, Y., Zhang, Y., Liu, Y., Zhang, G., Chen, Y.: On the spatial relationship between ecosystem services and urbanization: a case study in Wuhan, China. Sci. Total. Environ. **637–638**, 780–790 (2018)

29. MacKnight, H., Ohlms, P., Chen, T.D.: Curb ramp and accessibility element upgrade prioritization: a literature review and analysis of multi-state survey data. J. Accessibil. Design All **12**(1), 134–154 (2022)

30. Mora, R., Truffello, R., Oyarzún, G.: Equity and accessibility of cycling infrastructure: an analysis of Santiago de Chile. J. Transp. Geogr. **91**, 102964 (2021)

31. Pritchard, J.P., Tomasiello, D.B., Giannotti, M., Geurs, K.: Potential impacts of bike-and-ride on job accessibility and spatial equity in São Paulo, Brazil. Transp. Res. Part A: Policy Pract. **121**, 386–400 (2019)

Understanding the Gender Gap in the Acceptance of Automated Vehicles: International Mobility Study Across 17 Countries

Guilhermina Torrao[1]([⊠]) [iD] and Esko Lehtonen[2] [iD]

[1] Aston University, Aston Street, Birmingham B4 7ET, UK
g.torrao@aston.ac.uk
[2] VTT Technical Research Centre of Finland Ltd., P.O. Box 1000, 02044 Espoo, Finland

Abstract. The common assumption is that men are more likely to accept auto-mated vehicles (AVs) than women. However, studies have produced mixed results regarding this gender gap. Additionally, there is limited understanding of how the gender gap in the intention to use AVs might vary between countries.

This study aims to enhance the understanding of the gender gap in willingness to use AVs and how this gap might differ across various countries. To accomplish this, survey data from 18,631 respondents across 17 countries: Brazil, China, Finland, France, Germany, Hungary, India, Indonesia, Italy, Japan, Russia, Spain, South Africa, Sweden, Turkey, the UK, and the US, was analyzed. In this research, the gender gap in willingness to use AVs is defined as the difference in willingness to use AVs between men and women. The results indicate that gender differences in willingness to use AVs are not universal; some countries show opposing trends between men and women, while in others, the gender difference is not statistically significant. This study contributes to existing literature by examining the influence of gender and country on the willingness to use AVs. The findings have the potential to significantly impact policy development and transport planning by promoting gender inclusivity in future transport solutions, ensuring that all potential users can benefit from adopting AVs.

Keywords: Automated vehicles · country · gender gap · willingness to use · and future transport

1 Introduction

1.1 Background

Future mobility presents automated vehicles (AVs) as advantageous solutions for improv-ing road safety by preventing collisions and reducing human error, optimizing traffic flow, enhancing fuel efficiency, and generating environmental benefits. Additionally, AVs can increase accessibility for individuals who cannot drive and create opportuni-ties to improve transport equity across different user groups by enhancing accessibility

O. Gervasi et al. (Eds.): ICCSA 2025 Workshops, LNCS 15899, pp. 20–34, 2026.
https://doi.org/10.1007/978-3-031-97663-6_2

and mobility in underserved areas. Despite all these potential benefits, public acceptance remains critical for their successful integration into the transport systems. Public acceptance of AVs technology varies across different regions and demographic groups.

Men are often perceived as being more technologically inclined than women [1]. A study found that most enthusiasts of AVs were male, younger, and more knowledgeable about conditionally automated cars [2]. These individuals expected improvements in the productive use of travel time, comfort, and safety due to the adoption of AVs [2]. Other studies indicate that younger people of both genders tend to express more enthusiasm for AV technology; however, the gender gap persists across all age groups [3, 4].

Several research studies have reported gender differences in the acceptance of AVs, with men generally showing higher levels of acceptance than women. This difference is referred to as the "gender gap" in the acceptance of AVs, as defined in [5]. The following section presents literature that discusses this gender gap in the overall acceptance of AVs.

1.2 Previous Literature Studies

Studies conducted at the country level have shown that men generally have a higher acceptance of AVs compared to women. This trend suggests the possible impact that societal, cultural, and geographical factors can have on the adoption of AV technologies. The rapidly expanding market for AV technologies is particularly prominent in Europe, the US and China. Accordingly, this section highlights key studies conducted in various countries to provide a comparative perspective on public acceptance and behavioral intentions related to the acceptance of AVs.

Nordhoff and Lehtonen (2025) applied one of the most influential technology acceptance models, the Unified Theory of Acceptance and Use of Technology (UTAUT2), to investigate behavioral intentions toward conditionally automated vehicles. This study found that the influence of facilitating conditions, hedonic motivation, driver engagement, and the moderating effects of age and gender was not significant in most countries [6]. However, the existing literature continues to primarily focus on single-country contexts. For example, Zhu et al. (2024) also employed the UTAUT model to examine the factors influencing the intention to use fully automated taxis in China. Their findings indicated gender differences in the acceptance of autonomous vehicles (AVs). Social influence and perceived safety risks have a more significant impact on women, while men's intention to adopt AVs is notably influenced by their previous knowledge of the technology [7]. In Europe, several studies have explored public acceptance of AVs, with a particular focus on demographic factors such as age and gender. A study conducted in Hungary by Jászberényi et al. (2024) found that Hungarian respondents, particularly men and younger individuals from Generation Z or Y, are more likely to intend to try AVs technology on the roads. The study identified gender as a significant factor influencing the acceptance of AVs [8].

Similar results have been found in In Denmark [9]; in Finland [10]; and the Czech Republic [11]. Additionally, a study in Germany revealed that women rated the positive aspects of AVs lower than men and expressed greater concerns about the technology [12]. In the UK, research also indicated that men exhibited a more favorable attitude towards AVs compared to women [13]. Similarly, a study in the United States found that women felt less comfortable with AVs and were less willing to use them [14]. Interestingly, some studies indicate that this gender gap is not observed. In Greece, it was found no significant gender differences in the acceptance of autonomous shuttles [15]. Similarly, in Portugal no clear impact of gender on the adoption of AV technologies [16].

The general trend of men showing higher acceptance of AVs is not consistently observed across studies involving participants from various countries. These studies have yielded mixed results. Israelis were more likely to accept AVs, with men showing a more favorable attitude than women [17]. However, this gender gap was not found in North America (the US and Canada). Conversely, a study revealed that Indian women were more willing to ride in AVs than Indian men, whereas in the United States, the opposite was true [18].

The authors of this study have previously conducted a comprehensive analysis of the gender gap in the acceptance of AVs at SAE Level 3. Based on a questionnaire completed by 8,412 drivers across eight European countries, Torrao et al. (2024), found a significant gender gap in acceptance levels in Germany, the Netherlands, Sweden, and the UK [5]. In contrast, no such gap was identified in Italy, Poland, Romania, or Spain. Therefore, the authors concluded that the gender gap in the acceptance of AVs cannot be considered universal [5].

1.3 Research Gaps

Recent studies have increasingly focused on the influence of gender on the acceptance of AVs. Torrao et al. (2024) also conducted an extensive review of the literature relevant studies analyzing general attitudes and intention to use AVs, as well as how gender effects were addressed through different study design approaches [5]. The authors found that progress has been made in using more balanced datasets with respect to male and female participants. However, many studies continue to report gender differences in AV acceptance without offering clear explanations for these disparities. While some studies did propose potential explanations, those would benefit from more conclusive evidence. One commonly suggested explanation for the gender gap in acceptance of AVs relates to differences in knowledge and confidence; men generally report greater familiarity with AV technologies, which contributes to higher levels of acceptance [8].

Only a few studies have explored the reasons behind observed gender differences. For instance, two studies conducted in Germany offered the following insights. One study suggested that men experience anticipation of pleasure rather than anxiety when it comes to AVs, which may explain their higher willingness to use them. In contrast, women tend to experience anxiety instead [19]. Another study pointed out that women are more influenced by the perceived risks associated with AVs, while men appear less affected by such risks [20].

Emotional responses such as fear and anxiety can be influenced by broader societal and cultural factors that shape gender roles and expectations. For instance, women may be more risk-averse and cautious when approaching new technologies, while men may be more inclined to embrace innovation and take risks [3, 19]. However, Jászberényi et al. (2024) that gendered responses to AVs often arise from longstanding gender roles and socialization processes beginning in early life. In this context, gender influences the acceptance of AVs primarily through socially constructed experiences and expectations rather than inherent biological differences [8].

While public acceptance of AVs has been widely studied, relatively few investigations have addressed the gender gap in the acceptance of AV. Moreover, the limited studies that do explore this dimension report mixed and sometimes conflicting findings, as outlined in Sect. 1.2. Most of this research has been conducted in high-income countries, often with samples drawn from a single national context. Consequently, it remains unclear whether the observed gender differences along the explanations provided can be generalized globally or meaningfully account for cross-cultural variations in how men and women express their willingness to use AVs in the future.

Furthermore, to the authors' knowledge, the only study that has conducted an in-depth investigation of the gender gap in AV acceptance at a cross-country level is that of Torrao et al. (2024). This study found that the gender gap in the acceptance of AVs was observed in half of the countries analyzed (Germany, the Netherlands, Sweden, and the UK) but not in the other half (Italy, Poland, Romania, and Spain) [5].

This challenges the prevailing belief that men are more positive about AVs. The compelling evidence prompts the authors to extend their research beyond Europe to uncover valuable insights into the geographical differences in gender attitudes toward AV acceptance.

1.4 Study Aim

This study makes a relevant contribution to understanding the gender gap in willingness to use AVs by analyzing survey data collected from 17 countries across Africa, Asia, Europe, North America, and South America. While most existing research focuses on single-country or region-specific analyses, this study adopts a truly global perspective. It focuses on SAE Level 3 AVs, which are conditionally automated vehicles capable of managing all driving tasks within defined environments.

This research aims to enhance understanding of the gender gap in the acceptance of AVs through a unique cross-country analysis, measuring the willingness to use AVs between men and women in various geographic contexts. The breadth and diversity of the dataset offer insights into gender-based differences that have not been captured in the existing literature, making this one of the most comprehensive examinations to date.

2 Methods

2.1 Procedure and Recruitment

This study explored online data, which is available from the L3Pilot project, which tested conditionally automated driving functions for SAE Level 3 (L3) vehicles on European roads. The project evaluated the effects of conditionally automated vehicles on driving behavior and assessed their impacts on safety, efficiency, the environment, socioeco-nomics, and user acceptance. An extensive online survey was conducted with 18,631 respondents from 17 countries to investigate individual differences in the acceptance of conditionally automated vehicles. These countries include Brazil, China, Finland, France, Germany, Hungary, India, Indonesia, Italy, Japan, Russia, Spain, South Africa, Sweden, Turkey, the UK, and the US. The selected countries were chosen for their diverse car markets and geographical locations. The survey aimed to assess differences in age, gender, knowledge of conditionally automated vehicles, and their expected benefits.

Data collection took place from April 2019 to April 2020, targeting a sample repre-sentative of the country's population in terms of age and gender, specifically focusing on individuals who drive frequently. The data sample for each country was designed to reflect the demographics of age, gender, and income for their population and among frequent drivers.

The survey data is public available at Zenodo and details have been publish [21].

2.2 Procedure and Recruitment

This study uses data from the first data collection phase of the L3Pilot Global User Acceptance Survey.

Responders were first presented with instructions about what a conditionally auto-mated vehicle, SAE Level 3, could perform to ensure that they understood how this conditionally automated vehicle operated. The introduction to the survey included the following statement:

"Conditionally automated cars do the steering, acceleration and braking. They will stay in the lane and maintain a safe distance to the vehicle in front. They will also overtake slower moving vehicles or change lane. These are cars still have gas and brake pedals and a steering wheel." [21].

The questionnaire comprised five groups of questions:

1. Background information about participants, including age, gender, income, and travel habits.
2. Participants' understanding of the capabilities of conditionally automated cars (e.g., lane-keeping and autonomous overtaking).
3. Inquiries about whether participants had heard of automated cars before completing the questionnaire.
4. Participants' overall attitudes toward and acceptance of conditionally automated vehicles.
5. Participants express their intention to use conditional automation in various opera-tional design domains, such as urban roads and congested motorways.

Data were filtered for inconsistencies and the absence of important responses. For each questionnaire item, participants were presented with the option "I prefer not to respond." When selected, these responses were defined as missing values and excluded from the analysis.

Due to the focus on the means differences identified between men and women, the non-binary gender group (28 responders) was removed from the analysis. Due to the study's focus on mean differences between men and women, respondents who identified as non-binary (N = 28) were not included in the statistical analysis. However, the authors recognize that incorporating non-binary perspectives could offer valuable insights into the broader gender dynamics related to the acceptance of autonomous vehicles (AVs). This inclusion would be particularly relevant when the sample size is adequate to support reliable statistical analysis.

2.3 Data Analysis

Analyses were conducted using IBM SPSS Statistics version 29. To assess the intention to use conditionally automated vehicles (SAE Level 3), the two questionnaire items relevant to this study are:

- "I intend to use a conditionally automated car in the future".
- "I would use a conditionally automated car during my everyday trips".

Responses were measured on a five-point Likert scale, with a score between 1 (Strongly disagree) to 5 (Strongly agree). The mean ratings of these questions were calculated, with higher scores indicating a greater willingness to use AVs. Additionally, a new target variable "Willingness to use conditionally AVs" was computed to account for both intentions to use in the future and during everyday trips. This new target variable was computed as follows:

Willingness to use conditionally AVs = ("Intention to use conditionally AVs in the future" + "Intention to use a conditionally AVs in everyday trips")/2.

The gender gap in the willingness to use conditionally AVs was investigated as follows:

- Gender Means Difference of intention to use conditionally AVs in the future = Mean intention to use conditionally AVs in the future (men)-Mean intention to use conditionally AVs in the future(women).
- Gender Means Difference of intention to use conditionally AVs during everyday trips = Mean intention to use conditionally AVs during everyday trips (men)-Mean intention to use conditionally AVs during everyday trips (women).
- Gender Means Difference of willingness to use conditionally AVs = Mean intention to use conditionally AVs during everyday trips (men)-Mean intention to use conditionally AVs during everyday trips (women).

Non-parametric Mann-Whitney U tests and t-tests were conducted to assess the differences between men and women in the overall sample and within each country.

This study focuses on assessing the intention to use conditionally automated vehicles (SAE Level 3). This nomenclature is simplified by the abbreviation 'AVs,' which can represent any level of automation, including Level 3.

3 Results and Discussion

3.1 Participants

Table 1 provides an overview of the participants' ages and genders for the overall sample and for each country. After data filtering and curation, the final sample comprises 18,424 participants, with an average age of 40.73 years (SD = 13.62). Participants were recruited from each country to ensure a representative sample of the national population, along with a balanced representation of male and female participants. This balance enhances the reliability of the data analysis, which aims to investigate the gender gap in ratings concerning the intention to use AVs.

Table 1. Participants age and gender summary statistics (N = 18,424).

Country	Age (years)			Gender	
	N	M[a]	SD[b]	Male (%)	Female (%)
All countries	18424	40.73	13.62	50.10	49.90
Brazil	1050	37.50	12.42	49.50	50.50
China	997	37.22	11.88	50.60	49.40
Finland	1003	50.18	12.05	59.20	40.80
France	1148	42.72	13.84	47.60	52.40
Germany	1119	43.89	14.86	50.00	50.00
Hungary	1132	41.89	14.06	49.30	50.70
India	1044	35.45	11.83	51.60	48.40
Indonesia	1050	35.30	10.88	51.10	48.90
Italy	1161	42.73	13.24	50.30	49.70
Japan	1070	45.06	13.45	49.40	50.60
Russia	1067	37.69	11.80	46.30	53.70
South Africa	1063	35.50	12.74	47.50	52.50
Spain	1068	42.17	12.38	50.60	49.40
Sweden	1148	42.54	14.92	52.30	47.70
Turkey	1054	37.17	11.78	50.10	49.90
UK	1203	41.25	13.70	49.30	50.70
US	1046	43.58	14.44	47.80	52.20

[a] Mean; [b] Standard Deviation

3.2 Overall Willingness to Use Conditionally AVs

Overall, participants expressed a positive intention to use AVs, as indicated in Table 2. Men reported a higher intention to use AVs in the future, with a mean rating of M = 3.61 (SD = 1.13), compared to women, who had a mean rating of M = 3.50 (SD = 1.16). Additionally, male participants demonstrated a greater intention to use AVs for everyday trips compared to their female counterparts.

For this study, a new target variable was created to assess both the intention to use AVs in the future and the intention to use AVs for everyday trips. This variable, labelled "willingness to use AVs", was calculated as the average of the intention to use AVs in the future and the intention to use AVs for everyday trips. The results indicated that men exhibited a higher willingness to use AVs compared to women, with a mean rating of M = 3.64 (SD = 1.01) for men, while women had a mean rating of M = 3.54 (SD = 1.06).

The difference in ratings between genders was statistically significant (p < 0.001), as indicated in Tables 2 and 3. This finding highlights a gender gap in the intention to use AVs among the larger sample of 18,424 participants, which included 50.10% males and responders from 17 countries.

Table 2. Participants intention to use AVs (SAE Level 3) in the future and for everyday trips, based on overall data (N = 18,424).

Item	Males			Females			Gender Difference (Males – Females)	
	N	M[a]	SD[b]	N	M[a]	SD[b]	MD[c]	SED[d]
Intention to use AVs in the future	9232	3.61	1.13	9192	3.50	1.16	**0.11*****	0.02
Intention to use AVs for everyday trips	9232	3.68	1.11	9192	3.58	1.14	**0.09*****	0.02

[a] Mean; [b] Standard Deviation; [c] Mean Difference; [d] Standard Error Difference
***: p < 0.001

Table 3. Participants willingness to use AVs (SAE Level 3) computed as (Intention to use AVs in the future + Intention to use AVs for everyday trips)/2, based on overall data (N = 18,424).

Item	Males			Females			Gender Difference (Males – Females)	
	N	M[a]	SD[b]	N	M[a]	SD[b]	MD[c]	SED[d]
Willingness to use AVs	9232	3.64	1.01	9192	3.54	1.06	0.10***	0.02

[a] Mean; [b] Standard Deviation; [c] Mean Difference; [d] Standard Error Difference
***: p < 0.001

These findings corroborate previous literature indicating generally more positive attitudes towards the acceptance of AVs among men compared to women, as shown by previous studies [7, 8, 11, 13, 22].

3.3 Gender Gap in the Willingness to Use Conditionally AVs at Country Level

The previous section identified a significant difference in the mean ratings between men and women in their willingness to use conditionally automated vehicles, referred to as AVs for simplicity in this study. Subsequently, a comprehensive investigation was conducted to determine whether the overall gender gap in the willingness to AVs follows similar trends at the country level.

This study examines the ratings of willingness to use AVs among males and females across different countries. Table 4 presents summary statistics for gender ratings regarding the willingness to use AVs across 17 countries, organized alphabetically. While men generally exhibited higher ratings for their willingness to use AVs, it is noteworthy that in a few countries, women demonstrated greater willingness than men, and those are highlighted in bold in Table 4. This was observed in China, India, Indonesia, and Turkey. For instance, women in India reported higher willingness to use AVs compared to their male counterparts, with a mean of 4.29 (SD = 0.71) for women and a mean of 4.19

(SD = 0.78) for men. This finding is interesting because it does not follow the common trend of men exhibiting a higher willingness to use AVs, as is typically reported in the literature. Moreover, this aligns with a study by Anania et al. (2018), which found that Indian women were more willing to ride in AVs than men [18]. Across the 17 countries analyzed, it is noticed that in Russia, the willingness to use AVs was similar for both men and women, with both males and females showing a mean rating of 3.70 (Table 4), still clear expression of positive attitude towards the willingness to use AVs.

Table 4. Participants willingness to use AVs (SAE Level 3) computed as (Intention to use AVs in the future + Intention to use AVs for everyday trips)/2, based on overall data (N = 18,424).

Country	Males				Females			
	N	M[a]	SD[b]	SEM[c]	N	M[a]	SD[b]	SEM[c]
Brazil	520	4.18	0.74	0.03	530	4.16	0.77	0.03
China	504	4.03	0.63	0.03	493	**4.07**	0.66	0.03
Finland	594	2.94	1.19	0.05	409	2.64	1.03	0.05
France	547	3.27	1.12	0.05	601	3.06	1.16	0.05
Germany	560	3.54	0.89	0.04	559	3.38	0.98	0.04
Hungary	558	3.67	0.93	0.04	574	3.54	0.94	0.04
India	539	4.19	0.78	0.03	505	**4.29**	0.71	0.03
Indonesia	537	4.13	0.67	0.29	513	**4.15**	0.68	0.03
Italy	584	3.58	0.90	0.04	577	3.43	0.98	0.04
Japan	529	3.32	0.90	0.04	542	3.08	0.96	0.04
Russia	494	3.70	0.91	0.04	573	3.70	0.81	0.03
South Africa	505	3.98	0.83	0.04	558	3.85	0.90	0.04
Spain	540	3.68	0.93	0.04	528	3.47	1.02	0.04
Sweden	600	3.22	1.11	0.05	548	2.95	1.12	0.05
Turkey	528	4.12	0.84	0.04	526	**4.26**	0.80	0.04
UK	593	3.23	1.14	0.05	610	3.14	1.11	0.05
US	500	3.38	1.11	0.05	546	3.14	1.07	0.05

[a] Mean; [b] Standard Deviation; and [c] Standard Error of the Mean.

In the analysis of 17 countries, it was observed that both men and women exhibited a similar willingness to use AVs in Russia. Both genders had a mean rating of 3.70 (see Table 4), indicating an evident positive attitude toward the use of AVs.

Independent samples t-tests were conducted to investigate the identified gender gaps in willingness to use AVs at the country level. The relevance of this research is supported by the findings presented in Table 5, which reveal the gender gap in the willingness to use AVs expressed by the difference in means rating between men and women. Among the 17 countries analyzed, Indonesia exhibited the smallest gender gap in the willingness to use AVs (mean difference = −0.199, SE = 0.042), while Finland demonstrated the most significant gender gap (mean difference = 0.298, SE = 0.073), which is statistically significant (p < 0.001). These findings highlight the potential reluctance of Finnish women to adopt future mobility solutions based on automated vehicles technology, a trend also observed in Sweden, the US, Japan, Spain, France, Germany, Italy, Hungary, and South Africa.

Table 5. Gender gap in the willingness to use AVs (SAE Level 3) expressed by increasing order of mean difference between males and females across 17 countries.

Country	Independent Sample Test			Effect Sizes		
	MD[a]	SED[b]	Two-Sided p	Point Estimate	Lower	Upper
Indonesia	−0.199	0.042	0.633	−0.029	−0.150	0.092
Turkey	**−0.139***	**0.051**	**0.006**	**−0.170**	**−0.290**	**−0.049**
India	**−0.102***	0.046	0.029	−0.136	−0.257	−0.014
China	−0.04	0.041	0.324	−0.062	−0.187	0.062
Russia	0.003	0.052	0.947	0.004	−0.116	0.124
Brazil	0.014	0.047	0.770	0.018	−0.103	0.139
UK	0.097	0.065	0.133	0.087	−0.026	0.200
South Africa	**0.122***	0.053	0.022	0.141	0.020	0.261
Hungary	**0.130****	0.056	0.020	0.139	0.022	0.255
Italy	**0.157****	0.055	0.005	0.167	0.051	0.282
Germany	**0.165****	0.056	0.003	0.176	0.059	0.294
France	**0.205****	0.067	0.002	0.180	0.064	0.296
Spain	**0.212*****	0.060	0.000	0.217	0.096	0.337
Japan	**0.241*****	0.057	0.000	0.258	0.138	0.379
US	**0.243*****	0.068	<.001	0.223	0.101	0.344
Sweden	**0.271*****	0.066	< .001	0.242	0.126	0.359
Finland	**0.298*****	0.073	0.000	0.264	0.137	0.390

[a] Mean Difference; [b] Standard Error Difference
*** p < 0.001; ** p < 0.01; * p < 0.05

The results presented in Table 5 indicate that the gender gap in willingness to use AVs does not follow a consistent pattern. In most countries, a statistically significant gender gap was observed in willingness to use AVs. Notably, Finland, Sweden, the United States, Japan, and Spain exhibited significant gender gaps, with p-values of less than 0.001. Particularly in Finland, which has the highest gender gap in willingness to use AVs, previous studies [10, 23] found that men tend to have a more positive attitude toward AVs compared to their female counterparts. Similarly, in the US, the results of this study support a trend of greater willingness to use AVs among men than women [24]. In contrast, no statistically significant gender gap in willingness to use AVs was found in Indonesia, China, Russia, Brazil, and the UK. Nevertheless, it is interesting to note that in Indonesia and China, women's willingness to use AVs rated higher compared to men's. The direction of the gender effect size will be explored next.

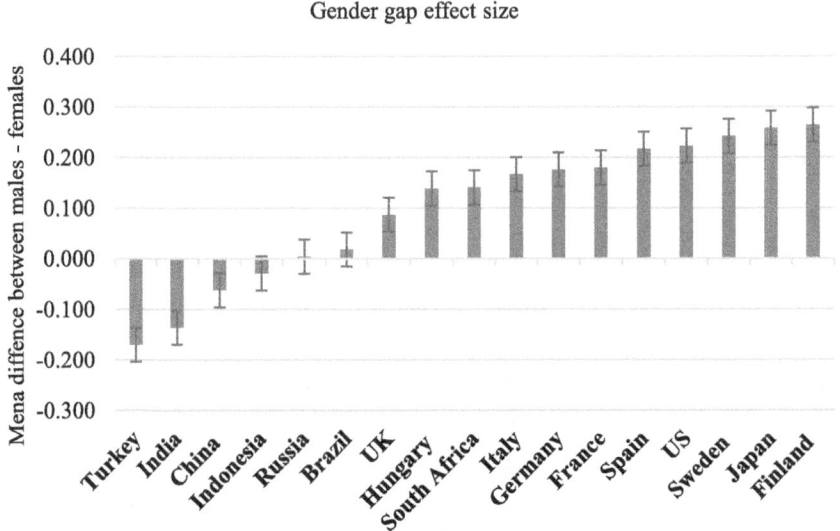

Fig. 1. Gender gap in the willingness to use AVs (SAE Level 3) and effect size across the 17 countries included in this study.

Figure 1 illustrates the effect size of the gender gap in willingness to use AVs based on Cohen's d-point estimate for the mean difference between males and females. It is evident that in most countries, the mean rating for men is higher than that for women. However, in Indonesia, Turkey, India, and China, the opposite is true, as indicated by the direction of the bars in Fig. 1. The effect size was very small for Russia, Brazil, Indonesia, and China, while it was more prominent in other countries. Although the effect size for all countries was below 0.3 (as shown by Cohen's d-point estimates in Fig. 1), the p-values indicate a statistically significant difference in willingness to use AVs between men and women in five of the 17 countries analyzed in this study. These countries: Finland, Sweden, the United States, Japan, and Spain, exhibited a significant gender gap, p-values of less than 0.001, as detailed in Table 5.

The findings gathered from this study, which covers a broader geographical representation involving 17 countries across five continents, align with a previous study by Torrao et al. (2024). That study involved participants from eight European countries and concluded that the gender gap in the acceptance of AVs did not follow a common trend; in fact, it was only observed in half of the countries [5]. As shown previously, no gender gap in the willingness to use AVs was found in Brazil, China, Indonesia, Russia, and the UK. These results corroborate the research by Nordhoff and Lehtonen (2025) gender was not significant for some countries [6]. These findings suggest that the gender gap in the acceptance of AVs cannot be considered universal and may be shaped by contextual, cultural, or societal factors specific to each country or region. These findings demonstrate that both individual characteristics and broader country-specific contexts shape gender differences in the acceptance of AVs. It is acknowledged that the intersection of other sociodemographic factors, such as age, education level, income, employment status, annual travel distance, and prior experience with driving assistance systems, may also significantly influence AV acceptance. These factors, however, were beyond the scope of the current analysis. Similarly, country-level indicators such as GDP per capita, road infrastructure quality, and road safety performance will likely affect individuals' willingness to use AVs. Although these variables were not directly examined in this study, the authors have previously conducted an in-depth analysis of gender differences in the acceptance of AVs that incorporated country indicators of societal equality and socioeconomic development. In particular, earlier work was among the first to explore the role of the Gender Equality Index (GEI) in influencing and impacting the acceptance of AVs, revealing that both GDP and GEI were strongly correlated with the gender gap.

While integrating additional sociodemographic and macro-level data would further enrich cross-national questionnaire studies, this research aimed to identify and map variations in the gender gap in willingness to use AVs across a large and diverse international sample. These findings provide a solid foundation for future research to examine the complex interplay between gender, individual attributes, and national contexts in shaping AV adoption.

3.4 Limitations

This study focused on conditionally automated vehicles, so the results may not apply to the acceptance of automated public transport, such as autonomous shared shuttles. Additionally, the analysis focused on binary gender differences (male and female) regarding the willingness to use AVs. It did not consider the diverse gender identities, including transgender and LGBTQ+ communities. It is acknowledged that other sociodemographic factors, such as participants' income, type of occupation, and country of residence, may influence the variations in the gender gap observed at the cross-country level. Nevertheless, this study benefits from a large sample of 18,424 participants who were carefully recruited to represent the demographic characteristics of each country's population, ensuring a balanced representation of gender. This enhances the reliability of the gender analysis presented in the study.

4 Conclusion

This study aimed to examine whether a gender gap exists in the willingness to use conditionally automated passenger cars (SAE Level 3) by conducting a questionnaire study across 17 countries: Brazil, China, Finland, France, Germany, Hungary, India, Indonesia, Italy, Japan, Russia, Spain, South Africa, Sweden, Turkey, the UK, and the US.

The results revealed significant gender differences in willingness to use automated vehicles in several countries. Specifically, women were found to be significantly less willing to use AVs than men in South Africa, Hungary, Italy, Germany, France, Spain,

Japan, the US, Sweden, and Finland. This indicates a gender gap in AV acceptance within these national contexts. In contrast, the pattern was reversed in Turkey and India, where women reported a higher willingness to use AVs than men. Conversely, no significant gender differences were observed in Brazil, China, Indonesia, Russia, or the UK. These findings highlight the nuanced and context-dependent nature of gender differences in the acceptance of AVs, underlining the importance of incorporating gender perspectives in future policy and design considerations related to future automated mobility.

Based on the findings of this study, three key recommendations are proposed.

- **Incorporate gender-sensitive design and testing in AVs development.** The design and testing of automated vehicles should account for comfort, communication interfaces, safety, and emergency features that address the needs of women and other underrepresented groups. This inclusive approach will help ensure that the design of AVs, user experience, and technological development are co-created with diverse user populations, ultimately enhancing accessibility and user trust.
- **Promote Gender-Inclusive Policy Strategies.** Policymakers and transport authorities should explicitly incorporate gender considerations into AV regulation, testing, deployment, and adoption strategies. Embedding gender equity within transport policy frameworks will contribute to the development of more inclusive, equitable, and socially sustainable mobility systems.
- **Conduct country-specific interventions and public engagement campaigns.** Interventions should be developed to reflect the cultural and specific perceptions within each country. Public engagement campaigns can help overcome barriers to the acceptance of AVs by addressing safety concerns, building trust, and communicating the broader benefits of AVs for diverse user groups. These efforts will support a more equitable and sustainable transition to future transport systems.

Future research will examine the underlying causes of gender differences in the willingness to use automated vehicles. Specifically, it will focus on understanding why women in some countries are less willing to use AVs, while in others, they demonstrate a greater willingness than men. Additionally, it will explore the intersectionality of gender with other demographic and contextual factors, such as income and urban or rural areas. Country-level indicators, such as GDP per capita and road safety performance, will also be considered to understand AV adoption in different contexts better.

Acknowledgments. The online survey leading to this study results was funded by the European Commission Horizon 2020 program under the project L3Pilot, grant agreement number 723051. Responsibility for the information and views set out in this publication lies entirely with the authors. The authors would like to thank partners within L3Pilot for their cooperation and valuable contribution.

Disclosure of Interests. The authors have no competing interests to declare that are relevant to the content of this article.

References

1. Kelan, E.K.: Tools and toys: communicating gendered positions towards technology. Inf. Commun. Soc. **10**(3), 358–383 (2007)
2. Nordhoff, S., et al.: Profiling the enthusiastic, neutral, and sceptical users of conditionally automated cars in 17 countries: a questionnaire study. J. Adv. Transp. **2022**(1), 8053228 (2022)
3. Tapia, J.L., Sánchez-Borda, D., Iniesta, C., Badea, F., Duñabeitia, J.A.: Shifting perceptions and emotional responses to autonomous vehicles using simulated experiences. Behav. Sci. **14**(1), 29 (2023)
4. Greenwood, P.M., Baldwin, C.L.: Preferred sources of information, knowledge, and acceptance of automated vehicle systems: effects of gender and age. Front. Psychol. **13**, 806552 (2022)
5. Torrao, G., Lehtonen, E., Innamaa, S.: The gender gap in the acceptance of automated vehicles in Europe. Transport. Res. F: Traffic Psychol. Behav. **101**, 199–217 (2024)
6. Nordhoff, S., Lehtonen, E.: Examining the effect of personality on user acceptance of conditionally automated vehicles. Sci. Rep. **15**(1), 1091 (2025)
7. Zhu, Y., Janssen, M., Pu, C.: Are men from Mars, women from Venus? Investigating the determinants behind the intention to use fully automated taxis. Transp. Lett. **16**(10), 1366–1377 (2024)
8. Jászberényi, M., Ásványi, K., Csiszár, C., Kökény, L.: Demographic and social differences in autonomous vehicle technology acceptance in Hungary. J. Eng. Tech. Manage. **72**, 101813 (2024)
9. Nielsen, T.A.S., Haustein, S.: On sceptics and enthusiasts: what are the expectations towards self-driving cars? Transp. Policy **66**, 49–55 (2018)
10. Liljamo, T., Liimatainen, H., Pöllänen, M.: Attitudes and concerns on automated vehicles. Transp. Res. F: Traffic Psychol. Behav. **59**, 24–44 (2018)
11. Havlíčková, D., Gabrhel, V., Adamovská, E., Zámečník, P.: The role of gender and age in autonomous mobility: general attitude, awareness and media preference in the context of Czech Republic. Trans. Transp. Sci. **10**(2), 53–63 (2019)
12. Weigl, K., Steinhauser, M., Riener, A.: Gender and age differences in the anticipated acceptance of automated vehicles: insights from a questionnaire study and potential for application. Gend. Technol. Dev. **27**(1), 88–108 (2023)
13. Hulse, L.M., Xie, H., Galea, E.R.: Perceptions of autonomous vehicles: relationships with road users, risk, gender and age. Saf. Sci. **102**, 1–13 (2018)
14. Wexler, N., Fan, Y.: Gauging public attitudes and preferences toward a hypothetical future public shared automated vehicle system: examining the roles of gender, race, income, and health. Transp. Res. Rec. **2676**(10), 588–600 (2022)
15. Madigan, R., Louw, T., Wilbrink, M., Schieben, A., Merat, N.: What influences the decision to use automated public transport? Using UTAUT to understand public acceptance of automated road transport systems. Transport. Res. F: Traffic Psychol. Behav. **50**, 55–64 (2017)
16. Rodrigues, R., Moura, F., Silva, A.B., Seco, Á.: The determinants of Portuguese preference for vehicle automation: a descriptive and explanatory study. Transport. Res. F: Traffic Psychol. Behav. **76**, 121–138 (2021)
17. Haboucha, C.J., Ishaq, R., Shiftan, Y.: User preferences regarding autonomous vehicles. Transp. Res. Part C: Emerg. Technol. **78**, 37–49 (2017)
18. Anania, E.C., Rice, S., Walters, N.W., Pierce, M., Winter, S.R., Milner, M.N.: The effects of positive and negative information on consumers' willingness to ride in a driverless vehicle. Transp. Policy **72**, 218–224 (2018)

19. Hohenberger, C., Spörrle, M., Welpe, I.M.: How and why do men and women differ in their willingness to use automated cars? The influence of emotions across different age groups. Transp. Res. Part A: Policy Pract. **94**, 374–385 (2016)

20. Kapser, S., Abdelrahman, M., Bernecker, T.: Autonomous delivery vehicles to fight the spread of Covid-19–How do men and women differ in their acceptance? Transp. Res. Part A: Policy Pract. **148**, 183–198 (2021)

21. Nordhoff, S., et al.: L3Pilot global user acceptance survey, first phase data (1.2). Zenodo (2023). https://doi.org/10.5281/zenodo.8389544

22. Moody, J., Bailey, N., Zhao, J.: Public perceptions of autonomous vehicle safety: an international comparison. Saf. Sci. **121**, 634–650 (2020)

23. Nordhoff, S., et al.: Using the UTAUT2 model to explain public acceptance of conditionally automated (L3) cars: a questionnaire study among 9,118 car drivers from eight European countries. Transport. Res. F: Traffic Psychol. Behav. **74**, 280–297 (2020)

24. Rice, S., Winter, S.R.: Do gender and age affect willingness to ride in driverless vehicles: if so, then why? Technol. Soc. **58**, 101145 (2019)

Spatiotemporal Analysis of e-scooter Demand in Lexington, Kentucky

Eleni Nalmpantidou[1], Dimitrios Sarafidis[1], Andreas Nikiforiadis[2](✉) (iD),
Nikiforos Stamatiadis[3] (iD), Grigorios Fountas[1] (iD), and Socrates Basbas[1] (iD)

[1] School of Rural and Surveying Engineering, Faculty of Engineering, Aristotle University of Thessaloniki, 54124 Thessaloniki, Greece
[2] School of Civil Engineering, Democritus University of Thrace, 67100 Xanthi, Greece
anikifor@civil.duth.gr
[3] Department of Civil Engineering, University of Kentucky, Lexington, KY, USA

Abstract. In the city of Lexington, Kentucky shared e-scooters made their appearance in the summer of 2019. This paper aims to examine which factors and how they affect the e-scooter demand based on data related to Lexington, KY. The data were obtained from two e-scooter sharing companies, Bird and Spin, and covered the entire year of 2022. Using this data, the characteristics influencing demand were analyzed, and behaviors and patterns were identified. Specifically, the analysis was conducted both in terms of the general and temporal characteristics of the recorded trips through graphs, and spatially through the creation of appropriate maps. The findings showed that e-scooter usage is greater in the city center and is affected by months, weather, days, and hours. In addition, by depicting points and areas of interest and comparing them with areas with increased demand, the main reason of a trip undertaken with an e-scooter, can be determined. The University of Kentucky community, although constituting 14% of the population, appears to represent a much larger percentage of e-scooter users, thus significantly influencing the demand profile.

Keywords: e-scooters · micromobility · demand analysis · spatial analysis

1 Introduction

In recent years, the use of shared electric scooters (e-scooters) has increased significantly, establishing them as a flexible and sustainable mode of transportation in urban centers [1]. Their introduction in the United States in 2017 marked a turning point in urban mobility, offering an efficient solution for short-distance travel [1]. The widespread adoption of e-scooters has been facilitated by the convenience of app-based rentals and the flexibility of parking options, which have contributed to their rapid expansion in the global micromobility market [2, 3]. As a result, shared e-scooters now play a crucial role in urban transport networks, effectively bridging the gap between residential areas, public transportation hubs, and other key destinations [2, 3].

The growing popularity of e-scooters is primarily driven by their practicality and environmental benefits. By providing an alternative to private vehicles, they help reduce

© The Author(s), under exclusive license to Springer Nature Switzerland AG 2026
O. Gervasi et al. (Eds.): ICCSA 2025 Workshops, LNCS 15899, pp. 35–47, 2026.
https://doi.org/10.1007/978-3-031-97663-6_3

traffic congestion and mitigate urban air pollution [1]. However, despite these advantages, integrating e-scooters into existing transportation systems presents several challenges. A comprehensive understanding of demand patterns and the factors influencing them is essential for the effective management and regulation of shared e-scooter services [1, 4].

Analyzing e-scooter demand is of critical importance for both micromobility service providers and policymakers [5]. For operators, demand data can be leveraged to optimize fleet distribution and ensure the availability of e-scooters in high-demand areas during peak hours [3]. Effective fleet management can improve service efficiency while minimizing operational costs. At the same time, policymakers can utilize demand analysis to develop appropriate regulatory frameworks and urban infrastructure, such as dedicated lanes and parking zones, to enhance safety, accessibility, and sustainability [6]. Ensuring a well-regulated e-scooter ecosystem requires data-driven decision-making processes that consider both user behavior and broader urban mobility trends.

A rigorous analysis of e-scooter demand necessitates the application of advanced statistical and spatial methodologies[7]. Statistical models help identify usage trends, assess the relationship between demand and key environmental variables, and evaluate the impact of external factors such as weather conditions [3, 7]. Meanwhile, spatial analysis techniques, including Geographic Information Systems (GIS) and spatial regression models, provide insights into the geographic distribution of e-scooter use and help identify high- and low-demand areas [8]. These analytical approaches contribute to a more comprehensive understanding of micromobility demand and inform evidence-based policy and business strategies.

The present study aims to investigate the key determinants of shared e-scooter demand, with a particular focus on spatial and temporal distribution patterns [1]. By examining factors such as weather conditions, temporal characteristics and points of interest, this research seeks to enhance understanding of e-scooter usage trends and provide insights for optimizing their integration into urban transport networks [7, 8]. The findings of this study are expected to support the development of policies and operational strategies that promote the efficient and sustainable use of shared e-scooters in contemporary urban environments.

2 Methodology

2.1 Data Collection

Lexington is the second-largest city in the state of Kentucky and the 57th largest city in the United States, with a population of approximately 320,000 (2022). The city is the seat of Fayette County and hosts significant business and educational activities. Electric scooters were introduced to the city in the summer of 2019, offering an alternative mode of transportation. As of 2022 (the year referenced in this paper), two electric scooter rental companies, Bird and Spin, were operating in the city. Bird was selected to provide electric scooter rental services within the University of Kentucky campus. The adoption of these new modes of transportation was expected to be particularly positive in a city like Lexington, where the only public transportation option is the city bus, with routes running from 5 a.m. to 9 p.m. (except for four routes that operate until midnight).

The data used for this study were obtained from the aforementioned companies. The files included information about the characteristics of each route (distance, duration), as well as the period in which the route was taken (month, day, start time, and end time). Additionally, they contained spatial information, such as the geographic longitude and latitude of the starting and ending points. By combining distance and duration data, the average speed for each route was calculated. It was necessary to check the quality of the recordings, as some entries contained incomplete or incorrect information or had anomalous values regarding speed, duration, or distance. Routes with a distance of zero, a duration under one minute or over 60 min, and speeds outside the range of 10–25 km per hour were removed (see Table 1).

Table 1. Data filtering process.

Data Filtering Process	Number of Records
Initial Data	178.287
Route Length = 0 km	3.154
Duration < 1 min	1.654
Duration > 60 min	6.384
Speed < 10 km/hr	52.032
Speed > 25 km/hr	229
Final Data	114.834

2.2 Data Analysis

The data were analyzed using two methods: statistical analysis and spatial analysis. For statistical analysis, bar charts were used to examine the general and temporal characteristics of the routes, identifying patterns and factors influencing demand. These charts depict the duration, distance, speed, and month, as well as the relationship between the month, mean temperature, and mean rainfall (in millimeters). Additionally, differences in trip characteristics between weekdays and weekends were examined.

For spatial analysis, starting and ending points were visualized and analyzed using two methods. The first method was deterministic spatial interpolation using IDW (Inverse Distance Weighting). This technique allowed for estimating the number of trips in areas with no recorded data, providing a more complete picture. Additionally, a graduated color scheme was applied, categorizing the number of trips and representing them with varying shades. Finally, to better understand areas of high demand, points of interest (POIs) were extracted from Open Street Map and mapped, including stadiums, theaters, universities, dining areas, retail stores, and parks.

3 Results

3.1 Statistical Analysis

In this subsection, selected charts produced during the analysis are presented. These charts highlight the most interesting results and the most significant findings.

Based on Fig. 1, approximately 77% of trips are between 0–2 km in length. Electric scooters are primarily used for the first and last segments of a journey ("first-mile and last-mile"). They often serve as a connection to public transportation, such as bus stops, or parking areas, allowing users to complete the rest of their trip by bus or private vehicles.

On weekdays, the highest percentage of trips last between 0–5 min, whereas on weekends, the majority of trips last between 5–10 min (see Fig. 2). The average duration and distance were calculated separately for weekdays and weekends. On weekdays, trips have an average duration of 6.6 min and an average distance of 1.6 km, while on weekends, the average duration is 10 min, and the average distance is two kilometers. This suggests that trips on weekends tend to be longer, possibly because people use electric scooters for recreational purposes, whereas on weekdays, trips are more purposeful and often linked to inflexible commitments.

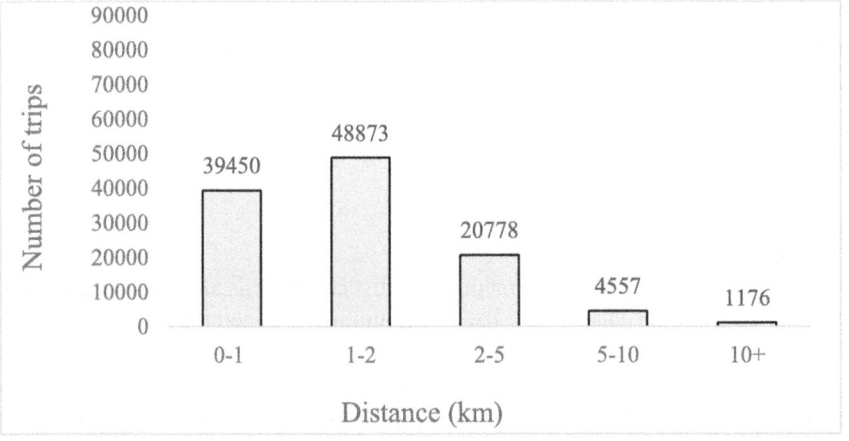

Fig. 1. Relationship between number of trips undertaken and distance measured in kilometers.

The number of trips cannot be described as directly proportional to temperature, but it is certainly influenced by it. In Fig. 3 is observed that from January to April, the number of trips and temperature increased together, showing a proportional relationship. However, from May to July, while the temperature continues to rise, the number of trips decreases. June and July record the highest temperatures and the fewest trips. From July to September, the temperature decreases while the number of trips increases. Finally, from September to December, both temperature and the number of trips decline.

Different weather conditions over these two months seem to impact electric scooter usage in an analogous way. However, when examining the average trip duration (in

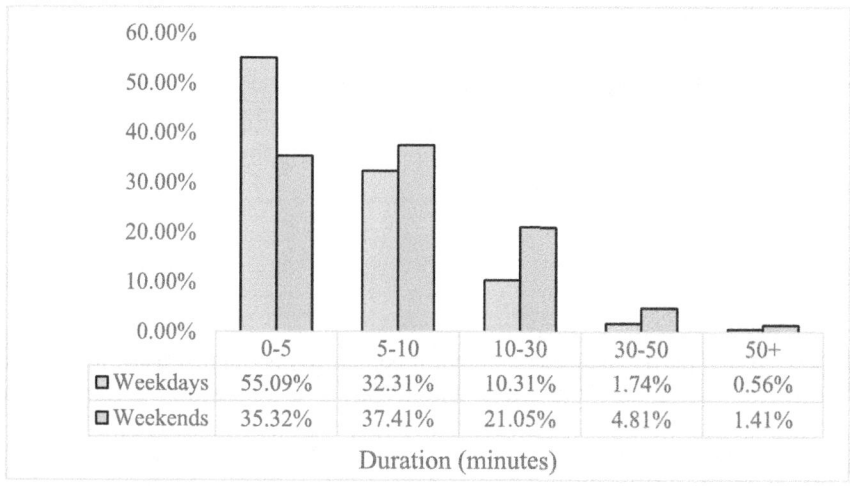

Fig. 2. Correlation between number of trips undertaken and duration measured in minutes.

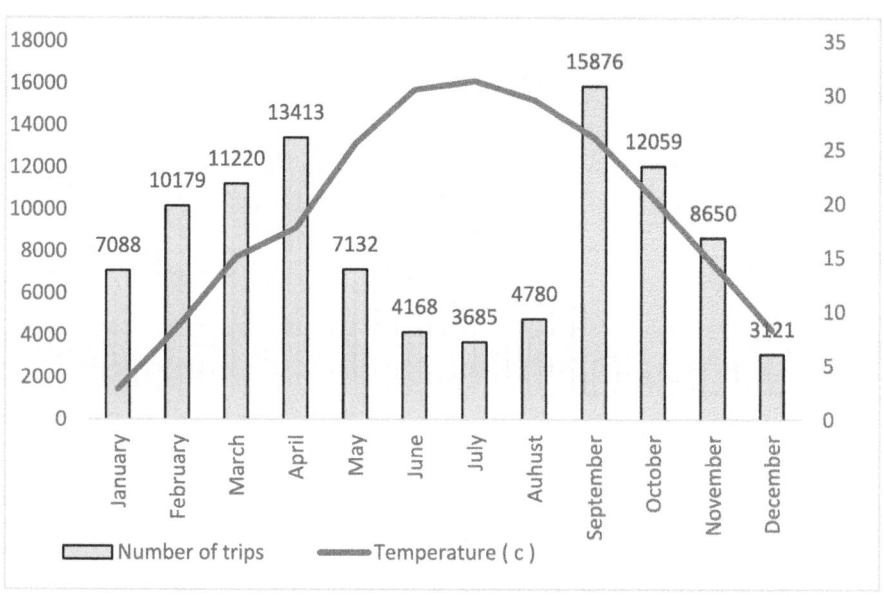

Fig. 3. Correlation among number of trips undertaken, mean temperature and month.

minutes) and the average distance traveled, it was observed that trips in July are significantly longer (see Fig. 3). Therefore, while the weather may not have influenced the total number of trips, it appears to have affected their characteristics (Table 2).

From Fig. 4 is becoming understood that on weekdays, higher percentages of trips occur during the morning and midday hours, between 09:00 and 16:00, whereas on weekends, peak usage is recorded between 17:00 and 00:00. Notably, between 16:00

Table 2. Comparison between July-December.

Comparing July – December

	Number of trips undertaken	Mean temperature (c)	Mean rainfall (mm)	Mean duration (minutes)	Mean distance (km.)
July	3685	31.3	5.3	14	3.2
December	3121	8.3	2.8	5.8	1.5

and 17:00, usage rates equalize. From that time until 04:00, higher usage is recorded on weekends, while from 05:00 to 16:00, usage is higher on weekdays. This suggests that on weekdays, electric scooter activity is more intense in the morning, likely due to work, university lectures, or other obligations. After 17:00, most people return home to rest. On weekends, morning demand is lower because people can start their day later, as they are not restricted by strict work schedules or university timetables. Finally, the increased demand in the afternoon and evening hours compared to weekdays is attributed to recreational outings, which are more frequent on Saturdays and Sundays.

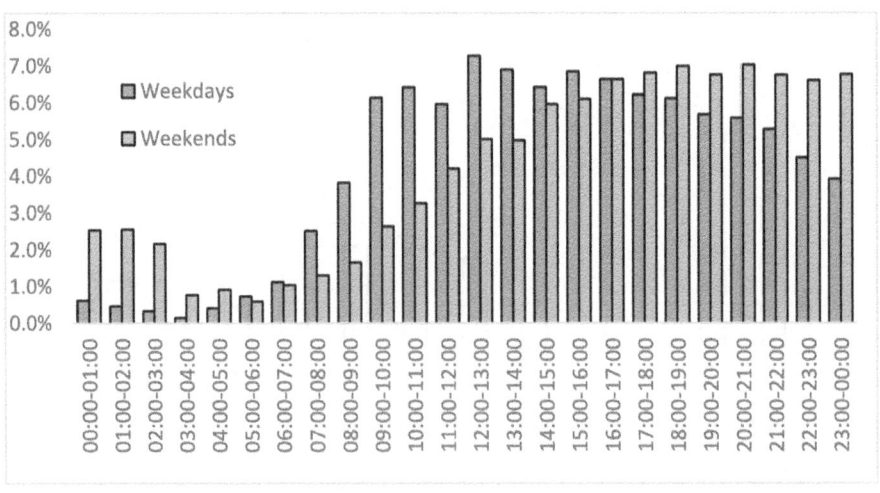

Fig. 4. Correlation among percentages of trips undertaken days and time.

3.2 Spatial Analysis

With regards to the spatial distribution of the demand, Figs. 5 and 6 depict the concentration of trip points on weekdays and weekends.

No significant differences are observed between the two maps, with the highest concentration in both cases found in the city center. On weekdays, the area with the highest demand is the University of Kentucky campus, as well as its northern side, where cafés, entertainment venues (bars), and restaurants are located. This suggests that most routes have either the campus as their destination, possibly due to lectures, or nearby dining establishments. On weekends, the routes concentrated within the university primarily relate to the Central Library. At the same time, increased activity is observed around the Central Bank Center (Opera House, Rupp Arena), where concerts, sporting events, and various other activities take place. Additionally, significant movement is recorded east of the center, in an area with theaters, cinemas, restaurants, and bars.

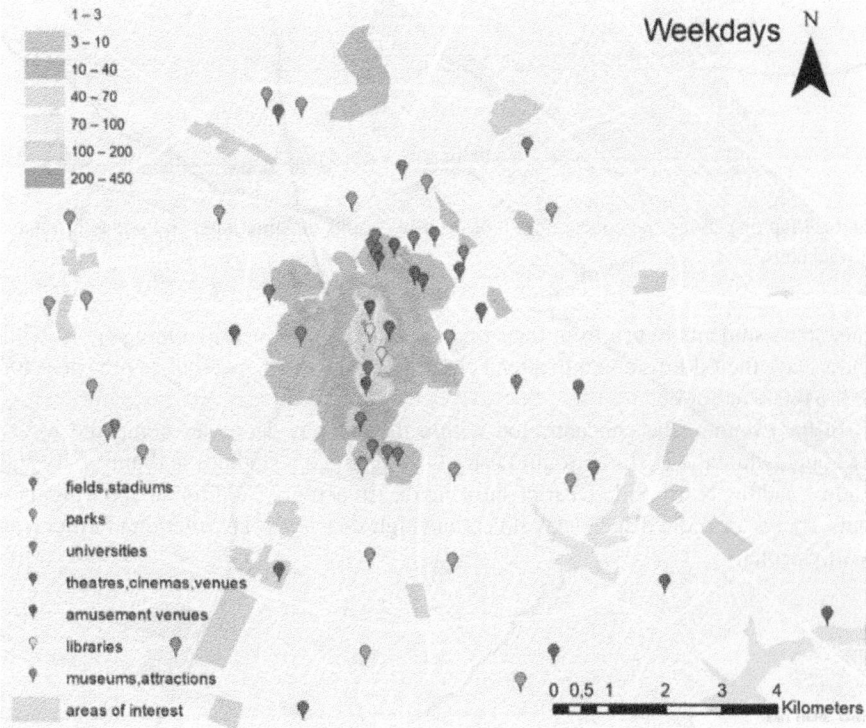

Fig. 5. Map displaying the concentration of drop-off points (destinations) and points of interest on weekdays.

With regards to the spatial distribution of the demand within the day, Figs. 7 and 8 are being presented. In the early morning hours, the highest demand is observed in the university dormitories and nearby areas of interest surrounding the campus. During this

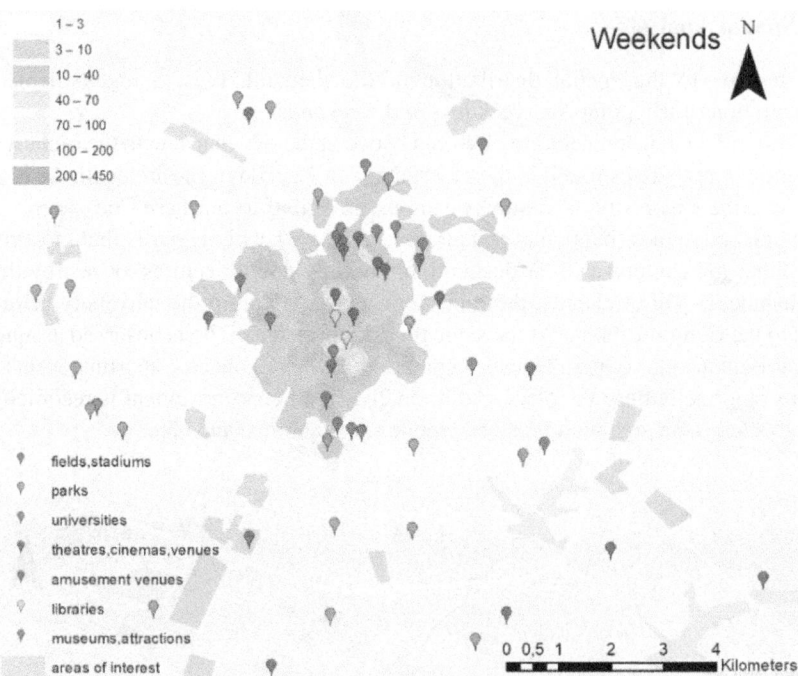

Fig. 6. Map displaying the concentration of drop-off points (destinations) and points of interest on weekends.

time, some students return from their night out and choose nearby dining spots, while others leave their dorms either to attend classes, engage in other activities or visit a store for breakfast or coffee.

In the evening, the concentration within the campus decreases compared to earlier hours, while the Historic South District—where many students and university staff reside—and the North Side District show increased activity. Additionally, during these hours, routes are more dispersed, with certain high-density points emerging farther from the city center.

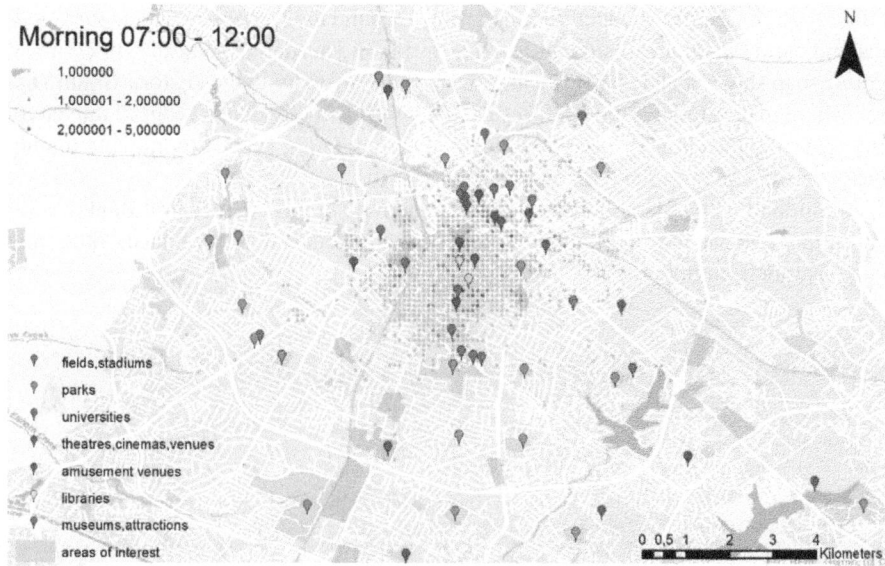

Fig. 7. Map displaying the distribution of drop-off points (destinations) and points of interest in the morning.

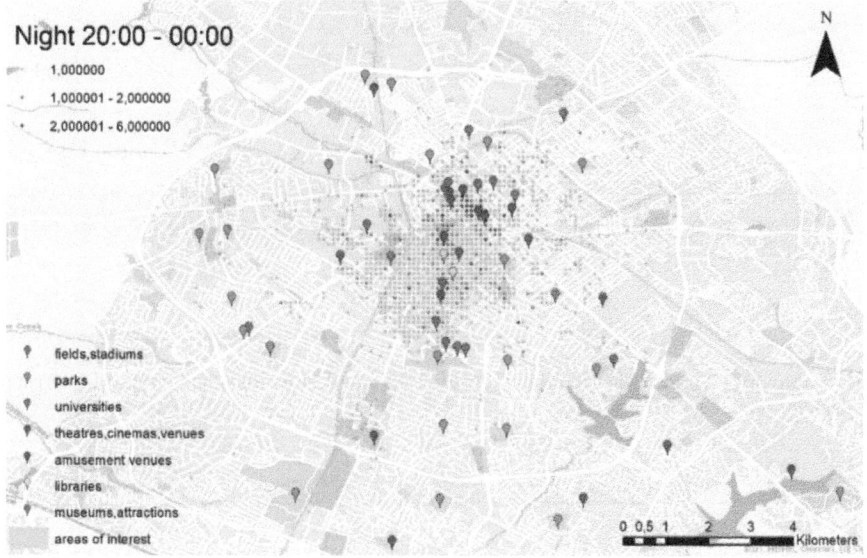

Fig. 8. Map displaying the distribution of drop-off points (destinations) and points of interest in the night.

Finally, the spatial distribution of the demand between a typical summer and a typical winter month is being explored (Figs. 9 and 10). The first map, which represents

February, shows a strong concentration of routes around the University and its surroundings, indicating heightened student activity during the academic semester. In contrast, the July map shows a clear shift in routes from the University to the Historic South District, where many students and staff reside. This shift is likely due to reduced university activity during the summer period, with students remaining in the city moving mainly towards residential areas and recreational spaces.

Additionally, there is noticeable increased activity around the Central Bank Center and Rupp Arena, as the stadium hosts numerous concerts and performances, attracting many visitors from both the city and beyond.

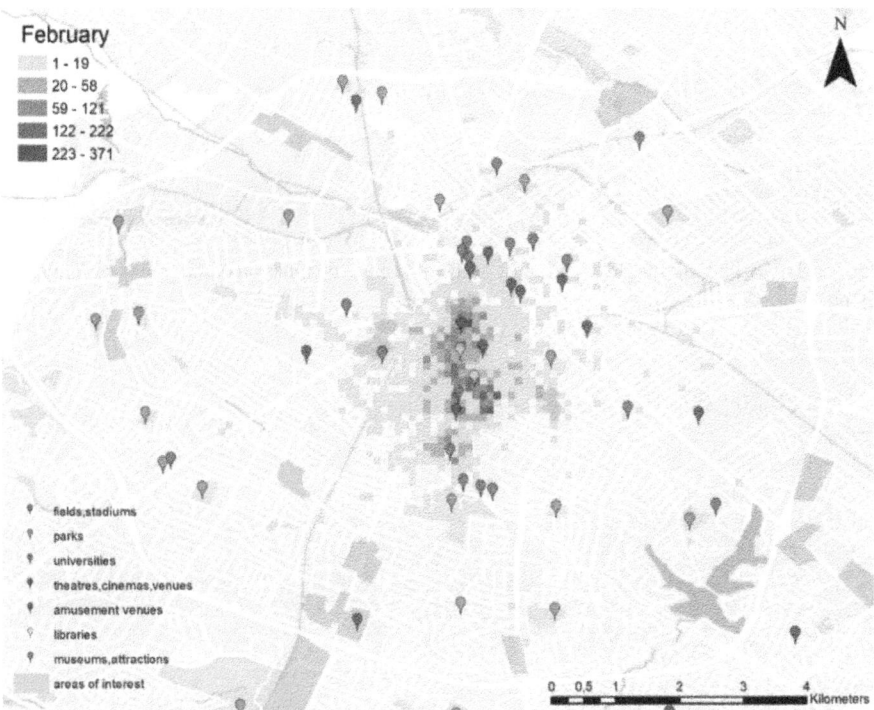

Fig. 9. Map displaying the distribution of drop-off points (destinations) and points of interest in February.

Fig. 10. Map displaying the distribution of drop-off points (destinations) and points of interest in July.

4 Conclusions

Trips at a speed of 10–15 km per hour account for 51% of the total, while those at a speed of 15–20 km per hour make up 40%. Overall, trips within the 10–20 km/h speed range represent 91% of all recorded trips.

Regarding distance, 77% of trips fall within the 0–2-km range, while in terms of duration, 84% of trips last between 0–10 min. These findings indicate that electric scooters are primarily used for short trips or to cover the "first-mile, last-mile" segment of a longer journey. Additionally, weekday trips tend to be shorter, whereas weekend trips have longer durations, suggesting a shift in usage patterns depending on the day of the week.

For the temporal characteristics, months, days, and hours were analyzed. September recorded the highest percentage of trips, while July had the lowest. To better understand the influence of months on demand, the average temperature and precipitation per month were examined. Regarding temperature, extreme conditions—whether excessively hot or cold—tended to reduce scooter usage, while milder temperatures encouraged it. However, the relationship between precipitation and demand was less clear. Some months with high rainfall recorded more trips than others with lower rainfall levels, and vice versa. Since rainfall is reported as a monthly average and can vary significantly over 30 days, it is reasonable that no clear trend emerges.

Regarding daily usage patterns, weekdays showed a higher number of trips compared to weekends, indicating greater commuting needs related to work, university lectures, and other obligations. In terms of hourly trends, the highest percentage of weekday trips occurred between 12:00 and 13:00, while on weekends, peak usage was recorded between 20:00 and 21:00. Comparing hourly demand across weekdays and weekends, trips were more frequent on weekdays from 05:00 to 17:00, whereas from 17:00 to 05:00, weekends exhibited higher demand.

From the demand maps depicting starting and ending points, the highest concentrations were observed in areas of interest in downtown Lexington, particularly within the University of Kentucky campus. However, starting and ending points did not show significant differences, as many of them overlapped. Most conclusions were drawn from demand visualization (by day, hour, and month) overlaid on a map with points of interest.

On weekdays, the highest number of trips was concentrated within the university campus and nearby areas of interest. Scooter usage appears to be driven primarily by commuting to lectures and short recreational activities (such as meals or coffee breaks) between classes. On weekends, hotspots shifted to areas with theaters, cinemas, bars, and restaurants, emphasizing the increased demand for leisure activities.

In terms of time-of-day patterns, mornings and midday hours showed a higher concentration of trips within the university campus and surrounding points of interest on weekdays. In the evening, at night, and even in the early morning hours, demand was significantly higher at weekends, particularly in entertainment districts.

Finally, it is worth noting that the university community (students, faculty, and staff), although comprising only 14% of the city's population, appears to represent a significantly higher proportion of electric scooter users. This highlights the considerable influence of the University of Kentucky on the overall demand profile for electric scooters in Lexington.

Disclosure of Interests. The authors have no competing interests to declare that are relevant to the content of this article.

References

1. Zhu, R., Zhang, X., Kondor, D., Santi, P., Ratti, C.: Understanding spatiotemporal heterogeneity of bike-sharing and scooter sharing mobility. Comput. Environ. Urban Syst. **81**, 101483 (2020)
2. Tuli, F.M., Mitra, S., Crews, M.B.: Factors influencing the usage of shared E-scooters in Chicago. Transp. Res. Part A: Policy Pract. **154**, 164–185 (2021)
3. Nikiforiadis, A., Paschalidis, E., Stamatiadis, N., Paloka, N., Tsekoura, E., Basbas, S.: E scooters and other mode trip chaining: preferences and attitudes of university students. Transp. Res. Part A: Policy Pract. **170**, 103636 (2023)
4. Shah, N.R., Guo, J., Han, L.D., Cherry, C.R.: Why do people take e-scooter trips? Insights on temporal and spatial usage patterns of detailed trip data. Transp. Res. Part A **173**, 103705 (2023)
5. McKenzi, G.: Spatiotemporal comparative analysis of scooter-share and bike-share usage patterns in Washington, D.C. J. Transp. Geogr. **78**, 19–28 (2019)

6. Hosseinzadeh, A., Algomaiah, M., Kluger, R., Li, Z.: Spatial analysis of shared e-scooter trips. J. Transp. Geogr. **92**, 103016 (2021)
7. Nikiforiadis, A., Paschalidis, E., Stamatiadis, N., Raptopoulou, A., Kostareli, A., Basbas, S.: Analysis of attitudes and engagement of shared e-scooter users. Transp. Res. Part D: Transp. Environ. **94**, 102790 (2021)
8. Caspi, O., Smart, M.J., Noland, R.B.: Spatial associations of dockless shared e-scooter usage. Transp. Res. Part D: Transp. Environ. **86**, 102396 (2020)

The Development of Integrated Public Transport and on Demand Services (PTs-DRTs) for Greater Flexibility and Complementarity of Transport Mode Choices

Tiziana Campisi[1]([⊠]) [ID], Chiara Spadaro[1]([⊠]) [ID], Antonio Russo[1] [ID], Giovanni Tesoriere[1] [ID], and Guilhermina Torrao[2] [ID]

[1] Department of Engineering and Architecture, University of Enna Kore, 94100 Enna, Italy
tiziana.campisi@unikore.it, chiara.spadaro@unikorestudent.it
[2] Department of Engineering Management, Aston University, Birmingham B4 7ET, UK

Abstract. Rapid urbanisation and technological developments in the mobility sector underline the importance of the deployment of flexible and complementary public transport services (PTs), such as Demand-Responsive-Transport (DRTs). The deployment of these services is strongly influenced by transport demand; hence it is shaped by socio-economic factors such as booking methods, reasons for travel, and time of travel. Additionally, travel habits and the specific needs of users as well as deployment in areas with low transport demand. This can include not only peripheral regions but also other locations. The integration of DRTs-PTs in Europe and the UK presents a significant opportunity to enhance mobility and sustainability in both urban and rural areas. DRTs have the potential to address the specific transport needs of different regions and contribute to reducing social and gender inequalities while avoiding service bias toward high-demand urban areas. The main goal of this research is to conduct an in-depth analysis of the current state of the art. It focuses on sustainability in the context of DRT mobility, and it also highlights benefits and criticalities through a SWOT analysis approach. This study analyses strengths and weaknesses, opportunities and strategies involved in implementing an integrated DRT-PT service. Ultimately, the findings of this research provide a foundational framework for better deployment of more flexible and complementary PTs, enhancing accessibility and ensuring service equity for all users.

Keywords: Public transport · DRT services · SWOT analysis · Integrated Transport System · Sustainable Mobility

1 Introduction

The European recommendations include the 2030 Agenda and in particular Goal 11 [1], "Make cities and human settlements inclusive, safe, durable and sustainable". By 2030 access to all transport systems must be ensured. The transportation system should be understood as safe, sustainable and affordable, especially for the most vulnerable groups.

O. Gervasi et al. (Eds.): ICCSA 2025 Workshops, LNCS 15899, pp. 48–64, 2026.
https://doi.org/10.1007/978-3-031-97663-6_4

In the logic of the 2030 Agenda goals, innovative approaches in the mobility sector are growing rapidly, and with them the inefficiencies and shortcomings of the traditional transportation context. Demand Responsive Transit (DRT) refers to flexible transportation services that can be adapted to different needs, based on digital technologies useful to optimize vehicle management and improve the accessibility of public transportation services. This increasing service is characterized not only by flexibility, but also by efficiency for the user, providing passengers with the ability to book transportation according to their desire/need, differently from traditional scheduled public transportation (PT). The introduction of this on-demand service can bring significant benefits in terms of environmental sustainability, by reducing private car dependency [2–4].

Additionally, it can foster economic sustainability, since DRT could optimize the cost of public transportation by working on the fuel efficiency and low-cost pair (i.e. pricing as a DRTs implicate costs between 5–15%, compared to 15–40% for public transport) [5]. Integration of PTs-DRTs therefore leads to significant cost savings, resulting in greater system efficiency. Benefits are also foreseen for social sustainability in terms of accessibility to sustainable mobility for all, especially for those with special needs. [6].

Such integration can be an effective strategy to address mobility challenges not only in urban but also rural areas by improving the efficiency and accessibility of the transportation system. In fact, PTs, based on pre-established routes and fixed timetable, are complementary to DRTs. In this way they can provide flexible and on-demand services, able to cover areas with low population density or low demand schedules.

In current scientific literature, are often analyses peculiarities of DRT, main drivers of demand and diffusion. However, despite the growing interest in this topic, the importance of synergies between DRTs and PTs, which is the focus of this study, is not sufficient. It is often thought that on-demand service can be the enemy of PTs, in fact DRTs, starting from their financial strategies, follow financial models that often rely on sub studies [7].

So, in terms of the innovative design of these services, the issue is to make DRT the most efficient/appropriate option compared to other modes of transportation (conventional buses, taxis). The ways in which DRT can operate compatibly with public transport are varied; it can propose itself, for example, as a service extended to PT therefore optimized [2, 8, 9].

The aim of the paper is to examine the characteristics of DRTs integrated with PTs, focusing on strategic planning by applying SWOT analysis.

This research paper introduces a state of art analysis in Sect. 2 and therefore aims to explore the characteristics of DRT transport service integrated to PT through a three steps analysis described in Sect. 3. The first introductory step is a literature review in the European Union and UK landscape; the second step aims to apply a strategic planning tool, SWOT analysis, to assess the strengths, weaknesses and opportunities for the implementation of an integrated DRT-PT service.

This SWOT analysis considers different viewpoints, from user to public administration and the operators, respectively, of the DRT and PT services. Finally, the analysis of application cases follows, which verify the stated assumptions. Section 4 additionally provides some suggestions for improving the integration of the above services for future research developments, introducing possible flexible and complementary transport solutions for passengers and small goods in order to improve public transport and last mile delivery.

2 Background

Previous studies have focused on transportation services, highlighting the peculiarities of DRTs; Brake et al. (2004) [10] describe it as "an intermediate form of public transport, somewhere between a regular service route that uses small low floor buses and variably routed, highly personalized transportation services offered by taxis".

As also mentioned by Lews et al. [11] DRTs can be defined as an intermediate and highly flexible mode of transportation that can give rise to a range of uses and functionalities thus representing a strategy to be deployed to address mobility challenges.

DRTs are able to cover transportation needs in weak demand areas and consequently ensure more efficient accessibility to all, especially for vulnerable users. This reflects a growing interest in improving and reducing social exclusion [10, 12].

At the same time, the service makes it possible to define forms of transportation that can be complementary and integrated with public transport by covering weak demand areas in the same way [6].

Papanikolaou et al. [13] analyses the gap between the public transportation market and DRT, proposing a possible framework so that integration between the two services is possible and successful. The innovative element of this research concerns the conceptualization and categorization of DRTs. It's based on the potential match with PTs and the possible optimization of transportation costs.

In agreement with Ryley et al. [14] several case studies emphasize the difficulties in terms of cost in the implementation and use of DRTs, also stressing the need for a combined transport service for an approach that is not only environmentally sustainable but also economically and socially sustainable.

Concerning social impact, the research conducted by [15] highlights social benefits of DRTs and the difficulties of implementing such services in the UK. They emphasize some critical issues related to economic self-independence.

Several demand models have been applied in literature for social and economic benefit assessments. In agreement with [16, 17] it is shown that the application of mixed logit models has generated interesting simulations that can build a DRT network model enabling the interaction between supply and demand, and between a rigid public transportation system with a flexible and efficient on-demand transport system.

Similarly, in the case of public transport services, it is crucial to define the benefits not only in terms of the environment, but also for the economy and society, which are often influenced by user satisfaction [18].

For both scheduled and flexible transport services, research conducted by [14] indicates that service frequency, travel time and flexibility are necessary not only to satisfy the user, but also to create the right conditions for using the service. This implies that all features must be available for each user cluster, so that no one is excluded and discouraged from using these services [19, 20].

There is no doubt that today's literature lacks studies related to the integration of DRTs, as pointed out by Desaulniers and Hickman [21], who emphasis the need to implement more integrated type services to strategically improve the service design, thus minimizing costs and ensuring the most comprehensive service possible.

The innovative design of a DRT integrated with the PTs, as suggested by Gorev et al. [22], could ensure flexible modes of public transport services implemented at the DRT by taking certain actions:

- an analysis of demand in the affected area not disregarding population density, condition of existing road and transport networks, income level and motorisation level;
- identification of factors that may adversely affect DRT;
- development of an organisational plan between DRT and PT;
- and calculation of necessary costs and the possibility of receiving subsidies from Local Authorities.

In accordance with their findings, the adoption of modern technologies could greatly increase PT integration and flexibility, allowing thus DRT to choose the best option that matches to user's needs.

In a last resort, in economic terms, costs could be balanced and contained, since DRTs require significant investment and subsidy. It is then recommended that combined solutions could be used to the benefit of users and service providers.

From the literature review, it is clear the importance of the complementarity of the two services, which integration through strategies and technologies can ensure environmental, economic and social sustainability.

This integration turns out to be efficient because first and foremost it helps PT to establish itself in weak demand areas, where it is lacking, supporting the principle of social sustainability in the first place and addressing issues of social exclusion and social needs [14]. It helps DRTs to establish itself and to sustain excessive costs as many of these results, show how difficult it is to make this service work economically, thus supporting an approach of economic sustainability and beyond.

This examination highlights the positive and negative aspects of the integration of the two services found in literature.

Unfortunately, it still does not emerge, through a SWOT analysis, the examination of strengths and weaknesses, therefore opportunities and threats on the topic of DRT-PT integration.

3   Methodology

The earlier sections have highlighted the growing need for deploying DRT services to meet 3 main objectives:

- Connect peri-urban areas to each other.
- Provide a first-last-mile mobility solution.
- Optimise operational costs by facilitating the digital transition of on-demand transportation services.

It is essential to understand the benefits and challenges that the implementation of a DRT services can offer. This understanding is fundamental not only for users of the transport system but also for Local Authorities and the management companies in the short, medium and long term.

This paper proposes a triple analysis, which could also be defined as a hybrid systematic literature review, as articulated and summarised in Fig. 1.

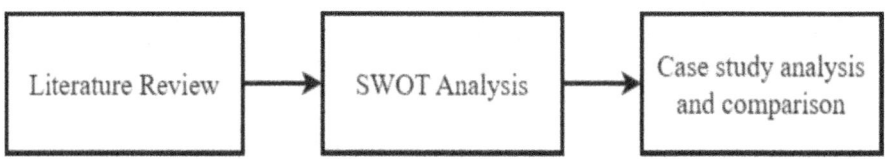

Fig. 1. Methodological steps applied in this study.

The first step, concerning literature analysis, involves defining specific keywords and searching on major search engines such as WOS, Science Direct.

Specifically, a smart literature search was conducted using the combination of keywords and Boolean operators used on search engines is of the type:

ALL = ("Public transport") AND (ALL = (DRT) OR ALL = ("Demand-responsive transit") OR ALL ("ON DEMAND BUS SERVICE")
ALL = (DRT) AND ALL = (PT) OR ALL ("Integrated transport system")

Among the criteria for selecting research results in this paper, the year of publication very important criterion in determining whether an article is included or excluded. This search targeted publications between 2014 and 2024.

From this analysis, 15 articles are selected that appear to be relevant related to the DRT-PT integration issue with spatial-temporal distribution defined in Table 1.

The second methodological step is SWOT analysis of the main elements of on-demand transport system integrated with PT. SWOT matrices inherent in the main elements of the on-demand transport system are then defined. A third and final step is the evaluation of selected application case studies in European Union and UK context in order to test the literature hypotheses.

Case studies from literature review are compared to verify scientific trends, models analysis and to better understand what has been demonstrated using the SWOT analysis technique.

SWOT analysis is a well-known technique for conducting a strategic study and consists of defining a matrix in which the main strengths, weaknesses, opportunities, and threats of a specific project alternative are stated.

In this case, the analysis involves determining the goal of the transportation service and identifying the internal and external factors for achieving the goal. The SWOT is useful when it is used to convert weaknesses into strengths and threats into opportunities [34, 35]. Several studies in the literature have applied the SWOT matrix definition for evaluating transportation mode choices [36, 37] and/or infrastructure planning [38, 39].

In recent years, the SWOT matrix has been used in different fields and has provided a good basis for strategy formulation when used correctly [40].

Table 1. Spatial-temporal distribution of main literature review analysed

Year	Reference	Spatial distribution
2014	[14]	UK
2015	[23]	Lincolnshire, UK
2017	[13]	–
2020	[24]	Amsterdam, NE
2020	[22]	Russia
2020	[25]	Baltic Region
2021	[26]	Styria
2022	[27]	Peri urban area
2023	[28]	Tampere, Genoa, Braunschweig
2023	[29]	Benevento, IT
2023	[30]	Netherlands
2023	[31]	Rural areas
2023	[32]	General planning strategy
2024	[33]	Sweden
2024		Tennesse, USA

However, inadequate application development of SWOT analysis leads to conclusions with long lists of generic, even meaningless and overly descriptive factors. Moreover, the results of the SWOT analysis are highly dependent on the knowledge and skills of the experts involved [41].

Therefore, this research aims to analyse various perspectives on implementing a DRT transport service, capturing both positive and negative aspects by considering users as customers, managers as service providers, and administrators as local authorities. The preliminary study of the benefits and criticalities deriving from a careful analysis of the literature and pilot cases from various parts of the world has made it possible to highlight some peculiarities of DRT services as well as some gaps to be filled for a wider dissemination of these modal choices.

4   Results and Discussions

4.1   The Main Advantages of PT-DRTs Integration

In general, scientific literature emphasises the most important advantages of DRTs, those are briefly described in the following:

- Potential high service flexibility i.e. convenient connections for large rural areas, support for citizens with reduced mobility, environmental benefits through reduction of private vehicles on the road.

- Improved quality of life in rural areas (in terms of accessibility, environmental, economic, and social impacts) and providing solutions for weak demand areas (increased coverage of areas, increased perception of transportation safety, increased user independence).

In summary the main impacts that should be paid attention to, include:

- Social impacts (road congestion, inclusion).
- Environmental impacts (reductions in air pollutants emissions and noise).
- Economic impacts (increased efficiency of PT in areas of weak demand).

This will encourage more businesses, tourism enterprises, commuters and families to access to sparsely populated areas with a lack of transport connectivity. Each new demand service responds to a customer challenge or need. By analysing past cases and considering a range of boundary situations, the service offered can be improved by optimising travel demand management and producing not only community benefits but also benefiting economic growth. To engage potential customers and encourage them to use DRTs, it is necessary to identify and understand their needs. Several studies in the literature point out that customers within the target group do not always share the same needs, which complicates efforts to maximise the impact of marketing strategies [42]. Therefore, Table 2 shows a SWOT analysis considering the users' point of view.

Table 2. Analysis SWOT Race-Sharing Services-Users

Strengths (S)	Weaknesses (W)
Flexibility	Costs
Dual evaluation system (client/driver)	Payment methods
"Independent" subjects	Type of reservation
Development of courtesy services (i.e.blablacar) and/or brokerage technology services with commercial purposes	
Opportunities (O)	Threats (T)
Increase in relational aspects	Drivers and customer switching platforms
Enhancing technological innovations	Frequent legal battles
Sharing on social media	Growing competition is leading to thinner profit margins
Sharing the costs of travel	Partial regulation of the industry
Automated matching of supply and demand	Self-driving cars

In this sense, parameters presented in the previous table serve as a guide to define the key aspects of the user needs, therefore supporting the evaluation of the optimal service performance that can be provided.

As next step, it is essential to investigate the behavioural aspects of the users through travel surveys and interviews, and integration of transport data, such as ticket prices to evaluate socio-economic and environmental impacts resulting from the use of a DRT.

The DRT Market Report for Europe and Beyond provides accurate market insights into trends in consumer preferences and behaviour, as well as an overview of market data and key companies.

Promotion and education are essential, and several key actions should be implemented by.

- Incentives for DRT mode choice- vouchers for a free trip and other incentives to encourage trials of the service, as well as encouraging user feedback and reviews.
- Reassurance regarding the reliability of travel service and building customer trust.
- Pairing technology (booking system based on App) with a call center to ensure accessibility to all the users.
- Strong partnerships collaboration between operators and local authorities to ensure the successful introduction and smooth operation of the service.
- Valuable role for DRT as part of the overall transport mix.

Regarding the factors related to local governments, Table 3 presents the most relevant attributes identified across the selected literature studies.

Table 3. SWOT Analysis Ride-Sharing Local Government

Strengths (S)	Weaknesses (W)
Flexibility	Costs
Reduced need for parking spaces	Informal and often disorganised service structure
Reduced pollution	Non-recurring service
Reduced traffic congestion	
Opportunities (O)	Threats (T)
Increasing modal choices	Limited regulation
MaaS enhancement	Potential safety problems on board
Automated matching of supply and demand	Pre-agreement between users

Regarding the Service Managers, it is possible to consider the viewpoint of the PT and DRT managers as defined in Table 4.

The presence of the two transport services as separated options could generate the following problems.

- Users will inevitably have two separate booking apps (one for DRT and one for public transport) or even more if shared mobility and micro-mobility are considered. This leads to user confusion and a reluctance to use alternative modes of transport.
- There is an unnecessary duplication of hardware and software solutions in the vehicle, with huge additional costs, especially for installation and maintenance.

Table 4. SWOT Analysis Ride-Sharing services PT and DRT Services Managers

Strengths (S)	Weaknesses (W)
Exclusive licences (taxis and NCCs)	Costs
Some platforms have global reach (such as Uber)	Potential privacy issues
Favourable contractual arrangement with drivers	The company failed to achieve consistent profitability
Company enjoys strong brand recognition	Unpredictable business model
Unique pricing system	Unethical working practices
Offers cheaper prices than its competitors	Low customer loyalty
Revolutionary business model	
Dual evaluation system (customer/driver)	
Low operating costs	
Opportunities (O)	Threats (T)
Enhancing one's reputation through greater responsibility and performance	Frequent legal battles
Investing in the future	Increasing competition is leading to thinner profit margins
Expand its operations	Partial regulation of the sector
Invest in green technology	Self-driving cars
Strengthen and diversify their products	

- Transport executives will continue to struggle to effectively manage day-to-day operations and successfully manage the overall mobility scenario for their organisation.
- Public administrations that subside the mobility ecosystem with taxpayers' money will suffer from the duplication of unnecessary costs to support both public transport and potentially unnecessary DRT services and vice versa; consider, for example, a user who books a door-to-door service with his DRT app, completely ignoring that a fixed-route bus is potentially just around the corner and would fully meet his needs.
- The use of both top-down and bottom-up approaches to evaluate past data of DRTs sales and revenue can improve the current market scenario. Therefore, evaluation of different service types, applications, end-users, major regions, and key industry participants is crucial.

The literature review also suggests addressing and mitigating some critical issues related to the lack of a regulatory framework and specific guidelines, as well as macroeconomic indicators that may influence the use of these services.

It is essential to understand the regional situation and the needs of citizens. This involves collecting data and analysing demographics and traffic patterns of the region, as well as the current modal split.

This data is needed to determine the best business model to implement.

- Public authorities can guide this data collection, but it should also be made available to transport operators so they can identify opportunities for implementing a new service.
- Although economic performance is important, the expected social impact of the service should be emphasised.

The key components of DRT implementation plans should include:

- Local user needs analysis: Conduct a thorough analysis of the mobility needs of local communities, taking into account demographic characteristics, travel habits and gaps in existing transport services. This will help identify areas that require priority intervention.
- Set accessibility standards: Setting minimum accessibility standards for transport services to ensure that all communities, regardless of size or location, have access to appropriate mobility options.
- Stakeholder involvement: Actively engage stakeholders, including citizens, local authorities, civil society organisations and businesses, in the planning process. This collaborative approach ensures that solutions are tailored to the actual needs of the community.
- Develop customised solutions: Creating mobility solutions tailored to the specific needs of different rural areas.

Therefore, greater user participation in service improvement could help to identify the main factors related to service deficiencies and develop short-, medium- and long-term strategies that can be implemented by service managers and local authorities to improve service and communication. For example, focusing on providing information and training on these modes, thereby reducing the use of private vehicles.

Public authorities can take the lead by bringing together the necessary stakeholders to initiate discussions and act as neutral partners to encourage collaboration. If properly implemented, communicated to users and integrated with traditional fixed services, DRT has the potential to shape the mobility of the future.

4.2 PTs-DRTs Integration: Case Studies

The best practices analysed underline how the DRT system is revolutionising. Indeed, this service would make it possible to respond to different mobility needs, not only in urban areas but also in rural areas. Among the different models of DRTs, three stand out: [43].

- LOCALISED DRT, capable of meeting targeted user needs with more flexible journeys, both in terms of timing and departure/arrival points.
- RURAL DRT, able to cover rural and low demand areas.
- FIRST- MILE/LAST-MILE, to meet the need to reach strategic hub areas.

The success of DRT integration with other transportation services, as noted by Pavanini et al. [28], relies on DRTs being recognised as one of the most efficient solutions to public transport challenges. This applies not only to rural areas but also to the various logistical difficulties that often compromise the effective use of traditional public transport services. This refers not only to rural settings but also to all the logistical difficulties that often make it difficult to use PTs.

Below, in Table 5 are described the peculiarities of each case study as an integrated DRT-TP service.

This research analyses the scientific literature and evaluates each case study in the European and UK context that has used an on-demand service integrated with public transport. Then through the discernment of said services, it is possible to confirm the hypotheses formulated using the SWOT analysis technique, which are useful for planning integrated services.

Table 5. Peculiarity of case studies analysed

Anno	City/Region	Context	Ref	Fleet type	Slot time	Reservation	Ticket price
2002	Genoa (IT)	Peripheral areas (4 areas not served by PT)	[28]	8 Minibus (14 seats)	07 am-08pm	App, call center, bus stop	There is only a €1 surcharge over the cost of an ordinary public transport ticket
2021	Tampere (FI)	8 on-demand services covering 18 peri-urban areas. Integrated service with LPT (72 bus lines, 2 tram lines, 3 railway lines) and 700 bicycles	[28]	Minibus (14–16 seats)	8.30 am 2.30 pm	Call center or bus stop	3.50 €, same price as PT
2020	Braunschweig (DE)	Suburban areas: Salzgitter, Helmstedt, Wolfsburg. (LPT consisting of buses and trams available in and around urban areas)	[28]	Taxi e minibus	Fixed timetable compatible with PT	Call center. App under development	Ticket and unit cost for both services

(continued)

Table 5. (*continued*)

Anno	City/Region	Context	Ref	Fleet type	Slot time	Reservation	Ticket price
2020	Morristown, Tennessee (USA)	Urban area	[33]	Minibus	Until 6 pm. Door-to-door service	Call center	Ticket of $3 for rides within the urban area. Ticket $6 for rides along the county boundaries
2020	Denmark (DK)	Rural areas	[25]	Minibus	Flexible timetable	Call center	
2020	Northway (NO)	Urban area, covering and replacing three PT lines	[25]	Taxi and minibus		Call center	
2015	Lincolnshire (UK)	Rural areas	[23]	Minibus (8–16 seats)	24hse-Monday-Sunday	App or bus stop	

The analysis of the case studies presented in Table 5 provides an insight into the services implemented in the European context and beyond, highlighting some of the optimal characteristics for defining better strategies and actions for the planning and design of integrated transport services.

In particular, the study carried out by Pavanini et al. [28], included in Table 5, explains how DRTs, when considered as an integral part of PTs, can be understood as a development strategy for less prosperous areas.

With reference to the considerations made within the SWOT analysis, the three cases of Genoa, Tampere and Braunschweig turn out to be emblematic because they describe most of the strengths for the user, from the flexibility of the service to the consolidation of the social dynamics of interrelations. It also emerges that the integration of the two DRT-PT services also has significant benefits for local authorities, i.e. strengths ranging from pollution reduction to better traffic management, thus the possibility of increasing modal choice and ensuring a more comprehensive, flexible and accessible offer.

In this way the economic sustainability problem about the case studies of Genoa, Tampere and Braunscweig present some differences about PTs' role. In Genoa, the PT is taking on more responsibility for DRT, and in both Genoa and Braunschweig, new service models are being implemented. Genoa is also the one that invests the most, has an efficient collaboration with PTs and has a DRTs valid in urban, rural and metropolitan levels [28].

Other results, such as the Benevento case study [29], also show how the integrated approach can create a beneficial and economically sustainable dynamic. The integration with the on-demand service could have a positive impact on the attractiveness of public transport, guaranteeing a reduction in journey times of up to 33%.

Regarding the Tennessee case study [33], the novelty that can be identified is the precision, i.e. the geo-localised method by which the area is represented. This allows not only to operators but also to customers to have a considerable accuracy of geographical coordinates. The novelty of the Morristown case study is that this paratransit service is designed to serve people with disabilities, as recommend by ADA, and it is not simply an on-call system for public.

In addition to the peculiarities already listed in Table 5, it is important to note that the reservation system records and collects data such as demographic variables, age and sex, travel distances and schedules. In this way it is possible to analyse the demand and the corresponding characteristics and then understand which user group is more likely to use DRTs.

Referring to the SWOT analysis, the strengths offered by this service are mainly related to the service operator, since the DRT operator himself has the ability to functionally reorganise the service. In this way, an advantageous contractual arrangement with DRT operators can be created. In this way, public transport would be given a high profile and be able to cover timetables and areas that were previously outside its scope.

At the same time, weaknesses could be identified from an economic point of view. Indeed, it should be noted that if economic resources came from private investors, i.e. DRT operators, the business risks and uncertainties of PT operators could be minimised [3].

The opportunities that can be considered are obviously future-oriented, because with an increase in supply, and thus in entry costs, it is possible to invest in the future and in sustainable/green technology right from the fleet.

Examining Table 5 and focusing on the best practices from the Baltic region [33], we can identify certain strengths and weaknesses that local governments and operators need to address. Enhancing user involvement could greatly improve the service operations. Additionally, by integrating the DRTs with the PTs in a flexible and efficient manner, the dependency on private cars use can be gradually reduced.

Beyond the European Union context, the UK County Councils Network reported that in 2023 several rural areas buses services have reached an historic low, with 344 million fewer journeys in 2022 because of reduced services [44]. As a result, several county authorities have acted to rolling out DRTs. The UK has had notable success with DRT, particularly in rural areas where public transport options are limited, and mobility challenges are significant. Transport policy in the UK [45] is facilitating the emergence of DRTs, as it can be seen these systems are also successful in solving social problems. Laws et al. [11] analyse the typical design and operating system that should be followed for the functional design of a DRT. These recommendations are drawn from a comprehensive of all flexible route bus systems operating in the UK. The survey, sent to 36 local authorities, resulted in approximately 99 registered systems offering detailed overview of each service, including geographical coverage, operational models and characteristics (e.g. routes), applied technologies and booking methods. The findings provided valuable guidelines and considerations for the design of a DRT system.

Within the UK context, the case of Lincolnshire stands out as a particularly noteworthy example, as detailed in Table 5.

Wang et al. [23], examining the case study of Lincolnshire in England, highlight the various difficulties and challenges facing PTs today. These factors that influence the use of the DRT system. Clearly, the most vulnerable users, those with specific needs that are not compatible with the rigid PT system, are more likely to use an on-demand system.

Identifying these data highlights the importance of offering valuable recommendations for designing services to include under-represented market segments.

It then becomes clear that the involvement of local authorities is important here, and also allows a further reference to the SWOT analysis developed above. As key stakeholders, local authorities play a crucial role in planning and coordinating integrated transport services. Their neutral position enables them to foster collaboration among operators and encourage greater acceptance among passengers. More importantly, their influence can drive significant positive impacts, including reduced congestion and the development of more flexible and adaptable transport systems. This integration also paves the way for innovative, technology-driven solutions—notably the advancement of Mobility as a Service (MaaS)—offering seamless, user-centric travel experiences through interconnected transport options.

5 Conclusions

This paper evaluates the integration of scheduled PT with flexible DRT services, an area that has seen limited academic research. Unlike traditional fixed-route systems, DRT offers dynamic routes that adapt to user demand. It is advantageous in low-demand areas like suburbs and rural regions where conventional public transport is often insufficient. DRT, with its potential to enhance access to essential services and combat social isolation, is a significant step towards addressing these pressing social issues in these areas.

This research paper conducted a hybrid systematic literature review to identify relevant studies. The results show that literature studies reveal an uneven distribution of DRT services due to various social, economic, and regulatory factors. It emphasises that integrating DRT with conventional transport can lead to technological advancements and improved cost management.

The research emphasises the need to implement SWOT analyses during the planning phase of these transport services, focusing on the categories of users (users, local administrations and service managers) trying to return a snapshot of the territory, its resources as well as its areas of particular fragility and that will be further deepened with in-depth surveys and greater citizen participation in local choices and reflections by technicians that will lead to the updating of the urban and mobility planning tool.

It is clear that the research presents an initial step of analysis that will have to provide for greater cohesion in the future between the results of the SWOT with respect to the partnership context that it realises in order to ensure greater cohesion on the theoretical and political levels of implementation.

Furthermore, this research study reviews relevant case studies in Europe and the UK and identifies strategies for enhancing integration. It concludes that this synergy can diversify transport options, improve economic and logistical efficiency, and create added environmental and social value. Key factors like service reliability an understanding transport demand are essential for developing adequate digital Mobility as a Service (MaaS) platforms and promoting sustainable urban mobility planning strategies and increasing accessibility for all users. Future steps will conduct a SWOT analysis through a participatory workshop, so that all aspects of the stakeholders are considered. In this way, strengths can be used for the benefit of all stakeholders.

Acknowledgments. Research is supported by the MUR (Italian Ministry of University and Research) through SMART3R-FLITS: SMART Transport for Travellers and Freight Logistics Integration Toward Sustainability (Project protocol:2022J38SR9_03, CUP Code: J53D23009330008), financed by the PRIN 2022(Research Projects of National Relevance) programme. We authorise the MUR to reproduce and distribute reprints for Governmental purposes, notwithstanding any copyright notations thereon. Any opinions, findings, and conclusions, or recommendations expressed in this material are those of the authors and do not necessarily reflect the views of the MUR.

Disclosure of Interests.   N.t.d.

Credit Author Statement.   This paper is the result of the joint work of the authors. In particular, the "Abstract" and "Conclusion" were jointly written by the authors. TC with CS wrote "Background". AR and CS wrote "Methodology". CS, GuT and TC wrote "Results and discussion" and related subparagraphs.

References

1. United Nations. Transforming our World: The 2030 Agenda for Sustainable Development (2015). https://sustainabledevelopment.un.org/post2015/transformingourworld/publication
2. Campisi, T., De Cet, G., Vianello, C., Garau, C.: Exploring economic and ethical challenges of implementing demand-responsive transport systems (DRT) in Italy. Eur. Transp./Trasp. Eur. (98) (2024)
3. Campisi, T., Garau, C., Acampa, G., Maltinti, F., Canale, A., Coni, M. Developing flexible mobility on-demand in the era of mobility as a service: an overview of the Italian context before and after pandemic. In: International Conference on Computational Science and Its Applications, pp. 323–338. Springer, Cham (2021)
4. Campisi, T., Canale, A., Tesoriere, G., Ali, N., Ignaccolo, M., Cocuzza, E.: An analysis of the integration of DRT services with local public transport in post-pandemic period: some of the preliminary insights in the Italian context. In: International Conference on Computational Science and Its Applications, pp. 496–508. Springer, Cham (2022)
5. Marsella, F., Visentin, A.: Trasporto pubblico locale: serve un cambio di marcia. Arthur Little, Viewpoint (2024)
6. Campisi, T., Cocuzza, E., Ignaccolo, M., Inturri, G., Tesoriere, G., Canale, A.: Detailing DRT users in Europe over the last twenty years: a literature overview. Transp. Res. Procedia **69**, 727–734 (2023)
7. Ruhlmann, A., Tauvel, M.: DRT: a key lever to bridge mobility gaps. Arthur Little, Viewpoint (2024)
8. Russo, A., Campisi, T., Tesoriere, G., Al-Rashid, M.A.: Sustainable rural mobility: integrating goods and passenger transportation–a systematic literature review (2024)

9. Ennas, S., Contu, F., Di Francesco, M., Maltinti, F., Zanda, S., Garau, C.: Best practices in integrated demand-responsive transport services for people and freight. In: International Conference on Computational Science and Its Applications, pp. 73–94. Springer, Cham (2024)

10. Brake, J., Nelson, J.D., Wright, S.: Demand responsive transport: towards the emergence of a new market segment. J. Transp. Geogr. **12**, 323–337 (2004)

11. Laws, R., Enoch, M., Ison, S., Potter, S.: Demand responsive transport: a review of schemes in England and Wales. J. Public Transp. **12**(1), 19–37 (2009)

12. Campisi, T., Basbas, S., Papanikolaou, A., Canale, A., Tesoriere, G.: Public transport versus demand responsive transport services in (extremely) low demand areas: the case of the sicilian hinterland. In: Nathanail, E.G., Gavanas, N., Adamos, G. (eds.) CSUM 2022. LNITI. Springer, Cham (2023). https://doi.org/10.1007/978-3-031-23721-8_90

13. Papanikolaou, A., Basbas, S., Mintsis, G., Taxiltaris, C.: A methodological framework for assessing the success of demand responsive transport (DRT) services. Transp. Res. Procedia **24**, 393–400 (2017)

14. Ryley, T.J., Stanley, P.A., Enoch, M.P., Zanni, A.M., Quddus, M.A.: Investigating the contribution of demand responsive transport to a sustainable local public transport system. Res. Transp. Econ. **48**, 364–372 (2014)

15. World commission on environment and development 1987 AND UN general assembly (2005)

16. Wang, C., Quddus, M., Enoch, M., Ryley, T., Davison, L.: Multilevel modelling of demand responsive transport (DRT) trips in Greater Manchester based on area-wide socio-economic data. Transportation **41**(3), 589e610 (2013)

17. Ambrosino, G., Nelson, J., Romananazzon, M. (eds.): Demand Responsive Transport: Towards the Flexible Agency. ENEA (Italian National Agency for New Technologies, Energy and sustainable economic development) (2003)

18. Le, H.T., Carrel, A.L., Li, M.: How much dissatisfaction is too much for transit? Linking transit user satisfaction and loyalty using panel data. Travel Behav. Soc. **20**, 144–154 (2020)

19. Gooze, A., Watkins, K.E., Borning, A.: Benefits of real-time transit information and impacts of data accuracy on rider experience. Transp. Res. Rec. **2351**(1), 95–103 (2013)

20. Khan, A.M., Etminani-Ghasrodashti, R., Kermanshachi, S., Rosenberger, J.M., Foss, A., Hladik, G.: Demand-responsive transit (DRT) services vs. fixed route transit: an exploratory study of university students. In: International Conference on Transportation and Development, pp. 77–87 (2022)

21. Desaulniers, G., Hickman, M.: Public transit (chapter 2), handbook in operations research and management science. Transportation **14**, 1–704 (2007)

22. Gorev, A., Popova, O., Solodkij, A.: Demand-responsive transit systems in areas with low transport demand of "smart city." Transp. Res. Procedia **50**, 160–166 (2020)

23. Wang, C., Quddus, M., Enoch, M., Ryley, T., Davison, L.: Exploring the propensity to travel by demand responsive transport in the rural area of Lincolnshire in England. Case Stud. Transp. Policy **3**(2), 129–136 (2015)

24. Coutinho, F.M., van Oort, N., Christoforou, Z., Alonso-González, M.J., Cats, O., Hoogendoorn, S.: Impacts of replacing a fixed public transport line by a demand responsive transport system: case study of a rural area in Amsterdam. Res. Transp. Econ. **83**, 100910 (2020)

25. Kirsimaa, K., Suik, K.: Demand-responsive transport (drt) in the Baltic Sea Region and beyond (2020)

26. Bauchinger, L., Reichenberger, A., Goodwin-Hawkins, B., Kobal, J., Hrabar, M., Oedl-Wieser, T.: Developing sustainable and flexible rural–urban connectivity through complementary mobility services. Sustainability **13**(3), 1280 (2021)

27. Thao, V.T., Imhof, S., von Arx, W.: Demand responsive transport: new insights from peri-urban experiences. Travel Behav. Soc. **31**, 141–150 (2023)

28. Pavanini, T., Liimatainen, H., Sievers, N., Heemsoth, J.P.: The role of DRT in European urban public transport systems—a comparison between Tampere, Braunschweig and Genoa. Future Transp. **3**(2), 584–600 (2023)
29. Marinelli, M., Gallo, M.: An integrated bus transit service for demand-responsive urban public transport. Transp. Res. Procedia **78**, 327–334 (2024)
30. Durand, A., Zijlstra, T.: Public transport as travel alternative for users of special transport services in the Netherlands. J. Transp. Health **29**, 101568 (2023)
31. Martí, P., Jordán, J., Julian, V.: A flexible approach for demand-responsive public transport in rural areas. Comput. Sci. Inf. Syst. **21**(1) (2024)
32. Wang, D., Araldo, A., Yacoubi, M.A.E.: AccEq-DRT: planning demand-responsive transit to reduce inequality of accessibility. arXiv preprint arXiv:2310.04348 (2023)
33. Guo, J., Mishra, S., Brakewood, C.: Analyzing gender and age differences in travel patterns and accessibility for demand response transit in small urban areas: a case study of Tennessee. J. Transp. Land Use **17**(1), 675–706 (2024)
34. Bull, J.W., et al.: Strengths, weaknesses, opportunities and threats: a SWOT analysis of the ecosystem services framework. Ecosyst. Serv. **17**, 99–111 (2016)
35. Bugheanu, A.M.: SWOT analysis of public transport system in Bucharest. Manage. Res. Pract. **7**(1), 14–31 (2015)
36. Hatefi, S.M.: Strategic planning of urban transportation system based on sustainable development dimensions using an integrated SWOT and fuzzy COPRAS approach. Glob. J. Environ. Sci. Manage. **4**(1), 99–112 (2018)
37. Campisi, T., Nikitas, A., Al-Rashid, M.A., Nikiforiadis, A., Tesoriere, G., Basbas, S.: The rise of e-scooters in Palermo: a SWOT analysis and travel time study. In: International Conference on Computational Science and Its Applications, pp. 469–483. Springer, Cham (2022)
38. Stoilova, S.D., Martinov, S.V.: Selecting a location for establishing a rail-road intermodal terminal by using a hybrid SWOT/MCDM model. In: IOP Conference Series: Materials Science and Engineering, vol. 618, no. 1, p. 012060. IOP Publishing (2019)
39. Campisi, T., Canale, A., Tesoriere, G.: SWOT analysis for the implementation of spaces and pedestrian paths at the street markets of Palermo. In: AIP Conference Proceedings, vol. 2040, no. 1. AIP Publishing (2018)
40. Comino, E., Ferretti, V.: Indicators-based spatial SWOT analysis: supporting the strategic planning and management of complex territorial systems. Ecol. Ind. **60**, 1104–1117 (2016)
41. Rauch, P., et al.: SWOT analysis and strategy development for forest fuel supply chains in South East Europe. For. Policy Econ. **61**, 87–94 (2015)
42. Amin, S.H., Yan, N., Morris, D.: Analysis of transportation modes by evaluating SWOT factors and pairwise comparisons: a case study. Multi-Criteria Methods Tech. Appl. Supply Chain Manage. **57** (2018)
43. MOVMI. https://movmi.net/blog/exploring-demand-responsive-transit-drt-the-history-business-models-benefits/
44. CCN. https://www.countycouncilsnetwork.org.uk/three-in-four-rural-authorities-roll-out-new-demand-responsive-transport-but-warn-that-they-are-not-a-substitute-for-traditional-bus-services/#:~:text=Analysis%20from%20the%20County%20Councils,a%20result%20of%20reduced%20services
45. GOV.UK. https://www.gov.uk/government/organisations/department-for-transport

Short Papers

Beyond Kaplan-Meier: A Comprehensive R Package for Interval-Censored Survival Analysis Using Turnbull's Approach

Marta Azevedo[1], Gustavo Soutinho[2], and Luís Meira-Machado[1]([✉])

[1] Centre of Mathematics, University of Minho, Braga, Portugal
lmachado@math.uminho.pt
[2] Research on Economics, Management and Information Technologies (REMIT),
Portucalense University, Porto, Portugal

Abstract. Interval-censored data frequently arise in survival analysis when the exact time of an event is unknown but is known to occur within a specific time interval. Traditional methods like the Kaplan-Meier estimator are inadequate for such data, necessitating specialized approaches. This paper presents an R library designed to handle interval-censored data, emphasizing the use of Turnbull's estimator for nonparametric survival estimation. The package offers flexible functionalities, including the calculation of survival estimates, the generation of both static and interactive plots, and the construction of bootstrap-based confidence bands. Additionally, the library provides users with detailed outputs such as Turnbull intervals and their corresponding weights, which are instrumental in understanding the survival distribution and serve as an analogue to Kaplan-Meier weights in right-censored contexts. These weights enable the extension of survival analysis methods to more complex models, including multi-state frameworks. The practical utility of the library is demonstrated using real-world datasets, highlighting its potential to support advanced survival analysis and foster the development of new estimators beyond traditional survival probabilities.

Keywords: survivalTB package · Intervalar censoring · Turnbull estimator

1 Introduction

Survival analysis is a cornerstone of statistical methodology, widely applied in medical research, reliability engineering, and social sciences to model the time until the occurrence of a specific event, such as system failure or disease progression [1–3]. While classical survival analysis methods, such as the Kaplan-Meier estimator [4], are tailored for right-censored data, where the exact event time is either observed or known to exceed a certain time point, many real-world scenarios involve more complex censoring mechanisms. One such instance is interval censoring, where the exact time of the event is unknown, but it is known to have

O. Gervasi et al. (Eds.): ICCSA 2025 Workshops, LNCS 15899, pp. 67–77, 2026.
https://doi.org/10.1007/978-3-031-97663-6_5

occurred within a specific time interval [5]. This type of censoring is common in longitudinal studies, medical follow-ups, and reliability testing, where the event of interest is only detectable at discrete inspection times.

Traditional methods like the Kaplan-Meier estimator are inadequate for interval-censored data as they cannot account for the uncertainty within the censoring intervals. To address this, Turnbull [6] proposed a nonparametric maximum likelihood estimator (NPMLE) that generalizes the Kaplan-Meier approach to handle interval-censored data. The Turnbull estimator iteratively computes survival probabilities over a set of non-overlapping intervals, known as Turnbull intervals, and assigns corresponding weights to these intervals to construct the survival curve. These weights serve as an analogue to Kaplan-Meier weights in right-censored data, facilitating further statistical analysis and enabling extensions to more complex models, such as multi-state frameworks.

Despite its theoretical robustness, the practical application of the Turnbull estimator remains challenging, particularly when it comes to integrating confidence bands, conducting bootstrap procedures, or visualizing results interactively. Existing R packages provide partial solutions for analyzing interval-censored data. The widely used `survival` package provides foundational tools for survival analysis, including Kaplan-Meier estimation and Cox proportional hazards models. While it does offer some support for interval-censored data, its capabilities remain limited. The `interval` package implements both parametric and nonparametric methods tailored for interval-censored data, while `icenReg` extends this functionality by supporting flexible parametric and semiparametric regression models. Additionally, `intcox` adapts the Cox model for interval-censored data, and `Icens` focuses on nonparametric estimation and allows for multiple imputation strategies to handle censoring uncertainty. Additionally, the `smicd` package offers a suite of statistical methods tailored for interval-censored data, particularly focusing on socioeconomic indicators and regression modeling using multiply imputed datasets. While valuable in applied contexts, it does not implement Turnbull's estimator or provide the same level of integration with visualization and confidence band functionalities as survivalTB.

However, these tools often lack features that facilitate comprehensive survival analysis, such as the ability to compute bootstrap confidence bands and not all directly extract Turnbull intervals and their corresponding weights. These components are crucial for extending survival analysis to more complex contexts, such as multi-state models, and for enabling the development of novel statistical estimators.

To address these gaps, this paper introduces the `survivalTB` package, an R library designed specifically for interval-censored survival data. The package focuses on enhancing user accessibility and analytical flexibility by providing tools for: (i) Estimating survival functions using Turnbull's estimator, (ii) Computing bootstrap-based confidence bands, (iii) Extracting Turnbull intervals and their corresponding weights, (iv) Generating both static and interactive survival plots.

The `survivalTB` package aims to simplify complex survival analysis tasks while maintaining methodological rigor, offering a valuable resource for researchers and practitioners dealing with interval-censored data.

The remainder of this paper is organized as follows. Section 2 describes the methodological framework for survival function estimation, with a focus on interval censoring and Turnbull's estimator. Section 3 introduces the `survivalTB` package, detailing its core functionalities and implementation. Section 4 presents a practical application of the package using a real biomedical dataset, while Sect. 5 discusses its applications beyond survival curve estimation. Finally, Sect. 6 provides concluding remarks.

2 Methods

2.1 Survival Function Estimation

The survival function, denoted as $S(t)$, represents the probability that an individual or object survives beyond a given time t, $S(t) = P(T > t)$ where T is a non-negative random variable representing the event time. Survival analysis plays a crucial role in various fields, including medical research, reliability engineering, and social sciences, as it allows for the estimation of event probabilities over time.

The survival function can be estimated using parametric or nonparametric approaches. Parametric methods assume that the survival times follow a specific distribution, such as exponential or Weibull, allowing for a model-based interpretation. While these methods can provide efficient estimates when the assumed distribution is appropriate, they may lead to biased results if the underlying distributional assumptions do not hold.

In contrast, nonparametric estimators make fewer assumptions about the underlying survival distribution, offering greater flexibility in modeling real-world data. A well-known example is the Kaplan-Meier estimator [4], widely used for right-censored data. This estimator calculates survival probabilities at observed event times, producing a stepwise survival function. It effectively adjusts for right-censored observations by incorporating only the individuals at risk at each event time.

Much of the work in survival analysis has focused on right-censored data. However, in many practical applications, event times are not exactly observed but are only known to lie within a given interval. This scenario, known as interval censoring, occurs frequently in clinical trials, reliability testing, and longitudinal studies where events are only detected at discrete inspection times.

Formally, for an individual i, the event time T_i is known to lie within an observation interval $[L_i, R_i)$, where $L_i \leq T_i < R_i$. If $R_i = \infty$, the observation is right-censored, meaning that the event has not been observed up to the last recorded time. If $L_i = R_i$, the exact event time is known. When $L_i < R_i < \infty$, the event is interval-censored, indicating that the event occurred within a specific time interval but without precise knowledge of the exact time.

A common but suboptimal approach to dealing with interval censoring is to approximate event times using imputation methods such as left, right, or midpoint imputation. These methods assign a single estimated event time within the censoring interval and then apply standard right-censoring techniques, such as the Kaplan-Meier estimator. However, this approach introduces bias and underestimates the variability of survival estimates, as it ignores the full uncertainty associated with the censoring interval.

A more appropriate method for interval-censored data is the Turnbull estimator [6], which generalizes the Kaplan-Meier approach by iteratively computing survival probabilities over non-overlapping intervals. This estimator constructs a nonparametric maximum likelihood estimate (NPMLE) of the survival function while properly accounting for interval censoring.

In this work, we focus on the Turnbull estimator for interval-censored data and its implementation within the `survivalTB` package, which facilitates the estimation of survival probabilities while providing additional analytical tools such as confidence bands and interval weight extraction.

2.2   Turnbull Estimator

The Turnbull estimator [6] extends the Kaplan-Meier estimator to interval-censored data through a nonparametric maximum likelihood estimation (NPMLE) approach. It is specifically designed to account for the uncertainty introduced by interval censoring by incorporating likelihood contributions from exact, right-censored, and interval-censored observations.

Construction of Turnbull Intervals. The first step in applying the Turnbull estimator involves determining a set of disjoint intervals, known as Turnbull intervals, over which the survival function will be estimated. These intervals are derived from the union of all observed censoring intervals. Let $\mathcal{D} = \{[L_i, R_i)\}_{i=1}^{n}$ represent the set of all observed intervals. The Turnbull intervals are constructed by identifying the distinct endpoints from $\mathcal{D}$, ordering them, and forming non-overlapping intervals that cover the support of T.

Specifically, these intervals are defined using the set of unique left and right endpoints, denoted as $I_j = [u_j, v_j)$, where u_j corresponds to a left endpoint, v_j to a right endpoint, and no other observed endpoint exists between them.

Likelihood Function and Weights. The NPMLE is obtained by maximizing the likelihood function over the discrete distribution of event times across the Turnbull intervals. Let p_j denote the probability that the event occurs in interval I_j.

For each interval $I_j = [u_j, v_j)$, the probability mass p_j, representing the probability that the event time T falls within that interval, is defined as $p_j = P(u_j \leq T < v_j)$. These probabilities must satisfy:

$$\sum_{j=1}^{m} p_j = 1, \quad p_j \geq 0 \tag{1}$$

The likelihood contribution for an observation i with censoring interval $[L_i, R_i)$ is:

$$l_i = \sum_{j:\, I_j \subset [L_i, R_i)} p_j \tag{2}$$

where the summation is taken over all Turnbull intervals $I_j = [u_j, v_j)$ that are fully contained within the observed censoring interval $[L_i, R_i)$ for individual i.

The total log-likelihood for the sample is:

$$\mathcal{L} = \sum_{i=1}^{n} \log \left(\sum_{j:\, I_j \subset [L_i, R_i)} p_j \right) \tag{3}$$

Maximizing this likelihood is typically achieved using the Expectation-Maximization (EM) algorithm. The iterative steps are as follows:

E-Step: Compute the expected number of events in each interval I_j based on the current estimates of p_j:

$$E_j = \sum_{i=1}^{n} \frac{p_j \mathbf{1}_{\{I_j \subset [L_i, R_i)\}}}{\sum_{k:\, I_k \subset [L_i, R_i)} p_k} \tag{4}$$

M-Step: Update the probability estimates:

$$p_j^{(t+1)} = \frac{E_j}{n} \tag{5}$$

These steps are repeated until convergence, typically when the change in the log-likelihood between iterations falls below a predefined threshold.

Estimating the Survival Function. Once the weights p_j for each Turnbull interval are obtained, the survival function is estimated as a step function. The survival probability at the right endpoint of each interval t_j is given by:

$$\hat{S}(t_j) = 1 - \sum_{k=1}^{j} p_k \tag{6}$$

This step function decreases at the endpoints of the Turnbull intervals, similar in structure to the Kaplan-Meier curve but adapted for the interval-censored data.

Properties and Interpretation. The Turnbull estimator is a nonparametric and consistent estimator for the survival function under interval censoring. The weights p_j represent the estimated proportion of failures within each Turnbull interval and play a role analogous to the Kaplan-Meier jump sizes at exact event times. The flexibility of the estimator allows it to accommodate various forms of censoring, including right-censoring and exact observations.

Confidence intervals for the survival estimates can be obtained using bootstrap resampling techniques, providing additional measures of uncertainty in the survival estimates.

3 The `survivalTB` Package

The `survivalTB` package provides a comprehensive and flexible workflow for conducting interval-censored survival analysis. It offers functions to preprocess interval-censored data, estimate survival functions using Turnbull's estimator, compute bootstrap-based confidence intervals, and create both static and interactive visualizations. The package is designed to address the complexities inherent in interval-censored data, which frequently arise in clinical trials, epidemiological studies, and reliability engineering. Its implementation in R [7] ensures reproducibility and seamless integration with other statistical packages, promoting efficient data analysis workflows.

The core functionality of the package is structured around three main functions:

- `TNBintervals`: Estimates survival distributions for interval-censored data using Turnbull's estimator, with optional bootstrap replications for confidence interval estimation.
- `TNBsurvival`: Provides time-specific survival estimates and allows for the calculation of confidence intervals at user-defined confidence levels.
- `plot.TB` and `plot.TBL`: Facilitate the visualization of survival curves, with `plot.TB` using base R graphics and `plot.TBL` offering interactive, Plotly-based visualizations.

These functions enable users to handle interval-censored survival data efficiently while providing flexibility in analysis and presentation.

A detailed summary of the arguments for each function is presented in Tables 1, 2, and 3.

Table 1. Summary of the arguments for the function `TNBintervals`.

Argument	Description
`left`	Numeric vector of left interval boundaries
`right`	Numeric vector of right interval boundaries (can include `NA` for right-censored data)
`nboot`	Integer specifying the number of bootstrap replications. Default is 1 (no bootstrap)

4 Example of Application

To illustrate the application of `survivalTB`, we use the `bcos` dataset from the `interval` package, which contains interval-censored survival times of breast cancer patients.

Table 2. Summary of the arguments for the function `TNBsurvival`.

Argument	Description
data	A list containing survival estimates (output of `TNBintervals`)
times	Numeric vector of time points for which survival estimates are required
conf	Logical indicating whether to calculate confidence intervals. Default is `FALSE`
conf.level	Numeric value specifying the confidence level for intervals (e.g., 0.95 for 95%). Default is 0.95

4.1   Loading the Package and Exploring the Data

Originally described by Finkelstein and Wolfe (1985) [8], this dataset consists of 94 observations and examines the time to cosmetic deterioration in breast cancer patients. The study includes two treatment groups: 46 patients who received radiotherapy alone and 48 patients who received both radiotherapy and chemotherapy. Since deterioration was only detected during clinical visits, 56 patients were interval-censored, while the remaining 38, who did not experience deterioration, were right-censored.

The dataset includes three variables. The variable `left` represents the lower boundary of the time interval during which the event was observed or censored, while `right` corresponds to the upper boundary. If `right` is Inf, the observation is right-censored. The variable `treatment` indicates the type of treatment received, distinguishing between radiotherapy alone (`Rad`) and a combination of radiotherapy and chemotherapy (`RadChem`).

We begin by loading the `survivalTB` package and importing the `bcos` dataset:

```
library(interval)
head(bcos)
```

```
  left right treatment
1   45   Inf       Rad
2    6    10       Rad
3    0     7       Rad
4   46   Inf       Rad
5   46   Inf       Rad
6    7    16       Rad
```

In this dataset, the `left` and `right` columns define the time interval within which the event was observed or censored. When `right` is Inf, the observation is right-censored, meaning the event was not recorded during the study period.

The presence of both interval and right censoring in the dataset makes it particularly valuable for assessing the flexibility and performance of survival analysis techniques, including those implemented in the `survivalTB` package.

Table 3. Summary of the arguments for the function `plot.TBL`.

Argument	Description
x	A list containing survival estimates (output of `TNBintervals`)
conf	Logical indicating whether to include confidence bands. Default is `FALSE`
conf.level	Numeric value specifying the confidence level for the bands (e.g., 0.95 for 95%). Default is 0.95
main	Character string specifying the title of the plot
xlab	Character string for the x-axis label
ylab	Character string for the y-axis label
line.col	Character string specifying the color of the survival curve. Default is "`blue`"
showlegend	Logical indicating whether to display the legend. Default is `TRUE`
main.line	Character string for the label of the main survival curve in the plot legend. Default is "`survival`"
filled	Character string for the label of the confidence interval ribbon in the legend. Default is "CI"
line.width	Numeric value specifying the line width for the survival curve. Default is 2
fillcolor	Character string specifying the color for the confidence band fill (e.g., "`rgba(128, 128, 128, 0.3)`"). Default is grey
. . .	Additional graphical parameters

4.2   Estimating the Survival Function

The `survivalTB` package enables estimation of survival probabilities from interval-censored data, supports bootstrap replication, and provides visualization tools.

To obtain survival estimates and generate the corresponding plots, it is essential to first use the `TNBintervals` function. This function identifies the set of all Turnbull intervals —the non-overlapping intervals used in the Turnbull estimator for interval-censored data. Additionally, it calculates the weights assigned to each Turnbull interval, which are crucial for deriving survival estimates.

```
library(survivalTB)
tbdata <- TNBintervals(bcos$left, bcos$right, nboot = 500)
tbdata$original
```

```
   left right weight survival
1     4     5 0.0449   0.9551
2     6     7 0.0226   0.9325
3     7     8 0.0560   0.8765
4    11    12 0.0790   0.7975
```

```
5    16    17 0.0605    0.7370
6    18    19 0.0216    0.7154
7    19    20 0.1441    0.5713
8    24    25 0.0497    0.5216
9    30    31 0.0911    0.4305
10   38    39 0.1264    0.3041
11   46    48 0.1869    0.1172
12   48    60 0.1170    0.0002
```

The output consists of three key components: Turnbull intervals, represented by the left and right columns; weights, which indicate the proportion assigned to each Turnbull interval; and cumulative survival estimates, which reflect the survival probability up to each interval.

We can compute survival probabilities at specific time points using the TNBsurvival() function:

```
times <- c(5, 10, 15, 20, 25, 30, 40, 45, 50)
est <- TNBsurvival(data = tbdata, times = times, conf = TRUE,
conf.level = 0.95)
print(est)
```

The resulting survival estimates are:

```
  time survival    ci_lower   ci_upper
1    5   0.9551   0.8951200 1.0000000
2   10   0.8765   0.8073350 0.9423600
3   15   0.7975   0.6939475 0.8776575
4   20   0.5713   0.4509125 0.7043875
5   25   0.5216   0.4234750 0.6416075
6   30   0.5216   0.3765175 0.6279675
7   40   0.3041   0.1888325 0.4364175
8   45   0.3041   0.1888325 0.4320300
9   50   0.0977   0.0000000 0.3350450
```

4.3   Visualizing the Survival Curve

To visualize the survival curve and include confidence bands, we use the plot() function:

```
plot(tbdata, conf = TRUE, conf.level = 0.95)
```

The plot (Fig. 1) displays the estimated survival curve alongside 95% confidence bands, enhancing the interpretability of the results. This visualization allows users to explore survival probabilities over time, providing insights into the progression of the event of interest.

An interactive plot, generated using the Plotly R package, can be obtained by setting the argument *interactive = TRUE*.

5   Applications Beyond Survival Curves

In recent years, several methods have been proposed in the literature for estimating key quantities in multi-state models, including the state occupation probabilities and transition probabilities. Notably, the work of Uña-Álvarez and Meira-Machado (2015) [9], published in *Biometrics*, introduced innovative techniques for estimating these probabilities under right-censored data. However, most of these methods are designed specifically for right-censored datasets and do not readily extend to interval-censored scenarios. Furthermore, the existing literature on multi-state models under interval censoring remains sparse, leaving a significant gap in methodological development.

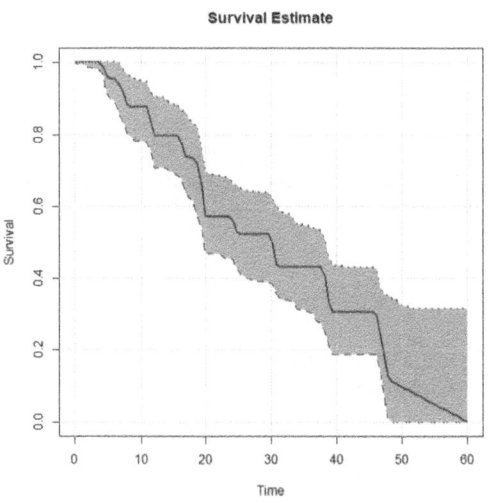

Fig. 1. Estimated survival curve using the Turnbull Estimator with 95% confidence bands.

Many of the existing methods for right-censored data rely on the Kaplan-Meier estimator or the associated Kaplan-Meier weights to derive occupation and transition probabilities. While effective in right-censored contexts, these methods cannot be directly applied to interval-censored data due to the inherent uncertainty in event times. However, the principles underlying these approaches can be adapted by substituting the Kaplan-Meier estimator with the Turnbull estimator and using the weights assigned to the Turnbull intervals. This substitution allows for the extension of existing multi-state analysis methods to interval-censored data, enabling more comprehensive and accurate modeling.

The `survivalTB` package provides researchers with the necessary tools to implement these adaptations. By offering access to both the survival estimates and the detailed structure of the Turnbull intervals along with their associated weights, the package equips users with the essential components needed for developing and applying advanced estimation methods in multi-state models under interval censoring.

Moreover, the versatility of the `survivalTB` package extends beyond simple survival analysis. Its functionalities can be applied to more complex frameworks, including recurrent event models and competing risks, broadening its utility across a range of research fields. Ongoing work is also focused on adapting and extending existing multi-state methods to fully accommodate interval-censored data, aiming to close the current methodological gaps and provide researchers with more robust analytical tools.

The survivalTB library, along with all its functionalities, is freely available at https://github.com/martaaaa/survivalTB. This repository provides access to the latest version of the library, documentation, and examples to facilitate its use.

6   Conclusion

The `survivalTB` package provides a robust and user-friendly framework for conducting survival analysis with interval-censored data. Leveraging Turnbull's estimator and bootstrap resampling techniques, it supports accurate survival probability estimation while offering tools for intuitive and interactive data visualization. Its comprehensive feature set makes it a valuable resource for researchers and practitioners in medical, epidemiological, and reliability studies.

Acknowledgments. This work is funded by national funds through FCT Fundação para a Ciência e a Tecnologia, I.P., under the UID/00013: Centro de Matemática da Universidade do Minho (CMAT/UM) Program Contract, and the project reference 2023.14897.PEX (DOI: 10.54499/2023.14897.PEX).

References

1. Klein, J., Moeschberger, M.: Survival Analysis - Techniques for Censored and Truncated Data. Springer, New York (1997)
2. Tableman, M., Kim, J.: Survival Analysis Using S. Chapman & Hall Ltd. (2003)
3. Kleinbaum, D., Klein, M.: Survival Analysis: A Self-Learning Text. Springer, New York (2012)
4. Kaplan, E.L., Meier, P.: Nonparametric estimation from incomplete observations. J. Am. Stat. Assoc. **53**, 457–481 (1958)
5. Radke, B.R.: A demonstration of interval-censored survival analysis. Prev. Vet. Med. **59**, 241–256 (2003)
6. Turnbull, B.W.: The empirical distribution function with arbitrarily grouped, censored and truncated data. J. Roy. Stat. Soc. Ser. B **38**, 290–295 (1976)
7. R Core Team. R: a language and environment for statistical computing. R Foundation for Statistical Computing, Vienna (2024). http://www.R-project.org/
8. Finkelstein, D.M., Wolfe, R.A.: A semiparametric model for regression analysis of interval-censored failure time data. Biometrics **41**, 731–740 (1985)
9. de Uña-Álvarez, J., Meira-Machado, L.: Nonparametric estimation of transition probabilities in the non-Markov illness-death model: a comparative study. Biometrics **71**(2), 364–375 (2015)

Imputation of the Response Variable in Survival Analysis with Interval-Censored Data

Gustavo Soutinho[1]([✉])[iD] and Luís Meira-Machado[2][iD]

[1] Research on Economics, Management and Information Technologies (REMIT), Portucalense University, Porto, Portugal
`gustavo.soutinho@upt.pt`
[2] Centre of Mathematics, University of Minho, Braga, Portugal

Abstract. Handling interval-censored data in survival analysis presents significant challenges, as the exact time to the event is only known to fall within predefined intervals. Common imputation strategies, such as those that use the lower bound, upper bound, or midpoint of the interval, often fail to capture the inherent uncertainty in the data, leading to biased or imprecise estimates. Prior studies have demonstrated the limitations of these approaches, particularly in accurately estimating survival probabilities and hazard ratios.

To tackle these issues, we propose the Scaled Linear Redistribution Method, a new imputation technique aimed at overcoming the limitations of existing methods. The method redistributes imputed values within the interval, keeping their variation and basic statistical behavior. While our approach has not yet been implemented, it represents a promising direction for future research. We plan to evaluate its performance through a comprehensive simulation study, comparing its performance to that of traditional imputation methods and the Turnbull estimator, a widely used nonparametric method for interval-censored data.

Keywords: Interval-censored data · Survival analysis · Imputation methods

1 Introduction

In survival analysis, the estimation of the survival function is important for understanding the time-to-event process under study. However, the presence of interval-censored data, where the exact timing of the event is unknown but known to fall within a specific interval $[L, R]$, poses significant analytical challenges. Interval censoring often arises in studies where individuals are assessed at predetermined intervals, leading to incomplete observations that are a particular case of interval-censored data. Properly handling this type of censoring is essential to avoid bias and obtain reliable estimates.

Despite the availability of specialized statistical methods for interval-censored data, many researchers continue to rely on the Kaplan-Meier estimator [1], which

© The Author(s), under exclusive license to Springer Nature Switzerland AG 2026
O. Gervasi et al. (Eds.): ICCSA 2025 Workshops, LNCS 15899, pp. 78–88, 2026.
https://doi.org/10.1007/978-3-031-97663-6_6

is designed for right-censored data. In this context, to deal with interval censoring, a typical approach is to assign a specific value within the interval, such as the lower limit, the upper limit, or the midpoint of the interval. While easy to apply, these methods ignore the uncertainty of interval-censored data, which may cause biased results, particularly when event rates vary between intervals [2, 4].

To overcome these challenges, nonparametric techniques like the Turnbull estimator [5] have been introduced as an extension of the Kaplan-Meier estimator for interval-censored data. This estimator employs an iterative self-consistency algorithm for survival function using maximum likelihood, which allows to effectively deal with interval censoring in the data. Despite its robustness and flexibility, the Turnbull estimator can be computationally intensive in cases with complex censoring schemes or large datasets [6]. In addition, it does not include covariates or offer hazard ratio estimates, which restricts its application in studies involving more comprehensive inferential insights.

Parametric and semiparametric regression models can be valid alternative approaches, enabling the inclusion of covariates and the modeling of the survival distribution. Among these, the parametric Weibull regression model and the Cox proportional hazards model [7] have been adapted to accommodate interval-censored data [2]. These techniques yield efficient estimates when their underlying assumptions hold. However, if these assumptions are violated or the model is misspecified, their performance can be poor.

Recently, imputation-based methods have become popular due to their adaptability and ability to work with a wide variety of models. As an example, we may refer multiple imputation, which uses covariate data to estimate missing or censored values. The smcfcs R package [8] (Substantive Model Compatible Fully Conditional Specification) highlights its ability to generate imputations that fit well with the survival model being studied. This capacity ensures that the imputed data set is in agreement with the structure of the survival process, becoming an effective tool for handling complex censoring situations [4].

Besides the conventional imputation approaches, we can also mention other new methods that were introduced to overcome the drawbacks of imputing a single value. Strapasson [2] conducted a simulation study to compare various imputation strategies, concluding that methods which explicitly account for interval censoring (such as the Turnbull estimator) tend to be more accurate. Recently, [3] proposed and validated through simulation extensions to SIMEX (Simulation-Extrapolation) that account for uncertainty in both event times and covariate trajectories. This involves modeling the joint distribution of the event and time-varying variables, or aligning imputed event times with the corresponding covariate values. However, when direct approaches are not feasible, the imputation of the midpoint can serve as a reasonable alternative, especially for narrow intervals or when event rates remain relatively stable.

In this study, we build upon these advancements by introducing the Scaled Linear Redistribution Method, a novel imputation approach that adjusts imputed values to fit within the interval bounds proportionally, preserving the variability of the original distribution.

Thus, this work represents a preliminary step, laying the groundwork for further research that extends beyond its current scope. In future work, we plan to conduct a comprehensive simulation study comparing the performance of this method against three traditional imputation strategies (lower bound, upper bound, and midpoint) as well as the Turnbull estimator. This forthcoming analysis will assess each method's ability to estimate survival probabilities and hazard ratios, offering insights into their strengths and limitations when handling interval-censored survival data. The results of these simulations, along with applications to real data, will be reported in a separate publication.

2   Notation

To facilitate the discussion of interval-censored data and the proposed methods, we introduce the following notation. Let T denote the true (unobserved) time of the event of interest. The event time is known to occur within a specific interval $[L, R]$, where L represents the lower bound and R represents the upper bound of the interval. If the event is only known to have occurred after a specific time L, we set $R = \infty$, indicating right-censoring. In cases where the event time is precisely observed, the interval reduces to a single point, such that $L = R$.

We define the censoring indicator δ to capture the type of observation, where: $\delta = 1$ corresponds to the situation in which the event time is observed exactly, meaning $L = R$; $\delta = 2$ if the observation is interval-censored, such that $L < R$; and $\delta = 0$ if the observation is right-censored, with $R = \infty$.

The estimated survival function, denoted by $\hat{S}(t)$, represents the probability that the event occurs after time t. This function plays a key role in evaluating the performance of the proposed methods and comparing them with existing approaches, such as the Turnbull estimator and the Kaplan–Meier estimator constructed using traditional imputation techniques. This notation will be used consistently throughout the study to describe the interval-censored data and the Scaled Linear Redistribution Method, and to facilitate comparisons among the methods under investigation.

3   Estimation of Survival

3.1   Kaplan-Meier Estimator

The Kaplan-Meier estimator [1], or product-limit estimator, is a well-known nonparametric technique designed to estimate the survival function $S(t)$. This method is especially useful for handling right-censored data. Accordingly, assume now that we have the event time is observed exactly $L = R$ or it is right-censored ($R = \infty$ or $\delta = 0$).

Let $L_1 < L_2 < \cdots < L_k$ denote the ordered, distinct event times of a sample with n individuals. The Kaplan-Meier product-limit estimator of the survival function can also be expressed using the Kaplan-Meier weights as follows [9]:

$$S(t) = 1 - \sum_{i=1}^{n} W_i I(L_{(i)} \leq t). \tag{1}$$

where W_i is the weight attached to $L_{(i)}$ that is defined as:

$$W_i = \frac{\delta_{[i]}}{n-i+1} \prod_{j=1}^{i-1} \left(1 - \frac{\delta_{[j]}}{n-j+1} \right), \tag{2}$$

Although the Kaplan-Meier estimator is widely used, it cannot directly accommodate interval-censored data. For such cases, the Turnbull estimator provides a more general approach, as described in the next section.

3.2 Turnbull Estimator

The Turnbull estimator [5] generalizes the Kaplan-Meier estimator to handle interval-censored data, where the exact event time T is unknown but lies within a specified interval $[L_i, R_i]$. Interval censoring commonly arises in longitudinal studies, when the occurrence of an event can only be established retrospectively, at the time of periodic clinical visits or assessments, so that its exact timing remains unknown.

Turnbull's method introduces the concept of *Turnbull intervals*, defined as the smallest set of disjoint intervals that contain all observed interval endpoints. For each interval $(u_j, v_j]$, the survival probability p_j is defined as:

$$p_j = P(u_j < T \leq v_j) = S(u_j) - S(v_j). \tag{3}$$

The likelihood function for interval-censored data is given by:

$$L(p_1, \ldots, p_m) = \prod_{i=1}^{n} \left(\sum_{j=1}^{m} \alpha_{ij} p_j \right), \tag{4}$$

where:

- $\alpha_{ij} = I\{(u_j, v_j] \subseteq [L_i, R_i]\}$ indicates whether the j-th interval is contained within the observation window $[L_i, R_i]$,
- $p_j, j = 1, \ldots, m$, are the survival probabilities to be estimated.

To maximize the likelihood, Turnbull's iterative self-consistency algorithm updates the estimates of p_j as follows:

$$p_j^{(r)} = \frac{1}{n} \sum_{i=1}^{n} \frac{\alpha_{ij} p_j^{(r-1)}}{\sum_{k=1}^{m} \alpha_{ik} p_k^{(r-1)}}, \tag{5}$$

where r denotes the iteration step. The algorithm continues until successive updates become negligible.

The estimated survival function is then defined as:

$$\hat{S}(t) = \begin{cases} 1, & t \leq u_1, \\ 1 - \sum_{j=1}^{k} p_j, & v_j < t \leq u_{j+1}, \\ 0, & t > v_m. \end{cases} \tag{6}$$

The Turnbull estimator has several notable characteristics. It accommodates exact, interval-censored, and right-censored observations within the same framework, making it highly versatile for a variety of survival data scenarios. The estimator converges to the nonparametric maximum likelihood estimate (NPMLE) of the survival function, ensuring statistical consistency and robustness. However, the iterative nature of the algorithm makes it computationally intensive, particularly when applied to large datasets with complex censoring patterns.

While the Kaplan-Meier estimator is suited for right-censored data, the Turnbull estimator extends its applicability to interval-censored scenarios by leveraging iterative maximum likelihood methods. The Kaplan-Meier estimator with (left, right or midpoint) imputation and the Turnbull estimator will serve as foundational methods in our comparative analysis of survival estimation approaches.

3.3 Illustrative Example

To illustrate the application of the Turnbull estimator and compare it with the Kaplan-Meier estimator using midpoint imputation, we consider a dataset of ten individuals evaluated at fixed time points $t = 2, 4, 6, 8$. The small dataset is presented in Table 1.

Table 1. Dataset of ten individuals evaluated at fixed time points (2, 4, 6, and 8). All subjects were assessed at each visit.

Id	Left	Right	Midpoint	Censoring Indicator (cens)
1	4	6	5	1
2	2	4	3	1
3	6	NA	6	0
4	4	6	5	1
5	2	NA	2	0
6	6	8	7	1
7	6	8	7	1
8	6	NA	6	0
9	4	6	4	1
10	6	8	7	1

Individuals represented in rows 3, 5, and 8 contribute with right-censored observations, as their event times are unknown beyond their last recorded assessment. These cases correspond to instances where the right endpoint (R_i) is missing (denoted as NA), and therefore, the individual does not experience the event by the end of the study's follow-up period. In contrast, the remaining individuals exhibit interval-censored data, which means, although having experienced the event, their corresponding event times are known only to lie within a specific observation window $[L_i, R_i]$. The Turnbull estimator effectively incorporates both right-censored and interval-censored observations within the same framework, making it a versatile approach for estimating the survival function in this dataset.

The Turnbull estimator requires determining a set of disjoint intervals $(u_j, v_j]$ where survival probability estimates are updated. These Turnbull intervals are constructed using all unique left and right endpoints from Table 1, ensuring that:

The intervals are obtained from the set of all left and right interval endpoints in such a way that u_j is a left endpoint, v_j is a right endpoint, and there is no other left or right endpoint between them.

By applying this rule to the dataset, we identify the following Turnbull intervals:

$$(2, 4], (4, 6], (6, 8]$$

These intervals represent the time periods where events may occur, and the survival function is estimated within them.

The probability mass associated with each of these Turnbull intervals is estimated iteratively using the self-consistency algorithm. For this dataset, the final estimated probabilities p_j corresponding to the intervals $(2, 4]$, $(4, 6]$, and $(6, 8]$ are 0.1481, 0.2963, and 0.5556, respectively. These values represent the proportion of total failures distributed across the intervals, ensuring that the sum of all interval probabilities equals one. The survival function may then be constructed stepwise using these probabilities, preserving the interval-censored nature of the data.

A common approach for handling interval-censored data is to apply the Kaplan-Meier estimator with midpoint imputation, where each interval $[L_i, R_i]$ is replaced by its midpoint, as shown in Table 1: $T_i = \frac{L_i + R_i}{2}$. The corresponding censoring indicator is provided in the last column of the table, where a value of 0 denotes a right-censored observation, while a value of 1 indicates that an event is assumed to occur at the midpoint of the interval.

Applying the Kaplan-Meier estimator to these imputed values provides an approximate survival curve, but at the cost of assuming that all events occur exactly at the midpoint rather than being distributed across the Turnbull intervals.

In this specific case, applying the `survfit` function from the `survival` package in R for interval-censored data, using the `interval2` method within the `Surv` function, produces the same survival estimates as those obtained through midpoint imputation. This equivalence occurs because the study design assumes fixed evaluation times for all individuals, with no missed assessments at any evaluation point. When all individuals are evaluated at identical, predetermined time points, the Turnbull estimator effectively distributes event probabilities in a manner that aligns with the midpoint imputation approach. For instance, considering the event times 2, 3, 5, 6, and 7, the survival estimates produced by both estimators are 1, 0.889, 0.556, 0.556, and 0.

However, this equivalence does not hold in more general cases. If the study includes individuals with variable assessment times or cases where participants miss scheduled evaluations, the two methods can yield different survival estimates. For instance, if we modify the first individual's observation by setting the lower bound to 2 instead of 4, this change would reflect a scenario where this individual missed the evaluation at time 4. Under this modification, the Turnbull estimator and the midpoint imputation method would produce distinct survival estimates, as the interval-censored model appropriately accounts for the uncertainty introduced by the missing assessment. Thus, in this case, the Turnbull estimator yields survival probabilities of 1, 0.852, 0.556, 0.556, and 0, while the midpoint imputation estimator gives 1, 0.889, 0.556, 0.556, and 0.

4   Imputation Methods

4.1   Usual Imputation Methods

For interval-censored observations, where $L_i < R_i$ and R_i is finite, imputation presents a unique challenge. Conventional methods for handling such observations often involve imputing a single representative value within the interval. Typical methods are:

- Left Imputation: Assigning the event time to the lower (L_i) limit of the interval, under the assumption that it occurred at the earliest possible time within the given range.
- Right Imputation: Assigning the event time to the upper bound (R_i) of the interval, assuming it occurred at the latest possible moment within the observed range.
- Midpoint Imputation: Assigning the event time to the midpoint interval ($(L_i + R_i)/2$) of the interval, assuming the event time is uniformly distributed within the interval.

Although these methods are simple, they fail when taking into consideration the variability and uncertainty within the interval. Furthermore, they may exhibit systematic bias, particularly when the event times do not follow a uniform distribution or are strongly influenced by covariates.

Another possible approach considers the response variable as missing and estimates its value based on the connections between the covariates and the survival outcome. This method treats the interval-censored response as a missing data point, which can be imputed using appropriate techniques. However, the difficulty lies in ensuring that the imputed value remains within the bounds of the observed interval $[L_i, R_i]$.

4.2   The Scaled Linear Redistribution Method

In this section, we introduce a new proposal that we call the Scaled Linear Redistribution Method. This new method ensures that imputed values stay within the interval and keeps the natural variation in the data.

Step-by-Step Procedure

The Scaled Linear Redistribution Method comprises the following step-by-step procedures:

Step 1: For each individual with interval-censored data, perform an initial random imputation by simulating a value $T_i^{(0)}$ from a uniform distribution:

$$T_i^{(0)} \sim U(L_i, R_i),$$

where L_i and R_i are the lower and upper bounds of the censoring interval.

Step 2: Estimate a regression model using a parametric Accelerated Failure Time (AFT) model [10–12] or a machine learning model such as XGBoost [13] using the initial imputed survival times. Then, use the trained model to predict new survival times for individuals with interval-censored data.

Predicted times may include values outside the interval bounds. For instance, if an individual's event is known to occur between $L = 4$ and $R = 5$, imputations may be observed over a broader range (e.g., $[2, 12]$).

Step 3: Iteratively perform the simulation and prediction process by repeating Step 1 and Step 2 M times (e.g., $M = 100$), each time generating new simulated values and refitting the predictive model. This results in a distribution of predicted survival times for each interval-censored observation.

Step 4: For each individual i, obtain the empirical distribution of predicted times $\hat{T}_i^{(1)}, \ldots, \hat{T}_i^{(M)}$ from the previous step. To ensure compatibility with the original censoring information, these predicted values are rescaled to fit within the interval $[L_i, R_i]$ using the following transformation:

$$T_i^{\text{scaled}} = L_i + \frac{\hat{T}_i - \min(\hat{T}_i)}{\max(\hat{T}_i) - \min(\hat{T}_i)}(R_i - L_i). \tag{7}$$

That way, all values stay within the interval while keeping their variability.

Step 5: Using the rescaled imputed times, re-run the regression model, using a parametric model or machine learning method on the updated dataset. The final imputed values for interval-censored observations are then obtained as the median of the predicted, scaled survival distributions:

$$T_i^{\text{final}} = \text{median}(\hat{T}_i^{(1)}, \ldots, \hat{T}_i^{(M)}). \tag{8}$$

To assess the uncertainty of this median, calculate the standard deviation (SD) of the M imputations for each individual. Finally, the SE for each individual is computed by dividing the SD by the square root of M, reflecting the variability and uncertainty in the estimated median across the replicates. This process is repeated for each individual, and the resulting SE values provide a measure of the precision of the imputations for each subject.

By redistributing values proportionally, this approach ensures that the variability of the initial imputed distribution is retained, while all values are constrained within the interval $[L, R]$. This avoids the artificial narrowing of the data range associated with imputing a single point such as midpoint while maintaining the stochastic nature of the imputations.

One of the advantages of the proposed Scaled Linear Redistribution Method lies in its ability to incorporate covariate information directly into the imputation process. Rather than treating censored intervals in isolation, the method used the relationship between covariates and the survival outcome to obtain informed imputations.

This ensures the model stays aligned with the way the data was imputed. This contrasts with simpler strategies, such as using the interval midpoint or one of its bounds (lower or upper), which can introduce bias or overlook essential information in the data.

The method also preserves the natural variability in the data. By redistributing values proportionally within the interval, it captures the available randomness of the process without flattening the distribution, resulting in more realistic and robust imputations.

Since the imputations rely on a survival model (Step 2), the method stays aligned with the later analysis, ensuring consistency between assumptions and imputations.

Table 2 provides a comparison of commonly used imputation approaches, including the well-known lower bound, upper bound, and midpoint imputations, as well as the proposed Scaled Redistribution method. While conventional methods such as lower and upper bound imputations are simple, they often lead to systematic biases by either underestimating or overestimating event times. The midpoint imputation assumes a uniform distribution within the interval, which may be unrealistic in many scenarios. In contrast, the Scaled Redistribution

Table 2. Comparison of different imputation methods for interval-censored data.

Method	Description	Limitations
Lower Bound Imputation	Impute L, the start of the interval.	Underestimates event times and ignores variability
Upper Bound Imputation	Impute R, the end of the interval.	Overestimates event times and ignores variability
Midpoint Imputation	Impute $(L + R)/2$, the midpoint of the interval.	Assumes uniform distribution within the interval; unrealistic
Scaled Redistribution	Adjusts imputed values to fit within $[L, R]$ while preserving variability.	Computationally intensive for very narrow intervals

method ensures that imputed values respect the interval bounds while preserving variability, although it can be computationally demanding for narrow intervals. Table 2 also summarizes these methods and highlights some of their advantages and limitations.

5   Conclusion

Interval-censored data is challenging because we don't know exactly when events happen. In this context, imputation techniques such as lower-bound, upper-bound, and midpoint methods, even though they provide straightforward and computationally efficient solutions, often overlook the natural variability within observed intervals, which can lead to biases and reduce the accuracy of survival estimates. To address these problems, we propose the Scaled Linear Redistribution Method, a new approach that keeps the variation in the data and respects the original interval boundaries.

The Scaled Linear Redistribution Method derives from imputations produced through the smcfcs library, which accounts for covariate information and ensures consistency with the survival model. This approach adjusts imputed values to stay within the observed interval, which helps reduce the reliance on arbitrary assumptions commonly found in simpler methods, such as the uniform distribution used in midpoint imputation.

The proposed methods are currently under investigation, meaning that the presented formulation has not yet been implemented or validated. Based on these early ideas, the method seems to offer advantages in flexibility and how it handles the data. However, no conclusion can yet be drawn regarding performance relative to existing imputation techniques. The proportional adjustment mechanism could also increase computational complexity, particularly when dealing with datasets that have narrow intervals or a high volume of observations. Additionally, since the method relies on initial imputations from smcfcs, its overall effectiveness is dependent on the accuracy of those imputations.

This remains an ongoing area of research. Future efforts will concentrate on implementing the method, improving its computational efficiency, and performing comprehensive simulation studies to evaluate its accuracy and robustness across various censoring scenarios, including left-censoring and mixed-censoring contexts. To this end, future work will include a thorough comparison of different methodologies, making use of both real-world datasets and simulation studies.

In summary, the Scaled Linear Redistribution Method holds potential as an innovative approach for addressing interval-censored survival data. While it aims to improve on existing methods, the approach still needs to be fully tested. If proven effective, this method could become a useful tool in survival analysis. Ongoing work and future findings will be presented elsewhere.

Acknowledgments. This work is funded by national funds through FCT – Fundação para a Ciência e a Tecnologia, I.P., under the UID/00013: Centro de Matemática da Universidade do Minho (CMAT/UM) Program Contract, and the project reference 2023.14897.PEX (DOI: 10.54499/2023.14897.PEX).

References

1. Kaplan, E.L., Meier, P.: Nonparametric estimation from incomplete observations. J. Am. Stat. Assoc. **53**(282), 457–481 (1958)
2. Strapasson, D.R.: Modelos para análise de sobrevivência com censura intervalar: Estudo de simulação e aplicação. Master's thesis, Universidade de São Paulo (2007)
3. Abrahamowicz, M., Beauchamp, M.-E., Moura, C.S., Bernatsky, S., Guerra, S.F., Danieli, C.: Adapting SIMEX to correct for bias due to interval-censored outcomes in survival analysis with time-varying exposure. Biom. J. **64**(8), 1467–1485 (2022)
4. Gomes, G., Giolo, S.R., Colosimo, E.A.: Survival analysis for interval-censored data: an R tutorial. Stat. Model. **9**(3), 269–287 (2009)
5. Turnbull, B.W.: The empirical distribution function with arbitrarily grouped, censored, and truncated data. J. Roy. Stat. Soc.: Ser. B (Methodol.) **38**(3), 290–295 (1976)
6. Lin, T.I., Lee, J.C., Yen, S.Y.: Finite mixture modelling for interval-censored survival data. Stat. Med. **29**(1), 7–20 (2010)
7. Cox, D.R.: Regression models and life-tables (with discussion). J. Roy. Stat. Soc.: Ser. B (Methodol.) **34**(2), 187–202 (1972)
8. Bartlett, J.W., Keogh, R., Bonneville, E.F., Ekstrøm, C.T.: smcfcs: substantive model compatible fully conditional specification. R package version 1.9.1 (2024). https://cran.r-project.org/package=smcfcs
9. Meira-machado, L.: The Kaplan-Meier estimator: new insights and applications in multi-state survival analysis. In: Lecture Notes in Computer Science, pp. 129–139 (2023)
10. Lawless, J.F.: Statistical Models and Methods for Lifetime Data, 2nd edn. Wiley, Hoboken (2003)
11. Kalbfleisch, J.D., Prentice, R.L.: The Statistical Analysis of Failure Time Data, 2nd edn. Wiley, Hoboken (2002)
12. Wei, L.J.: The accelerated failure time model: a useful alternative to the Cox regression model in survival analysis. Stat. Med. **11**(14–15), 1871–1879 (1992)
13. Wang, H., Li, B., Ghosh, D.: A gradient boosting approach for censored survival data. Stat. Med. **38**(23), 4834–4846 (2019)

Cutting-Edge Malware Detection in Healthcare: Leveraging Cascaded-AlexNet Model

Sania Akhtar[1]([⊠]), Muhammad Hanif[1], Muhammad Waqas Arshad[2]([⊠]),
and Faryal Farooq[3]

[1] Aerial Robotics and Vision Laboratory, GIK Institute of Engineering Sciences and Technology, Topi 23460, Pakistan
{sania.akhtar,muhammad.hanif}@giki.edu.pk

[2] Department of Computer Science and Engineering, University of Bologna, 40136 Bologna, Italy
muhammadwaqas.arsha2@unibo.it

[3] Faculty of Computing and AI, Air University, Islamabad, Pakistan
faryal.farooq@students.au.edu.pk

Abstract. The rapid expansion of 5G and IoT has increased security risks in e-health applications, where malware threats pose significant challenges to patient data protection. Traditional malware detection methods rely on conventional classifiers, limiting adaptability to evolving threats. This study introduces a deep learning-based malware detection approach utilizing Convolutional Neural Networks (CNNs) to enhance classification accuracy in e-health environments. A cascaded classification framework was developed, where an optimized AlexNet model in Stage-1 performs initial classification, followed by a Stage-2 three-tier classifier for fine-grained malware family detection. The performance of our approach was evaluated on the Malimg and Malvis datasets, which include 25 and 26 malware families, respectively. Experimental results demonstrate that the Stage-1 optimized AlexNet achieves 100% accuracy on Malimg and 93% on Malvis, outperforming standard AlexNet (96% and 88%), VGG16 (93% and 81%), and ResNet50 (85% and 79%). Future work will extend the cascaded classification framework by integrating the three-tier classifier results from Stage-2 to further improve detection precision.

Keywords: Malware Detection · Deep Learning · CNN · Health-Care · Data

1 Introduction

The integration of 5G networks and Internet of Things (IoT) technologies has revolutionized e-health systems that enhanced to real time patient monitoring and cloud based medical data management. However, this digital revolution has

© The Author(s), under exclusive license to Springer Nature Switzerland AG 2026
O. Gervasi et al. (Eds.): ICCSA 2025 Workshops, LNCS 15899, pp. 89–100, 2026.
https://doi.org/10.1007/978-3-031-97663-6_7

made the healthcare infrastructure more vulnerable to advanced malware threats that target patient's records and vital medical equipment [1]. The conventional signature based detection methods are failing steadily to detect polymorphic and zero day attacks in these connected ecosystems [2]. Achieving automated feature extraction for malware analysis has become possible with recent developments in deep learning. Although VGG16 and ResNet [3] have been successful in image classification tasks, their application to malware detection in healthcare systems is still unexplored. Many current approaches are inadequate because they fail to consider the hierarchical structure of the malware classification task, in which identifying the type of malware should come before identifying the family the malware belongs to [4].

This paper presents three key contributions:

– A cascaded AlexNet architecture employing sequential classification of malware types and families.
– Comprehensive evaluation of CNNs (VGG16, Inception, ResNet) on medical malware datasets.
– Hybrid training methodology combining transfer learning with custom dense-flatten layers.

Based on the emerging research in medical cybersecurity [5], we develop the use of convolutional neural networks for the detection of e-health malware in the three critical challenges: Encrypted medical IoT traffic, the classification of evolving ransomware variants, and the efficiency of the detection device on constrained resources. The proposed model achieves 97% accuracy on the Malimg dataset, which is 14% better than other methods [6].

2   Literature Review

The integration of cloud computing and the Internet of Things (IoT) has revolutionized various domains, particularly in healthcare, by facilitating seamless connectivity among smart devices. However, this advancement has also introduced new security vulnerabilities, necessitating robust defense mechanisms. Several researchers have investigated associative rules mining and API calls sequences for malware classification [7] and also deep learning-based malware detection models, including Recurrent Neural Networks (RNNs), Long Short-Term Memory (LSTM), Convolutional Neural Networks (CNNs), Deep Belief Networks (DBNs), and Deep Reinforcement Learning (DRL), to improve threat identification accuracy and mitigate false positives [8]. In [10], authors conducted a PRISMA-based SLR on security threats in AI-driven healthcare, analyzing studies from Scopus and Web of Science. They examined vulnerabilities in NLP, computer vision, and acoustic AI, highlighting blockchain's role in ensuring dataset integrity, secure training, and trusted deployment.

In [11], authors proposed EIDS-HS for intrusion detection in Industry 5.0 healthcare. Evaluated on a benchmark dataset, it achieved high accuracy and resilience against cyber threats, ensuring robust security. In [12], authors introduced a hybrid ransomware detection framework combining heuristic profiling with machine learning.

Table 1. Malware Detection Techniques in 2023

Ref	Year	Model	Dataset	Accuracy	Challenges	Limitations
[13]	2023	EoT Framework	EMNIST, X-IIoTID, Federated TON$_{IoT}$	98%	Secure EoT-cloud integration for attack detection via federated transfer learning	Performance relies on training parameters; Edge IoT distribution is limited
[14]	2023	SFMR-SH	BitcoinHeist Ransomware Dataset	99.33%	Real-time access & ransomware protection	Blockchain may cause latency, scalability issues, and false positives
[15]	2023	Review and Analysis	N/A	N/A	Hospital cyberattacks risk data breaches and reputational damage	Reliance on outdated security and lack of real-time protection
[16]	2023	Custom CNN model	Malimg dataset	98.26%	Overfitting in pretrained models	Data imbalance issues in training
[17]	2023	AutoML with CNNs	SOREL-20M & EMBER-2018 datasets	SOTA performance	High overhead in model optimization	Difficulty in tuning neural architecture search

A summary of the 2023 literature on malware detection is presented in Table 1. The reviewed studies underscore the critical role of deep learning and optimization techniques in securing IoMT and healthcare infrastructures [9]. Current works emphasize feature selection, hyperparameter tuning, and adaptive threat detection to enhance malware identification. However, challenges such as feature dependency, computational complexity, and evolving attack strategies necessitate further research into lightweight and scalable cybersecurity solutions for real-time IoMT security. Unlike previous works that rely on flat classification or complex models prone to false positives, our proposed cascaded AlexNet architecture introduces a two-stage hierarchical classification, first by malware type, then by family enhancing detection precision, reducing false alarms, and offering a lightweight solution suitable for real-time IoMT deployment.

3   Methodology

The proposed system integrates an AI-driven malware detection module into healthcare infrastructure to safeguard E-Health records from unauthorized access, malware threats, and cyberattacks. The methodology follows a structured pipeline, leveraging deep learning models for threat detection and classification. The workflow of the proposed system is depicted in Fig. 1.

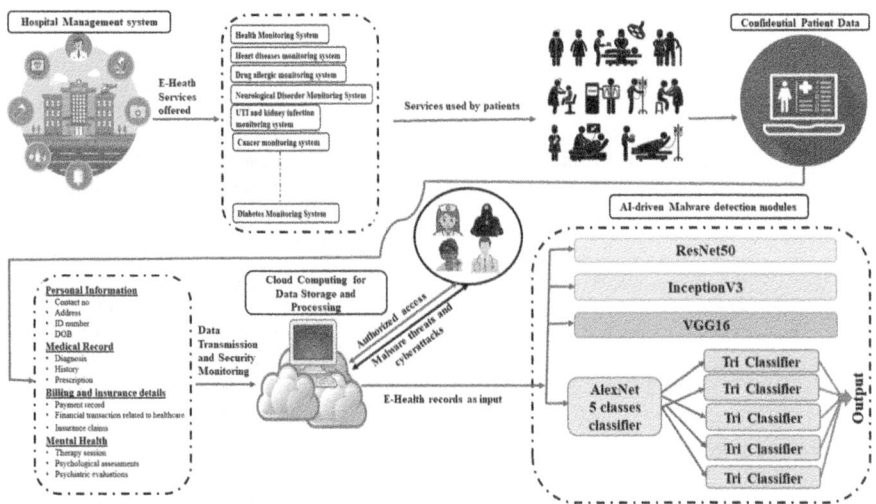

Fig. 1. Workflow of the proposed methodology.

3.1   Data Acquisition and Processing

The system processes E-Health records, which include personal information, medical history, billing details, and mental health assessments. These records are transmitted and stored via a cloud-based infrastructure, ensuring efficient data management. However, this cloud-based environment is vulnerable to various security threats, necessitating a robust intrusion detection mechanism.

3.2   AI-Driven Malware Detection Module

To identify malware threats, the system employs deep learning-based malware detection models, including ResNet50, InceptionV3, and VGG16. These pre-trained CNN architectures extract critical features from E-Health data to detect anomalies related to malware signatures, encryption patterns, and unauthorized access attempts. We developed a cascaded AlexNet architecture and detection process is divided into two key stages which is represented in Fig. 2.

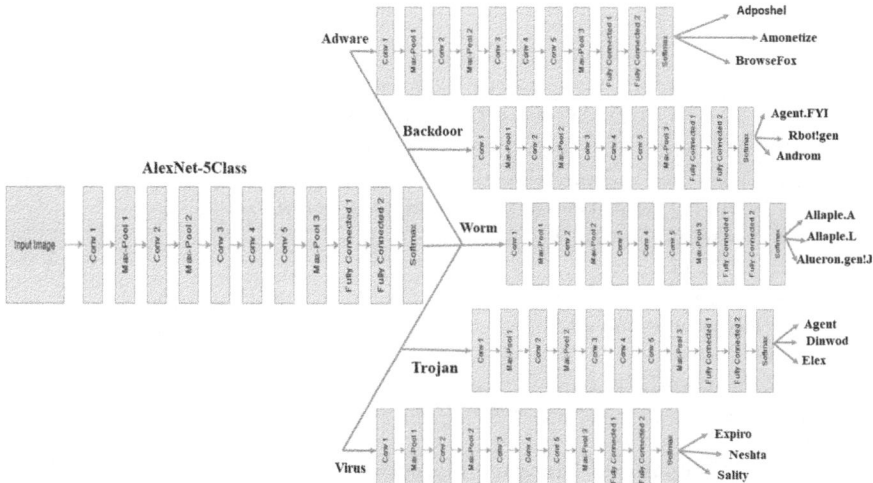

Fig. 2. Cascaded Model for Malware Classification: Stage one categorizes malware types, while stage two further classifies them into respective families.

Stage 1: AlexNet5 Classes Classifier : In the first stage, we developed a Cascaded AlexNet Model to classify malware into five primary types. AlexNet, a widely used CNN architecture, is optimized for recognizing distinct malware patterns by analyzing file system modifications, network anomalies, and execution behaviors. This initial classification enhances the model's ability to detect broad malware categories efficiently.

Tri-Class Family Classification: Following the primary classification, a Tri-Classifier framework is applied to further categorize each malware type into three specific families. This hierarchical classification enables fine-grained threat detection, ensuring precise differentiation between benign, suspicious, and malicious activities. The multi-stage approach enhances detection accuracy and security robustness, mitigating threats in real-time and reducing false positives.

3.3   Security and Deployment

The proposed framework ensures the confidentiality, integrity, and availability of patient data. The AI-driven malware detection module operates in real-time, continuously monitoring data transmission and cloud security. By integrating multi-stage classification and deep learning-based anomaly detection, the system strengthens the security of Industry 5.0-driven healthcare infrastructures, preventing unauthorized access and cyber threats effectively. Algorithm 1 illustrates the functioning of the cascaded AlexNet architecture, which detects five primary malware types and further classifies each type into three distinct malware families.

Algorithm 1. AI-Driven Malware Detection in E-Health Systems

1: **Input:** Confidential patient data stored in the cloud
2: **Output:** Classified malware threats, Classifier weights
3: **Cloud Security Monitoring & Threat Detection:**
4: **for** $i = 1$ to max-iteration **do**
5:      Perform **UAD**.
6:      **if** UAD_a **then**
7:          Flag as potential **MT**.
8:      **else**
9:          Exit_Loop = 1
10:     **end if**
11: **end for**
12: **Deep Learning-Based Malware Detection:**
13: Apply DLMC:
14: - ResNet50, InceptionV3, VGG16, Cascaded AlexNet.
15: **Two-Stage AlexNet-Based Malware Classification:**
16: **Stage 1 (Main Module):** AlexNet 5 classes classifier.
17: **Stage 2 (Submodule):** Tri-classifer:
18: **Evaluation:**
19: **for** $i = 1$ to max-iteration **do**
20:     **if** Malware_Correctly_Classified in Stage 1 = 1 **then**
21:         Proceed to Stage 2 classification.
22:         **if** Families_Correctly_Classified in Stage 2 = 1 **then**
23:             Stop = 1
24:         **else**
25:             Continue training.
26:         **end if**
27:     **end if**
28: **end for**
29: **Security Assessment & Response:**
30: **if** Malware detected **then**
31:     Generate a SAR.
32:     INSM.
33: **end if**
34: **Return:** Classified MT and SAR.

UAD = Unauthorized Access Detection, UAD_a = Unauthorized Access Attempt, SAR = Security Assessment Report, INSM = Implement Necessary Security Measures, DLMC = Deep Learning Malware Classification, Malware Threat = MT

---

4   Experimental Evaluation

4.1   Experimental Setup

The experiments were conducted on a 64-bit Windows 11 Pro operating system (Version 23H2) with 16 GB of RAM, an Intel Core i5-1334U CPU @ 1.30 GHz, and a storage capacity of 256 GB. For model training and evaluation, we utilized Google Colab's GPU resources. The proposed model was developed using various Python packages, including TensorFlow, Sci-Kit Learn, Pandas, NumPy, Seaborn, and Matplotlib.

4.2   Dataset Description

In this research article, we have presented experiments on two different datasets, malimg and melvis comprised of information regarding malware attack detection. Experimentation has been conducted by implementing four different architectures of CNN including VGG16, ResNet, Inception model, and cascaded AlexNet architecture. This section presented the effectiveness of the proposed technique by evaluating different CNN architectures on two different datasets.

Malimg: The Malimg Dataset consists of 9,339 malware images categorized into five major malware types and 25 families. However, the dataset is highly imbalanced as represented Fig. 3. A significant proportion of images belong to the Worm category, with over 30% from the Allaple.A family and 17% from the Allaple.L family. This imbalance poses challenges for deep learning model training, potentially leading to biased classification. To mitigate this issue, techniques such as selective sampling from the overrepresented families or augmenting underrepresented families with synthetic data could be employed. However, for compatibility and comparability with existing works, we retained the original Malimg dataset structure in this study. For better organization, we categorized the dataset into five major malware types and further grouped each sample into its respective malware family and it is represented in Table 2.

Table 2. Categorization of Malware Types and Their Families in the Malimg Dataset

Malware Type	Family Names
Adware	Dialplatform.B, Instantaccess, Swizzor.gen!E, Swizzor.gen!I
Worm	Allaple.A, Allaple.L, Autorun.K, VB.AT
Trojan	Agent.FYI, Alueron.gen!J, C2LOP.P, C2LOP.gen!g, Dontovo.A, Fakerean, Lolyda.AA1, Lolyda.AA2, Lolyda.AA3, Lolyda.AT, Malex.gen!J, Obfuscator.AD, Wintrim.BX
Backdoor	Rbot!gen
Virus	Adialer.C, Skintrim.N

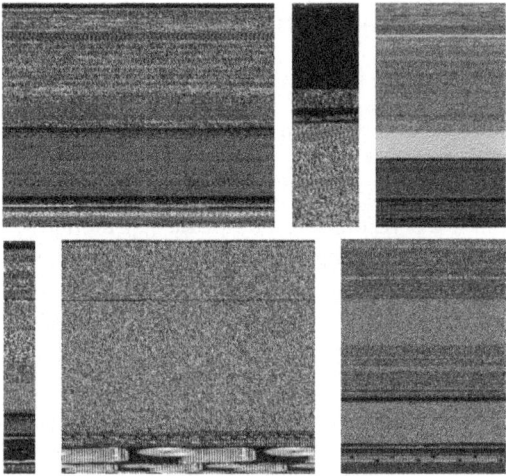

Fig. 3. Representative visualized malware images.

Malevis: A total of 26 families (25 malware + 1 cleanware) and 14,226 RGB byte images make up the MaleVis dataset shows in Fig. 4.

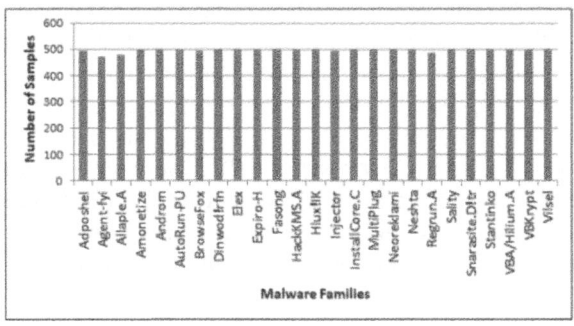

Fig. 4. Visualized malware images of malevis dataset.

4.3 Experimental Setup

The experiments were conducted on a 64-bit Windows 10 operating system with 8GB of RAM, a storage capacity of 930GB, an Intel Core i7-6700 CPU, and an NVIDIA Tesla T4 GPU. The implementation of our proposed malware detection system utilized the Keras v0.1.1 deep learning library within the Python framework. The model was trained for 100 epochs with a learning rate of 0.0001 and a batch size of 32. To evaluate its effectiveness, the dataset was randomly divided into 70% training and 30% validation sets. Two malware datasets, along with 1,043 clean-ware samples, were used for performance assessment. Specifically, for the Malimg dataset, which contained 9,339 malware and 1,043 clean-ware samples, training was performed on 7,268 samples, while 3,115 samples were allocated for evaluation. Similarly, for the MaleVis dataset, 9,958 samples were used for training and 4,268 for testing. Binary input images of different sizes (32 × 32 and 64 × 64) were utilized in the experiments. Notably, images reshaped to 64 × 64 preserved more information and exhibited improved prediction accuracy.

4.4   Performance Metrics

The effectiveness of the dataset utilized to produce the best and most secure outcomes affects performance indicators. After the model has been trained, testing is carried out as described in the previous section.

Accuracy: The ratio of the model's true positive forecasts to its correct predictions.

where TP, TN, FP, and FN stand for *True Positive* Class Prediction, *True Negative* Class Prediction, and *False Positive* Class Prediction. The Eq. (1) represents the loss and accuracy curve for each architecture on malimg dataset.

$$Accuracy = \frac{TP + T}{TP + TN + FP + F} \tag{1}$$

4.5   Results and Discussion

The accuracy of all models represents how much the proposed model is accurate. Table 3 shows the comparison of the performance of all four architectures on two different malware attack detection datasets. The experimental results compare the performance of **AlexNet, Optimized AlexNet, ResNet50, and VGG16** on **Malming and Malvis** datasets, focusing on convergence, generalization, and stability.

Stage 1: Optimized AlexNet 5-Class Classifier: In Stage 1, Optimized AlexNet outperforms the standard version, achieving faster convergence, smoother loss curves, and improved stability across both datasets. **ResNet50 and VGG16** demonstrate strong feature extraction but exhibit higher sensitivity to dataset variations, especially in Malvis, where fluctuations in validation accuracy indicate potential overfitting. Optimized AlexNet provides a lightweight yet effective alternative for malware classification. The Performance is represented in Fig. 5 and 6.

Future Work: Future work will address Malimg dataset imbalance and assess cascaded AlexNet's inference time for real-time E-Health monitoring. A Three-Tier Classifier (ResNet50, InceptionV3, VGG16) will be introduced to improve detection accuracy and reduce false positives. Further directions include multi-model integration, ensemble learning, lightweight edge computing, and explainable AI to enhance malware detection in healthcare systems and ensure robust IoMT security.

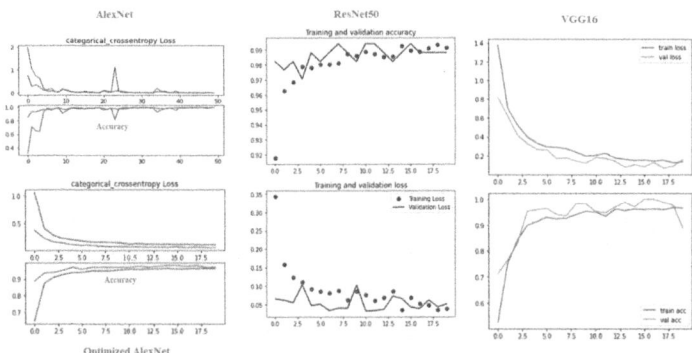

Fig. 5. Loss and accuracy curves of AlexNet (upper left), Optimized AlexNet (lower left), ResNet50 (middle), and VGG16 (right) models on the Malimg dataset.

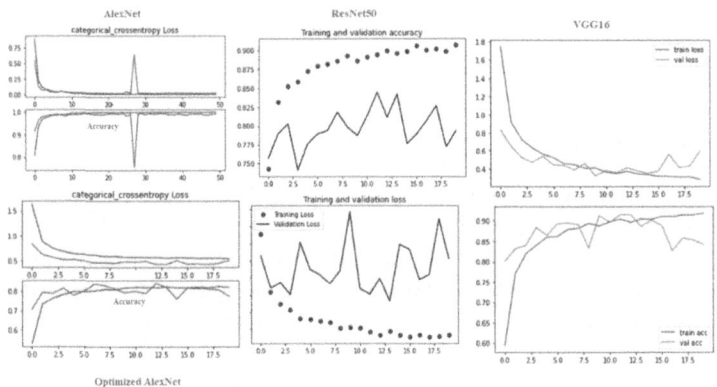

Fig. 6. Loss and accuracy curves of AlexNet (upper left), Optimized AlexNet (lower left), ResNet50 (middle), and VGG16 (right) models on the Malvis dataset.

Table 3. Results of Four Architectures on Two Datasets

Models	Malimg Dataset	Malvis Dataset
Cascaded (Optimized AlexNet Stage-1)	100%	93%
Cascaded (AlexNet Stage-1)	96%	88%
VGG16	93%	81%
ResNet50	85%	79%

5   Conclusion

This research demonstrates how AI-based solutions protect Internet of Medical Things (IoMT) environments by securing E-Health records against malware threats. The proposed system achieved better malware detection accuracy through its multi-stage deep learning approach that used an optimized Cascaded AlexNet architecture to outperform ResNet50 and VGG16 across various datasets. The hierarchical classification approach delivered precise threat identification, which reduced false positives and improved real-time security capabilities. The research demonstrates how advanced AI methodologies can effectively solve existing problems with dataset imbalance and computational complexity, and evolving attack strategies.

References

1. Maniriho, P., Mahmood, A.N., Chowdhury, M.J.: Deep learning models for detecting malware attacks. arXiv preprint arXiv:2209.03622 (2022)
2. Lu, J., Ren, X., Zhang, J., Wang, T.: CPL-net: a malware detection network based on parallel CNN and LSTM feature fusion. Electronics **12**(19), 4025 (2023)
3. Simonyan, K., Zisserman, A.: Very deep convolutional networks for large-scale image recognition. In: ICLR (2014)
4. Aucoin, A., Lin, K.K., Gothard, K.M.: Detection of latent brain states from baseline neural activity in the amygdala. bioRxiv (2024)
5. Zhang, S., Gao, M., Wang, L., Xu, S., Shao, W., Kuang, R.: A malware-detection method using deep learning to fully extract API sequence features. ElectronicsD **14**(1), 167 (2025)
6. Wang, L., Chen, Q., Song, C.: Anomaly detection model of network dataflow based on an improved grey wolf algorithm and CNN. Electronics **12**(18), 3787 (2023)
7. D'Angelo, G., Ficco, M., Palmieri, F.: Association rule-based malware classification using common subsequences of API calls. Appl. Soft Comput. **105**, 107234 (2021)
8. D'Angelo, G., Palmieri, F.: Enhancing COVID-19 tracking apps with human activity recognition using a deep convolutional neural network and HAR-images. Neural Comput. Appl. **35**(19), 13861–13877 (2023)
9. D'Angelo, G., Rampone, S.: Towards a HPC-oriented parallel implementation of a learning algorithm for bioinformatics applications. BMC Bioinform. **15**, 1–15 (2014)
10. Shinde, R., Patil, S., Kotecha, K., Potdar, V., Selvachandran, G., Abraham, A.: Securing AI-based healthcare systems using blockchain technology: a state-of-the-art systematic literature review and future research directions. Trans. Emerg. Telecommun. Technol. **35**(1), e4884 (2024)
11. Wazid, M., Singh, J., Das, A.K., Rodrigues, J.: An ensemble-based machine learning-envisioned intrusion detection in industry 5.0-driven healthcare applications. IEEE Trans. Consum. Electron. **70**(1), 1903–1912 (2024). https://doi.org/10.1109/TCE.2023.3318850
12. Fuller, R., Moore, C., Taylor, T., Anderson, C.: A novel hybrid machine learning approach for real-time ransomware detection using behavior-driven heuristic features (2024)

13. Chakraborty, C., Nagarajan, S.M., Devarajan, G.G., Ramana, T.V., Mohanty, R.: Intelligent AI-based healthcare cyber security system using multi-source transfer learning method. ACM Trans. Sens. Netw. (2023)
14. Alenizi, J., Alrashdi, I.: SFMR-SH: Secure framework for mitigating ransomware attacks in smart healthcare using blockchain technology. Sustain. Mach. Intell. J. **2**, 4-11 (2023)
15. Al-Qarni, E.A.: Cybersecurity in healthcare: a review of recent attacks and mitigation strategies. Int. J. Adv. Comput. Sci. Appl. **14**(5) (2023)
16. Jabra, M. B., Cheikhrouhou, O., Atitallah, N., Amor, A. B., Hamam, H.: Malware detection using deep learning and CNN models. In: 2023 International Conference on Cyberworlds (CW), pp. 432-439. IEEE (2023)
17. Brown, A., Gupta, M., Abdelsalam, M.: Automated machine learning for deep learning based malware detection. Comput. Secur. **137**, 103582 (2024)

Comparative Analysis of Participatory Urban Regeneration in Italy: From Small Towns to Metropolitan Areas

Alessia Brisdelli(✉) (iD)

University of Studies "G. D'Annunzio" of Chieti-Pescara, Viale Pindaro 42, 65127 Pescara, Italy
alessia.brisdelli@phd.unich.it

Abstract. In recent years, participatory urban regeneration has undergone significant evolution in Italy, consolidating itself as a key tool for territorial transformation, both at the scale of small and medium-sized towns and metropolitan areas. This process has been characterized by the adoption of innovative approaches that encourage co-design between institutions, citizens, and local associations, alongside the shared management of public spaces. These intervention models not only promote the physical and functional redevelopment of urban spaces but also create new opportunities to strengthen a sense of belonging, improve quality of life, and support local development through greater democratic participation. This paper aims to analyze the differences between the participatory urban regeneration models adopted in small and medium-sized cities, characterized by a stronger community cohesion, and those implemented in large metropolitan areas, where complex dynamics require multilayered strategies and greater integration between traditional planning and active participation. Specifically, the paper proposes a comparative analysis of two cases of "Tactical Urbanism" at very different scales to identify differences and similarities: the "Ca.Fè." initiative in San Nicolò a Tordino, a small town in the province of Teramo, where ten local associations collaborated to transform a former school into a multifunctional center for cultural, educational, and social activities, and the "Piazze Aperte" case in the metropolitan city of Milan, which stood out for the adoption of an integrated strategy combining various participatory approaches. The analysis, which seeks to identify the conditions that promote the scalability and replicability of participatory models, will conclude with a reflection on co-design practices and participatory approaches necessary to build more resilient and inclusive urban spaces at different territorial scales and under varying economic and social conditions.

Keywords: Social Innovation · Participatory Urban Regeneration · Scalability

© The Author(s), under exclusive license to Springer Nature Switzerland AG 2026
O. Gervasi et al. (Eds.): ICCSA 2025 Workshops, LNCS 15899, pp. 101–110, 2026.
https://doi.org/10.1007/978-3-031-97663-6_8

1   Active Participation and Social Innovation

From small towns to large cities, urban transformation processes today face multidimensional challenges: from combating climate change to reducing social inequalities and addressing housing marginality. In this scenario, the active participation of citizens has acquired a central role in public policies, no longer considered a mere accessory element but a key factor for building inclusive and resilient cities. Many Italian cities have adopted innovative tools to encourage such participation. One example is the "Collaboration Pacts" (Patti di Collaborazione), introduced by the Municipality of Bologna in collaboration with Labsus [6] and later formalized by Regional Law 24/2017 of Emilia-Romagna. As highlighted by Arena [1], directly involving communities not only enhances the quality of public spaces but also strengthens the sense of collective responsibility, fostering constructive interaction between institutions and citizens. This approach has generated concrete experiences of regeneration [6], some of which have produced innovative governance models, while others have highlighted their limitations. Active participation can be interpreted as a form of "social innovation", as it addresses needs inadequately met by traditional approaches. Social innovations, in fact, include both organizational models and collaborative processes aimed at improving quality of life, fostering inclusion, and accelerating the transition toward sustainability. A distinctive feature of such innovations is scalability, i.e., the ability to expand their impact through replication or adaptation to new contexts. As emphasized by Gabriel [13], «a social innovation achieves scalability when its impact grows to match the scale of the need». Scalability primarily refers to the number of beneficiaries, achievable through the diffusion of methodological principles or the reproduction of interventions (quantitative scaling). It requires distinguishing between "core" elements (fixed and indispensable) and flexible aspects adaptable to local contexts. It must be differentiated from replicability, which implies the faithful reproduction of an original model in different environments [15]. To explore these concepts further, the article examines two case studies that, while sharing the goal of promoting social innovation, differ in approach, scale, and territorial dynamics.

2   Case studies

2.1   Innovation from Below, Challenges fro Above: The "Ca.Fè." Case in Abruzzo

San Nicolò a Tordino (Abruzzo), located in the Tordino River valley, represents an emblematic example of participatory urban regeneration in small-to-medium-sized contexts. The transition from a rural village to a residential area, accelerated by the 2009–2016 earthquakes, highlighted the urgency for public spaces suited to socialization and civic participation. A symbol of this transition is the former Carlo Febbo School, damaged by seismic events, which was repurposed in 2022 into the multifunctional cultural center "Ca.Fè.", thanks to the involvement of ten local associations. The project, included in the "Teramo Città Capoluogo" program [4] and aligned with the National Recovery and Resilience Plan (PNRR), combined architectural restoration with sociocultural valorization, returning to the community not just a building but an identity space. The initiative transcended the physical dimension: the Municipality's adoption of "Collaboration Pacts" formalized a shared governance model, strengthening the dialogue between institutions and citizens. This bottom-up model anticipated official urban policies, demonstrating the role of local associations in planning. However, challenges persist, such as reliance on volunteer work and the lack of structural funding, risking relegating the project to an isolated episode.

Key Dimensions and Institutional Challenges. A crucial step was the launch of the Municipal Urban Plan (PUC) in 2024, which introduced a participatory approach to planning, replacing the former General Regulatory Plan (PRG). Linked to this is the 2021 Referendum for the redevelopment of the historic center, promoted by local committees, reflecting a desire for active participation, encapsulated in the slogan: «The city can no longer wait […] it is the citizens' duty to demand a serious debate». The administration responded with collaborative governance tools, such as the Participatory Budget (Bilancio Partecipativo), still in its initial phase, encouraging inclusive decision-making processes. However, the Regional Urban Planning Law (LUR) 2023 has drawn criticism from the Orders of Architects of L'Aquila, Pescara, and Teramo, who denounce the lack of tools for effective public participation. The transferability of participatory models, like the one tested in San Nicolò, depends on the ability to adapt innovative tools to local specificities. In small towns, community cohesion and simplified bureaucracy facilitate direct participatory processes, but scarce financial resources and dependence on local administrations remain critical challenges. As highlighted by Montanari et al. [15], the scalability of such models requires contextual adaptability and adequate resources. A pilot-project-based approach and progressive institutionalization of processes could mitigate these limitations, transforming isolated experiences into systemic policies. In Teramo, urban regeneration focuses on the recovery of existing heritage, avoiding land consumption, and enhancing peripheral infrastructure. Concurrently, environmental initiatives aim to reduce soil sealing and expand green areas, aligning with the PNRR's climate resilience goals. The adoption of the Municipal Urban Plan (PUC) in 2024 represents a decisive step toward integrating these interventions into participatory urban planning.

A Laboratory of Participatory Regeneration. The experience of the "Ca.Fè." cultural center demonstrates how participatory urban regeneration processes, even when born in small-scale contexts, can trigger profound and lasting transformations, provided they combine community spontaneity and institutional structuring. The restoration of the former Carlo Febbo School returned to the community not only a physical space but also a collective identity, strengthened by the synergistic action of ten local associations. This case offers significant insights for the replicability of participatory models in small towns, highlighting three key dimensions. First, the value of community cohesion proved indispensable as a driver: the spontaneous mobilization of local associations compensated for the lack of economic and institutional resources, transforming an abandoned building into a cultural hub. This approach, based on the territory's social capital, aligns with the OECD 2022 recommendations on rural resilience, where trust among local actors and shared common goals are enabling factors for sustainable projects. Second, adaptability to crises characterized the entire process. The post-earthquake repurposing of the former school reflects a "resilient by design" approach, integrating physical regeneration with social regeneration, consistent with the National Recovery and Resilience Plan (PNRR) goals for inner areas. The ability to turn an emergency into an opportunity demonstrates how small towns can become laboratories of innovation. Finally, the anticipatory experimentation of "Ca.Fè." played a pioneering role: the bottom-up project inspired the adoption of tools like the "Collaboration Pacts" and influenced Teramo's new Municipal Urban Plan. This dynamism confirms what was observed by De Luca et al. (2023) in the study "Bottom-Up Urbanism in Southern Europe", where informal practices often act as precursors to structured public policies, especially in resource-limited contexts. However, to prevent such initiatives from remaining isolated episodes, it is necessary to translate local successes into systemic actions. First, by allocating dedicated funds for small municipalities, with PNRR quotas aimed at creating territorial "skill banks" (banche delle competenze), as proposed by the CNR (2023) to map associative resources, train professionals, and facilitate access to funding, overcoming current fragmentation. Additionally, adopting inclusive digital platforms, modeled on the Living Labs tested in L'Aquila [7], would enable citizens to engage in the management of regenerated spaces, even in peripheral areas, democratizing processes often dominated by Top-Down logics. Lastly, formalizing institution-community pacts, inspired by British Community Land Trusts [22], would ensure project continuity by defining shared responsibilities and transparent governance mechanisms.

From Space to Place. The impact of the "Ca.Fè." initiative transcends mere physical regeneration, touching upon deep-rooted identity and social dimensions. As evidenced by resident testimonies, the repurposing of the former Carlo Febbo School has transformed "a wound of abandonment into a laboratory of hope" (Marcattili, 2023), restoring to the community not just a physical space but a *locus* imbued with collective memory. Former students who once occupied its classrooms now engage in intercultural workshops or music events, reaffirming the value of a space that envisions the future while preserving its historical legacy. The ten associations within the ATS Ca.Fè. Consortium, from neighborhood committees to Autism Abruzzo APS, have fostered a cross-sectoral ecosystem of practices, engaging children, migrants, and athletes in sustained dialogue. Journalist Veronica Marcattili, in her project reportage, highlights how the "Ca.Fè." initiative has "restored agency to a dormitory suburb, transforming it into a living community," while Chiara Ciminà, President of the ATS Ca.Fè., emphasizes its role as an "intergenerational bridge where elders share oral histories and children teach digital literacy." The municipal administration acknowledges the project as a model of "grassroots regeneration" capable of prefiguring public policies, as demonstrated by the integration of Collaboration Pacts into Teramo's Urban Plan. The current challenge lies in transitioning this *experiment* into an enduring paradigm, where the three pillars identified, community cohesion, crisis adaptability, and proactive planning, synergistically reinforce one another, ensuring the "seed of optimism" planted in San Nicolò evolves into systemic, inclusive policies (Fig. 1).

2.2   The Complexities of Urban Regeneration in Milan

With 1.3 million inhabitants and a metropolitan area of over 3 million, Milan embodies a dual transition: from an industrial hub to a global center of finance and design, and from a centralized model to a laboratory of urban democracy. This development, however, has

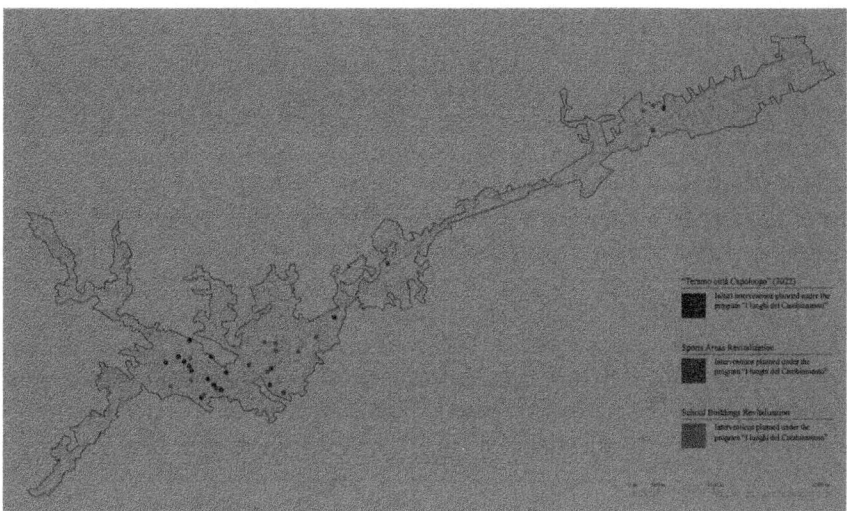

Fig. 1. Map of urban regeneration interventions in the territory of Teramo and its hamlets: Teramo Città Capoluogo urban regeneration projects, revitalization of sports facilities and cultural buildings, historic heritage restoration. Source: Author's elaboration based on data from the Municipality of Teramo [4, 10].

accentuated socio-spatial inequalities, requiring "hybrid" planning that integrates top-down and bottom-up approaches. At the heart of this transformation lies the Territorial Governance Plan (PGT) 2019, the result of 14 months of citizen consultations. The plan formalizes the "Milano 2030" vision, based on polycentrism, sustainability, and participation, encapsulated in the concept of "88 neighborhoods to be named", which aims to decentralize services and improve quality of life. This vision has been translated into concrete interventions such as 30 km of cycle paths and 12 new nurseries. Tools like "Collaboration Pacts", active since 2017 with over 120 projects) and the "Atlas of Urban Regeneration" (Atlante della Rigenerazione Urbana) promote public-private co-design. Examples include the repurposing of historic farmsteads into cultural centers co-designed by citizens and the "Open Squares" (Piazze Aperte) project, based on tactical urbanism, which transformed 25 spaces through tactical interventions involving 15,000 residents. Another innovative tool is the Participatory Budget, introduced in 2015 as Italy's first large-scale experiment and institutionalized in 2020 as a structural instrument of the Municipality of Milan, with €20 million annually allocated to projects proposed and voted on by citizens. Concurrently, grassroots initiatives flourish: "Social Street", a network of over 60 neighborhood groups promoting skill and resource exchanges, thrives in semi-peripheral areas but fails in the city center; "Milano da Vivere" (2021), with 10 km of pedestrianized streets during the pandemic, exemplifies how citizens reinvented public spaces, confirming Michel de Certeau's insight: "The city is practiced, not just planned".

European Models and Systemic Challenges. Milan, however, draws on European experiences, adapting them to its context with mixed results: while Barcelona's "Decidim" platform (engaging 7% of citizens in digital decision-making) inspired Milan to use open data for transparency, Turin's "Co-City" project regenerates abandoned spaces through public-community pacts in railway yards, reserving 50% of housing for vulnerable groups—compared to Milan's 15% [9]. Lisbon's BIP/ZIP program allocates 70% of funds to peripheries, financing 120 micro-projects/year, whereas only 15% of Milan's PNRR funds target marginal areas. Fragmentation among institutions, private actors, and the third sector remains a systemic challenge for Milan, despite the 2017 White Paper (Libro Bianco 2017) identifying "collaboration among diverse actors" (p. 12) as the key to an innovative ecosystem. A case in point is the "Riutilizzasi" project, launched in 2019 to repurpose 50 disused buildings into social spaces, stalled since 2021 due to governance conflicts. As Italy's first Smart City, Milan has chosen to promote social innovation as a central pillar: an intelligent city is not just one that adopts new technologies but one that leverages innovation to address socially relevant problems through novel methods. In this, Milan has demonstrated a willingness to experiment with solutions favoring community welfare, sharing economy, start-ups, FabLabs, and smart working. However, these elements form an organic whole only when they converge toward shared goals while retaining their identities. The challenge lies in transforming heterogeneity into a resource, replacing competitive logic with integrated governance.

Dynamism and Contradictions of a Smart City. Milan plays a leading role in the context of social innovation, driven by a desire to experiment and conceive innovation as a tool capable of contributing to the development of new methods for solving socially relevant problems, using technologies to support collaborative processes. "Milano che cambia" (Milan in Transition) is a concept that aptly encapsulates the city's evolution in recent years: a metropolis that has undergone radical transformation since Expo 2015, becoming an international benchmark for innovation and urban development. However, this exponential growth also brings challenges, including the need to reduce inequalities between the center and peripheries, ensuring equitable distribution of resources and services. On one hand, Milan's dynamism echoes the Futurist energy of Umberto Boccioni's "La città che sale" (The City Rises), where industrial progress was depicted through a whirlwind of colors and movement. On the other hand, the city struggles to bridge increasingly stark socio-spatial disparities. Today, Milan continues to transform rapidly, reshaping its skyline with modern towers and reconfiguring urban spaces (Panarella, 2020). The city's contemporary identity emerges from transformations in response to the Covid-19 emergency, where it reclaimed public spaces by reinventing everyday ways of inhabiting them. This practical resilience parallels Michel de Certeau's reflections in "L'invenzione del quotidiano" (The Practice of Everyday Life): cities are designed according to strategic models, but it is the daily practices of citizens that generate opportunities for freedom and creativity. The Milanese Smart City model embodies this duality: on one hand, the ambition to be a technological and social vanguard; on the other, the risk of "variable-geometry innovation" that primarily benefits already central areas.

Open Data and Hybrid Models. To become truly "intelligent," Milan must transform civic participation and inclusion from mere slogans into operational drivers, integrating peripheries into a cohesive urban ecosystem. The Milan case highlights the need for systemic actions to reconcile technological innovation and socio-spatial equity. For example: inspired by the aforementioned BIP/ZIP program, establishing a "Social Innovation Fund" with public-private co-financing mechanisms, aimed at co-designed microinterventions; transforming the "Atlas of Urban Regeneration" into an open-source dashboard with real-time data on fund allocation and socio-spatial indicators, modeled on Amsterdam's monitoring system; adopting hybrid (online/offline) platforms based on the Living Lab model [2], with physical access points in libraries and senior centers. Such actions aim to systemically restructure urban policies by prioritizing allocative equity, social performance indicators, and structured participation. Innovation must be understood as a co-evolutionary socio-technical process [12], rather than the mere adoption of prefabricated solutions (Fig. 2 and Table 1).

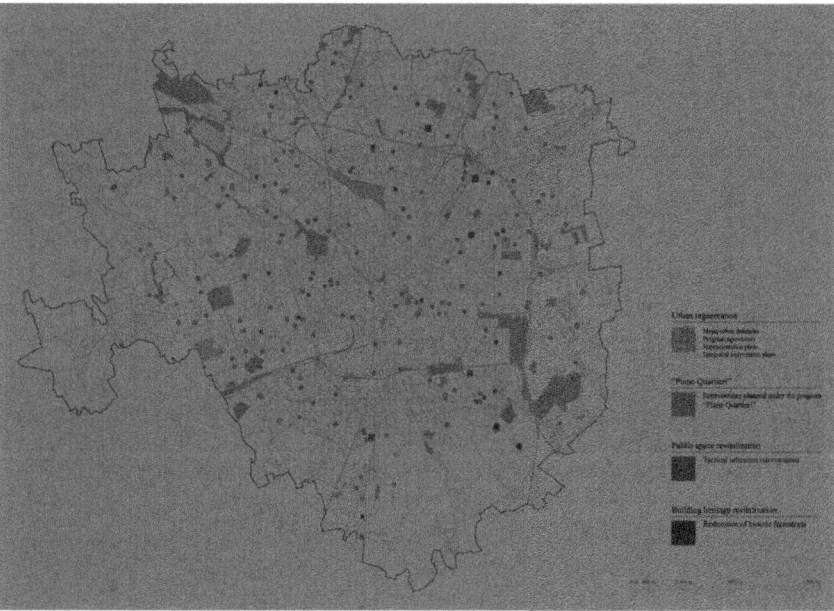

Fig. 2. Map of urban regeneration interventions in Milan: Tactical urbanism projects ("Piazze Aperte"/Open Squares), revitalization of public spaces, restoration of historic farmsteads, and geographical distribution of the "Bilancio Partecipativo" (Participatory Budget). Source: Author's elaboration based on data from the Municipality of Milan [8, 9].

Table 1. Comparison of Participatory Regeneration Models in Milan and Teramo. (Source: Author's elaboration based on analyzed case studies)

Category	Milan	S. Nicolò a Tordino (TE)
Socio-territorial Context	Metropolitan area (>3M inhabitants), transition from industrial hub to global center. Center-periphery inequalities	Small town in Abruzzo, post-seismic transition (2009–2016). Need for identity spaces for a transforming community
Key Tools	• PGT 2019 and "Milano 2030" vision • Collaboration Pacts, CSR • Bilancio Partecipativo (Participatory Budget, €20M/year) • Tactical Urbanism ("Piazze Aperte"/Open Squares)	• PUC 2024 (Municipal Urban Plan) • Collaboration Pacts • "Ca.Fè." project (former school) • Citizen referendum (2021)
Social Innovation	Smart City with FabLabs, sharing economy, digital Living Labs. Public-private-third sector collaboration	Post-earthquake community resilience. Anticipatory experimentation (e.g., Ca.Fè. as a model for national policies)
Critical Issues	• Management fragmentation • Inequality in fund access	• Reliance on volunteer work • Limited financial resources • Lack of effective participation (LUR 2023)

3   Cities in Motion

3.1   Regenerating Spaces as Living Ecosystems

Participatory urban regeneration is confirmed not as a universal formula but as a process of contextual translation, where success depends on the ability to hybridize global models with local identities. The analysis of the two case studies discussed above reveals a constructive dichotomy: in small communities, a single symbolic intervention, such as the conversion of the former Carlo Febbo school into "Ca.Fè.", can catalyze identity-driven regeneration, transforming an abandoned building into a space of collective resonance. This effect, typical of small-scale contexts, is rooted in relational proximity and the community's capacity for self-organization, bridging institutional gaps through associative networks (OECD, 2022). However, such initiatives require institutional grafting: integration into the Municipal Urban Plan (PUC) and the adoption of Collaboration Pacts represent crucial steps to translate grassroots enthusiasm into structured policies supported by dedicated funding and shared expertise (CNR, 2023). In metropolises like Milan, by contrast, participatory regeneration demands a networked logic: isolated interventions, though significant, dissolve within the complex urban fabric. The Milanese model lies in an ecosystem of interconnected practices, creating a pervasive social infrastructure capable of engaging multiple actors (citizens, private entities, third-sector organizations) in complementary processes. However, this approach is not without challenges: management fragmentation (e.g., the stalled "Riutilizzasi" project) and the unequal distribution of PNRR funds between central and peripheral areas reveal how quantitative scalability does not automatically ensure equity. Thus, replicability in metropolitan contexts must be measured not by the number of projects but by their capacity to generate synergies and correct spatial asymmetries.

The Participatory Continuum in the Osmotic Process. A key emerging element of this analysis is the redefinition of participatory continuity as a critical factor. Urban regeneration cannot be confined to the planning phase but must evolve through adaptive mechanisms responsive to shifting community needs. In Milan, tools like the Atlas of Urban Regeneration and digital Living Labs exemplify how hybrid platforms—bridging physical and digital realms—can sustain cyclical engagement, transforming citizens from users into co-managers of spaces (De Luca et al., 2023). These tools are not static but evolving prototypes, turning cities into open-air laboratories where each intervention is an iterative experiment fueled by real-time data and collective feedback. In small towns, continuity is built through relational technologies: social capital becomes a strategic resource, as demonstrated by the "Ca.Fè." project, which activated a shared stewardship of space, even anticipating national PNRR policies. Scalability can be defined as a "decomposition-recomposition" process, where model transfer is nonlinear. In Milan, metropolitan strategies must be "disassembled" into micro-actions adaptable to neighborhoods (e.g., Social Street), while small towns need to "expand" local practices through regional networks, such as the proposed "skill banks" [5]. Tools like co-design are not mere project methodologies but listening devices to decode invisible needs. The experience of Seoul and Malmö with Urban Living Labs [3] shows that adaptability thrives on continuous dialogue between technical expertise and everyday practices. Hybrid Metrics for Impact Evaluation: Beyond physical parameters (e.g., regenerated square meters), qualitative indicators—such as increased social capital and reduced decision-making asymmetries—are essential to measure transformative effectiveness, especially in marginal areas. Looking ahead, Italy's challenge lies in leveraging PNRR funds as a driver for widespread spatial democracy. For small municipalities, this means creating territorial hubs to map associative resources and facilitate funding access; for metropolises, it requires reimagining governance as a nervous system where institutions, citizens, and private actors co-design flexible responses to crises (climate, social, housing). In conclusion, participatory regeneration is not an endpoint but a permanent laboratory: a dynamic equilibrium between planning and improvisation, institutions and communities. As suggested by Michel de Certeau's legacy, cities reinvent themselves daily through inhabitants' practices. Embracing this complexity and translating it into fluid policies is the only way to build resilient, vibrant cities capable of transforming vulnerabilities into collective opportunities.

References

1. Arena, G.: I custodi della Bellezza. Prendersi cura dei beni comuni [The Guardians of Beauty: Caring for Common Goods]. Donzelli, Rome (2020)

2. Amsterdam Smart City Dashboard. https://amsterdamsmartcity.com. Accessed 15 June 2024
3. Cho, E.J.: Urban Living Labs: Innovazione Sociale nelle Città Globali [Urban Living Labs: Social Innovation in Global Cities]. Springer, Berlin (2018)
4. Ciminà, C.: Inaugurato Spazio Multiculturale Ca.Fè. Teramo città capoluogo [Multicultural Space Ca.Fè. Inaugurated. Teramo as Provincial Capital] (2022). https://teramocittac apoluogo.it/news/20210844/Inaugurato-Spazio-Multiculturale-Ca-Fe-
5. CNR: Linee guida per la rigenerazione delle aree interne [Guidelines for the Regeneration of Inner Areas]. PNRR Report, Rome (2023)
6. Comune di Bologna, Labsus: Patti di Collaborazione [Collaboration Pacts] (2017). https://www.labsus.org
7. Comune de L'Aquila: Living Lab per la partecipazione digitale [Digital Participation Living Lab] (2022). https://comune.laquila.it
8. Comune di Milano: Atlante della Rigenerazione Urbana [Atlas of Urban Regeneration]. Milan (2023)
9. Comune di Milano: PGT 2019 – Relazione Generale [Territorial Governance Plan 2019 – General Report]. Milan (2019)
10. Comune di Teramo: Teramo Città Capoluogo [Teramo as Provincial Capital]. (2022). https://teramocittacapoluogo.it
11. De Certeau, M.: L'invenzione del quotidiano [The Practice of Everyday Life]. Edizioni Lavoro, Rome (2001)
12. De Luca, G., et al.: Bottom-up urbanism in southern Europe. J. Urban Plan. **10**(2), 112–130 (2023)
13. Gabriel, M.: Making it Big: Strategies for Scaling Social Innovation. NESTA, London (2014)
14. Mizzau, L., Montanari, F.: Open innovation, città e luoghi di innovazione: una visione integrata di ecosistema di nnovazione [Open innovation, cities, and innovation hubs: an integrated vision of innovation ecosystems]. In: Montanari, F., Mizzau, L. (eds.) I luoghi dell'innovazione aperta. Modelli di sviluppo territoriale e inclusione sociale [Places of Open Innovation: Models of Territorial Development and Social Inclusion]. Quaderni Fondazione Brodolini, vol. 55, pp. X–Y. Fondazione Brodolini, Rome (2016)
15. Montanari, F., Razzoli, D., Rinaldini, M.: Diffondere innovazione: verso un modello di scalabilità per i progetti di innovazione sociale [Spreading innovation: toward a scalability model for social innovation projects]. Impresa Sociale **13**, 45–60 (2019)
16. OECD: Rural Resilience and Community-Led Innovation. OECD Publishing, Paris (2022)
17. OECD: Urban Policies for Inclusive Growth. OECD Publishing, Paris (2021)
18. Ordine degli Architetti di Teramo: La LUR 2023 in Abruzzo: criticità e prospettive [The 2023 Regional Urban Planning Law in Abruzzo: Critical Issues and Perspectives]. Technical report, Teramo (2023)
19. Panarella, A.: Milano che cambia [Milan in Transition]. Il Giornale dell'Archit. **45**, 22–30 (2020)
20. Panarella, A., Roda, M.: Maran: dobbiamo conciliare i grandi piani con la Milano policentrica degli 88 quartieri [Maran: reconciling large-scale plans with Milan's polycentric 88 neighborhoods]. Il Giornale dell'Archit. **45**, 22–30 (2020)
21. Sgaragli, F., Montanari, F.: Libro Bianco sull'Innovazione Sociale a Milano [White Paper on Social Innovation in Milan]. Comune di Milano (2017)
22. Italiana, U.: Community land trust: modelli di co-gestione per spazi pubblici [Community land trust: co-management models for public spaces]. Urbanistica Ital. **12**(3), 45–60 (2023)

Exploring Slow Tourism: Integration Between Mobility, Heritage, and Landscape Regeneration

Chiara Correra[(✉)] [iD]

University of Rome "La Sapienza", 00185 Rome, Italy
chiara.correra@uniroma1.it

Abstract. Exploring Slow Tourism: Integrating Mobility, Heritage, and Landscape Regeneration
This study explores the feasibility of slow and sustainable **tourism** to enhance cultural and natural heritage while fostering connections between coastal and inland territories. By promoting **non-motorized mobility**, such as cycling and walking, slow tourism offers an alternative to conventional car-based travel, encouraging deeper engagement with landscapes, local traditions, and historical sites. Focusing on different environments, the study examines how slow itineraries can cross mountainous regions, rural areas, and coastal ecosystems, creating a seamless link between urban centres and remote landscapes. These routes reveal the hidden potential of underutilized spaces, transforming abandoned sites into rest stops, cultural hubs, or meditation areas, while also supporting local economies and community-led initiatives. **Slow travel itineraries** revitalize fragile landscapes and promote environmental awareness and responsible tourism practices by integrating natural conservation with sustainable tourism. From forested reserves to coastal lagoons and historic villages, these journeys immerse travellers in the ecological and cultural richness of the territory. Beyond recreation, the study highlights how investing in infrastructure, safety and services can strengthen vulnerable regions, fostering resilient and interconnected communities. Slow tourism thus emerges as a powerful tool for territorial regeneration, sustainable mobility, and heritage conservation, redefining how people engage with places and local cultures.

Keywords: Coastal resilience · fragile land regeneration · slow mobility strategy

1 Introduction

Slow and Sustainable Tourism: Connecting Coast and Hinterland for Territorial Regeneration

Sustainable tourism has gained increasing attention as an alternative to conventional, car-dependent travel, offering a means of balancing the preservation of the surrounding environment with cultural and economic development. Within this framework, slow tourism emerges as a model that fosters deep engagement with local landscapes, heritage and communities while minimizing environmental impact. This paper explores the feasibility and sustainability of routes that easily connect inland areas with coastal cities. The

O. Gervasi et al. (Eds.): ICCSA 2025 Workshops, LNCS 15899, pp. 111–121, 2026.
https://doi.org/10.1007/978-3-031-97663-6_9

ability to connect two different environments also implies the ability to provide services, places for overnight stays and entertainment for different target intercepted population. This research evaluates the potential of the trail understood co-as **ecosystem infrastructure** in fostering local economic revitalization, cultural preservation, and environmental sustainability. Key considerations include infrastructure development, safety measures, and accessibility of services, ensuring that the route meets the needs of both visitors and host communities. By assessing the implications of slow tourism on regional resilience, the study contributes to broader discussions on sustainable mobility, heritage preservation, and territorial cohesion.

Slow tourism, often associated with walking or cycling, is a contemporary travel practice rooted in sustainability and place-based engagement. It promotes a deeper, more conscious interaction with the landscape, local culture, and heritage. While it responds to modern environmental and social challenges, its foundations can also be traced back to historical forms of movement, such as religious pilgrimages and seasonal migrations. In ancient times, travel was often a transformative act—whether heroic, spiritual, or existential—marking a personal encounter with the unknown and the surrounding world. Concepts such as *genius loci*, the "spirit of place", help frame this deeper connection, where the act of moving through a landscape becomes an immersive and reflective experience. This study explores how these values of slowness and connection are revived today through sustainable tourism models that link coastal and inland territories, highlighting their potential for environmental stewardship, cultural preservation, and economic revitalization. By the spirit of places is meant that feeling of being lost in unfamiliar environments in which one comes to find a part of oneself that appears hidden, concealed. Schulz asserts that "through the interaction of surface relief, vegetation and water, characteristic totality or places are formed that constitute the fundamental elements of landscapes," those landscapes that from prospective backgrounds become the protagonists, together with the individual walking, of an emotional and sensory interaction. In every civilization, era, and geographical place, traveling, migrating, habitually moving represents a "human invariant," not universal but characterizing every context and culture to which it belongs.[1]

In recent years, numerous projects and studies have highlighted the potential of soft mobility routes, such as hiking trails and cycle paths, in connecting coastal areas with inland areas. The possibility of strategically connecting the coastal cities, with all their advantages from an economic, viability and social point of view with the less valued and known inland areas, allows the movement of the mass tourist flow to destinations of high historical-cultural value, less known, making them more visible and enriching them, consequentially, from multiple points of view. The coastal road system, in fact, presents a completely different logic from that of hilly or mountainous areas, especially along the Adriatic coast, where settlements follow a **comb-like pattern**, linked to the river components scattered along the territory. The river, therefore, connotes the landscape but also represents a means of transportation, a line that divides the territory and at the same time unites it, with bridges or connections that emphasize its fundamental

---

[1] Author, Raimon Pannikar: Book title Peace and Interculturality: A Philosophical Reflection- Publisher. Jaca Book (2002).

importance. Numerous are examples of soft mobility that connects the territory precisely by exploiting the potential of river nature as an ecosystem infrastructure.

Parallel to the presence of water, which closely connotes the coast and river basins, initiatives such as the Regional Natural Park of the Coastal Dunes in Apulia[2] or the OMNIS project aims to promote sustainable and inclusive tourism in the coastal and inland regions of Italy and Croatia[3], demonstrate how it is possible to develop routes that not only allow the exploration of the natural and cultural heritage, but also support local economies. The importance of such routes lies in their ability to **revitalize marginal territories**, fostering the rediscovery of historic villages, local agricultural production and landscapes often neglected by mass tourism flows. Revitalization for tourism purposes consequently implies an organizational engagement of the entire local co-munity, which is consequently driven to consider the ecosystem-ca network as a source of economic and social enrichment.

A key aspect of coastal and inland integration is the valorisation of ecosystem services, i.e. those benefits provided by natural ecosystems that support quality of life and environmental sustainability. As reported in the study presented in Chapter 3 of The GEO Handbook on Biodiversity Observation Networks "At national and sub-national scales, ecosystem services can be an effective tool for informing decisions about the use and management of the planet's resources, especially when trade-offs and synergies need to be considered. Without this information, decisions that determine the fate of terrestrial, coastal and marine systems, and the benefits they provide, are made in the dark, with little understanding of the ecosystem service outcomes (benefits and costs) of a given decision or its consequences for the different stakeholders that depend on these services".

A key aspect of coastal and inland integration is the valorisation of **ecosystem services**, i.e. those benefits provided by natural ecosystems that support quality of life and environmental sustainability. As reported in the study presented in Chapter 3 of "*The GEO Handbook on Biodiversity Observation Networks*" "At national and sub-national scales, ecosystem services can be an effective tool for informing decisions about the use and management of the planet's resources, especially when trade-offs and synergies need to be considered. Without this information, decisions that determine the fate of terrestrial, coastal and marine systems, and the benefits they provide, are made in the dark, with little understanding of the ecosystem service outcomes (benefits and costs)

---

[2] Natural Park of the Coastal Dunes in Puglia: The Regional Natural Park of the Coastal Dunes from Torre Canne to Torre San Leonardo extends over approximately 1,100 hectares, along eight kilometres of coastline and into inland agricultural areas, occupied by centuries-old olive groves and ancient farms. The perimeter measures a total of fifty-five kilometres; within it lies the Site of Community Importance (SIC) "Littoral brindisino", included in the European network "Natura 2000", SCI characterised by coastal wetlands which have an important value for rare and endangered species of flora and fauna. [Source : https://www.parks.it/parco.dune. costiere/par.php].

[3] OMNIS Project: The OMNIS project aims to promote sustainable and inclusive tourism in coastal and inland regions of Italy and Croatia, with a strong focus on accessibility for people with special needs. By promoting inland destinations and fostering collaboration between coastal and hinterland tourism operators, OMNIS improves travel experiences for travellers with dogs and blind people. [Source: https://omnistourism.it/it/].

of a given decision or its consequences for the different stakeholders that depend on these services"[4]. The reforestation of degraded areas, the protection of coastal wetlands and the creation of ecological corridors can contribute to mitigate the effects of climate change, improve biodiversity, and favour the development of a more environmentally aware and conservation-conscious tourism. In this context, as elaborated also by the previously mentioned research, land management policies are called to stimulate the constructive collaboration between local actors, institutions, and tourism operators, promoting regenerative tourism practices able to guarantee a balance between fruition and ecosystem protection.

The functional integration between the coast and inland areas is both a challenge and an opportunity to rethink the **sustainable** management of the connection between green areas and more urbanised areas. Through the creation of soft mobility networks, the enhancement of ecosystem services and greater involvement of local communities, it is possible to develop a model that is truly inclusive and capable of generating positive long-term impacts. The future of sustainable tourism therefore passes through a broader, large-scale vision that recognises the value of territories in their complexity and favours a harmonious connection between nature, landscape, culture, and economic development. To move towards the realisation of this model, the intrinsic integration and interdependence of the landscape mosaic of these areas must be considered as fundamental. The possibility of linking these types of territories carries with it a highly important historical significance, which has its roots in the era of the Transhumance, the seasonal migration of flocks, herds and shepherds from hilly or mountainous areas to the plains (in the winter season) or vice versa (in the summer season) along the natural sheep-tracks. Transhumance, recognised by UNESCO as an Intangible Cultural Heritage, is an emblematic example of how the landscape and social relations have been shaped over the centuries by practices of displacement. Retracing the ancient shepherds' paths through dedicated itineraries means not only preserving a centuries-old tradition but also offering opportunities for experiential tourism that allow visitors to enrich their experience with local stories, landscapes, and flavours. In Italy, two examples of routes that enhance transhumance are the Regio Tratturo Pescasseroli-Candela and the Tratturo Magno, which connect the Apennine regions with coastal areas. Another example is **cycle tourism along waterways**, such as the Rimini-Marecchia route. (Rimini-Marecchia), shows how the territory can be rediscovered through routes that connect the coastline with the hinterland. Following the course of rivers, they pass through historic villages, protected natural areas and ancient production sites, fostering in-depth knowledge of the territory and its ecological and cultural dynamics. These itineraries are part of a wider network of **European greenways**, such as EuroVelo 5 (Via Romea Francigena), which connects different nations promoting sustainable mobility.

Cultural ecosystem services, mentioned earlier, include all the intangible benefits that derive from the interaction between man and the environment, such as the beauty

---

[4] K. Thonicke Potsdam Institute for Climate Impact Research, Potsdam, Germany e-mail: Kirsten.Thonicke@pik-potsdam.de F. Villa Basque Centre for Climate Change (BC3); IKER-BASQUE, Basque foundation for Science, Burlington, Bilbao, Spain e-mail: ferdinando.villa@bc3research.org A. Walz Institute of Earth and Environmental Science, University of Potsdam, Potsdam, Germany e-mail: ariane.walz@pik-potsdam.de 3 Ecosystem Services 43.

of the landscape, the spiritual value of certain places and the recreational experiences offered by nature. Integrating these elements into tourism planning makes it possible to develop destinations that foster psychophysical wellbeing and social cohesion, encouraging regenerative tourism practices. Tourists and pilgrims can meet local communities, participate in traditional events, discover handicrafts, and taste typical products, thus helping to support local economies and learn more about the history of these places. Projects such as the European Union's 'Green Infrastructure Strategy' promote the integration of tourism, environment, and economic development, encouraging the creation of green corridors and the preservation of historic natural and agricultural areas.

The integration of slow tourism, soft mobility and the enhancement of cultural eco-system services can become a key strategy for harmonious territorial development. Through the creation of thematic itineraries, the recovery of historical routes and the enhancement of light infrastructures, it is possible to build a tourism system capable of connecting coast and hinterland, preserving the cultural heritage, and improving the quality of life of local communities. In this context, European strategies such as the Natura 2000 Network and the Green Infrastructure Business Plan aim to strengthen the environmental resilience and economic value of territories, creating opportunities for experiential tourism and landscape regeneration. Investing in tourism that focuses on people's well-being and the enhancement of social relations means not only fostering more authentic and conscious travel experiences but also ensuring sustainable land management in the long term.

2   Creation of Network Between Coastal Cities and Inner Territories

2.1   Strategic Models of Cohesion of Different Habitats

As mentioned in the introduction, there are already contemporary models of action-strategies aimed at the "**hooking**" gesture, between coastal and inland landscapes, or at least typically associated with inland landscapes. In the Italian panorama, some examples can be found in the region of Apulia, where the land conformation already in itself allows a strong contact between the natural elements of water and land. One only must think of the nature parks that have sprung up near the Adriatic coastal lakes of Varano and Lesina. The possibility of walking through their landscapes, experiencing heterogeneous habitats, immediately connected to the Gargano National Park, which is characterised by further peculiar landscape nuances, makes this area rich in naturalistic elements of considerable importance. From the richness of the landscape and nature, therefore, arises the need to connect the economic nerve centres -the town centres- with the numerous settlements scattered throughout the territory, also on an economic and road network level.

An interesting model of approach to the act of connecting such different areas is represented by the Regional Natural Park "Dune Costiere da Torre Canne a Torre S. Leonardo." Established in 2006, it represents a significant example of how the enhancement of coastal areas can extend inland, creating an ecological and cultural continuum. ISPRA's study "Italy's sandy coastal habitats: ecology and conservation problems" highlight the importance of Italian dune habitats, underlining how coastal dunes play a crucial role in the conservation of biodiversity and the protection of the coastline from erosion (see Fig. 1). The document reports that the typical physical environment of coastal dune landscapes 'is dynamic and unstable, being dominated by natural forces such as storm surges and fierce winds. The habitat is based on sandy beaches and/or with gravel of small grain size near the foreshore, where the organic material carried by the waves accumulates and decomposes, enriching the substrate with nutrients and salts. The vegetation consists of very short-cycled communities (therophytic-which-alonitrophilic formations) that germinate in autumn or winter, flower and produce fruits in a noticeably short vegetative period (sometimes only 1–2 months in late spring), then dry up in summer. The fruits open in early summer and the seeds, covered with sand, remain dormant until the autumn rains. Due to its peculiarities, the vegetation has an exceptionally low cover (often only 5% of the total), however this is already sufficient to hinder the wind transport of the sand, favouring its accumulation instead'"[5].

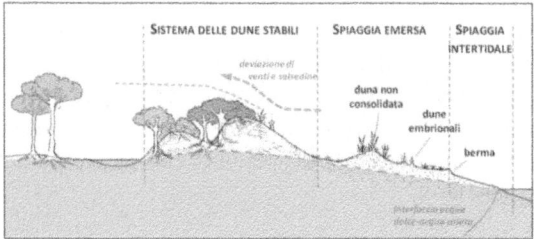

Fig. 1. Beach-dune system profile (drawing by C. Percopo, off scale)

Within the park, routes have been developed that connect the coastal strip with the hinterland, allowing visitors to explore a variety of natural and cultural environments. These itineraries encourage the discovery of ancient hypogenous oil mills, historical farms and water channelling systems, integrating the seaside experience with the rural one.

In parallel, the example of the OMNIS project, aims to promote sustainable and inclusive tourism in the coastal and inland regions of the two countries. The OMNIS project, launched in 2023 under the Italy-Croatia Interreg programme, aims to create a network of inclusive and sustainable itineraries. According to the official monitoring report (2024), over 120 km of trails have been mapped and 18 municipalities involved across both countries. Preliminary data from the first tourist season show a 17% increase in visitors to lesser-known inland destinations compared to the previous year. Furthermore, 63% of surveyed tourists reported that the combined coastal-hinterland routes positively influenced their decision to explore the region beyond the shoreline. These findings suggest that integrated mobility and tourism strategies can support both territorial cohesion and economic diversification. The project areas are located in Italy and Croatia, encouraging tourism that combines coastal attractions with the rich offerings of the hinterland: in Italy, from the Pesaro-Urbino coastal area to the lower Apennines of Pesaro and Ancona,

---

[5] The habitats of the Italian sandy coasts: ecology and conservation issues [Source: ISPRAMBIENTE.GOV.IT].

encompassing nine municipalities: Acqua-lagna, Apecchio, Arcevia, Cagli, Cantiano, Piobbico, Frontone, Sassoferrato and Serra Sant'Abbondio; in Croatia; from the coastal area of Split to the lively hinterland of Split-Dalmatia County. According to an article published by Ri-sposte Turismo, the main objective of the project is to create a network of accessible itineraries connecting coastal areas with the hinterland, enhancing local natural and cultural resources. Through the collaboration between Italian and Croatian partners, OMNIS intends to develop thematic routes that include historical sites, protected natural areas and local communities, offering tourists authentic and sustainable experiences. This approach not only diversifies the tourism offer but also contributes to the strengthening of local economies and the preservation of shared cultural heritage. As stated on the project's official website, OMNIS was created with the objective of promoting accessible and sustainable tourism, with a focus on groups that encounter barriers in traditional tourism. It aims to enhance inland destinations by highlighting the lesser-known areas of the Italian and Croatian hinterland, encouraging travel outside the most popular coastal regions. A key priority is the improvement of accessibility, especially for visually impaired travelers, pet owners and individuals with special needs. By developing inland itineraries, OMNIS contributes to reducing environmental and social pressures by mitigating overtourism in coastal areas, benefiting local communities and ecosystems. Furthermore, the project establishes a scalable model that can be replicated in future initiatives to support other groups, including the elderly, people with disabilities and people with food restrictions.

3   Methodologic Approaches and Objectives

Spatial Regeneration Through Ecosystem Services

The research adopts a qualitative case study approach, combining document analysis, spatial interpretation, and project evaluation. Case studies were selected based on three criteria: (1) demonstrable integration between coastal and inland areas; (2) inclusion of ecosystem services and soft mobility strategies; (3) alignment with European sustainability frameworks (e.g., Natura 2000, LIFE SAM4CP). Data were gathered from institutional reports, scientific publications, and technical documentation of projects such as the OMNIS initiative and the Regional Natural Park of the Coastal Dunes. Geographic Information Systems (GIS) were used to map existing routes and identify potential ecological corridors, while content analysis was applied to policy documents and community engagement strategies. The objective was to evaluate how slow tourism infrastructures can serve as catalysts for spatial regeneration by linking ecosystem value, mobility, and heritage.

3.1   Relevance of Ecosystem Services Mapping

The theme of integration between coastal and inland areas also introduces the topic from the exploitation of ecosystem services, which is those benefits provided by natural ecosystems that support the quality of life and environmental sustainability. This typology of services can be scaled according to the context in which they are inserted. The study "Urban regeneration and good land use", part of the Life Sam4cp project, highlights the importance of mapping and assessing ecosystem services to support spatial planning and promote sustainable land use. This approach aims to identify precisely the areas with the greatest potential for slow tourism, facilitating the creation of routes that link the coast and inland in a strategic and sustainable way. The use of GIS tools and environmental assessment models allows to identify critical areas for biodiversity, high cultural value routes and spaces to be recovered for cycling routes and historical trails. Integrating this information into tourism development plans helps to maximise socio-economic benefits and ensure balanced land management (see Fig. 2).

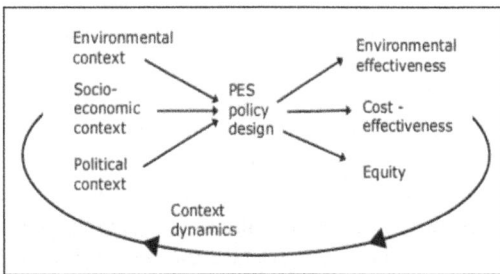

Fig. 2. Payments for ecosystem services placed in the context of criteria for their definition and assessment (Jack et al., 2008). INSPRA Report: towards the national strategy for biodiversity - Definition of the method for classification and quantification of ecosystem services in Italy

3.2   Connection with European Strategies

The approach to land regeneration through ecosystem services is in line with several European sustainable development strategies. The European Union's Green Infrastructure Action Plan and the Natura 2000 Network are key tools to strengthen environmental resilience and improve the economic value of marginal areas. In particular, the project Life Sam4cp - Soil Administration Models 4 Community Profit (SAM4CP)-, funded by the European LIFE + programme, was created to make available some tools for better soil management over the four years of its operation, With particular emphasis on the assessment and mapping of ecosystem services, understood as the tangible and intangible benefits that humans can derive from this natural resource. The project demonstrates how mapping of ecosystem services can contribute to the identification of a network of green corridors and can promote the conservation of historic natural and agricultural areas, With the parallel aim of making these currently unusable areas more visible and comprehensible. These strategies not only protect the landscape but also provide opportunities for regenerative tourism by encouraging local communities to become involved in the management and development of their territory.

A realistic example of the application of these principles is represented by cycling along waterways, such as the Rimini-Marecchia route. The offer proposed to discover the villages and large spaces overlooking the valley of the river Marecchia ranges from routes dedicated to food, those of landscape discovery to those for more experts, with areas to cross through climbing or rough stretches. Starting from the source of the river, on the Alpe della Luna, you can proceed keeping the sea of Rimini behind and looking at the coastal hills of ancient towns, villages, and castles. "The Valmarecchia is a border territory, *"romagnola"* for its approach and hospitality, but nestled between Tuscany and the Marches, a territory more designed by history together with the Montefeltro than by the bureaucracy of the regions." Territorial regeneration can be achieved through the exploitation of sustainable connecting ecosystem services. ' Bike Marecchia", a parallel route to the one that can be taken on foot, starts from the banks of the iver Marecchia, extending to Ponte Messa for a length of 45.7 km. The cycle path of Val Marecchia, Threcorded a 25% increase in usage between 2020 and 2023 (source: Bike Marecchia Project Report). In the same period, local businesses along the route reported an 18% rise in tourist-related income, suggesting a direct economic benefit from the soft mobility infrastructure. It stretches from the coast to the inland along the banks of the river Marecchia, offering a route immersed in nature that connects Rimini to Novafeltria. This track has no significant differences in level, but the unpaved ground adds a slight degree of difficulty and an element of charm that differentiates the route from the linear slopes of the Riviera Romagnola.

Similarly, transhumance routes such as the Regio Tratturo Pescasseroli-Candela and the Tratturo Magno can benefit from an accelerated mapping of ecosystem services to identify strategic locations for refreshment, Equipped rest areas and landscape interpretation centres. The recognition of transhumance as UNESCO Intangible Cultural Heritage further strengthens the importance of these routes for the enhancement of local traditions and the promotion of experiential and sustainable tourism. Migration has played a key role in the modelling of landscape and social relations in central Italy. In the period between 1600 and 1800, it is estimated that between 5 and 6 million sheep moved annually from Abruzzo to Puglia, with revenues representing a third of the entire state budget. The tracts, the ancient ways of transhumance, covered a total extension of about 3,000 km, constituting a fundamental network for the pastoral economy of the time. [elearning.unite.it] Recently, the practice of transhumance has been reassessed not only for its social and cultural value, but also as a factor in the conservation of the rural landscape and agro ecosystem. Studies have shown how the reactivation of transhumance routes can contribute to the enhancement of ecosystem services and the strengthening of local communities. These examples show how the exploitation of the old ways of transhumance and the development of cycling routes can be integrated into a sustainable tourism model, promoting the rediscovery of the territory and collective well-being (see Fig. 3).

3.3   Towards Integrated Land Management

Integrating ecosystem assessment into regional tourism development plans ensures balanced management between environmental conservation and the creation of new economic opportunities for local communities. European spatial planning strategies, such as the **Green Infrastructure Strategy**, demonstrate how an integrated approach to landscape regeneration can generate long-term positive impacts. The creation of soft mobility networks and green corridors not only improves the quality of life of the inhabitants but also promotes greater tourist attractiveness based on sustainability and respect for the territory. Through these strategies, slow tourism can become an engine of development

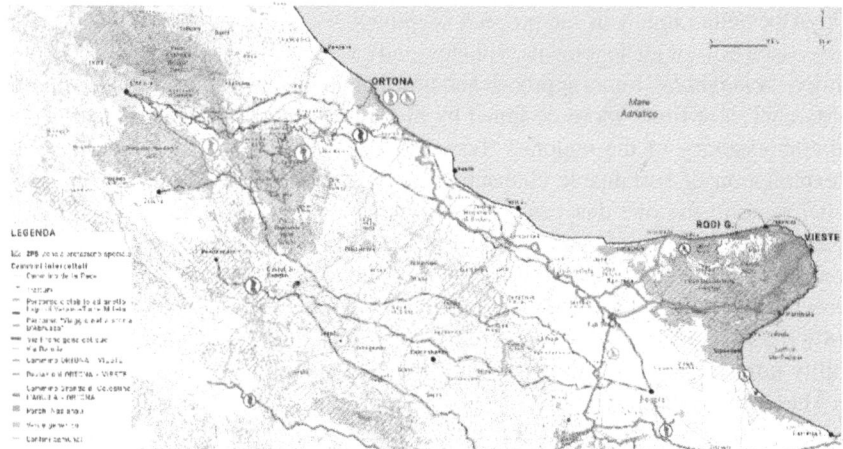

Fig. 3. Analysis of soft mobility along the Adriatic coast, from Abruzzo to Puglia. In the analysis are highlighted the tracts of the tracts, the Via Francigena and the Via Micaelica. There are also overlays of paths that trace in an analogous way the ancient tracks of the Transhumance. (Source: Chiara Correra).

for inland areas, contributing to economic revitalization, conservation of the natural heritage and promotion of a more responsible and inclusive tourism model.

4   Conclusions

The analysis shows that slow and sustainable tourism represents a strategic opportunity for territorial regeneration through coastal-inland connection. The ecosystem approach to soft mobility network planning highlights how the protection of cultural and natural heritage and the involvement of local communities can be the pillars of an integrated and resilient development model. The infrastructure of routes that exploit pre-existing landscape elements, such as rivers, old transhumance routes and cycling networks, contributes to the decongesting of coastal destinations, distributing tourist flows over often marginalised inland areas. This approach, in addition to mitigating the environmental impacts of conventional tourism, is part of a broader framework for adaptation to climate change, where the recovery of ecological connections and the preservation of biodiversity play a significant role (Thonicke et al., 2018). The results of the study highlight the need for multi-level governance strategies, where coordination between institutions, tourism operators and local stakeholders is crucial to the creation of a sustainable tourism offer. In particular, the importance of adopting land-use planning tools incorporating predictive models on the carrying capacity of territories, ensuring a balance between use and protection of the landscape, emerges. However, while slow tourism presents multiple benefits, it also raises potential risks that must be acknowledged. These include green gentrification—where increased attractiveness of slow routes may lead to displacement of local populations—as well as conflicts over land use between conservation goals and economic interests. Furthermore, maintenance of soft infrastructure (e.g., unpaved trails, signage, resting areas) often lacks stable funding, threatening long-term viability. A more critical and balanced approach is therefore essential to ensure equitable and durable outcomes.

References

1. Norberg-Schulz, C.: Genius Loci: Towards a Phenomenology of Architecture. Rizzoli, New York (1979)
2. Pannikar, R.: Peace and Interculturality: A Philosophical Reflection. Jaca Book, Milano (2002)
3. Springer: LNCS Homepage. http://www.springer.com/lncs. Accessed 25 Oct 2023
4. Almheiri, A., Montenegro, J.F., Ewane, E.B., Mohan, M.: Climate change hazards and the resilience of coastal cities in the gulf cooperation council countries: a systematic review – art01 (PDF)
5. Giaimo, C., Salata, S.: Rigenerazione urbana e buon uso del suolo: mappare e valutare i servizi ecosistemici alla scala locale. Esperienze dal Progetto Life Sam4cp. Università di Napoli
6. Balvanera, P., et al.: Chapter 3 Ecosystem services. In: Walters, M., Scholes, R.J. (eds.) The GEO Handbook on Biodiversity Observation Networks. Springer, Cham
7. Angrilli, M.: La ciudad Adriatica. Paisajes costeros (2023)
8. ISPRA: Rapporto sulle dune e sui servizi ecosistemici. ISPRA, Roma
9. Progetto Bike Marecchia: Report Finale. https://www.fiumemarecchia.it/wp-content/uploads/Report-Finale-progetto-Bike-Marecchia.pdf
10. Thompson, C.W.: Linking landscape and health: the recurring theme. Landsc. Urban Plann. **99**(3–4), 187–195 (2011)
11. Orff, K.: Toward an Urban Ecology. Princeton Architectural Press, New York (2016)
12. Corner, J.: The Landscape Imagination: Collected Essays of James Corner, 1990–2010. Princeton Architectural Press, New York (2014)
13. Fleming, B.: Design and the green new deal. Places J. (2019)
14. Laboratorio del Cammino - DIST, Dipartimento Interateneo di Scienze, Progetto e Politiche del Territorio del Politecnico di Torino e dell'Università degli Studi di Torino: Walking the shrinkage. 21 parole chiave e 5 temi per descrivere la contrazione in cammino (2022)
15. Taraborrelli, L., Caramanico, L.: Il cammino della Pace. Dall'Aquila a Monte Sant'Angelo. Guida del Pellegrino. Il Viandante (2021)
16. Collana Ricerche e Studi Territorialisti: Spazi e corpi in Movimento. Fare urbanistica in cammino. SDT Edizioni (2020)
17. Latino, A.F.P.: L'Abbazia benedettina della SS. Trinità di Monte Sacro in Mattinata: Leggende, fatti e misfatti. Gargano Studi – Rivista del Centro Studi Garganici, II ristampa, Mattinata (2012)
18. Russo, S.: Dialoghi di storia. Claudio Grenzi Editori (2002)
19. Leccisotti, P.T.: Documenti di Capitanata. Tra le Carte di S. Spirito del Morrone
20. Savinio, A.: Dico a te, Clio. Adelphi (1992)
21. Grenzi, G.: Gargano. Sacro di Natura. Claudio Grenzi Editore (2002)
22. Fulloni, S.: L'Abbazia dimenticata. La Santissima Trinità sul Gargano tra Normanni e Svevi. Liguori Editore (2006)
23. Fulloni, S.: Die Abtei SS. Trinitm auf dem Monte Sacro. Gargano (APULIEN). Edizioni del Museo Nazionale Germanico di Norimberga
24. European Institute of Cultural Routes: Cultural Routes of the Council of Europe Programme Activity Report 2022. Abbaye de Neumünster Bâtiment Robert Bruch, Luxembourg
25. Vie e civiltà della Transumanza Patrimonio dell'Umanità: "Sentieri dello spirito in Abruzzo" - Paths of the Spirit in Abruzzo. Guida ai cammini storici fra Gran Sasso e Marsica. Terre di Mezzo Editore (2015)
26. Cammini di Europa: Linee Guida per l'avvio, lo sviluppo e la gestione di Itinerari Culturali in Italia. Manuale operativo di progetto (2015)

Renewable Energy Communities Monitoring, Optimization, and Planning. The RECMOP Research Project

Alessandra Marra[1]([✉]) [iD], Michele Grimaldi[1] [iD], Isidoro Fasolino[1] [iD], and Monica M. L. Sebillo[2] [iD]

[1] Department of Civil Engineering, University of Salerno, Fisciano, Italy
almarra@unisa.it
[2] Department of Computer Science, University of Salerno, Fisciano, Italy

Abstract. The concentration of anthropogenic activities in cities has made them more and more energy-intensive, with an increase in climate-changing emissions and local temperature, seriously threatening the quality of life and, more generally, urban sustainability. Urban planning cannot fail to address these needs, which must be placed among its primary objectives. Renewable Energy Communities (RECs) are a promising tool for tackling these global challenges, as well as energy poverty. However, despite promotion policies at both European and national level, RECs are struggling to spread across Member States, mainly due to the absence of transparent and accessible data on the benefits provided, the territorializability of projects and the absence of incentives at local level. This contribution aims to describe an ongoing research project, titled "Renewable Energy Communities Monitoring, Optimization and Planning (RECMOP)", intended to design a monitoring network to address the above-mentioned open questions. It is aimed at optimizing the space-time configurations of RECs, in order to maximize its social, environmental and economic benefits. The same network will support urban planning through the construction of cognitive frameworks that provide transparent and accessible information, to citizens and stakeholders, of the relevant parameters for the optimization of existing and future RECs. The monitoring network is based on a WEB platform and GeoAI technology, integrated with data from satellites, in situ and shared by citizens and stakeholders.

Keyword: Renewable Energy Communities · GeoAI · Urban Planning

1 Introduction

Numerous international agendas call for urgent action to contain global temperature, reduce dependence on fossil fuels and promote renewable energy [1, 2]. In this framework, cities, which have doubled globally from 1975 to 2020, are increasingly energy-intensive, with a demand for energy from homes equal to 22% of the total needs for the building sector, second only to that of transport. In Italy, half of residential buildings are

O. Gervasi et al. (Eds.): ICCSA 2025 Workshops, LNCS 15899, pp. 122–132, 2026.
https://doi.org/10.1007/978-3-031-97663-6_10

energy inefficient and, energy poverty, given by a combination of high energy expenditure, poor energy performance of homes and low income [3], is on average double that of Europe [4, 5]. The latter, amounting to about 31 million people in 2019, is set to increase due to the pandemic and the Russia-Ukraine conflict [6, 7].

Faced with these challenges, EU countries are obliged by 2030 to reduce emissions by 55% compared to 1990 levels, and to achieve carbon neutrality by 2050 [8]. In this scenario, urban planning becomes essential to increase sustainability and address climate-changing emissions and local temperature in urban areas [9, 10]. Therefore, it cannot fail to take into account these needs, to be placed among its primary objectives.

As a promising tool to combat these global challenges, Renewable Energy Communities (RECs) emerge. Intended as coalitions of citizens, SMEs and local authorities, capable of producing, consuming and sharing locally produced energy from renewable sources, RECs have the main aim of providing environmental, economic and social benefits to the community itself or to the areas in which it operates [11].

In support of this solution, experiments in the USA and Europe show the advantages of RECs obtained in specific areas, including the energy efficiency of existing buildings, the impact of the use of renewable energy, the consequent reduction of emissions and the fight against energy poverty [12–17].

The link with the areas in which they operate differentiates RECs from other configurations of collective self-consumption, making RECs an important tool for achieving the above-mentioned urban planning objectives.

Directive EU/2001/2018 (RED II), part of the Clean Energy for all Europeans regulatory package, obliges Member States to promote RECs, assessing their barriers and development potential in their territories, as well as facilitating them with an appropriate support framework [11].

In Italy, RECs were introduced by Decree-Law No. 162 of 30 December 2019, subsequently updated by Legislative Decree No. 199 of 8 November 2021, which implemented the aforementioned Directive. Italian RECs must comply with specific constraints to obtain economic incentives, such as connection to the same primary substation, i.e. medium-high voltage, and renewable plants with a power not exceeding 1 MW each. Some Italian Regions have anticipated European legislation, financing RECs establishment, often in the most disadvantaged areas. In addition, the National Recovery and Resilience Plan reserves additional incentives for RECs in municipalities with a population of less than 5000 inhabitants, to counter demographic decline [18]. In order to simplify the verification process about the eligibility for incentives and the feasibility in terms of energy capacity of REC projects, the National Energy Service Operator (GSE) has released the map of the areas served by the primary substations [19] and the map of the critical areas in terms of grid saturation [20].

In addition, several applications useful for the optimal RECs design are developed internationally, e.g. Procsimulator [21] and LoadProfileGenerator [22].

Examples of Italian design support platforms are the following: a simulator by GSE [23]; the RECON, DHOMUS, and CruISE applications by ENEA [24–26]; the e-360 platform by Sistematica company [27].

2 Barriers to the RECs Deployment in Europe and Italy

Despite the RECs promotion in the framework of the European Green Deal and Repower EU initiatives, their uptake in the Member States is limited.

As shown by a recent EU report on this issue, among the main obstacles are the following: the difficulty of involving potential community members; the lack of expertise to localize REC projects; urban planning obstacles, in terms of constraints, intended use and previous building rights, in the authorization process of projects; the absence of incentives at local level [28].

Notwithstanding these aspects, a review of the international literature has shown that energy/technological and cost-effectiveness aspects prevail in the search for optimal RECs spatial configurations, while those related to urban planning, as well as the phenomenon of energy poverty, have received little attention [29, 30].

This picture does not differ much from the Italian one, in which, despite the efforts made by both the national government and the Regions, there are still few RECs fully implemented [31], which are disconnected from planning processes. Furthermore, from the analysis of the municipal urban planning instruments of the 109 Italian provincial capitals, the concept of REC is included in only seven cases, highlighting an obsolescence of the plans examined with respect to this issue, particularly in the South [32–35].

These trends are also reflected in the currently available applications, which facilitate the optimal RECs design from an energy/technological and economic point of view, but do not support the pre-project or planning phase.

Exceptions are the maps of primary substations and existing grid capacity [19, 20]. However, the maps are drawn up at an inadequate level of spatial detail to address these issues at the local level.

Therefore, general urban planning is considered a probable obstacle if not properly updated on the subject [36–38].

On the contrary, it can play a relevant role in overcoming these barriers, especially if integrated with local energy planning, contrary to what happens historically [39, 40].

In particular, the general plan should be integrated with the Sustainable Energy and Climate Action Plan (SECAP), which pursues common objectives, such as the reduction of climate-changing emissions and the fight against energy poverty to ensure a sustainable and fair transition, providing for the citizens active participation in decision-making processes.

This path can also be followed by considering the role of Local Authorities both as potential members of RECs and as institutions that can lead the process of activating RECs, facilitating the involvement of citizens, even in the planning process of their competence [41, 42].

3 Open Questions and Scope of the Work

From the analysis conducted on the state of the art, some open questions emerge from a scientific point of view (OQ):

OQ1) in the experiments carried out there is often the difficulty of involving citizens as potential RECs members, due to their lack of information and/or perception about the potential benefits brought by the RECs themselves - a problem that is not secondary since the ERC activation process is based on their open and voluntary participation;

OQ2) in the search for optimal spatial configurations of RECs there is a prevalent attention to energy/technological aspects and economic convenience, while aspects related to urban sustainability have received little attention, as well as the phenomenon of energy poverty, with the risk of a non-territorializability of projects, or of a limited RECs performance;

OQ3) RECs are disconnected from urban planning processes, making planning itself a possible obstacle to their development, as well as determining the lack of incentives at the local level.

As a result, it emerges that, despite promotion policies at both European and national level, RECs are struggling to take off in the Member States, mainly due to the absence of transparent and accessible data on the benefits brought by the territorializability of projects and the absence of incentives at the local level [28].

These trends are reflected in the currently available applications and maps, which do not support the pre-design phase, which is useful for the projects territorialization, planning and the involvement of potential REC members. This limitation represents the main technological gap found that can become a significant business opportunity.

This contribution aims to describe an ongoing research and development project, titled "Renewable Energy Communities Monitoring, Optimization and Planning (REC-MOP)", intended to design a monitoring network to address the above-mentioned open questions from a scientific and technological point of view, in order to promote the rapid deployment of RECs, in line with European and national policies.

The scientific approach, with reference to OQ1, is to monitor existing RECs to measure their social, economic and environmental benefits, to increase the awareness of potential members about these benefits, through appropriate participatory processes, as well as to evaluate the impacts of RECs promotion policies in terms of achieving the expected results.

With reference to OQ2, it is necessary to optimize the RECs configurations from a spatial point of view, but also temporarily, both by minimizing the obstacles, also with reference to urban and territorial constraints, and by maximizing the benefits, not only in terms of technological or economic performance, but also with reference to the objectives of adaptation to climate change and reduction of energy poverty in urban areas.

With reference to OQ3, it is necessary to strengthen the role of Local Authorities and urban planning to promote RECs, aiming to overcome the historically difficult integration between energy planning and city planning (Fig. 1).

Overall, the main objective of RECMOP is to develop a RECs monitoring network, aimed at optimizing their spatio-temporal configurations, in order to maximize their performance, understood in terms of social, environmental and economic benefits. The same network will support urban planning through the construction of cognitive frameworks that provide transparent and accessible information, to citizens and stakeholders, of the relevant parameters for the optimization of existing and future RECs.

Based on a cyclical process of Monitoring-Optimization-Planning, the network represents a new technological solution, not present on the market, to effectively promote

RECs as tools for achieving the ambitious European decarbonization goals, as well as combating energy poverty.

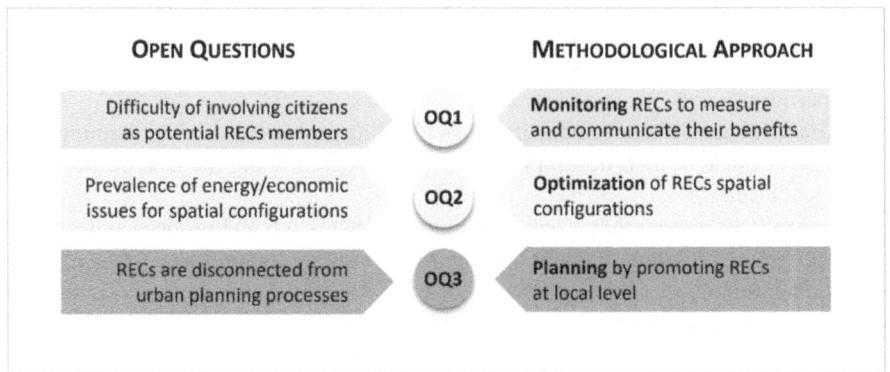

Fig. 1. The scientific approach behind the RECMOP project.

4   The Structure of the RECMOP Project

The monitoring network is based on a WEB platform and GeoAI technology integrated with data from satellites, in situ and shared by citizens / stakeholders, thanks to the partnership with the companies Latitudo 40 and Nexsoft. More precisely, the monitoring network will allow the drafting and consultation of cognitive frameworks, supplementary to those already available at national level [19, 20], which may concern the following parameters, by way of example:

- the spatial perimeter of existing RES plants;
- the suitable sites for the location of new RES plants or, in other words, the urban and territorial constraints on the location of new RES plants;
- the RES local potential, in terms of the most suitable renewable energy sources;
- the most energy-intensive buildings, with particular reference to predominantly residential urban areas;
- urban areas inhabited by low-income households;
- the areas of greatest energy poverty;
- any building and urban planning incentives differentiated by areas;
- any projects approved or under construction that may have shared objectives;
- the barriers faced by citizens who are REC members or who have failed to become members.
- The data necessary to build this knowledge will be taken from:
- official datasets periodically updated by public bodies and entities (e.g. Italian Institute of Statistics, Italian Institute for Environmental Protection and Research, Regional Agencies for Environmental Protection, Regions, Provinces);
- data ordinarily available in municipal urban planning processes;
- data derived from satellite images.

The overall structure of the project is divided into Work Packages (WP), within which specific Activities are envisaged, useful for the implementation and validation of the proposed methodology, which consists of the workflow described in subsequent sentences.

WP1 concerns the recognition of sources, the collection and analysis of the data necessary to build the cognitive frameworks.

Starting from these data, it will be possible, through appropriate processing already consolidated in the experience of the partnership, to build further data, through analysis and simulation algorithms, such as spatial analysis in a GIS environment and Machine Learning, in particular the use of innovative analysis solutions applied to satellite images (Sentinel 2 super-resolution at 1mt, models for the analysis of environmental phenomena and for the identification of solar panels), will allow the creation of an expert system to support the identification of the most suitable areas for the RECs establishment and to monitor their environmental benefits (WP3).

The aforementioned data will also be supplemented with data directly provided by citizens. The latter will be acquired through appropriate information and awareness of the population, involved through the same network and with the help of an integration of participation techniques, during the entire period of the project implementation, also in synergy with municipal authorities, professional associations and stakeholders (WP5).

The network will be designed and developed in its architecture (WP2) and functionality (WP3).

The network will be tested in a selected case study (WP4), but will be designed to be transferable to other geographical contexts (Fig. 2).

The cognitive frameworks built within the RECMOP project are intended to be useful to support:

- with reference to OQ1, participatory processes for the information and awareness of citizens, individually or in association, SMEs and institutions, as current or potential members of RECs, or even leaders who can lead the process of activating RECs, with particular reference to Local Authorities;
- with reference to OQ2, professionals and companies engaged in the ecological and energy transition in the pre-feasibility studies of REC projects, minimizing the risk of non-territorializability of the projects;
- with reference to OQ3, the choices of political decision-makers in the promotion of RECs in municipal, general and sectoral urban planning tools, also through incentive mechanisms, reducing the risk that urban planning that is not up-to-date on the subject or not integrated could be among the obstacles to the spread of RECs.

Examples of such incentives for private initiative in support of public action are the following: volume or surface increases; discount on urbanization charges; local tax advantages; green credits [43–45]. So, municipal authorities will be able to respond, at local level, to the European Commission obligation to identify the obstacles and development potential in their territories, promoting RECs dissemination through the provision of transparent and accessible knowledge frameworks, as well as through an appropriate support framework and incentives, to be made explicit in urban planning instruments. Finally, the updating of the knowledge framework (ex post) is a way to monitor the impacts of RECs on the territory with respect to the individual issues in which this knowledge is articulated (ex ante), allowing the outcome of the political and technical choices made to be assessed, with particular reference to the achievement of the expected social, economic and environmental benefits, to be taken into account in the updating of plans and projects.

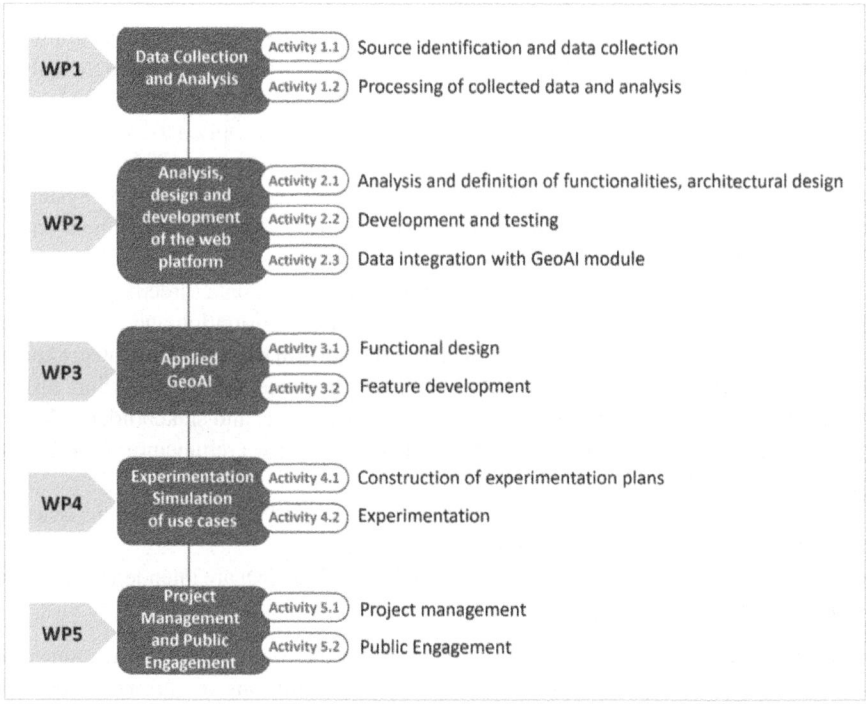

Fig. 2. The proposed workflow according to the WPs and related Activities.

5   Conclusion

The concentration of anthropogenic activities in cities has made them more and more energy-intensive, with an increase in climate-changing emissions and local temperature, seriously threatening the quality of life and, more generally, urban sustainability. In addition, the escalation of poverty, due to the recent pandemic, and the rise in energy prices are significantly increasing the risk of experiencing energy poverty, which was already a concern in Europe before the spread of Covid-19.

Renewable Energy Communities are a promising tool for tackling these global challenges.

Despite promotion policies at both European and national level, RECs are struggling to spread across Member States, mainly due to the absence of transparent and accessible data on the benefits provided, the territorializability of projects and the absence of incentives at local level, often due to urban plans not updated on the topic. This contribution aims to present an ongoing research and development project, titled "Renewable Energy Communities Monitoring, Optimization and Planning (RECMOP)", intended to design a monitoring network to address the above-mentioned open questions. The monitoring network is based on a WEB platform and GeoAI technology integrated with data from satellites, in situ and shared by citizens.

The main expected results concern the repercussions of the knowledge framework produced, which will be made accessible through the platform, promoting:

- information, awareness and involvement of citizens, SMEs, institutions and stake-holders, all potential members of a REC;
- professionals and companies in the energy transition sector in pre-feasibility studies, reducing the risk of projects not suited to the territory;
- policy makers in the integration and promotion of CERs in urban planning, also through incentives and reward measures aimed at encouraging private initiative in support of public action.

The ultimate goal of RECMOP research and development project is to promote the rapid development of RECs, as tools to achieve climate neutrality and combat energy poverty in urban areas, in line with European and Italian decarbonization policies.

Acknowledgments. The present study fits within the Research and Development Project titled "Renewable Energy Communities: Monitoring, Optimization and Planning (RECMOP)", funded by Italian National Recovery and Resilience Plan (NRRP) and selected in the Cascata Call by Extended Partnership NEST "Network 4 Energy Sustainable Transition", SPOKE 8 University of Roma Sapienza (CUP: B53C22004070006).

Authors Contributions.   Conceptualization, A.M., M.G., I.F. and M.M.L.S; methodology, A.M., M.G., I.F. and M.M.L.S.; investigation, A.M.; data curation, A.M.; writing—original draft preparation, A.M.; writing—review and editing, A.M., M.G., I.F. and M.M.L.S.; visualization, A.M.; project administration, M.G. All authors have read and agreed to the published version of the manuscript.

Disclosure of Interests.   The authors have no competing interests to declare that are relevant to the content of this article.

References

1. UNFCCC. The Paris Agreement. In: Proceedings of the Paris Climate Change Conference. COP 21, Paris, France (2015)
2. UN, United Nations. Transforming Our World: The 2030 Agenda for Sustainable Development. New York, USA (2015)
3. EU, European Commission. Introduction to the Energy Poverty Advisory Hub (EPAH) Handbooks: A Guide to Understanding and Addressing Energy Poverty. Energy Poverty Advisory Hub, Bruxelles (2022)
4. ENEA, Agenzia Nazionale per le Nuove Tecnologie, l'Energia e lo Sviluppo Economico Sostenibile. Sistema Informativo degli Attestati di Prestazione Energetica - SIAPE (2021). https://siape.enea.it. Accessed 03 Mar 2025

5. ISTAT, Istituto Nazionale di Statistica. Statistical Information for 2030 Agenda in Italy. 2021 SDGs Report. Roma (2021)
6. EU, European Commission. State of the Energy Union 2021 – Contributing to the European Green Deal and the Union's recovery (2021)
7. EU, European Commission. State of the Energy Union 2022 (2022)
8. EU, European Commission. Regulation 2021/1119 of the European Parliament and of the Council of 30 June 2021 establishing the framework for achieving climate neutrality and amending Regulations (EC) No 401/2009 and (EU) 2018/1999 («European Climate Law») (2021)
9. UN-Habitat, United Nations Human Settlements Programme: World Cities Report 2020: The Value of Sustainable Urbanization. UN-Habitat, San Francisco, CA, USA (2021)
10. UN-Habitat, United Nations Human Settlements Programme. World Cities Report 2022: Envisaging the Future of Cities. United Nations, Nairobi, Kenya (2022)
11. EU, European Commission. Directive (EU) 2018/2001 of the European Parliament and of the Council of 11 December 2018 on the promotion of the use of energy from renewable sources. EU, Brussels (2018)
12. Colombo, G., Ferrero, F., Pirani, G., Vesco, A.: Planning local energy communities to develop low carbon urban and suburban areas. In: Proceedings of the IEEE International Energy Conference (ENERGYCON), Dubrovnik, Croatia, 13–16 May 2014, pp. 1012–1018 (2014)
13. Brummer, V.: Community energy – benefits and barriers: a comparative literature review of community energy in the UK, Germany and the USA, the benefits it provides for society and the barriers it faces. Renew. Sustain. Energy Rev. **94**, 187–196 (2018)
14. McCabe, A., Pojani, D., Broese van Groenou, A.: Social housing and renewable energy: community energy in a supporting role. Energy Res. Soc. Sci. **38**, 110–113 (2018)
15. Koltunov, M., Bisello, A.: Multiple impacts of energy communities: conceptualization taxonomy and assessment examples. In: Bevilacqua, C., Calabrò, F., Della Spina, L. (eds.) New Metropolitan Perspectives. NMP 2020. Smart Innovation, Systems and Technologies, vol. 178, pp. 1081–1096. Springer, Cham (2021). https://doi.org/10.1007/978-3-030-48279-4_101
16. Wierling, A., Zeiss, J.P., Lupi, V., Candelise, C., Sciullo, A., Schwanitz, V.J.: The contribution of energy communities to the upscaling of photovoltaics in Germany and Italy. Energies **14**, 2258 (2021)
17. Marra, A.: A model to detect low income urban areas to plan renewable energy communities against energy poverty. In: Gervasi O., et al. (eds.) Computational Science and Its Applications – ICCSA 2023 Workshops. Proceedings, Part IX. Lecture Notes in Computer Science, vol. 14112, pp. 353–363. Springer, Cham (2023). https://doi.org/10.1007/978-3-031-37129-5_29
18. Italian Government. Italian National Revovery and Resilience Plan (NRRP) (2022)
19. GSE, National Energy Service Operator. Mappa delle aree servite dalle cabine primarie [Map of the areas served by the primary substations] (2024). https://www.gse.it/servizi-per-te/autoconsumo/mappa-interattiva-delle-cabine-primarie. Accessed 03 Mar 2025
20. E-distribuzione. Mappa delle aree critiche in termini di saturazione della rete [Map of the critical areas in terms of grid saturation] (2023). https://www.e-distribuzione.it/a-chi-ci-rivolgiamo/produttori/aree-critiche.html. Accessed 03 Mar 2025
21. Velosa, N., Gomes, E., Morais, H., Pereira, L.: PROCSIM: an open-source simulator to generate energy community power demand and generation scenarios. Energies **16**(4), 1611 (2023). https://doi.org/10.3390/en16041611
22. Pflugradt, N.: Load Profile Generator (2015). https://www.loadprofilegenerator.de/. Accessed 03 Mar 2025
23. GSE. GSE simulator (2025). www.autoconsumo.gse.it. Accessed 03 Mar 2025

24. ENEA. RECON (2025). https://recon.smartenergycommunity.enea.it/. Accessed 03 Mar 2025
25. ENEA. DHOMUS (2025). https://dhomus.smartenergycommunity.enea.it/. Accessed 03 Mar 2025
26. ENEA. CruISE (2025). https://www.smartenergycommunity.it/strumenti/cruise/. Accessed 03 Mar 2025
27. Sistematica Spa. e-360 (2025). https://www.e-360.it/simulazione-e-gestione-comunita-ene rgetiche/. Accessed 03 Mar 2025
28. EU, European Commission. Energy Communities repository. Barriers and action drivers for the development of different activities by Renewable and Citizen Energy Communities. EU, Brussels (2024)
29. Gerundo, R., Marra, A., Grimaldi, M.: A preliminary model for promoting energy communities in urban planning. In: Calabrò, F., Della Spina, L., Mantiñán, M.J.P. (eds.) New Metropolitan Perspectives: Post COVID Dynamics: Green and Digital Transition, Between Metropolitan and Return to Villages Perspectives. Lecture Notes in Networks and, Systems, vol. 482, pp. 2833–2840. Springer, Cham (2022). https://doi.org/10.1007/978-3-031-06825-6_270
30. Gerundo, R., Marra, A.: A decision support methodology to foster renewable energy communities in the municipal urban plan. Sustainability **14**(23), 16268 (2022). https://doi.org/10. 3390/su142316268
31. Legambiente. Comunità Rinnovabili. Sole, Vento, Acqua, Terra, Biomasse. Lo Scenario Della Generazione Distribuita Nel Territorio Italiano. Lo Sviluppo Dei Nuovi Modelli Energetici Nei Territori in Attesa del Completo Recepimento Della Direttiva Europea (2021)
32. Huang, Z., Yu, H., Peng, Z., Zhao, M.: Methods and tools for community energy planning: a review. Renew. Sustain. Energy Rev. **42**, 1335–1348 (2015)
33. Gerundo, R., Marra, A. (eds.): Le Comunità Energetiche Rinnovabili. Progetti e Piani. Urbanistica Inf. **306**, 777–801 (2022)
34. Gerundo, R., Marra, A. (eds.): Renewable energy communities: urban research and land use planning. BDC. Bollettino Centro Calza Bini **22**(2), 160–311 (2022)
35. Marra, A.: Exploring the integration of renewable energy communities in urban planning. The case of Italy. Scienze Territorio **12**(2), 18–31 (2024). https://doi.org/10.36253/sdt-15751
36. Ministero dello Sviluppo Economico, Ministero dell'Ambiente, della Tutela del Territorio e del Mare, Ministero delle Infrastrutture e dei Trasporti. Piano Nazionale Integrato per l'Energia e il Clima (PNIEC) (2019)
37. De Lotto, R., Micciché, C., Venco, E.M., Bonaiti, A., De Napoli, R.: Energy communities: technical, legislative, organizational, and planning features. Energies **15**, 1731 (2022). https:// doi.org/10.3390/en15051731
38. Balletto, G., Ladu, M., Camerin, F., Ghiani, E., Torriti, J.: More circular city in the energy and ecological transition: a methodological approach to sustainable urban regeneration. Sustainability **14**(22), 14995 (2022). https://doi.org/10.3390/su142214995
39. Brunetta, G., Mutani, G., Santantonio, S.: Planning for territorial resilience. The citizen energy communities model. Archivio Studi Urbani Regionali LII **131**, 44–70 (2021)
40. Curreli, S., Zoppi, C.: Coal and spatial planning: Rhetoric of decline and critical issues within the energetic transition of Sardinia (Italy). Archivio Studi Urbani Regionali LII **131**, 166–185 (2021)
41. Candelise, A., Ruggieri, A.: Status and evolution of the community energy sector in Italy. Energies **13**, 1888 (2020). https://doi.org/10.3390/en13081888
42. Friends of the Earth Europe, REScoop.eu, Energy Cities. Municipalities & Local Authorities: an ideal partner. In: Community Energy. A practical guide to reclaiming power (2020)
43. Macchiaroli, M., Dolores, L., De Mare, G., Nicodemo, L.: Tax policies for housing energy efficiency in Italy: a risk analysis model for energy service companies. Buildings **13**(3), 582 (2023). https://doi.org/10.3390/buildings13030582

44. Dolores, L., Giannattasio, O., Macchiaroli, M., De Mare, G., Caprino, R. M.: Medium-long term economic sustainability for public utility works. In: Calabrò, F., Della Spina, L., Piñeira Mantiñán, M. J. (eds.) New Metropolitan Perspectives. Lecture Notes in Networks and Systems, vol. 482, pp. 1319–1327. Springer, Cham (2022). https://doi.org/10.1007/978-3-031-06825-6_128

45. EEA, European Environment Agency. Energy prosumers and cities. Briefing no. 19/2022 (2022). https://doi.org/10.2800/371424

Integrating the Ecosystem Approach into Urban and Landscape Planning: Enhancing Ecosystem Services for Sustainable Development

Francesca Perrone[1], Rachele Vanessa Gatto[2](✉) ⓘ, and Catherine Vandermeulen[3]

[1] Department of Planning, Design and Technology of Architecture (PDTA),
Sapienza University of Rome, Rome, Italy
francesca.perrone@uniroma1.it
[2] School of Engineering, University of Basilicata, Viale Dell'Ateneo Lucano 10,
85100 Potenza, Italy
rachelevanessa.gatto@unibas.it
[3] Hafen City Universität, Henning-Voscherau-Platz 1, 20457 Hamburg, Germany
catherine.vandermeulen@hcu-hamburg.de

Abstract. The ecosystem approach can potentially increase political-administrative interest in environmental issues. Pending further exploration (through identification tools and specific indicators) of the value of Ecosystem Services (ESs), urban-territorial and landscape planning tools undertake a path to identify and evaluate ESs. Reevaluating and reconsidering the role of ecological functions of environmental components in terms of anthropogenic benefits (ESs), can allow urban planning tools to give useful indications to reduce the damage caused to ecosystems and natural resources of reference, through the development of strategic choices aimed at reducing or qualifying sustainably the interventions of soil artificialization. From this point of view, the ecosystem approach adopted by land-use and landscape planning tools could allow for focusing attention on the increasing dependence between the stability of landscapes and the balance of ESs. The maintenance and enhancement of ESs in a given landscape area maximizes, in fact, their level of sustainability. At the same time, the ability of a landscape scope to provide ESs allows ecosystem components to be maintained in a given state of balance.

Keywords: Ecosystem approach · Land take · Urban planning tools

1 Introduction

The growing theoretical and conceptual interest in Ecosystem Services (ESs) reflects an increasing awareness of the interdependence between humans and natural systems. This awareness spans various dimensions, including ecological-environmental (regulating ESs), physical-structural (supporting ESs), productive agribusiness (provisioning ESs), and social-ecological and cultural-historical (cultural ESs) aspects.In terms of scientific applications, the focus on ESs is primarily cognitive and analytical. Researchers aim to assess the following aspects [1]:

© The Author(s), under exclusive license to Springer Nature Switzerland AG 2026
O. Gervasi et al. (Eds.): ICCSA 2025 Workshops, LNCS 15899, pp. 133–140, 2026.
https://doi.org/10.1007/978-3-031-97663-6_11

- conceptual interpretation (to circumscribe and/or further detail the field of investigation);
- interdisciplinary studies (to quantify and qualify the presence of distinct types of ESs);
- studies aimed at further investigating the role of ESs (and contextual variables);
- Cognitive feedback informs intervention needs at the policy, administrative, and decision-making levels as research advances and concepts in the field of ESs become systematized.

1.1 The Reason for an Ecosystem Approach

Despite the current awareness of humans' strong and unavoidable dependence on various ecosystem functions, the planning-decision-making level experiences severe difficulties in introducing ES issues pertaining to ESs into the defection and organization of the contents of urban planning tools [2].

Indeed, analysis and interpretation work are indispensable for understanding the system of relationships between ecological functions and ESs. Yet, *"many investigations still focus on a few selected ecosystem services and exclude trade-off analyses. Assessments of ecosystem services tend to be tailor-made to respond to the scale level of analysis and goal of the case study, making the comparison of different study outcomes difficult. As a result, scientifically focused ecosystem services assessments are often too complex and thus too complicated to be directly used in practical application, such as eco-audits or environmental impact assessments"* [3] (p. 55). This means that it is not enough to set up methodologies and define data analysis toolsbecause cognitive details and increasingly in-depth and specific information will not necessarily enable planning tools to enhance their strategic operational role. It is necessary to investigate the end to which the derived results tend: interpretative cognitive purpose and strategic function. In many cases, moreover, the sometimes anachronistic planning tools are unable to respond quickly to the problems and transformation needs that arise daily. The result is a scenario that leads to continuous consumption of natural resources and potentially exceeding environmental carrying capacity [4].

2   The Ecosystem Approach and the Governance of Land Take in Urban Planning Tools

The analytical and strategic contents of planning tools must first protect ESs and then manage the drivers of land use change (i.e. land consumption), as alterations in ecosystems are largely driven by these factors [5, 6]. The identification and assessment of ESs allows for strong consideration of the ecological-environmental value of specific land areas. This provides the opportunity: on the one hand, to better understand the characteristics and ecosystem role of natural components and, on the other hand, to protect these components and related ESs from compromising processes of anthropogenic origin, first and foremost, the artificialization of soils. Indeed, *"changes in land use play a central role in the delivery of ESs and urban planning, in turn, has a significant influence on their conservation or enhancement [...]"* [6] (p. 2).

2.1 Literature Review

The operational function of plan instruments plays a crucial role in sustainable land use management by integrating assessments on ESs.

As highlighted by Karrasch, Klenke, and Woltjer (2014) [7], the approach to ESs,], is a key element in promoting sustainable development whichrequires adaptive planning strategies and spatially explicit actions. A significant example is the methodology applied in the Krummhörn region of Germany, which combines ESs analysis and social impact assessment, providing a sound basis for establishing sustainable land use strategies.

Albert et al. (2016) [1] propose two integrated analytical models: the DPSIR and ES evaluation models. The former schematizes the interactions between anthropogenic pressures and responses to improve environmental conditions. At the same time, the latter proposes a distinction between ESs offered and used, facilitating a detailed assessment of ecological and social dynamics. This approach provides crucial information to curb land consumption, a factor that negatively affects ESs.

The integration of ESs in urban planning decisions, according to Cabral et al. (2016) [8], is essential to improvingawareness of the importance of sustainable land management. The study on the Urban Community of Bordeaux shows how a quantitative spatial assessment of ESs can support planning decisions, particularly through urban planning tools such as the Plan Local d'Urbanisme (PLU), which aim to balance urbanization and ecosystem protection.

Nin et al. (2016) [9] propose a structured method for integrating ESs into land use transformation planning through a process that includes human activity selection, land suitability modeling, and spatial prioritization. This approach makes it possible to identify areas for protection and areas for sustainable transformation while minimizing environmental impacts.

Van der Biest et al. (2020) [10] outline a step-by-step process for integrating ESs into land use planning, considering external factors, habitats, and natural and anthropogenic processes. This approach allows for the identification of areas where land consumption could compromise the availability of ESs, guiding decisions toward sustainable interventions.

At the national level, the LIFE SAM4CP project, analyzed by Salata et al. (2020) [11], applied the approach to ESs in three municipalities in the Metropolitan City of Turin, Italy, intending to limit land consumption and promote sustainable management strategies. The analysis highlighted the need to conserve areas with high capacity to provide ESs and to plan urban development consciously.

A further contribution is made by the SOS4LIFE project, studied by Calzolari et al. (2020) [12], which focuses on the city of Carpi (Italy) and aims to integrate soil knowledge into urban planning. The ESs maps developed showed how different soils can provide ESs of varying quality depending on the degree of sealing, underscoring the importance of wise urban area management to preserve natural capital.

In conclusion, the integration of ESs into planning tools is an essential strategy for sustainable land management, enabling the balancing of urban development needs with environmental protection. The adoption of advanced analytical models and spatial assessment of ESs provides concrete operational tools to guide planning policies toward a more sustainable future.

3   Assessment Process and Steps for Governing ESs and Land Take

To participate in the initiated discussion, a scheme focused on the interdependent relationship between the assessment process and the steps of "governing" ESs and land take was developed in the form of a conceptual map (Fig. 1). The concept map aims to systematize the relationship between governance of ESs and governance of land consumption. Urban planning tools take on the task of:

1. circumscribe the ecosystem components (cognitive-analytic status), by the ecosystem functions involved (different in types and characteristics), by the processes highlighted (environmental, social, economic), and by the interactions and connections (between components);
2. analyze its ESs (cognitive-analytical status) in relation to values (actual or potential), presence (more or less widespread and/or relevant), aggregation characters (in terms of quantity and quality), recognized at the territorial level;
3. to define, accordingly, strategies to govern ESs (operational-decisional status) in relation to the implications called into question in (1) and (2) and to the translation of ecosystem benefits into functional values for the qualification of processes and activities of sustainable governance of urban-territorial transformations;
4. finally, define strategies to govern land consumption, starting with monitoring of ESs and ecosystem strategies adopted, in relation to the status of the values considered (supporting, regulating, supplying, cultural, etc.) and their conditions of use (for particular purposes and objectives).

4   ESs and Decision-Making Processes

The factors of anthropization (on which land take depends), so that the limits of ecosystem resilience are not exceeded, must respect the general guidelines for the preservation and enhancement of available natural capital.

The added value of concretely introducing the ecosystem approach within urban planning tools allows [13]:

– consider all ESs, supportive, regulatory, procurement and cultural. *"Implementing the ES concept in a systematic and holistic manner in landscape planning processes fosters integration between the environmental, social and economic aspects of ecosystem utilization"* [14] (p. 119);
– recognizing differentiated and interrelated ESs within territories understood as "open systems," linked by deep ecological-structural dynamics;
– operate at an appropriate spatial scale of intervention to consider and include different types of ESs, both in analysis and in strategic and operational planning;
– adopt adaptive management and governance strategies that take into account, not only, the long-term state and dynamics of ecosystems, but are able to maintain the energy flows derived from ESs in a state of equilibrium;
– provide specific information on ESs dynamics to define "[…] *(1) current land-use/land cover and (2) its change over time, although the relationship may be nonlinear"* [15] (p. 12).

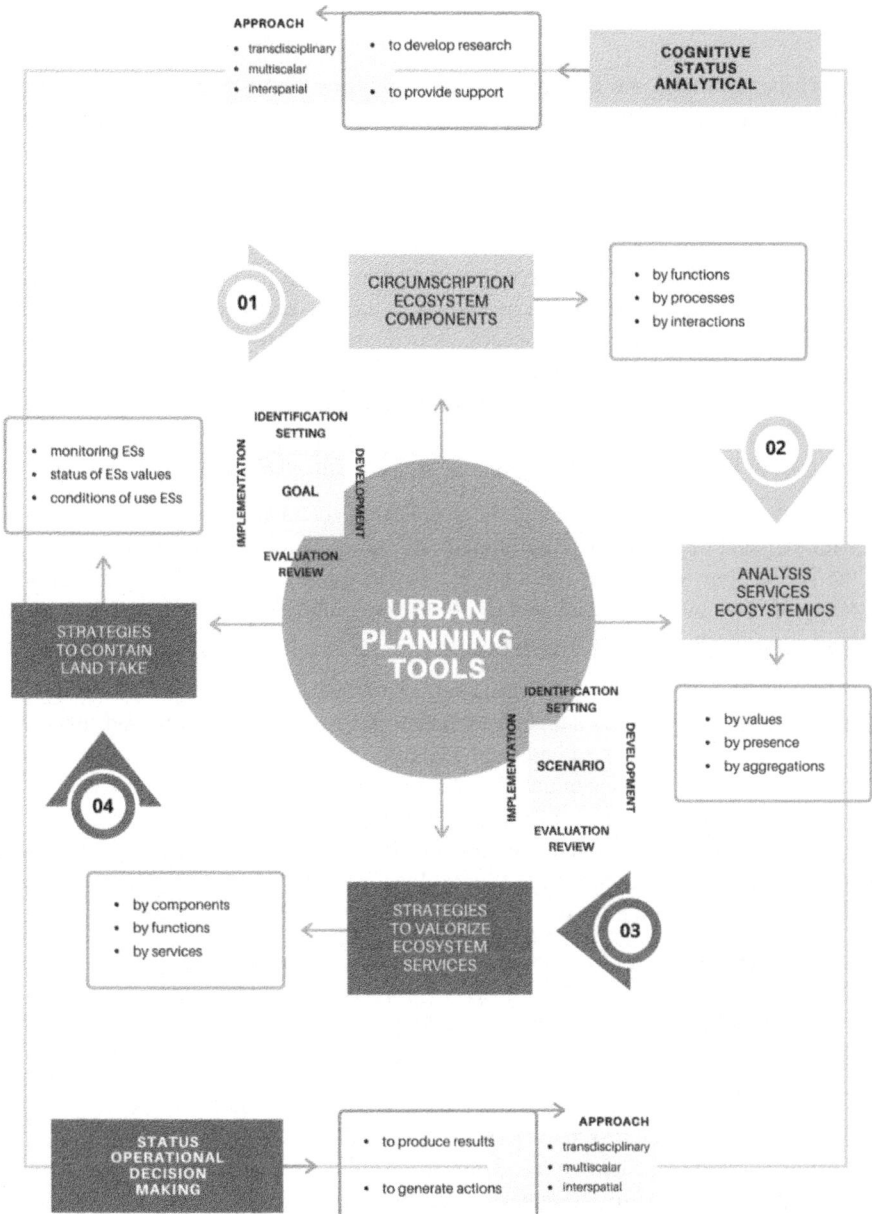

Fig. 1. The role of urban planning tools in circumscribing ecosystem components, analyzing ESs, enhancing I ESs, and containing land take.

5 Conclusions

Research pertaining to the identification and assessment of ESs has been established and has continued to receive attention and in-depth study, starting with the scientific feedback given by the Millennium Ecosystem Assessment (MEA), a research project that, between 2001 and 2005, engaged numerous experts in the field on the topic at hand: the challenge accepted by the ecosystem approach in reversing the course of the degradation of ESs components, functions and related ESs. The utility of adopting such an approach lies in the fact that the way ecosystems are managed and governed can be improved by having full and greater awareness of the link between the benefits provided to humans by nature (as a function of ecosystem quality) and the conditions of ecosystem integrity of which nature is composed.

"The ES approach provides one way of categorizing characteristics of ecosystems to improve legibility for decision makers in a way that remains more comprehensive in scope" [2]. In the context of urban planning tools, it aims to support:

- the strategies aimed at integrating the demands of social and economic development with the need to protect the environment, its components and functions;
- the actions put in place to influence the conservation and enhancement of a wide range of ESs, and to contain, as a result, the interventions that cause the increase in land consumption (and its resources).

Yet, although the results of the case study examination presented are promising, we are still far from having truly satisfactory data to propose homogeneous and functional ecosystem approaches in the context of planning tools [16]. The results open a new space for dialogue on a conceptual and scientific basis related to the approach to ESs [17, 18], which presents different scenarios and development perspectives for urban planning tools [19]. Work on the integration of ESs, both in the analytical phase and in the proposal phase of the plans [20], will no longer be able to be ignored, starting with the fine-tuning of certain issues:

1. the systematic nature of the recognition and evaluation process of ESs;
2. the gradualness of the inclusion of ESs in urban planning instruments;
3. the integrability of the values of ESs in urban planning instruments;
4. the adaptability of urban planning tools to the ecosystem issue;
5. the reliability of ESs monitoring processes.

Beyond the issues addressed in this study, the challenge will be to continue to work on the usefulness of the ESs approach and how it can effectively influence decision-making activities in urban, land use and landscape planning, contributing to the maintenance of functioning soils and ecosystems in general.

References

1. Albert, C., Galler, C., Hermes, J., Neuendorf, F., Von Haaren, C., Lovett, A.: Applying ecosystem services indicators in landscape planning and management: the ES-in-planning framework. Ecol. Ind. **61**, 100–113 (2016)

2. Wilkinson, C., Saarne, T., Peterson, G.D., Colding, J.: Strategic spatial planning and the ecosystem services concept. An historical exploration. Ecol. Soc. **18**(1) (2013)
3. Koschke, L., Fürst, C., Frank, S., Makeschin, F.: A multi-criteria approach for an integrated land-cover-based assessment of ecosystem services provision to support landscape planning. Ecol. Ind. **21**, 54–66 (2012)
4. Murgante, B., Borruso, G., Balletto, G., Castiglia, P., Dettori, M.: Perchè prima l'Italia? Aspetti medici, geografici e pianificatori del Covid-19. GEOmedia **24**(1) (2020)
5. Arcidiacono, A., Ronchi, S., Salata, S.: Managing multiple ecosystem services for landscape conservation: a green infrastructure in Lombardy region. Procedia Eng. **161**, 2297–2303 (2016)
6. Colavitti, A.M., Floris, A., Serra, S.: Urban standards and ecosystem services: the evolution of the services planning in Italy from theory to practice. Sustainability **12**(6), 2434 (2020)
7. Karrasch, L., Klenke, T., Woltjer, J.: Linking the ecosystem services approach to social preferences and needs in integrated coastal land use management. A planning approach. Land Use Policy **38**, 522–532 (2014)
8. Cabral, P., Feger, C., Levrel, H., Chambolle, M., Basque, D.: Assessing the impact of land-cover changes on ecosystem services: a first step toward integrative planning in Bordeaux, France. Ecosyst. Serv. **22**, 318–327 (2016)
9. Nin, M., Soutullo, A., Rodríguez-Gallego, L., Di Minin, E.: Ecosystem services-based land planning for environmental impact avoidance. Ecosyst. Serv. **17**, 172–184 (2016)
10. Van der Biest, K., Meire, P., Schellekens, T., D'hondt, B., Bonte, D., Vanagt, T., Ysebaert, T.: Aligning biodiversity conservation and ecosystem services in spatial planning: focus on ecosystem processes. Sci. Total Environ. **712**, 136350 (2020)
11. Salata, S., Giaimo, C., Alberto Barbieri, C., Garnero, G.: The utilization of ecosystem services mapping in land use planning: the experience of LIFE SAM4CP project. J. Environ. Planning Manage. **63**(3), 523–545 (2020)
12. Calzolari, C., Tarocco, P., Lombardo, N., Marchi, N., Ungaro, F.: Assessing soil ecosystem services in urban and peri-urban areas: from urban soils survey to providing support tool for urban planning. Land Use Policy **99**, 105037 (2020)
13. Mooney, P.: A systematic approach to incorporating multiple ecosystem services in landscape planning and design. Landsc. J. **33**(2), 141–171 (2015)
14. Bezák, P., Mederly, P., Izakovičová, Z., Špulerová, J., Schleyer, C.: Divergence and conflicts in landscape planning across spatial scales in Slovakia: an opportunity for an ecosystem services-based approach? Int. J. Biodivers. Sci. Ecosyst. Serv. Manag. **13**(2), 119–135 (2017)
15. Bürgi, M., Silbernagel, J., Wu, J., Kienast, F.: Linking ecosystem services with landscape history. Landscape Ecol. **30**, 11–20 (2015)
16. Pilogallo, A., Saganeiti, L., Scorza, F., Murgante, B.: Ecosystem services approach to evaluate renewable energy plants effects. In: Misra, S., et al. (eds.) Computational Science and Its Applications – ICCSA 2019, pp. 281–290. Springer, Cham (2019). https://doi.org/10.1007/978-3-030-24311-1_20
17. Pilogallo, A., Scorza, F.: Ecosystem services multifunctionality: an analytical framework to support sustainable spatial planning in Italy. Sustainability **14**(6), 3346 (2022). https://doi.org/10.3390/SU14063346
18. Annunziata, A., Scorza, F., Corrado, S., Murgante, B.: Unveiling intra-rural divides: investigating decline and prosperity in rural areas. The case study of southern Italy. Eur. Plann. Studies **32**(7), 1478–1505 (2024). https://doi.org/10.1080/09654313.2024.2335312;WGROUP: STRING:PUBLICATION

19. Scorza, F., Pilogallo, A., Saganeiti, L., Murgante, B., Pontrandolfi, P.: Comparing the territorial performances of renewable energy sources' plants with an integrated ecosystem services loss assessment: a case study from the Basilicata region (Italy). Sustain. Cities Soc. **56**, 102082 (2020). https://doi.org/10.1016/j.scs.2020.102082
20. Pilogallo, A., Scorza, F.: Mapping regulation ecosystem services specialization in Italy. J. Urban Plann. Dev. **148**(1) (2022). https://doi.org/10.1061/(ASCE)UP.1943-5444.0000801

Renewable Energy and Landscape Transformation: A GIS-Based and Ecosystem Services Assessment

Shiva Rahmani$^{(\boxtimes)}$ ⓘ, Beniamino Murgante, and Mariacristina Marino ⓘ

School of Engineering, University of Basilicata, Viale Dell'Ateneo Lucano 10, 85100 Potenza, Italy
shiva.rahmani@unibas.it

Abstract. Although increasing the use of renewable energy is a crucial step in reducing the effects of climate change, assessments of sustainable energy can be supported by the lens of ecosystem services to guarantee the sustainability of renewable energy production at the regional level. Land use policy plays a crucial role in this context, as it has the primary power to transform land from the planning stage to implementation. Furthermore, an environmental policy-based analysis supports urban planners in proposing more sustainable and innovative interventions. Compared to traditional planning approaches, these interventions are relatively new, and there is limited time for trial and error due to the urgency of addressing climate change. Ecosystem service indicators can support urban planners, policymakers, and other stakeholders in fostering win-win collaborations. In this study, we investigate renewable energy sources as a phenomenon that has gained significant importance in urban and energy planning. To geographically examine the integration of renewable energy with habitat quality—one of the primary components of ecosystem services—this article suggests a GIS-based methodology by considering Basilicata region as the case study. Three major sections comprise the methodological approach: First, the regional energy plan's specified policy limits. Second, the sprinkling index was used to geographically analyze the energy landscape fragmentation to evaluate how land use changes were affected by renewable energy installations. Lastly, the ecosystem services lens will guarantee the sustainability of renewable energy production at the regional level.

Keywords: Sprinkling index · Spatial analysis · Ecosystem services · Habitat quality · Renewable energy sources

1 Introduction

Global energy demand is projected to double over the 21st century, posing a significant challenge for energy security and sustainability. COP27 placed significant emphasis on securing low-cost financing to facilitate the transition to clean energy. To limit global warming to 1.5 °C, countries must electrify all energy sectors and achieve a complete transition to wind, water, and solar (WWS) power by 2050 [1]. To meet this growing

O. Gervasi et al. (Eds.): ICCSA 2025 Workshops, LNCS 15899, pp. 141–151, 2026.
https://doi.org/10.1007/978-3-031-97663-6_12

demand while mitigating environmental impacts, the expansion of renewable energy sources (RES), particularly solar photovoltaic panels and wind turbines, is considered essential. These technologies play a crucial role in reducing dependence on fossil fuels, lowering greenhouse gas emissions, and supporting the transition toward a more sustainable energy system [2]. Furthermore, ambitious climate goals are increasingly interconnected with rising energy prices, driven by the Russia–Ukraine conflict and the global surge in energy demand following the COVID-19 pandemic recovery. Consequently, accelerating the transition to renewable energy has become more critical than ever [3]. Despite the clear economic and environmental benefits of solar and wind energy production, their installation can face local opposition due to concerns about their impact on the landscape [4]. The increasing installation of solar panels and wind turbines raises concerns about its impact on land use and ecosystem services. Understanding how solar energy development influences land use patterns over time is crucial for balancing renewable energy growth with environmental sustainability. Without regulations, RES plants could cause unintended social, environmental, and economic problems, which could slow down the transition to clean energy. To ensure sustainable and balanced implementation of RES plants, focusing on policy constraints which are not meant to block renewable energy projects, but to improve their efficiency is mandatory step in energy plan. Engaging many social, environmental and energy experts to prepare this regulation makes it more reliable as a reference for other projects and plans in urban planning. On the other hand, usually regional and national plans update periodically, so using other innovative tools beside policy-based regulation makes the process more sustainable. Ecosystem services indicators, as a tool that well defined the human-nature relationship can help planners and other stakeholders to do assessment of RES impact on environment and human life. This study investigates the evolution of land use in the Basilicata region due to solar panel and wind turbine installations over different time intervals. Using maps, spatial analysis, and statistical methods, the research examines the extent of land use changes, particularly focusing on habitat quality, landscape fragmentation, and energy dispersion. The findings aim to provide valuable insights for policymakers, planners, and researchers working on sustainable land management and renewable energy planning.

2   Materials and Methods

This study follows a multi-step approach within a GIS framework, tested on the Basilicata region as the case study. The methodological approach is structured into three main sections: Firstly, policy constraints defined in the regional energy plan (PER) are mapped to identify suitable areas for energy production from solar plants and wind turbines, considering existing regulatory limitations [5]. Secondly, the energy landscape fragmentation was spatially analysed using the sprinkling index (SPX) to assess the impact of renewable energy installations on land use changes. Lastly, to ensure the sustainability of renewable energy production on a regional scale, the lens of ecosystem services applied to support sustainable energy assessments. In this work we focus on habitat quality and degradation model of ecosystem by InVEST that combines information on LULC and threats to biodiversity to produce habitat quality maps. By integrating all these steps, we aim to predict the impact of renewable energy sources (RES) on habitat quality in Basilicata and determine whether the relationship between RES and ecosystem services (RES-ES) is a trade-off or an asymmetrical one.

2.1 Case Study: Basilicata Region, Italy

Basilicata is an administrative region in Southern Italy, bordered by Campania to the west, Apulia to the north and east, and Calabria to the south (Fig. 1). The region spans approximately 10,000 km^2 (3,900 sq mi) and had a population of just over 540,000 in 2021. (istat2024) Basilicata is the most mountainous region in the south of Italy, with 47% of its area of 9,992 km^2 (3,858 sq mi) covered by mountains. Of the remaining area, 45% is hilly, and 8% is made up of plains (https://www.istat.it/). At the spatial level, Basilicata offers relatively favorable conditions compared to central and northern Italy. This is even more evident when contrasted with central and northern European countries, where renewable energy technologies are widely adopted despite less favorable environmental conditions [5]. Furthermore, in 2018, the Basilicata Regional Authority in southern Italy approved the regional law on "Decarbonisation and Regional Policies on Climate Change (Basilicata Carbon Free)." This law aims to minimize climate change risks, preserve natural heritage, and protect public health, well-being, and assets. To achieve ambitious greenhouse gas (GHG) emission reduction targets, the law supports measures that encourage the adoption of Kyoto Protocol mechanisms, technological innovation, and improvements in energy efficiency across both the private and public sectors [7].

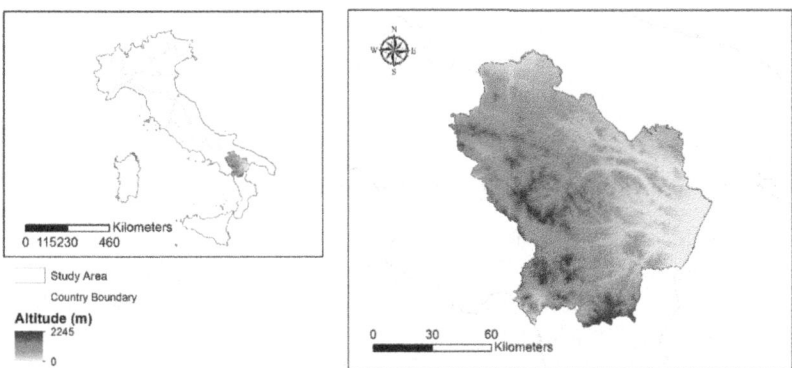

Fig. 1. Introduction map of Basilicata in Italy

2.2 Suitable Areas for RES Production Through Policy Lenses

To ensure sustainable and balanced implementation of RES plants, this part focuses on policy constraints which are not meant to block renewable energy projects, but to improve their efficiency. Without regulations, RES plants could cause unintended social, environmental, and economic problems, which could slow down the transition to clean energy. In the PER of the Basilicata region, the "suitability of land for energy production" is defined through a set of constraints specific to each renewable energy source RES. However, this study considers suitable areas for RES production through policy lenses. The following map presents the constraint elements used to identify suitable land for energy production from wind turbines and solar farms. The suitability map is the result of overlaying multiple vector shapefiles, we downloaded from the geoportal website and filtered to exclude areas outside the study region. The Fig. 2 Shows the proportion of both restricted areas, and suitable areas.

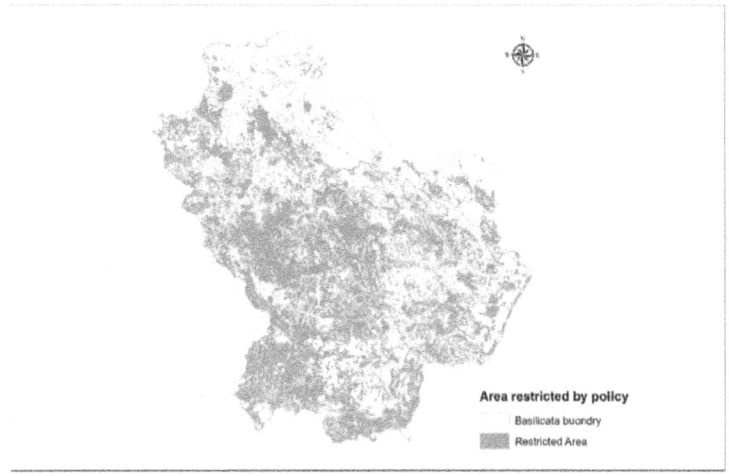

Area restricted by policy
Basilicata buondry
Restricted Area

Fig. 2. Prohibited area by law for RES intervention

2.3   How is Fragmentation Trend of RES in Basilicata Region?

Creating a reliable data set for assessment on RES impact on environment is the very beginning and the most important step. The fundamental geographical information structure consists of a database of RES installations, gathered from TRC (https://rsdi.regione. basilicata.it/dbgt-ctr/), produced by the Basilicata Region and distributed through OGC standards within the RSDI; additionally, GSE (https://www.gse.it/). Due to missing or outdated data, we conducted the digitization of installations using aerial photogrammetric surveys carried out at different times, incorporating orthophotos. In the final year of the survey, 1,819 wind turbines and 327 solar panels were identified.

The methodology is applied across three different time intervals to analyze both spatial and temporal aspects. The selected time periods are: (i) 2008–2012, (ii) 2012–2018, and (iii) 2018–2021. Additionally, for a more comprehensive analysis, wind turbines are classified into three main categories based on their installation power and size: mini, medium, and large. Firstly, the study area is divided by a 1 km^2 grid. SPX index assumes that the most compact form of agglomeration growth is the circular one and is based on the Euclidean distance between two or more geometries within each cell. Secondly, to assess the land take of wind turbines and photovoltaic fields, we considered the area surrounding each RES installation within an influence radius proportional to its power output. For solar panels, we applied a 25-m buffer, as their large surface area allows for effective spatial analysis, and this buffer enhances the comprehensiveness of the assessment. Given the relatively small footprint of wind turbines, we analyzed their distribution patterns using a two-step buffering approach. The first buffer was applied around each installation based on its power capacity: 15 m for micro turbines, 25 m for medium-sized turbines, and 35 m for large turbines. Since the expected effects (e.g., loss of habitat quality) extend beyond the immediate footprint of individual installations, wind turbines were aggregated within a maximum distance of 250 m. It is therefore assumed that this entire area is permanently repurposed from its previous land uses. Thirdly, the energy landscape fragmentation was spatially calculated by using the sprinkling index (SPX) [10]. The SPX index assumes that the most compact form of agglomeration growth follows a circular pattern. It quantifies spatial clustering by measuring the Euclidean distance between multiple geometries within each cell. In this analysis, these geometries correspond to photovoltaic fields and clusters of wind turbines. The index is calculated using the following formula:

$$SPX = \frac{\sum \sqrt{(xi - x*)^2 + (yi - y*)^2}}{R}$$

where xi and yi are the centroid coordinates of each polygon, representing photovoltaic fields and clusters of wind turbines within a 1 km^2 grid cell. $x*$ and $y*$ correspond to the centroid coordinates of the largest concentration of installations within the cell. R represents the radius of a circular area with a total surface equivalent to the combined area of all RES installations in the cell. Furthermore, after computing the SPX for all RES clusters, we joined the SPX values to the corresponding grid cells containing each cluster to enhance visualization (Fig. 3).

2.4   How Does the Expansion of RES Affect Habitat Quality?

After analysis of the previous part that shows the noticeable expansion of RES, during years of study, in this part we are going to figure out how it affected the environment. Maintaining biodiversity is an important ecosystem service that is closely linked to other services [11]. It can directly affect other ecosystem services, like pollination and pest control, which depend on specific species communities [12]. It can also indirectly affect ecosystem services related to biological processes, like carbon and nutrient sequestration, by influencing internal ecosystem processes and species activities. [13] For this study we selected habitat quality as a representative of ecosystem services. This can help with land-use planning and identifying areas for ecological conservation [14].

    Current habitat quality (HQ) assessments often concentrate on regional species evaluations, but these can be constrained by the high costs associated with data collection, limiting their applicability for large-scale analyses. To address these challenges, the InVEST model has emerged as a practical and efficient tool for conducting spatiotemporal HQ assessments [15]. The InVEST model defines HQ as the ability of ecosystems to support species' survival, reproduction, and activities [16]. The changes in HQ were

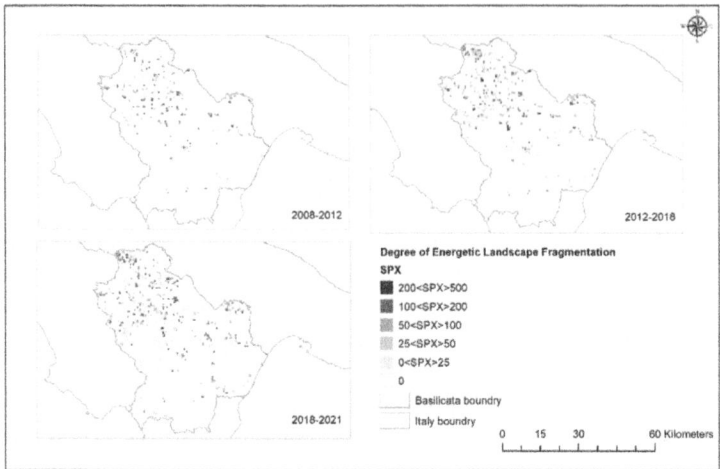

Fig. 3. Energy fragmentation index changes

used to explain variations in habitat area, a key process in habitat loss and fragmentation. The formula for HQ is as follows: the HQ of patch x, in land use type j (LULCj), is represented by Qxj:

$$Qxj = Hxj(1 - (Dxj/(k + Dxj)))$$

where z and k are scaling parameters, and Hj represents the suitability of land use type j for the species. Generally, natural areas are considered to have relatively high suitability, while human-dominated lands are much less suitable [13]. The InVEST Habitat Quality model uses LULC data and biodiversity threats to generate habitat quality maps. For this study, we analyzed changes between 2008 (pre-renewable energy installations in Basilicata) and 2021 (significant growth in renewable energy sources) and using Copernicus Corin land cover data. (https://www.copernicus.eu/en) The model also considers threats, here we consider agriculture, urbanization, industry, mining, roads, and renewable energy installations as threatening elements for habitat quality. The Fig. 4 shows the result of habitat quality for the year 2008, and year 2021, additionally their differences. The map shows a general view of changing trends during the period of study for both years' result shows lower quality in upper side of area.

3   Result

The comparative analysis of data from 2012, 2018, and 2021 reveals a notable increase in the territorial impact of renewable energy installations (RES) in the Basilicata region. The findings underscore that, without proper governance through spatial planning instruments, the energy transition can lead to increasingly pronounced dynamics of landscape fragmentation. This critical issue aligns with the concerns raised by Murgante and Scorza, who emphasized the importance of integrating energy planning with landscape planning—particularly in environmentally vulnerable regions such as Basilicata.

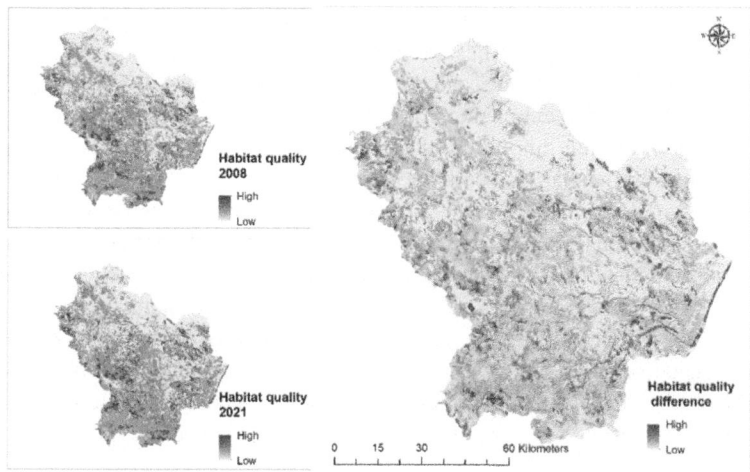

Fig. 4. Habitat quality differences of Basilicata region

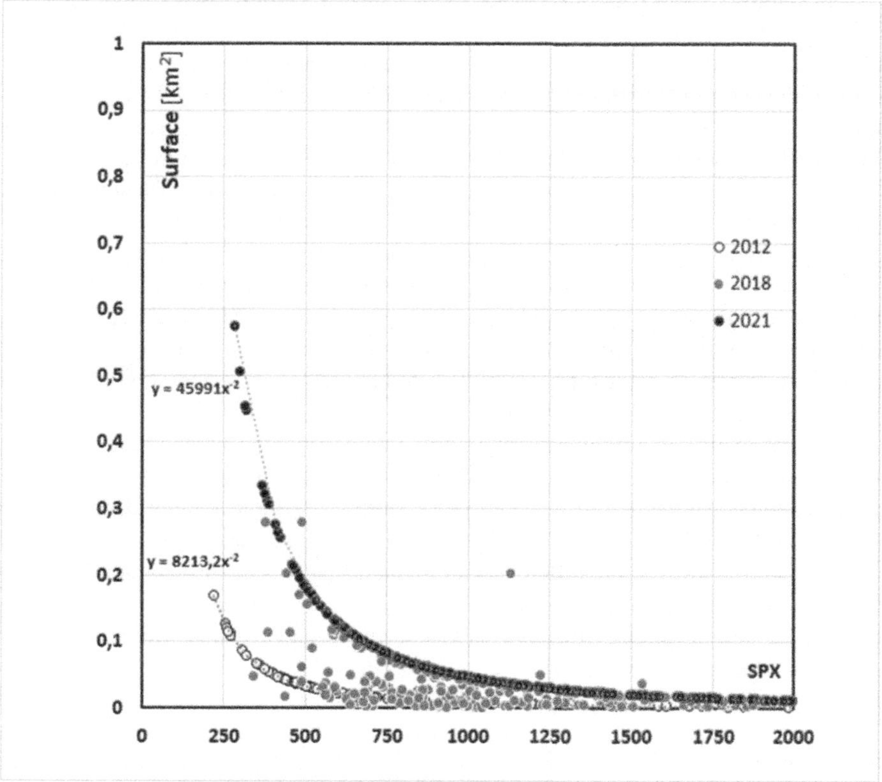

Fig. 5. Comparison of SPX and aggregates surface variation between 2012 and 2021

Figure 5 illustrates the relationship between the fragmentation index (SPX) and the area occupied by RES in the Basilicata region across three time points: 2012, 2018, and 2021. In 2012, both the SPX values and the occupied area were relatively low, indicating an early stage of development characterized by concentrated installations and minimal spatial dispersion. During this initial phase, the impact on the landscape was limited, as installations were primarily located near existing infrastructure or in areas already modified by human activity. The year 2018 marks a noticeable transitional phase. The intermediate positioning of the 2018 data between the 2012 and 2021 clusters indicates a significant shift in installation dynamics. During this period, three key trends emerge: (i) a progressive saturation of the most suitable sites for renewable energy development, (ii) the beginning of a shift toward more dispersed spatial distribution of installations (iii) a noticeable escalation in SPX values, reflecting emerging fragmentation. This transitional phase may reflect the early effects of energy policies—especially those introduced by the 2010 PIEAR—even though their full impact had not yet reached the critical level seen in 2021.

The 2021 data present a stark contrast, revealing a significantly altered situation. The sharp increase in both SPX values and the occupied area confirms the establishment of an increasingly dispersed settlement model. Notably, the comparison of the quadratic regression equations is telling: In 2012, the equation was $y = 8E + 06x2$, whereas in 2021 it had risen to $y = 5E + 07x2$. The increase in the quadratic coefficient of more than six times indicates that, for the same increase in SPX, the area needed for new plants has become significantly larger. This quantitative data confirms a fundamental qualitative trend: the fragmentation of the territory does not grow linearly with the expansion of plants but accelerates disproportionately as new installations are made. The implications of this evolution are particularly relevant for territorial planning: The intermediate phase of 2018 could have been a wake-up call to intervene with corrective policies. The absence of adequate regulatory tools has allowed the continuation of increasingly less sustainable settlement dynamics. The quadratic relationship between SPX and occupied area suggests the existence of critical thresholds beyond which territorial impacts become particularly severe. About habitat quality Fig. 6 shows a general trend of RES effect on habitat quality. The x-axis in the graph represents habitat quality scores, ranging from 0 (poor habitat quality) to 1 (high habitat quality), while the y-axis indicates the frequency of pixels with each value. A peak at 0 suggests that a significant portion of the area experienced low habitat quality for both years. Both years show a major concentration of values around 0.3 to 0.4, indicating that habitat quality remained relatively stable in certain regions. However, the differences in frequency across the distribution highlight shifts in habitat conditions over time. The overlapping areas reveal the extent to which the two distributions align or differ. This visualization suggests that while some areas retained similar habitat quality, others experienced a decline, potentially due to land use changes or anthropogenic impacts.

These results highlight the pressing need to balance the goals of the energy transition with the protection of landscapes and ecosystems. The study illustrates how temporal comparative analysis can uncover key turning points in territorial evolution, providing valuable insights for more informed and sustainable energy transition planning.

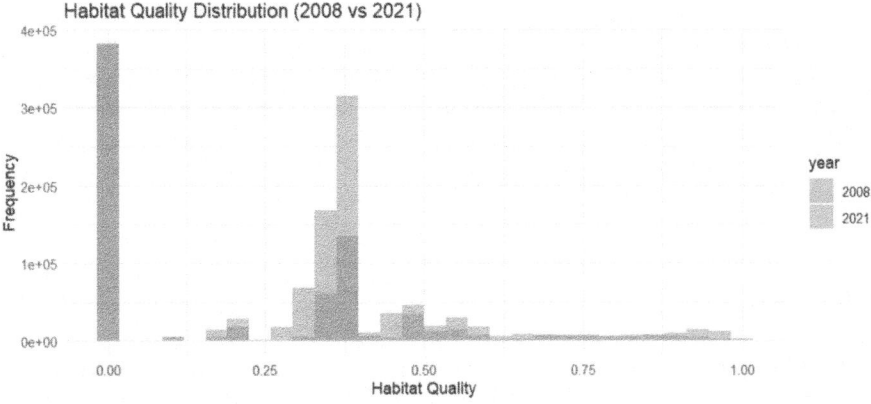

Fig. 6. Comparison of habitat quality between 2008 and 2021

4   Conclusion

In conclusion, the results indicate that to meet the increasing demand for clean energy and achieve the goals set at COP27 [19], traditional planning approaches are not inherently efficient. Basilicata in this work consider as an example, the increasing trend of RES in Basilicata shows, that although policy-based interventions in somehow can significantly prevent the scattered expansion of renewable energy infrastructures, but in terms of examining environmental factors, it requires more precise tools and equipment. In other words, effective implementation of energy and climate policies necessitates the development of new models of multilevel governance. [20] In this work ecosystem services lenses, and specifically habitat quality as a key concept in ecology, conservation biology, and environmental planning, is presented as an innovative tool. Combining the result of both traditional and new methods can help us for having more clear prediction of future impact of RES intervention on human-nature relation and ecosystem services. Furthermore, from a governance perspective, the findings advocate for the development of new multilevel and cross-sectoral planning models that integrate ecological data with socio-economic objectives. These models must enable cooperation between local authorities, regional planners, environmental scientists, and energy stakeholders. By doing so, it is possible to better align RES development with both sustainability goals and landscape resilience.

Future research should focus on enhancing habitat models to include species-specific responses to different types of RES infrastructures. Exploring the socio-cultural dimensions of landscape change due to energy transitions. Developing integrated planning platforms that merge spatial, ecological, and policy data in real-time to support adaptive governance. By refining planning strategies through the lens of ecosystem services, and promoting interdisciplinary collaboration, the transition to renewable energy can be better managed to ensure it is not only technologically feasible and economically viable but also ecologically and socially just.

Acknowledgments. This work was supported by the National Recovery and Resilience Plan (NRRP), Mission 4, Component 2, Investment 1.1, under the Call for Tender No. 1409 (published on 14.09.2022) by the Italian Ministry of University and Research (MUR). Funding was provided by the European Union – NextGenerationEU, as part of the project "Definition of a guidelines handbook to implement climate neutrality by improving ecosystem service effectiveness in rural and urban areas" (CUP F53D23010760001). The authors acknowledge the Grant Assignment Decree No. 1378 (adopted on 01.09.2023 by MUR) for its financial support.

References

1. Jacobson, M.Z., et al.: 100% clean and renewable wind, water, and sunlight all-sector energy roadmaps for 139 countries of the world. Joule 1(1), 108–121 (2017). https://doi.org/10.1016/j.joule.2017.07.005
2. Lewis, N.S., Nocera, D.G.: Powering the planet: Chemical challenges in solar energy utilization (2006). https://www.pnas.org/doi/abs/10.1073/pnas.0603395103
3. Liao, S.: The Russia–Ukraine outbreak and the value of renewable energy. Econ. Lett. 225 (2023). https://doi.org/10.1016/j.econlet.2023.111045
4. Minelli, A., Marchesini, I., Taylor, F.E., De Rosa, P., Casagrande, L., Cenci, M.: An open source GIS tool to quantify the visual impact of wind turbines and photovoltaic panels. Environ. Impact Assess. Rev. 49, 70–78 (2014). https://doi.org/10.1016/j.eiar.2014.07.002
5. Consiglio Regionale di Basilicata Piano di Indirizzo Energetico Ambientale Regionale
6. https://www.istat.it/
7. Di Leo, S., Pietrapertosa, F., Salvia, M., Cosmi, C.: Contribution of the Basilicata region to decarbonisation of the energy system: results of a scenario analysis. Renew. Sustain. Energy Rev. 138 (2021). https://doi.org/10.1016/j.rser.2020.110544
8. https://rsdi.regione.basilicata.it/dbgt-ctr/
9. https://www.gse.it/
10. Romano, B., Zullo, F., Fiorini, L., Ciabò, S., Marucci, A.: Sprinkling: an approach to describe urbanization dynamics in Italy. Sustainability 9(1) (2017). https://doi.org/10.3390/su9010097
11. Mace, G.M., Norris, K., Fitter, A.H.: Biodiversity and ecosystem services: a multilayered relationship. Elsevier Ltd. (2012). https://doi.org/10.1016/j.tree.2011.08.006
12. Penvern, S., et al.: Farmers' management of functional biodiversity goes beyond pest management in organic European apple orchards. Agric. Ecosyst. Environ. 284 (2019). https://doi.org/10.1016/j.agee.2019.05.014
13. Li, D., Sun, W., Xia, F., Yang, Y., Xie, Y.: Can habitat quality index measured using the invest model explain variations in bird diversity in an urban area? Sustainability 13(10) (2021). https://doi.org/10.3390/su13105747
14. Zhang, D., et al.: Land use/cover predictions incorporating ecological security for the Yangtze River Delta region, China. Ecol. Indic. 119 (2020). https://doi.org/10.1016/j.ecolind.2020.106841
15. Jiao, A., Xu, J., Deng, M., Ling, H.: How does ecological water conveyance promote the improvement of habitat quality in the lower reaches of inland rivers in arid regions? A 'past-future' perspective. J. Clean. Prod. 502 (2025). https://doi.org/10.1016/j.jclepro.2025.145374
16. Terrado, M., Sabater, S., Chaplin-Kramer, B., Mandle, L., Ziv, G., Acuña, V.: Model development for the assessment of terrestrial and aquatic habitat quality in conservation planning. Sci. Total. Environ. 540, 63–70 (2016). https://doi.org/10.1016/j.scitotenv.2015.03.064
17. https://www.copernicus.eu/en

18. Scorza, F., Las Casas, G.B., Murgante, B.: Spatializing open data for the assessment and the improvement of territorial and social cohesion. ISPRS Ann. Photogram. Remote Sens. Spatial Inf. Sci. Copernicus GmbH 145–151 (2016). https://doi.org/10.5194/isprs-annals-IV-4-W1-145-2016

19. The Theme of the Issue: Environmental Governance and Climate Change Post-COP27, Key Takeaways and Next Steps Governance for Sustainable Development Review. http://nigsd.gov.eg

20. Betsill, M.M., Bulkeley, H.: Cities and the Multilevel Governance of Global Climate Change (2006)

Serious Play for a Safer World: An Analysis of Geogames at the Nexus of Cybersecurity, and Disaster Management

Zhenhua Yang[1]([⊠]) [iD], Ema Odra Raščan[2] [iD], Alenka Poplin[1] [iD],
and David I. Schwartz[3] [iD]

[1] Iowa State University, Ames, IA 50011, USA
{aayang,apoplin}@iastate.edu
[2] University of Ljubljana, 1000 Ljubljana, Slovenia
[3] Rochester Institute of Technology, Rochester, NY 14623, USA
david.i.schwartz@rit.edu

Abstract. In an era marked by rapidly evolving cyber threats and increasing disaster risks, geogames offer innovative approaches to education and training. Motivated by the need to understand the current landscape, this paper systematically maps the landscape of 92 geogames at the intersection of cybersecurity and disaster management. This study examines the availability of these games, their application areas, genres, target audiences, and other design characteristics, such as medium and publisher type. By categorizing games based on these criteria, we offer a comprehensive overview of what is currently available in this domain. Notably, this paper provides a structured resource that highlights trends and gaps in the market, thereby serving as a valuable reference for researchers and developers seeking to understand and enhance the role of geogames in cybersecurity and disaster management training.

Keywords: Serious Games · Geogames · Cybersecurity · Disaster Mangement · Critical Infrastructure

1 Introduction

Serious games have been increasingly used as powerful tools for education and training across diverse domains. Among them, geogames – games that real-world location or spatial context fundamentally shapes gameplay [10, 11] – demonstrates their unique advantages for addressing the complex interplay between cybersecurity and disaster management. These games have shown their effectiveness in awareness education and training for geographic exploration, cybersecurity, and disaster response [2, 3, 11, 16]. The rationale for connecting these seemingly disparate game categories stems from the increasingly interconnected nature of our world, where cyber threats can have tangible impacts on physical infrastructure and the effectiveness of disaster response efforts. Addressing complex real-world challenges requires interdisciplinary approaches, and

O. Gervasi et al. (Eds.): ICCSA 2025 Workshops, LNCS 15899, pp. 152–164, 2026.
https://doi.org/10.1007/978-3-031-97663-6_13

the integration of spatial, security, and disaster-related concepts within geogame environments offers theoretically grounded potential for enhancing systems thinking, spatial reasoning, and situated learning.

The integration of cybersecurity considerations and disaster management learning and training is becoming increasingly critical [17] due to the evolving threat landscapes and the growing dependence on interconnected cyber-physical systems [18]. Geogames can uniquely illustrate the place-based consequences of cyberattacks by embedding scenarios within specific urban environments, infrastructure systems, or policy ecosystems. This approach may support co-creation and localized learning, mirroring how disaster games emphasize community-level preparedness [2]. On the other hand, by leveraging spatial mechanics, geogames can translate abstract cyber scenarios such as network intrusion and data breaches into concrete, place-based consequences (e.g., localized power outages, disruption of geographically dispersed services), enhancing players' understanding of vulnerability and impact. For instance, a geogame may involve defending a city's power grid from a simulated ransomware attack or coordinating municipal services during a breach of emergency communication networks. Such designs can bridge the gap between abstract technical skills and tangible societal impact of cybersecurity, promoting both technical literacy and civic responsibility.

The growing convergence of these gaming applications highlights important considerations for game developers and educators. Geogames must address privacy and security challenges related to user location data [19]. Meanwhile, representations of critical infrastructure in disaster simulations provide valuable opportunities to demonstrate the cascading effects of security breaches across physical and digital systems [20].

This paper systematically analyzes 92 serious geogames across application areas including their characteristics, educational approaches, and accessibility. The goal is to map how these selected geogames are being utilized as teaching tools in cybersecurity, disaster management, and other risk-related domains, providing insights into effective design strategies for these increasingly interconnected educational contexts.

This rest of the paper is organized as following. Section 2 provides a brief overview of related work. Section 3 clarifies our research focus. Section 4 describes the methodology used in this paper. Section 5 presents the result of the data collection. Section 6 and 7 discuss and summarize the main findings and further research directions.

2 Related Work

Several studies have explored the landscape of serious games for both crisis/disaster management and cybersecurity education and training, providing valuable insights into the field. Loreto et al. [1] conducted an overview of collaborative serious games for crisis management, aiming to characterize crisis management and analyze existing games based on these characteristics. Their analysis focused on understanding the strengths and weaknesses of these environments. Solinska-Nowak et al. [2] provided an overview of 45 non-commercial serious games and simulations, analyzing their characteristics, target groups, and potential for developing disaster risk management (DRM) skills. While highlighting the promise of these tools for raising awareness and simulating disaster scenarios, their research also pointed to a lack of robust scientific evidence regarding their effectiveness from the surveyed publications. In the domain of cybersecurity, multiple survey papers have examined serious games. Alotaibi et al. [3] reviewed the effectiveness of mobile gaming applications in raising cybersecurity awareness in Saudi Arabia. While most studies show positive results in using games for awareness and training, there is a need for more robust evaluations with larger sample populations and issue-specific games tailored to user needs. Jr., W. A. H. et al. [4] provides a survey of cybersecurity serious games targeting various audiences from K-12 students to college students and cybersecurity professionals. The study highlights that while many games focus on general cybersecurity awareness, some address more specialized technical topics. Hill et al. [5] examined twenty cybersecurity games and found that most games focus on cybersecurity awareness rather than technical topics, with privately developed games generally offering better interactivity and visual quality. The authors concluded that most publicly available options are either too basic for higher education curriculum needs or they lack the engagement value that makes game-based learning effective. Calvano et al. [6] reviewed 15 cybersecurity serious games and found that most games prioritize educational content over gaming elements, potentially reducing players' engagement and hindering learning outcomes. The research recommends a design approach using standardized methodologies that balance educational and gaming aspects to help educators select more effective training tools for cybersecurity education. Chattopadhyay et al. [7] presents a novel analysis of cybersecurity educational games by examining their alignment with established industry and academic standards and provides a reference that helps educators and industry professionals make informed choices about which games to use for specific educational purposes. Ng & Hasan [8] systematically analyzed 53 cybersecurity games development from 2014 to 2024 and identified several gaps of the research such as limited attention to common threats like social media scams, overreliance on quiz-style formats despite their limited effectiveness, and lack of customizable content to address evolving threats. Tioh et al. [9] surveyed serious games in cybersecurity training, emphasizing the need to educate users as they are often the weakest link. The authors concluded that current cyber security games and products show promise but lack rigorous, large-scale evaluation to show their effectiveness.

Previous studies reveal a well-established research landscape for serious games in both crisis management and cybersecurity domains. While the analysis of those games show promise for training and awareness, common limitations emerge across studies: insufficient evidence of effectiveness, imbalance between educational content and gameplay elements, and lack of rigorous large-scale evaluations. Many cybersecurity games focus primarily on general awareness rather than technical skills, and are often either too basic for higher education or lack engaging elements. Different from existing work, this paper specifically investigates the under-explored category of *geogames*, providing a systematic overview of how they are currently employed at the intersection of cybersecurity and disaster management education and training.

3　Research Focus

While previous research has provided valuable overviews of serious games within the distinct domains of crisis/disaster management and cybersecurity, highlighting aspects such as their characteristics, effectiveness, and alignment with standards, a significant gap remains. Specifically, existing literature reviewed serious games for disaster management or cybersecurity separately, but not the combination within the specific category of geogames. Also, there was no systematic analysis on current state of development on such geogames in terms of game characteristics, learning objectives, audiences, and their sources. Therefore, this short paper aims to bridge these gaps by providing a comprehensive overview of the currently available geogames in these specified application areas from academic research, general education, and commercial game market. Our research questions are listed as below:

- What is the current landscape of available geogames at the intersection of cybersecurity and disaster management?
- What is the current state of development of geogames in cybersecurity and disaster management in terms of game characteristics, learning objectives, audiences, and their sources?

4 Methodology

The research methodology includes literature review, definitions of the selected types of games, identification of geogames that fall into the intersection of disaster management and cybersecurity.

4.1 Definitions

Geogames. Geogames represent a compelling intersection of gaming and geography, fundamentally defined as games where a player's real-world location and spatial context directly influence the gameplay [10]. This initial definition of geogames has been recently widened to include all games that concentrate on the well-being and regeneration of planet Earth. They are designed with a purpose beyond mere fun and entertainment. Often, they are designed as teaching and learning tools [11]. Geogames can be analog, digital, or hybrid mixing analog and digital principles. Examples for geogames come from a variety of application areas such as architecture, urban planning, community engagement, geography, disaster management, cybersecurity, history, religious studies and more.

Cybersecurity Games. In this paper, cybersecurity games are geogames that span physical and virtual mechanisms in which the player explores and interacts with systems typically involving security education and simulation. For example, Cyber Ready Community Game is a strategy board game developed by FEMA in collaboration with cybersecurity experts to help communities understand and prepare for cyber incidents [12].

Disaster Management Games. Disaster management games are geogames designed to educate and train participants in various aspects of disaster preparedness, response, and recovery. These geogames simulate disaster scenarios to improve decision-making skills and enhance community resilience. They often focus on risk assessment, resource allocation, evacuation planning, and coordination among different stakeholders. Spatial awareness is a key component, as disasters inherently have geographical impacts. There have been many games created under this category [2].

4.2 Game Selection

The selection of games follows a systematic search process across multiple platforms to ensure comprehensive coverage of geogames in cybersecurity and disaster management. Searches were conducted through literature review of academic papers and online game platforms. The keywords used included "geogame", "cybersecurity game", "disaster management" and "risk management". Games were included in the ludography if they contain educational elements, cybersecurity or disaster management awareness learning or skill training.

4.3 Data Analysis Framework

To analyze all selected geogames, the following categories of information were considered: game characteristics [2], source, knowledge characteristic, and audience. Table 1 shows the categorized terms and their definitions.

Table 1. Data Analysis Framework.

Category	Term Name	Definition
Knowledge Characteristic	Application Area	The knowledge area this game is applied to
Game Characteristics	Genre	A category or classification of games based on their gameplay mechanics, themes, or style
	Medium	The format of the game
	Medium Type	Physical or digital
	No. of Players	The number of player(s) can play at the same time
Audience	Target Audience	The player groups this game is designed for
Game Source	Is Accessible	Is the game available for play by the date of collection
	Publication Type	The purpose of the game publication
	Publisher Type	The classification of the entity based on its primary role and function in producing or distributing the game

5 Results

Altogether 92 geogames were analyzed based on their application area, genre and platform used for the implementation. The full list of collected games is presented in Appendix A. Table 2 provides a summary with respect to the number of games found in each of the respective categories. The collection includes 47 games in cybersecurity &

digital defense and 45 in disaster management & resilience. All collected games were created for various audiences. Most frequently mentioned audiences include students and educators, cybersecurity and IT professionals, military and defense personnel, and business roles. The typical example of cybersecurity game is CIST, which is a single-player online game designed to raise awareness about cybersecurity threats within the hardware supply chain. Players analyze attack scenarios, categorize them using the CIST model, identify potential adversaries and vulnerable stages, and select appropriate defenses. The study found the game useful for learning and promoting self-study regarding supply chain threats [22]. DisCoord is a serious game designed as a public pedagogy tool for Disaster Risk Reduction (DRR). It functions as a collaborative space to connect diverse perspectives and knowledge from various DRR stakeholders who might be separated by location or socio-cultural differences. The study concluded that the game is a useful intervention for bringing different types of knowledge together and enabling co-learning among participants [23].

Table 2. Application areas of the games analyzed.

Application area	Number of games
Cybersecurity & Digital Defense	47
Disaster Management & Resilience	45

5.1 Game Characteristics

Genre. There are no unified definitions for the list of game genres. After analyzing the game types on our ludography, we identified following game genres: Role-playing, Strategy, Interactive fiction, Simulation, Puzzle, and Quiz. Table 3 demonstrates the numbers of games found in our dataset. Some games can be categorized into multiple genres. The result shows that the most frequently created game genres are strategy (39.13% of total) and simulation (55.43% of total).

Table 3. Game genres of the games analyzed.

Genre	Number of games
Role-playing	15
Strategy	36
Interactive fiction	2
Simulation	51
Puzzle	11
Quiz	4

Game Medium. In our collection, 40 games are browser-based, taking 43.48% of total 92 games. 18 are board games, 16 are card games, 13 of them are live events, and desktop and mobile downloadable has 5 and 2 games, respectively. In summary, 48 games have digital mediums, and 49 has physical medium. Among all of them, 5 games include both digital and physical mediums (Table 4).

Table 4. Game mediums of the analyzed games

Game Medium	Number of games
Browser-Based	40
Board	18
Card	16
Live Event	13
Desktop Downloadable	5
Mobile Downloadable	2

Number of Players. To better understand scale of game play, the minimum number of players supported by each game was examined. For 86 games it was possible to identify the number of players, out of which 46.51% are single-player games and 58.14% are multi-player games. This includes four games supporting both single and multiple players. Most multi-player games need at least 2–8 players play at the same time, and seven need nine or more players. It is worth noting that several games support very large group of learners play together. For example, PHUSICOS NBS Simulation supports up to 40 players [13], Extreme Event allows maximum of 48 players [14]. Table 5 summarizes these statistics.

Table 5. Minimum number of players required to play the game.

Min. No. of Players	Games
1	44
2–8	33
9 and more	7
Multiple players not specified	7
Unknown	6

5.2 Game Sources

Finally, the source of the games was analyzed. As shown in Table 6, among all analyzed geogames, 68 are still available on the date of date of data collection. In this section, the type of publisher and the purpose of the game publication was analyzed. Most games, about 65.22% games were created for public education, 31.52% were created as part of academic research. In addition, 30 game, taking 32.61% games were commercialized in forms of purchased copies or paid training sessions. In addition, several games were created in the research project, then later successfully implemented for public education or commercial game publication.

Table 6. Purposes of the games.

Purpose	Game Count
Public Education	60
Academic Research	29
Paid Training Session	11
Commercial	19

Publisher Type. This breakdown is useful for understanding the landscape of educational game development and which types of organizations are most active in creating educational gaming content. As shown in Table 7, 28 games were published by non-education organizations, leading publishers, followed by private company. Most publishers are non-profit entities, which take 72.94% of all 85 known publishers. Amount 67 games that are still accessible, 21 of them are paid games in forms of digital, physical, or in person activities, and 46 games in our collection are free to play.

Table 7. Publisher types of games

Publisher Type	Game Count
Non-profit Organization	28
Private Company	23
Educational Institution	16
Government Agency	13
Individual/Research Team	5
Unknown	7

6 Discussion

The analysis of knowledge characteristics revealed a significant disparity between games focused on awareness learning and those on skill development. As shown in Table 8, 79 games provide focus on awareness education, while only 17 games emphasize the practice of technical skills, including four that provide both awareness education and practice of technical skills. This strong emphasis on risk awareness suggests that the current landscape of serious geogames in this intersection prioritizes educating a broad audience about the potential threats, vulnerabilities, and consequences associated with cybersecurity and disaster management [3]. A potential reason for this imbalance is that knowledge learning may be technically easier to implement and evaluate than skill learning. On the other hand, the training of technical skill practice requires more sophisticated simulation environments and feedback mechanisms [15]. Researchers and designers may benefit from emerging technologies to address this gap. For instance, the Metaverse offers significant potential as a platform for more dynamic, realistic, and immersive environments for teaching and learning how to handle diverse threats [21]. Such virtual environments could provide scalable and engaging settings for practicing complex decision-making in both cybersecurity breach scenarios and simulated disaster response situations, potentially bridging the gap between abstract knowledge and practical application.

Table 8. Learning Focuses of Collected Games

Learning Focus	Game Count
Awareness Education	79
Technical Skills	17

In our collection, 25 of all games are not accessible, taking 27.17% the total numbers. All of them were created for public education or academic research. This indicates the sustainability issue of such geogames that might limit their accessibility to their audiences. This attrition rate raises concerns about the long-term viability of such initiatives. Non-profit projects, while ideally positioned to deliver free resources, often depend on unstable funding streams, volunteer labor, or short-term grants, which may impede ongoing maintenance, updates, or server hosting.

A further challenge identified in the analysis is the lack of language and cultural adaptability across the geogames. Natural disaster games are often highly localized, designed to reflect the specific risks, infrastructure, and response systems of a particular region or city. These geogames incorporate local hazards such as floods, earthquakes, or wildfires and often embed community-specific emergency planning into gameplay. This localized approach enhances relevance for players and strengthens context-specific risk awareness. In contrast, cybersecurity games are typically designed with a universal user in mind. They focus on globally recognized threats like phishing, malware, and system breaches, and generally avoid references to specific national or institutional settings. This broader framing reflects the transnational nature of cyber threats and supports wider applicability across organizational and geographical boundaries.

7 Conclusions

This study provided an initial overview of 92 geogames at the intersection of cybersecurity and disaster management based on the selected characteristics. Given the importance of safety and security in critical infrastructure, designing a safe and secure geogame requires the consideration of cybersecurity principles. This study shows that disaster management games tend to be localized, often incorporating community-specific emergency planning and reflecting regional hazards, while cybersecurity games are more universally applicable, focusing on global threats like phishing and malware. This difference reflects the place-based nature of disaster response and the transnational nature of cyber threats.

Moving forward, this research will deepen the analysis of game implementation, learning objectives, and narrative structures, with a focus on how location-aware design and place-based scenarios can enhance the educational value of both cybersecurity and disaster management games. Additionally, while this short paper focuses on mapping the current landscape based on readily available characteristics (genre, medium, audience, etc.), exploring functional characteristics like customization and collaboration potential would also be beneficial. Furthermore, we will investigate the potential of immersive technologies like the Metaverse in creating dynamic learning environments to bridge cybersecurity and disaster management games.

Appendix A

- CyberProtect by Department of Defense
- Crypto Go by Universidad Carlos III de Madrid and Universidad Rey Juan Carlos
- Sticker Heist by Sinclair College
- Cyber Threat Defender by Center for Infrastructure Assurance and Security (CIAS), UTSA
- Cyber Awareness Challenge by Defense Information Systems Agency (DISA) - U.S. Department of Defense (DoD)
- The Cyber Challenge by Department of Defense
- Targeted Attack: The Game by The Fugle Company
- CyberEscape Online by LivingSecurity
- Cyber Attack (Publisher is not clear)
- LUXO Interactive (Publisher is not clear)
- CyberCIEGE by Naval Postgraduate School
- Be-aware by Taif University, Al-Ha
- Agile App Security Game by BCS, Secure Development Initiative, and Lancaster University
- Decisions & Disruptions by Ben Shreeve and Awais Rashid (University of Bristol Cyber Security Group)
- CyberStart by SANS Institute
- Cyber Crisis Simulation by Cyberbit
- Cybersecurity Lab by PBS
- Game of Threats by PwC France

- Jack Voltaic by Army Cyber Institute at West Point
- CIST: A Serious Game for Hardware Supply Chain by Hart, Halak, Sassone
- Elevation of Privilege (EoP) Threat Modeling Card Game by Adam Shostack
- Backdoors and Breaches by Black Hills Information Security
- OWASP Cumulus by TNG Technology Consulting
- CIA: Collect It All by Diegetic Games (co-designed with Techdirt)
- Cybersecure: Contingency Planning by Office of the National Coordinator for Health Information Technology USA
- Data Heist by Dataprotectionpal
- LINDDUN GO by DistriNet, KU Leuven
- Cyber Security by JeopardyLabs
- Power Surge: Cyber Security Academy – The Card Game by ZmYchE
- Cyber-Ready Community Game by FEMA (Federal Emergency Management Agency), CISA, UTSA
- Anti-Phishing Phil by Wombat Security
- Exploited In The Wild by WIZ Research
- FTC Phishing Scam Game by Federal Trade Commission
- Safe Online Surfing by FBI
- NOVA Cybersecurity lab by PBS NOVA
- Interland by Google
- HackShield by Flavour and KraBé Academy
- HackTale by Komodo Consulting
- Control-Alt-Hack by University of Washington
- Phishing IQ Test or Phishing Simulator by PhishingBox, LLC
- Enter The Spudnet by Potato Pirates
- World of Haiku by Haiku Inc.
- Data Breach by Three Hundred Spears
- Cryptomancer RPG by Land of NOP
- [d0x3d!] by Gamewright
- Byte Club by Michael Novack
- PASDJO by Seitz and Hussmann
- Squally by CS420 Team
- Ekos: The Path to resilience by Urban Systems Lab
- Information meeting about evacuation scheme Greenwood by FLOODsite
- Disaster in My Backyard by Campus Vesta, Belgian First Aid & Support Team
- Disaster Imagination Game (DIG) by Japan International Cooperation Agency (JICA)
- Beat the Quake by Southern California Earthquake Center (SCEC)
- Battle of Flooding Protection by Hwa Hsia University of Technology, Taiwan
- Disaster Awareness Game (DAG) by Gunma University, University of the West Indies
- Decisions for the Decade by Red Cross Red Crescent Climate Centre
- Cultural Memory Game by Centre for Systems Solutions
- Disaster Master by FEMA, Department of Homeland Security
- Before the Storm by Red Cross Red Crescent Climate Centre
- Cards Against Calamity by Environmental Law Institute, NOAA Sea Grant
- Rolling the dice (Infrastructure resilience in Cabo Verde) by Global Facility for Disaster Reduction and Recovery, Government of Japan

- Earthquake Response by Save The Children Australia, Enabled Solutions
- Disaster Hero by American College of Emergency Physicians
- Game of Floods by Marin SLR / The Game Crafter
- DisCoord – The Disaster Coordination game by Visayas State University
- Downpour! by Playfuel & Oropendola Productions
- Bosai Duck by T. Kikkawa, K. Yamori
- PRECINCT Serious Game by PRECINCT Project (EU Funded)
- Shaping your Shelter: A game on post-disaster reconstruction of homes by Red Cross / Red Crescent Climate Centre
- Flood Resilience Game by Centre for Systems Solutions & IIASA
- Disaster Master Game by U.S. Department of Homeland Security
- Be a Hero… build a kit! by Ready.gov
- Dice & Disasters by Emergency Management Division Washington
- inSIGHT by ICCROM
- Stop Disasters! by UNDRR
- Storm Struck: Protect Your Home Against Natural Disasters by FLASH
- Sai Fah! The Flood fighter! by UNESCO Bangkok
- The Disaster Response Game by International Science Reserve
- Master that Disaster by Red Cross Red Crescent Climate Centre
- Riskland by UNISDR
- Story Go Round by Red Cross; Jane Friedhoff, Mike Susol, Kelly Tierney
- Ready! by Red Cross Red Crescent Climate Centre
- Inside the Haiti Earthquake by PTV Productions Inc.
- Extreme Event by LabX
- Pandemic by Z-Man Games
- Meltdown 2020 by SimplyFun
- Hazagora: Will You Survive the Next Disaster? by Vrije Universiteit Brussel
- Evacuation board game by Flood Site Project
- Hurricane Strike! by National Hurricane Center
- ERU: Emergency Response Unit by Big Fish Games
- Act to Adapt by Red Cross Red Crescent Climate Centre
- Disaster zone by Christian Aid
- PHUSICOS NBS Simulation by Centre for Systems Solutions (CRS), funded by EU Horizon 2020

References

1. Di Loreto, I., Mora, S., Divitini, M.: Collaborative serious games for crisis management: an overview. In: 2012 IEEE 21st International Workshop on Enabling Technologies: Infrastructure for Collaborative Enterprises, pp. 352–357. IEEE (2012)
2. Solinska-Nowak, A., et al.: An overview of serious games for disaster risk management – prospects and limitations for informing actions to arrest increasing risk. Int. J. Disaster Risk Reduction **31**, 1013–1029 (2018)
3. Alotaibi, F., Furnell, S., Stengel, I., Papadaki, M.: A review of using gaming technology for cyber-security awareness. Int. J. Inf. Secur. Res. **6**(2) (2016)

4. Hill Jr, W., Fanuel, M., Yuan, X., Zhang, J., Sajad, S.: A Survey of Serious Games for Cybersecurity Education and Training (2020)

5. Hill, W., Fanuel, M., Yuan, X.: Comparing Serious Games for Cyber Security Education (2020)

6. Calvano, M., Caruso, F., Curci, A., Piccinno, A., Rossano, V.: A Rapid Review on Serious Games for Cybersecurity Education: Are "Serious" and Gaming Aspects Well Balanced?

7. Chattopadhyay, A., Maschinot, C., Nestor, L.: Mirror mirror on the wall - what are cybersecurity educational games offering overall: a research study and gap analysis. In: 2021 IEEE Frontiers in Education Conference (FIE), pp. 1–8. IEEE (2021)

8. Ng, C., Hasan, M.: Cybersecurity serious games development: a systematic review. Comput. Secur. **150**, 104307 (2025)

9. Tioh, J., Mina, M., Jacobson, D.: Cyber security training a survey of serious games in cyber security. In: 2017 IEEE Frontiers in Education Conference (FIE), pp. 1–5. IEEE (2017)

10. Geogames Lab. www.geogameslab.net. Accessed 12 Feb 2025

11. Marahatta, D., Ghimire, J., Poplin, A.: Designing and evaluating games for landslides, earthquakes, and fires: lesson learned from schools in Nepal. Sustainability **16**(23), 10296 (2024)

12. Federal Emergency Management Agency. https://www.fema.gov/emergency-managers/nat ional-preparedness/exercises/tools#PrepToolkit. Accessed 07 May 2025

13. The PHUSICOS NBS Simulation. https://phusicos.socialsimulations.org/. Accessed 07 May 2025

14. LabX Evtreme Event. https://labx.org/our-programs/extreme-event/. Accessed 07 May 2025

15. Hendrix, M., Al-Sherbaz, A., Bloom, V.: Game based cyber security training: are serious games suitable for cyber security training? Int. J. Serious Games **3**(1) (2016)

16. Tomaszewski, B., et al.: Supporting disaster resilience spatial thinking with serious GeoGames: project lily pad. ISPRS Int. J. Geo Inf. **9**(6), 405 (2020)

17. Prisilla, G.: The cyber security issues over emergency management. In: ICTCS 2016: Proceedings of the Second International Conference on Information and Communication Technology for Competitive Strategies, pp. 1–8 (2016)

18. Loukas, G., Gan, D., Vuong, T.: A review of cyber threats and defence approaches in emergency management. Future Internet **5**(2), 205–236 (2013)

19. Chaubey, C., Raj, S., Kaswan, S.: Security and privacy issues in location dependent services for mobile communication: a synergistic review. IOP Conf. Ser. Mater. Sci. Eng. **1149**(1), Article 012007 (2021)

20. Palleti, V., Adepu, S., Mishra, V.: Cascading effects of cyber-attacks on interconnected critical infrastructure. Cybersecurity **4**(1), Article 3 (2021)

21. Al-Karaki, J., Itradat, A., Mekonen, S.: Immersive cybersecurity teaching/training using gamification on the metaverse: a hands-on case study. In: 2023 IEEE International Conference on Dependable, Autonomic and Secure Computing, International Conference on Pervasive Intelligence and Computing, International Conference on Cloud and Big Data Computing, International Conference on Cyber Science and Technology Congress (DASC/PiCom/CBDCom/CyberSciTech), pp. 0101–0108. IEEE (2023)

22. Hart, S., Halak, B., Sassone, V.: CIST: a serious game for hardware supply chain. Comput. Secur. **122**, 102912 (2022)

23. Delima, G., et al.: DisCoord: co-creating DRR knowledge in Uganda through interaction in a serious game. Int. J. Disaster Risk Reduction **60**, 102303 (2021)

PalmCity: An Emerging Benchmark Dataset for Semantic Segmentation of Panoramic Street View Images in Under-Represented Developing Countries

Muzaffer Can Iban[1]([📧])(iD), Onur Can Bayrak[2](iD), Serkan Kartal[3](iD),
Dogu Ilmak[4](iD), and Dursun Zafer Seker[5](iD)

[1] Department of Geomatics Engineering, Mersin University,
33343 Mersin, Turkey
caniban@mersin.edu.tr
[2] Department of Geomatics Engineering, Yildiz Technical
University, Istanbul, Turkey
onurcb@yildiz.edu.tr
[3] Department of Computer Engineering, Cukurova University, Adana, Turkey
skartal@cu.edu.tr
[4] Department of Remote Sensing and GIS, Mersin University, Mersin, Turkey
[5] Department of Geomatics Engineering, Istanbul Technical
University, Istanbul, Turkey
seker@itu.edu.tr

Abstract. Street View Imagery (SVI) offers detailed, street-level data for urban analysis, enabling the study of green spaces, sky, buildings, and other urban elements through semantic segmentation. Techniques like Green/Sky/Building View Indexes link urban morphology, climate, socio-economic factors, and public health. However, pre-trained models such as Cityscapes and ADE20K, designed for cities in developed countries, often fail to represent the diverse architectural and land-use patterns of developing countries like Türkiye, resulting in poor segmentation performance. To address this, the PalmCity project introduces a tailored benchmark dataset for Türkiye's unique urban characteristics. Using 360-degree action cameras, PalmCity will collect at least 5,000 panoramic SVI images from Mersin City, chosen for its representative urban typologies. The dataset aims to improve SVI semantic segmentation and support urban studies in under-represented regions. PalmCity is going to evaluate the state-of-the-art deep learning models, including FCN, PSPNet, DeepLabV3 and Transformer-based models, using ResNet as the primary backbone. Models trained on PalmCity are going to be compared to Cityscapes-trained models to assess segmentation performance. Preliminary results show that Cityscapes weights perform well for general classes like sky, road, building and trees but struggle with urban objects, vehicles, and panoramic distortions in PalmCity images, underscoring the need for dataset-specific training.

O. Gervasi et al. (Eds.): ICCSA 2025 Workshops, LNCS 15899, pp. 165–175, 2026.
https://doi.org/10.1007/978-3-031-97663-6_14

Keywords: Street View Imagery · Benchmark Dataset · Semantic Segmentation · Deep Learning

1   Introduction

1.1   Street View Imagery

In recent years, Street View Imagery (SVI) has become a pivotal tool in urban studies, offering street-level, panoramic views of urban environments [1]. The rise of services like Google Street View (GSV), advancements in deep learning and computer vision, and increased computational power have driven the widespread adoption of SVI in academic research [2]. Unlike aerial or satellite imagery, SVI provides a horizontal, human-eye perspective, enabling detailed, human-centric analysis of urban features. This has proven invaluable in urban planning, environmental assessment, traffic optimisation, and city management, supporting sustainable urban development.

Google is the largest global SVI provider, with GSV covering over 90 countries. GSV images, captured by vehicle-mounted multi-directional cameras, offer panoramic views. Researchers can download GSV images in bulk via the Google Maps API, though limitations exist. For instance, GSV is unavailable in China, where Tencent Street View and Baidu Total View dominate [2]. Volunteer-based platforms like Mapillary and KartaView complement GSV by hosting user-contributed images, particularly useful for areas inaccessible to vehicles, such as pavements and pedestrian paths. These platforms are especially beneficial for studying developing or remote regions [3].

However, both commercial and volunteer-based SVI providers have limitations. The Google Maps API restricts access to historical images and often provides lower-resolution downloads. GSV update frequencies vary, with some areas having outdated or seasonally inconsistent images, and weather conditions further affect data quality [4]. Volunteer-based platforms, while valuable, often rely on non-panoramic dashcam images, offering less comprehensive perspectives [3]. Despite these challenges, SVI remains a critical resource for urban research, bridging gaps in traditional data collection methods.

1.2   Information Extraction from SVI

SVI data is widely used to derive key indicators like the Green View Index (GVI) and Sky View Factor (SVF), essential for assessing urban environmental conditions. GVI measures vegetation proportion in SVI images, reflecting greenery from a human perspective, while SVF quantifies visible sky, influencing urban microclimates. Together, they help monitor urban heat islands and evaluate thermal comfort. A 2022 review of 135 studies found that 62% used deep learning, 23% relied on unsupervised RGB/HSV classification, and 13% employed manual digitisation [4]. Deep learning techniques rely on semantic segmentation, which groups pixels by extracted features, to predict their position and class. Widely used in autonomous driving, medical imaging, and remote sensing, it enables precise object identification. Popular architectures for semantic segmentation of SVI include Fully Convolutional Networks (FCN), Pyramid Scene Parsing Networks (PSPNet), SegNet, DeepLabV3, and DeepLabV3+. These semantic segmentation techniques group pixels by object, effectively extracting GVI and SVF from SVI data.

1.3   Limitations of Current Benchmark Datasets

The majority of SVI studies rely on pre-trained deep learning models that have been trained on benchmark datasets. Among these, Cityscapes and ADE20K are the most commonly used. However, these datasets have notable limitations that affect their applicability to urban research, particularly in developing countries.

ADE20K. Developed by MIT's Computer Science and Artificial Intelligence Laboratory, ADE20K contains scenes representing various environments but is not specifically focused on street views [5]. It includes 150 semantic classes, many of which pertain to indoor objects, making it less suitable for street-level analysis.

Cityscapes. Created by TU Darmstadt, the Max Planck Institute for Informatics and Daimler, Cityscapes is designed for autonomous vehicle navigation and includes 30 object classes relevant to driving scenarios. It comprises 5,000 finely annotated and 20,000 coarsely annotated images captured from vehicle-mounted cameras in 50 cities in Germany and neighbouring countries [6]. While Cityscapes is the first benchmark dataset dedicated to street views, it has several limitations. The images in the data set are captured using a 2-megapixel camera, which may not provide sufficient resolution for detailed segmentation tasks. Furthermore, the fixed perspective of the camera limits the generalisation ability of models trained on this dataset, particularly for urban research requiring panoramic views. Additionally, Cityscapes does not include semantic classes for water bodies, staircases, overpasses, or certain types of vegetation, which are critical for comprehensive urban analysis.

Other Datasets. Such as CamVid, KITTI, Mapillary Vistas, DarkZurich, and BDD100K, are also used for the semantic segmentation of street scenes. However, these data sets are primarily focused on driving and traffic scenarios, limiting their applicability to pedestrian-focused urban research. Moreover, the variability in image quality due to the use of different devices and the imbalance in class distribution further constrain their utility [7].

1.4   PalmCity Project

Benchmark datasets are often pre-trained on models that include weights for the classes present in the dataset. Although this allows users to predict semantic classes in their own images without additional annotation, the generalisation of these models to different urban contexts, particularly in developing countries, remains a challenge [8]. For example, Cityscapes and similar datasets predominantly represent European and North American urban patterns, which may not adequately capture the architectural and land use diversity found in cities in developing countries [9]. This highlights the need for region-specific datasets that reflect the unique urban characteristics of these areas.

Urban areas in developing countries, particularly Türkiye, exhibit common patterns in land use and architectural diversity. This study identifies six distinct typologies present in Turkish cities: market areas, planned residences, planned apartments, informal settlements, industrial urban areas, and coastal areas [10]. Mersin has been selected as the primary case study, as it contains all six typologies and serves as a suitable representative for other Turkish cities. The SVI data collected from Mersin will be used to develop transferable and generalisable models applicable to other urban areas in developing countries. Additionally, SVI scenes from other cities may be integrated into the dataset through voluntary contributions or related projects, enhancing research on semantic segmentation, object detection, and scene classification in urban environments.

Each typology reflects varying densities of urban objects, materials, human and vehicle behaviours, and distributions of green spaces and sky visibility. However, current datasets used for autonomous vehicle navigation lack consideration of these architectural and land-use typologies, primarily focusing on pedestrian and vehicle detection. Moreover, large-scale datasets are often deemed necessary for generalisation in real-world applications, yet their preparation and processing present significant challenges. Recent studies suggest that domain adaptation and few-shot learning offer effective alternatives, reducing dataset size while maintaining model performance. Few-shot learning enables deep learning models to generalise from limited training examples, while domain adaptation allows models trained on one dataset to perform effectively in different environments [11,12].

The PalmCity project aims to create an urban dataset that addresses the limitations of existing semantic segmentation datasets by capturing a diverse range of urban patterns rather than a monotonous built environment. It ensures the structured collection and annotation of urban scenes to reflect typological variations. Additionally, it provides a more efficient and adaptable dataset, reducing the need for extensive manual annotation while maintaining high model performance.

The PalmCity dataset, derived from Mersin, is designed to offer a richer variety of object classes and urban features compared to existing datasets, particularly in developing countries. Key differences include: (i) PalmCity includes streets with inconsistent lane markings, variable pavement widths, and unpaved surfaces. (ii) Developing countries exhibit greater visual variability in vehicles due to wear, modifications, and informal traffic behaviours. Pedestrians frequently cross outside designated areas, and motorcycles are widely used. (iii) PalmCity features dense advertising billboards, informal vendors, and horse-drawn carts, reflecting local urban life.

By capturing these elements, the PalmCity dataset enhances autonomous vehicle research, urban transformation studies, and security assessments in complex urban environments. Unlike traditional datasets that prioritise large-scale image collection, PalmCity focuses on strategic scene selection, ensuring greater typological representation and efficiency in model training.

2   Materials and Methods

2.1   Field Work

The fieldwork for PalmCity project was meticulously planned and executed to ensure the collection of high-quality 360° panoramic SVI across selected neighbourhoods in Mersin, Türkiye. The primary objective was to capture a diverse range of urban landscapes, reflecting variations in land use and architectural typologies, as indicated in the previous section. Four districts within Mersin city centre—Yenişehir, Akdeniz, Toroslar, and Mezitli—were prioritised, with specific neighbourhoods such as Hürriyet, Çiftlikköy, İnönü, Çankaya, Sağlık, and Viranşehir identified as key locations for data collection. At least 5000 panoramic SVI images will be obtained.

The fieldwork is being conducted using GoPro Max 360 action cameras, chosen for their dual-lens design and ability to capture 16.6-megapixel 360° panoramic images. The camera is mounted on a selfie stick attached to a waist harness, mimicking human eye-level perception (see Fig. 1). This configuration allows for stable and consistent image capture while moving through urban environments. To ensure accurate geotagging, the camera is synchronised with smartphones to record location data in real time. Images are stored on Micro SD cards and later transferred to computers via Type-C cables or Wi-Fi.

Field activities are carried out during clear weather conditions, avoiding rainfall or overcast skies, to maintain image quality. Shooting takes place during midday when sunlight was optimal, ensuring minimal shadows and consistent lighting. The camera is positioned at approximately 2.2 m above ground level. A team of assistants accompanies the operator to ensure safety, particularly when capturing images from the centre of roads. A distance of 15-âĂŞ20 m is maintained between consecutive shots, with adjustments made at intersections or curved streets to ensure comprehensive coverage of the urban landscape.

2.2   Annotation Protocol

The annotation protocol for this project was designed to ensure the accurate and consistent semantic annotation of at least 1,000 selected SVI images, reflecting the complexity and diversity of urban environments in Mersin, Türkiye. The annotation process is being conducted using the Supervisely web platform, which supports simultaneous collaboration among multiple users and allows for the annotation of up to 5,000 images. It also enables the export of annotated mask files in multiple formats, including COCO, Pascal VOC, and Cityscapes, ensuring compatibility with various machine learning frameworks.

Fig. 1. Image collection with a 360-degree action camera.

The annotation process involves a team of researchers and project assistants (8 annotators, 2 admins), who meticulously annotate each image using a predefined protocol. The annotation begins with background objects and progressed to foreground elements to avoid redundant annotations. Each image requires approximately 2 h and 30 min for annotation, followed by an additional 30 min for quality control. To ensure accuracy, a subset of 20 randomly selected images will be re-annotated by different team members, and the results were compared using metrics such as the Intersection over Union (IoU) for boundary precision and F1 score for label (class) consistency.

Two class hierarchies are being established: a general first-level hierarchy (e.g., buildings, sky, vegetation) and a detailed second-level hierarchy for segmentation model development. The first-level classes will be used for factor calculations (GVI and SVF), while the second level will support advanced segmentation tasks. Table 1 provides a detailed list of second-level semantic classes. A *void* category was included to account for unlabellable or negligible objects, ensuring that segmentation models were not trained on irrelevant pixels. Standard RGB colour codes were assigned to each class to maintain visual consistency and facilitate comparison with datasets like Cityscapes.

Post-annotation, statistical analyses will be conducted to evaluate the dataset's quality and diversity. These included volumetric and density calculations to determine the spatial distribution of semantic classes, object count analyses to assess diversity, and the calculation of void pixel percentages.

Table 1. The semantic object classes considered in the labelling studies, along with their descriptions.

Semantic Class	Description
Road	The surface on which vehicles are driven. Includes all lanes, directions, and street types. Areas separated by texture changes and markings (e.g., bicycle lanes) are also roads. Does not include kerbstones.
Sidewalk	Surfaces separated by kerbstones, posts, or markings for pedestrians to walk on.
Parking Lot	Areas marked with distinct patterns and designated for vehicle parking, different from roads.
Parking Barrier	The products applied in all places to prevent vehicle parking violations.
Soil	Bare soil cover found in empty plots or under plants at the base of pavements.
Pedestrian	Only people walking or standing still in the scene. Includes people carrying handcarts and pushchairs.
Driver	People on or inside vehicles in the scene (drivers, visible passengers, etc.)
Car	Cars, jeeps, SUVs, small vans, open and closed commercial vehicles, and caravans.
Truck	Heavy-duty trucks and lorries carrying loads and containers (includes loads and containers).
Bus	All buses, minibuses, and midibuses carrying more than 9 passengers (includes public transport vehicles).
Motorcycle	Motorcycles, mopeds, and scooters. Excluding riders.
Bicycle	Bicycles and tricycles powered by muscle. Excluding riders.
Traffic Light	All illuminated traffic signs and lights, excluding poles.
Traffic Sign	All direction, parking, and traffic rule signs. Front faces of signs with text and symbols will be annotated. Back faces are void.
Pole	Vertically and rarely horizontally positioned poles carrying traffic lights, signs, and urban lighting.
Garbage Box	Street waste containers and small rubbish bins.
Sitting Bench	Benches and seats mounted on streets for resting purposes.
Infrastructure Cover	Covers on the ground providing access to electricity, water, natural gas, sewage, and clean water infrastructure.
Infrastructure Box	Electricity, natural gas, and telephone infrastructure boxes on the ground.
Building	Includes all windows, glass surfaces, doors, railings, awnings and umbrellas, signs, external air conditioning units, satellite dishes, roofs, terraces, balconies, clotheslines, and all objects on them that make up a building.
Wall	Includes retaining walls and protective walls built around buildings. Does not include walls forming the exterior surface of the building.
Fence	All fences made of metal wire or wood.
Stairs	Stairs visible in the scene, located on streets and building entrances.
Railing	All types of railings and roadside crash barriers.
Overpass	Overpasses designated for pedestrian use over roads. Does not include highway overpasses.
Water Surfaces	Sea surfaces found in coastal panoramas. Includes boats.
Sky	Open sky and clouds. Includes electrical wires in front of the sky and birds that may be present in the view.
Tree	Trees, plant-based hedges, and all types of vertical vegetation. Does not include pots on balconies and windows. Includes vegetation covering a significant portion of a wall or building surface.
Grass	Herbaceous and horizontal vegetation found in undeveloped plots.
Pruned Tree	Trees specifically pruned or deciduous.
Operator	The head and body of the operator carrying the camera appear at the bottom of the image due to cylindrical projection. These pixels are not annotated as pedestrians.
Void	Objects that will not be in the scene the next day/hour. Suitcases and bags, rubbish bags, chairs, street animals, wheelchairs. Indistinguishable scattered objects in the image. Mountains, hills, small objects that are very difficult to annotate, backs of signs.

2.3   Training Semantic Segmentation Models on PalmCity Data Set

After the labelling process is completed, the images will be divided into training, testing, and validation subsets at a ratio of 0.60:0.30:0.10. This division will not be random but will ensure an even distribution based on image locations, land use/architectural typologies, and capture times. The goal is to obtain at least 600 training, 300 testing, and 100 validation samples, though these ratios are flexible and can be optimised to meet the project's objectives. A key step in developing a semantic segmentation system is selecting the ourperforming model. To achieve this, the performance of various model architectures and backbone variations will be thoroughly evaluated. The architecture determines the neural network's structure and design, enabling the system to identify and classify image segments. Encoder-decoder structures are commonly used, with convolutional layers extracting features and decoders merging these features to make predictions.

A total of nine deep neural network architectures is going to be tested on the PalmCity dataset, including established models like FCN, PSPNet, DeepLabV3, and DeepLabV3+, as well as novel architectures such as DDRNet, PIDNet, Mask2Former, K-Net, and SegFormer. The project will also remain open to incorporating emerging architectures. Training is going to primarily use ResNet as the backbone, with controlled experiments conducted using alternative backbones for comparison. The models is going to be trained using leading deep learning libraries like PyTorch and TensorFlow, with the training set teaching the models to distinguish segmentation classes. The validation set will prevent overfitting, while the test set will evaluate performance using metrics like Pixel Accuracy and Intersection over Union (IoU). Trained model weights is going to be shared for top-performing models. Additionally, models trained on the Palm-City dataset will be compared with pre-trained Cityscapes models to assess segmentation performance, with mIoU values used as a benchmark. This comparison will help determine the effectiveness of the PalmCity dataset relative to Cityscapes.

3   Preliminary Results

As of March 2025, the PalmCity project, which began in November 2024, has completed 50% of the fieldwork for image acquisition and 30% of the annotation tasks. The exported annotation files have been tested for suitability in semantic segmentation tasks.

Using weights pre-trained on the Cityscapes benchmark dataset, semantic segmentation predictions were generated for 10 images from the PalmCity dataset, and their performance was assessed using the IoU metric. Segmentation was performed for 17 semantic classes, compatible with both the Cityscapes and PalmCity datasets, using 13 different deep learning models. An example of segmented images and their results are shown in Fig. 2, while the IoU values for specific semantic classes and the mean IoU (mIoU) values across all classes are presented in Fig. 3.

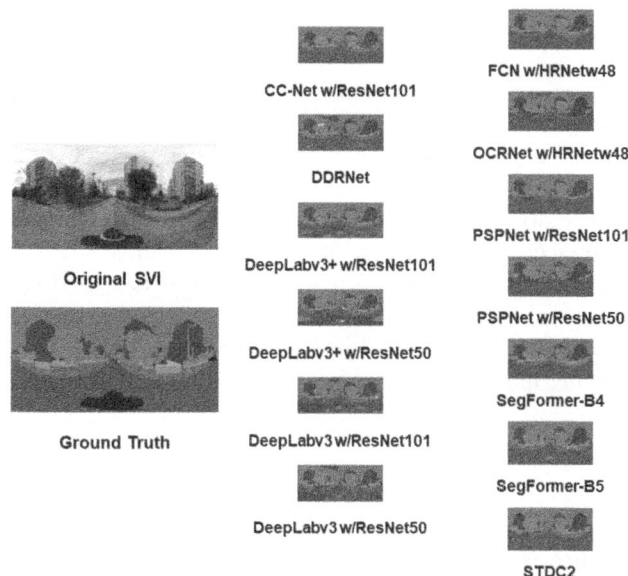

Fig. 2. Semantic segmentation predictions on PalmCity images using deep learning models pre-trained on the Cityscapes benchmark dataset.

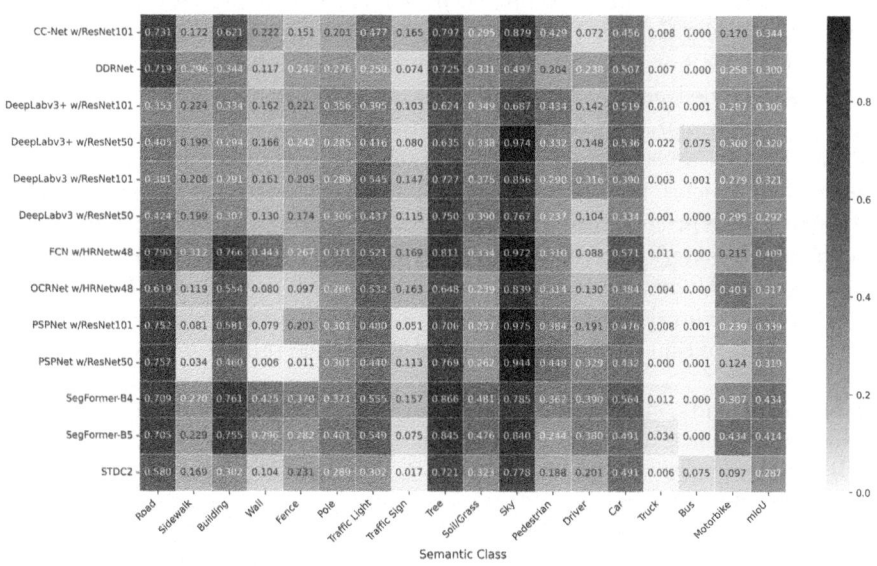

Fig. 3. Class-based semantic segmentation results.

As evident from the performance results in Fig. 3, the weights from the Cityscapes benchmark dataset provide acceptable performance for generalised semantic classes such as sky, road, building and trees in the PalmCity dataset images. However, for classes like various vehicle types, urban objects, traffic signs, pavements, and parking areas, the generalisation capability of the Cityscapes dataset falls short when applied to PalmCity images. Additionally, the panoramic nature of PalmCity SVI images, which causes certain objects to appear distorted due to cylindrical projection, further limits the generalisation potential of the Cityscapes dataset. Therefore, the need for the PalmCity dataset is justified by several factors: the diversity of urban objects in developing countries, the presence of panoramic scenes, and the fact that the action cameras used for PalmCity offer eight times higher resolution detail compared to those used for Cityscapes. Moreover, the semantic segmentation performance of classes unique to the Palm-City dataset, which are not included in Cityscapes, can only be evaluated after training and testing models specifically on the PalmCity dataset.

4   Impact

A competition will be organized to introduce and promote the PalmCity dataset in the data science community, with the goal of increasing its use in model development, practical applications, and academic connections. The dataset will be split into training, validation (with images and annotation files) and test sets (with raw images). Participants will use the training set to develop models, and their predictions will be compared to hidden test segmentation annotations on a platform like Kaggle. Results will be evaluated on a leader board, with a secondary leader board kept secret to prevent participants from manipulating outcomes. Detailed information about the competition, rules, and data sharing is going to be available on the project website.

Additionally, several events will be organized: a training session at Mersin University to discuss the dataset's contributions, a meeting at Istanbul Technical University to promote open access with stakeholders (Mapillary, WikiMedia, OpenStreetMap etc.), an online meeting with international researchers, a workshop at Mersin University to integrate PalmCity with datasets from other disciplines, and presentations at both national and international conferences. These activities will continue from the 18th month until the project's conclusion.

Acknowledgments. This study was supported by the Scientific and Technological Research Council of Türkiye (TÜBİTAK) 3501 - Career Development Program (CAREER) under the Grant Number 124Y224. We would like to thank TÜBİTAK for their support in the project.

Disclosure of Interests. The authors have no competing interests to declare that are relevant to the content of this article.

References

1. Biljecki, F., Ito, K.: Street view imagery in urban analytics and GIS: a review. Landsc. Urban Plan. **215**, 104217 (2021)

2. Zhang, F., Wu, L., Zhu, D., Liu, Y.: Social sensing from street-level imagery: a case study in learning spatio-temporal urban mobility patterns. ISPRS J. Photogramm. Remote. Sens. **153**, 48–58 (2019)

3. Juhász, L., Hochmair, H.H.: User contribution patterns and completeness evaluation of Mapillary, a crowdsourced street level photo service. Trans. GIS **20**(6), 925–947 (2016)

4. Lu, Y., Ferranti, E., Chapman, L., Pfrang, C.: Assessing urban greenery by harvesting street view data: a review. Urban Forestry Urban Green. **83**(6), 127917 (2023)

5. Zhou, B., et al.: Semantic understanding of scenes through the ADE20K dataset. Int. J. Comput. Vision **127**, 302–321 (2019)

6. Cordts, M., et al.: The Cityscapes dataset for semantic urban scene understanding. In: 2016 IEEE Conference on Computer Vision and Pattern Recognition (CVPR), Las Vegas, NV, USA, pp. 3213–3223. IEEE (2016)

7. Ülkü, I., Akagündüz, E.: A survey on deep learning-based architectures for semantic segmentation on 2D images. Appl. Artif. Intell. **36**(1), 2032924 (2022)

8. Varma, G., Subramanian, A., Namboodiri, A., Chandraker, M., Jawahar, C. V.: IDD: a dataset for exploring problems of autonomous navigation in unconstrained environments. In: IEEE Winter Conference on Applications of Computer Vision (WACV), Waikoloa Village, HI, USA, pp. 1743–1751. IEEE (2019)

9. Baheti, B., Innani, S., Gajre, S., Talbar, S.: Semantic scene segmentation in unstructured environment with modified DeepLabV3+. Pattern Recogn. Lett. **138**, 223–229 (2020)

10. Çalışkan, O., Temizel, N.P., Akay, M., Mashhoodi, B.: Typological diversity and morphological continuity in the modern residential fabric: the case of Ankara. Turkey. Habitat Int. **142**, 102950 (2023)

11. Zhang, J., Ma, C., Yang, K., Roitberg, A., Peng, K., Stiefelhagen, R.: Transfer beyond the field of view: dense panoramic semantic segmentation via unsupervised domain adaptation. IEEE Trans. Intell. Transp. Syst. **23**(7), 9478–9491 (2021)

12. Ankareddy, R., Delhibabu, R.: Dense segmentation techniques using deep learning for urban scene parsing: a review. IEEE Access **13**, 34496–34517 (2025)

Forecasting Tourism Services Exports for Sustainable Development: A Case Study of Uzbekistan

Kozimbek Tuxtabekov[1] (ID), Makhina Buzrukova[2] (ID), Habibullo Hasanov[3](✉) (ID), and Elena Salnikova[4] (ID)

[1] Oriental University, Shota Rustaveli Street. 154/a, Tashkent 100121, Uzbekistan
[2] Sharof Rashidov Samarkand State University, Boulevard, 15, Samarkand 140100, Uzbekistan
[3] Samarkand Institute of Economics and Service, A.Temur Street. 9, Samarkand 140105, Uzbekistan
khabibulloeco@gmail.com
[4] "Silk Road" International University of Tourism and Cultural Heritage, Boulevard 17, Samarkand 140100, Uzbekistan

Abstract. Tourism service exports play an important role in the economic growth and sustainable development of many countries. This study aims to forecast Uzbekistan's tourism services exports and identify the main economic factors affecting them. The analysis was conducted using log-log and semi-log regression models based on official statistical data for 2010–2023. The results show that the number of inbound tourist and hotel beds is the main driver of services exports, and their growth has a significant positive impact. Passenger transport, trade and accommodation services also have a positive impact on the growth of tourism exports. The forecast was made based on the semi-logarithmic model ($R2 = 0.785$), which has the highest accuracy among the models studied, and it was determined that Uzbekistan's tourism services exports could reach 2.85 billion USD by 2028. The results of the study confirm that the development of tourism infrastructure and increasing the flow of foreign tourists are important factors for sustainable development. These results serve as a scientific basis for the formulation of Uzbekistan's tourism policy, investment decisions and long-term strategic planning.

Keywords: Tourism Services Export · Forecasting · Regression Analysis · Foreign Tourist Flows · Hotel Capacity · Sustainable Development

1 Introduction

Tourism is one of the most important sectors of the world economy today, playing an important role in ensuring economic growth, employment and foreign exchange earnings in many countries [1]. Especially for developing countries, the tourism sector is one of the main factors in increasing national income, developing infrastructure and deepening international integration [2–4]. Uzbekistan is also strengthening its position in the international tourism market due to its rich historical and cultural heritage, natural beauty and convenient geographical location [4, 5].

© The Author(s), under exclusive license to Springer Nature Switzerland AG 2026
O. Gervasi et al. (Eds.): ICCSA 2025 Workshops, LNCS 15899, pp. 176–186, 2026.
https://doi.org/10.1007/978-3-031-97663-6_15

In recent years, the tourism sector in Uzbekistan has been developing rapidly, and the government is implementing comprehensive reforms aimed at supporting this sector. In particular, the simplification of visa procedures, the expansion of the hotel network and the improvement of logistics infrastructure are contributing to a significant increase in the flow of international tourists [6]. At the same time, the development of the export of tourism services and its forecasting remain one of the urgent issues today.

Tourism services exports are foreign exchange earnings that a country earns through services provided to foreign tourists, which contribute to the sustainable development of the country's economy. Accurate forecasting of such earnings is of great importance for national economic planning, investment decision-making, and tourism strategy development. Therefore, there is an increasing need to predict the future volume of tourism services exports using scientifically based methods.

This study aims to forecast tourism services exports and assess the impact of key economic indicators on tourism services exports using regression analysis and time series models. The results of the study serve as a scientific basis for developing effective strategies in the tourism sector, improving the investment climate, and ensuring sustainable development.

2 Literature Review

The issue of forecasting tourism revenues is one of the most relevant topics for economists and researchers today. In recent years, a lot of research has been conducted on the development of forecasting models in the tourism sector and their practical application. Most of this research is aimed at assessing the impact of tourism on economic development, forecasting tourist flows, and improving the methods used in formulating tourism policy.

As posited by Dwyer and Forsyth [7], local consumers have been identified as a primary catalyst for tourism. In their study, Allaberganov and Preko [8] demonstrated a positive correlation between tourists' travel motivations and the frequency of their visits. The researchers administered a questionnaire to 563 international tourists, though it should be noted that the study's findings are based on a single moment in time. The impact of ownership forms and management efficiency on economic growth and tourism development has also been studied previously [9], where the balance between the public and private sectors is shown as an important factor in sustainable development. Safarov et al. [10] utilized the ARDL and ARIMA methods, which are dynamic statistical techniques, to forecast the volume of tourist services in Uzbekistan, with the number of incoming tourists serving as the primary variable. Witt [11] asserts that three distinct methods are employed in the field of tourism forecasting: cause-and-effect models, time series models, and qualitative models. Goh and Law [12] identify three main types of quantitative forecasting models: time series models, econometric models and artificial intelligence (AI) based models. In time series models, future values are usually predicted based on changes in data in past periods. Although time series models are widely used in practice, they are often difficult to explain in economic theory. Time series models can be categorized into two broad types: simple models (e.g. simple moving averages, one-way exponential smoothing) and complex models (e.g. two-way exponential smoothing, autoregressive moving averages, simple structural time series). Peng et al. [13] employed econometric models in their research to identify cause-and-effect relationships between factors affecting tourism demand. In essence, econometric models do not function as mere extrapolation methods, rather, they are designed to identify influential factors. Common types of econometric models include simple linear regression, gravity models, vector autoregression, error correction models, cointegration, and autoregressive distributed lag models.

Since the early 2000s, the utilization of AI for forecasting purposes has gained significant traction within the tourism industry [14]. It has become evident that AI-based models, such as artificial neural networks, support vector machines, random time series, genetic algorithms, and expert systems, have proven to be more efficacious than conventional forecasting methodologies [15]. While AI-based models yield more accurate forecast values, the rationale behind the selection of weights during the learning process remains opaque [14]. Consequently, the employment of artificial intelligence-based models is predominantly observed in scenarios involving classification or identification challenges posed by voluminous data sets. In contemporary research practices, a prevalent approach entails the concurrent utilization of diverse forecasting methods to calculate forecast values [15].

Milenkovski et al. [16] conducted a study on the impact of road infrastructure on inbound tourism in the Republic of Macedonia, finding that environmental conditions and safety had a significant impact on inbound tourism. Breda et al. [17] also studied the impact of safety measures on inbound tourism in China, finding that political and social stability and fashion trends had a significant impact on inbound tourism demand. However, Biagi et al. [18] found that tourism development led to an increase in crime. Sunlu's [12] study found that when the number of tourists visiting a destination exceeds its capacity, it hurts the environment of that destination.

The factors influencing the development of tourism vary from country to country. Some studies have found that transport infrastructure [19], safety [16] and environmental conditions [20–22] have a direct impact on tourist flows. In the case of Uzbekistan, tourism infrastructure, hotel capacity and the flow of foreign tourists are considered to be the main drivers of the export of tourism services.

3 Materials and Methods

The study used official statistical data from the Agency for Statistics of the Republic of Uzbekistan from 2010–2023. This data covers various aspects of the tourism sector and allows us to identify key important variables for the study. Table 1 describes these variables.

The main object of the study was chosen as the export of tourism services (TourExp), as it reflects the economic potential of the country in the tourism sector and its position in the international market. This indicator serves as a key indicator for assessing the development of the tourism sector.

The study used economic and statistical analysis methods. Correlation analysis was conducted to determine the relationship between factors, the results of which are presented in (Fig. 1).

According to the results of the correlation analysis, there is a strong relationship between the factors CollAccPlaces, HotelPlaces, PassTrans, AccFoodServ, TradeServ

Table 1. Description of variables used in the analysis.

Symbol	Variable name	Unit of measure
TourExp	Volume of tourism services export	Million USD
TourFirms	Number of operating travel companies and organizations (tour operators, travel agents)	Units
InbTourism	Inbound tourism	Persons
CollAccPlaces	Number of places in collective accommodation facilities (total)	Thousand units
HotelPlaces	Number of places in hotels	Thousand units
PassTrans	Number of passengers transported (total)	Million persons
AccFoodServ	Volume of accommodation and food services	Billion UZS
TradeServ	Volume of trade services	Billion UZS
TranspServ	Volume of transport services	Billion UZS
TourClients	Number of people served by tourist companies and organizations	Thousand units
MuseumVisits	Number of visits to museums	Thousand units

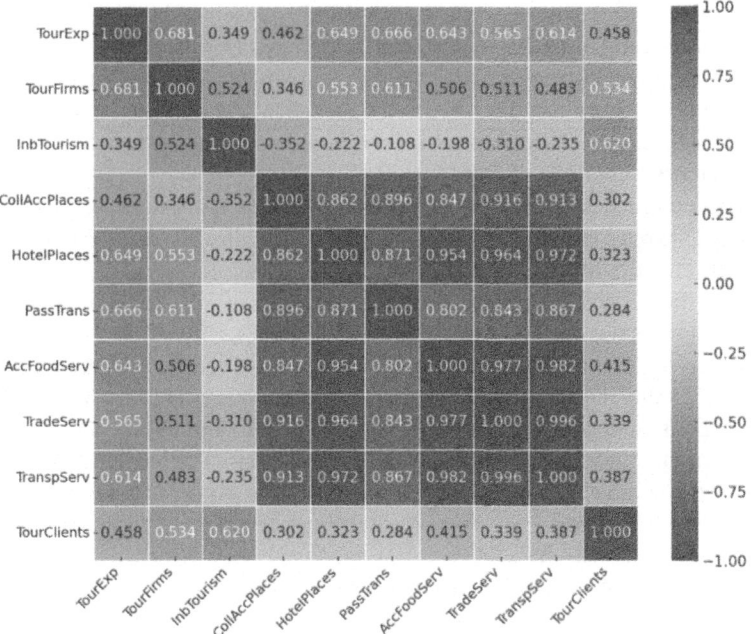

Fig. 1. Correlation matrix of variables.

and TranspServ, which may cause the problem of multicollinearity. To eliminate these problems, each variable is expressed in separate regression equations.

In addition, since the relationship between factors was found to be nonlinear during the study, all variables were log-transformed and a log-log regression model was constructed. The log-log regression model was expressed as follows:

$$log(TourExp) = \beta_0 + \beta_1 \, log(X_1) + \beta_2 \, log(X_2) + \ldots + \beta_n \, log(X_n) + \varepsilon \qquad (1)$$

where: $log(TourExp)$ – the logarithmic value of tourism services exports; $X1, X2,\ldots, Xn$ – independent variables affecting tourism services exports; β_0 – the regression model intercept (constant term); $\beta_1,\ldots, \beta_n$ – elasticity coefficients of the independent variables; ε – random error term.

As a result of applying the log-log model, the elasticity coefficients of the factors are determined, that is, they show how much a 1% change in each independent variable affects the export of tourism services.

4   Results and Discussion

According to the results of the study, a log-log regression model was used to identify the main factors affecting the export of tourism services (Table 2).

This model allowed us to estimate their elasticity coefficients, taking into account nonlinear relationships between factors. The results presented in Table 2 demonstrate that factors such as InbTourism, HotelPlaces, PassTrans, TradeServ and TradeServ exert a significant positive influence on the export of tourism services ($p < 0.01$). In a similar vein, the CollAccPlaces factor proved to be statistically significant at the 95 percent confidence interval ($p < 0.05$), while AccFoodServ demonstrated statistical significance at the 90 percent confidence interval ($p < 0.1$).

Also, factors such as TourFirms and TourClients were not statistically significant in the model. This may indicate that these factors do not directly affect tourism exports or that their effect is manifested through other mediating factors. The results showed that none of the variables exceeded the threshold value of VIF < 5, which means that multicollinearity is not a serious problem.

Of all the regression models analyzed, model 2 had the highest accuracy ($R2 = 0.78$). The R2 value indicates that this model explains 78% of the variability in tourism services exports, indicating a good fit of the model. In addition, Prob > F = 0.004 confirms that the model is statistically significant overall. The results show that a 1% increase in the number of foreign tourists increases the export of tourism services by an average of 1.048%, and a 1% increase in the number of hotel beds can increase the export of tourism services by 2.402%.

The results of Table 2 show that the main driving forces of exporting tourism services are Inbound Tourism and Hotel Places. Therefore, the factors of Inbound Tourism and Hotel Places were selected to forecast the export of tourism services. Although the log-log model is suitable for analyzing elasticity, the semi-log model is more convenient for directly expressing the quantitative change in the export of tourism services. This allows us to express the forecast results more accurately in quantitative terms and bring

Table 2. Estimation results of log-log regression models.

	I	II	III	IV	V	VI
TourFirms	0.080	−1.357	−0.585	−0.620	−0.882	−0.826
	(0.09)	(−1.32)	(−0.64)	(−0.49)	(−0.91)	(−0.85)
InbTourism	0.814**	1.048***	0.659**	0.868**	1.042***	0.983***
	(2.65)	(3.53)	(2.83)	(2.29)	(3.38)	(3.25)
CollAccPlaces	2.306**					
	(2.75)					
HotelPlaces		2.402***				
		(3.63)				
PassTrans			4.453***			
			(3.35)			
AccFoodServ				0.428*		
				(2.24)		
TradeServ					0.828***	
					(3.45)	
TradeServ						1.007***
						(3.35)
TourClients	−0.380	−0.317	−0.091	−0.201	−0.340	−0.378
	(−0.97)	(−0.98)	(−0.28)	(−0.50)	(−1.01)	(−1.09)
Constant	−12.260**	−4.986	−35.562***	−2.346	−7.402**	−8.861**
	(−0.97)	(−1.66)	(−3.82)	(−0.56)	(−2.36)	(−2.72)
Prob > F	0.017**	0.004***	0.007***	0.034**	0.006***	0.007***
R-squared	0.71	0.78	0.76	0.65	0.77	0.76
Mean VIF	2.52	3.49	2.32	3.48	3.24	3.13

*Note: *** $p < 0.01$, ** $p < 0.05$, * $p < 0.1$*

Table 3. The results of (TourExp | log(InbTourism), log(HotelPlaces)) semi-log regression model.

TourExp	Coef.	St.Err.	t-value	p-value	[95% Conf	Interval]	Sig
log(InbTourism)	501.812	110.639	4.54	0.001	258.296	745.327	***
log(HotelPlaces)	1464.44	256.628	5.71	0.000	899.606	2029.274	***
Constant	−10386.733	1859.294	−5.59	0.000	−14479.01	−6294.455	***
Mean dependent var		937.064	SD dependent var		560.107		
R-squared		0.785	Number of obs		14		
F-test		20.129	Prob > F		0.000		
Akaike crit. (AIC)		200.335	Bayesian crit. (BIC)		202.252		

*Note: *** $p < 0.01$, ** $p < 0.05$, * $p < 0.1$*

them into a format convenient for use in economic decisions. Therefore, this model was developed to forecast TourExp until 2028 (Table 3).

According to the results in Table 3, the semi-log model has high reliability for forecasting tourism services exports. The factors of Inbound Tourism and Hotel Places are statistically significant ($p < 0.01$), which have a significant impact on tourism services exports. The model shows that in general, it can generally explain 78.5% of the variability in tourism services exports ($R2 = 0.785$). The overall statistical significance of the model is ($Prob > F = 0.000$), and the results indicate that the model is reliable for forecasting until 2028 and can be used to predict the future development of the tourism sector.

Based on the results in Table 3, TourExp can be forecasted using the following regression Eq. (2):

$$TourExp = 501.812 \times log(InbTourism) + 1464.44 \times ln(HotelPlaces) - 10386.733$$
$$(2)$$

To forecast the future values of TourExp, the forecast of InbTourism and HotelPlaces was determined by identifying the trend line of their values. As shown in Fig. 2, the 14-year dynamic of InbTourism shows fluctuations that make it difficult to identify the trend line. However, it was hypothesized that this variable is more suitable for a third-order trend and the trend Eq. (3) is given below:

$$InbTourism = 385.96 \times t^3 - 8992.8 \times t^2 + 51431 \times t + 146787 \qquad (3)$$

$$HotelPlaces = 0.1552 \times t^2 + 0.6875 \times t + 23,588 \qquad (4)$$

Here t is the number of years (time) since the calculation period.

We have also constructed the above trend Eq. (4) assuming that HotelPlaces changes according to the trend as shown in Fig. 3.

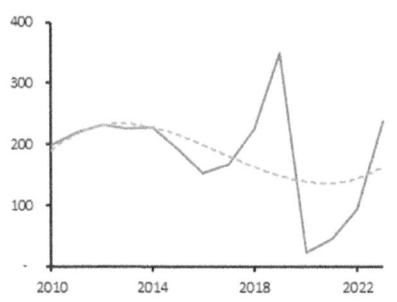 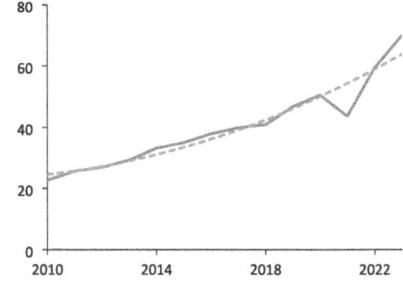

Fig. 2. Trend of InbTourism (thousand people) in Uzbekistan

Fig. 3. Trend of HotelPlaces (thousand units) in Uzbekistan

Based on the above analysis, we calculated the forecast values for the variables TourExp, InbTourism, and HotelPlaces until 2028 using Eqs. (2), (3) and (4) (Table 4).

The semi-log model with the highest accuracy was used to calculate forecast values for the factor TourExp until 2028. According to the results, if tourist flows and hotel infrastructure continue to grow, tourism services exports could reach 2.85 billion USD

Table 4. Forecast values for TourExp, InbTourism and HotelPlaces (2024–2028).

Years	Inbound tourism, persons	Number of places in hotels, thousand units	Volume of tourism services export, million USD
2024	197 487.00	68.82	1 928.84
2025	248 418.36	74.32	2 156.57
2026	318 416.28	80.13	2 391.37
2027	409 796.52	86.25	2 625.76
2028	524 874.84	92.68	2 855.26

by 2028 (Table 4). These forecasts serve as a scientific basis for formulating Uzbekistan's tourism strategy and making investment decisions.

The results of the analysis show that the forecast values are in line with historical trends, which confirms the accuracy and reliability of the model created. The forecast results, which are within the 95% confidence interval, increase the likelihood that exports of tourism services will have a stable growth trend until 2028 (Fig. 4). This indicates that the modeling process was chosen correctly and that the forecasts developed based on the model are reliable for strategic planning.

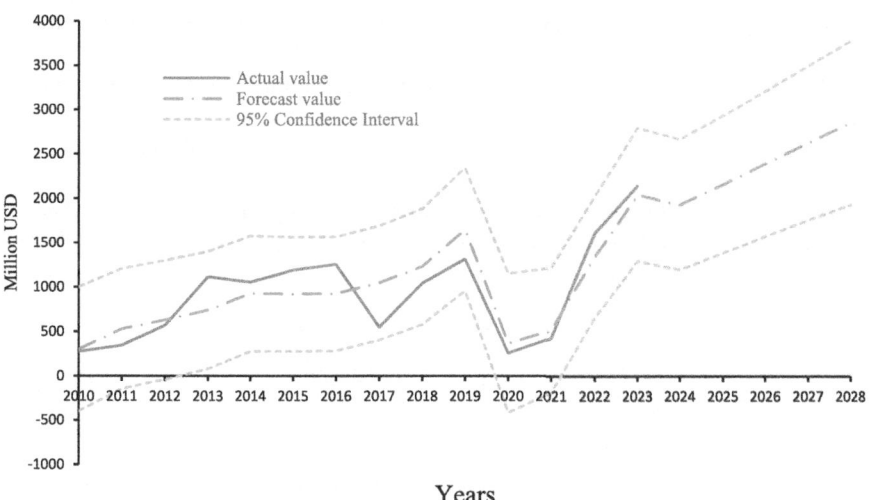

Fig. 4. Actual and forecasted values of tourism services export (2010–2028) with 95% confidence interval.

The results show that the growth of tourism services exports is mainly related to factors such as InbTourism and HotelPlaces. Analyses based on log-log and semi-log regression models confirmed that these factors have a significant impact on tourism services exports. These results are in line with previous studies. For example, a study by Safarov et al. [4] on the tourism sector in Uzbekistan also found that tourist flows and the development of tourism infrastructure have a significant impact on tourism receipts. While Endo [23] confirmed the role of the tourism sector in foreign investment and service exports, the results of this study provide a detailed explanation of the internal effects of tourism infrastructure.

In addition, Table 2 shows that the variables PassTrans, AccFoodServ, TradeServ and TranspServ also have a positive impact on the export of tourism services. These results are in line with Kevin Li [1] theory of the relationship between tourism development and economic growth. However, the variables TourFirms (number of tourism firms operating) and TourClients (number of people served by tourism firms) were found to be statistically insignificant, which means that these factors have an indirect rather than a direct effect on export volumes.

5 Conclusion

This study aims to forecast Uzbekistan's tourism services exports and identify the main factors influencing them. Official statistical data for 2010–2023 were analyzed and log-log and semi-log regression models were used. The results of the study showed that inbound tourism and the number of hotel beds are the most important factors in the export of tourism services, and their growth significantly increases tourism exports. It was also found that passenger transport, accommodation and food services and trade and transport services also have a positive impact on the growth of tourism exports.

According to the forecast results, if tourist flows and hotel infrastructure continue to grow, the volume of tourism services exports could reach 2.85 billion USD by 2028. The model results are within the 95% confidence interval, confirming the reliability of the forecasts. These results serve as a scientific basis for formulating Uzbekistan's tourism policy, making investment decisions and ensuring the sustainable development of the tourism sector.

We believe that future research could explore the impact of digital technologies on tourism exports and regional differences. It could also be useful to examine the impact of government policies and private sector participation on tourism services export performance.

Acknowledgments. The research undertaken was made possible by the equal scientific involvement of all the authors concerned.

Disclosure of Interests. The authors have no competing interests to declare that are relevant to the content of this article.

References

1. Li, K.X., Jin, M., Shi, W.: Tourism as an important impetus to promoting economic growth: a critical review. Tour. Manag. Perspect. **26**, 135–142 (2018). https://doi.org/10.1016/j.tmp.2017.10.002
2. Ghimire, K.B.: The Growth of National and Regional Tourism in Developing Countries: An Overview. In: The Native Tourist. Routledge (2001)

3. Christie, I., Fernandes, E., Messerli, H., Twining-Ward, L.: Tourism in Africa: harnessing tourism for growth and improved livelihoods (2013)
4. Safarov, B., et al.: Prospects of agrotourism development in the region. Economies **12** (2024). https://doi.org/10.3390/economies12120321
5. Safarov, B., Janzakov, B.: Measuring competitiveness in tourism enterprises using integral index. Geo J. Tourism Geosites **37**, 768–774 (2021). https://doi.org/10.30892/gtg.37305-707
6. Khujaev, K.: The development of Uzbekistan's tourism contributes to the growth of the people's welfare. https://uzbekistan.org/the-development-of-uzbekistans-tourism-contributes-to-the-growth-of-the-peoples-welfare/4597/. Accessed 14 Feb 2025
7. Dwyer, L., Forsyth, P.: Assessing the benefits and costs of inbound tourism. Ann. Tour. Res. **20**, 751–768 (1993). https://doi.org/10.1016/0160-7383(93)90095-K
8. Allaberganov, A., Preko, A.: Inbound international tourists' demographics and travel motives: views from Uzbekistan. J. Hosp. Tourism Insights **5**, 99–115 (2021). https://doi.org/10.1108/JHTI-09-2020-0181
9. Mukhammedov, M., Safarov, B., Hasanov, H., Isxakova, S., Buzrukova, M., Hassan, T.H.: Methods for optimizing property relations as a key aspect of stimulating the development of the tourism industry. Geojournal Tourism Geosites **58**, 484–491 (2025). https://doi.org/10.30892/gtg.58145-1430
10. Safarov, B., et al.: Forecasting the volume of tourism services in Uzbekistan. Sustainability **14**, 7762 (2022). https://doi.org/10.3390/su14137762
11. Witt, S.F., Witt, C.A.: Forecasting tourism demand: a review of empirical research. Int. J. Forecast. **11**, 447–475 (1995). https://doi.org/10.1016/0169-2070(95)00591-7
12. Goh, C., Law, R.: The methodological progress of tourism demand forecasting: a review of related literature. J. Travel Tourism Mark. (2011)
13. Peng, B., Song, H., Crouch, G.I.: A meta-analysis of international tourism demand forecasting and implications for practice. Tour. Manage. **45**, 181–193 (2014). https://doi.org/10.1016/j.tourman.2014.04.005
14. Li, S., Chen, T., Wang, L., Ming, C.: Effective tourist volume forecasting supported by PCA and improved BPNN using Baidu index. Tour. Manage. **68**, 116–126 (2018). https://doi.org/10.1016/j.tourman.2018.03.006
15. Hong, W.-C., Dong, Y., Chen, L.-Y., Wei, S.-Y.: SVR with hybrid chaotic genetic algorithms for tourism demand forecasting. Appl. Soft Comput. **11**, 1881–1890 (2011). https://doi.org/10.1016/j.asoc.2010.06.003
16. Milenkovski, A., Gjorgievski, M., Nakovski, D.: The impact of the traffic infrastructure on the tourist destination. UTMS J. Econ. **11**, 43–47 (2020)
17. Breda, Z., Costa, C.: Safety and security issues affecting inbound tourism in the People's Republic of China. In: Tourism, Security and Safety. Routledge (2005)
18. Biagi, B., Brandano, M.G., Detotto, C.: The effect of tourism on crime in Italy: a dynamic panel approach. Economics **6**, 20120025 (2012). https://doi.org/10.5018/economics-ejournal.ja.2012-25
19. Khadaroo, J., Seetanah, B.: Transport infrastructure and tourism development. Ann. Tour. Res. **34**, 1021–1032 (2007). https://doi.org/10.1016/j.annals.2007.05.010
20. Caciora, T., et al.: Digitization of the built cultural heritage: an integrated methodology for preservation and accessibilization of an art nouveau museum. Remote Sens. **15** (2023). https://doi.org/10.3390/rs15245763
21. Wendt, J.A., et al.: Natural sources in preventive conservation of naturally aged textiles. Fibres Text. East. Europe (2021). https://doi.org/10.5604/01.3001.0014.9309

22. Ilies, D.C., et al.: Indoor air quality perception in built cultural heritage in times of climate change. Sustainability **15** (2023). https://doi.org/10.3390/su15108284
23. Endo, K.: Foreign direct investment in tourism—flows and volumes. Tour. Manage. **27**, 600–614 (2006). https://doi.org/10.1016/j.tourman.2005.02.004

Strategic Development of Tourism and Hospitality for Sustainability in Uzbekistan

Bahodirhon Safarov[1] , Nargiza Mansurova[2] , Habibullo Hasanov[3](✉) ,
and Siroj Samiyev[2]

[1] Samarkand Branch of Tashkent State University of Economics, Professors Street. 51,
Samarkand 140147, Uzbekistan
[2] "Silkroad" International University of Tourism and Cultural Heritage, Boulevard 17,
Samarkand 140100, Uzbekistan
[3] Samarkand Institute of Economics and Service, A.Temur Street. 9, Samarkand 140105,
Uzbekistan
khabibulloeco@gmail.com

Abstract. This study comprehensively analyzed the economic, environmental, and social factors that affect the sustainable development of tourism and hospitality in Uzbekistan. The study conducted an analysis using semi-logarithmic regression models based on statistical data for the period 2000–2023. The results showed that the growth rate of gross domestic product, the use of renewable energy sources, the well-being of the population, the level of use of public transport, and the ecological footprint index have a positive impact on the number of tourists visiting the country. In particular, an increase in the share of renewable energy improves the country's image in the international tourism market by ensuring environmental sustainability. However, the impact of the level of drinking water supply was not significant. Based on the results of the study, practical recommendations were developed for the development of green hotels, ecological transport systems, and digital technologies in Uzbekistan.

Keywords: Sustainable Tourism · Tourist Demand · Economic Growth · Ecological Footprint · Renewable Energy · Social Well-Being

1 Introduction

Uzbekistan is one of the most ancient and culturally rich countries in Central Asia, attracting tourists with its unique architectural monuments, rich historical heritage and natural beauty. The country's strategic location, the presence of ancient cities as an important center of the Silk Road, and the measures taken in recent years to develop tourism infrastructure are bringing Uzbekistan to an important place in the global tourism market.

According to the World Travel and Tourism Council, by 2028, the tourism sector in Uzbekistan is expected to create more than 1.2 million jobs and contribute $16.147 billion to the country's GDP [1]. At the same time, a significant increase in the number of international tourists in 2023 indicates that the country's tourism potential is growing.

O. Gervasi et al. (Eds.): ICCSA 2025 Workshops, LNCS 15899, pp. 187–196, 2026.
https://doi.org/10.1007/978-3-031-97663-6_16

However, along with the economically efficient development of tourism, it is important to analyze its environmental and social impacts. The concept of sustainable tourism involves the development of tourism by protecting the environment, taking into account the interests of the local population, and ensuring long-term economic stability. Especially in countries with limited natural resources but high tourism potential, such as Uzbekistan, the development and implementation of a sustainable tourism model is an important strategic direction.

This study aims to identify the main factors influencing the formation of sustainable tourism demand in Uzbekistan, analyzing them, including economic, environmental, and social aspects. The results of the study will serve to study the possibilities of ensuring long-term sustainability through the use of renewable energy sources, reducing the ecological footprint, and modernizing infrastructure, which are important for tourism development.

2 Literature Review

Sustainable tourism is a strategic approach aimed at ensuring a balance between people and the environment, and its main goal is to harmonize the social, economic and ecological aspects of tourism activities. This concept has been widely recognized since the end of the 20th century and is now considered an integral part of sustainable development. The World Tourism Organization defines sustainable tourism as tourism that increases the well-being of local populations and preserves cultural heritage, while causing minimal damage to the environment [2].

Tourism is one of the important factors of economic development, and its growth has a significant impact on the overall well-being of a country [3–5]. According to studies conducted based on the gravity model, the economic stability of countries, transport costs and exchange rates directly affect the flow of tourists [6]. At the same time, increasing consumer spending, improving the quality of services and modernization of tourist facilities also lead to an increase in tourism demand [7].

Climate change and environmental factors are among the main factors affecting the long-term development of tourism [8]. Research shows that rising temperatures and an increase in extreme weather events can reduce the attractiveness of tourism in some regions [9]. For example, research conducted in Kazakhstan found that regions with moderate temperature conditions are more preferred by tourists [10]. Therefore, environmental protection and reducing carbon emissions are important aspects of sustainable tourism development.

The impact of tourism on local culture and infrastructure is also important. Involving local communities in tourism development and increasing their economic benefits is essential for sustainable development. Research shows that tourists tend to use environmentally friendly and socially responsible services [11–14]. Therefore, the introduction of ecotourism, green hotels and ecological transport systems can help increase tourism demand.

Digital technologies and innovations are playing an important role in shaping the demand for sustainable tourism today. For example, artificial intelligence, blockchain, and IoT technologies can be used to effectively manage tourism services, provide personalized services to tourists, and use natural resources wisely [15]. These innovations can help increase the sustainability of the tourism industry and reduce environmental impact.

Thus, the scientific basis of sustainable tourism includes economic, environmental, and social factors that shape tourism demand. By managing these factors in a balanced way, sustainable tourism development in Uzbekistan can be ensured.

3   Data and Methodology

In the study, we use time series data, which includes extensive data from 2000 to 2023, to assess the factors influencing the number of tourists arriving in Uzbekistan.

The level of economic development is assessed based on statistical indicators collected in the Sustainable Development Goals database. In this process, the GDPgrowth variable is used, which reflects the annual growth rate of GDP per capita and plays an important role in assessing economic development. The relationship between economic growth and sustainable development has been widely covered in modern economic research. In particular, Armeanu et.al [16] have confirmed the effectiveness of this methodology in their scientific works and substantiated the inextricable link between economic growth and sustainable development.

Renewable energy use is an important issue in sustainable development discussions and is measured by the variable RenewableEnergy (the variable that measures the share of renewable energy sources in total energy consumption). This approach is consistent with the analytical models developed by C.Hall et.al [17].

Additionally, the study evaluates natural resource availability through WaterResources and DrinkingWater, which measure available freshwater resources and the proportion of freshwater biodiversity areas, respectively. These variables are critical for understanding environmental sustainability in tourism, as Eagles [18] discuss in the broader context of ecological conservation. The proportion of mountain key biodiversity areas, represented by MountainArea, is also included to underscore the region's unique ecological attributes.

The environmental impact is analyzed through CO_2 emissions, where data on emissions are taken from the Sustainable Development Goals database. Safarov et.al [8] have studied in detail how CO_2 emissions from tourism and economic activities contribute to global climate change. Their research highlights the need for measures to reduce the negative impact on the environment and increase environmental responsibility in the tourism sector.

Social wellbeing and support mechanisms are captured through LifeLadder, the indicator based on the Gallup World Poll that assess subjective wellbeing and the availability of social support, which have been widely used in social research to evaluate quality of life and community support networks [19].

The variable used in this analysis, Ecological Footprint per Tourist (EFT), serves as a key sustainability metric for Uzbekistan's tourism sector. EFT is calculated as the ratio of the total number of tourist arrivals in Uzbekistan to the ecological footprint index, providing a quantitative measure of the environmental impact associated with tourism activities. The data obtained from the United Nations World Tourism Organization database, ensuring a robust basis for international tourism analysis. Complementarily, the ecological footprint index, derived from the Happy Planet Index database, provides a measure of environmental impact relative to biocapacity, which has been previously validated in sustainability research [20].

Furthermore, this study incorporates the Human Development Index (HDI) to reflect broader socio-economic dimensions within each country, including health, education, and standard of living. The HDI ranges from 0 to 1, with higher values indicating better living conditions.

This comprehensive approach not only aligns with established methodologies in the literature but also introduces a nuanced framework for evaluating the multifaceted impacts of tourism on sustainable development in Uzbekistan. This comprehensive approach not only aligns with established methodologies in the literature but also introduces a nuanced framework for evaluating the multifaceted impacts of tourism on sustainable development in Uzbekistan.

In our study, we construct the following Semi-Log regression model to assess the factors affecting the number of tourists visiting Uzbekistan:

$$Ln(TouristArrivals)_t = \beta_0 + \sum_{i=1}^{12} \beta_i X_{i,t} + \varepsilon_t \tag{1}$$

This model serves to assess the relationship between the number of tourists and 12 main independent variables that affect it. The components of the model are explained as follows: $Ln(TouristArrivals)_t$ — the number of tourists arriving in Uzbekistan (thousand people); β_0 — a constant value, which indicates the initial level of the number of ourists when all independent variables are zero; $X_{i,t}$ — independent variables in Table 1.

The natural logarithm is a mathematical transformation widely used in econometric research. It is important for overcoming various methodological problems and for interpreting research results. Since economic data in most cases have non-linear relationships, the use of the natural logarithm helps to solve this problem. Firstly, the natural logarithm can be used to linearise non-linear relationships between economic variables, allowing the effective use of linear regression models. As Wooldridge [21] noted, in economic research the non-linearity of data can cause difficulties in its analysis. In such circumstances, the logarithmic transformation simplifies these relationships and facilitates their analysis in statistical models. Secondly, the natural logarithm serves to stabilise the variance of the variables, i.e. it reduces the problem of heteroscedasticity, since in this case the diversity of the variables is reduced and they become closer to each other. Thirdly, the estimated coefficients obtained as a result of logarithmisation can be interpreted as elasticities. This allows a more meaningful interpretation of the research results in economic terms. Fourth, the natural logarithm reduces the scale of large numbers, which allows for the creation of economic models that are comparable and convenient for analysis.

Taking these aspects into account, the use of natural logarithms in this study ensures the stability and interpretability of the results and simplifies the analysis process. The results obtained using natural logarithms are used to better understand economic relationships and to make effective policies and decisions.

Table 1. Variables used in the analysis.

Abbreviation	Full name	Description
GDPgrowth	Gross Domestic Product Growth	The growth rate of a country's GDP expressed as a percentage
CPI	Consumer Price Index	An index that reflects changes in the prices of consumer goods and services
CO2	CO_2 Emissions	The amount of carbon dioxide emissions released into the atmosphere
HDI	Human Development Index	An index measuring a country's level of health, education, and economic development
RenewableEnergy	Renewable Energy Consumption	The share of renewable energy sources in total energy consumption
PubTranPop	Population Using Public Transport	The proportion of the population using public transportation
LifeLadder	Life Quality Index	An index reflecting the quality of life and well-being of the population
ForestSize	Forest Area	An index reflecting the quality of life and well-being of the population
DrinkingWater	Drinking Water Supply	The proportion of the population with access to safe drinking water
MountainArea	Mountainous Area Share	The share of mountainous land in a country's total area
WaterResources	Water Resources	The availability of drinking water and other natural water resources
EFT	Ecological Footprint per Tourist	Represents the environmental impact per tourist in Uzbekistan. It is calculated as the number of tourist arrivals divided by the ecological footprint index, measuring sustainability in tourism

4 Results and Discussion

At the initial stage of the study, we constructed a correlation matrix (Fig. 1) to further analyze the relationships between the factors under study. This matrix allows us to determine the degree of correlation between the factors.

Correlation coefficients of 0.7 or higher indicate that there is a strong relationship between the factors [22]. This can lead to the problem of multicollinearity, which is avoided by analyzing highly correlated independent variables in separate regression equations.

Additionally, variables exhibiting strong multicollinearity were carefully reviewed and selected based on their theoretical importance and statistical significance to maintain the accuracy of the regression results. To further ensure the reliability of our findings, VIF tests were also performed, confirming that all selected variables fell within acceptable multicollinearity thresholds. Consequently, this approach strengthened the validity and interpretability of the econometric analysis conducted in this study.

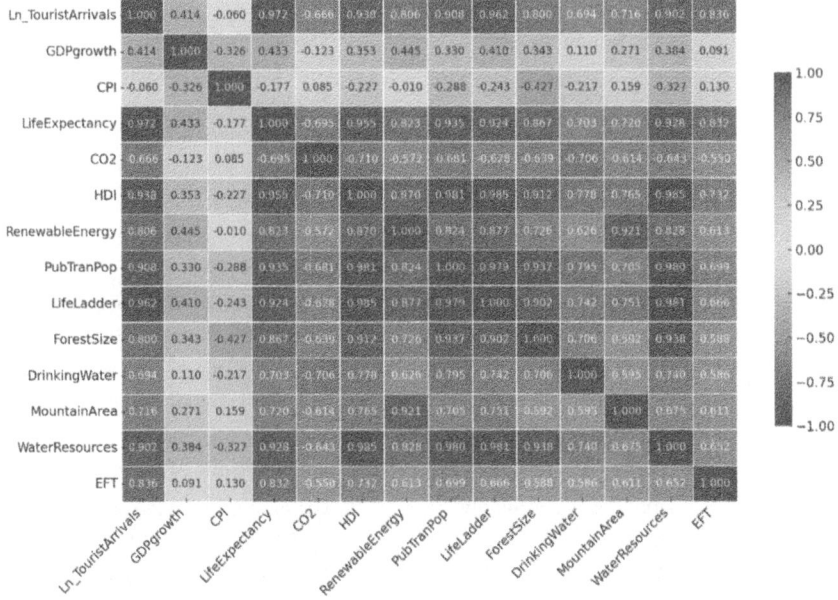

Fig. 1. Correlation matrix of variables

During the analysis, 6 regression models were built and their results were compared (Table 2). In each model, independent variables were tested in different combinations and the level of statistical significance was assessed. In addition, the robust standard error method was used in the regression analysis to reduce the problem of heteroscedasticity and stabilize the results. This approach helped ensure the reliability and accuracy of the relationships between variables.

Variance Inflation Factor (VIF) is widely used to measure the degree of correlation of a factor with other independent variables (degree of multicollinearity) [23]. If the VIF value is high, this factor is strongly correlated with other factors, which can make the results of the regression model unreliable. Typically, VIF < 5 is considered an acceptable indicator [24]. The highest VIF value is 3.80 (PubTranPop), which is also in the acceptable range. Also, the average VIF values range from 1.18 to 2.37 (Table 2), which confirms that the independent variables are not strongly correlated and the reliability of the regression results. Thus, multicollinearity does not pose a significant problem in the model and indicates that all variables are suitable for reliable analysis.

Table 2. Results of semi-log regression models.

	I	II	III	IV	V	VI
GDPgrowth	0.049** (2.13)	0.074*** (3.17)	0.074*** (7.15)	0.056*** (3.99)	0.079*** (7.68)	0.064*** (5.62)
CPI	0.39*** (4.55)	−0.003 (0.20)	0.028** (2.67)	0.016* (1.76)	0.029 (1.63)	0.030*** (3.44)
CO2			−0.007 (−0.93)	−0.012 (−1.59)		−0.009 (−1.33)
HDI	24.200*** (11.46)					
RenewableEnergy		0.204*** (2.97)				
PubTranPop			0.102*** (5.77)			
LifeLadder				0.548*** (5.58)		
ForestSize					0.010*** (4.42)	
DrinkingWater		0.054 (1.31)				
MountainArea					250.621 (0.77)	
WaterResources						0.449*** (6.59)
EFT		0. 00038*** (4.25)	0.00024*** (3.32)	0.00027*** (4.63)	0.00034*** (4.05)	0.00026*** (4.45)
Constant	−13.931*** (−6.76)	1.130 (0.22)	−4.257 (−1.53)	2.877 (1.66)	−7601.244 (−0.77)	−22.05 (−4.45)
Prob > F	0.000***	0.000***	0.000***	0.000***	0.000***	0.000***
R-squared	0.923	0.888	0.953	0.953	0.908	0.962
Mean VIF	1.18	2.06	2.21	1.97	2.37	2.07

Note: *** $p < 0.01$, ** $p < 0.05$, * $p < 0.1$

According to the results of the study, factors affecting the number of tourists coming to Uzbekistan were identified and the interrelationships between them were assessed. Based on the conducted correlation and regression analyses, it was found that factors such as economic growth (GDPgrowth), human development index (HDI), renewable energy consumption (RenewableEnergy), PubTranPop, and ecological footprint index (EFT) have a statistically significant positive impact on the flow of tourists. In particular, it was shown that a 1% increase in the level of economic growth increases the number of tourists coming to the country by an average of 0.049–0.079%. These results confirm that economic stability and prosperity in the country play an important role in shaping the demand for tourism.

In assessing environmental sustainability, it was shown that an increase in the share of renewable energy sources in total energy consumption helps to increase the environmental awareness of tourists and improve the image of the country. Also, when assessed through the EFT, the lower the environmental impact of each tourist visiting Uzbekistan, the more opportunities it creates for long-term sustainable tourism development.

At the same time, indicators of local population well-being (LifeLadder), forest area (ForestSize) and water resources (WaterResources) also had a significant positive impact on the number of tourists visiting the country. Through these factors, the improvement of local environmental conditions and the increase in the quality of life of the population serve to increase the attractiveness of the tourism sector.

However, some factors, such as the level of drinking water supply (DrinkingWater), were found to be statistically insignificant. This may indicate that the availability of drinking water in the country does not directly affect the decision of tourists to come to Uzbekistan. This is because the level of development of tourism infrastructure is more related to the quality of infrastructure and the level of services, and water supply may not be considered a key factor. It is also possible that the statistical insignificance of some factors is also due to the short data period or variability in data quality.

Based on the identified factors, the following recommendations were developed for the development of sustainable tourism in Uzbekistan: expand the use of renewable energy sources; development of environmentally friendly hotels and transport systems; implementation of programs that take into account the interests of the local population; improvement of tourism service management systems through digital technologies.

5 Conclusion

The results of the study showed the interdependence of economic, environmental and social factors and their joint importance for the development of sustainable tourism in Uzbekistan. Economic development, especially increasing the well-being of the population and rational use of environmental resources, play a key role in increasing the country's tourist attractiveness. This requires supporting economic growth, widespread introduction of environmentally friendly technologies, digital innovations and the development of green tourism infrastructure.

However, it was noted during the study that some factors, such as the level of drinking water supply, do not have a significant impact on tourist flows. A more in-depth study of the mechanisms of influence of such factors is considered one of the main directions of future research. Also, by continuing the study based on data collected over a longer period, it will be possible to develop specific policy recommendations aimed at ensuring sustainability in the tourism sector.

Thus, it was noted that a comprehensive strategic approach that combines economic, environmental and social directions is necessary for the sustainable development of the tourism sector in Uzbekistan. This will help increase the country's competitiveness in the international tourism market, as well as achieve long-term economic and social prosperity.

Acknowledgments. The research undertaken was made possible by the equal scientific involvement of all the authors concerned.

Disclosure of Interests. The authors have no competing interests to declare that are relevant to the content of this article.

References

1. Uzbekistan - EIR Factsheet | WTTC Research Hub. https://researchhub.wttc.org/factsheets/uzbekistan. Accessed 07 Mar 2025
2. Chirieleison, C., Rizzi, F.: Sustainable tourism. In: Idowu, S.O., Schmidpeter, R., Capaldi, N., Zu, L., Del Baldo, M., Abreu, R. (eds.) Encyclopedia of Sustainable Management, pp. 3607–3613. Springer, Cham (2023). https://doi.org/10.1007/978-3-031-25984-5_135
3. Safarov, B., et al.: Prospects of agrotourism development in the region. Economies **12** (2024). https://doi.org/10.3390/economies12120321
4. Kuvandikov, S., Khasanov, K.: The impact of government performance indicators on the business environment: the case of Uzbekistan. Mod. J. Soc. Sci. Humanit. **1**, 98–103 (2022). https://doi.org/10.51699/mjssh.v1i9.489
5. Mukhammedov, M., Safarov, B., Hasanov, H., Isxakova, S., Buzrukova, M., Hassan, T.H.: Methods for optimizing property relations as a key aspect of stimulating the development of the tourism industry. Geojournal Tourism Geosites **58**, 484–491 (2025). https://doi.org/10.30892/gtg.58145-1430
6. Ibragimov, K., Perles-Ribes, J.F., Ramón-Rodríguez, A.B.: The economic determinants of tourism in Central Asia: a gravity model applied approach. Tour. Econ. **28**, 1749–1768 (2022). https://doi.org/10.1177/13548166211009985
7. Safarov, B., Janzakov, B.: Measuring competitiveness in tourism enterprises using integral index. Geo J. Tourism Geosites **37**, 768–774 (2021). https://doi.org/10.30892/gtg.37305-707
8. Safarov, B., et al.: Forecasting the volume of tourism services in Uzbekistan. Sustainability **14**, 7762 (2022). https://doi.org/10.3390/su14137762
9. Sharpley, R.: Host perceptions of tourism: a review of the research. Tour. Manage. **42**, 37–49 (2014). https://doi.org/10.1016/j.tourman.2013.10.007
10. Pashkov, S., Mazhitova, G., Sedelnikov, I., Ospan, G., Sagatbayev, Y.: Assessment of tourism and climate potential of territories of northern Kazakhstan. GeoJournal Tourism Geosites **48**, 725–732 (2023). https://doi.org/10.30892/gtg.482spl06-1072
11. Caciora, T., et al.: Digitization of the built cultural heritage: an integrated methodology for preservation and accessibilization of an art nouveau museum. Remote Sens. **15** (2023). https://doi.org/10.3390/rs15245763
12. Wendt, J.A., et al.: Natural sources in preventive conservation of naturally aged textiles. Fibres Text. East. Europe (2021). https://doi.org/10.5604/01.3001.0014.9309
13. Ilies, D.C., et al.: Indoor air quality perception in built cultural heritage in times of climate change. Sustainability **15** (2023). https://doi.org/10.3390/su15108284
14. Ilieş, D.C., et al.: Preserving cultural heritage: enhancing limestone durability with nano-TiO2 coating. Heritage **7**, 4914–4932 (2024). https://doi.org/10.3390/heritage7090232
15. Siddik, A.B., Forid, M., Yong, L., Du, A.M., Goodell, J.W.: Artificial intelligence as a catalyst for sustainable tourism growth and economic cycles. Technol. Forecast. Soc. Chang. **210**, 123875 (2025). https://doi.org/10.1016/j.techfore.2024.123875
16. Armeanu, D.Ş., Vintilă, G., Gherghina, Ş.C.: Empirical study towards the drivers of sustainable economic growth in EU-28 countries. Sustainability **10** (2018). https://doi.org/10.3390/su10010004
17. Hall, C.M., Gössling, S., Scott, D.: The Routledge Handbook of Tourism and Sustainability. Routledge Abingdon (2015)
18. Eagles, P.F.J.: Research priorities in park tourism. J. Sustain. Tour. **22**, 528–549 (2014). https://doi.org/10.1080/09669582.2013.785554
19. Helliwell, J., Layard, R., Sachs, J.: World happiness report. London School of Economics and Political Science, LSE Library (2012)

20. Buckley, R.: Ecological indicators of tourist impacts in parks. J. Ecotour. **2**, 54–66 (2003). https://doi.org/10.1080/14724040308668133
21. Wooldridge, J.M.: Econometric Analysis of Cross Section and Panel Data. MIT Press (2010)
22. Chaddock, R.E.: Principles and Methods of Statistics. Houghton Mifflin (1925)
23. Thompson, C.G., Kim, R.S., Aloe, A.M., Becker, B.J.: Extracting the variance inflation factor and other multicollinearity diagnostics from typical regression results. Basic Appl. Soc. Psychol. **39**, 81–90 (2017). https://doi.org/10.1080/01973533.2016.1277529
24. O'brien, R.M.: A Caution Regarding Rules of Thumb for Variance Inflation Factors. Qual. Quant. **41**, 673–690 (2007). https://doi.org/10.1007/s11135-006-9018-6

Regeneration and Reuse of Heritage in Basso Sangro Trigno: An Opportunity for the Sustainable Development of Inner Areas

Ilaria Matta[✉] [ID]

University "G. d'Annunzio" Chieti-Pescara, Viale Pindaro 42, 65127 Pescara, Italy
ilaria.matta@unich.it

Abstract. The Basso Sangro Trigno area in Abruzzo is one of the 72 pilot areas identified by the National Strategy for Inner Areas, a national policy introduced in 2014 aimed at reducing social, economic, and demographic disparities between urban centers and the more marginal regions of the country.

The out-migration towards urban centers and the aging population have had significant repercussions on both the quality and availability of services, leading to increased management costs, particularly in key sectors such as education, healthcare, and mobility. However, the progressive depopulation of these areas has also deeply impacted the surrounding landscapes - both natural and built. Nevertheless, the regeneration of these territories through the reuse of existing heritage can represent a vital opportunity for their revitalization.

Although often underestimated, neglected, or abandoned, heritage remains a fundamental resource for the sustainable development of these territories. The concept of reuse emerges as an approach that preserves the identity and uniqueness of places while counteracting urban sprawl and fostering local community involvement in heritage management practices. This aligns with the principles outlined in the United Nations' Global Agenda for Sustainable Development.

This paper analyzes territorial regeneration models applicable to inner areas, with a focus on the case study of Basso Sangro Trigno. In this context, strategies are proposed based on the reuse of abandoned assets and the strengthening of community networks, seen as key actors in the shared management of recovered resources, with the aim of returning them to the public good.

Keywords: Inner areas · Reuse · Regeneration · Community

1 Introduction

Inner areas are often characterized by demographic, economic, and social fragility. However, they also hold a vast and diverse environmental, historical, and cultural heritage. With the introduction of the National Strategy for Inner Areas, Basso Sangro Trigno has gained particular significance as one of the 72 pilot areas targeted for initiatives aimed at curbing depopulation, improving access to essential services, and bridging the socio-economic gap with more urbanized centers.

O. Gervasi et al. (Eds.): ICCSA 2025 Workshops, LNCS 15899, pp. 197–207, 2026.
https://doi.org/10.1007/978-3-031-97663-6_17

In this context, regeneration and the reuse of existing heritage represent crucial opportunities to trigger sustainable development processes. Inner areas are undergoing profound transformations, suspended in a phase of "no longer and not yet" (Salvatore, Chiodo, 2017). Once seen as symbols of decline and abandonment, these territories are now beginning to emerge as places of potential.

2 Methodology

This research adopts a qualitative approach aimed at exploring and understanding the social, cultural, and spatial dynamics related to regeneration processes in inner areas, with a particular focus on the Basso Sangro Trigno area. The methodology employed is based on the integrated use of various research tools: document analysis, case studies from the Italian context, direct field observation, and exploratory interviews conducted with local administrators and community representatives.

The document analysis phase focused on an in-depth examination of the main national and regional strategic planning tools (National Strategy for Inner Areas, Regional Laws, Local Development Plans, Framework Program Agreements), as well as academic literature, press articles, and documents produced by local actors and institutions.

This phase made it possible to reconstruct the regulatory and strategic framework for inner areas, to understand how policies are received and implemented in the territories, and to identify guiding concepts useful for the analysis of case studies, thereby informing the subsequent phases of the research.

Some case studies were selected based on characteristics comparable to the Basso Sangro Trigno context: small population size, presence of underused or abandoned building stock, and experimentation with reuse models based on participatory approaches. The selection of case studies was determined both by the availability and accessibility of data and information, and by direct field observations, including site visits and conversations with local actors and residents, which enriched the understanding of the analyzed contexts.

Direct field observation was carried out through site inspections, participation in public events and workshops, exploration of places, photographic surveys, and conversations with local actors and residents. This enriched the overall understanding, allowing for the identification of aspects often not detectable otherwise, and highlighting hidden challenges and potentialities within the analyzed contexts.

Interviews were conducted with local administrators, third sector representatives, and residents. The interviews with local administrators explored policy-related aspects, with the aim of investigating the effects and impacts generated in the territories.

The interviews with third sector representatives (associations, community cooperatives) examined the role of ongoing or completed initiatives in processes of territorial regeneration and/or socially driven reactivation, with particular attention to shared management practices and the main operational challenges encountered.

Cartographic representations were created using official institutional, regulatory, and ministerial sources, selected based on criteria of reliability, relevance, and consistency with the objectives of the analysis.

In addition, statistical data and materials from previous research carried out at the Master's Lab of Professor Massimo Angrilli, Department of Architecture in Pescara, were also consulted.

3   From Urban Areas to Inner Areas

Non-urban areas - those we often simplistically refer to as rural or natural - make up 98% of the Earth's surface. These territories, particularly what we call the countryside, are undergoing profound transformations and are increasingly being viewed as places of possibility and experimentation. In his work Countryside. A Report (2020), architect Rem Koolhaas, presents the result of a wide-ranging investigation that culminated in the exhibition of the same name at the Guggenheim Museum in New York, offers a critical reflection on the evolving role of the countryside. The work explores development dynamics affecting extra-urban areas, highlighting the often-invisible, profound changes occurring within them, and proposing these territories as strategic spaces for experimentation and innovation. Our culture is deeply rooted in the city/countryside, urban/rural dichotomy, but we must move beyond the idea of rurality as the opposite of the city. It would be more fruitful, in fact, to think of space as a site where relationships occur—as the product of practices, trajectories, and social and relational interactions (Massey, 2005). Within the dense and diverse mosaic of territories and landscapes that make up the European Union, a predominant portion consists of non-urban areas. Rural zones are a fundamental part of the EU, recognized and valued for their food production and resource management, as well as for the breadth and variety of natural and cultural landscapes (European Commission, 2021). However, it cannot be denied that these uneven and vulnerable areas—shaken by deep social and economic changes, including globalization and urbanization—have seen their roles called into question in recent decades and face significant challenges related to access to and the provision of services. The issue of service accessibility has become increasingly central in the European regional political agenda, resulting in a shift of focus toward those inner areas that face the greatest challenges in terms of well-being and social inclusion, bringing to light concerns related to equity and social justice, especially in terms of access to basic services. In Italy, the debate on so-called "inner areas"—understood as territories significantly distant from centers providing essential public services (healthcare, education, mobility) and rich in environmental and cultural resources (DPS, 2014)—has reemerged strongly in the last decade, reviving a line of thought that, albeit intermittently, has influenced political, public, and academic discourse for at least a century. Since the second decade of the 2000s, conditions have become favorable in Italy and across Europe for the development and testing - perhaps for the first time - of territorial (place-based) policies aimed at addressing "the persistent underuse of resources" and "reducing persistent social exclusion in specific places" (Barca, 2009).

In March 2010, the European Council in Brussels approved the Territorial Agenda 2020, which set out the important goal of bringing territorial cohesion policies back to the heart of European decisions. It emphasized the need to ensure all citizens have access to adequate services, promoting a program focused on knowledge and innovation that is both sustainable and inclusive. With the aim of promoting harmonious development and enhancing economic, social, and territorial growth within the European Union - and in accordance with Article 174 of the Treaty on the Functioning of the European Union, which calls for "special attention to be paid to rural areas, areas affected by industrial transition, and regions with severe and permanent natural or demographic handicaps, such as the northernmost regions with very low population density and island, cross-border, and mountain regions" - Italy, like other member states, introduced specific policies aimed at increasing livability and social cohesion in these territories, with a focus on citizenship rights.

Today, policies targeting inner areas are implemented through the National Strategy for Inner Areas (DPS, 2014). Introduced in 2014 by the then Minister for the South and Territorial Cohesion, Fabrizio Barca, the strategy aims to counter depopulation and improve quality of life in terms of social inclusion, employment, and reducing the long-term costs of territorial abandonment. This is a public policy for development and territorial cohesion based on a place-based approach. It aims to revitalize development in areas characterized by socioeconomic marginalization by enhancing their opportunities and addressing the main obstacles - particularly access to public services (healthcare, education, mobility): the longer the travel time to service-providing municipalities, the greater the gap affecting those communities. From a methodological standpoint, the territorial classification of inner areas begins by identifying "hub" or "inter-municipal hub" municipalities, i.e., those that serve as centers for public service provision. The remaining municipalities are categorized into four groups - belt, intermediate, peripheral, and ultra-peripheral - based on the travel time required to reach a hub. Starting in 2015, within the national context, a transparent and rigorous territorial planning process was launched to select the areas in which to concentrate interventions (Mantino, Locatelli, 2016). The 55 areas initially selected in July 2015 increased to 68 in December 2016 and were formalized as 72 in 2017, as reported in the Annual Report on the National Strategy for Inner Areas (December 2018). These areas encompass a total of 51,366 km^2, comprising 1,077 municipalities spread across the country, with a total population of 2,072,718 (as of 2016). Of the 1,077 municipalities, 57.7% are classified as peripheral or ultra-peripheral. The selection of project areas resulted from a public investigation process, facilitated by cooperation among the Inner Areas Technical Committee (CTAI), the State, Regions, local governments, inter-municipal unions, and local associations. Among the project areas proposed by each Region, one is designated as the prototype area, which begins the process of implementing the National Strategy for Inner Areas (SNAI) ahead of the others. The prototype area - and subsequently the others - develops its own area strategy, which sets out the principles for action to counter the negative trends affecting each specific territory.

4   The Inner Areas of Abruzzo and the Basso Sangro Trigno Area

In the Abruzzo region, within the framework of the National Strategy for Inner Areas, four project areas were identified starting in 2015[1]: Val Fino–Vestina, Valle Subequana–Gran Sasso, Valle Giovenco–Roveto, and Basso Sangro–Trigno. These were joined in

---

[1] As established by Regional Council Resolution No. 290 of 14/04/2015.

2016[2] by the Alto Aterno–Gran Sasso Laga area and, later, in 2022[3], by the inner areas of Piana del Cavaliere Alto Liri and Valle del Sagittario e dell'Alto Sangro.

Out of a total of 305 municipalities, as many as 230 are classified as inner areas, of which 115 fall into the categories of peripheral and ultra-peripheral areas. These municipalities are mainly concentrated in the mountainous zones along the Apennine ridge (Department for Cohesion Policies and the South – Presidency of the Council of Ministers). Moreover, in 253 of these municipalities, the resident population is fewer than 5,000 inhabitants (ISTAT, Permanent Population Census – Abruzzo, May 2024) (Fig. 1).

Fig. 1. SNAI classification of inner areas in Abruzzo (left), SNAI project areas (right). Source: Author's elaboration based on data from the Department for Development and Economic Cohesion - Ministry of Economic Development and the Abruzzo Region.

In total, the seven inner areas of Abruzzo (2021–2027 programming cycle) are home to a resident population of 464,843 inhabitants, representing 37% of the region's total population. Within this framework lies the Basso Sangro Trigno Area.

This area includes 37 municipalities[4] in the province of Chieti, located between the eastern Maiella and the border with Molise, and is home to 21,778 inhabitants (ISTAT 2024), accounting for 5.7% of the population of the province of Chieti and 1.7% of the regional population (Fig. 2).

---

[2] Regional Council Resolution No. 613 of 26/09/2016.

[3] Regional Council Resolution No. 857 of 27/12/2022.

[4] Borrello, Carunchio, Castelguidone, Castiglione Messer Marino, Celenza sul Trigno, Civitaluparella, Civitella Messer Raimondo, Colledimacine, Colledimezzo, Fallo, Fara San Martino, Fraine, Gamberale, Gessopalena, Lama dei Peligni, Lettopalena, Montazzoli, Montebello sul Sangro, Monteferrante, Montelapiano, Montenerodomo, Palena, Palombaro, Pennadomo, Pietraferrazzana, Pizzoferrato, Quadri, Roccascalegna, Roccaspinalveti, Roio del Sangro, Rosello, San Giovanni Lipioni, Schiavi di Abruzzo, Taranta Peligna, Torrebruna, Torricella Peligna e Villa Santa Maria.

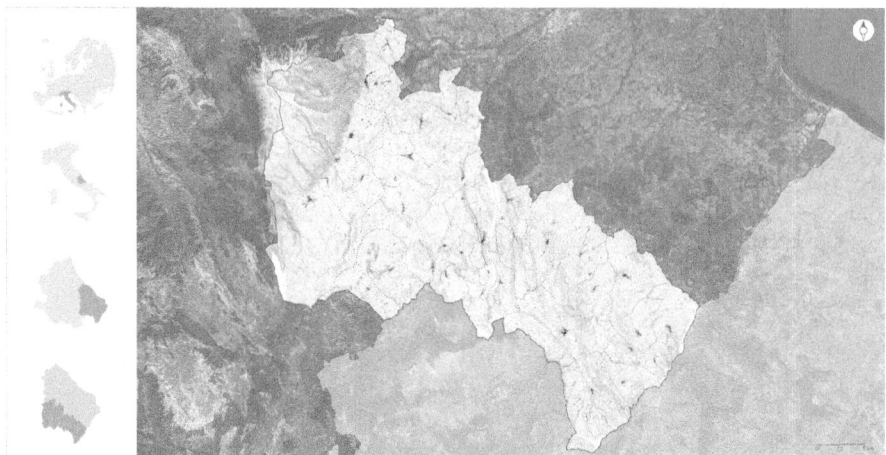

Fig. 2. Overview of the Basso Sangro-Trigno Area. Source: Author's elaboration based on GIS data.

In the Basso Sangro Trigno area, a steady demographic decline has been observed for some time, largely attributable to depopulation dynamics linked to the migration of residents toward valley-floor urban centers and coastal areas. This phenomenon is primarily driven by a lack of essential services and employment opportunities, as well as the selective outmigration of young people. Once they leave for educational purposes, they tend not to return after completing their studies, thus contributing to the erosion of local human capital. This process leads, among other effects, to a significant aging of the resident population, with elderly people making up 32% of the total—substantially higher than both the regional average (23.4%) and the national average for inner areas (21.2%). This demographic imbalance exacerbates the area's social and economic vulnerability, further diminishing the capacity for community stewardship and regeneration. Moreover, the outflow of residents and the associated aging process have a notable impact on the quality and quantity of public services, leading to a significant increase in their management costs. Outward migration flows are particularly intense in inner areas, primarily directed toward major urban centers and foreign countries, while inward migration trends are weak and insufficient to offset the negative population balance. This imbalance accelerates demographic thinning and further weakens territorial resilience.

As a result, on the one hand, urban and metropolitan areas are experiencing growing congestion, becoming increasingly exclusive and, in many cases, unaffordable for residents due to rising rental costs. On the other hand, entire inner territories are becoming depopulated, leaving behind numerous vacant and unused buildings.

One of the key challenges we face, therefore, concerns the reuse and sustainable management of this vast abandoned building stock, which should be addressed in conjunction with the enhancement of rural and forested open spaces.

5   Regeneration Through the Reuse of Built Heritage

The regeneration of inner areas through the reuse of the built heritage represents a crucial strategy for sustainable and inclusive development, in line with the goals of the 2030 Agenda, specifically the aim to make cities and communities sustainable (Goal 11) and to achieve land degradation neutrality (Goal 15).

In many territories - particularly in mountainous and rural areas - there exists a vast building stock made up of structures, small constructions, and workshops that are largely abandoned or unused due to the depopulation affecting these regions.

However, the recovery of abandoned or underused assets in fragile areas offers a tangible opportunity for revitalization, both socioeconomically and environmentally. It helps reduce land consumption and environmental impact, improves planning and management (SDG 11.3.1), and restores degraded environments while preserving ecological balance (SDG 15.3.1). Moreover, as Angrilli and Morrica (2016) highlight, *"approaches based on recycling and reinterpretation of buildings and territories are particularly relevant - if not the only viable option - in contexts where traditional top-down interventions are not feasible"*. Such an approach promotes local resources and stimulates a regeneration process that is genuinely sustainable and participatory. In this context, innovative tools such as collaboration pacts between citizens and institutions, co-design workshops, and community cooperatives enable residents to actively participate in regeneration efforts. These tools support the creation of services and foster the management of shared spaces that truly respond to the needs of the local territory. In rural settings in particular, Community Cooperatives play a crucial role. These are social enterprises aimed at producing goods and services that have a stable and lasting impact on the social and economic well-being of the community.

The International Cooperative Alliance already emphasized their mission in 1995: "Cooperatives work for the sustainable development of their communities through policies approved by their members". Thus, the concept of community care becomes a fundamental task of cooperative action, taking shape through shared and participatory management. Community cooperatives are increasingly emerging as key actors in the management and redevelopment of properties, offering alternative models based on active participation and inclusiveness - "taking architecture away from the architects and returning it to the people who use it" (De Carlo, 1972, p. 60) - highlighting that it is the communities themselves who create architecture.

In small Italian towns, successful experiments have been carried out using participatory management models for local heritage, transforming disused buildings into multifunctional spaces, artist residencies, cultural centers, artisan workshops, or facilities for experiential and sustainable tourism. A well-known example is Ostana, a small mountain municipality located in the Western Alps, in the province of Cuneo, about 1300 m above sea level, dominated by the spectacular Monviso mountain group, in the Piedmont region. One of the pillars of Ostana's revival was the restoration of its existing building stock. In the 1980s, Ostana had been reduced to just a handful of residents (five permanent inhabitants) and seemed destined for abandonment and obscurity. However, thanks to a visionary mayor, that outcome was avoided. Starting in the mid-1980s - during a time marked by reckless construction - Mayor Lombardo chose to prohibit the construction of new buildings and to promote the restoration of existing ones in line with the local architectural style and the unique characteristics of the place, believing that beauty would generate more beauty. This process was enriched through collaborations with research centers and universities, such as that with Professor Antonio De Rossi and the Polytechnic University of Turin, who since 2008 have worked to support the architectural recovery of Ostana's built environment. Demographic decline was effectively reversed by enhancing the architectural and landscape heritage: cultural spaces were created, including a center for the Occitan language and facilities for sustainable tourism. These spaces, developed based on the community's needs through a participatory design process, are now managed by the local community cooperative. Indeed, in Ostana, the birth of the community cooperative *Viso a Viso* in the spring of 2020—during the height of the pandemic—was crucial in preventing the final abandonment of the village and enabling the management of the regenerated structures. Today, Ostana stands as a model for alpine regeneration.

Another example is Grottole, in the Basilicata region, where since 2018 the *Wonder Grottole* project has initiated the mapping and regeneration of abandoned buildings through a proactive collaboration between the local community and external stakeholders. This regeneration effort, which includes artist residencies, the renovation of abandoned homes, and experiential tourism activities linked to local traditions, has triggered a virtuous cycle of economic and territorial revitalization. Other successful cases are scattered throughout Italy, where local communities - supported by public and private stakeholders - have initiated virtuous actions that actively contribute to the revitalization of local economies (notable examples include the community cooperatives of Castel del Giudice in Molise, and those of San Leo and Succiso in Emilia-Romagna).

Although these cases show encouraging results, *"for the participatory approach to work, certain contextual conditions must exist, which are not always present and not always replicable"* (Giusti, 2001). Challenges often involve the lack of competent leadership in managing such processes, the scarcity of consistent long-term financial resources, the difficulty in directly engaging stakeholders, and a potential disengagement of the local community (Maino, Cau, 2023). It is therefore essential to understand whether the contextual conditions in each setting are genuinely adequate and whether they represent the most appropriate choice for applying participatory models.

6   Abandonment and the Applicability of Heritage Recovery in the Basso Sangro Trigno Area

The history of Abruzzo is inextricably intertwined with the theme of the abandonment - partial or total - of historic centers, often due to the consequences of the Second World War and the succession of natural disasters such as earthquakes and landslides, which over time have drastically affected the livability of many towns.

Whether it concerns the abandonment of large or small buildings, agricultural areas, pastures, or agrarian landscapes, or even the complete or partial desertion of ancient villages and their relocation[5] just a few kilometers away, the Basso Sangro Trigno area

---

[5] Law No. 445 of July 9, 1908, established for the first time the relocation of settlements due to hydrogeological or seismic instability.

is no exception. One such example is the village of Buonanotte, which in the mid - 1950s was relocated due to a landslide that threatened the settlement and is now completely abandoned. Montebello sul Sangro, the new town founded further downstream in a flatter, more accessible area, is one of the many examples of relocation seen across Abruzzocases in which, as elsewhere, the new housing settlements failed to retain the population (Varagnoli, Serafini, Verazzo 2020).

Similarly, the ancient settlement of Gessopalena, carved into and shaped by gypsum, was abandoned and relocated due to a series of catastrophic events: in 1850, a landslide caused the collapse of the old town and split the village in two; the 1933 Majella earthquake caused extensive damage, prompting residents to move to a safer location; and the destruction from World War II marked its definitive decline. The geological fragility of the Abruzzo region has been a key factor in the abandonment of these ancient settlements in favor of more accessible and safer areas, often immediately adjacent to the critical zones. As a result, we see that the inland areas of Abruzzo are composed of a series of new settlements that stand alongside ruins. Abandonment particularly affects small rural villages and hamlets, where it may involve clusters of contiguous buildings (known as "pocket abandonment") - as is the case in Fallo, Rosello, Pietraferrazzana, and Monteferrante - or total abandonment of the built fabric, affecting all other settlements where at least one in three houses is unoccupied. In Colledimacine, out of a total of 443 residential buildings, 106 are in a state of ruin. Of the remaining buildings, only 150 are permanently inhabited, while 24 are used only sporadically (Serafini 2016). A similar situation can be found in Lettopalena, Palena, San Giovanni Lipioni, and other towns throughout the area. Beginning in 2020, the small village of San Giovanni Lipioni saw the launch of urban regeneration initiatives thanks to the commitment of the social promotion association Riabitare San Giovanni, as part of a project supported by GAL Maiella Verde. The initiative aimed to counteract the ongoing depopulation of the village through the functional and architectural rehabilitation of disused buildings and the promotion of new forms of living, actively involving both the resident community and external actors. One of the key elements of the intervention was the survey of abandoned properties, conducted by the Faculty of Architecture at the University of Bologna.

Fifteen vacant building clusters within the town center were identified. However, only one of these clusters - composed of nine housing units - met the necessary conditions to initiate the project: the traceability of the owners and their willingness to participate. In this block, a full restoration of the housing units was carried out, creating favorable conditions for stable residency and the settlement of new, either temporary or permanent, inhabitants. The adopted strategy focused on enhancing both explicit and latent territorial assets, promoting their reinterpretation and transformation into visible, accessible, and activatable resources. The Riabitare San Giovanni project community operates with a systemic vision of territorial regeneration, using an integrated approach that combines the recovery of abandoned buildings with the socioeconomic reactivation and cultural promotion of the area, all in line with the principles of sustainable development and environmental compatibility. The results already observed - though still in the early stages - are significant relative to the village's demographic size (approximately 137 inhabitants): six individuals have chosen to relocate to the village because of the interventions, including four foreigners (a British couple and an American couple) and two locals returning from the province of Parma. This initial signal of demographic reversal highlights the potential of regeneration models based on conscious reuse practices and community participation. The initiative has also received international attention, as evidenced by a New York Times article published on January 22, 2024: *"An Italian Town Full of the Elderly Wants to Feel Young Again"*, emphasizing the symbolic and replicable value of this experience in Italy's inland areas.

With these foundations, there are real opportunities for applying the process of recovery and reuse of abandoned buildings across the Basso Sangro Trigno area, supporting the revitalization of the local economy and ensuring the habitability of the region. It is important to emphasize that the recovery process should focus on buildings located in the so-called "new settlements", which already offer the structural safety and habitability required. Meanwhile, a separate and more complex discussion is needed to address the future of the ruins.

7 Conclusions

The regeneration and reuse of built heritage represent a strategic tool to counter depopulation and promote sustainable development in Italy's inner areas.

The case of Basso Sangro Trigno, which is part of the National Strategy for Inner Areas, demonstrates how restoring abandoned buildings - combined with active community involvement - can revitalize territories, improve quality of life, and strengthen local identity. Successful experiences in towns like Ostana (Piemonte), Grottole (Basilicata), Castel del Giudice (Molise), Succiso (Emilia-Romagna), confirm the effectiveness of participatory management models in these contexts. In an area as fragmented and fragile as Italy's inner regions, unused heritage can become a valuable resource—one that should be responsibly invested in, in line with the goals of Agenda 2030. By recovering abandoned buildings and avoiding land consumption, these territories can shift from being marginal to becoming engines of economic and social development. Additionally, Italy's inner areas - rich in potential and adaptable to change - can serve as an inspiration for urban centers, where the right to housing is increasingly under threat due to rising rents and housing shortages. Participatory management models thus emerge as a crucial path for the social and economic revitalization of these regions, ensuring that the universal right to housing is preserved a right that, in urban areas, is increasingly becoming a privilege. The cooperative management of restored buildings can serve as a structural, economic, and social regeneration tool, reinforcing territorial identity and fostering community cohesion.

In conclusion, heritage valorization in inner areas is not merely a preservation measure—it is a concrete strategy to combat depopulation, generate new local economies, and rebuild a sense of community. To ensure the success of these processes, an integrated approach is needed—one that combines environmental sustainability, social innovation, and active participation.

References

Angrilli, M., Morrica, M.: Condizione della fragilità in Abruzzo. In: Quaderno RE-CYCLE No. 23, Aracne Editore, Rome (2016)

Barca, F.: An Agenda for a Reformed Cohesion Policy: A Place-Based Approach to Meeting European Union Challenges and Expectations, Independent Report, European Parliament, Brussels (2009)

De Carlo, G.: L'architettura della partecipazione. Quodlibet, Macerata (2013)

De Rossi, A. (a cura di): Riabitare l'Italia. Le aree interne tra abbandoni e riconquiste. Donzelli, Rome (2019)

DPS - Dipartimento per lo Sviluppo e la Coesione economica: Strategia Nazionale per le Aree Interne: definizioni, obiettivi, strumenti e governance. Accordo di Partenariato 2014–2020 (2013)

European Commission: A Long-Term Vision for the EU's Rural Areas – Towards Stronger, Connected, Resilient, and Prosperous Rural Areas by 2040, Brussels (2021)

Giusti, M.: Modelli partecipativi di interpretazione del territorio, in A. Magnaghi (a cura di), Rappresentare i luoghi, Alinea, Firenze (2001)

Koolhaas, R., Therrien, T.C., Maak, N.: Countryside. A Report. Taschen, Berlin (2020)

Maino, G., Cau, M.: Coprogrammare e coprogettare: alcune considerazioni sugli approcci partecipativi, in Impresa Sociale n. 3/2023, Iris Network Editore (2023)

Mantino, F., Lucatelli, S.: Le aree interne in Italia: un laboratorio per lo sviluppo locale. Agriregionieuropa **45**, 1–3 (2016)

Massey, D.: For Space. Sage, London (2005)

Regione Abruzzo: APQ – Accordo di Programma Quadro, 2017. "Area Interna - Basso Sangro Trigno", Rome (2017)

Regione Abruzzo: Relazione di Avanzamento Annuale, 2019, Accordo di Programma Quadro "Area Basso Sangro Trigno" Regione Abruzzo – Avanzamento 31 dicembre (2019)

Salvatore, R., Chiodo, E.: Non più e non ancora. Le aree fragili tra conservazione ambientale, cambiamento sociale e sviluppo turistico, Franco Angeli, Milan (2017)

Trivilino, R., Di Lorenzo, M.: Strategia Area Basso Sangro Trigno. Comunità generative all'opera. Accordo di partenariato 2014–2020, Rome (2017)

Unione Europea: Trattato sul funzionamento dell'Unione Europea, art. 174, Gazzetta Ufficiale dell'Unione Europea, L 326/47, Brussels (2012)

Varagnoli, C., Serafini, L., Verazzo, C.: I luoghi dell'abbandono. I centri minori dell'Abruzzo e del Molise, pp. 260–291, ARCHISTOR (2020)

Flexible Textile Antenna for IoT Applications at 2.4 GHz Analyzed with Characteristic Modes

Carlos Ramiro Peñafiel-Ojeda[1]([⊠])[iD], Alex Eduardo Guambaña-Tapia[1][iD],
Jose Luis Jínez-Tapia[2][iD], Hugo Oswaldo Moreno Aviles[3][iD],
and Gabriela Tubon-Usca[4][iD]

[1] Facultad de Ingeniería, Carrera de Telecomunicaciones, Grupo de Investigación en Telecomunicaciones, Informática, Industria y Construcción (TEIIC), Universidad Nacional de Chimborazo, Riobamba, Ecuador
carlospenafiel@unach.edu.ec
[2] Facultad de Ingeniería, Carrera de Telecomunicaciones, Grupo de Investigación GI(CT), Universidad Nacional de Chimborazo, Riobamba, Ecuador
[3] Facultad de Informática y Electrónica, Carrera de Telecomunicaciones, Grupo de Investigación en Electromagnetismo y Microondas, Escuela Superior Politécnica de Chimborazo (ESPOCH), Riobamba, Ecuador
[4] Facultad de Ciencias, Carrera de Ingeniería Química, Grupo de Investigación en Materiales Avanzados (GIMA), Escuela Superior Politécnica de Chimborazo (ESPOCH), Riobamba, Ecuador

Abstract. In this paper, the design of a flexible textile antenna operating at a frequency of 2.4 GHz is presented. The structure has been inspired by the e vowel and has dimensions close to a $\lambda/4$ resonator. The structure has been then analysed using the Characteristic Mode Theory (CMT) to understand the structure's operation in the absence of the feed point. The characteristic angles, radiation patterns, and modal current distributions are represented. The S-parameter results of the proposed antenna using different types of conductive materials such as copper tape, silver ink, and buddy paint are presented below. Finally, the process used to manufacture the antennas and how the materials impact the antenna's performance are described.

Keywords: Characteristic modes theory · conductive materials · flexible antenna · IoT systems

1 Introduction

The accelerated development of wearable electronics and the Internet of Things (IoT) highlights a revolution in real-time human performance monitoring and analysis [8]. With the advancement of the fourth and fifth generation of wireless mobile communications, antennas have taken on a central role in the evolution of wearable technology, favoring the development of more compact antennas [17]. This technological synergy, particularly relevant in the field of high-performance sports, has generated an exponential demand for flexible and efficient antennas. The ability to collect and transmit

© The Author(s), under exclusive license to Springer Nature Switzerland AG 2026
O. Gervasi et al. (Eds.): ICCSA 2025 Workshops, LNCS 15899, pp. 208–218, 2026.
https://doi.org/10.1007/978-3-031-97663-6_18

critical biomedical data, such as heart rate, body temperature, and oxygen saturation, during physical activity opens up a range of possibilities to optimize training, prevent injuries, and improve the health of athletes.

Within this context, the 2.4 GHz of the Industrial, Scientific, and Medical (ISM) frequency bands has established itself as the preferred spectrum for wearable applications, thanks to its widespread adoption in ubiquitous wireless technologies such as Wireless Fidelity (Wi-Fi) and Bluetooth [4,6]. This standardization facilitates interoperability and global connectivity, crucial elements for real-time data transmission. However, integrating antennas into textiles poses significant engineering challenges that require innovative solutions [7].

The dynamic nature of physical activity requires antennas to maintain stable electromagnetic performance under bending, torsion, and stretching conditions [3,11]. Furthermore, the proximity of the antenna to the human body introduces absorption and tuning effects that must be taken into account. The need to ensure device comfort and durability without compromising radiation efficiency imposes additional constraints on design and material selection.

Although textile antennas are highly appreciated for their physical appearance, the design and manufacturing process, as well as limitations in conductive materials that adhere to the textile correctly, make the evolution of this class of antennas slow. The appropriate antenna design for integration into wearable technology operating in the ISM band is the patch antenna, either rectangular or circular, with different types of slots, which allows the control of surface waves and improves impedance matching [5,10]. Textile antennas use different woven fibers as substrates; therefore, it is necessary to know their electromagnetic properties (ϵ_r, $\tan(\delta)$) for efficient antenna design. However, each textile has its own dielectric values and these must be measured through a methodical material characterization process [16]. The most commonly used textile substrates for textile antennas are: silk, felt, nylon, polyester, among others [9,18].

Therefore, the main objective of this scientific article is to optimally design and implement a textile antenna using commercial conductive inks. Characteristic Mode Theory has been used to understand its operation. To achieve this objective, the antenna design, behavioral analysis, and manufacturing process are described; the results measured and obtained through simulation are discussed in detail below. Finally, the final section describes the conclusions of this research work.

2 Flexible Textile Antenna Design

The design of the proposed antenna is inspired by a geometry shaped like the letter "e" as shown in Fig. 1. The structure has been optimized to dimensions of length $\lambda/4$ to resonate at the 2.4 GHz frequency, a crucial ISM band for interoperability with Wi-Fi and Bluetooth devices. The geometric configuration of the antenna is the result of a parametric simulation process, achieving an antenna with dimensions of $0.2088\,\lambda_0 \times 0.156\lambda_0$ at the resonance frequency, which can be easily integrated into any work environment. This shape is chosen because the electrical length can be increased without increasing the physical area; the "e" shape allows reducing the size of the antenna while maintaining a low resonant frequency compared to a patch type.

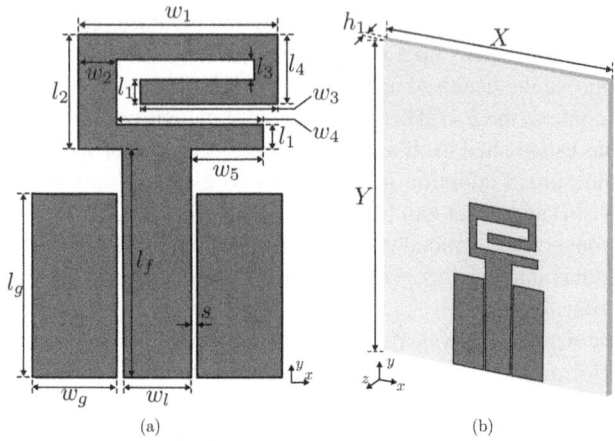

Fig. 1. Proposed flexible textile antenna. a) Frontal view and, b) 3D view.

Table 1. Optimized parameters of proposed flexible textile Antenna

Variable	Value [mm]	Variable	Value [mm]
X	50.00	Y	50.00
s	0.25	l_g	14.30
l_f	17.60	l_1	1.50
l_2	8.50	l_3	2.00
l_4	5.70	w_g	6.80
w_l	5.70	w_1	14.50
w_2	1.50	w_3	10.50
w_4	13.50	w_5	5.75

Table 1 provides a detailed summary of the values for each of the variables that make up the proposed structure.

The antenna is fed through a coplanar waveguide (CPW) line, a strategic choice that addresses the need for stable impedance matching and easy integration on flexible substrates [2, 15]. The CPW structure, characterized by a conductive center line flanked by two parallel ground planes, offers several intrinsic advantages. First, it simplifies the manufacturing process by eliminating the need for metallic layers on the back of the substrate. Second, it provides greater stability in the frequency response against mechanical deformations, a crucial factor in wearable electronics applications where the antenna is subject to bending and twisting. However, although this type of antenna may present certain disadvantages in specific environments—particularly in the presence of the human body—such as increased energy absorption (high Specific Absorption Rate SAR values), a reduction in radiation efficiency due to coupling with lossy biological tissues, and possible detuning caused by the body's dielectric charge, these effects do not represent a significant limitation when the textile antenna is used for off-body communication applications. This is the case of the proposed antenna, whose potential application contemplates its integration into hospital textile elements, such as gowns, sheets or pillows, in which an omnidirectional radiation diagram is required that allows the efficient location of patients within the hospital environment, without the antenna necessarily being in direct contact or in immediate proximity to the human body.

Furthermore, the selection of the Lycra textile substrate is based on its exceptional mechanical and dielectric properties. Lycra, with its high flexibility and mechanical strength, is perfectly suited to the demands of wearable electronics. Its dielectric properties, characterized by a relative permittivity $\varepsilon_r = 1.50$ and a loss tangent $\tan \delta = 0.0093$ and a height $h = 0.65\ mm$, allow an optimal balance between material flexibility and electromagnetic performance. The low loss tangent minimizes energy dissipation in the substrate, improving the antenna radiation efficiency. Furthermore, the low relative permittivity facilitates impedance matching, contributing to a better overall device performance [1].

To understand the structure's operation and corroborate the location of an excitation point to achieve the desired resonance, the CMT is used.

3   Characteristics Modes Analysis

In recent years, Characteristic Mode Theory (CMT) has grown considerably, becoming a very powerful tool for antenna design. This is because it provides important information about an arbitrary structure in the absence of excitation [13].

The mathematical formulation that describes the characteristic modes or characteristic currents J_n involve the impedance matrix of the structure, these modal currents are obtained as the eigenfunctions of the weighted eigenvalue equation which is shown below:

$$X(J_n) = \lambda_n R(J_n) \tag{1}$$

where R and X are the real and imaginary parts of the impedance operator, while λ_n are the eigenvalues and J_n are the eigenfunctions or eigencurrents [12].

The characteristic modes form a complete set of orthogonal modes, which allow to decompose any induced current and the far fields generated by an external source. In this way, the induced currents on a Perfect Electrical Conductor (PEC) surface can be described as a linear combination of characteristic currents [14]:

$$\mathbf{J} = \sum_n a_n \mathbf{J}_n \tag{2}$$

The physical interpretation of characteristic modes can be done in various ways, but for this study, it will be done through characteristic angles. Therefore, a structure is in resonance when the characteristic angle value is equal to $180°$.

In Fig. 2, the characteristic angle of the proposed structure can be seen for the frequency range of 1.5 to 3.5 GHz obtained by the Altair FEKO electromagnetic computational solver can be seen. It is evident that there is a resonant mode at a frequency very close to 2.4 GHz. The representation of the modal current distribution and its characteristic angle have been inserted within Fig. 2. From the shape of the radiation pattern

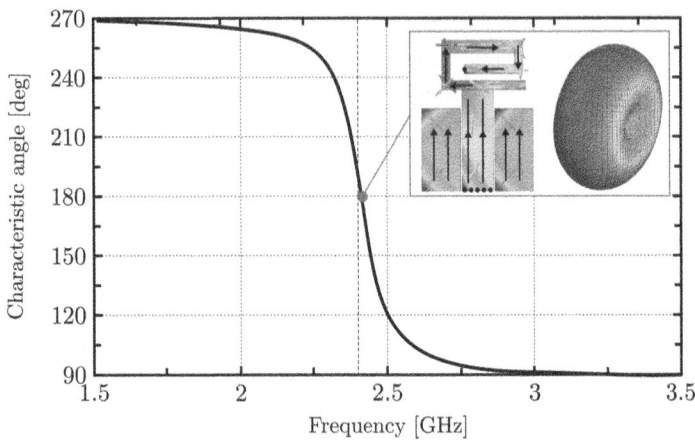

Fig. 2. Characteristic Angle of proposed antenna without feeding point.

and the direction in which the currents flow on the surface of the structure and the pair of current nulls generated at the bottom and inner end of the "e" shape, it is clear that the excited mode is the fundamental mode J_1. Furthermore, with the generation of the current null at the bottom of the structure, it is confirmed that it is the optimal position to locate the power port, this is because the excitation of a structure can be forced at a point where the current is maximum through an inductive power supply, or at a point of zero current using a capacitive power supply [12].

4   Results and Discussion

To generate the results presented in this section, a full-wave analysis was performed using the commercial electromagnetic simulator CST Studio Suite. The conductive material used for the modelling and simulation processes is the copper tape conductive material with the following conductive properties $\sim 5.8 \times 10^7$ S/m (seems the pure copper). The results of the reflection coefficient S_{11} obtained through the simulation are shown in Fig. 3, which represents a well-marked resonance at 2.4 GHz, with an impedance coupling of less than <-10 dB of 10.28 %.

The radiation pattern and total currents of the proposed antenna at the resonant frequency are presented in Fig. 4. The shape of the current flow over the surface of the structure is similar to that of the J_1 fundamental mode shown in the previous section, therefore, the radiation pattern will be omnidirectional with a directivity of about 1.778 dBi and 1.50 dB in gain in the direction of maximum radiation, which represents a radiation efficiency close to 94%

Subsequently, to contrast the results and verify the correct operation of the proposal, the antenna was manufactured using a commercial copper adhesive tape placed over the dielectric material (lycra). The S_{11} reflection coefficient is shown in Fig. 3. As can be seen, the simulated and measured dispersion parameters are very similar. Within the frequency range analyzed, there is a minimal shift toward a higher frequency of around

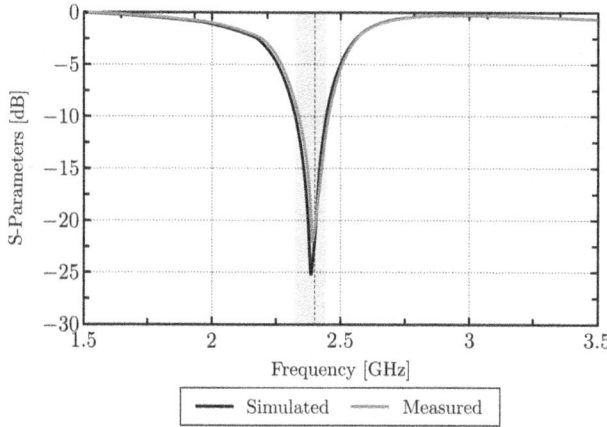

Fig. 3. Comparative plot of reflection coefficient between simulated and measured results of the proposed antenna.

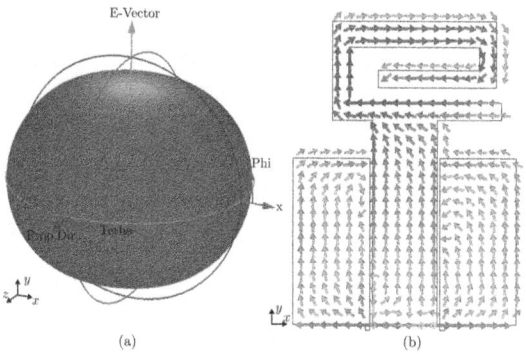

Fig. 4. 3D view of radiation pattern and total current distribution at 2,4 GHz of the proposed antenna.

20 MHz and an increase in return loss of approximately -3dB relative to the minimum value generated in the simulation. This variation is linked to the manufacturing quality and process used. However, the material used for manufacturing is not the most appropriate, as it is very fragile and will easily come off over time, causing the properties obtained through simulation and optimization to be lost.

5   Experimental Manufacture

Despite having successfully designed an antenna integrated into a textile and operating at a 2.4 GHz frequency, it is essential to seek alternatives that improve versatility and user comfort, especially considering its exposure to liquids and fluids. Therefore, experiments have been conducted with different conductive materials to improve the antenna's characteristics, such as silver ink, Buddy Paint, and bare conductive ink.

Working with liquid conductive materials and to prevent these materials from running through the textile material, a thin layer of textile vinyl was deposited on the Lycra fabric. This vinyl has plastic properties that prevent the conductive ink from seeping through the substrate without compromising the system's flexibility.

To impregnate the conductive materials (silver ink, Buddy Paint) onto the textile substrate, a technique based on transparent vinyl molds was used. First, the antenna design is replicated on the vinyl, and then the excess material is removed before applying the conductive ink. This process requires precise and uniform application, as any unevenness in distribution affects the antenna's performance.

In all cases, after depositing the inks on the material, they must undergo a drying process at room temperature. This ensures that their physical and electrical properties are not affected and that they do not impact the antenna's performance. Figure 5 shows the front views of the antennas manufactured with various materials. The first one used as a reference is the one made with copper tape, followed by the one made with silver ink, and finally, the one made with Buddy Paint.

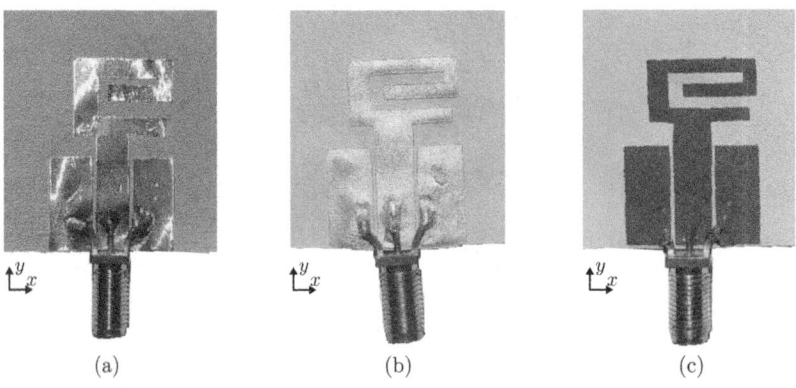

    (a)   (b)   (c)

Fig. 5. Front view of the proposed manufactured antenna made from different materials. a) Copper tape, b) silver ink and c) buddy paint.

A comparative graph of the S-Parameters obtained through the RIGOL RSA5065N Vector Network Analyzer (VNA) using the SOLT (Short-Open-Load-Through) calibration method for each of the fabricated antennas is shown in Fig. 6. As can be seen, in all cases the operating frequency remains at 2.4 GHz; however, a significant improvement in bandwidth is evident when using Buddy Paint. This increase in bandwidth appears to be related to the conductivity of the materials used. In the case of silver ink and Buddy Paint, conductivity is not constant, as it depends on factors such as the thickness of the applied layer, the type and amount of binder, and the curing process. These variations can affect radiation efficiency and, therefore, influence the frequency behaviour of antennas made with these materials.

However, despite this performance optimization, the next challenge lies in ensuring the antenna's flexibility and fluid resistance without compromising its performance or

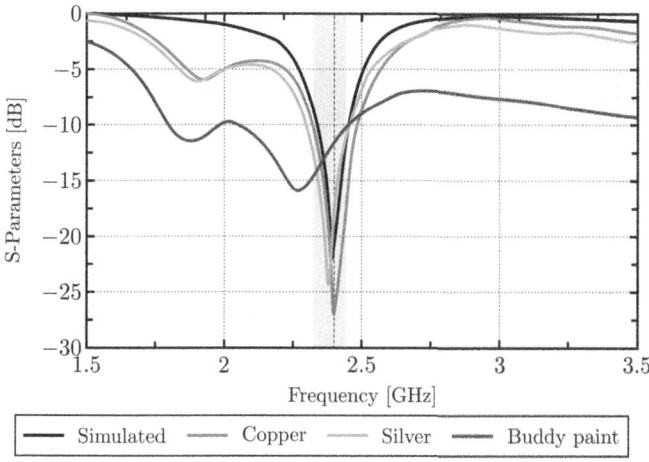

Fig. 6. A comparative plot of the reflection coefficient of the proposed manufactured antenna with different materials.

its electrical and mechanical characteristics. To address this challenge, several empirical experiments were conducted, as shown in Fig. 7. In this experiment, a flexibility test was performed; each of the antennas, with its different conductive materials, was subjected to a variation in shape. To this end, the structures were mounted on a cylindrical substrate with $\varepsilon_r = 1.0$ and a variable radius R, which is linked to the following equation:

$$R = \frac{L \times 360^0}{2\pi \times \phi} \tag{3}$$

where L represents the physical length of the antenna and ϕ describes the angle generated between both ends of the structure. As the radius decreases, the antenna will deform into a cylindrical shape. However, when the cylinder is extraordinarily large, the antenna deforms minimally, i.e., the antenna will have a flat shape.

The results revealed that, among all the inks used, silver ink is the only one that shows no significant changes in its properties after exposure to adverse conditions (see Fig. 8). The S-parameters measured before and after testing indicate that the antenna fabricated with silver ink maintains stable behaviour, without any degradation in performance. This is due to its rapid drying and the ability of its components to repel liquids, thus preventing moisture absorption and preserving its structure and operational efficiency. These findings represent an important advance in design optimisation, enabling the development of more robust textile antennas suitable for applications in demanding environments.

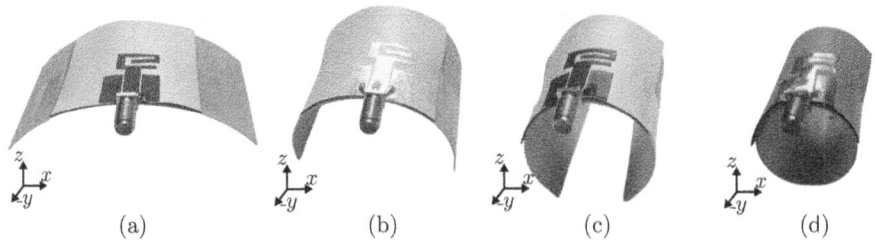

Fig. 7. Progressive flexibility test of the implemented textile antennas over a cylindrical shape. (a) at 100° setup, (b) at 200° setup, (c) at 300° setup and (d) at 360° setup.

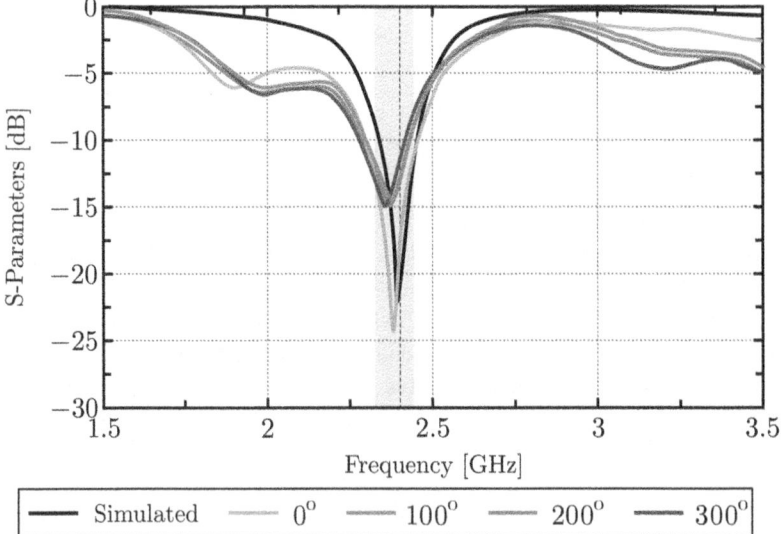

Fig. 8. Antenna manufacturer's reflection coefficient with silver ink at different angle variations.

6   Conclusions

The paper shows the design of a flexible textile-integrated antenna for IoT applications. Its dimensions are linked to a resonator with a length of $\lambda_0/4$ at a frequency of 2.4 GHz and a characteristic impedance of 50 Ω.

An "e"-shaped geometry is used because it allows the antenna's physical dimensions to be reduced without altering its operating frequency. This configuration is complemented by a CPW (coplanar waveguide) feed, which facilitates impedance matching.

To understand the operation of the proposed structure, an analysis using the characteristic modes theory was used, where the fundamental mode J_1 was represented, forcing the generation of an omnidirectional radiation pattern, where the resonance directly depends on the physical dimensions of the antenna.

The results of the S-parameters, both simulated and measured, were presented for various antennas made from different conductive materials. While all resonated at the desired operating frequency, the antenna made with buddy paint showed the best performance in terms of bandwidth. However, its usefulness is limited when in contact with fluids due to its solubility.

The silver ink demonstrated greater stability, as its electrical properties did not undergo significant changes either when exposed to mechanical deformation conditions.

The results of the simulated and measured S-parameters of several types of antennas manufactured with different conductive materials were shown. Each of them resonates at the working frequency, but the one with the best characteristics in relation to bandwidth is the buddy paint material. However, the material that has not changed its properties when exposed to fluids and deformation is that which has been manufactured with silver ink.

Acknowledgments. This work has been supported by the funds of the research projects with resolution N° 12-CIV-1-2-2023 and N° 12 267-CIV-23-11-2023 at Universidad Nacional de Chimborazo in Ecuador, also project named Desarrollo de Materiales y Nanomateriales multifuncionales para aplicaciones de Ingeniería y Tecnologías Verdes en la provincia de Chimborazo at Escuela Superior Politécnica de Chimborazo in Ecuador. Finally, the authors would like to thank everyone who contributed to this project, including our colleagues and partners.

Disclosure of Interests. The authors have no competing interests to declare that are relevant to the content of this article.

References

1. Ali Khan, M.U., Raad, R., Tubbal, F., Theoharis, P.I., Liu, S., Foroughi, J.: Bending analysis of polymer-based flexible antennas for wearable, general IoT applications: a review. Polymers **13**(3), 357 (2021)
2. Balanis, C.A.: Antenna Theory: Analysis and Design. Wiley (2016)
3. El Gharbi, M., Fernández-García, R., Ahyoud, S., Gil, I.: A review of flexible wearable antenna sensors: design, fabrication methods, and applications. Materials **13**(17), 3781 (2020)
4. Gao, G.P., Hu, B., Wang, S.F., Yang, C.: Wearable circular ring slot antenna with EBG structure for wireless body area network. IEEE Antennas Wirel. Propag. Lett. **17**(3), 434–437 (2018)
5. Gao, G., Zhang, B., Dong, J., Dou, Z., Yu, Z., Hu, B.: A compact dual-mode pattern-reconfigurable wearable antenna for the 2.4-Ghz WBAN application. IEEE Trans. Antennas Propag. **71**, 1901–1906 (2023). https://api.semanticscholar.org/CorpusID:254300766
6. Hasni, U., Piper, M.E., Lundquist, J., Topsakal, E.: Screen-printed fabric antennas for wearable applications. IEEE Open J. Antennas Propag. **2**, 591–598 (2021)
7. Li, Z., et al.: All-organic flexible fabric antenna for wearable electronics. J. Mater. Chem. C **8**(17), 5662–5667 (2020)
8. Meena, J.S., Choi, S.B., Jung, S.B., Kim, J.W.: Electronic textiles: new age of wearable technology for healthcare and fitness solutions. Mater. Today Bio 100565 (2023)
9. Memon, A.W., de Paula, I.L., Malengier, B., Vasile, S., Van Torre, P., Van Langenhove, L.: Breathable textile rectangular ring microstrip patch antenna at 2.45 Ghz for wearable applications. Sensors **21**(5), 1635 (2021)

10. Musa, U., et al.: Design and analysis of a compact dual-band wearable antenna for WBAN applications. IEEE Access **11**, 30996–31009 (2023)
11. Paracha, K.N., Rahim, S., Soh, P.J., Khalily, M.: Wearable antennas: a review of innovative materials, structures and features for autonomous communication and sensing. IEEE Access **7**, 56694–56712 (2019)
12. Peñafiel Ojeda, C.R.: Design of Multi-feed UWB Antennas using the Theory of Characteristic Modes. Ph.D. thesis, Universitat Politècnica de València (2021)
13. Peñafiel-Ojeda, C.R., Ortíz-Cruz, A., Tubón-Usca, G., et al.: Antena textil para aplicaciones de internet de las cosas analizada con la teoría de modos característicos. Tesla Revista Científica **3**(2), e180–e180 (2023)
14. Perotoni, M.B., Silva, F.A.A.D., Silva, L.A.D.: Characteristic mode analysis applied to antennas. Revista Brasileira de Ensino de Física **42**, e20200119 (2020)
15. Pozar, D.M.: Microwave Engineering. Wiley (2011)
16. Santiso Bellón, J.: Diseño de una antena multimodo sobre substrato textil para aplicaciones corporales. Ph.D. thesis, Universitat Politècnica de València (2012)
17. Sharon Giftsy, A.L., Kommuri, U.K., Dwivedi, R.P.: Flexible and wearable antenna for biomedical application: progress and opportunity. IEEE Access **12**, 90016–90040 (2024). https://doi.org/10.1109/ACCESS.2023.3343154
18. Yan, S., Soh, P.J., Vandenbosch, G.A.: Low-profile dual-band textile antenna with artificial magnetic conductor plane. IEEE Trans. Antennas Propag. **62**(12), 6487–6490 (2014)

Rethinking Peatland Futures for Latvia: Life Cycle Thinking Approach Integrated Within Multicriteria Analysis

Maksims Feofilovs$^{(\boxtimes)}$ ⓘ, Dace Araja, and Francesco Romagnoli ⓘ

Institute of Energy Systems and Environment, Faculty of Electrical and Environmental Engineering, Riga Technical University, Riga, Latvia
`info.videszinatne@rtu.lv`

Abstract. Latvia relies on its peat resources economically, environmentally, and culturally, but with increasing pressure from climate targets and biodiversity commitments, there is a growing urgency to rethink how degraded peatlands are managed. This study evaluates various restoration and after-use strategies for extracted peatlands by applying an integrated Life Cycle Sustainability Assessment (LCSA) framework that combines environmental (LCA), economic (LCC), and social (S-LCA) evaluation dimensions. A Multi-Criteria Decision Analysis (MCDA) approach using the TOPSIS method is employed to compare ten after-use scenarios, including renaturalization, afforestation, water body creation, wetland crop cultivation, and renewable energy installations. The analysis highlights trade-offs across sustainability dimensions and supports informed land-use planning by identifying which options deliver the most balanced performance. The proposed method provides a structured and adaptable tool for policymakers and land managers to guide post-extraction peatland recovery in line with national and EU sustainability goals.

Keywords: Life cycle thinking · peat exctraction · sustainability · multi-criteria analysis

1 Introduction

Peatlands are unique and long-evolving ecosystems formed by the accumulation of partially decomposed plant matter in waterlogged environments. These ecosystems develop slowly [1]. The constantly saturated conditions limit decomposition, allowing peat to build up over thousands of years, layer by layer. As a result, peatlands have become one of the most carbon-dense terrestrial ecosystems on Earth [2]. Although they cover only about 3% of the planet's land surface, peatlands store an estimated 30% of the world's soil carbon, far more than any other ecosystem relative to their size [3]. However, when peatlands are drained (e.g. for extraction or agricultural use) this carbon stock becomes a source of emissions. As oxygen reaches the peat layers, microbial activity accelerates decomposition, releasing large quantities of CO_2 into the atmosphere.

© The Author(s), under exclusive license to Springer Nature Switzerland AG 2026
O. Gervasi et al. (Eds.): ICCSA 2025 Workshops, LNCS 15899, pp. 219–229, 2026.
https://doi.org/10.1007/978-3-031-97663-6_19

The scale of this problem is particularly evident in the European Union, which emits around 220 million tonnes of CO_2 equivalent annually from drained peatlands, equal to 15% of global peatland related emissions. In 2017, this accounted for roughly 5% of the EU's total greenhouse gas emissions [4]. Major emitting countries include Germany, Finland, Poland, Ireland, Romania, Sweden, Latvia, Lithuania, and the Netherlands. In many of these nations, drained peatlands are responsible for more than a quarter of emissions from the land use, agriculture, and forestry sectors [5]. Restoration strategies for degraded peatlands are now embedded in both EU and national-level planning. However, decisions about the most appropriate type of restoration are still typically guided by climate and biodiversity outcomes, while the economic and social cycle dimensions remain underrepresented in actual policy and planning frameworks [6].

In Latvia, peatlands have been both ecologically significant and economically utilized. As of the early 21st century, fully or partially extracted peatlands covered more than 37,000 hectares, which is about 0.57% of national territory [7]. Of these, 36% are classified as degraded and no longer in active use, at the same time lacking a clear after-use strategy. Meanwhile, 30% are still under extraction. Only a small portion, about 5%, is undergoing natural regeneration. The remaining land has been converted into forests, meadows, water bodies, or in rare cases, commercial berry cultivation [8].

According to researchers, the resource has not been used to its full potential. Inefficiencies in processing, lack of innovation, and missed opportunities in land reuse suggest that peat could be managed more intelligently. This includes developing new peat-based products, modernizing extraction practices, and restoring or repurposing exhausted peatlands through sustainable land-use strategies [7].

While sustainability has become a key guiding principle in both national policy and business strategy, the challenge often lies in its practical implementation. Over recent decades, the focus of environmental science has gradually expanded—from pollution control and resource conservation to a broader understanding of sustainability that integrates environmental, economic, and social dimensions. This shift has led to the development of Life Cycle Sustainability Assessment (LCSA), a comprehensive approach for evaluating long-term impacts across the full life cycle of a product, service, or land-use option [9].

Given peatlands' critical role in carbon storage, biodiversity support, and water regulation, their degradation poses risks not only to local environments but also to broader climate stability. Thus, this study addresses helps to tackle the challenges related to sustainable peatland management by assessing different restoration and after-use scenarios for Latvian peatlands, using life cycle-based sustainability methods to inform better decisions for the future.

2 Methodology

To address the gaps identified in literature, the present study applies the full LCSA approach [10], evaluating three core dimensions: environmental impacts through Life Cycle Assessment (LCA), social effects through Social impact indicators, and economic performance through Life Cycle Costing (LCC). Together, these provide a multi-layered understanding of how different peatland after-use options perform in sustainability terms.

The study methodology is structured in alignment with the ISO 14040 and 14044 standards, which define the LCA process in four interlinked stages: goal and scope definition, life cycle inventory analysis, impact assessment, and interpretation. To capture all relevant aspects of peatland recovery strategies, the study follows the conceptual model of Professor Walter Klöpffer, who in 2008 proposed the integration of LCA, LCC, and S-LCA sustainability assessment [11].

The sustainability evaluation covers ten peatland after-use scenarios identified through literature analysis and real-world case studies in Latvia. These are:

- Renaturalisation,
- Creation of water bodies,
- Afforestation,
- Cultivation of paludiculture (wetland crops),
- Cultivation of large-berry cranberries,
- Cultivation of blueberries (Vaccinium species),
- Establishment of perennial grasslands,
- Conversion to arable land,
- Installation of wind farms, and
- Installation of solar farms.

Each scenario is analyzed across all three sustainability dimensions, with specific indicators selected based on published sources and context-specific expertise.

To compare the alternatives and determine which restoration strategies offer the best balance of long-term sustainability, the study uses a Multi-Criteria Decision Analysis (MCDA) approach, applying the TOPSIS (Technique for Order of Preference by Similarity to Ideal Solution) method [12]. TOPSIS calculates how close each option is to an ideal solution and ranks them accordingly. The results of this approach helps landowners, peat extraction site managers, and policymakers identify the most viable, science-based paths for peatland recovery.

The combination of LCSA and MCDA enables a comprehensive yet practical framework grounded in international standards and adaptable to various peatland contexts. This integrated method not only supports evidence-based decisions but also ensures that ecological, economic, and social factors are considered together, as part of a truly sustainable strategy for restoring degraded peat landscapes.

2.1 Environmental Life Cycle Assessment

The environmental LCA in this study is carried out using the ReCiPe method, applied through the SimaPro software and using the Ecoinvent database. The LCA examined ten peatland after-use scenarios, assessing their environmental impacts based on three key indicators: human health impact, effects on ecosystems, and resource depletion are assessed at the endpoint level from midpoint categories as foreseen in ReCiPe method (Fig. 1). The developed approach allows to consider the avoided emissions from renewable energy production. For instance, in scenarios involving wind turbines or solar panels, the benefit of replacing fossil-based electricity in the national grid is accounted for in the total climate impact value.

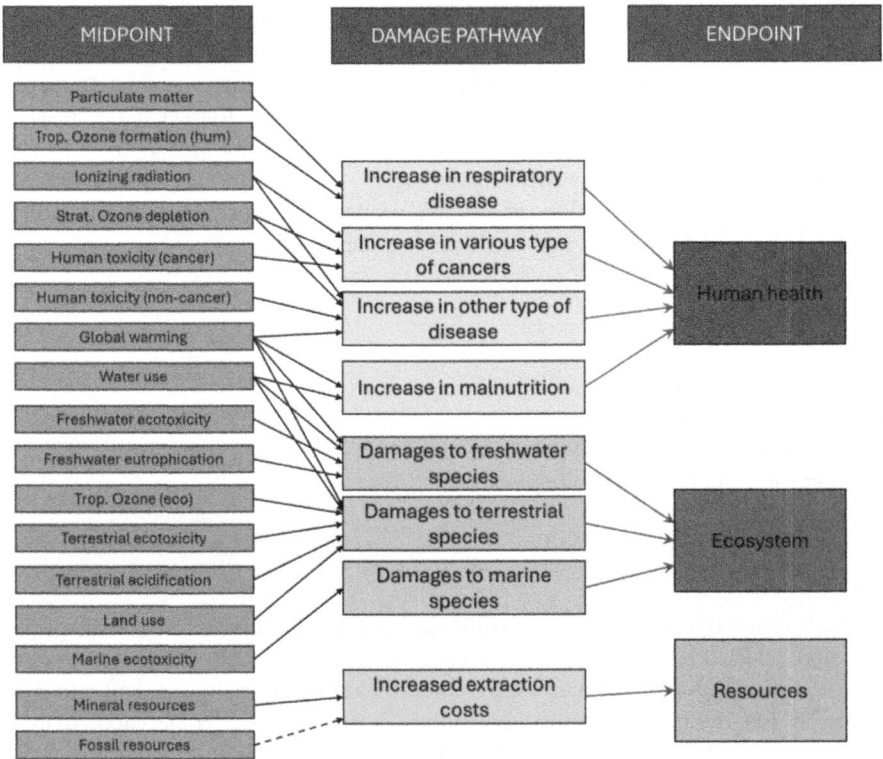

Fig. 1. Overview of the impact categories that are covered in the ReCiPe2016 method, adopted from [13].

Impacts on human health were measured in disability-adjusted life years (DALYs), representing years of life lost due to exposure to harmful environmental effects. Ecosystem damage was calculated in terms of species loss per year, while resource use was evaluated as future economic costs of resource depletion, presented in USD (2013 value).

2.2   Life Cycle Costing

The LCC in this study evaluates the long-term financial feasibility and value generation of various peatland after-use strategies. Four key indicators were selected for this purpose: net present value (NPV), internal rate of return (IRR), profitability index (PI), and the monetary value of ecosystem services. Together, these indicators offer a multi-perspective view of how economically viable each scenario is over its operational lifespan.

The selection of economic indicators was guided by three key criteria: relevance to sustainability decision-making, data availability and consistency, and comparability across land use alternatives. Relevance ensures that each indicator meaningfully reflects long-term economic performance under varying after-use conditions. Indicators such as NPV and IRR provide clear signals about financial viability, while profitability index offers a normalized basis for comparing projects of different scales. The inclusion of ecosystem service valuation reflects an effort to integrate non-market economic contributions of restored peatlands.

The NPV was calculated to assess whether the investment in a given land-use option would generate positive returns over time according to Eq. (1):

$$NPV = \sum_{t=0}^{n} \frac{C_t}{(1 + r)^t} \tag{1}$$

where:

C_t is the net cash flow in year t.
r is the discount rate (in this case, the weighted average cost of capital),
n is the number of periods in the analysis timeframe, and
t is the year index, starting from 0 (the initial investment).

This formula allows for a time-adjusted comparison of future economic returns, accounting for the cost of capital and risk over time. It ensures that scenarios with delayed or uncertain cash inflows are appropriately evaluated in terms of present-day value. The standard discounted cash flow formula was used, taking into account future cash flows adjusted by a discount rate, which in this case corresponds to the weighted average cost of capital (WACC). WACC was determined based on both equity and borrowed capital components, reflecting realistic financing conditions for land rehabilitation projects.

In addition to NPV, the IRR used to evaluate the expected return rate generated by each scenario's projected cash flow. The profitability index, defined as the ratio between total NPV and the initial investment, provided an additional metric to compare different investment options with varying cost levels.

The fourth component of the LCC—ecosystem service valuation—addressed the broader economic benefits delivered by restored peatlands. Although detailed economic valuations for Latvian peatland ecosystem services are limited in scientific literature, which estimated values for provisioning, regulating, and cultural ecosystem services across several land use types. For renewable energy scenarios (solar and wind), no ecosystem service value was assigned, due to lack of data and methodological limitations.

2.3 Social Dimension

The social dimension of sustainability is often considered the least developed within life cycle-based assessments. Nonetheless, it remains a vital component for understanding the broader impacts of land use strategies. In this study, a assessment of social indicators was applied to evaluate ten peatland use scenarios, using four indicators: direct employment, employment generated over the life cycle, workplace injuries, and dependence on external suppliers. The combination of data from public literature, national statistics, professional databases is used.

The direct employment indicator reflects the number of workers engaged during implementation and operation phases, rated on a qualitative scale from 1 (very low) to 5 (very high). Labor-intensive options, such as blueberry and cranberry cultivation, received high scores due to the significant manual effort required for planting, maintenance, and harvesting. In contrast, renaturalization, wetland restoration, and afforestation were associated with minimal labor needs.

The life cycle employment indicator measures job creation across the entire operational timeline, including seasonal labor and value-chain effects. For example, forest-based scenarios considered employment in nursery operations, planting, forest management, and harvesting. Agricultural options are evaluated based on typical labor input per hectare, while job creation in solar and wind energy is estimated using international conversion factors per MW of installed capacity, due to the lack of Latvian-specific data.

Worker safety is assessed using the annual number of occupational injuries reported in each sector. For agriculture, data from the State Labour Inspectorate were used. For solar and wind energy sectors, international statistics were applied to approximate typical injury rates, acknowledging that sector-specific data in Latvia is currently unavailable. This approach enabled a relative risk comparison across all land use scenarios.

The supply chain dependency indicator highlights risks linked to sourcing materials or services from outside Latvia, particularly from regions with lower labor rights standards or political instability.

2.4 Life Cycle Sustainability Assessment

To determine which peatland after-use strategy offers the most sustainable outcome, a multi-criteria decision analysis (MCDA) was carried out using the TOPSIS method. This approach compares each option against an ideal solution across three key dimensions: environmental, economic, social.

Each option is assessed across several indicators, forming a matrix where each element represents the performance of a specific alternative according to a particular criterion. The importance of each criterion is reflected through assigned weights, ensuring the total influence across all criteria sums to one.

Initially, the data is normalized to eliminate scale effects, followed by multiplying each normalized value by the respective criterion weight. The weights assigned to each sustainability criterion (environmental, economic, and social) were derived through a qualitative scoring process informed by expert judgment and iterative internal discussions within the research team. Each dimension was evaluated for its relative importance in the context of post-extraction peatland restoration in Latvia. In this study, equal weights were initially assumed for the environmental, economic, and social dimensions to ensure a balanced assessment in the absence of conclusive stakeholder priorities. This approach provides a neutral baseline, allowing each dimension to contribute equally to the composite sustainability score. Future applications of this method may incorporate context-specific weighting derived from stakeholder engagement or policy-driven prioritization. This produces a weighted decision matrix, forming the basis for the analysis.

Next, two benchmark solutions are determined: one representing the most favorable outcome across all criteria, and the other representing the least favorable. Each alternative is then compared to these benchmarks by calculating the distance to both the best and worst theoretical solutions.

Finally, a relative performance score is derived for each alternative as given in Eq. 1, indicating its closeness to the optimal solution and distance from the least desirable one:

$$(P_i) = \frac{A_i^-}{A_i^+ + A_i^-} \text{ with } i = 1, \ldots, m \tag{1}$$

Pi – Relative closeness of alternative i to the ideal solution. This is the final score that indicates how good an alternative is compared to others. It ranges between 0 and 1. The closer it is to 1, the better (closer to the ideal solution).

Ai+ represents the ideal value of alternative i.

Ai− represents the anti-ideal value of alternative i.

i− index of the alternative. The variable i goes from 1 to m, where m is the total number of alternatives being evaluated.

This enables a ranking of the options, supporting informed decision-making on the preferred course of action. In this context, it helps identify the most suitable approach for peatland reclamation, guided by sustainability criteria and life cycle considerations.

3 Results

These LCA finddings shown in Table 1 confirm that renewable energy recovery best solution in environmental dimension due to higher avoided impact benefits in energy sector for fossil-based electricity generations, while agricultural and grassland conversion carry the highest ecological costs. The moderate environmental performance of renaturalization, afforestation, and wetland crop scenarios supports their consideration as environmentally viable strategies for post-extraction peatland management.

Table 1. Life Cycle Assessment Results

Indicator/Land Use Type	Global Warming Potential kg CO2 eq ha-1 y-1	Human Health DALY	Ecosystem Impact species/year	Resources USD2013
Renaturalisation	6,70E+03	3,53E−05	−3,33E−04	1,36E+00
Paludiculture	5,61E+03	5,03E−03	8,20E−06	7,25E+02
Water Bodies	2,38E+03	4,12E−03	6,10E−06	3,02E+02
Solar Panels	−1,02E+07	−5,42E+00	−2,59E−03	−1,23E+06
Wind Turbines	−2,45E+07	−2,27E+01	−3,60E−02	−2,59E+06
Agriculture (Winter Wheat)	1,94E+06	3,42E+00	2,81E−02	1,08E+05
Grasslands	6,53E+05	1,70E+00	5,61E−04	5,31E+04
Afforestation	1,74E+04	7,23E−04	−3,23E−03	1,47E+01
Blueberries	1,84E+05	4,82E−01	3,66E−03	1,51E+04
Cranberries	−1,04E+03	3,19E−03	3,25E−03	3,02E+02

The findings from LCC shown in Table 2 emphasize the tension between direct financial returns and broader ecosystem value. While infrastructure and market-driven strategies such as energy production and berry cultivation offer revenue potential, nature-based solutions like renaturalization and afforestation deliver substantial non-market benefits. This highlights the need for supportive financial and policy instruments, such as carbon credits or agri-environmental schemes to make ecologically valuable strategies more economically attractive for landowners and investors.

Table 2. Lice Cycle Costing Results

Indicator/Land Use Type	NPV EUR	IRR %	PI %	Monetary value of ecosystem services EUR/ha
Renaturalisation	−4,95E+03	0,00E+00	0,00E+00	2,20E+05
Paludiculture	−2,13E+03	0,00E+00	8,00E−02	1,80E+05
Water Bodies	−5,29E+03	0,00E+00	0,00E+00	1,37E+05
Solar Panels	−6,24E+04	5,00E−02	8,40E−01	0,00E+00
Wind Turbines	7,46E+04	8,40E−02	1,15E+00	0,00E+00
Agriculture (Winter Wheat)	4,66E+03	1,40E−01	3,10E−01	3,12E+03
Grasslands	−2,79E+03	0,00E+00	−2,30E−01	4,50E+03
Afforestation	−4,64E+03	0,00E+00	0,00E+00	1,98E+05
Blueberries	4,72E+04	2,70E−01	3,70E−01	4,65E+04
Cranberries	6,48E+03	9,00E−02	3,60E−01	5,74E+04

The results of social impacts (see Table 3) show renewable energy options were having high a dependency on external suppliers due to their reliance on imported components like turbines and solar panels, often sourced from China, Germany, and other EU countries. Conversely, land uses such as renaturalization, water bodies, and afforestation scored low on this indicator, as they require minimal external inputs. Moderate dependence was identified for berry plantations and paludiculture, largely due to the need for quality planting materials sourced abroad. Labor-intensive land uses, particularly berry cultivation, stand out for their job creation potential. On the other hand, low-intervention solutions like renaturalization and wetland restoration score well in terms of safety and supply chain autonomy but contribute less to employment.

After calculating the combined normalized scores across all three sustainability dimensions (Fig. 2), wind energy development emerges as the most sustainable solution, with a Pi value of 0.750, clearly closest to the ideal. This was followed by solar panels (Pi = 0.426) and blueberry plantations (Pi = 0.416), both of which offered a balanced trade-off between ecological and economic performance.

Conversely, converting peatland into arable farmland, specifically for winter cereals, was found to be the least sustainable option (Pi = 0.251), with grassland establishment (Pi

Table 3. Social Life Cycle Assessment Results

Indicator/Land Use Type	Direct Employment (Employed Persons)	Life Cycle Employment (Jobs Created)	Workplace Injuries (Number of Injuries)	Dependence on External Suppliers (Rating from 1 to 5)
Renaturalisation	1,00E+00	0,00E+00	0,00E+00	1,00E+00
Paludiculture	1,00E+00	0,00E+00	0,00E+00	3,00E+00
Water Bodies	1,00E+00	0,00E+00	0,00E+00	1,00E+00
Solar Panels	3,00E+00	4,25E+02	1,10E+01	5,00E+00
Wind Turbines	3,00E+00	3,27E+02	1,02E+01	5,00E+00
Agriculture (Winter Wheat)	2,00E+00	1,00E+01	5,50E+01	2,00E+00
Grasslands	2,00E+00	5,00E+00	5,50E+01	1,00E+00
Afforestation	2,00E+00	8,50E+01	3,20E+01	1,00E+00
Blueberries	4,00E+00	6,30E+01	5,50E+01	3,00E+00
Cranberries	4,00E+00	4,20E+01	5,50E+01	3,00E+00

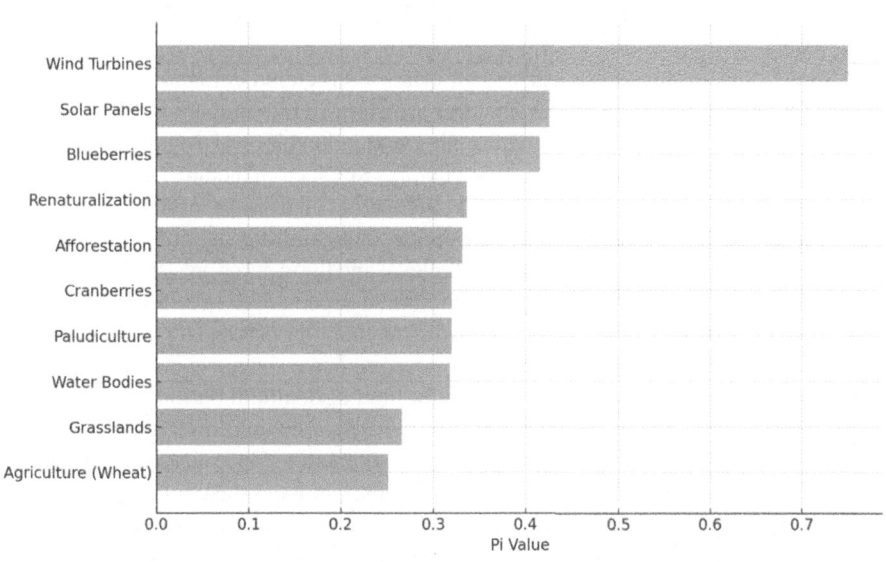

Fig. 2. Ranking of Peatlant Use Alternatives Based on Relative Closeness to the Ideal Solution

= 0.266) ranking only slightly higher. These land uses had relatively poor environmental and social outcomes, despite modest economic returns.

In the context of this assessment, the Pi value represents how close each after-use option comes to the ideal sustainability scenario, as defined by the highest performance across all evaluated criteria. A higher Pi value indicates better overall sustainability, meaning the option performs well across environmental, economic, and social dimensions. Conversely, a lower Pi value reflects a greater distance from the ideal and suggests trade-offs or shortcomings in one or more areas of performance.

4 Conclusion

This study developed a new analytical tool for assessing peatland restoration strategies using a life cycle sustainability approach. The tool integrates environmental, economic, and social dimension, offering a comprehensive evaluation method that had not previously been applied to the full range of potential after-use options for degraded peatlands. Its novelty lies in unifying all three sustainability perspectives into a single assessment. Among the ten evaluated options, wind turbine installation emerged as the most sustainable solution, followed by solar energy, renaturalization, and paludiculture. However, the potential to combine or layer multiple strategies, such as integrating natural rewetting with energy infrastructure, should also be considered in broader planning.

One of the study's key challenges was assessing the social dimension, particularly due to limited available data and the evolving nature of S-LCA methodologies. As such, part of the analysis was guided by expert judgment based on practical experience and literature. A second difficulty was the valuation of ecosystem services, which remains under-researched in Latvia, especially in the peatland context. The study relied on results from the LIFE Restore project, but this area clearly requires further empirical development.

Although the sustainability assessment offers a structured comparison of peatland after-use strategies, local site characteristics play a crucial role in shaping which options are actually feasible or beneficial. These physical and ecological conditions can vary widely and should be considered during planning. Key factors include the type of peatland, peat layer thickness, and degree of decomposition, all of which affect suitability for specific land uses like paludiculture, afforestation, or technical installations. Soil pH and hydrological conditions, such as groundwater level and flood duration, are also critical—particularly for rewetting or cultivation. Additional aspects like terrain roughness and underlying soil structure can influence both implementation costs and long-term stability. For instance, uneven or root-dense ground may complicate solar or wind infrastructure, while poor drainage or substrate instability can limit agricultural options.

Looking forward, the inclusion of a sensitivity analysis would strengthen the robustness of the proposed approach for its application in practice. Since sustainability priorities may vary across policy agendas, funding schemes, or local stakeholder preferences, testing how changes in indicator weightings affect the final rankings would help assess the model's stability. This would also make the tool more adaptable to different planning contexts by revealing how outcomes shift when greater emphasis is placed on environmental, economic, or social criteria. Incorporating such an analysis could further support its use in participatory decision-making and policy development.

Acknowledgments. The work has been developed as part of the Fundamental and Applied Research Project "Sustainable Strategies for the Restoration of Peat Mining Sites (Peat4Res)", project no. lzp-2022/1-0405, within the framework financed by Latvian Science Council.

References

1. Ozola, I.: Holocēna organogēnie nogulumi un to uzkrāšanās apstākļu izmaiņas purvos Ziemeļvidzemē. Latvijas Universitāte (2013). https://dspace-dev.lu.lv/server/api/core/bitstr eams/a88c3d25-d715-43d7-aaa4-3566fcfa50cf/content
2. Salimi, S., Almuktar, S., Scholz, M.: Impact of climate change on wetland ecosystems: a critical review of experimental wetlands. J. Environ. Manage. **286** (2021). https://doi.org/10. 1016/J.JENVMAN.2021.112160
3. Lefèvre, C., Rekik, F., Alcantara, V., Wiese, L.: Carbone organique du solrichesse invisible une (2017)
4. EUKI. Reporting Greenhouse Gas Emissions from Organic Soils in the European Union: Challenges and Opportunities. https://www.euki.de/en/euki-publications/greenhouse-gas-emissi ons-from-organic-soils/
5. O'Brolchain, N., Peters, J.: CAP Policy Brief Peatlands in the new European Union Version 4.8 (2022). https://www.researchgate.net/publication/340829681_CAP_Policy_Brief_Peatla nds_in_the_new_European_Union_Version_48
6. International Peatland Society. Peatlands. https://peatlands.org/peatlands/
7. Kalniņa, L.: https://enciklopedija.lv/skirklis/27677-purvi-Latvij%C4%81
8. Life Restore. Latvijas degradēto kūdrāju inventarizācija un datu bāzes izveide. https://res tore.daba.gov.lv/public/lat/jaunumi/e_zinotajs1/e_zinotajs_nr_3_par_degradeto_kudraju_i nventarizaciju_latvija/
9. LIFE REstore - Rokasgrāmata "Kūdras ieguves ietekmētu teritoriju atbildīga apsaimniekošana un ilgtspējīga izmantošana. https://restore.daba.gov.lv/public/lat/aktivi tates_un_rezultati/rokasgramata_kudras_ieguves_ietekmetu_teritoriju_atbildiga_apsaimnie kosana_un_ilgtspejiga_izmantosana/
10. UNEP. Towards a life cycle sustainability assessment: making informed choices on products/UNEP - UN Environment Programme (2011). https://www.unep.org/resources/report/ towards-life-cycle-sustainability-assessment-making-informed-choices-products
11. Finkbeiner, M., Schau, E., Lehmann, A., Traverso, M.: Towards life cycle sustainability assessment. Sustainability **2**(10), 3309–3322 (2010). https://doi.org/10.3390/SU2103309
12. Krohling, A., Pacheco, A.: A-TOPSIS – an approach based on TOPSIS for ranking evolutionary algorithms. Procedia Comput. Sci. **55**, 308–317 (2015). https://doi.org/10.1016/J.PROCS. 2015.07.054
13. Huijbregts, M.A.J., Steinmann, Z.J.N., Elshout, P.M.F., et al.: ReCiPe2016: a harmonised life cycle impact assessment method at midpoint and endpoint level. Int. J. Life Cycle Assess. **22**, 138–147 (2017). https://doi.org/10.1007/s11367-016-1246-y

Variance-Guided Structured Pruning for Optimized Convolutional Neural Networks

Dildar Shah$^{(\boxtimes)}$ ⓘ, Muhammad Hanif ⓘ, and Naveed Razzaq Butt ⓘ

Ghulam Ishaq Khan Institute of Engineering Sciences and Technology,
Swabi, Pakistan
dildarsyed711@gmail.com, {muhammad.hanif,naveed.butt}@giki.edu.pk

Abstract. Deep learning (DL) has changed the landscape of various fields, but its high computing needs make it hard to use in places with limited resources. To address these limitations, this paper presents a novel structured pruning approach that dynamically identifies and removes nonsignificant filters during training using a variance-based threshold. Unlike conventional pruning methods that permanently eliminate filters, our approach applies soft pruning by temporarily deactivating filters with low activation variance, setting their weights to zero, while preserving the original network structure. We retain filters that contribute to some fixed percentage of the total variance in each layer, pruning the rest. Although the variance percentage is fixed, the pruning threshold varies across layers. Importantly, pruned filters remain in the network but are not updated, as their gradients are masked to zero. Experimental evaluations on CIFAR-10, CIFAR-100, and Tiny ImageNet datasets demonstrate that our method reduces computational cost by approximately 58.09% with minimal impact on accuracy.

Keywords: Deep Learning · Resource-constrained AI · Neural network pruning · Structured pruning · Variance · train-time pruning

1 Introduction

Convolutional Neural Networks (CNNs) are commonly applied in areas like image and speech recognition, but they usually need a lot of computing power, such as GPUs or TPUs [12]. In resource-limited environments such as embedded systems, IoT, and mobile devices, model training is often constrained by the lack of computational power [14]. To efficiently utilize these models, it is essential to maintain a proper balance between the network architecture and the number of parameters. The key tunable parameters in neural networks are weights and biases. Adjusting these parameters determines how the network processes input data to achieve the desired outcome. Moreover, the number of parameters significantly impacts performance. Too many parameters increase tuning costs and require more memory, while too few parameters can limit the learning capacity

© The Author(s), under exclusive license to Springer Nature Switzerland AG 2026
O. Gervasi et al. (Eds.): ICCSA 2025 Workshops, LNCS 15899, pp. 230–240, 2026.
https://doi.org/10.1007/978-3-031-97663-6_20

of the network, leading to suboptimal performance [3]. Therefore, optimizing the model structure while keeping computational constraints in mind is crucial for achieving efficiency and accuracy.

Considering these limitations, researchers are focusing on developing high-performing, lightweight networks that ensure better generalization and efficient parameter storage within a single-chip memory [9]. In Machine Learning (ML), finding an optimal network architecture for a specific task remains a challenging and less-understood problem. Additionally, computational overhead in CNNs is often caused by multiple convolutional layers, which significantly increase processing requirements.

Pruning methods can be broadly divided into two categories: structured and unstructured. Individual weights depending on magnitude thresholds are eliminated via unstructured pruning, which frequently results in high compression rates with negligible effect on accuracy [7]. On the other hand, structural pruning reduces computational cost and speeds up inference by eliminating entire sets of weights, such as filters or channels [1].

Researchers are focusing on optimally selecting the features and passing them to the next layer. This helps reduce energy consumption and memory usage. Methods like knowledge distillation, quantization, and pruning are used to make this possible. These methods optimize the model's size and complexity with minimal loss in accuracy. Particularly, network pruning is the most popular as it not only removes unnecessary and redundant connections but maintains the performance as well [1].

1.1   Network Pruning

Network pruning is a technique used to reduce the size and complexity of a trained model by removing nonsignificant parameters, such as connections or neurons. Pruning can be represented mathematically as follows.

$$\tilde{f}(x) = f(x; \mathcal{T}(W)) \quad \text{where} \quad \mathcal{T}(W) = M \odot W, \tag{1}$$

where $\tilde{f}(x)$ is the pruned model, $f(x; W)$ is the vanilla input model with parameters W, M is a binary mask, $\odot$ denotes element-wise multiplication, and $\mathcal{T}$ is a pruning operation. If fine tuning is employed, then Eq. (1) can be updated as:

$$\tilde{f}(x) = f(x; W'), \tag{2}$$

where W' are the weights obtained by fine-tuning $M \odot W$. Likewise, if the pruning is applied iteratively, then for $t \in \{1, ..., T\}$ pruning steps, we have

$$\tilde{f}_t(x) = f(x; \mathcal{T}_t(W)) \quad \text{where} \quad \mathcal{T}_t(W) = M_t \odot W'_t \tag{3}$$

where M_t represents a binary mask by thresholding the fine-tuned weights W'_{t-1} from the previous step, and W'_t denote the updated weights by applying the fine tuning to the masked weights.

Pruning can be performed at different stages of model training: pre-training, post-training, or during training. Pruning during training is the most effective as it allows the network to adapt to the pruning process. Various rules can be applied to decide which connections to remove, like pruning based on weight magnitude or how sensitive the model is to certain weights [4]. Previous studies have shown that many weights can be made close to zero without seriously impacting the model's performance [5]. Various pruning techniques in the literature rely on L_1 and L_2-norm-based loss functions to evaluate the importance of weights [13]. Some researchers focus on sensitivity analysis to identify and retain the most critical parameters, pruning the rest [11]. One of the most widely used criteria is loss-change-based pruning, where parameters are evaluated based on their impact on the overall loss, and the less important ones are removed accordingly [15]. However, most of the existing methods either apply hard pruning, which permanently removes weights from the network architecture, potentially degrading model performance, or use global thresholds that are not layer-specific, which may lead to the loss of important weights across several layers [10].

1.2   Contributions

To overcome these limitations, this work introduces a dynamic soft pruning technique that uses a variance-based threshold to remove less significant parameters during training. Unlike traditional pruning methods, our approach triggers pruning after every few iterations, with a specific threshold set for each layer. We maintain the original network topology while softly removing non-significant parameters, allowing us to achieve true sparsity without the risk of reactivation. Below is a list of our main contributions.

- We employ soft pruning inside the epoch, which differs from conventional methods where pruning typically occurs on an epoch-to-epoch basis.
- We retain only the filters that account for some predefined percentage of the total variance and discard the rest.
- Although the target variance percentage is fixed, each layer has its own threshold. This layer-specific approach ensures that useful information is retained across all layers.
- Depending on the model's complexity, we do not apply pruning after every epoch. Instead, pruning is triggered only after a few epochs, starting from a predefined point in training.

The rest of the paper is structured as follows. In Sect. 2, the idea of variance and its importance in pruning are covered. In the context of pruning, the ResNet-50 architecture is summarized in Sect. 3. Section 4 presents our variance-driven threshold-based pruning method. Results from experiments comparing ResNet-50's performance with and without pruning are reported in Sect. 5. The investigation is finally concluded, and the main findings are summed up in Sect. 6.

2   Variance

It is a statistical measure that illustrates how much the values in a dataset deviate from the mean. It reflects the degree of spread or variability of the data points. Mathematically, it is defined as:

$$\sigma^2 = \frac{1}{N} \sum_{i=1}^{N} (x_i - \mu)^2, \tag{4}$$

where σ^2 is the variance, x_i are the data points, μ is the mean, and N is the total number of samples. In Eq. 2, we use division by N because the variance is computed over all available data, not a sample.

2.1   Significance of Utilizing Variance in Pruning

In CNNs, different filters capture different levels of abstraction. High-variance filters indicate strong responses to diverse input patterns, while low-variance filters remain inactive or redundant. Let each convolutional layer L_i contain a set of filters:

$$\mathbb{F}_i = \{F_1, F_2, \ldots, F_{n_i}\} \tag{5}$$

where n_i represents the total number of filters in the i-th layer. Each filter $F_j \in \mathbb{R}^{C \times K \times K}$ is a tensor with C input channels and spatial dimensions $K \times K$. The importance of a filter is determined based on the variance of its activation outputs across the batch and spatial dimensions. The variance of the i-th filter's activation outputs is computed as:

$$\sigma_i^2 = \frac{1}{BHW} \sum_{b=1}^{B} \sum_{h=1}^{H} \sum_{w=1}^{W} \left(A_i(b, h, w) - \mu_i \right)^2, \tag{6}$$

where $A_i(b, h, w)$ is the activation value of filter i for batch index b and spatial position (h, w), and μ_i is the corresponding mean. Once the variance is computed, all the filters in layer L_i are arranged in ascending order, as given below in Eq. 7.

$$\sigma_{(1)}^2 \leq \sigma_{(2)}^2 \leq \cdots \leq \sigma_{(n_i)}^2. \tag{7}$$

This ordering enables the identification of filters with the lowest variance, which should be pruned. For a given pruning percentage p, we define the number of filters to be retained as follows.

$$k_i = \lfloor n_i \cdot p \rfloor. \tag{8}$$

The floor function $\lfloor \cdot \rfloor$ in Eq. 8 returns the greatest integer less than or equal to the input. The number of filters to be pruned is:

$$r_i = n_i - k_i = \lfloor n_i \cdot (1 - p) \rfloor. \tag{9}$$

The pruning threshold for layer L_i is the variance of the r_i-th filter in the sorted list as given in Eq. 10 below.

$$\tau_i = \sigma^2_{(r_i)}. \tag{10}$$

All filters with variances lower than τ_i are pruned by setting their weights to zero. Since each layer has a different number of filters and a different variance distribution, the threshold τ_i varies from layer to layer. i.e., some layers may lose more filters than others, depending on their variance distribution.

3   Residual Network in the Context of Pruning

This section gives a short overview of ResNet-50 concerning pruning. ResNet-50 is a deep CNN consisting of 50 layers, which include convolutional, pooling, and fully connected layers. Its key innovation, residual connections, helps bypass intermediate layers, improving gradient flow and addressing the vanishing gradient problem [6]. Originally, CNNs were used for tasks like handwritten digit recognition, but ResNet-50 significantly enhanced their depth and efficiency [8]. The huge amount of multiply-and-accumulate (MAC) operations in the convolutional and fully connected layers makes the architecture computationally demanding, even though it is successful. Optimization techniques, such as converting convolutions to matrix-matrix multiplications, have been proposed to mitigate this [2]. Our approach reduces this cost by dynamically pruning filters during training, using variance-based thresholding to remove less significant filters. The architecture is shown in Fig. 1, and the next section explains the pruning method in detail.

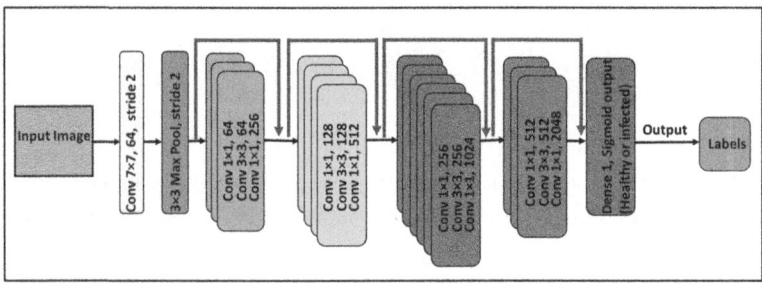

Fig. 1. ResNet-50 architecture with skip connections.

4   Methodology

This section describes our variance-based soft pruning approach for CNNs. The technique prunes the least significant convolutional filters after assessing each filter's significance based on its low activation variance.

4.1   Overview of the Pruning Methodology

The proposed method computes the variance of each filter's activation output and prunes the least significant ones. We employ soft pruning, i.e., pruned filters are set to zero rather than removed from the network architecture. A binary mask M is applied to enforce pruning:

$$M_k = \begin{cases} 1, & \text{if } I_k > \tau, \\ 0, & \text{otherwise.} \end{cases} \tag{11}$$

where I_k represents the importance of the k-th filter computed as the variance of its activation outputs. The pruning mask is applied in-place on the convolutional layer weights to zero out pruned filters after computing activations.

During the forward pass, the masked filters are used for computation:

$$\hat{F}_k = M_k \cdot F_k,$$

where F_k and $\hat{F}_k$ represent weights of original and masked filters respectively. The layer output is then computed as given below in Eq. 12.

$$Y = \mathcal{F}(X * \hat{F}), \tag{12}$$

where $\hat{F}$ represents the masked filter tensor, X is the input tensor, $\mathcal{F}$ is the activation function, and $*$ denotes the convolution operation. During the backward pass, gradients are only computed for unpruned filters as given in Eq. 13. For pruned filters, the gradients are explicitly set to zero.

$$\frac{\partial \mathcal{L}}{\partial \hat{F}_k} = M_k \left(\frac{\partial \mathcal{L}}{\partial F_k} \right). \tag{13}$$

The pruning process is adaptive and dependent on the variance distribution in each layer. It ensures that filters contributing the least to the model's learned representation are removed while preserving high-variance filters that encode more essential features. Algorithm 1 presents the pseudo-code for the proposed method.

Algorithm 1: VarianceâĂŚBased Soft Filter Pruning

Input: Model, optimizer, loss function, pruning parameters
Output: Pruned filters

1 **for** *epoch = 1* **to** `num_epochs` **do**
2   **for** *each miniâĂŚbatch* (x, y) *in training data* **do**
3   forward pass; compute $\mathcal{L}$;
4   backward pass; compute gradients;
5   apply pruning mask M; update weights;
6   **for** *each convolutional layer in model* **do**
7   compute activation variance per filter;
8   sort filters ascending by variance;
9   set threshold τ from `pruning_fraction`;
10   update pruning mask M;
11   **end**
12   **end**
13   update learning-rate scheduler;
14   check early stopping on validation;
15 **end**
16 compute and store pruning stats;

$$T_{train} = t_{end} - t_{start}. \tag{14}$$

where t_{start} and t_{end} are the timestamps recorded at the beginning and end of training, respectively. A stochastic gradient descent (SGD) optimizer with a learning rate of 0.003, momentum of 0.9, and weight decay of 0.0001 is used for training. During training, a step-based scheduler modifies the learning rate. Data augmentation methods like horizontal flipping, random cropping, and normalization are used to improve generalization.

5   Results and Discussion

This section presents the experimental results from training a ResNet-50 model on the publicly available datasets[1]: CIFAR-10, CIFAR-100, and Tiny ImageNet. datasets. We use ResNet-50 as a baseline dense model and train it on the two datasets. For the experiments, we utilized a system with an AMD Ryzen 9 7950X 16-Core Processor @ 4.50 GHz, 64.0 GB of RAM (63.1 GB usable), running a 64-bit operating system with an x64-based processor. Initially, we train the baseline model on CIFAR-10, adjusting the final fully connected layer to have 10 output units to match the number of classes in the dataset. The training lasted for 105 epochs, resulting in a final validation accuracy of 97.02%, as shown in Fig. 2 (top).

---

[1] https://www.cs.toronto.edu/~kriz/cifar.html,   https://huggingface.co/datasets/ Maysee/tiny-imagenet.

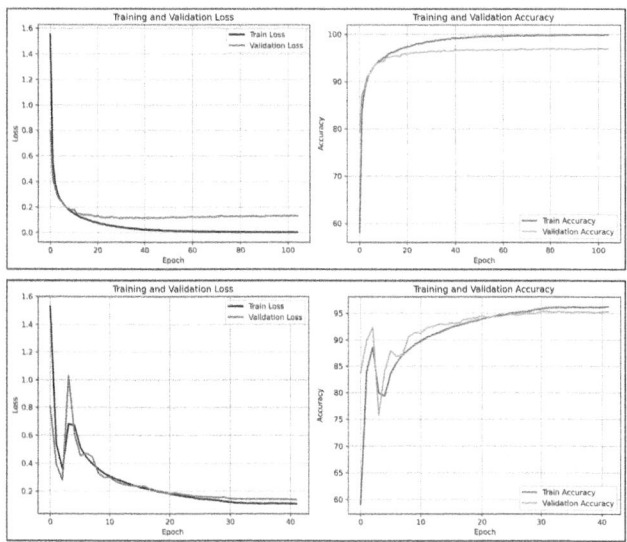

Fig. 2. Training and validation loss and accuracy of the baseline dense model (top) and the pruned model (bottom) on the CIFAR-10 dataset.

The baseline model consists of 23,528,522 trainable parameters, and the training process was completed in 4055.16 s. We significantly reduce computation time by integrating iterative variance-based pruning into the training process while maintaining high accuracy, as shown in Fig. 2 (bottom). The pruned model achieves a final validation accuracy of 96.66% on CIFAR-10, with a reduced training time of 1699.38 s. The initial performance drop in Fig. 2 (bottom) is due to structured pruning, where entire filters along with their associated connections are removed at once. This causes an abrupt drop in accuracy, which stabilizes over subsequent epochs as the model adapts.

After achieving strong results on CIFAR-10, we extend our experiments to the more complex CIFAR-100 dataset, which contains 100 classes. Similar to the previous setup, we modify the final fully connected layer to include 100 units to match the number of classes. The model is trained for 95 epochs, achieving a final validation accuracy of 84.47%, as shown in Fig. 3 (top).

The baseline model consists of 23,712,932 trainable parameters, with the training process completing in 3,671.78 s. By incorporating iterative pruning during training, the model achieves a significant reduction in training time with minimal accuracy loss. The pruned model attains a final validation accuracy of 83.37%, while the total training time is reduced to 2175.45 s, as illustrated in Fig. 3 (bottom).

Finally, we evaluate the baseline model on the Tiny ImageNet dataset, which comprises 200 classes and presents higher complexity and greater variability compared to CIFAR-10 and CIFAR-100. To accommodate the increased number of classes, the model architecture was adapted by modifying the final fully

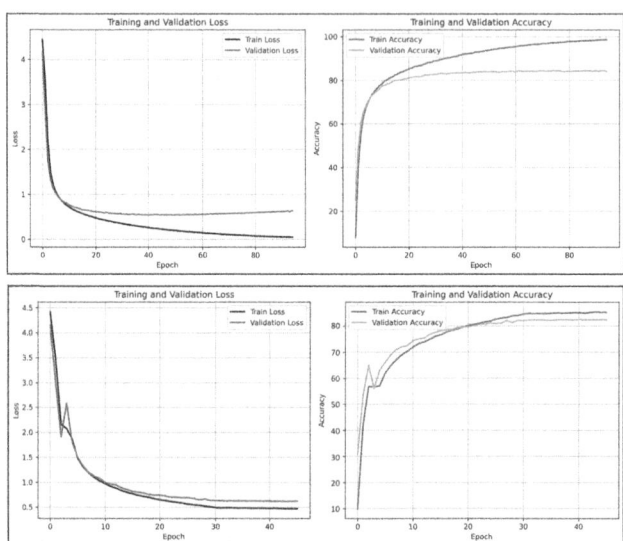

Fig. 3. Training and validation loss and accuracy of the baseline dense model (top) and the pruned model (bottom) on the CIFAR-100 dataset.

connected layer to produce 200 output logits. The model was trained for 60 epochs, achieving a final test accuracy of 82.36%, as illustrated in Fig. 4 (top). These results demonstrate the model's robustness and capacity to generalize effectively to large-scale, fine-grained image classification tasks.

The baseline model comprises $25,966,832$ trainable parameters, with the complete training process requiring $5,810.56$ s. By integrating pruning into the training pipeline, consistent with the methodology used in previous experiments, the model achieves a final validation accuracy of 81.37% on the Tiny ImageNet dataset with a substantial reduction in training time to 3496.15 s, as shown in Fig. 4 (bottom).

The baseline model and its pruned counterpart are compared on CIFAR-10, CIFAR-100, and Tiny ImageNet datasets to evaluate the effect of pruning. The outcomes demonstrate the benefits of pruning, particularly its ability to reduce training times without compromising accuracy too much. Notably, there is very little accuracy loss between datasets, indicating that the suggested trimming technique works. Since this kind of work is rarely explored in the literature, we can not find a direct comparison with any method in the literature. Table 1 provides a thorough comparison of our baseline and pruned models' performance.

On CIFAR-10, pruning reduced the training duration from 4055.16 s to 1699.38 s, reflecting an approximate 58.09% reduction. Despite this significant computational improvement, the test accuracy declined only slightly from 97.02% to 96.66%, resulting in a minimal accuracy drop of 0.36.

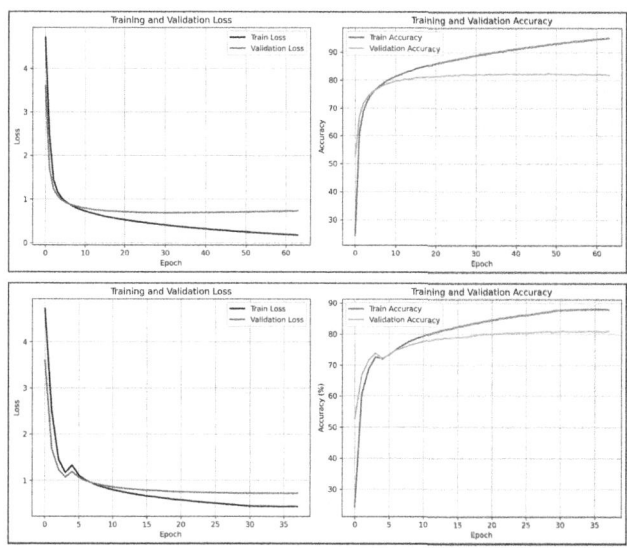

Fig. 4. Training and validation loss and accuracy of the baseline dense model (top) and the pruned model (bottom) on the Tiny ImageNet dataset.

Table 1. Results comparison of baseline model and its pruned counterpart

Dataset	Model	Training Time (s)	Time Reduction (%)	Test Accuracy (%)	Accuracy Drop (Baseline − Pruned)
CIFAR-10	Baseline	4055.16	58.09	97.02	0.36
	Pruned	1699.38		96.66	
CIFAR-100	Baseline	3671.78	40.75	84.47	1.1
	Pruned	2175.45		83.37	
Tiny ImageNet	Baseline	5810.56	39.83	82.36	0.99
	Pruned	3496.15		81.37	

On CIFAR-100, the pruning approach lowered the training time from 3671.78 s to 2175.45 s, marking a 40.75% reduction. The test accuracy decreased marginally from 84.47% to 83.37%, yielding a modest drop of 1.1.

On Tiny ImageNet, the training time reduced to 3496.15 s, showing a total training time reduction of 39.83% with a minimal loss of 0.99 in the final test accuracy.

These results demonstrate that the pruning technique effectively minimizes computational demands while preserving model performance.

6 Conclusion

In this article, we proposed a dynamic soft-pruning method based on variance analysis to address the computational challenges of deep learning models. Unlike conventional pruning techniques that permanently remove weights, our method identifies and prunes less important weights during training. This layer-wise pruning approach, which does not depend on a global criterion, ensures precise pruning tailored to each layer's specific characteristics. Our experiments on the CIFAR-10, CIFAR-100, and Tiny ImageNet datasets show that this method significantly reduces training time with minimal impact on accuracy. The results demonstrate the effectiveness of our approach in producing efficient neural networks suitable for environments with limited computational resources.

References

1. Anwar, S., Hwang, K., Sung, W.: Structured pruning of deep convolutional neural networks. ACM J. Emerg. Technol. Comput. Syst. **13**(3), 1–18 (2017)
2. Chellapilla, K., Puri, S., Simard, P.: High-performance convolutional neural networks for document processing. In: Tenth International Workshop on Frontiers in Handwriting Recognition. Suvisoft (2006)
3. Dauphin, Y.N., Bengio, Y.: Big neural networks waste capacity. arXiv preprint arXiv:1301.3583 (2013)
4. Han, S., Mao, H., Dally, W.J.: A deep neural network compression pipeline: pruning, quantization, Huffman encoding. arXiv preprint arXiv:1510.00149 **10** (2015)
5. Han, S., Pool, J., Tran, J., Dally, W.: Learning both weights and connections for efficient neural networks. In: Advances in Neural Information Processing Systems, vol. 28 (2015)
6. He, K., Zhang, X., Ren, S., Sun, J.: Deep residual learning for image recognition. In: Proceedings of the IEEE Conference on Computer Vision and Pattern Recognition, pp. 770–778 (2016)
7. Lazarevich, I., Kozlov, A., Malinin, N.: Post-training deep neural network pruning via layer-wise calibration. In: Proceedings of the IEEE/CVF International Conference on Computer Vision, pp. 798–805 (2021)
8. LeCun, Y., Bottou, L., Bengio, Y., Haffner, P.: Gradient-based learning applied to document recognition. Proc. IEEE **86**(11), 2278–2324 (1998)
9. Li, Z., Li, H., Meng, L.: Model compression for deep neural networks: a survey. Computers **12**(3), 60 (2023)
10. Liu, J., Zhang, X., Guo, Y., Lin, D., Hu, H.: Dynamic sparse training: Find efficient sparse network from scratch. arXiv preprint arXiv:2005.06870 (2020)
11. Santacroce, M., Wen, Z., Shen, Y., Li, Y.: What matters in the structured pruning of generative language models? arXiv preprint arXiv:2302.03773 (2023)
12. Simonyan, K., Zisserman, A.: Very deep convolutional networks for large-scale image recognition. arXiv preprint arXiv:1409.1556 (2014)
13. Sun, M., Liu, Z., Bair, A., Kolter, J.Z.: A simple and effective pruning approach for large language models. arXiv preprint arXiv:2306.11695 (2023)
14. Thompson, N.C., Greenewald, K., Lee, K., Manso, G.F.: The computational limits of deep learning. arXiv preprint arXiv:2007.05558 (2020)
15. You, Z., Yan, K., Ye, J., Ma, M., Wang, P.: Gate decorator: global filter pruning method for accelerating deep convolutional neural networks. In: Advances in Neural Information Processing Systems, vol. 32 (2019)

YOLOv11-SAMNet: A Hybrid Detection and Segmentation Framework for Urine Sediment Analysis

Sania Akhtar[1]([✉]), Muhammad Hanif[1], Hamdi Melih Saraoglu[2], Sham Lal[3], and Muhammad Waqas Arshad[4]([✉])

[1] Aerial Robotics and Vision Laboratory, GIK Institute of Engineering Sciences and Technology, Topi 23460, Pakistan
{sania.akhtar,Muhammad.hanif}@giki.edu.pk
[2] Department of Electrical and Electronics, Kutahya Dumlupinar University, Kutahya, Turkey
hmelih.saraoglu@dpu.edu.tr
[3] Faculty of Computing and AI, Air University, Islamabad, Pakistan
231183@students.au.edu.pk
[4] Department of Computer Science and Engineering, University of Bologna, 40126 Bologna, Italy
muhammadwaqas.arsha2@unibo.it

Abstract. Urinalysis plays a vital role in diagnosing kidney diseases and urinary tract infections, but conventional manual analysis is often subjective, time-intensive, and prone to variability. Existing detection and segmentation methods struggle with accurately identifying small and irregularly shaped urine sediment particles, leading to inconsistencies in results. To overcome these limitations, we introduce YOLOv11-SAMNet, a novel one-stage instance segmentation model that combines the YOLOv11 detector with the Segment Anything Model (SAM) for 14 classes. Our approach enhances both detection precision and segmentation accuracy by leveraging a feature extraction backbone for capturing key image details, a multi-scale fusion neck for integrating diverse feature representations, and a detection and segmentation head to refine instance segmentation, followed by a bounding box. The model performs exceptionally well on well-defined structures, such as Leukocytes (94.3% *mAP@50*) and Epithelial cells (92.5% *mAP@50*), but encounters challenges when segmenting small and irregular elements like bacteria (33.8% *mAP@50*) and mucus (27.2% *mAP@50*). To further enhance model performance, we developed an expert-assisted data preprocessing pipeline to improve the quality of training data. Our findings highlight the potential of YOLOv11-SAMNet in automating urinalysis, offering a more efficient and objective alternative to traditional manual analysis, ultimately contributing to improved clinical diagnostics.

Keywords: Yolov11 · Urine Sediment Analysis · SAM · Detection · Segmentation

© The Author(s), under exclusive license to Springer Nature Switzerland AG 2026
O. Gervasi et al. (Eds.): ICCSA 2025 Workshops, LNCS 15899, pp. 241–251, 2026.
https://doi.org/10.1007/978-3-031-97663-6_21

1 Introduction

Urinalysis plays a vital role in diagnosing kidney diseases and urinary tract infections (UTIs), helping detect conditions such as leukocyturia, proteinuria, and hematuria [1]. Microscopic examination of urinary sediment, comprising red blood cells (RBCs), white blood cells (WBCs), crystals, and other particles—provides essential insights into underlying medical conditions [2]. However, manual sediment analysis is often time-consuming, labor-intensive, and prone to observer variability, underscoring the need for reliable automated solutions. In recent years, deep learning has emerged as a powerful tool for automating urine sediment analysis, particularly through object detection and segmentation techniques. Nonetheless, most existing methods focus exclusively on either detecting particles or segmenting their boundaries, rarely addressing both simultaneously. This narrow focus limits the diagnostic value of such systems, as effective urinalysis requires not only accurate localization but also detailed morphological interpretation of sediment particles. For instance, previous studies using YOLOv5 variants [3] have achieved notable detection performance but did not incorporate instance-level segmentation, leaving a critical gap in comprehensive analysis.

To overcome this limitation, we propose YOLOv11-SAMNet, a novel one-stage instance segmentation model that seamlessly integrates the YOLOv11 detector with the Segment Anything Model (SAM). Unlike two-stage approaches such as Mask R-CNN, which achieve high accuracy at the cost of complex post-processing and longer inference times, our method offers a real-time, end-to-end solution that is well-suited for clinical workflows. One-stage instance segmentation models are gaining momentum in medical imaging for their ability to balance speed and precision, qualities essential for time-sensitive diagnostics. The proposed framework further incorporates expert-assisted data preprocessing strategies, including label verification, image quality enhancement, and data validation. These measures help ensure the robustness of the training dataset, thereby improving both detection and segmentation outcomes. YOLOv11-SAMNet features a three-part architecture: a backbone for hierarchical feature extraction, a neck for multi-scale feature fusion, and a head designed for simultaneous detection and segmentation. To the best of our knowledge, this is the first one-stage YOLO-based model tailored specifically for 14 urine sediment classes, achieving significant improvements in classification and localization accuracy. The key contributions of this paper are as follows:

- **Development of YOLOv11-SAMNet:** We present a novel one-stage instance segmentation framework that integrates the YOLOv11 object detector with the Segment Anything Model (SAM). This hybrid design is tailored to provide accurate and efficient segmentation of urine sediment particles in microscopic imagery.
- **Expert-Assisted Data Pre processing:** We introduce a systematic pre-processing pipeline involving domain expert validation, accurate labeling, quality enhancement, and data integrity checks to ensure high-quality inputs that enhance overall model performance.

– **Multi-Class Segmentation for Urine Sediment Analysis:** This work pioneers the application of a one-stage YOLO-based instance segmentation framework for 14 distinct urine sediment classes, significantly enhancing the accuracy of both detection and classification.

The remainder of this paper is organized as follows: Sect. 2 reviews the relevant literature. Section 3 outlines the proposed methodology and model architecture. Section 4 presents the output generation process. Section 5 discusses the experimental setup and results. Finally, Sect. 6 concludes the paper with key findings and future directions.

2   Related Work

One-stage models like YOLO perform detection and segmentation in a single pass, offering speed and efficiency. In contrast, two-stage models such as Mask R-CNN provide higher accuracy but with greater computational cost. Our proposed YOLOv11-SAMNet integrates the speed of one-stage detection with the segmentation precision of SAM, aiming for balanced, real-time performance in urinalysis. Table 1 and 2 One-stage models like YOLO perform detection and segmentation in a single pass, offering speed and efficiency.

Table 1. Summary of One-Stage Instance Segmentation Methods for Cell Segmentation

Reference	Problem Addressed	Method Used	Dataset/Domains	Performance
[1]	Slow, subjective manual urine sediment analysis; existing methods lack accuracy and speed for small, dense targets	YOLOv5n with FCN-enhanced head, multi-scale feature fusion	Custom urine sediment dataset (500 images)	mAP50 = 91.8%, FPS = 63.3
[5]	Speed and efficiency limitations in cell segmentation	Cell-DETR (Transformer + CNN)	Cell segmentation dataset	Jaccard 0.82 (A), 0.84 (B)
[6]	Heterogeneity in breast tumor cells	SOLOv2 for tumor cell instance segmentation	Breast tumor dataset	mAP$_{50}$ = 68.00%

Table 2. Summary of Two-Stage Instance Segmentation Methods for Cell Segmentation

Reference	Problem Addressed	Method Used	Dataset/Domains	Performance
[7]	Weak boundaries, overlapping cells	Mask R-CNN with anchor box adjustment	Cancer cell dataset	IoU 87.9%
[8]	Variation in cell shape	Mask R-CNN with contour refinement	Live cell dataset	F1-score 89.5%
[9]	Clumped objects, high overlap	Mask R-CNN with attention mechanism	Histopathology images	IoU 92.3%
[10]	Small objects in microscopy images	Mask R-CNN with feature fusion	Fluorescence microscopy dataset	Mean IoU 84.6%, Error Rate 2.7%

3   Methodology

The proposed approach, illustrated in Fig. 1, integrates YOLOv11 with the Segment Anything Model (SAM) to enable accurate instance segmentation of urine sediment particles. It comprises three main stages: expert-assisted data preprocessing, feature extraction, and instance segmentation.

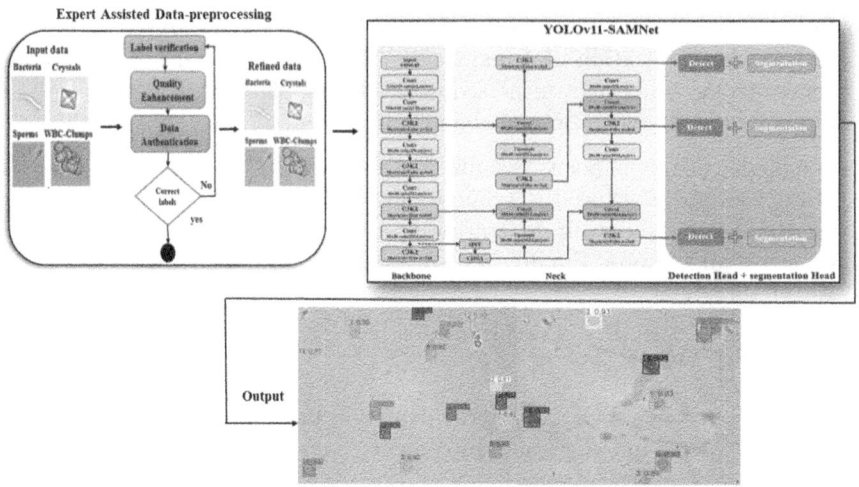

Fig. 1. Workflow of the proposed methodology

3.1 Expert-Assisted Data Preprocessing

The first stage ensures high-quality data labeling and refinement through verification by medical experts, allowing for the correction of inaccurate labels before advancing to the next phase.

3.2 YOLOv11-SAMNet Architecture

The YOLOv11-SAMNet architecture is composed of three key components: the backbone, neck, and head.

Backbone Network: The Conv Block processes input of size $C \times H \times W$ using a 2D convolution, Batch Normalization, and SiLU activation.

Neck Network: The neck network enhances feature fusion across multiple scales to improve detection and segmentation performance. It employs upsampling and down sampling operations to integrate shallow and deep features.

Head Network: The head network comprises two primary branches:

- Object Detection Head: Responsible for bounding box regression and object classification. It includes three detection heads operating at different spatial resolutions (32×32, 64×64, and 128×128), as shown in Fig. 1.
- Instance Segmentation Head: This branch integrates the Segment Anything Model (SAM) for precise instance-level segmentation. It processes features from the C3 layers of the neck using a lightweight fully convolutional network

(FCN) composed of three convolutional layers followed by an upsampling module. The FCN refines deep feature maps to generate high-resolution segmentation masks.

The overall loss function of YOLOv11-SAMNet consists of four components and is defined as follows:

$$L_{\text{total}} = L_{\text{box}} + L_{\text{cls}} + L_{\text{obj}} + L_{\text{seg}}. \tag{1}$$

where L_{box} is the bounding box regression loss, L_{cls} is the classification loss, L_{obj} is the object confidence loss, and L_{seg} is the segmentation loss.

3.3 Bounding Box Regression Loss

The bounding box regression in YOLOv11 utilizes the Complete Intersection over Union (CIoU) loss, which integrates additional components to account for aspect ratio consistency and center point distance, thereby improving localization accuracy:

$$L_{\text{bbox}} = 1 - \text{CIoU}(d, d_{gt}) + \frac{\psi^2(d, d_{gt})}{s^2} + \gamma u. \tag{2}$$

where d and d_{gt} represent the predicted and ground truth bounding box coordinates, respectively; ψ^2 denotes the squared Euclidean distance between the center points; s is the diagonal length of the smallest enclosing box; and u is a penalty term for aspect ratio discrepancy, modulated by a weighting factor γ.

3.4 Classification and Object Loss

In YOLOv11, both the classification lossL_{class} and $L_{\text{obj\_conf}}$ are computed using Distribution Focal Loss (DFL). This loss function is specifically designed to enhance classification accuracy in dense object detection tasks by modeling the distribution over continuous regression targets. The DFL effectively balances confidence learning and class prediction, and is defined as:

$$L_{\text{class}} = -\frac{1}{M} \sum_{j=1}^{M} \left[(1 - q_j)^\delta z_j \log(q_j) \right]. \tag{3}$$

where M is the total number of predictions, q_j is the predicted probability of class j, z_j is the ground truth label, and δ is the focusing parameter that downweights easy examples to focus on hard-to-classify instances.

Similarly, the object confidence loss is formulated as:

$$L_{\text{obj\_conf}} = -\frac{1}{M} \sum_{j=1}^{M} \left[z_j \log(\sigma(r_j)) + (1 - z_j) \log(1 - \sigma(r_j)) \right]. \tag{4}$$

where r_j is the objectness score for the predicted bounding box, and $\sigma(.)$ is the sigmoid function.

3.5 Segmentation Loss

The segmentation loss incorporates pixel-wise loss with instance-based refinement from SAM-generated masks:

$$L_{\text{seg}} = -\frac{1}{M} \sum_{k=1}^{M} \frac{1}{B_k} \sum_{l=1}^{D_k} \left[\beta g_k^r \log(g_k^q) + (1-\beta)(1-g_k^r) \log(1-g_k^q) \right] \times v_l \times \text{Trim}(c_l).$$

(5)

where B_k is the area of the predicted mask, g_k^r and g_k^q represent the ground truth and predicted masks, β is a balancing factor, v_l is a weight term emphasizing boundary regions, and $\text{Trim}(c_l)$ ensures loss computation only within the bounding box:

$$\text{Trim}(c_l) = \begin{cases} 1, & \text{if } c_l \in S_k \text{ and } g_k^q > \delta \\ 0, \text{otherwise} \end{cases}.$$

(6)

where S_k is the predicted bounding box, and δ is a mask confidence threshold to filter low-confidence regions.

4 Output Generation

The final output of YOLOv11-SAMNet, illustrated in Fig. 4, includes:

- Bounding boxes annotated with classification scores for detected urine sediment particles.
- High-resolution instance segmentation masks for each identified particle, enabling precise localization and shape delineation.

This integrated methodology delivers a robust and real-time solution for automated urine sediment analysis, effectively balancing detection precision and segmentation accuracy for clinical use.

5 Experimental Analysis

5.1 Dataset

The dataset used in this study, as described in [2], was carefully curated with meticulous annotation and validation by medical professionals to ensure accuracy. Labeling was performed using the Roboflow platform, which enabled the creation of high-quality annotations essential for reliable model training and evaluation. Over a period of five months, 7,201 microscopic images were annotated, representing 14 distinct classes of urine sediment. These classes include Miscellaneous, Bacteria, Mucus, Budding Yeast, Sperm, Yeast, RBC-Clumps, WBC-Clumps, Cast, Crystals, Leukocytes, Epith, Erythrocytes, Epithin, and Mycete. Figure 2 illustrates representative labeled samples from the dataset. To facilitate robust training and validation, the dataset was divided into 70% for training, 20% for validation, and 10% for testing. This stratified split ensures effective performance evaluation across all categories.

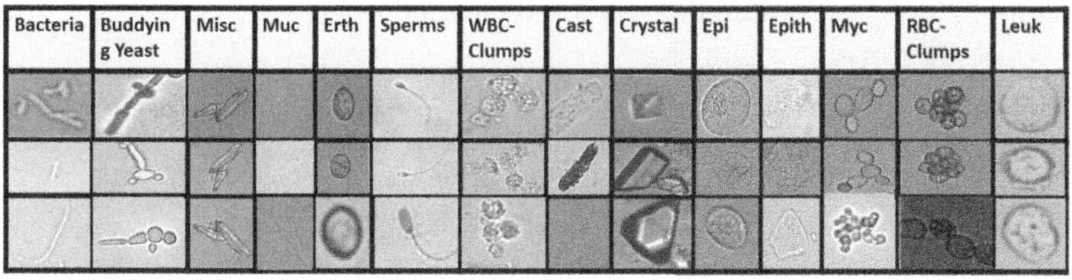

Bacteria	Buddyin g Yeast	Misc	Muc	Erth	Sperms	WBC-Clumps	Cast	Crystal	Epi	Epith	Myc	RBC-Clumps	Leuk

Fig. 2. Sample images labeled using the Roboflow

5.2 Performance Metrics and Implementation Details

In this study, we evaluate the performance of the YOLOv11-SAMNet model using several metrics: precision (P), recall (R), F1-score, and mean Average Precision at 0.5 IoU ($mAP@50$). These metrics are divided into two main categories: object detection quality and segmentation quality. Object detection quality is measured using precision (P(box)), recall (R(box)), and F1-score (F1(box)), while segmentation quality is assessed using precision (P(seg)), recall (R(seg)), and F1-score (F1(seg)). In contrast to models like Mask R-CNN, where detection quality is typically measured with P(box), R(box), and F1(box) while segmentation performance is evaluated using $mAP@50$, YOLOv11-SAMNet separately evaluates both tasks. The object detection performance is assessed using P(box), R(box), and F1(box), whereas segmentation performance is measured with P(seg), R(seg), and F1(seg). The YOLOv11-SAMNet model is trained using the AdamW optimizer, with a learning rate of 0.000556 and momentum set to 0.9. Weight decay parameters include 81 weight parameters with a decay of 0.0, 88 weight parameters with a decay of 0.0005, and 87 bias parameters with a decay of 0.0.

5.3 Experimental Results of YOLOv11-SAMNet

This section presents the performance results of the YOLOv11-SAMNet model across 14 classes of urine sediment, as summarized in Table 3. The model demonstrates its highest performance for Leukocytes (Leuko), achieving a recall of 94.6% and an $mAP@50$ of 94.3%. It is closely followed by Epithelial cells (Epith), which reach an $mAP@50$ of 92.5%. These results highlight the model's strong capability to accurately detect well-defined and common cell types. In contrast, bacteria and mucus exhibit the lowest performance, with $mAP@50$ values of 38.0% and 27.2%, respectively. These lower results suggest difficulties in detecting irregularly shaped and smaller particles, likely caused by their overlapping structures and variability in appearance. Figure 3 illustrates the confusion matrix, providing deeper insights into the model's performance. It shows a high true positive rate for well-classified particles such as leukocytes (0.94) and epithelial cells (0.92). However, there is noticeable misclassification of smaller and less distinct particles. Specifically, bacteria (0.56) and mucus (0.17) exhibit

Table 3. Performance metrics per class

Class	Images	Instances	Box(P)	R	mAP50	mAP50-95
all	1440	11082	0.593	0.576	0.589	0.295
Bacteria	42	1578	0.480	0.318	0.338	0.0977
Budding yeast	4	29	1.000	0.0478	0.384	0.107
Miscellaneous	66	95	0.466	0.537	0.484	0.204
Mucus	120	532	0.482	0.205	0.272	0.092
RBC-Clumps	16	116	0.526	0.534	0.494	0.177
Sperms	9	91	0.342	0.514	0.514	0.143
WBC-Clumps	118	298	0.540	0.595	0.566	0.216
Yeast	10	50	0.281	0.350	0.400	0.210
Cast	282	726	0.557	0.815	0.754	0.456
Cryst	172	342	0.760	0.854	0.858	0.545
Epith	293	1269	0.721	0.925	0.911	0.598
Epithn	85	124	0.746	0.855	0.871	0.390
Eryth	202	4695	0.904	0.822	0.860	0.507
Leuko	264	1185	0.782	0.946	0.943	0.590

significant confusion with the background and other sediment classes, indicating challenges in differentiating them from artifacts or noise present in the dataset. Furthermore, classes such as budding yeast (0.27) and miscellaneous particles (0.54) show moderate levels of confusion, suggesting that these categories could benefit from further refinement in future iterations.

5.4   Comparison With SOTA Models

In the comparison of state-of-the-art models for object instance segmentation, as shown in Table 4, our YOLOv11-SAMNet model demonstrates competitive performance on a specialized urine sediment dataset containing 14 distinct classes. While YOLOv5n achieves the highest *mAP@50* score of 91.8% on a 3-class dataset, our model attains a *mAP@50* of 60%, but shows strong precision metrics, with 93% bounding box precision and 85% segmentation precision. These results highlight the model's high confidence in positive detections, even with the more complex multi-class urine dataset. In comparison, other models such as Mask R-CNN and MaskDis R-CNN, both trained on the extensive 91-class COCO dataset, achieve mAP scores of 87.4% and 88.8%, respectively. Despite the difference in mAP performance, YOLOv11-SAMNet demonstrates its potential for specialized medical imaging applications, with precision and recall F1 scores of 82% for bounding boxes and 81% for segmentation tasks. To the best of our knowledge, this is the first work to apply instance segmentation on 14 distinct classes using the Urinalysis dataset. Moreover, there is limited research on

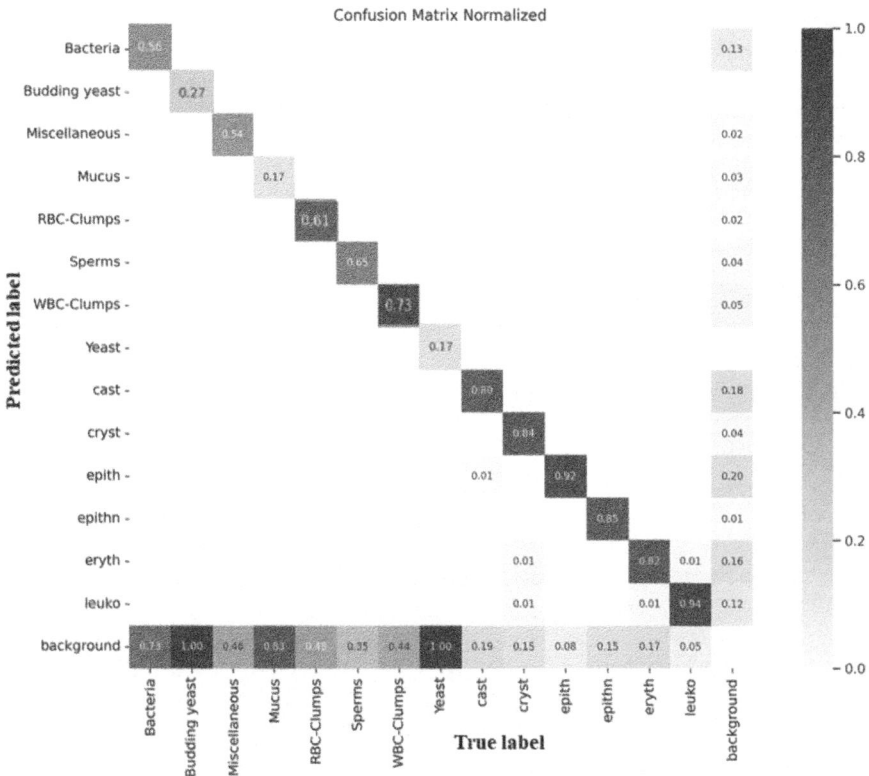

Fig. 3. Confusion matrix of the YOLOv11-SAMNet

instance segmentation in this domain, primarily due to the challenges associated with pixel-level labeling. Urine particles are typically small and share similar morphological characteristics, making precise annotation particularly challenging.

Figure 4 illustrates the prediction results of YOLOv11-SAMNet for urine sediment analysis. Each detected particle is enclosed within a bounding box, with distinct colors representing different sediment classes. The numerical values beside the bounding boxes correspond to the model's confidence scores for each detection. In the first image, the model accurately detects 65 Red Blood Cells (RBCs), highlighting its ability to localize small, densely packed particles. In the second image, the model identifies 21 epithelial cells, which are comparatively larger and more distinct. In the third image, the model successfully localizes 8 casts, demonstrating its proficiency in detecting elongated structures within urine samples.

It is important to note that particles of the same class do not share a uniform color. Instead, the visualization adopts an instance segmentation approach, where distinct colors are assigned to each individual particle based on its loca-

Table 4. Comparison of mAP and Inference Time Across Existing Object Instance Segmentation Methods

Method/Technique	Dataset	mAP@50	P(box)	R(box)	F1(box)	P(seg)	R(seg)	F1(seg)
YOLOV5n [1]	3 classes	91.8	84.5	89.5	86.8	86.5	91.5	88.8
Mask R-CNN [1]	91 classes (COCO dataset)	87.4	88.2	84.82	84.6	–	–	–
MaskDis R-CNN [1]	91 classes (COCO dataset)	88.8	91.5	85.9	88.4	–	–	–
YOLOv11-SAMNet	14 classes	**60**	**93**	**82**	51	**85**	**75**	**81**

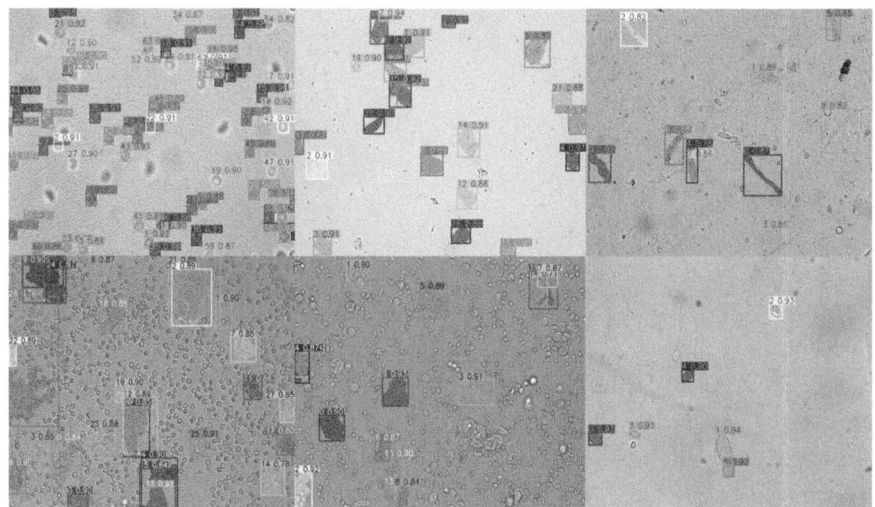

Fig. 4. Prediction results of YOLOv11-SAMNety

tion, not its class. This strategy facilitates the clear differentiation of overlapping or closely positioned objects, enhancing the interpretability of the detection results. These findings emphasize the effectiveness of YOLOv11-SAMNet in detecting and classifying various sediment types in microscopic images. However, challenges such as variations in image contrast and overlapping structures may still affect detection accuracy for certain classes.

6   Conclusion

In this study, we introduce YOLOv11-SAMNet, a novel one-stage instance segmentation model tailored for automated urine sediment analysis. By combining YOLOv11 with the Segment Anything Model (SAM), our approach significantly improves detection precision and segmentation accuracy across 14 distinct urine sediment classes. The model architecture includes a feature extraction backbone, a multi-scale fusion neck, and a specialized detection and segmentation head, optimizing instance segmentation performance. Experimental results show strong performance in detecting well-defined structures such as Leukocytes

(94.3% *mAP@50*) and Epithelial cells (92.5% *mAP@50*). However, challenges persist in segmenting smaller and irregularly shaped particles, such as bacteria (33.8% *mAP@50*) and mucus (27.2% *mAP@50*). To address these challenges, we developed an expert-assisted data preprocessing pipeline to refine the quality of training data, thus enhancing overall model performance. The encouraging results of YOLOv11-SAMNet demonstrate its potential to automate urinalysis, offering a more efficient and objective alternative to traditional manual analysis, ultimately supporting improved clinical diagnostics.

References

1. Tu, S., et al.: The urine formed element instance segmentation based on YOLOv5n. Sci. Rep. **14**(1), 28658 (2024)

2. Akhtar, S., et al.: An optimized data and model centric approach for multi-class automated urine sediment classification. IEEE Access (2024)

3. Suhail, K., et al.: Microscopic urinary particle detection by different YOLOv5 models with evolutionary genetic algorithm based hyperparameter optimization. Comput. Biol. Med. **169**, 107895 (2024)

4. Bai, B., et al.: YUSEG: YOLO and UNet is all you need for cell instance segmentation. Competitions in Neural Information Processing Systems. PMLR (2023)

5. Prangemeier, T., Reich, C., Koeppl, H.: Attention-based transformers for instance segmentation of cells in microstructures. In: 2020 IEEE International Conference on Bioinformatics and Biomedicine (BIBM). IEEE (2020)

6. Priego-Torres, B.M., et al.: Deep learning-based instance segmentation for the precise automated quantification of digital breast cancer immunohistochemistry images. Expert Syst. Appl. **193**, 116471 (2022)

7. Ren, X., et al.: Mask-RCNN for cell instance segmentation. IEEE Trans. Med. Imaging (2020)

8. Loh, D.R., et al.: A deep learning approach to the screening of malaria infection: automated and rapid cell counting, object detection and instance segmentation using Mask R-CNN. Comput. Med. Imaging Graph. **88**, 101845 (2021)

9. Qiu, X., et al.: Segmentation of multiple myeloma cells using feature selection pyramid network and semantic cascade mask R-CNN. In: 2022 IEEE 19th International Symposium on Biomedical Imaging (ISBI). IEEE (2022)

10. Mitate, E., et al.: Application of the sliding window method and Mask-RCNN method to nuclear recognition in oral cytology. Diagn. Pathol. **17**(1), 62 (2022)

Split-and-Merge Segmentation of Biomedical Images Using Graph Wedgelet Decompositions

Wolfgang Erb$^{(\boxtimes)}$ (ID)

Department of Mathematics "Tullio Levi-Civita", University of Padova,
Via Trieste 63, 35121 Padua, Italy
wolfgang.erb@unipd.it
https://www.math.unipd.it/~erb/

Abstract. Graph wedgelets are a novel tool for the fast decomposition of images in geometrically meaningful, wedge-shaped, subregions. In this work, we study the usage of graph wedgelets as a promising splitting method in a split-and-merge segmentation scheme for images. We combine adaptive wedgelet splits of images with a simple and classical merging strategy for subregions, and obtain in this way an efficient and robust segmentation of relevant subdomains, that can be used in the segmentation of biomedical images obtained by modalities as, for instance, Magnetic Resonance Imaging.

Keywords: Graph Wedgelets · Geometric Wavelets on Graphs · Split-and-merge Segmentation · Biomedical Imaging

1 Introduction

Combined split-and-merge schemes for image segmentation have been introduced by Horowitz & Pavlidis [12] in the seventies of the last century. The principal idea of these region-based segmentation schemes is to recursively partition an image into small homogeneous parts and then to merge these small building blocks into larger homogeneous segments of the image. The merging step of these schemes is usually more cost intensive since the computational load required for the comparison and the combination of subregions is high. Therefore, a key aspect and at the same time also the challenge of split-and-merge strategies is to implement a splitting scheme that decomposes an image efficiently into a relatively small but geometrically significant number of subblocks, as for instance discussed in Correa-Tome & Sanchez-Yanez [5] and Salembier & Garrido [14].

In this work, we explore the usage of graph wedgelets, as introduced in [9], for the initial geometric partitioning of images within a split-and-merge segmentation framework. In this graph-based approach, an image is represented as a discrete graph that is then divided into a set of geometrically significant subgraphs. These partitions can be encoded easily using a binary wedge partitioning

(BWP) tree and efficiently stored as a corresponding sequence of center nodes. The primary advantages of such a discrete splitting strategy lie in its computational efficiency, its simplicity in terms of coding, as well as its adaptability to diverse domains and imaging scenarios.

In the following sections, we will recapitulate the fundamental properties of graph wedgelets for image decomposition and show how this wedgelet-based splitting can be effectively combined with a classical merging procedure to yield a final segmentation of images. We will further analyze the computational complexity and storage requirements of the proposed combined scheme. Finally, we illustrate the practical utility of this approach by applying it to the segmentation of white matter or the extraction of tumor areas in biomedical images obtained from Magnetic Resonance Imaging (MRI).

2   Methodology for Image Splitting and Merging

2.1   The Splitting Procedure Based on Graph Wedgelets

To split the image into geometrically relevant subregions, we use a graph wedgelet decomposition as introduced in [9]. Graph wedgelets interpret the image as a graph signal and efficiently approximate it with piecewise constant functions on partitions that are encoded in a binary graph partitioning tree and constructed upon hierarchical adaptive wedge splits. This structure allows to store and process the image partitions cost-efficiently by a sequence of graph nodes that encode the entire tree. In [9], tests showed that with identical partition sizes graph wedgelets, similarly to their continuous analogs [8,10] or to binary space partitioning trees [13] lead to a higher adaptivity and, thus, to an improved approximation quality compared to quadtree decompositions or hierarchical Haar wavelet decompositions. A key advantage of graph wedgelets is their flexibility. The graph structure can be easily adapted to different imaging scenarios. This allows the same approach to be applied not only for rectangular images, but also for the decomposition of more complex data such as 3D scans of magnetic particles [2], vector fields on simplicial grids [1], or distorted images captured by hyper-hemispherical cameras [15]. As graph wedgelets rely on a discrete imaging model, they contrast with continuous approaches that often offer stronger theoretical guarantees, see [4,6,7]. In the following, we provide a brief review of graph wedgelets, the details and further references can be found in [9].

Modeling Images as Graphs. In a graph-based approach to image processing, we interpret an image as a graph $G = (V, E, \mathbf{A}, d)$ in which the single pixels of the image are identified as nodes $V = \{v_1, \ldots, v_n\}$, and neighboring pixels v_i and $v_{i'}$ are connected through edges $e_{i,i'} = (v_i, v_{i'})$. We assume that the edges are undirected and denote the set of all edges by E. The symmetric matrix $\mathbf{A} \in \mathbb{R}^{n \times n}$ is referred to as adjacency matrix, and contains as entries $\mathbf{A}_{i,i'}$ the connection weights of the edges $e_{i,i'} \in E$. We further require a metric distance d on the vertex set V. As standard distance d on V we use the graph geodesic distance, i.e., the length of the shortest path connecting two graph vertices. We will further assume that G is connected, i.e., that the distance between two nodes is always finite.

This graph-based approach is very versatile and allows the usage of different neighborhood models for the pixels in the image. If only the closest neighbors in the image grid get connected to a pixel, this leads to a graph with a sparse adjacency matrix $\mathbf{A}$, yielding fast graph-based algorithms if image processing tasks have to be performed locally in subregions. On the other hand, sometimes it is more useful to model an image as a complete graph in which the edge weights are linked to the inverse of the euclidean distance between two pixels.

In this work, we are interested in the decompositions of images, i.e. of functions $f : V \to \mathbb{R}$ representing images on the vertex set V of the graph G. The functions f on the discrete set V can be also interpreted as vectors $f = [f(v_1), \ldots, f(v_n)]^\mathsf{T} \in \mathbb{R}^n$ and are referred to as *graph signals*. This graph-based approach is very versatile and allows the usage of different neighborhood models for the pixels in the image. If only the closest neighbors in the image grid get connected to a pixel, this leads to a graph with a sparse adjacency matrix $\mathbf{A}$, yielding fast graph-based algorithms if image processing tasks have to be performed locally in subregions. On the other hand, sometimes it is more useful to model an image as a complete graph in which the edge weights are linked to the inverse of the euclidean distance between two pixels.

In this work, we are interested in the decompositions of images, i.e. of functions $f : V \to \mathbb{R}$ representing images on the vertex set V of the graph G. The functions f on the discrete set V can be also interpreted as vectors $f = [f(v_1), \ldots, f(v_n)]^\mathsf{T} \in \mathbb{R}^n$ and are referred to as *graph signals*.

This graph-based approach is very versatile and allows the usage of different neighborhood models for the pixels in the image. If only the closest neighbors in the image grid get connected to a pixel, this leads to a graph with a sparse adjacency matrix $\mathbf{A}$, yielding fast graph-based algorithms if image processing tasks have to be performed locally in subregions. On the other hand, sometimes it is more useful to model an image as a complete graph in which the edge weights are linked to the inverse of the euclidean distance between two pixels.

In this work, we are interested in the decompositions of images, i.e. of functions $f : V \to \mathbb{R}$ representing images on the vertex set V of the graph G. The functions f on the discrete set V can be also interpreted as vectors $f = [f(v_1), \ldots, f(v_n)]^\mathsf{T} \in \mathbb{R}^n$ and are referred to as *graph signals*.

Wedge Splits. Graph wedgelets rely on an adaptive recursive binary partitioning of the vertex set V in which geometric information of the signal f is included. For this, a binary partitioning tree is generated which depends on the topology of the graph G as well as on the signal f. As elementary splittings of a vertex set, we consider wedge splits.

We call a dyadic partition $\{V_q, V_{q'}\}$ of the vertex set V a *wedge split* of V if there exists a pair of nodes $\{q, q'\}$ in V such that V_q and $V_{q'}$ have the form

$$V_q = \{v \in V \mid d(v, q) \le d(v, q')\}, \quad V_{q'} = \{v \in V \mid d(v, q) > d(v, q')\}.$$

The center nodes q and q′ uniquely determine the wedge split $\{V_q, V_{q'}\}$ of V. This allows to code the splittings very efficiently in terms of their center nodes. Further, if the metric d is the graph geodesic distance and V is connected, then also V_q and $V_{q'}$ are connected subsets of the graph G. A recursive wedge splitting leads to a binary partitioning tree of the graph.

Binary Wedge Partitioning (BWP) Trees. A BWP tree $\mathcal{T}_Q$ of the graph G with respect to the ordered set $Q = \{q_1, \ldots, q_M\} \subset V$ of centers is a binary tree consisting of subsets of the vertex set V that can be ordered recursively in partitions $\mathcal{P}^{(m)}$ of V according to the following steps:

1. The root of the tree $\mathcal{T}_Q$ is the entire set V forming the trivial partition $\mathcal{P}^{(1)} = \{V_{q_1}^{(1)}\} = \{V\}$. The root is linked to the first node q_1 of Q.
2. Let $\mathcal{P}^{(m)} = \{V_{q_1}^{(m)}, \ldots, V_{q_m}^{(m)}\}$ be a partition of V in $\mathcal{T}_Q$ linked to the nodes $q_i \in V_{q_i}^{(m)}$, $i \in \{1, \ldots, m\}$, $m < M$. Then, the new node q_{m+1} contained in one subset $V_{q_j}^{(m)}$ together with the center node q_j define a new wedge split of $V_{q_j}^{(m)}$ resulting in a new partition $\mathcal{P}^{(m+1)}$ of V into $m + 1$ disjoint sets.

The ordered set Q of graph vertices uniquely determines the BWP tree $\mathcal{T}_Q$. This allows to encode the entire BWP tree compactly in terms of the M elements of the set Q. A BWP tree $\mathcal{T}_Q$ contains $2M - 1$ subdomains of V, 1 root and $2M - 2$ children regions. The M leaves of the tree $\mathcal{T}_Q$ correspond to the sets of the final partition $\mathcal{P}^{(M)} = \{V_{q_1}^{(M)}, \ldots, V_{q_M}^{(M)}\}$ of V.

Graph Wedgelets. The characteristic functions

$$\omega_{q_i}^{(m)}(v) = \chi_{V_{q_i}^{(m)}}(v), \quad i \in \{1, \ldots m\}, \ m \in \{1, \ldots, M\},$$

of the sets $V_{q_i}^{(m)}$ in a BWP tree $\mathcal{T}_Q$ are referred to as *graph wedgelets*. The wedgelets $\{\omega_{q_i}^{(m)} : i \in \{1, \ldots, m\}\}$ form an orthogonal basis for the piecewise constant functions on the partition $\mathcal{P}^{(m)}$.

Adaptive Greedy Calculation of BWP Trees. In order to determine the BWP tree $\mathcal{T}_Q$, at each level m one of the subdomains $V_{q_j}^{(m)}$, $j \in \{1, \ldots, m\}$, has to be chosen and a respective new node $q_{m+1} \in V_{q_j}^{(m)}$ selected. In order to approximate a signal f best possible, these selections can be performed in an f-adaptive way. We consider the following two-step iterative greedy procedure for the generation of the BWP trees. A simple example of this procedure applied to a gray-scale image can be found in Fig. 1. The entire wedgelet decomposition scheme to generate a BWP tree is summarized in Algorithm 1.

Step 1: Selection of the Subdomain: at level m, we consider the mean values

$$\bar{f}_{V_{q_i}^{(m)}} = \frac{1}{|V_{q_i}^{(m)}|} \sum_{v \in V_{q_i}^{(m)}} f(v)$$

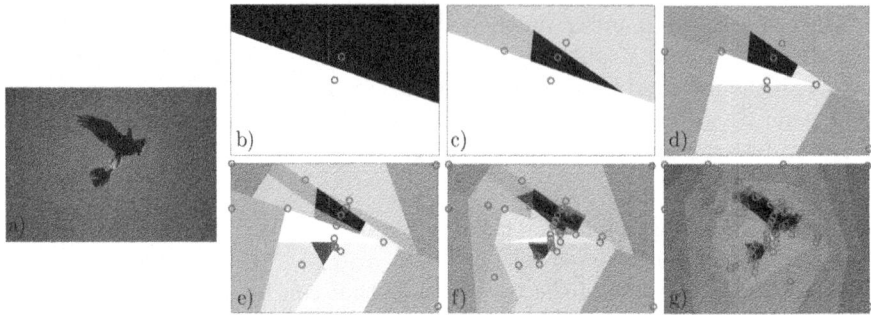

Fig. 1. Adaptive BWP splitting of a 481×321 gray-scale image using Algorithm 1a) The original image; b) c) d) e) f) g) Graph wedgelet decomposition of the image using 2, 4, 8, 16, 32 and 64 wedgelet domains, respectively. The center nodes Q of the BWP tree are marked with a red circle. (Color figure online)

of the function f over the subsets $V_{q_i}^{(m)}$. Then, the domain $V_{q_j}^{(m)}$ with the maximal $\mathcal{L}^2$-error

$$j = \underset{i \in \{1,\dots,m\}}{\operatorname{argmax}} \|f - \bar{f}_{V_{q_i}^{(m)}}\|_{\mathcal{L}^2(V_{q_i}^{(m)})}, \tag{1}$$

is selected. Inside this domain, the next wedge split is defined in terms of the center node q_j and an additional node q_{m+1}.

Step 2: Adaptive Selection of the Second Node q_{m+1}. The second node q_{m+1} is chosen according to an adaptive rule such that the resulting split provides a best possible approximation of the function f in terms of piecewise constant components. If $\{V_{(q_j,q)}^{(m)+}, V_{(q_j,q)}^{(m)-}\}$ denotes the partition of $V_{q_j}^{(m)}$ according to the wedge split given by the node q_j and a second node q, we determine q_{m+1} such that the quantity

$$\|f - \bar{f}_{V_{(q_j,q)}^{(m)+}}\|_{\mathcal{L}^2(V_{(q_j,q)}^{(m)+})}^2 + \|f - \bar{f}_{V_{(q_j,q)}^{(m)-}}\|_{\mathcal{L}^2(V_{(q_j,q)}^{(m)-})}^2 \tag{2}$$

is minimized over all $q \in S \subset V_{q_j}^{(m)}$. As a set S of admissible nodes, one can for instance take $S = V_{q_j}^{(m)} \setminus \{q_j\}$. It is however generally advisable to reduce the computational complexity of the optimization problem (2) by selecting a relatively small set S. One way to do this is by picking $|S|$ nodes uniformly at random from the domain $V_{q_j}^{(m)} \setminus \{q_j\}$.

Acceleration Possibilities. For very large images, the adaptive strategy described in 1) and 2) might be too costly from a computational point of view, even if the size $|S|$ of the selected nodes in (2) is relatively small. To reduce the computational expenses, one can additionally split the image in a preliminary step in J subblocks. This can be done by hand by selecting proper subblocks. Alternatively, a clustering algorithm, as for instance k-center clustering [11], can be applied in order to extract subregions of the image, similarly as described for

---

Algorithm 1: Wedgelet decomposition of the image

Input: A graph signal f, a starting node $q_1 \in V$, the starting partition $\mathcal{P}^{(1)} = \{V\} = \{V_{q_1}^{(1)}\}$ and a final partition size $M \geq 1$.

for $m = 2$ *to* M **do**

> 1) **Greedy selection of subset:** calculate j according to the rule (1) as
>
> $$j = \arg\max_{i \in \{1,\ldots,m-1\}} \left\| f - \bar{f}_{V_{q_i}^{(m-1)}} \right\|_{\mathcal{L}^2(V_{q_i}^{(m-1)})};$$
>
> 2) **Determine new node** q_m such that the squared $\mathcal{L}^2$-error term (2) is minimized over all nodes in S and add it to the node set Q;
> 3) Generate **new partition** $\mathcal{P}^{(m)}$ from the partition $\mathcal{P}^{(m-1)}$ by a wedge split of the subset $V_{q_j}^{(m-1)}$ into the children sets $V_{(q_j,q_m)}^{(m-1)\,+}$ and $V_{(q_j,q_m)}^{(m-1)\,-}$;
> 4) Compute **mean values** $\bar{f}_{V_{q_i}^{(m)}}$, $i \in \{1,\ldots,m\}$, for the new partition $\mathcal{P}^{(m)}$ by an update from $\mathcal{P}^{(m-1)}$.

Output: node set $Q = \{q_1,\ldots,q_M\}$, mean values $\left\{ \bar{f}_{V_{q_1}^{(M)}}, \ldots, \bar{f}_{V_{q_M}^{(M)}} \right\}$.

---

partition of unity methods on graphs in [3]. After this preliminary splitting, the described greedy method in 1) and 2) can be applied separately to each cluster, providing also a direct way to parallelize the computations.

From an implementation point of view, this preliminary splitting into J sub-blocks results in J disjoint BWP trees instead of a single tree, and the respective selected center nodes generally differ from the ones generated by the single BWP scheme. This modification will therefore also have an impact on the final splitting of the image, as well as for the subsequent merging procedure.

2.2   The Merging Procedure

Once the image is decomposed into M wedgelet domains $\{V_{q_1}^{(M)}, \ldots, V_{q_M}^{(M)}\}$ with a sufficient homogeneity which can be measured in terms of the $\mathcal{L}^2$-errors in (1), a merging scheme needs to be applied to the subdomains in order to obtain a segmentation of the image. For this, we will consider as starting information the mean values $\{\bar{f}_{V_{q_1}^{(M)}}, \ldots, \bar{f}_{V_{q_M}^{(M)}}\}$ of the function f on the M subdomains and proceed similarly as described in Salembier & Garrido [14] to generate with a bottom-up strategy a second binary partitioning tree for the merging part. For this merging partitioning tree a *merging order* and a *region model* is required. As a model for the image value $f_{R_1 \cup R_2}$ on the union $R_1 \cup R_2$ of two regions R_1 and R_2 we use the upper median of the function values f_{R_1} and f_{R_2} on the regions R_1 and R_2. The similarity between two regions R_1 and R_2 is measured by the quantity

$$O(R_1, R_2) = \min(|R_1|, |R_2|)(f_{R_1} - f_{R_2})^2.$$

According to this measure, the merging starts with those regions where the quantity $O(R_1, R_2)$ is minimal. The merging scheme is completed, and the image

---

Algorithm 2: Merging part of the split-and-merge segmentation

---

Input: A partition of the vertex set V in M regions $\mathcal{R}^{(M)} = \{R_1, \ldots R_M\}$ with $R_i = V_{q_i}^{(M)}$ and initial values $f_{R_i} = \bar{f}_{V_{q_i}^{(M)}}$ for $i \in \{1, \ldots, M\}$.

for $m = M$ **to** $L + 1$ **do**

    1) **Selection of regions:** determine the regions R_i, R_j in $\mathcal{R}^{(m)}$ such that

$$O(R_i, R_j) = \min(|R_i|, |R_j|)(f_{R_i} - f_{R_j})^2$$

    gets minimal.

    2) **Merge** regions R_i and R_j to $R_i \cup R_j$ and calculate **high median**

$$f_{R_i \cup R_j} = \begin{cases} f_{R_i} & \text{if } |R_i| > |R_j|, \\ f_{R_j} & \text{if } |R_i| < |R_j|, \\ \max\{f_{R_i}, f_{R_j}\} & \text{if } |R_i| = |R_j|. \end{cases}$$

    3) **Update** $\mathcal{R}^{(m-1)} = \mathcal{R}^{(m)} \setminus \{R_i, R_j\} \cup \{R_i \cup R_j\}$ and the values $f_{R_1}, \ldots, f_{R_{m-1}}$ for the sets in the new partition $\mathcal{R}^{(m-1)}$.

Output: Partition $\mathcal{R}^{(L)} = \{R_1, \ldots, R_L\}$ of V and values $f_{R_1}, \ldots, f_{R_L}$.

---

segmentation terminates if a selected partition size L of composed subregions is reached. This merging procedure is summarized in Algorithm 2.

Computational Complexity and Storage Costs. As outlined out in [9], the computational complexity for the calculation of the adaptive BWP tree given in Sect. 2.1 can be bounded by $\mathcal{O}(M|S|n)$. On the other hand, the simple merging scheme in Sect. 2.2 requires $\mathcal{O}(M^2)$ operations for the calculation of the merging tree. For this, the complete split-and-merge segmentation remains cost-efficient as long as the number M of calculated wedgelet domains remains of moderate size.

It is further shown in [9] that the storage costs of the adaptive BWP tree can be bounded by $\lceil \log_2(n) \rceil M/n$ bits per pixel. In order to store the segmentation of the image in L subregions, only additional $\lceil \log_2(L) \rceil M/n$ bits per pixel have to be invested. If, on top, also the region values $f_{R_1}, \ldots, f_{R_L}$ are stored, further $\lceil \log_2(K) \rceil L/n$ bits per pixel are required if the values f_{R_i} are quantized in terms of K different values.

3 Results and Discussions

We test our split-and-merge scheme on two gray-scale images and two MRI data sets. The 481×321 gray-scale images in Fig. 2 a) and Fig 3 a) are used as simple test sets to obtain an initial assessment of the method and a rough indication on how the number M of domains and the choice of the set S in the initial BWP splitting influence the final segmentation of the image. For this, we generate

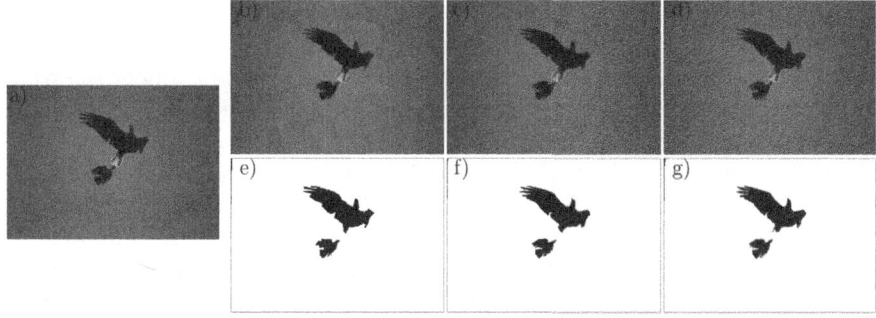

Fig. 2. Split-and-merge segmentation of a gray-scale image a) original image with 481×321 pixels; b) c) d) BWP decomposition of the image using 200, 500 and 1000 domains; e) f) g) Image segmentation based on the application of Algorithm 2 to the BWP decompositions in b) c) d). Segmentations with 2 components are created.

in Fig. 2 b) c) d) a BWP decomposition of the image using 200, 500 and 1000 wedgelet domains, and subsequently apply the merging procedure in Algorithm 2 to obtain respective segmentations of the image with $L = 2$ components. Further, in Fig. 3, Algorithm 1 is applied with the following parameter configuration. The subfigures b) c) d) illustrate the wedgelet decomposition of the image into $M = 1000$ regions, where b) the sets S consist of a single node located farthest away from the center node q_j, c) the sets S consist of 1000 randomly selected nodes, and d) the selection sets S are the same as in c) but a preliminary partitioning of the image in $J = 25$ subblocks is used. In the subfigures e) f) g) of Fig. 3 the respective segmentation provided by Algorithm 2 is shown.

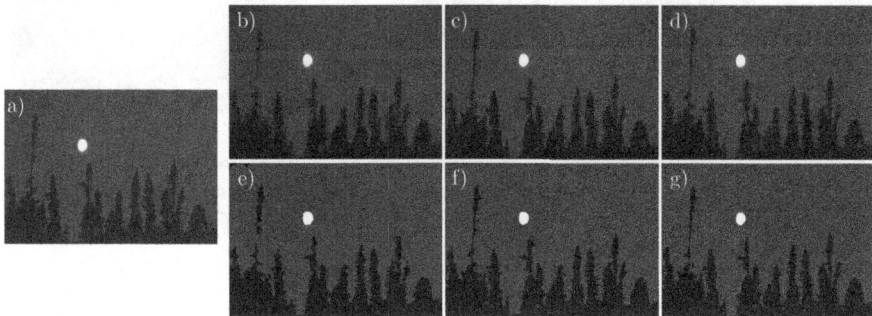

Fig. 3. Split-and-merge segmentation of a gray-scale image a) original image with 481×321 pixels; b) c) d) BWP decomposition of the image using $M = 1000$ domains and b) sets S consisting of a single node, c) sets S with 1000 randomly selected nodes, and d) an additional preliminary partitioning of the image in $J = 25$ blocks; e) f) g) Image segmentation based on the application of Algorithm 2 to the BWP decompositions in b) c) d). Segmentations with 3 components are created.

The third data set is an artificial MRI image of the brain (in Fig. 4a)) generated by the simulator BrainWeb (http://www.bic.mni.mcgill.ca/brainweb/). Using the presented split-and-merge approach, our goal is to segment the white matter from the rest of the surrounding brain tissue. Using the graph wedgelet algorithm, we split the original MRI image in 2500 subdomains (Fig. 4b), PSNR 33.19). Then, we apply the merging procedure of Algorithm 2 and obtain a segmentation of the image in terms of $L = 4$ different grayscales (Fig. 4c)). The segment related to the white matter is afterwards colored in blue (Fig. 4d)).

In Fig. 5, we additionally compare the wedgelet-based extraction of the white matter (Fig. 5c)) with the ground truth of the white matter downloaded from BrainWeb (Fig. 5a)). As the ground truth contains different gray-scales, we extract the domain representing the white matter by a simple thresholding strategy (Fig. 5b)). The absolute difference between the domains in the subfigures b) and c) is then illustrated in Fig. 5d).

The forth test image is an MRI scan containing a glioma (in Fig. 6a)) taken from a dataset on Kaggle (https://www.kaggle.com/sartajbhuvaji/brain-tumor-classification-mri/). The aim of this final experiment is to see whether our approach can segment the glioma from the rest of the image. Again, we conduct a wedgelet decomposition (Fig. 6b), PSNR 27.68) to split the image in 2500 subregions. After the application of the merging algorithm, we obtain a segmentation of the image in $L = 4$ grayscales (Fig. 6c)). The segment describing the region with the glioma is colored in blue (Fig. 6d)).

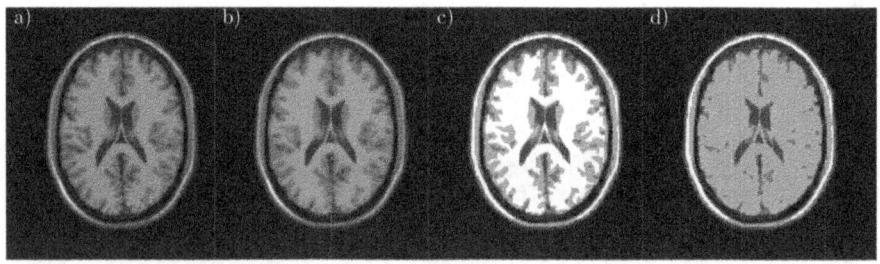

Fig. 4. Wedgelet split-and-merge segmentation for biomedical images: a) Original artificial MRI image; b) Wedgelet BWP split into 2500 regions; c) Segmentation with the presented method; d) Blue colored segmented white matter (Color figure online)

In all four experiments, it is visible that the wedgelet algorithm provides a piecewise constant approximation of the original image and a splitting into a moderate number of geometrically significant wedge-shaped subregions. These preselected subregions can then be easily processed with the given merging method to obtain a simple and fast segmentation of the aimed-at regions. An advantage of the used wedgelet decomposition in the splitting procedure is that the original image is automatically denoised, leading to a more robust final segmentation. On the other hand, it is also visible that some details of the image get

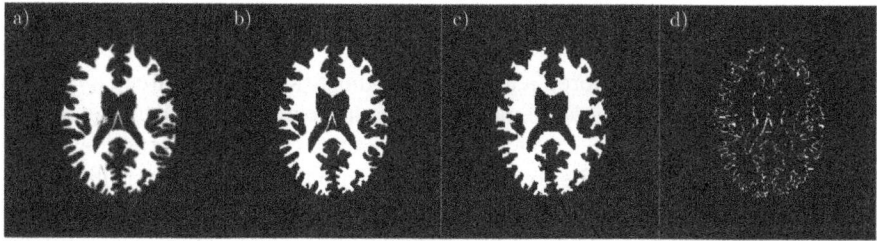

Fig. 5. Comparison of wedgelet split-and-merge segmentation with ground truth of white matter: a) Ground truth of white matter of MRI image in Fig. 4; b) Extraction of segmentation domain from ground truth by thresholding; c) Segmentation of white matter with the presented method; d) Absolute difference between b) and c)

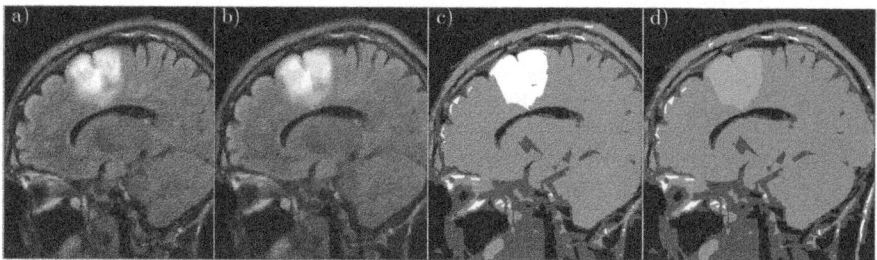

Fig. 6. Wedgelet split-and-merge segmentation for biomedical images: a) Original MRI image with glioma b) Wedgelet split into 2500 regions c) Segmentation with the presented method d) Blue colored segmented glioma. (Color figure online)

lost in those regions where the wedgelet approximation is not accurate enough. This is particularly visible in Fig. 2 where different numbers M of wedgelet splits are compared, and in Fig. 5 where differences at the border of the extracted white matter domain get visible in comparison to the ground truth.

The wedgelet algorithm itself allows to select the number M of adopted wedge splits and the sets S of nodes which are taken into consideration for the Greedy selection of the splits. This allows to control the number of considered subregions and the accuracy of the wedgelet approximation. The role of the number M is, for instance, visualized in Fig. 2, while in Fig. 3 it gets visible that large selection sets S lead to a more accurate partitioning of the domain and a refined segmentation. The usage of a preliminary splitting of the domain in J subblocks has only a relatively small impact on the final segmentation. The selection of these parameters and the trade-off between accuracy and robustness plays an important role also for the computational complexity of the method and needs to be investigated further to guarantee significant but also computationally efficient segmentations of medical images. Furthermore, in this study we used only a very simple model for the merging step. This leaves a lot of potential for further improvements.

4   Conclusion

In this short study, we explored a graph-based image splitting strategy as part of an integrated split-and-merge segmentation framework with particular emphasis on applications in biomedical imaging. The presented splitting method leverages discrete adaptive wedge splits to divide images into a set of geometrically mean-ingful subregions that can be described by a binary wedge partitioning tree and encoded efficiently by a sequence of graph centers. This graph-based splitting scheme together with a classical merging procedure yields a robust and computa-tionally efficient split-and-merge segmentation scheme for images. The presented numerical experiments demonstrate that the method has strong potential and can be applied practically to segmentation tasks in medical imaging.

Acknowledgments. The author of this article is funded by the Università degli Studi di Padova - Dipartimento di Matematica under the project SID BIRD 2023 entitled "ALISIA - ALgorithms for Immersive Stereoscopic Imaging with Applications to the Daedalus camera system", and by the European Union - NextGenerationEU under the National Recovery and Resilience Plan (NRRP), Mission 4 Component 2 Investment 1.1 - Call PRIN 2022 No. 104 of February 2, 2022 of Italian Ministry of University and Research; Project 2022FHCNY3 (subject area: PE - Physical Sciences and Engi-neering) "Computational mEthods for Medical Imaging (CEMI)". Further support by the Indam research group GNCS (Indam-GNCS project CUP_E53C24001950001), the Italian Research Network on Approximation (RITA), and the Italian Mathematical Union (research group UMI-TAA) is gratefully acknowledged.

References

1. Alonso Rodríguez, A., Bruni Bruno, L., Rapetti, F.: Computing weights for high order Whitney edge elements. Dolomites Res. Notes Approx. **15**, 1–12 (2022)
2. Bringout, G., Erb, W., Frikel, J.: A new 3D model for Magnetic Particle Imaging using realistic magnetic field topologies for algebraic reconstruction. Inverse Prob. **36**, 124002 (2020)
3. Cavoretto, R., De Rossi, A., Erb, W.: Partition of unity methods for signal pro-cessing on graphs. J. Fourier Anal. Appl. **27**(4), 1–29 (2021). https://doi.org/10.1007/s00041-021-09871-w
4. Cohen, A., Dyn, N., Hecht, F., Mirebeau, J.-M.: Adaptive multiresolution analysis based on anistropic triangulations. Math. Comput. **81**(278), 789–810 (2012)
5. Correa-Tome, F.E., Sanchez-Yanez, R.E.: Integral split-and-merge methodology for real-time image segmentation. J. Electron. Imaging **24**(1), 013007 (2015)
6. Dekel, S., Leviatan, D.: Adaptive multivariate approximation using binary space partitions and geometric wavelets. SIAM J. Numer. Anal. **43**(2), 707–732 (2005)
7. Demaret, L., Iske, A.: Optimal N-term approximation by linear splines over anisotropic Delaunay triangulations. Math. Comput. **84**(293), 1241–1264 (2015)
8. Donoho, D.L.: Wedgelets: nearly minimax estimation of edges. Ann. Stat. **27**(3), 859–897 (1999)
9. Erb, W.: Graph wedgelets: adaptive data compression on graphs based on binary wedge partitioning trees and geometric wavelets. IEEE Trans. Image Process. **9**, 24–34 (2023)

10. Friedrich, F., Demaret, L., Führ, F., Wicker, K.: Efficient moment computation over polygonal domains with an application to rapid wedgelet approximation. SIAM J. Sci. Comput. **29**(2), 842–863 (2007)
11. Gonzalez, T.F.: Clustering to minimize the maximum intercluster distance. Theoret. Comput. Sci. **38**, 293–306 (1985)
12. Horowitz, S., Pavlidis, T.: Picture segmentation by a tree traversal algorithm. J. ACM **23**, 368–388 (1976)
13. Radha, H., Vetterli, M., Leonardi, R.: Image compression using binary space partitioning trees. IEEE Trans. Image Proc. **5**(12), 1610–1624 (1996)
14. Salembier, P., Garrido, L.: Binary partition tree as an efficient representation for image processing, segmentation, and information retrieval. IEEE Trans. Image Process. **9**(4), 561–576 (2000)
15. Simioni, E., et al.: A-central model for the geometric calibration of hyper-hemispherical lenses. Opt. Express **32**(20), 34777–34795 (2024)

Adriatic Ports of the Future: Trieste and Koper Towards Circularity

Francesca Sinatra[1]([⊠]) [iD] and Marina Zanne[2] [iD]

[1] University of Trieste, Alfonso Valerio 4/1 Street, Trieste, Italy
francesca.sinatra@phd.units.it
[2] University of Ljubljana, Pot pomorščakov 4, Portorož, Slovenia
marina.zanne@fpp.uni-lj.si

Abstract. The present study aims to investigate the effects of applying circular and industrial symbiosis models within the maritime sector, with a focus on logistics and transport. The intention is to focus on location decisions and the reduction of emissions. The rationale underpinning this study is to integrate strategies that facilitate the reutilisation of waste as a secondary raw material. The paper will analyse and examine how such circular practices can promote the sustainability of port infrastructures. The present study investigates and compares circular economy and industrial symbiosis initiatives integrated in the activities of port systems. The investigation will concentrate on two ports, Trieste and Koper, given their geographic proximity, in order to identify the actions and decisions taken by the ports with regard to the relationship between territorial location, territorial development and the various collaborations between actors. It is anticipated that the implementation of circular initiatives will result in a reduction of emissions, an enhancement of the competitive advantages held by the two analysed ports, and the promotion of activities and strategies that are aimed at efficient traffic management in accordance with European sustainability standards.

Keywords: Maritime transport · Port of Koper · Port of Trieste

1 Introduction

The advent of the circular economy (CE) can be attributed to the necessity of transitioning from linear economic models to more circular and sustainable ones in an era of globalisation. The objective of this phenomenon is to reduce and minimise the creation of waste, as well as to achieve a more conscious and efficient use of available resources. The Ellen Macarthur Foundation is a prominent proponent of the circular economy, a concept which emphasises the necessity of transitioning towards more sustainable economic practices. As posited by this foundation, the concept of the circular economy has been subjected to rigorous analysis, resulting in the observation and study of its application across various sectors and disciplines. This analysis has highlighted the potential of the circular economy to be integrated with new digital technologies. As demonstrated in the relevant literature, reuse and recycling practices have been shown to play a crucial role in waste management, with a concomitant decrease in negative externalities generated by human activities [1, 2].

O. Gervasi et al. (Eds.): ICCSA 2025 Workshops, LNCS 15899, pp. 264–272, 2026.
https://doi.org/10.1007/978-3-031-97663-6_23

Furthermore, it has emerged how the circular economy and industrial symbiosis (IS) can generate advantages and benefits, both economically and socially, in the creation of new jobs and social equity. Recent studies have also focused on the transport and logistics sector, highlighting how waste reduction and efficient use of resources are important in creating sustainable ecosystems, leading to a reduction in environmental footprint [3, 4].

As a result, it is possible to state that the circular economy and industrial symbiosis are now important in the development of long-term sustainable strategies.

In this context, the present paper aims to investigate the influence and impact that circular economy and industrial symbiosis strategies can have in the maritime transport sector. The rationale behind the selection of this sector is twofold. Firstly, ports are of pivotal significance in the realm of international trade, serving as pivotal nodes for the convergence of transport networks. Even more, they represent pivotal points of confluence for these networks, thus underscoring their role as critical infrastructure. Secondly, in recent years, environmental sustainability has become a concept of significant interest to ports, which have sought to adopt various circular economy and industrial symbiosis strategies in order to mitigate the negative externalities generated by their activities and achieve efficiency in the use of resources [1–4].

The present work considers two ports: The two locations under discussion are Trieste, located in Italy, and Koper, in Slovenia. The selection and investigation of these two areas of interest is represented by their geographical proximity. The objective of this study is to compare the various strategies that have been implemented for the purpose of achieving circular practices in order to facilitate a sustainable transition.

The paper is organized as follows: Sect. 2 Metodology; Sect. 3 Data; Sect. 3.1 Port of Trieste; Sect. 3.2 Port of Koper; Sect. 4 Discussion; Sect. 5 Conclusion.

2 Methodology

The present study employs a qualitative approach to identifying strategies implemented in the port sphere with reference to the circular economy and industrial symbiosis. To develop this analysis, a thorough review of existing literature in the port sphere has been carried out. This includes institutional documents and environmental reports issued by the ports themselves. The review also includes official documents and releases as well as web sources. The objective of this study is to identify and analyse the waste management, reusable material recovery and treatment, water and energy resources management, and collaborative efforts implemented by the Port of Trieste and the Port of Koper.

3 Data

The circular economy represents an economic model that moves from a linear to a circular model by adopting strategies that are aimed at minimising waste and making efficient use of available resources. For this reason, this model includes the recycling and reuse of materials and waste, and the use of renewable energy sources. Alongside the circular economy, industrial symbiosis is also an integral part of it, through collaboration and exchanges between companies, where waste for one company can become a resource for another, leading to the creation of an interconnected and sustainable ecosystem. These concepts can also be applied in the port sphere, as they are crucial nodes for the development of a given territory and territorial economic development. In fact, CE and IS allow the reduction of impacts on the environment and constitute competitive advantages for the optimisation of processes and activities carried out within port areas, as well as the reduction of operating costs.

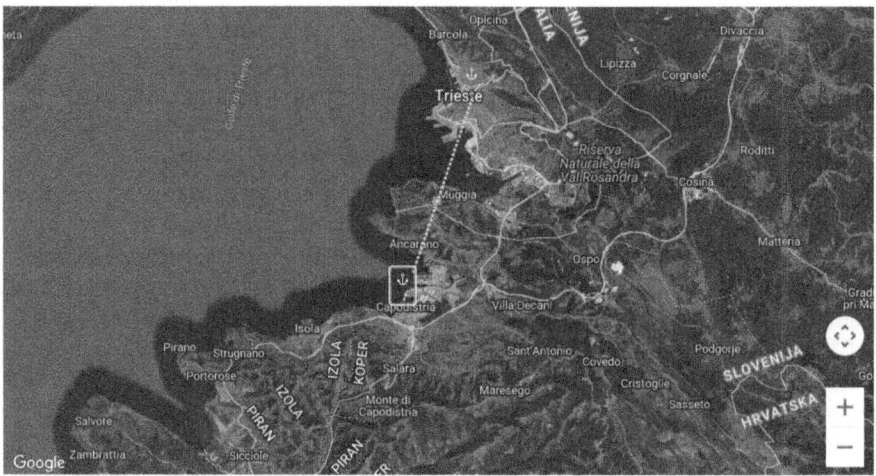

Fig. 1. Distance between the port of Trieste and the port of Koper [5]

The distance between the two ports is approximately 22 km by land and 6 nautical miles by sea. So, due to their proximity, the port of Trieste and the port of Koper were chosen for the analysis by the authors.

3.1 The Port of Koper Through Circular Economy and Industrial Symbiosis

The port of Koper, is a commercial port located in Slovenia, in the northern part of the Adriatic Sea and mainly connects the markets of the Mediterranean Sea with Central and South-Eastern Europe and the Far East. It is the main port of call in the North Adriatic for container traffic and vehicle handling, handling approximately 2/3 of the total national maritime traffic (Fig. 1). It is part of the North Adriatic Ports Association (NAPA) together with the port of Venice, Trieste and Rijeka and is connected to the main road and rail infrastructure. The port is managed by the company Luka Koper, whose capital is 100% owned by Slovenia (Fig. 2).

In relation to circular operations, the Port of Koper is implementing a proactive approach towards a sustainable transition through the Solar Power for Reducing Emissions (SOPOREM) project. This project involves the construction of a large solar power plant with a total capacity of 3.3 MW.

This involves the construction of a large solar power plant with a total capacity of 3.3 MW. The power plant, situated on the roofs of the cargo terminal's warehouses,

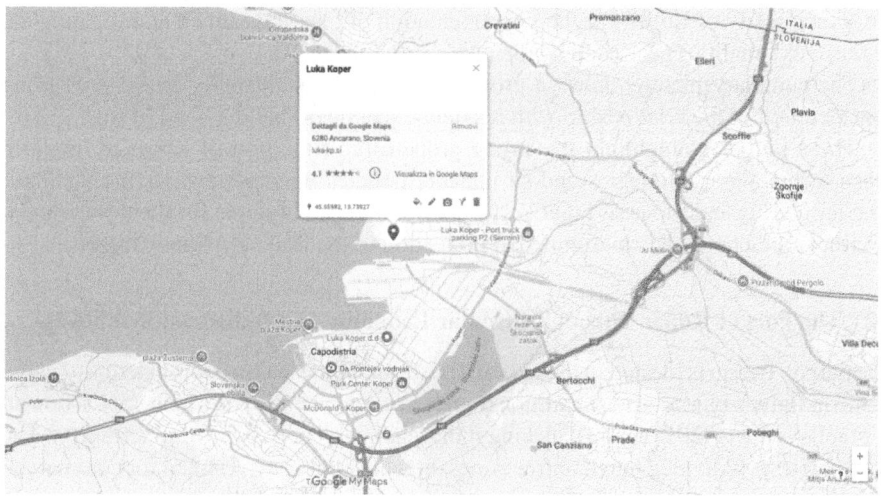

Fig. 2. The Port of Koper

is designed to reduce CO_2 emissions into the atmosphere by 1,500 tonnes per year, thereby contributing to the achievement of sustainability objectives. In addition, the port has made substantial investments in recent years in the electrification of port operations, notably through the replacement of diesel cranes with electric cranes and the utilisation of low-emission vehicles for internal activities [6, 7]. These measures are intended to enhance the energy efficiency and reduce the ecological impact of the port's operations, thereby aligning with the sustainability objectives outlined in the 2030 Agenda at both the national and European levels.

As is evident in the published annual report, there has been a notable emphasis on sustainable policies. Consequently, the port has been identified as one of the most active in the Adriatic region in terms of sustainability.

Indeed, a range of strategies have been implemented for the purpose of measuring and monitoring various environmental indicators. These indicators include, but are not limited to, the following [6, 7]:

- air quality,
- energy consumption,
- water management,
- waste management,
- greenhouse gas emissions,
- and noise pollution.

With reference to waste management, activities aimed at separate waste collection have been implemented, reaching 60% of recycled products, thanks to the monitoring of waste, the port is able to optimise waste disposal and implement strategies of circular economy and industrial symbiosis. Furthermore, the Luka koper association has committed to contributing annually, by donating funds in excess of 700,000 euro to the Municipality of Koper, for the implementation of measures aimed at mitigating the negative externalities generated by the port's activities [6, 7].

The summary picture shows a growing focus on sustainability but also a strong consideration of the relationship with residents, seeking to build a bond of trust.

These initiatives highlight the strong propensity of the port of Koper to invest in green technologies, strategies and sustainable policies oriented towards the medium-long term. This leads to assert that Port Luka Koper is an example for the development of circular practices and environmental protection in the Balkan-Adriatic region.

3.2   The Port of Koper Through Circular Economy and Industrial Symbiosis

The port of Trieste is located in the gulf of Trieste and is the leading port in terms of cargo traffic in Italy, with a total of 62 million tonnes of cargo per year, of which 75% is related to preoil products (2017 figure), making it the leading oil port in the Mediterranean. The port of Trieste is divided into five free zones, of which three are destined for commercial activities [8]:

- The Old Free Port
- The New Free Port
- The timber terminal,
- The Mineral Oils Free Port (from which the oil pipeline originates)
- Zaule Canal, utilised for industrial activities.

The port of Trieste is distinguished by its deep water, which facilitates efficient nautical accessibility. Additionally, it boasts well-developed rail and road connections, further enhancing its logistical capabilities. This infrastructure is part of the main TEN-T network, where the port is identified as a core node between the European Baltic-Adriatic and Mediterranean corridors. Likewise the port of Koper, also the port of Trieste is a constituent of the NAPA. The port of Trieste is overseen by the Trieste Port Authority (L.84/94); in conjunction with the ports of Nogaro and Monfalcone, it constitutes the Eastern Adriatic Sea System Authority (Decree implementing L.124/2015). Further information can be found at [9] (Fig. 3):

In terms of environmental sustainability, the Port of Trieste is engaged in the enhancement and advocacy of practices within the framework of the circular economy. Specifically, the National Recovery and Resilience Plan (NRRP) has allocated funding for the primary sustainable measure, the cold ironing project.

This initiative involves the electrification of docks, with the objective of reducing emissions and noise pollution. The cold ironing project enables moored ships to disconnect from their engines and connect to the port's electricity grid. Moreover, projects encompass the initiation of the electrification of the quays belonging to Pier V and Pier VII, with the objective of supplying energy to cargo ships during their period of stay in port [10].

In addition to the aforementioned measures, the Port of Trieste has committed itself to the implementation of systems aimed at environmental monitoring. The objective of these systems is to obtain measurements of air quality and the management of waste generated by port activities. Furthermore, the integration of circular economy strategies into the daily operations of the port is a key commitment, often in collaboration with

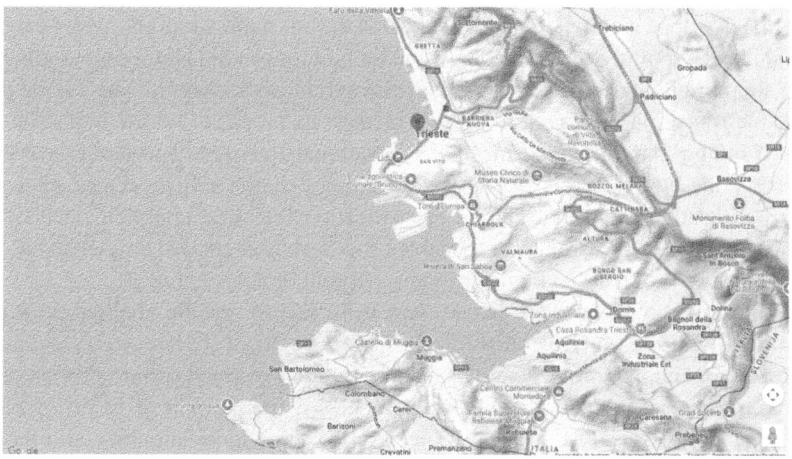

Fig. 3. The Port of Trieste [8]

the industries present in the area. Moreover, in collaboration with ARPA FVG, the environmental impact of maritime traffic will be monitored, encompassing not only emissions but also the risks of hydrocarbon spills and underwater noise [11].

In consideration of the circular economy, the Port of Trieste has initiated collaborative endeavours with companies that possess specialized knowledge in this domain. In collaboration with the Crismani Group, a partnership has been established with the objective of enhancing the recycling and material recovery activities of waste materials from port activities [12]. This initiative is designed to contribute to the active implementation of circular practices and industrial symbiosis within the port's area of responsibility.

4 Discussion

In this brief overview, it is evident that the approaches of the two ports considered are distinct. Despite this, they appear complementary in that, on the one hand, the port of Trieste focuses more on infrastructural energy transition and on building an industrial ecosystem that is able to support circular practices and industrial symbiosis strategies. The proximity to the industrial zone and the funding obtained from the PNRR-national recovery and resilience plan-supports the sustainable transition of the port itself. On the other hand, the Port of Koper is focusing more toward renewable energy production, through solar and internal electrification facilities, along with sustainable governance, allows for the development and implementation of solutions that are sustainable and allow for the measurement of achieved goals.

In consideration of the circular economy, the Port of Trieste has initiated collaborative endeavours with companies that possess specialized knowledge in this domain. In collaboration with the Crismani Group, a partnership has been established with the objective of enhancing recycling and material recovery activities related to waste materials from port activities. This initiative is designed to contribute to the active implementation of circular practices and industrial symbiosis within the port's area of responsibility.

So, the two appear complementary in that, on the one hand, the port of Trieste focuses more on infrastructural energy transition and on building an industrial ecosystem that is able to support circular practices and industrial symbiosis strategies. The Trieste port's sustainable transition is supported by two factors: its proximity to the industrial zone and the funding obtained from the PNRR (National Recovery and Resilience Plan). Conversely, the Port of Koper has adopted a strategy that prioritizes renewable energy production through solar and internal electrification facilities, complemented by sustainable governance. This approach enables the development and implementation of sustainable solutions and facilitates the measurement of achieved goals.

Despite this, both ports, are not exempt from facing specific challenges in order to best deal with the current transition. In fact, the port of Trieste needs to improve and strengthen collaboration, synergies, and integration with industrial logistics system actors to implement industrial symbiosis strategies while the port of Koper, thanks to its involvement in several European projects in the circular economy, could increase cross-border.

5 Conclusion

The analysis highlighted the differences between the two ports analyzed, highlighting how the two ports, which are geographically close, can develop and adopt distinctly different circular economy and industrial symbiosis practices, akin to the same field.

Trieste implements a systemic approach that is aimed at the organization and integration of infrastructure, industry and logistics. The reduction of emissions can be carried out by the port thanks to the projects developed in the field of cold ironing and industrial symbiosis initiatives, with the aim of waste minimization. Trieste also, due to its proximity to the industrial zone can promote industrial symbiosis strategies.

The analysis highlighted the differences between the two ports analyzed, highlighting how the two ports, which are geographically close, can develop and adopt distinctly different circular economy and industrial symbiosis practices, akin to the same field.

Trieste implements a systemic approach that is aimed at the organization and integration of infrastructure, industry and logistics. The reduction of emissions can be carried out by the port thanks to the projects developed in the field of cold ironing and industrial symbiosis initiatives, with the aim of waste minimization. Trieste also, due to its proximity to the industrial zone can promote industrial symbiosis strategies.

Koper, on the other hand, seems to focus more on energy self-production and electrification of inland operating assets, for example by investing large sums in photovoltaic systems, highlighting how it focuses more on energy efficiency and giving more weight.

We can state that both ports are trying to implement good practices of circular economy, despite the differences between the two realities, where more collaboration between the two ports, would bring benefits and advantages as well as stronger cross-border cooperation.

Furthermore, given the proximity of the two ports, they could implement circular strategies to enhance their competitiveness and foster international cooperation and cohesion between ports.

Therefore, the need to implement shared strategies in the Upper Adriatic Area emerges, in order to share synergies, knowledge, strategies and technologies that could turn into a reference model for other ports in Europe.

The cases considered represent different but virtuous examples, although still improvable, of the environmental transition taking place in the Mediterranean port area, overcoming barriers to achieve not only environmental but also economic and social transition.

Acknowledgments. PhD programme in Circular Economy at the University of Trieste, Cycle XXXVIII, with the support of a scholarship financed by the Ministerial Decree no. 351 of 9th April 2022, based on the NRRP - funded by the European Union - NextGenerationEU - Mission 4 "Education and Research", Component 1 "Enhancement of the offer of educational services: from nurseries to universities" - Investment 4.1 "Extension of the number of research doctorates and innovative doctorates for public administration and cultural heritage".

Authors' Contribution. Conceptualization, methodology, formal analysis, materials and resources, data curation and validation: all authors. In particular: Sinatra wrote Sect. 2, 3 and 4, Zanne wrote Sect. 1 and 5.

Disclosure of Interests. The authors have no competing interests to declare that are relevant to the content of this article.

References

1. Okumus, D., Gunbeyaz, S.A., Kurt, R.E., Turan, O.: Circular economy approach in the maritime industry: barriers and the path to sustainability. Transport. Res. Procedia **72**, 2157–2164 (2023)
2. Jensen, H.H., et al.: Digitalisation in a maritime circular economy. In: Lind, M., Michaelides, M., Ward, R. (eds.) Maritime Informatics: Additional Perspectives and Applications, pp. 17–37. Springer, Cham (2021)
3. Gallo, M., Moreschi, L., Mazzoccoli, M., Marotta, V., Del Borghi, A.: Sustainability in maritime sector: waste management alternatives evaluated in a circular carbon economy perspective. Resources **9**(4), 41 (2020)
4. Ellen MacArthur Foundation. https://www.ellenmacarthurfoundation.org/topics/circular-eco nomy-introduction/overview. Accessed 28 Apr 2025
5. BednBlue – Sailing Distance Calculator: Trieste, Italy – Marina Koper, Slovenia. https://www.bednblue.it/sailing-distance-calculator?map=%5B%7B%22latLng%22%3A%2245.649526%2C13.776818%22%2C%22name%22%3A%22Trieste%2C%20Italy%22%7D%2C%7B%22latLng%22%3A%2245.549849%2C13.727792%22%2C%22name%22%3A%22Marina%20Koper%2C%20Slovenia%22%7D%5D. Accessed 10 May 2025
6. Luka Koper – Annual Reports, https://www.luka-kp.si/en/investors/annual-reports/, last accessed 2025/05/05
7. Luka Koper Business Report 2023. https://www.luka-kp.si/wp-content/uploads/2024/04/06-Luka-Koper_Business-Report_2023.pdf. Accessed 05 May 2025
8. Porto di Trieste – Trail. https://trail.unioncamereveneto.it/infrastrutture/porto-di-trieste/. Accessed 15 Apr 2025

9. Shipping Italy: Aggiudicato a Nidec ASI il cold ironing nei moli V e VII del porto di Trieste. https://www.shippingitaly.it/2023/10/09/aggiudicato-a-nidec-asi-il-cold-ironing-nei-moli-v-e-vii-del-porto-di-trieste/. Accessed 10 Apr 2025

10. Gemmo – Acquisition of a cold ironing construction contract for the Port of Trieste. https://www.gemmo.com/en/home-en/acquisition-of-a-cold-ironing-construction-contract-for-the-port-of-trie-ste/. . Accessed 05 May 2025

11. ARPA FVG – Porto di Trieste. https://www.arpa.fvg.it/temi/temi/sviluppo-sostenibile/notizie-in-evidenza/porto-di-trieste/. Accessed 13 Apr 2025

12. Gestione rifiuti, Itelyum acquisisce il gruppo triestino Crismani. https://www.adriaports.com/it/logistica/rifiuti-itelyum-trieste-crismani/. Accessed 02 May 2025

Semantic 3D City Models as a Catalyst for Circular Construction Practices

Burak Bek[✉], Mehmet Akif Ortak, and Jörg Rainer Noennig

HafenCity University Hamburg, Henning-Voscherau-Platz 1, 20457 Hamburg, Germany
burak.bek@hcu-hamburg.de

Abstract. Rapid global urbanization and escalating environmental challenges demand innovative strategies to reduce waste and enhance resource efficiency. As a major resource consumer, the construction industry requires a transformative shift toward sustainable practices through improved material stock assessments and efficient management of construction and demolition waste (CDW). Semantic 3D city models, utilizing the CityGML standard, provide a structured framework for capturing and analyzing building-related data across various levels of detail (LOD). This paper demonstrates how semantic 3D models could empower stakeholders to perform rapid stock inventories, assess reuse potential, and plan waste-minimizing demolition or renovation scenarios, through a sample system architecture for a Web GIS application built on open-access LOD2 CityGML data enriched with material-specific, recyclability, and life-cycle metadata. This framework underscores the role of semantic information in bridging geometric data and circular-economy decision support, supporting more resilient and resource-efficient urban development.

Keywords: Circular Economy · Construction and Demolition Waste · CityGML

1 Introduction

1.1 Construction and Demolition Waste in Circular Economy

The growing pressure to make the urban environment more sustainable has led to an increased focus on the principles of circular economy in the construction sector. Circular economy prioritizes the reuse, recycling and recovery of materials in order to minimize waste and reduce resource consumption [1]. The construction industry, responsible for more than 30% of global waste generation and significant resource extraction, faces critical challenges in managing construction and demolition waste (CDW) due to its volume, diversity, and complex handling requirements [2, 3]. Effective CDW management is pivotal for reducing environmental impacts, such as landfill overuse and greenhouse gas emissions, while also yielding economic benefits through material recovery and cost savings. By adopting circular economy practices, cities can mitigate environmental footprints, optimize resource use, and foster resilient urban infrastructure [4, 5].

Digital technologies are emerging as facilitative tools in this process. The semantic 3D city model, especially CityGML, has become a prominent standard to model, analyze,

O. Gervasi et al. (Eds.): ICCSA 2025 Workshops, LNCS 15899, pp. 273–282, 2026.
https://doi.org/10.1007/978-3-031-97663-6_24

and manage urban environments digitally [6]. By holding geometric as well as semantic attributes of buildings, meticulous material stock assessments can be conducted, which is essential for proper the management of CDWs [7]. Such specifics are useful for decisions on recycling, reuse plans, and environmentally friendly practices that align urban growth with circular economy endeavors.

The aim of this paper is to demonstrate how semantic 3D city models, especially a CityGML-based model, can serve as a catalyst for circular construction practices. The objective is to illustrate how a system architecture of such a Web GIS application possibly could be structured to support urban stakeholders in visualizing, querying, and evaluating building materials at scale. The proposed system emphasizes interoperability, real-time visualization, and semantic querying through a modular architecture, and a user-friendly frontend interface. This prototype can help assess reuse potential, map recyclable elements, and inform material recovery strategies for urban renovation or demolition projects.

By providing detailed semantic information in 3D models, CityGML-based models enable stakeholders to identify recyclable materials and effectively make plans for material reuse optimization. It highlights the dual benefit of semantic enrichment: to improve the accuracy of material inventories and to facilitate interdisciplinary cooperation between urban planners, geospatial analysts and sustainability experts. In this respect, this paper aims to lay the foundation for analyzing how advanced digital models can fill the gap between conceptual models of the circular economy and practical application in urban building and demolition processes.

This paper is organized into four chapters. In Sect. 1, we introduce the concepts of circular economy in construction and demolition waste, define the scope and objectives of our study, and emphasize the value of semantic 3D urban models in facilitating the assessment and management of material stocks. Section 2 explores CityGML as a semantic information holder and explains its structure, the concept of levels of detail and its benefits in providing detailed material properties for effective circular economy applications. In Sect. 3, we present the sample architecture of a web portal for material management showing how geospatial data is used, and visualized by an interactive front-end to facilitate decision-making in sustainable urban development. Finally, the last section summarizes the key conclusions, discusses limitations, and indicates future research directions to further improve the integration of semantic 3D models into circular construction practices.

2   CityGML as a Semantic Information Holder

CityGML is a standard data model and exchange format for 3D urban models, which integrates geometric and semantic information [8]. Its structure is organized into core modules and thematic modules that define together the spatial and non-spatial characteristics of urban objects [9]. One of the most important aspects of CityGML is the concept of level of detail (LOD) [10]. LODs provide a formal framework for representing urban models at varying granularities, ranging from simple block models (LOD1) to detailed models of architectural elements and material characteristics (LOD3).

The semantic enrichment provided by CityGML is particularly useful for applications in the circular economy. By associating detailed material properties and construction elements with their geometric counterparts, CityGML makes it possible to conduct comprehensive material stock analyses. Within CityGML, building components such as walls, roofs, windows, and doors can be enhanced with semantic attributes describing their material attributes [7]. This is facilitated by utilizing predefined attribute classes and, if required, Application Domain Extensions (ADEs) through which additional domain-specific information can be added [11]. Material attributes such as thermal conductivity, recyclability, or life expectancy can be appended to the data. This capability is important in CDW management. This information allows planners and engineers to assess the extent of material recycling, reduce waste and the environmental impact of construction activities.

Besides, the standardization through CityGML also increases data interoperability across disciplines and platforms which helps promote cooperation among urban planners, environmental scientists, and policy makers. CityGML is a semantic information source that not only provides transparency and access to urban data but also enables innovative solutions for circular construction practice.

3 Use Case: Web Portal for Material Management

Recent advancements in web technologies, data formats, and increased internet speed have significantly enhanced Web GIS solutions, positioning them as primary interfaces between geospatial data and end-users. While traditional GIS systems have predominantly provided solutions based on two-dimensional (2D) datasets, contemporary developments have enabled more realistic and detailed visualizations using three-dimensional (3D) data. Specifically, the growing importance of CityGML standards and the adoption of urban digital twins have underscored the critical role that 3D geospatial data plays in sustainable urban development and management. Yao et al. highlight how CityGML significantly extends analytical capabilities beyond conventional 2D GIS by enabling realistic simulations, detailed visualizations, and comprehensive spatial analyses [12, 13].

The number of cities utilizing CityGML datasets, particularly at LOD 2, has been increasing. Planners, engineers, managers, and administrators, increasingly rely on web-based GIS platforms designed to leverage geometric and semantic information for informed decision-making. Examples include the Hamburg Geoportal, the Berlin Economy Overview Map, or the Helsinki's Energy and Climate Atlas [14–16]. Such platforms offer interactive visualization, advanced querying functions, and enhanced accessibility for diverse stakeholders involved in urban material management and circular economy initiatives. On this background, this paper proposes a system architecture, illustrated by the modern Web GIS architecture depicted in Fig. 1, for effectively publishing CityGML data in a web environment.

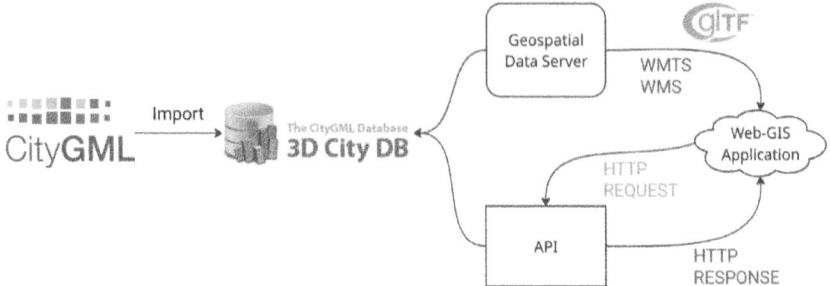

Fig. 1. System Architecture of a conceptual Web GIS Portal. *Source: authors*

3.1 Data Processing

Before being utilized in web applications or machine and deep-learning analyses, raw geospatial data require extensive preprocessing. Depending on data types and target applications, preprocessing tasks may vary significantly. CityGML data produced through surveying must undergo validation processes using dedicated tools such as FZKViewer [17].

CityGML's raw XML-based format is generally not efficient for direct use in interactive web applications. Therefore, the data must be converted into formats compatible with browser-based visualization technologies such as WebGL. Among the most suitable standards for this purpose is the Graphics Library Transmission Format (glTF), developed by the Khronos Group. glTF provides a compact, self-contained format optimized for real-time online rendering, enabling rapid data loading and reduced computational demands [18]. The core of glTF comprises a JSON file that describes the structure and composition of 3D models, combined with binary blocks containing vertex, index, and animation data in raw byte arrays [19]. Using the 3DCityDB, CityGML data can be efficiently exported into glTF format, establishing a secure and streamlined data processing pipeline from raw data to visualization-ready datasets [13] (Fig. 2).

3.2 Backend Infrastructure

Backend systems in Web GIS applications serve as intermediaries between data storage layers and frontend visualization platforms, primarily through Application Programming Interfaces (APIs) and geospatial data servers. Although modern tech stacks often conceptualize backend systems purely as APIs, handling geospatial data requires specialized data servers that comply with standards set by organizations such as the Open Geospatial Consortium (OGC). Standardized communication protocols, like Web Mapping Service (WMS), allow backend systems to deliver geospatial data consistently to various frontend clients, including both web and desktop GIS applications, ensuring sustainability and broad interoperability [20].

Additionally, APIs manage critical functions such as user authentication and authorization. APIs enable user-specific data access, ensuring that data security and privacy regulations are strictly adhered to, particularly important in circular economy contexts.

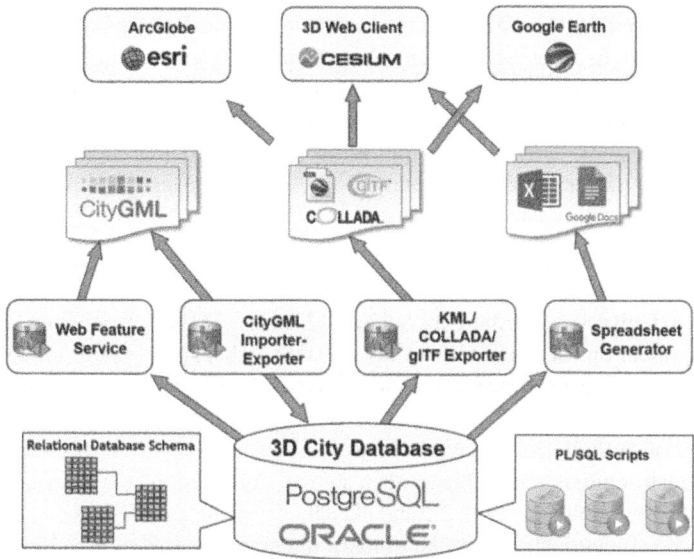

Fig. 2. Key components of the 3DCityDB Software Suite. *Source: Yao et al.* [12]

A common approach for backend implementation involves using Python-based frameworks, which offer extensive libraries for geospatial data handling. When integrated with databases like 3DCityDB, Python frameworks can securely manage SQL interactions via libraries such as SQLAlchemy, facilitating efficient database processing capabilities directly accessible to frontend users [12].

For serving large-scale 3D datasets, scalable geospatial servers are essential. One prominent example is Cesium Ion, an online platform offering streamlined handling of 3D data formats compatible with web and game-engine applications [21]. Although its free tier has limitations, Cesium Ion is ideal for proof-of-concept (POC) projects due to minimal initial backend investment. Larger projects, however, might require deploying a dedicated, scalable 3D Tiles server. Literature such as Yao et al. [12] and Liu [22] provide valuable insights into implementing on-premise tile servers, highlighting the importance of careful backend design to ensure smooth frontend interactions and efficient data transfer.

3.3 Frontend Design Considerations

Frontend interfaces are the primary points of interaction between geospatial data and end-users, enabling visualization, filtering, and analysis functionalities. Given the broad application scope of GIS, designing Web GIS interfaces tailored to specific user profiles through user experience (UX) and user interface (UI) design principles has become a standard practice. A common pattern includes the implementation of side panels (left and right) to facilitate intuitive information navigation, especially effective in map-centered applications. Two primary approaches exist for frontend implementation:

Fully Customized Development. This involves building a bespoke frontend architecture from scratch, allowing full control over interface design and functionalities. A popular technology choice for 3D visualization in this scenario is Cesium.js, an open-source library enabling streaming and rendering of extensive heterogeneous geospatial datasets through its 3D tiles specification. While this offers comprehensive flexibility, it demands substantial time, human resources, and financial investment, which might not be feasible for limited-resource scenarios.

Framework-Based Rapid Development. Alternatively, projects can leverage existing open-source frameworks designed specifically for Web GIS, such as the TOSCA initiated by HafenCity University Digital City Science [23]. The TOSCA is an open source and full stack application for WEB GIS solution. TOSCA backend system utilizes Python Django API, a Postgre database and GeoServer, a geospatial data server solution [23–25]. The frontend of TOSCA uses Vue-3 Js web framework and the Maplibre GL mapping library based on WebGL. Including its underlying subsystems, the entire codebase of the TOSCA infrastructure is accessible as open source. Furthermore, the system infrastructure is suitable for publishing both 2D and 3D data. By using established documentation, project-specific functionalities can be quickly integrated, significantly reducing initial development effort and facilitating early stakeholder testing and feedback (Fig. 3).

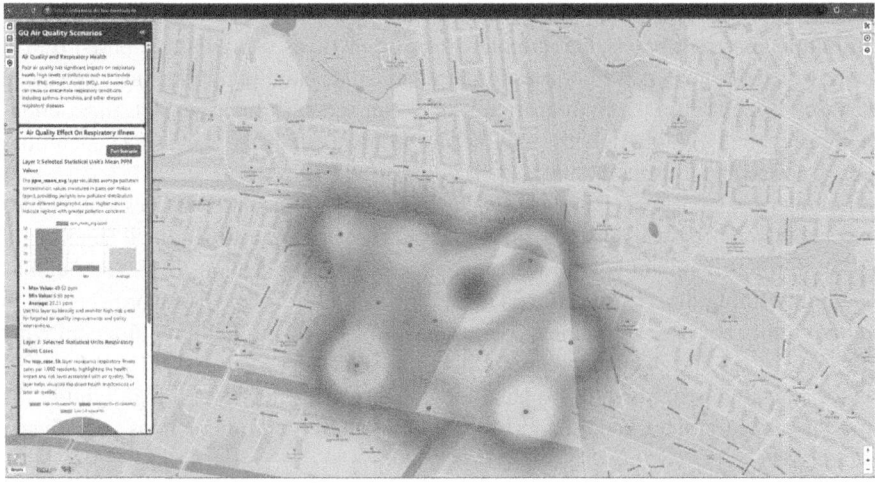

Fig. 3. TOSCA for public health use case. *Source: authors* [26]

Regardless of whether a fully customized frontend or a framework-based approach is employed, the effectiveness of a Web GIS application in supporting circular construction practices largely depends on its interface design and functional responsiveness. Figure 1 illustrates the shared conceptual foundation underlying both development strategies. Central to this foundation is the prioritization of user-centered design, where interface components such as side panels and interactive map elements must be tailored to the specific analytical needs of end-users. Filtering functionalities represent a core component of such platforms. Both attribute-based filtering (e.g., by material type, construction year, or reuse potential) and spatial filtering are fundamental for enabling users to extract relevant subsets of the building stock. In addition, the integration of essential geospatial processing functions such as buffer, dissolve, and intersection can enhance the platform's analytical capabilities, supporting scenario-based analyses of demolition, renovation, and resource recovery. These foundational functions enable stakeholders to derive actionable insights from complex urban datasets and are critical for the implementation of circular economy strategies in the built environment.

When geospatial data is produced and published according to standardized formats, the integration of new scenarios into existing Web GIS systems is significantly facilitated. In particular, adopting a framework-based development approach allows for the seamless inclusion of additional use cases as requirements evolve. For example, the Digital City Science team at HafenCity University has developed the AGORA Web GIS platform for the LIG (Hamburg Real Estate and Land Property Management Authority) using the TOSCA base system [26, 27]. This platform supports urban planning workflows compatible with German geospatial standards such as ALKIS and XPlanung and enables experts to identify the most suitable land parcels [28] (Fig. 4).

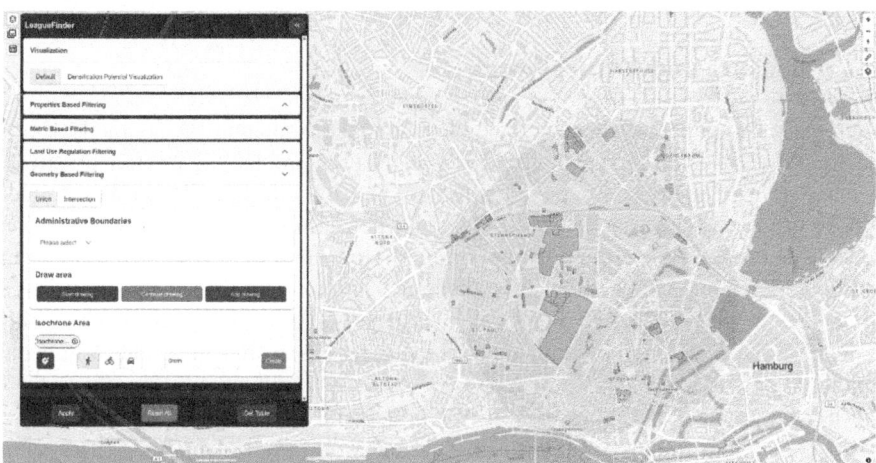

Fig. 4. AGORA property (include general real estate and exclude roads) and geometry (15 min concept) based filtering. *Source: authors* [27]

Within the AGORA system, users can apply both attribute-based filters (e.g. zoning category, land use type) and spatial filters (e.g. drawn area of interest, administrative/statistical boundaries or isochrone-based catchment areas generated via a routing engine) to efficiently query and analyze land parcel data within the city of Hamburg.

The same modular filtering logic combining attribute and geometric constraints can be applied to other domains. For example, in the context of the circular economy use case, the same filtering mechanisms can be reused to produce relevant insights, provided that the underlying geospatial data is published in accordance with defined standards. As demonstrated in the AGORA system, such filters are not hard-coded but abstracted in a reusable manner, allowing them to be flexibly adapted to different application scenarios with minimal front-end changes. Given these examples, we present a sample feature set for a Web GIS application for circular economy focus.

Exemplary Feature Set for a Circular Economy Web GIS Application
To support decision-makers in quickly performing analyses related to circular economy metrics, the proposed Web GIS solution should include:

- *Material Query & Filtering:* Query buildings by material type, quantity, and reuse/recycle potential.
- *Material Inventory Analysis:* Assess buildings based on recyclability, reuse potential, and sustainability scores.
- *Spatial Querying:* Filter buildings by attributes such as type, construction year, and materials.
- *Dashboard & Reporting:* Visualize key circular economy indicators, including recycling potentials and potential CO_2 savings.
- *Scenario Simulation:*Simulate building demolition and renovation scenarios, emphasizing material reuse.
- *Export & Sharing:*Provide options to export analysis results in standard formats (e.g., PDF, CSV) to facilitate stakeholder communication.

4   Conclusion and Future Work

In summary, this paper has demonstrated the potential of semantic 3D city models, particularly those based on CityGML, to act as a catalyst for circular construction practices. By integrating geometric and semantic information, CityGML provides a robust framework for accurately assessing material stocks and managing construction and demolition waste. This capability is critical in supporting the transition to a circular economy in urban environments, where efficient resource use is important. The detailed semantic enrichment in CityGML-based models enables experts to collaborate effectively, facilitating informed decisions regarding material reuse, recycling strategies, and sustainable demolition practices.

The system showcased how modern Web GIS solutions can bridge the gap between theoretical circular economy models and their real-world implementation. The system architecture, which includes backend infrastructure and user-friendly frontend interfaces, serves as an example of how digital tools can support experts in sustainable urban development.

Despite the advantages of CityGML-based semantic 3D city models in supporting circular construction, several limitations remain. First, the accuracy and completeness of these models heavily depend on the availability and quality of input data, which can vary significantly across different municipalities and regions. Inconsistencies in data collection methods, sensor precision, and classification standards can lead to discrepancies in material assessments and hinder interoperability. Additionally, while the web-based material management system presented in this paper facilitates visualization and decision-making, the complexity of ensuring real-time data updates and cross-platform compatibility remains an ongoing issue.

Looking ahead, several avenues for future work are apparent. First, further refinement of data processing workflows and the integration of more detailed semantic attributes could enhance the accuracy and utility of material stock assessments. Expanding the use case to incorporate additional datasets from different cities or higher Levels of Detail (e.g., LOD3) would allow for more comprehensive analyses, despite the associated challenges in data acquisition and processing costs. Moreover, the development of standardized protocols for semantic enrichment across various urban contexts could foster greater interoperability and data sharing among municipalities, researchers, and industry practitioners.

Additionally, exploring the integration of other sustainability metrics—such as life cycle assessment (LCA) or carbon footprint estimation—into CityGML models could provide a more holistic view of urban environmental performance. These enhancements would not only support better planning decisions but also encourage wider adoption of circular economy practices. Ultimately, continued interdisciplinary research and collaboration are essential to advance these digital solutions, ensuring that they meet the evolving needs of sustainable urban development in the 21st century.

References

1. Ghaffar, S.H., Burman, M., Braimah, N.: Pathways to circular construction: an integrated management of construction and demolition waste for resource recovery. J. Clean. Prod. **244**, 118710 (2020). https://doi.org/10.1016/j.jclepro.2019.118710
2. Soto-Paz, J., Arroyo, O., Torres-Guevara, L.E., Parra-Orobio, B.A., Casallas-Ojeda, M.: The circular economy in the construction and demolition waste management: a comparative analysis in emerging and developed countries. J. Build. Eng. **78**, 107724 (2023). https://doi.org/10.1016/j.jobe.2023.107724
3. Pomponi, F., Moncaster, A.: Circular economy for the built environment: a research framework. J. Clean. Prod. **143**, 710–718 (2017). https://doi.org/10.1016/j.jclepro.2016.12.055
4. Adams, K.T., Osmani, M., Thorpe, T., Thornback, J.: Circular economy in construction: current awareness, challenges and enablers. Proc. Inst. Civil Eng. Waste Res. Manag. **170**, 15–24 (2017). https://doi.org/10.1680/jwarm.16.00011
5. Benachio, G.L.F., Freitas, M.D.C.D., Tavares, S.F.: Circular economy in the construction industry: a systematic literature review. J. Clean. Prod. **260**, 121046 (2020). https://doi.org/10.1016/j.jclepro.2020.121046
6. Biljecki, F., Stoter, J., Ledoux, H., Zlatanova, S., Çöltekin, A.: Applications of 3D city models: state of the art review. ISPRS Int. J. Geo Inf. **4**, 2842–2889 (2015). https://doi.org/10.3390/ijgi4042842
7. Kolbe, T.H.: Representing and exchanging 3D city models with CityGML. In: Lee, J., Zlatanova, S. (eds.) 3D Geo-Information Sciences. pp. 15–31. Springer, Heidelberg (2009). https://doi.org/10.1007/978-3-540-87395-2_2
8. Kolbe, T.H., Gröger, G., Plümer, L.: CityGML: interoperable access to 3D city models. In: van Oosterom, P., Zlatanova, S., Fendel, E.M. (eds.) Geo-information for Disaster Management, pp. 883–899. Springer, Heidelberg (2005). https://doi.org/10.1007/3-540-27468-5_63
9. Kutzner, T., Chaturvedi, K., Kolbe, T.H.: CityGML 3.0: New functions open up new applications. PFG. **88**, 43–61 (2020). https://doi.org/10.1007/s41064-020-00095-z
10. Biljecki, F., Ledoux, H., Stoter, J.: An improved LOD specification for 3D building models. Comput. Environ. Urban Syst. **59**, 25–37 (2016). https://doi.org/10.1016/j.compenvurbsys.2016.04.005

11. Rosser, J.F., Long, G., Zakhary, S., Boyd, D.S., Mao, Y., Robinson, D.: Modelling urban housing stocks for building energy simulation using CityGML EnergyADE. ISPRS Int. J. Geo Inf. **8**, 163 (2019). https://doi.org/10.3390/ijgi8040163

12. Yao, Z., et al.: 3DCityDB - a 3D geodatabase solution for the management, analysis, and visualization of semantic 3D city models based on CityGML. Open Geospat. Data Softw. Stand. **3**, 5 (2018). https://doi.org/10.1186/s40965-018-0046-7

13. Santhanavanich, T., et al.: Enabling interoperability of urban building energy data based on OGC API standards and CityGML 3D city models. ISPRS Ann. Photogram. Remote Sens. Spatial Inf. Sci. **X-1-W1–2023**, 97–105 (2023). https://doi.org/10.5194/isprs-annals-X-1-W1-2023-97-2023

14. Geoportal Hamburg. https://geoportal-hamburg.de/. Accessed 29 Mar 2025

15. virtualcitySYSTEMS: Helsinki 3D Atlas - Helsinki 3D city model viewer. https://kartta.hel.fi/3d/atlas/#/. Accessed 29 Mar 2025

16. Berlin Economy Overview Map. https://www.businesslocationcenter.de/wab/maps/main/#/. Accessed 29 Mar 2025

17. webmaster, I.A.I.: KIT - IAI - Downloads – FZKViewer. https://www.iai.kit.edu/english/1648.php. Accessed 29 Mar 2025

18. Schilling, A., Bolling, J., Nagel, C.: Using glTF for streaming CityGML 3D city models. In: Proceedings of the 21st International Conference on Web3D Technology, pp. 109–116. Association for Computing Machinery, New York (2016). https://doi.org/10.1145/2945292.2945312

19. glTF - Runtime 3D Asset Delivery. https://www.khronos.org/gltf/. Accessed 29 Mar 2025

20. Web Map Service (WMS) Standard | OGC Publications. https://www.ogc.org/publications/standard/wms/. Accessed 08 May 2025

21. Cesium ion. https://cesium.com/platform/cesium-ion/. Accessed 08 May 2025

22. Liu, T.: A Prototype Architecture for Interactive 3D Maps on the Web (2024). https://dspace.library.uvic.ca/bitstreams/648e0937-d91c-44c7-a689-1277ba4ef935/download

23. Digital City Science: TOSCA-2 Wiki Github Repository. https://github.com/digitalcityscience/TOSCA-2/wiki/Home. Accessed 08 May 2025

24. Implementation Partnership: Masterportal: The Open Source Geoportal, https://www.masterportal.org/en/partnership/about-us. Accessed 29 Mar 2025

25. Moleiro, M., Mukherjee, A., Noennig, J.R.: The TOSCA case: how open-source spatial and digital decision support tools help urban agglomerations to leapfrog towards smart sustainable cities. Int. J. E-Plan. Res. **12** (2023). https://doi.org/10.4018/IJEPR.319370

26. TOSCA: Toolkit for Open and Sustainable City Planing & Analysis India. https://india.tosca.dcs.hcu-hamburg.de/. Accessed 08 May 2025

27. Digital City Science: LIGFinder. https://agora.dcs.hcu-hamburg.de/. Accessed 08 May 2025

28. XPlanung | XLeitstelle. https://xleitstelle.de/xplanung. Accessed 08 May 2025

Evaluation of the Performance of the Global Weather Dataset AgERA5 for Sustainable Water Management in Agriculture: A Focus on Reference Evapotranspiration

Anna Pelosi[1]([⊠]) [iD], Gianmarco Aceto[1], Angeloluigi Aprile[2], and Giovanni Battista Chirico[2] [iD]

[1] Università degli Studi di Salerno, Via Giovanni Paolo II 132, Fisciano, SA, Italy
apelosi@unisa.it
[2] Università degli Studi di Napoli "Federico II", Via Università 100, Portici, NA, Italy

Abstract. Assessing water withdrawal for crop irrigation at large scale is a decisive step for arranging a sustainable development in the agriculture sector toward an optimal allocation and management of water resources. Since direct measurements of irrigation volumes are very often not available, indirect estimates are needed. These require the use of consistent time-series of gridded weather data for implementing crop-water balance models. So far, advances in meteorological numerical modelling have been encouraging the use of their outputs, including reanalysis data, as gridded weather data sources for similar purposes. As interest in meteorological weather reanalysis data increases, the need to evaluate their performance and compare the suitability of different databases for various sites becomes central. This study evaluates the performance of the weather dataset AgERA5, which was lately derived from ERA5 reanalysis with a finer resolution, for agricultural water management applications. The AgERA5 is compared with the ERA5-Land dataset, as well as with ground-based weather interpolated observations, which are the primary alternative weather database. The study focuses on the weather variables needed for computing the FAO Penman-Monteith reference evapotranspiration, ET_0, such as wind velocity, surface shortwave radiation, temperature and relative humidity of air: key variables for irrigation volume estimates. The target area for the analyses is the Campania Region, a mediterranean-climate region in the South of Italy. The performances of the databases are evaluated from April to September, when irrigation occurs, respect to the years 2008–2024. Results show that AgERA5 is a reliable dataset for assessing agricultural indicators in regional studies by simply applying a local correction of the bias and it outperforms the weather dataset alternatives for assessing ET_0.

Keywords: Reanalysis data · FAO-56 Penman-Monteith reference evapotranspiration · irrigation season

1   Introduction

An important goal of the current European policies for climate change adaptation regards the identification of water management strategies and actions able to guarantee water supply for food production, in accordance with the principles of sustainability, under which the environment and ecosystems obtain a central role along with the social and economic development. Then, agricultural water management assumes a significant role toward this goal, since in many European regions, especially in the Mediterranean area, the consumption and quality degradation of water for irrigating crops is the primary stressor on hydrological cycle. In these areas, evaluating water use for irrigation is crucial for designing sustainable policies and making rational and optimal decisions in water resource management [1]. Above all, agricultural water management planning entails the assessment of irrigation water volumes to program suitable actions by identifying priorities and specific needs in single district. Quantifying irrigation and water uses is indeed a condition set by the Water Framework Directive (2000/60/EC), that was later implemented in Italy according to the MiPAAF (i.e., Ministry of Agricultural, Food and Forestry Policies) Ministerial Decree issued on 31 July 2015. The said Decree establishes a set of guidelines to meet the following objectives: (1) build an updated knowledge framework about the irrigation needs of the Italian agricultural context, (2) propose tools and methodologies for quantifying the volumes withdrawn used for irrigation purposes, (3) start setting up a unique and shared platform for collecting and processing the information acquired about irrigation use. Since direct measurements of irrigation volumes are very often not available over a region and for an adequate long span time, indirect estimates are needed. Following the experiences of various irrigation consulting systems, operating across some Italian regions, over Europe and around the globe [2–5], several studies [6–8] proposed to accept the net irrigation requirement for crops under "standard" conditions as defined by the FAO - Food and Agriculture Organization of the United Nations - [9] as operative proxy of the irrigation water volume. In Mediterranean regions, such as Italy and the target area, where precipitations can be assumed negligible in the period April-September, when irrigation is indeed needed, evapotranspiration remains the fundamental variable for assessing crop water requirements [6]. It depends on weather information, such as wind velocity, surface shortwave radiation, temperature and relative humidity of air as well as crop parameters, like LAI (i.e., Leaf Area Index).

In recent years, satellite-based estimates of crop parameters with very high spatial resolution (e.g., 20 m for Sentinel-2) were used to obtain the actual crop development with satisfying reliability [8, 10, 11]. On the other hand, evapotranspiration estimates require gridded weather data as input source for regional analyses [12–14]. A classical approach to address the need for gridded weather dataset is to use advanced geostatistical interpolation techniques [15] applied to ground-based weather data observed at a restricted number of places along a district. However, although ground-based weather observations may be considered a weather truth at the site of measurement, elsewhere these data are affected by estimation errors that depend on both the geometry and consistency of the observation system and the variability over space of the weather variable itself [6, 12, 14]. Therefore, due to the great development of numerical weather modelling in the last decades, gridded weather data from reanalysis datasets have been becoming an interesting opportunity for agricultural water management applications and, in particular, for evapotranspiration estimates. In recent years, many studies evaluated reanalysis datasets, such as ERA5 and ERA5-Land, developed by European Centre for Medium-Range Weather Forecasts (ECMWF), for evapotranspiration studies and it was found that these datasets provide a consistent and global source of meteorological data for this purpose [6, 8, 10, 12, 16]. Freely available and easily accessible, reanalysis datasets span extensive time periods and offer high spatial resolution, making them an attractive solution for applications in data-sparse regions [6, 13]. Here, we evaluate the performance of the latest released reanalysis dataset, AgERA5 over a data-sparse region located in Southern Italy. The focus is on the weather variables that have a key role in the assessment of reference evapotranspiration (ET_0) and then, in agricultural water management applications. A recent study was conducted for evaluating ET_0 by employing AgERA5 over the Jucar River system in Spain and Sicily Region in Italy [17]. Interesting discussions are then proposed for comparison among these Mediterranean areas, crucial sites for investments and actions in sustainable water management to prevent water scarcity.

2 Target Region and Weather Datasets

2.1 Target Region

The target region of the study is Campania, depicted in Fig. 1, which is a mediterranean-climate region located in South of Italy. The territory has an extension of 13671 km^2 from the Southern Apennines to the Tyrrhenian Sea. It is mostly characterized by the Mediterranean climate with very warm and semi-arid summers, rainy and cold winters and mild autumns and springs. Although it depends on the specific crops and their cycles, the irrigation season can be set in the span time of the year from April to September [6]. Therefore, in the present study, the analyses are being referred to these months for the years 2008–2024.

2.2 Weather Datasets

In the target area, a monitoring network composed of 18 complete ground-based automatic weather stations (AWSs) is available. The reanalysis data from ERA5-Land and AgERA5 databases cover the area as well. Figure 1 shows the region, with some information about the weather data availability, whose details are described below.

Ground-Based Weather Dataset. The current weather monitoring network has been managing by the Multi-Risk Service of the Regional Civil Protection Department in Campania Region. It is composed of 18 complete ground-based AWSs that sparsely cover the region with an average density of about one station over 750 km^2. The network is very uneven, resulting in some portions of the region that appear not monitored at all, such as the southern coast and the center of the region (Fig. 1). The AWSs have been working continuously since 2008, measuring, with a time resolution of 10 min, the following weather variables: (i) wind velocity at 10 m height, hereinafter denoted as WS, (ii) surface shortwave radiation, hereinafter denoted as RS, (iii) air temperature, hereinafter denoted as T, (iv) air relative humidity, hereinafter denoted as RH, and (v)

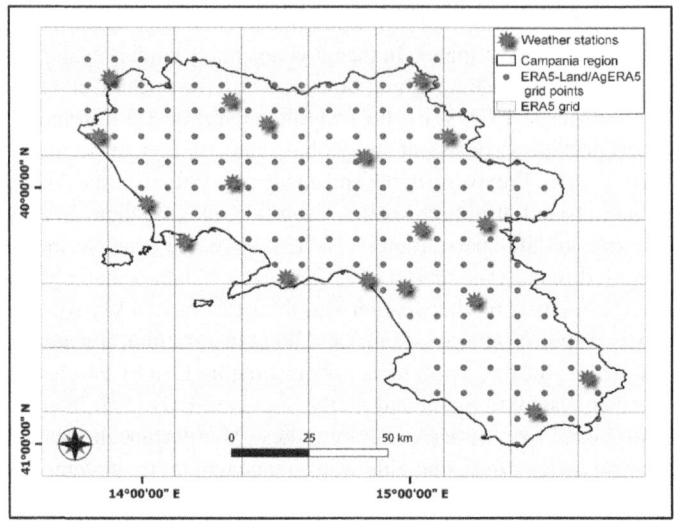

Fig. 1. Target area, ground-based weather stations in red and grid points of ERA5-Land and AgERA5 datasets in blue, in comparison with the mesh of the global ERA5 reanalysis database.

atmospheric pressure. Table 1 reports some regional statistics about observations in the analyzed period that spans from April to September of 2008–2024. Since in the following analyses the interest is in the daily minimum and maximum temperatures (T_{min} and T_{max}, respectively), their statistics are also reported as follows.

Table 1. Means and coefficients of variation referred to the daily weather observations within the period April-September of 2008–2024 for the target area, i.e., Campania Region.

Weather Variable	Mean	Coefficient of variation
T	20.5 °C	0.0041
T_{max}	27.0 °C	0.24
T_{min}	14.7 °C	0.21
RS	244.9 W m^{-2}	0.31
RH	69.3%	0.18
WS	2.4 m s^{-1}	0.38

Interpolated Ground-BASED Data (IGD). Ground-based weather observations are generally available in discrete points over a region. Spatial interpolation permits us to assess the values of the observation elsewhere in unmonitored sites and, eventually, on a regular grid for obtaining a gridded weather dataset. Among the spatial interpolation methods, geostatistical interpolation by kriging is one of the most used and advanced techniques [15]. Here, ordinary kriging is employed for interpolating the daily observations of wind velocity, surface shortwave radiation, air relative humidity and atmospheric pressure. Daily minimum and maximum air temperature are interpolated with regression kriging, using elevation as predictor for improving the estimates [6, 12, 14]. The interpolated ground-based data, after in the text referred to as IGD, are computed at each AWS site by means of the leave-one-out crossvalidation method, which allows to assess the interpolated value in a point where the measure is available by applying the interpolation technique on the remaining set of observations obtained by excluding the measure at the point of interest.

Reanalysis Data. The reanalysis databases considered in this study are ERA5-Land and AgERA5, developed by ECMWF and available for free downloading on the web application Copernicus Climate Data Store. Both of them cover a period from 1979 to the near present (few days back) and both are derived product from ERA5 data for land and agricultural applications, respectively. However, while the resolution in space of ERA5 is $0.25 \times 0.25°$, the horizontal resolution for ERA5-Land and AgERA5 is $0.10 \times 0.10°$. The temporal resolution of data is always one hour. Figure 1 shows the grid points of these datasets, compared with the native grid of ERA5. The weather outputs of the datasets are WS at 10 m height, RS, then T, atmospheric pressure, dew point temperature (T_{dew}), all available at a height of 2 m above ground. To have consistent datasets with ground-based observations, the dew point temperature is converted to relative humidity by applying the following formula [9]:

$$RH = 100\frac{e_a}{e_s} \tag{1}$$

where e_s is the mean saturation vapor pressure [9], while e_a is the actual vapor pressure computed by Eq. (2) as function of T_{dew}:

$$e_a(T_{dew}) = 0.6108 exp\left[\frac{17.27T_{dew}}{T_{dew} + 273.3}\right] \tag{2}$$

Both ERA5-Land and AgERA5 data are corrected with a simple and efficient bias correction technique [12, 18], which consists of subtracting the monthly regional mean bias for each variable of interest. For the objectives of the current analysis, the correction bias is computed over the same span time of the analyses, by assuming that the ground-based observations are available and for testing the case that, despite this availability, the gridded reanalysis data represent a good alternative data source for weather observations in regional studies.

3   Methods

FAO-56 ET$_0$. The reference evapotranspiration, ET$_0$ was here calculated by employing the Penman–Monteith formula proposed by the paper FAO-56 [9], as stated in the next equation:

$$ET_0 = \frac{1}{0.408}\frac{\Delta(R_n - G) + \gamma \frac{900}{T+273} WS(e_s - e_a)}{\Delta + \gamma(1 + 0.34 \, WS)} \tag{3}$$

where γ is the psychometric constant; Δ is the slope of the vapor pressure law; T is the daily mean air temperature at 2 m height that has to be determined by averaging T_{min} and T_{max}; WS is the wind velocity related to an height of 2 m above the ground; e_s (kPa) and e_a (kPa) are, respectively, the daily saturation vapor pressure and daily actual vapor pressure; R_n is the net solar radiation at the crop surface and G is the soil heat flux density. The net solar radiation (R_n) is the difference between the incoming net shortwave radiation and the outgoing net longwave radiation. The incoming net shortwave radiation is a fraction of the incoming shortwave solar radiation, called RS, by means of the albedo (i.e., equal to 0.23 for the hypothetical grass crop for the computation of ET_0). The wind velocity at 2 m, WS (m s^{-1}), is given by the wind velocity at 10 m that is the available information, by using a very common logarithmic wind velocity profile as also proposed by the paper FAO-56 [9]. Detailed information on input data can be found in [9].

In the following, Table 2 reports some regional statistics about daily ET_0 computed by using observations in the analyzed period (April-September of 2008–2024).

Evaluation of the Performance. Let V_j be the observed daily value of each variable of interest for the analyses at the ground-based network and F_j the corresponding daily value as predicted by the different databases, i.e., AgERA5, ERA5-Land and IGD data, the two statistical indicators here applied to assess the performance of AgERA5, compared with the one of the remaining datasets of interest are:

$$PBIAS(\%) = \frac{1}{\overline{V}} \frac{\sum_{j=1}^{m}(F_j - V_j)}{m} 100 \qquad (4)$$

$$PRMSE(\%) = \frac{1}{\overline{V}} \sqrt{\frac{\sum_{j=1}^{m}(F_j - V_j)^2}{m}} 100 \qquad (5)$$

where $\overline{V}$ is the average value of ground-based observations in the period of interest made of m days.

Table 2. Means and coefficients of variation of the ET_0 calculated by using ground-based observations as input data, within the period April-September of 2008–2024 for Campania.

Daily ET_0	Mean (mm day^{-1})	Coefficient of variation
April	2.7	0.20
May	3.5	0.18
June	4.5	0.15
July	5.0	0.15
August	4.5	0.17
September	3.0	0.24

4 Main Outcomes and Discussion

In the current section, the major outcomes of the analyses are given. Primarily, in Figs. 2, 3, 4, 5, 6 and 7 are proposed the performance of all the weather variables proposed for the ET_0 assessment. In particular, the results refer to bias corrected reanalysis data. Wind speed is the most biased variable, which is also affected by the highest values of PRMSE, followed by solar radiation and then, air relative humidity.

Air temperature is the best predicted variable, however the T_{max} estimates outperform the T_{min} estimates that show an average regional PRMSE equal to about 16%–17% for the IGD, ERA5-Land and AgERA5 data, compared with the 6%–7% related to T_{max}.

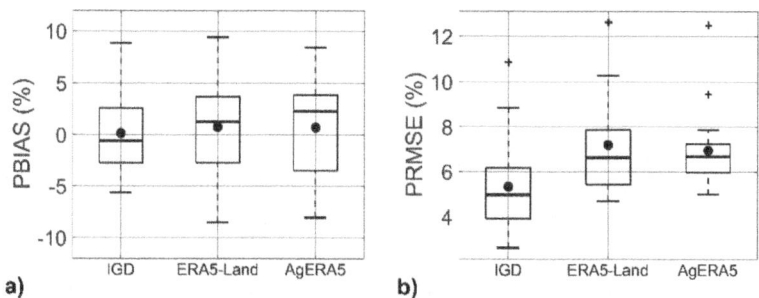

Fig. 2. Boxplot of the regional a) PBIAS and b) PRMSE for T

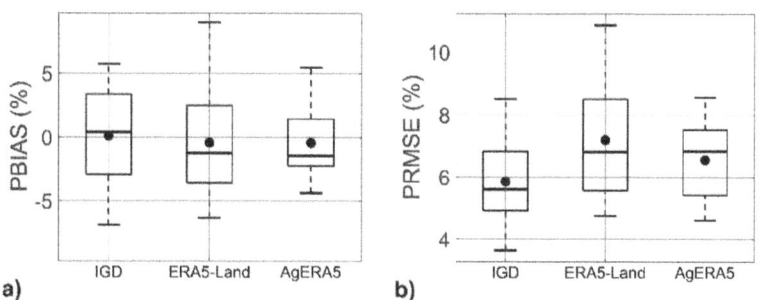

Fig. 3. Boxplot of the regional a) PBIAS and b) PRMSE for T_{max}

Solar radiation estimates show average regional PRMSE equal to 18.6%, 22.4% and 18% respectively for the IGD, ERA5-Land and AgERA5 databases while the same statistics equal values of 10%, 12.5% and 14% for the IGD, ERA5-Land and AgERA5 relative humidity estimates.

Wind speed estimates show average regional PRMSE equal to 60.5%, 49.1% and 48.2% respectively for the IGD, ERA5-Land and AgERA5 databases.

For all the variables, the three databases, i.e., IGD, ERA5-Land and AgERA5, slightly differ each other by supporting the hypothesis that gridded reanalysis is a good proxy for weather observations if a bias correction technique is applied. However, it is noted that AgERA5 outputs slightly outperform ERA5-Land data for air temperature

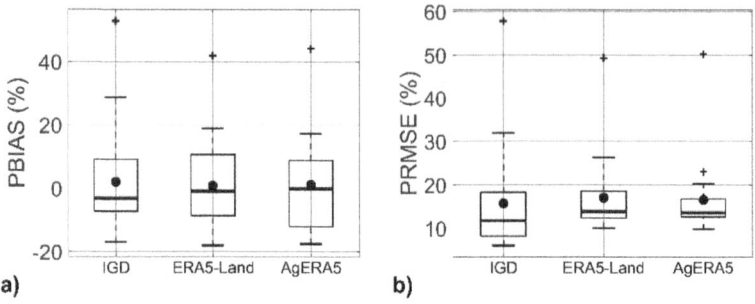

Fig. 4. Boxplot of the regional a) PBIAS and b) PRMSE for T_{min}

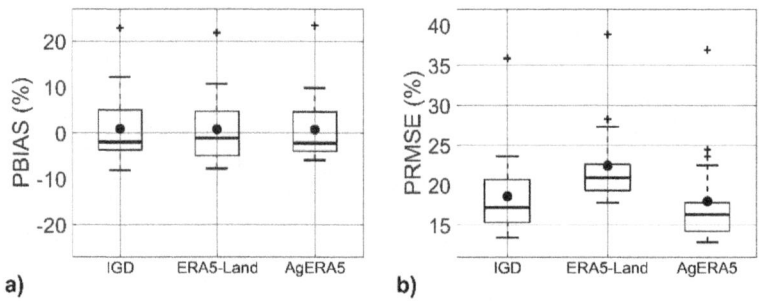

Fig. 5. Boxplot of the regional a) PBIAS and b) PRMSE for RS

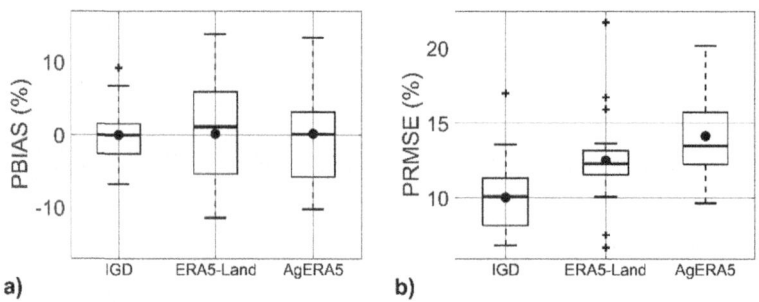

Fig. 6. Boxplot of the regional a) PBIAS and b) PRMSE for RH

and solar radiation. Similar results were also found by [17] in two area located in Spain and Italy as well: in that study wind speed also remained the most biased meteorological variable.

Figure 8 exhibits the performance of the three different analyzed input weather databases for the assessment of the FAO ET_0 by means of Eq. (3). It is clear that both of the reanalysis datasets are excellent proxy of weather observations for this purpose, showing a regional average mean PBIAS equal to 0.8% and 1.6% for ERA5-Land and AgERA5 estimates, respectively, compared with the 1.5% showed by the IGD estimates. The maximum absolute PBIAS values for the IGD, ERA5-Land and AgERA5 ET_0 estimates

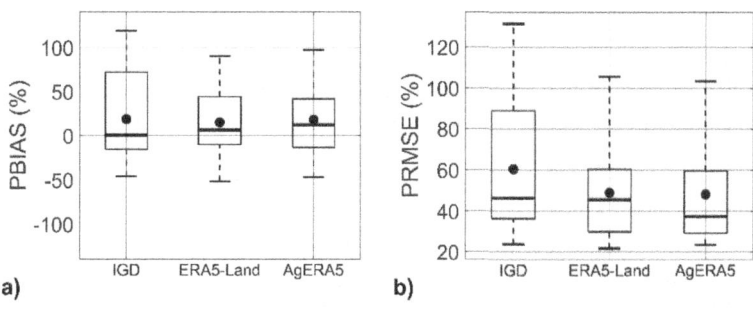

Fig. 7. Boxplot of the regional a) PBIAS and b) PRMSE for WS

are 17.7%, 13.6% and 15.9% respectively. The average values of the PRMSE are 18.2%, 19.4% and 18.3% respectively for the IGD, ERA5-Land and AgERA5 ET_0 estimates while the maximum values of the PRMSE are 29.7%, 31.4% and 28.9% respectively.

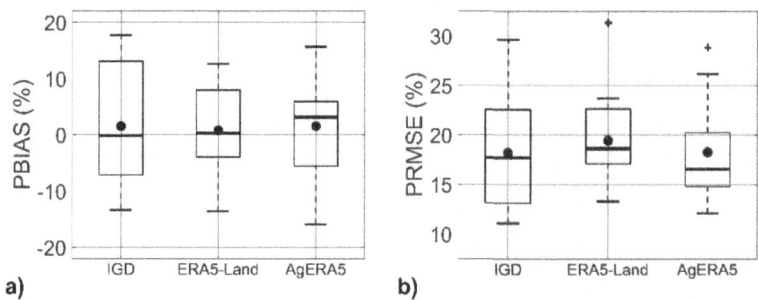

Fig. 8. Boxplot of the regional a) PBIAS and b) PRMSE for ET_0

As also pointed out by [17], AgERA5 showed superior performance than ERA5-Land.

5   Conclusions

Sustainable agricultural water management requires knowledge of irrigation water volumes for planning investment and actions as well as for identifying critical areas and preventing water scarcity. Since direct measurements of water volumes for irrigation purposes are unavailable at the level of analysis, alternative methods that use gridded weather data to implement crop-water balance models are necessary.

To obtain gridded data at a regional scale, sparse ground-based weather observations must be spatially interpolated, which introduces interpolation errors that depend on the variable of interest and the density of the monitoring network. On the other hand, in recent years the development of numerical weather modeling provides the opportunity to use weather reanalysis data as gridded data in regional applications.

The proposed analyses demonstrate that gridded reanalysis datasets, such as ERA5-Land and the latest AgERA5, are accurate and reliable alternative of weather observations when a bias correction technique is applied. In particular, their use for assessing reference evapotranspiration—a key variable for estimating irrigation water volumes—appears to be a promising possibility. Indeed, both ERA5-Land data and AgERA5 data, derived from ERA5 with a finer spatial resolution for specific land and agricultural applications, are acceptable substitutes of weather data observed at the ground-based monitoring network as data input for the assessment of ET_0 at the district scale.

Acknowledgments. The content of the present paper was part of the project "Integrated Monitoring & Modelling for the Sustainability of Irrigated Crops" (I-MOSAIC), funded by the European Union - Next Generation EU within the PRIN 2022 call promoted by the Italian Ministry of University and Research. As stated above, the reanalysis datasets were downloaded from the ECMWF Copernicus Climate Data Store (cds.climate.copernicus.eu). Weather observations were provided by the Regional Civil Protection Department in Campania Region (centrofunzionale.regione.campania.it).

Disclosure of Interests. The authors state that they do not have any competing interests, which can be significant to the matter of the present paper.

References

1. Wriedt, G., van der Velde, M., Aloe, A., Bouraoui, F.: A European irrigation map for spatially distributed agricultural modelling. Agric. Water Manag. **96**, 771–789 (2009). https://doi.org/10.1016/j.jhydrol.2009.05.018
2. Consoli, S., Vanella, D.: Comparisons of satellite-based models for estimating evapotranspiration fluxes. J. Hydrol. **513**, 475–489 (2014). https://doi.org/10.1016/j.jhydrol.2014.03.071
3. Vuolo, F., D'Urso, G., De Michele, C., Bianchi, B., Cutting, M.: Satellite-based irrigation advisory services: a common tool for different experiences from Europe to Australia. Agric. Water Manag. **147**, 82–89 (2015). https://doi.org/10.1016/j.agwat.2014.08.004
4. Chirico, G.B., Pelosi, A., De Michele, C., Falanga Bolognesi, S., D'Urso, G.: Forecasting potential evapotranspiration by combining numerical weather predictions and visible and near-infrared satellite images: an application in Southern Italy. J. Agric. Sci. **156**, 702–710 (2018). https://doi.org/10.1017/S0021859618000084
5. Pelosi, A., Villani, P., Falanga Bolognesi, S., Chirico, G.B., D'Urso, G.: Predicting crop evapotranspiration by integrating ground and remote sensors with air temperature forecasts. Sensors **20**, 1740 (2020). https://doi.org/10.3390/s20061740
6. Pelosi, A., Terribile, F., D'Urso, G., Battista Chirico, G.: Comparison of ERA5-Land and UERRA MESCAN-SURFEX reanalysis data with spatially interpolated weather observations for the regional assessment of reference evapotranspiration. Water **12**, 1669 (2020). https://doi.org/10.3390/w12061669
7. Belfiore, O.R., et al.: Monitoring of irrigation water use in Italy by using IRRISAT methodology: the INCIPIT project. In: Ferro, V., Giordano, G., Orlando, S., Vallone, M., Cascone, G., Porto, S.M.C. (eds.) AIIA 2022: Biosystems Engineering Towards the Green Deal. AIIA 2022. LNCE, vol. 337, pp. 41–49. Springer, Cham (2022). https://doi.org/10.1007/978-3-031-30329-6_4
8. Longo-Minnolo, G., D'Emilio, A., Vanella, D., Consoli, S.: Advancing in satellite-based models coupled with reanalysis agrometeorological data for improving the irrigation management under the European Water Framework Directive. Agric. Water Manag. **301**, 108955 (2024). https://doi.org/10.1016/j.agwat.2024.108955

9. Allen, R.G., Pereira, L.S., Raes, D., Smith, M.: Crop evapotranspiration. Guidelines for Computing Crop Water Requirements. Paper 56 FAO Irrigation and Drainage. FAO, Rome (1998)

10. Pelosi, A., Belfiore, O.R., D'Urso, G., Chirico, G.B.: Assessing crop water requirement and yield by combining ERA5-Land reanalysis data with CM-SAF satellite-based radiation data and Sentinel-2 satellite imagery. Remote Sens. **14**, 6233 (2022). https://doi.org/10.3390/rs1 4246233

11. Er-Rami, M., D'Urso, G., Lamaddalena, N., D'Agostino, D., Belfiore, O.R.: Analysis of irrigation system performance based on an integrated approach with Sentinel-2 satellite images. J. Agric. Eng. **52** (2021). https://doi.org/10.4081/jae.2021.1170

12. Pelosi, A., Chirico, G.B.: Regional assessment of daily reference evapotranspiration: can ground observations be replaced by blending ERA5-Land meteorological reanalysis and CM-SAF satellite-based radiation data. Agric. Water Manag. **258**, 107169 (2021). https://doi.org/10.1016/j.agwat.2021.107169

13. Nouri, M.: Drought assessment using gridded data sources in data-poor areas with different aridity conditions. Water Res. Manag. **37**, 4327–4343 (2023). https://doi.org/10.1007/s11269-023-03555-4

14. Pelosi, A.: Performance of the Copernicus European Regional Reanalysis (CERRA) dataset as proxy of ground-based agrometeorological data. Agric. Water Manag. **289**, 108556 (2023). https://doi.org/10.1016/j.agwat.2023.108556

15. Journel, A.G., Huijbregts, C.J.: Mining Geostatistics. Academic Press, London (1978)

16. Vanella, D., et al.: Comparing the use of ERA5 reanalysis dataset and ground-based agrometeorological data under different climates and topography in Italy. J. Hydrol. Reg. Stud. **42**, 101182 (2022). https://doi.org/10.1016/j.ejrh.2022.101182

17. Garcia-Prats, A., et al.: High-resolution spatially interpolated FAO penman-monteith crop reference evapotranspiration maps using Agera5 and Era5-land reanalysis datasets (2024). SSRN: https://ssrn.com/abstract=5065028 or https://doi.org/10.2139/ssrn.5065028

18. Paredes, P., Martins, D.S., Pereira, L.S., Cadima, J., Pires, C.: Accuracy of daily estimation of grass reference evapotranspiration using ERA-Interim reanalysis products with assessment of alternative bias correction schemes. Agric. Water Manag. **210**, 340–353 (2018). https://doi.org/10.1016/j.agwat.2018.08.003

Engaging Citizens in Public Transit Choice: Insights from Vietnam and Italy

Martina Carra$^{(\boxtimes)}$ ⓘ, Roberto Ventura ⓘ, and Benedetto Barabino ⓘ

Department of Civil, Environmental, Architectural Engineering and Mathematics,
University of Brescia, 25123 Brescia, Italy
martina.carra@unibs.it

Abstract. Recently, Multi-Criteria Decision-Making methods (MCDMs) have become increasingly relevant in public transport planning, offering structured ways to assess complex alternatives that involve both technical and human-centered criteria. Despite their widespread use, previous studies have often overlooked the involvement of citizens in the decision-making process. Moreover, the wide variety of available MCDMs can pose challenges in selecting the most appropriate method for a given context. To address these gaps, this study introduces an integrated framework that combines five MCDM techniques: AHP, SAW, TOPSIS, VIKOR, and PROMETHEE II. The approach incorporates both expert assessments and user preferences to provide a comprehensive assessment of transit alternatives. Applied to two case studies, Ho Chi Minh City (Vietnam) and Brescia (Italy), the framework highlighted how citizen input can meaningfully contribute to public transport planning while also enabling the comparison of methodological outcomes across diverse urban contexts. The proposed framework provides a flexible, transparent, and replicable tool for policymakers and transport planners aiming to evaluate and prioritize public transport solutions in both developing and developed countries.

Keywords: Decision-making · Public transport planning · Citizen participation

1 Introduction

Efficient transportation is a vital component of cities. It enables mobility, supports economic growth, and shapes the daily lives of people. Currently, mobility systems are increasingly strained in many developing cities, where private vehicles dominate. Congestion, air and noise pollution, and deteriorating public health are becoming common consequences. These issues are particularly severe in metropolis, where urbanization and centralized economic activities highly pressure on infrastructure and services [1]. As cities aim to become smarter, safer, and more sustainable, public transportation systems are emerging as key enablers of this transformation. Well-designed public transport reduces dependency on cars, improves air quality, enhances safety, and ensures equitable access to services [2]. However, choosing the most suitable public transport mode is a complex task. Each city faces unique challenges, ranging from demographic and spatial

© The Author(s), under exclusive license to Springer Nature Switzerland AG 2026
O. Gervasi et al. (Eds.): ICCSA 2025 Workshops, LNCS 15899, pp. 294–305, 2026.
https://doi.org/10.1007/978-3-031-97663-6_26

characteristics to socio-economic and cultural factors. Therefore, any transport investment must consider both technical feasibility, local needs, and long-term sustainability [3, 4]. A challenge in transport planning is how to evaluate and prioritize alternative systems. Should a city invest in metro, bus rapid transit, trams, buses, etc.? Which solution offers the best balance among cost, efficiency, environmental impact, and user satisfaction? Researchers increasingly turn to MCDM methods to address these questions and support the decision-making process [5–7]. These are structured approaches used to compare and rank options based on a combination of quantitative and qualitative criteria.

MCDM methods are promising in the urban transport sector, where decision-making involves multiple stakeholders, conflicting objectives, and uncertainty. These methods enable for the inclusion of diverse evaluation criteria, such as travel time, cost, emissions, accessibility, comfort, and safety. Moreover, they can incorporate both objective performance indicators and subjective preferences from users and experts alike. Various MCDMs have been developed, each with different structures, assumptions, and applications. Broadly, they can be grouped into three categories [8]. *Value-based methods* (e.g., Simple Additive Weighting – SAW, Analytic Hierarchy Process – AHP, Multi-Attribute Utility Theory – MAUT) assign weights to each criterion and compute overall scores for each alternative based on additive models [9]. For instance, in SAW, alternatives are ranked by summing weighted scores across all criteria [10]. *Outranking methods* (e.g., ELECTRE, PROMETHEE) compare alternatives pairwise for each criterion to determine preferences [11–13]. Unlike value-based approaches, they do not require all criteria to be on the same scale and are better suited for handling vague or imprecise judgments. *Goal-based methods* (e.g., TOPSIS, VIKOR) assess how close each alternative is to an ideal solution [9, 10]. For instance, TOPSIS identifies the option with the shortest distance from the best-case scenario and the furthest from the worst-case. VIKOR uses compromise programming to balance performance and regret.

Each method has advantages and limitations [9, 14]. While value-based methods are intuitive and easy to communicate, they may oversimplify complex trade-offs. Outranking methods better reflect human decision-making but may yield inconclusive or ambiguous rankings that are less transparent to non-experts. Goal-based models offer more flexibility but rely heavily on the definition of the "ideal" alternative.

MCDM methods have been widely used in public transport planning to: (i) select project alternatives, such as comparing different transport modes or technologies [15–17]; (ii) evaluate service quality [18, 19]; (iii) support planning by identifying the most efficient or user-preferred transport systems [20, 21].

Despite their usefulness, some key limitations remain in current research. (i) Comparative analysis of MCDM methods across different city types or contexts is lacking, making it difficult to identify recurring patterns or best practices. (ii) The best-performing alternative is not always the most feasible for implementation as contextual factors, such as funding, social acceptance, and long-term maintenance, are often under-considered [22]. (iii) Assessments tend to rely solely on expert opinions, with limited stakeholder engagement, a key point for legitimacy, acceptance, and successful implementation, as highlighted in the EU's SUMP principles [23, 24].

To overcome these challenges, this study proposes a hybrid MCDM framework that integrates five methods: AHP, SAW, TOPSIS, VIKOR, and PROMETHEE. It enables decision-makers to: (i) combine the strengths of each method while mitigating individual limitations; (ii) cross-validate results across techniques to identify converging or diverging outcomes; (iii) incorporate both expert knowledge (via literature and technical standards) and user preferences (collected through surveys).

The framework is applied to two case studies representing different urban contexts, Ho Chi Minh City (Vietnam) and Brescia (Italy). By comparing outcomes in these cities, the study explores how the decision-making tools may lead to different conclusions depending on the urban scale, transport needs, and stakeholder priorities.

The results highlight the relevance of an integrated participatory approach for selecting public transport systems that are technically valid, economically viable, socially accepted, and environmentally sustainable. Involving citizens improves the quality of the decision and helps build trust, reduce resistance, and encourage public transport adoption. In the context of smart, safe, and healthy cities, this approach offers a transparent, adaptable, and user-inclusive decision support model that is data-driven for evidence-based planning and focused on sustainable and equitable mobility. It provides valuable insights and practical tools for urban planners, transport authorities, and policymakers aiming to build more livable cities.

2   Methodology

This study applied an integrated methodology to support the selection of the most appropriate public transport system across different urban contexts. The framework consists of three main steps, as shown in Fig. 1.

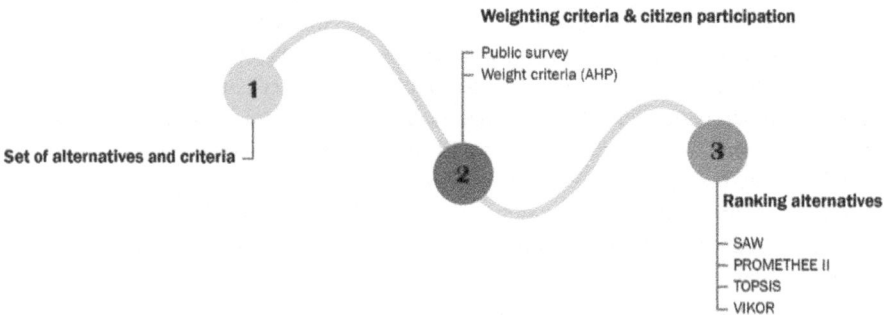

Fig. 1. The structure of integrated methodology.

2.1   Step 1. Defining Alternatives and Criteria

The first step identifies a set of public transport alternatives and assessment criteria. Alternatives are derived from an extensive literature review, ensuring that each one represents a viable solution within the scope of urban mobility planning. Alternatives range across different performance levels, from basic to high-capacity systems, and reflect various degrees of investment, sustainability, and technological advancement. A set of criteria is also defined to assess these options meaningfully. They represent alternative characteristics such as cost, efficiency, and environmental impact. Criteria may be split into sub-criteria to make the decision process more structured and manageable, i.e., to ensure that alternatives can be measured, compared, and prioritized effectively. While many studies do not categorize alternatives to prevent bias, this framework explicitly includes such classification to illustrate that lower-performance options may sometimes be more appropriate, depending on the context. This helps decision-makers remain open to a broader range of solutions and avoid over-prioritizing high-end systems that may not align with local needs or resources [11].

2.2 Step 2. Weighting Criteria and Citizen Participation

The second step determines the relevance of the assessment criteria by applying the AHP. This widely applied MCDM method decomposes complex decisions into simpler pairwise comparisons within a hierarchical structure.

Citizens and experts are involved through surveys via Google forms and the AHP-OS platform. Specifically, AHP-OS enables participants to provide immediate feedback on their response consistency, enabling them to revise their judgments and improve the reliability of their input. Generally, AHP is applied using the expert's judgment. However, this study also includes citizens' input in the weighting process to reflect broader stakeholder values and ensure greater transparency and social legitimacy, e.g., affordability vs environmental impact when choosing public transportation.

Once responses are collected, AHP processes the pairwise comparisons to derive a normalized weight $\widehat{w}_j$ for each criterion and sub-criterion. Let D and J be the sets of participants and criteria, respectively. For each participant $d \in D$, a pairwise comparison matrix $A_{j,d}$ is built. The relative importance of criterion $j \in J$ compared to another $k \in J$ is expressed as a ratio $a_{jk,d}$. Weights are computed using the geometric mean method and normalized as follows:

$$\widehat{w}_{j,d} = \frac{\left(\prod_{k \in J} a_{jk,d}\right)^{1/|J|}}{\sum_{j \in J}\left(\prod_{k \in J} a_{jk,d}\right)^{1/|J|}} \tag{1}$$

To ensure coherence in judgments, the AHP checks the Consistency Ratio (CR) for each matrix [25] as follows:

$$CR_{J,d} = \frac{\left(\lambda_{maxJ,d} - |J|\right)}{RI \cdot (|J| - 1)} \tag{2}$$

where λ_{max} is the eigenvalue of the matrix, and RI is a random index based on the number of criteria. In this study, a relaxed threshold of CR ≤ 0.15 was adopted to accommodate non-expert participants (compared to the standard 0.10 used for experts) [26, 27]. Valid responses are then aggregated into a final group judgment using the Weighted Geometric Mean Aggregation method, ensuring that all valid judgments contribute proportionally to the final result [28]. To obtain the overall weight for each terminal node in the decision hierarchy, the sub-criteria weights were multiplied by their respective parent criteria weights. This provided a comprehensive ranking of all elements involved in the evaluation process.

2.3 Step 3. Ranking Alternatives

The third stage ranks the alternatives using four widely used MCDM methods: SAW, TOPSIS, VIKOR, and PROMETHEE II. Let I be the set of alternatives. Each method builds a decision matrix based on the performance of each alternative $i \in I$ containing performance values x_{ij} for each alternative $i \in I$ and criterion $j \in J$. When data are qualitative, they are translated into numerical values using predefined scales. Next, the decision matrix is normalized into a utility matrix $\hat{x}_{ij}$, , considering whether the criterion is a benefit (to be maximized) or a cost (to be minimized). The weights $\hat{w}_j$, computed in the previous step, are then applied to reflect the relevance of each criterion. The normalized and weighted values are subsequently used to compute a global score G_i for each alternative, which reflects its overall suitability. Finally, the global score determines the rank from most to least appropriate alternative.

Each method follows a different computational logic. SAW aggregates performance by summing all weighted normalized values [Eq. 3]. It is straightforward and intuitive but may oversimplify complex decisions. TOPSIS compares each alternative's distance from an ideal best Δ^+_i and an ideal worst Δ^-_i solution. Alternatives are ranked based on their relative closeness CC_i to the ideal solution, making the method useful when both optimality and risk minimization are relevant [Eq. 4]. VIKOR identifies a compromise solution, balancing between the collective satisfaction (group utility S_i) and regret R_i of individuals who are most affected by poor performance on specific criteria. A parameter $\beta = 0.5$ is used to weigh these two aspects equally, although it can be adjusted according to decision-makers preferences [Eq. 5]. PROMETHEE II is an outranking method that performs pairwise comparisons between alternatives. It calculates positive $\emptyset^+(i)$ and negative $\emptyset^-(i)$ preference flows to reflect how much each alternative outranks or is outranked by others. The resulting net flow score offers insight into dominance relations among the options, which is especially useful for visual analysis [Eq. 6].

$$G_{SAW,i} = \sum_{j \in J} \hat{w}_j \hat{x}_{ij} \tag{3}$$

$$G_{TOP,i} = CC_i = \frac{\Delta^-_i}{\Delta^-_i + \Delta^+_i} \tag{4}$$

$$G_{VIK,i} = \beta \frac{S_i - S_{min}}{S_{max} - S_{min}} + (1 - \beta) \frac{R_i - R_{min}}{R_{max} - R_{min}} \tag{5}$$

$$G_{PRO,i} = \emptyset(i) = \emptyset^+(i) - \emptyset^-(i) \tag{6}$$

While SAW, TOPSIS, and PROMETHEE generate positively oriented rankings (where higher scores indicate better alternatives), VIKOR produces a negatively oriented score, where lower values reflect more balanced and satisfactory options.

This combined approach enables for comparison and validation of results across methods, offering robust insights into the most appropriate public transport alternatives.

3 Results

The method was applied in two different urban contexts to explore how public transport systems can be selected more effectively. Ho Chi Minh City (Vietnam), with its rapid growth and ageing infrastructure, faces major challenges in handling its daily traffic. In contrast, Brescia is a mid-sized Italian city where a metro system already supports part of the network, but further expansion is needed. By applying the assessment framework, the research offers useful insights for cities with different scales and needs.

3.1 Step 1. Defining Alternatives and Criteria

In Step 1, criteria were grouped into two main categories: Individual criteria (IC), which reflect the needs and preferences of public transport users, and Provider-public criteria (PP), which relate to broader considerations relevant to service providers and the public interest (Table 2). *ID* were assessed by users via survey, as they pertain to elements that influence passengers' choices in everyday travel. Six criteria and related sub-criteria were identified from existing study [18, 30, 31]: (i) vehicle-related (comfort, capacity), (ii) safety (at stops, onboard, of vehicle), (iii) travel time (access, waiting, in-vehicle), (iv) availability (operating hours, ticket characteristics), (v) reliability (punctuality, tracking), and (vi) directness (connectivity, transfers, stop distance). In contrast, the *PP criteria* were intended to capture strategic planning concerns. Among these, two sub-criteria were selected: (i) investment cost and (ii) city development, according to [29].

The transport modes alternatives were classified by performance level following [30] framework: low (Regular Buses, trams), medium (Bus Rapid Transit, Ligh Rail Transit), and high (metro, Automatic Light Rail Transit). Categories informed the selection of alternatives for the two case studies. The alternatives for Ho Chi Minh City included RB, BRT, LRT, and Metro. For Brescia, the selection comprised RB, BRT, ALRT, and Tram, aligning with lower demand and different infrastructural contexts. Each alternative was characterized through a mix of quali-quantitative criteria. Technical data were drawn from official sources/reports, while qualitative performance was evaluated using a linguistic scale based on prior research [31]. Finally, assumptions were standardized to ensure comparability; e.g., access times were longer for high-performance modes, assuming greater walking distances in exchange for faster services.

3.2 Step 2. Weighting Criteria and Citizen Participation

The Step 2 weighting criteria through AHP, informed by a public survey distributed across both case studies. 174 responses were collected, 157 from Ho Chi Minh and 17 from Brescia, reflecting the population sizes of the two cities. Moreover, individual criteria were weighted based on survey responses, while the Provider-public criteria weights were derived from previous studies due to their technical nature.

The results showed that in Ho Chi Minh, a larger share of importance was placed on public and strategic dimensions (60.4%), while in Brescia, users gave slightly more weight to individual and user-centered criteria (47%). The most relevant criteria across both cases included Travel time and Directness (Table 2), suggesting that users favor transport options that offer save time and connected experiences. In contrast, Availability and Vehicle comfort or capacity criteria were rated less critical. City development emerged as the highest priority for the Provider-public criteria, followed by Investment cost. This highlights the significance of long-term urban benefits in the public transport decision-making process (Table 1).

Table 1. Set and normalized weights of the criteria.

Categories	Criterion	#	Sub-criterion	Overall normalized weight	
				Ho-Chi-Min	*Brescia*
Individual	Vehicle	1.1	Comfortability	0.027	0.032
		1.2	Passenger capacity	0.014	0.017
	Safety	2.1	On board	0.034	0.040
		2.2	At stops	0.022	0.026
		2.3	Of vehicle	0.021	0.025
	Travel time	3.1	Access time	0.033	0.039
		3.2	Waiting time	0.019	0.022
		3.3	In-vehicle time	0.028	0.033
	Availability	4.1	Operating hours	0.040	0.047
		4.2	Ticket	0.018	0.021
	Reliability	5.1	Regularity	0.040	0.047
		5.2	Tracking availability	0.024	0.029
	Directness	6.1	Transfer	0.031	0.037
		6.2	Integration	0.030	0.036
		6.3	Distance	0.016	0.019
Provider-public	Investment cost	7.1	-	0.128	0.138
	City development	7.2	-	0.476	0.392

3.3 Step 3. Ranking Alternatives

The final step applied four MCDM methods to rank the public transport alternatives for each case study.

Each method involved the construction of a decision matrix, where the performance of each transport mode was assessed against each sub-criterion. Qualitative values were translated into numerical scores using established linguistic scales to enable normalization and comparison.

Results were largely consistent across the different methods. In Ho Chi Minh City, Metro emerged as the top-ranked solution in all four approaches. The gap between Metro and other alternatives was significant, reaffirming its suitability in a high-density urban environment. In Brescia, ALRT and Tram alternated in the top positions depending on the method used. According to SAW and PROMETHEE II, ALRT was the most preferred, while TOPSIS and VIKOR gave a slight edge to the Tram. However, the differences in scores between these two options were marginal. The VIKOR method also applied additional acceptance criteria to assess whether the best-ranked alternative

Table 2. Decision matrix.

#	Unit	±	RB		BRT		LRT	Metro	ALRT	Tram
			*	**	*	**	*	*	**	**
1.1	–	+	A	A	G	G	E	O	E	G
1.2	space/h/line	+	3000	3000	6000	6000	10000	50000	17000	10000
2.1	–	+	A	A	VG	VG	VG	O	O	VG
2.2	–	+	A	A	VG	VG	VG	O	O	G
2.3	–	+	A	A	G	G	VG	O	O	VG
3.1	Mins	–	5	5	10	10	10	10	10	10
3.2	Mins	–	20	15	10	12	10	5	6	9
3.3	Mins	–	42	25	29	15	18	10	10	16
4.1	Hours	+	16	16	17	18	19	19	18	18
4.2	$	–	0.5	1.4	1	1.4	2	2	1.4	1.4
5.1	–	+	G	A	VG	VG	VG	O	E	VG
5.2	–	+	A	G	VG	E	VG	O	O	E
6.1	–	–	2	2	1	1	1	1	1	1
6.2	Times	+	O	O	G	G	A	O	G	G
6.3	Km	+	0.2	0.2	0.3	0.4	0.5	1.2	0.5	0.5
7.1	Mil-$/km	–	1	1	11.5	10	45	100	78	31
7.2	–	+	A	A	G	VG	VG	O	E	E

* Ho Chi Min case and ** Brescia case; + (Benefit) and - (Cost); A (Average), G (Good), VG (Very good), E (Excellent), O (Outstanding).

could be considered a valid compromise. Metro clearly satisfied both conditions in Ho Chi Minh, confirming its dominance. In Brescia, Tram and ALRT failed to meet all the compromise criteria, suggesting that both should be considered as co-leading options (Table 3).

4   Discussion and Conclusion

The application of multiple MCDM methods across two contrasting city contexts highlights several insights regarding public transport planning and method suitability. In Ho Chi Minh City, all methods consistently ranked the Metro as the top alternative. This result aligns with expectations. Previous studies have similarly found metro and light rail options preferable in megacities, emphasizing their capacity to meet large-scale demand efficiently [29, 31]. Although all four methods produced similar rankings overall, VIKOR showed a slight shift, placing BRT above LRT. This divergence is likely due to VIKOR's focus on balancing group utility and individual regret, which may highlight relative performance differences overlooked by traditional methods. In contrast, Brescia

Table 3. Global scores and ranking.

Method	Case	#	Bus	BRT	LRT	Metro
SAW	Ho-Chi-Min	G_{saw}	0.371	0.385	0.480	0.831
		Rank	4	3	2	1
	Brescia	G_{saw}	0.425	0.581	0.795	0.713
		Rank	4	3	1	2
TOPSIS	Ho-Chi-Min	G_{top}	0.247	0.339	0.503	0.756
		Rank	4	3	2	1
	Brescia	G_{top}	0.368	0.690	0.632	0.785
		Rank	4	2	3	1
VIKOR	Ho-Chi-Min	G_{vik}	1.000	0.359	0.393	0.000
		Rank	4	2	3	1
	Brescia	G_{vik}	1.000	0.251	0.124	0.039
		Rank	4	3	2	1
PROMETHEE II	Ho-Chi-Min	G_{vik}	-0.343	-0.104	-0.008	0.455
		Rank	4	3	2	1
	Brescia	G_{vik}	-0.487	0.046	0.223	0.219
		Rank	4	3	1	2

presented a more complex scenario with no dominant alternative. While TOPSIS and VIKOR identified the Tram as the most balanced option, SAW and PROMETHEE II favored ALRT. However, the performance gap between the two modes was minimal across all methods, suggesting that both could be considered viable solutions. This variability reflects the challenges of decision-making in medium-sized cities, where several alternatives can perform similarly across criteria [22, 29, 32]. Moreover, it demonstrates how different MCDM approaches may yield slightly different preferences depending on the evaluation focus. Interestingly, the regular bus system was consistently ranked last in both case studies. Its lower performance confirms existing evidence about the limited potential of basic transit modes in addressing contemporary urban mobility challenges.

The comparison of methods also provides insight into which tools are most suitable for different contexts. In straightforward situations like Ho Chi Minh, where one mode clearly outperforms others, any of the four methods can provide useful guidance. However, in more nuanced cases like Brescia, VIKOR and PROMETHEE II are recommended. VIKOR's adjustable parameter (β) enables for tailored assessments based on stakeholder preferences, while PROMETHEE II enables flexible preference modeling and visual comparisons of alternatives. Still, even these robust methods rely on the quality and clarity of input data.

In this study, citizen participation through the AHP survey proved challenging, especially in Brescia, due to the complexity of pairwise comparisons and the survey length. Several participants found it difficult to evaluate abstract criteria, leading to inconsistent data. This highlights the need for future research to explore simplified, user-friendly tools for involving non-experts in complex decision processes. Furthermore, the conversion of qualitative criteria into numerical values remains a potential source of imprecision. More structured approaches to quantifying indicators like "city development" would enhance the robustness of results. Breaking this down into measurable sub-criteria, e.g., real estate growth, user modal shift, or long-term environmental benefits, could lead to more accurate assessments.

To conclude, this study offers an integrated MCDM framework that blends expert input with citizen opinion to support transport planning in diverse urban settings. Applying the approach in both a metropolis and a medium-sized city demonstrates how contextual differences shape mobility needs and influence decision outcomes. The research contributes to the literature in several ways. It emphasizes the value of including citizen perspectives in decision-making, which are often underrepresented in traditional MCDM applications. It also shows how method selection matters, mainly when alternatives perform similarly, and offers practical guidance on choosing the most appropriate MCDM method based on scenario complexity. Moreover, this is one of the first studies to apply such methods to Vietnam's urban transit system, adding valuable regional insight to the global conversation on transport planning. Finally, it provides a replicable model for other cities, particularly in developing countries, facing similar challenges and leading to smarter, more sustainable, and citizen-oriented urban mobility systems.

Nevertheless, the model should be considered a support tool, not a prescriptive solution. Future studies should seek to improve data accuracy, expand public participation through more intuitive interfaces, and incorporate additional criteria related to construction impacts, operational constraints, and technological developments. An expert-only survey for technical parameters is also advisable to avoid inconsistencies in weight attribution.

Acknowledgments. This study was partially funded by the University of Brescia within the Grant "CUP: D75F21002920001" PON R&I 2014–2020 (FSE REACT-EU). Special thanks to Phan Nguyen Minh Tan for their preliminary work carried out as part of his thesis.

CRediT Authorship Contribution Statement. Conceptualization: B.B.; Methodology: All; Formal analysis: M.C., R.V.; Data curation: M.C., R.V.; Visualization: All; Writing-Original Draft: All; Writing-review & editing: All; Supervision: B.B.

Disclosure of Interests. The authors have no competing interests to declare that are relevant to the content of this article.

References

1. Lee, S., Lee, S., Lee, Y.I.: Innovative public transport oriented policies in Seoul. Transportation **33**, 189–204 (2006)
2. Barabino, B.: Transit bus route network design: a model and its application in a real network. WIT Trans. Built Environ. **107**, 369–382 (2009)

3. Dulce, F., Murillo-Hoyos, J., Caicedo, E.: Comparative analysis of the performance, environmental impact, and costs of electric, combustion, and gas buses in an operating context of a mid-sized city of an emerging country. Transport. Res. Interdisc. Perspect. **25**, 101113 (2024)

4. Kronprasert, N., Talvitie, A.: Use of reasoning maps in evaluation of transport alternatives: inclusion of uncertainty and "I Don't Know": demonstration of a method. Transportation **42**, 389–406 (2015)

5. Beria, P., Maltese, I., Mariotti, I.: Multicriteria versus cost benefit analysis: a comparative perspective in the assessment of sustainable mobility. Eur. Transp. Res. Rev. **4**(3), 137–152 (2012)

6. Marleau Donais, F., Abi-Zeid, I., Waygood, E.O.D., Lavoie, R.: A review of cost–benefit analysis and multicriteria decision analysis from the perspective of sustainable transport in project evaluation. EURO J. Decis. Processes **7**(3–4), 327–358 (2019). https://doi.org/10. 1007/s40070-019-00098-1

7. Samani, Z.N., et al.: Advancing urban healthcare equity analysis: integrating public participation GIS with fuzzy best-worst decision-making. Sustainability **16**, 1745 (2024)

8. Carra, M., Pavesi, F.C., Barabino, B.: Sustainable cycle-tourism for society: Integrating multicriteria decision-making and land use approaches for route selection. Sustain. Cities Soc. **99**, 104905 (2023)

9. Broniewicz, E., Ogrodnik, K.: Multi-criteria analysis of transport infrastructure projects. Transport. Res. Part D: Transp. Environ. **83**, 10235 (2020)

10. Ciardiello, F., Genovese, A.: A comparison between TOPSIS and SAW methods. Ann. Oper. Res. **325**(2), 967–994 (2023)

11. Yannis, G., Kopsacheili, A., Dragomanovits, A., Petraki, V.: State-of-the-art review on multicriteria decision-making in the transport sector. J. Traffic Transport. Eng. **7**(4), 413–431 (2020)

12. Brans, J.P., Vincke, P., Mareschal, B.: How to select and how to rank projects: the promethee method. Eur. J. Oper. Res. **24**(2), 228–238 (1986)

13. Brans, J.P., De Smet, Y.: PROMETHEE methods. Int. Ser. Oper. Res. Manag. Sci. **233**, 187–219 (2016)

14. Velasquez, M., Hester, P.T. An analysis of multi-criteria decision making methods. Int. J. Oper. Res. **10**(2) (2013)

15. Hamurcu, M., Eren, T.: Electric bus selection with multicriteria decision analysis for green transportation. Sustainability **12**(7), 2777 (2020)

16. Borghetti, F., Carra, M., Besson, C., Matarrese, E., Maja, R., Barabino, B.: Evaluating alternative fuels for a bus fleet: an Italian case. Transp. Policy **154**, 1–15 (2024)

17. Manzolli, J.A., Trovão, J.P., Antunes, C.H.: Scenario-Based Multi-criteria decision analysis for rapid transit systems implementation in an urban context. ETransportation **7**, 100107 (2021)

18. Moslem, S., Alkharabsheh, A., Ismael, K., Duleba, S.: An integrated decision support model for evaluating public transport quality. Appl. Sci. **10**(12), 4158 (2020)

19. Shabani, A., Shabani, A., Ahmadinejad, B., Salmasnia, A.: Measuring the customer satisfaction of public transportation in Tehran during the COVID-19 pandemic using MCDM techniques. Case Stud. Transp. Policy **10**(3), 1520–1530 (2022)

20. Le Pira, M., Inturri, G., Ignaccolo, M., Pluchino, A.: Analysis of AHP methods and the Pairwise Majority Rule (PMR) for collective preference rankings of sustainable mobility solutions. Transport. Res. Procedia **10**, 777–787 (2015)

21. Güner, S.: Measuring the quality of public transportation systems and ranking the bus transit routes using multi-criteria decision making techniques. Case Stud. Transp. Policy **6**(2), 224 (2018)

22. Ventura, R., Bonera, M., Carra, M., Barabino, B., Maternini, G.: Evaluating the viability of a tram-train system: a case study from Salento (Italy). Case Stud. Transp. Policy **10**(3), 1945–1963 (2022)
23. Taylor, B.D., Morris, E.A.: Public transportation objectives and rider demographics: are transit's priorities poor public policy? Transportation **42**, 347–367 (2015)
24. Rupprecht Consult (ed.): Guidelines for Developing and Implementing a Sustainable Urban Mobility Plan, Second Edition (2019)
25. Saaty, T.L.: The Analytical Hierarchy Process: Planning, Priority Setting, Resource Allocation. McGraw-Hill, New York (1980)
26. Carrara, E., Ciavarella, R., Boglietti, S., Carra, M., Maternini, G., Barabino, B.: Identifying and selecting key sustainable parameters for the monitoring of e-powered micro personal mobility vehicles: evidence from Italy. Sustainability **13**(16), 9226 (2021)
27. Wedley, W.C.: Consistency prediction for incomplete AHP matrices. Math. Comput. Model. **17**(4–5), 151–161 (1993)
28. Grošelj, P., Zadnik Stirn, L., Ayrilmis, N., Kuzman, M.K.: Comparison of some aggregation techniques using group analytic hierarchy process. Expert Syst. Appl. **42**(4), 2198–2204 (2015)
29. Lee, D. J. A multi-criteria approach for prioritizing advanced public transport modes (APTM) considering urban types in Korea. Transportation Research Part A **111** (2018)
30. Vuchic, V.R.: Urban Transit Systems and Technology. Wiley, Hoboken (2007)
31. Nassereddine, M., Eskandari, H.: An integrated MCDM approach to evaluate public transportation systems in Tehran. Transport. Res. Part A **106**, 427–439 (2017)
32. De Aloe, M., Ventura, R., Bonera, M., Barabino, B., Maternini, G.: Applying cost–benefit analysis to the economic evaluation of a tram-train system: evidence from Brescia (Italy). Res. Transport. Bus. Manag. **47**, 100916 (2022)

Artificial Intelligence and Sustainable Tourism: An Integrated Model for Impact Assessment

Giovanna Acampa[1] , Fabrizio Finucci[2] , Mariolina Grasso[3(✉)] ,
and Daniele Mazzoni[2]

[1] University of Florence, 50121 Florence, Italy
[2] University of Roma Tre, 00153 Rome, Italy
[3] University of Enna "Kore", 94100 Enna, Italy
mariolina.grasso@unikore.it

Abstract. In recent years, among the various potential applications of Artificial Intelligence (AI), its ability to serve as a useful tool for data implementation and analysis in various monitoring and impact assessment processes has become increasingly evident. This paper presents an example of AI being used as an integration and support tool for impact assessment in the context of sustainable tourism. In 2023, it is estimated that there were 1.286 billion international tourists worldwide. Specifically, Europe was the most visited region, largely due to domestic demand and travel from the United States. In 2013, the European Commission launched the European Tourism Indicator System (ETIS), consisting of a set of indicators designed to assess tourism sustainability, support destinations, and monitor and measure their performance. This research aims to define an evaluation model that considers these indicators through a weighted system. To determine the specific weight of each indicator and assess the usefulness of AI systems, the paper presents the results of a study aimed at identifying discrepancies and convergences in output data obtained in two ways:

a) Using a traditional model, (stakeholders' consultation).
b) Through AI-based interrogation.

In the proposed case study, a questionnaire will be used and administered to stakeholders in the sector as well as to major AI software systems. The input data will be carefully structured to enable AI to function as a knowledgeable expert in the tourism sector.

Keywords: Artificial Intelligence · Sustainable Tourism · Impact Assessment

1 Introduction

1.1 International Tourism: Trends and Challenges

In 2020, international tourism experienced its worst crisis due to the outbreak of the COVID-19 pandemic. For this reason, the latest reports published by major global agencies monitoring tourist flows refer to annual data compared to the year 2019. According to

O. Gervasi et al. (Eds.): ICCSA 2025 Workshops, LNCS 15899, pp. 306–317, 2026.
https://doi.org/10.1007/978-3-031-97663-6_27

the World Tourism Barometer of the UNWTO, in 2024, 1.4 billion international tourists were recorded, recovering 99% of pre-pandemic levels and marking an 11% increase compared to 2023. Thus, 2024 marks a global recovery in tourist flows, but results vary by region.

Compared to the pre-pandemic period (2019), the Middle East recorded the most significant increase worldwide, with a 32% growth in international arrivals. With 74 million arrivals, Africa saw a 7% increase compared to 2019, driven by increases in Ethiopia (+40%), Morocco (+35%), Tunisia (+9%), and Kenya (+9%). The last region to surpass pre-pandemic levels was Europe, reaching 747 million international arrivals (+1%), mainly supported by strong intra-regional demand. All European countries exceeded 2019 levels, except for Central and Eastern Europe, where many destinations are still affected by the lingering impacts of the Russia-Ukraine conflict [1].

Specifically, 21 European destinations have surpassed 2019 levels. Among the countries that recorded the highest increases, one country saw a remarkable 80% rise in international arrivals in the first 10–12 months of 2024, followed by Andorra (+35%), Malta and Serbia (+29%), Portugal (+18%), Denmark (+17%), Greece and Turkey (+14%), and Spain (+10%). The Americas recovered 97% of pre-pandemic arrivals, with the Caribbean and Central America already surpassing 2019 levels, thanks to strong outbound travel from the United States [1].

In addition to the growth of international tourism, 2024 set record levels for total tourism-related export revenues (including transport and accommodation), reaching $1.9 trillion, approximately 3% more than in 2019. According to the latest estimates, in the first nine to eleven months of 2024, several destinations reported significant revenue growth. Specifically, El Salvador tripled its earnings, recording a 206% increase, followed by Saudi Arabia with a 148% increase, Albania (+136%), Serbia (+98%), and Canada (+70%). This trend is also confirmed among the world's major tourist destinations; for example, the United Kingdom saw a 40% revenue increase, Spain 36%, France 27%, and Italy 23%.

According to the first forecasts for international tourist arrivals in 2025, these levels are expected to grow between 3% and 5% compared to 2024, assuming a continued recovery in Asia and the Pacific. Confirming these expectations, the latest United Nations Tourism Confidence Index (UN TCI) predicts "better" or "much better" prospects for 2025 compared to 2024 for approximately 64% of respondents. Specifically, the TCI aims to assist governments, business leaders, and other decision-makers worldwide in shaping tourism policies [2].

However, as industry experts highlight, economic difficulties and geopolitical risks (in addition to ongoing conflicts) represent a set of factors that could jeopardize these forecasts. Balancing growth and sustainability will be crucial in 2025, as highlighted by two main trends identified: the search for sustainable practices and the discovery of lesser-known destinations [1].

1.2 Aim and Scope of Study

The expansion of the Internet, coupled with the emergence of Artificial Intelligence (AI) and autonomous mobility [3], is significantly influencing many sectors, including tourism, by offering substantial opportunities. Although tourism is known as an interdisciplinary field, research methodologies have long been constrained by classical approaches [4].

As reported by Ciano, Alderighi, and Ferrara in the era of digitalization, data appears in new unstructured forms [5]. This, together with traditionally structured datasets, has led to the rise of Big Data. Consequently, thanks to advancements in computing and, above all, the rapid development of algorithms, advanced analytical tools and methods have emerged, enabling more accurate and in-depth insights, including those related to urban policy, planning, design, and the management of urban transformation, and ultimately, systemic approaches to decision-making support [6].

In recent years, some of these new methods have been applied to the study and forecasting of tourism, such as route optimization, predictive and forecasting analysis, alert and monitoring systems, and much more [7]. Tourism is, therefore, an extremely complex and multidimensional sector, making it an ideal field for the application of Artificial Intelligence systems. The use of AI could be beneficial in investigating both tourism supply and demand, including marketing strategies, managing overtourism [7] and, most importantly, designing policies focused on sustainable tourism.

Since providing a comprehensive review of all significant proposals and projects on AI applications in the tourism sector is complex, an excerpt from the guidelines provided by Ciano, Alderighi, and Ferrara on possible applications is presented below:

"Innovative tourism strategies can only be designed with new visions and ideas. Creativity techniques can then be applied by considering insights obtained from the analysis of large datasets. Alternatively, new ways to visualize them could be used; among the latest principles of the circular economy, sustainable development, and environmental economics can inspire governments, destination managers, local tourism entities, and tourism stakeholders in general. [6]."

To determine the specific weight of each indicator and assess the usefulness of AI systems, the paper presents the results of a study aimed at identifying discrepancies and convergences in output data obtained in two ways:

a) Using a traditional model, (stakeholders' consultation).
b) Through AI-based interrogation.

In the proposed case study, a questionnaire will be used and administered to stakeholders in the sector as well as to major AI software systems. The input data will be carefully structured to enable AI to function as a knowledgeable expert in the tourism sector.

2   Literary Review: Tools and Methods for Impact Assessment of Tourists Flows

For the analysis of sustainable tourism, there are no sources providing references for assigning weight values.

De Marchi et al. introduce the Tourism Sustainability Index (TSI), which provides a scalable and georeferenced assessment of tourism sustainability based on ETIS criteria, focusing on tourist satisfaction through sentiment analysis [8].

Liu et al. present a comprehensive analysis of regional tourism sustainability using the TOPSIS method to evaluate the level of sustainable tourism development in the Yangtze River region [9]. They establish a system of scientific indicators to assess economic, social, resource-related, and environmental aspects of tourism, offering insights into the coordination between tourism and various factors in the region.

Troise et al. propose an interpretative model that uses multiple case studies to assess sustainable tourism initiatives, highlighting stakeholder approaches and tourists' perceived quality [10].

Park & Yoon focus on developing indicators for evaluating sustainable rural tourism, emphasizing the importance of these indicators in measuring progress and enhancing community capacity development [11].

Epifani introduces the Sustainable Tourism Assessment Index (STAI), a synthetic index designed to assess a destination's preparedness for sustainable tourism development trajectories with a holistic approach [12].

Budeanu discusses the impacts and responsibilities of sustainable tourism from the perspective of tourism operators, emphasizing the need for a preventive approach to mitigate the consequences of rapid tourism growth [13].

Weiler et al. conduct a bibliometric analysis of trends and research models in sustainable tourism, highlighting the evolution of theoretical and methodological approaches over time [14].

In conclusion, the assessment of tourism is crucial for ensuring long-term sustainability and the positive impacts of tourism activities on destinations and communities.

Below is a summary table listing additional authors who have used methods and tools to evaluate tourism in different application fields (Table 1).

Table 1. Reference papers

Paper	Objective	Method/Tool
Chen, C. L., & Bau, Y. P. (2016). Establishing a multi-criteria evaluation structure for tourist beaches in Taiwan: A foundation for sustainable beach tourism. Ocean & Coastal Management, 121, 88–96. [15]	Identify the factors influencing beach environments and establish a multi-criteria evaluation framework for tourist beaches; Inform beach managers on where and how to invest resources to achieve sustainable beach tourism	Critical review of the literature on beach quality criteria. Interviews with experts to identify the factors related to a highly frequented tourist beach. The fuzzy Analytical Hierarchy Process (AHP), a decision-making method based on pairwise comparisons between criteria, was then used to construct a three-level evaluation framework with associated criteria and weights for beach managers

(continued)

Table 1. (*continued*)

Paper	Objective	Method/Tool
Hatipoglu, B., Ertuna, B., & Salman, D. (2019). Corporate social responsibility in tourism as a tool for sustainable development: An evaluation from a community perspective. *International Journal of Contemporary Hospitality Management, 31*(6), 2358–2375	Analyze corporate social responsibility (CSR) programs in tourism as a tool for sustainable development within the CSR program of a multinational company in Turkey	Qualitative research on a single company, including content analysis of corporate documents, participant observations, questionnaires for tourism project coordinators, and follow-up interviews with company directors and project managers
Cernat, L., & Gourdon, J. (2011). Is the concept of sustainable tourism sustainable? Developing the Sustainable Tourism Benchmarking Tool	Provide a unified methodology to assess the sustainability of tourism, based on a set of quantitative indicators	The Sustainable Tourism Benchmarking Tool (STBT) will provide a set of benchmarks to assess the sustainability of tourism activities in various countries A model development procedure is proposed: identifying the dimensions (economic, socio-ecological, infrastructural) and indicators, scaling method, graphical representation, and evaluation in three Asian countries
Montis, A. D., Deplano, G., & Nijkamp, P. (2007). Multicriteria evaluation and local environmental planning for sustainable tourism. In *Advances in modern tourism research: Economic perspectives* (pp. 207–232). Heidelberg: Physica-Verlag HD	Decision-making process of a hypothetical institutional entity interested in developing an objective and standardized procedure for evaluating the spatial dimension of sustainable tourism development	The methodology belongs to the family of multicriteria tools and was developed by integrating the regime method with AHP (Analytic Hierarchy Process)
García-Melón, M., Gómez-Navarro, T., & Acuña-Dutra, S. (2012). A combined ANP-delphi approach to evaluate sustainable tourism. *Environmental Impact Assessment Review, 34*, 41–50	The evaluation of sustainable tourism strategies promoted by stakeholders in National Parks	Methodology based on the Analytic Network Process and a Delphi-type evaluation procedure. The approach aims to engage stakeholders in a participatory process and consensus building

(*continued*)

Table 1. (*continued*)

Paper	Objective	Method/Tool
Blancas, F. J., Lozano-Oyola, M., González, M., & Caballero, R. (2018). A dynamic sustainable tourism evaluation using multiple benchmarks. *Journal of cleaner production*, *174*, 1190–1203	Designing more effective benchmarking practices among different tourist destinations Differentiated evaluation based on the type of territory to define a comprehensive benchmarking practice	Creation of a composite vector indicator defined through two components: one dynamic, to grade the evolution of the destination in relation to its sustainability; the other static, to contextualize its position relative to other territories, evaluating the status achieved in the social, economic, and environmental parameters that influence the level of sustainability
Rita, S. E., Ferreira, F. A. F., & Rosa, L. (2019). A socio-technical approach to the assessment of sustainable tourism: Adding value with a comprehensive process-oriented framework [J]. *Journal of Cleaner Production*, *236*(5), 117487–17489	Create a system for evaluating sustainable tourism by providing a rational and transparent basis for the selection and weighting of evaluation criteria	A technique that combines the use of cognitive maps with Choquet integral (CI), developed through group meetings with a panel of tourism experts
Punzo, G., Trunfio, M., Castellano, R., & Buonocore, M. (2022). A multi-modelling approach for assessing sustainable tourism. *Social Indicators Research*, *163*(3), 1399–1443	Build and validate a composite sustainable tourism indicator (SusTour-Index), which recognizes the economic, environmental, and social dimensions as the three main interconnected aspects of sustainable tourism	The SusTour-Index is composed of 75 elementary indicators, appropriately structured into pillars and sub-pillars within each dimension: economic (34), environmental (21), and social (20) A multi-model approach verifies the hierarchical structure of the SusTour-Index by combining various weighting and aggregation methods within each dimension of sustainability to select the most appropriate model once the uncertainty analysis has been conducted

(*continued*)

Table 1. (*continued*)

Paper	Objective	Method/Tool
Wang, S. H., Lee, M. T., Château, P. A., & Chang, Y. C. (2016). Performance indicator framework for evaluation of sustainable tourism in the Taiwan coastal zone. *Sustainability*, 8(7), 652	The evaluation of coastal tourism performance, using a framework of indicators to facilitate sustainable development and improve the effectiveness of coastal resource utilization	Through a literature review and expert surveys using the fuzzy Delphi method (FDM) and fuzzy analytic hierarchy process (FAHP), this study constructs a performance indicator framework and identifies key factors influencing the sustainable development of coastal tourism in Taiwan
De Marchi, D., Becarelli, R., & Di Sarli, L. (2022). Tourism sustainability index: measuring tourism sustainability based on the ETIS toolkit, by exploring tourist satisfaction via sentiment analysis. *Sustainability*, 14(13), 8049	Measuring the sustainability of tourism and developing a composite indicator based on the use of sentiment analysis techniques to assess e-reputation and tourist satisfaction, combining this analysis with other open data sources	Starting with the ETIS and developing new TSI indicators

3 Materials and Methods

3.1 Weighing ETIS Indicators: AI and Stakeholders Consultation

The weighting process of the ETIS sustainability indicators adopted in this study is based on a participatory approach that combines stakeholder involvement with the use of Artificial Intelligence (AI). The goal is to achieve a balanced assessment that integrates both the subjective perceptions of stakeholders and a quantitative analysis based on predictive models. The process unfolds through six key stages, outlined below (Fig. 1).

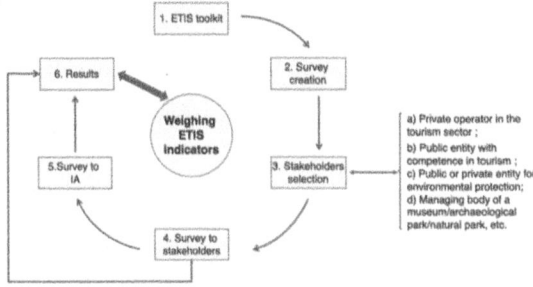

Fig. 1. Weighing ETIS indicators (Source: created by the authors)

Initially, the ETIS toolkit, a tool developed by the European Commission to measure the sustainability of tourism in various destinations, was studied. This phase allowed for the identification of the 43 sustainability indicators to be assessed, covering economic, social, cultural, and environmental aspects. Subsequently, a structured questionnaire was developed, consisting of 43 questions, corresponding to the 43 ETIS indicators. Each participant was asked to assign a score from 1 to 5, using an ascending importance scale, where 1 indicated minimal importance and 5 indicated maximum importance. The questionnaire was created using the Google Forms platform, ensuring easy and intuitive access for participants and facilitating data collection and analysis.

The next phase involved the selection of stakeholders, divided into four main categories: (a) private tourism operators, (b) public tourism bodies, (c) public and/or private environmental protection bodies, and (d) park management organizations or archaeological site authorities. The questionnaire was distributed to representatives from each category, ensuring broad participation and collecting various perspectives on the importance of each indicator. At the same time, AI was involved to perform an autonomous assessment of the indicators. The AI model was trained to "simulate" each stakeholder category, replicating their viewpoint and assigning a score to each indicator based on available data and the specific criteria of the relevant sector. This process provided an additional weighting based on objective analysis, mitigating the subjectivity of human assessments. The data collected from both the stakeholders and the AI were then analyzed and compared to determine the final weight of each indicator. Finally, the results obtained were used to define a ranking of the most relevant indicators, contributing to an improvement in the monitoring and evaluation system for sustainable tourism.

4 Results

Regarding the results of the weighting process, the data collected show significant differences between the assessments provided by AI and those given by stakeholders.

As seen in Fig. 2, private tourism operators (category a) attributed greater importance to economic indicators and destination management, while environmental and cultural aspects were rated with slightly lower scores. This result is consistent with their role in the sector, which focuses on profitability and efficient resource management. The AI, when queried as stakeholders in category a), instead assigned a balanced weight to all four macro-categories of indicators (destination management, social aspects and cultural impacts, economic aspects, and environmental aspects), giving similar scores across them.

On the other hand (Fig. 3), public tourism authorities (category b) placed greater emphasis on destination management and social and cultural aspects, reflecting their responsibility in ensuring balanced and sustainable tourism growth. Environmental aspects, while considered important, received a lower rating compared to the other areas. The results from the AI, again, provided a more balanced view, although indicators related to destination management were still considered more relevant than others.

The comparative analysis between the AI ratings and those of the stakeholders in category c, namely public and private environmental protection bodies, highlights key differences in the priorities assigned to sustainability indicators. The AI assigned a

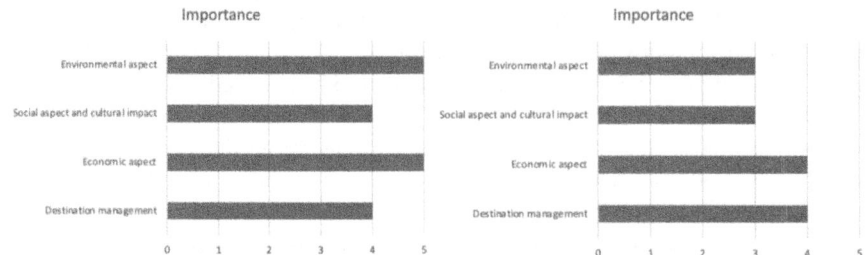

Fig. 2. Degree of preference among indicators – AI cat. a) and stakeholders cat.a) (from left to right) (Source: created by the authors)

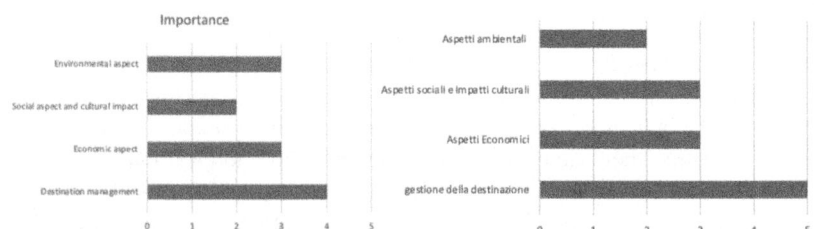

Fig. 3. Degree of preference among indicators – AI cat. b) and stakeholders cat. b) (from left to right) (Source: created by the authors)

balanced evaluation across the four macro-categories, with a slight preference for environmental aspects and destination management. However, the stakeholders placed significant emphasis on environmental aspects, giving them the highest rating among all categories. This result aligns with the mission of the organizations involved, which prioritize environmental protection in their activities. Additionally, compared to the AI, the stakeholders assigned a slightly lower rating to the economic aspects, considering them less relevant than the other dimensions of sustainability (Fig. 4).

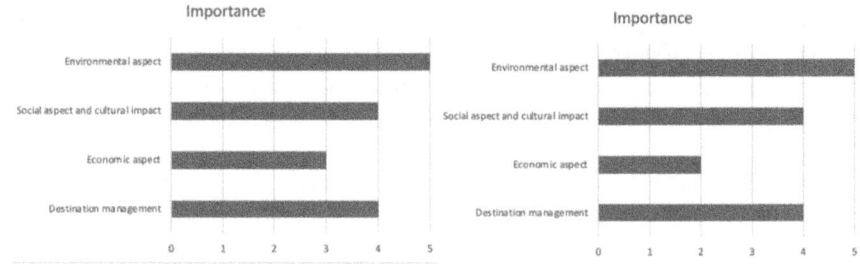

Fig. 4. Degree of preference among indicators – AI cat. c) and stakeholders cat. c) (from left to right) (Source: created by the authors)

Regarding category d, which includes the managers of nature parks or archaeological sites, some specificities are evident in the responses. The AI assigned a uniform evaluation to the indicators, with similar scores across all aspects of sustainability. However, stakeholders in category d gave the highest score to destination management, recognizing its crucial role in the preservation and enhancement of natural and cultural heritage. Environmental and social aspects were also rated highly, while economic aspects received slightly lower consideration. This reflects the nature of the institutions involved, which prioritize heritage conservation over economic performance [19] (Fig. 5).

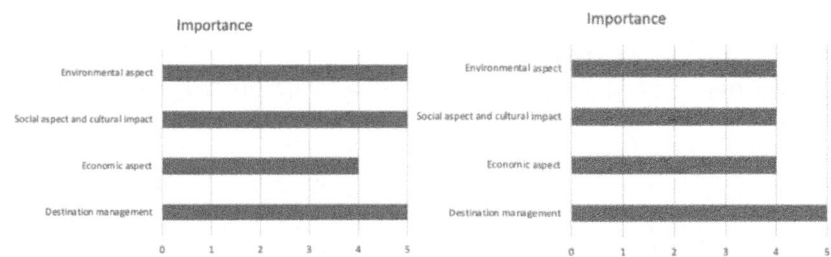

Fig. 5. Degree of preference among indicators – AI cat. d) and stakeholders cat. d) (from left to right) (Source: created by the authors)

5 Discussion and Conclusion

The analysis of the collected data highlights a general trend in the priorities perceived by the various actors involved. The AI, regardless of the stakeholder category "interpreted," showed a uniform distribution of weights across the four macro-categories, demonstrating a balanced approach based on historical data and analytical models. "Real" stakeholders, on the other hand, tended to highlight different preferences depending on their category of involvement.

For instance, destination management received high scores from both private tourism operators and public tourism entities, emphasizing its central role in the planning and management of tourism activities. In contrast, environmental aspects received lower scores from private operators compared to public entities and environmental organizations, highlighting the need for policies that encourage sustainability without compromising economic competitiveness.

Another significant difference concerns social and cultural aspects, which were rated more highly by public entities than by private operators. This suggests that public institutions perceive a key role in ensuring the respect of local traditions and the well-being of host communities, while tourism operators tend to focus more on economic profitability and operational management.

These results underline the importance of continuous dialogue between all actors in the tourism sector to define shared and sustainable strategies.

In summary, the weighting process of the ETIS indicators has allowed for highlighting the priorities and divergences among the various stakeholders, providing a solid foundation for developing more effective and sustainable tourism policies. The combined use of empirical data and human evaluations represents an innovative approach to improving tourism governance and promoting more responsible development of tourist destinations.

The integration between the judgment of stakeholders and the evaluations provided by AI has enabled a more comprehensive and multidimensional view of sustainable tourism.

Finally, below are listed the strengths and weaknesses of the research, as well as possible future developments.

1) The focus on AI is timely and aligns with ongoing trends making the research applicable to current challenges
2) the effectiveness of AI assessments depends on the quality and comprehensiveness of the underlying algorithms and data. Any inherent limitations in these algorithms could impact the validity of the AI-generated results
3) the reliance on existing tools like the ETIS toolkit may limit the exploration of innovative or emerging sustainability metrics that could provide additional insights
4) train the AI models on more comprehensive datasets and refining how they simulate different stakeholder views.

References

1. UNWTO. World Tourism Barometer, vol. 23, no. 1 (2025). https://pre-webunwto.s3.eu-west-1.amazonaws.com/s3fs-public/2025-01/UNWTO_Barom25_01_January_EXCERPT_v3.pdf?VersionId=AzILN6U4VW.RbM2oMF2DBpGQreisL4Xa. Accessed 25 Feb 2025
2. Croce, V.: Can tourism confidence index improve tourism demand forecasts? J. Tour. Fut. **2**(1), 6–21 (2016)
3. Epasto, S., Galdelli, A.: L'intelligenza artificiale per la gestione sostenibile delle risorse idriche. Caso di studio: gorgovivo, ancona. Documenti geografici **1**, 271–302 (2024)
4. Egger, R., Luger, K.: Tourismus und mobile Freizeit: Lebensformen, Trends, Herausforderungen. BoD–Books on Demand (2014)
5. Ciano, T., Alderighi, M., Ferrara, M.: Metodi e Strumenti di Intelligenza Artificiale per il forecasting dei flussi della mobilità turistica spaziale e temporale. In: Stampa di Ateneo (2023)
6. Finucci, F., Masanotti, A.G.: Crowdmapping: inclusive cities and evaluation. In: Lecture Notes in Computer Science (including subseries Lecture Notes in Artificial Intelligence and Lecture Notes in Bioinformatics), 2023. LNCS, Vol. 14112, pp. 80–90 ((2023))
7. Egger, R., Yu, C.-E.: Epistemological challenges. In: Egger, R. (ed.) Tourism on the Verge. Applied Data Science in Tourism, pp. 17–34. Springer, Cham (2022a)
8. De Marchi, D., Becarelli, R., Di Sarli, L.: Tourism sustainability index: measuring tourism sustainability based on the ETIS toolkit, by exploring tourist satisfaction via sentiment analysis. Sustainability **14**(13), 8049 (2022). https://doi.org/10.3390/su14138049
9. Liu, C., Zhang, R., Wang, M., Xu, J.: Measurement and prediction of regional tourism sustainability: an analysis of the yangtze river economic zone, China. Sustainability **10**(5), 1321 (2018). https://doi.org/10.3390/su10051321
10. Troise, C., et al.: Entrepreneurship and sustainability in tourism: an interpretative model. J. Manag. Sustainabil. (2020)

11. Park, D.B., Yoon, Y.S.: Developing sustainable rural tourism evaluation indicators. Int. J. Tour. Res. **13**(5), 401–415 (2011). https://doi.org/10.1002/jtr.804

12. Epifani, F., Valente, D.: Sustainable governance of tourism-based social-ecological landscapes. Sustainability **15**(22), 15967 (2023). https://doi.org/10.3390/su152215967

13. Budeanu, A.: Impacts and responsibilities for sustainable tourism: a tour operator's perspective. J. Clean. Prod. **13**(2), 89–97 (2005). https://doi.org/10.1016/j.jclepro.2003.12.024

14. Weiler, B.: Trends and patterns in sustainable tourism research: a 25-year bibliometric analysis. J. Sustain. Tour. (2014)

15. Chen, C.L., Bau, Y.P.: Establishing a multi-criteria evaluation structure for tourist beaches in Taiwan: a foundation for sustainable beach tourism. Ocean Coast. Manag. **121**, 88–96 (2016). https://doi.org/10.1016/j.ocecoaman.2015.11.004

16. Hatipoglu, B., Ertuna, B., Salman, D.: Corporate social responsibility in tourism as a tool for sustainable development: an evaluation from a community perspective. Int. J. Contemp. Hosp. Manag. **31**(6), 2358–2375 (2019). https://doi.org/10.1108/IJCHM-10-2018-0803

17. Cernat, L., Gourdon, J.: Is the concept of sustainable tourism sustainable? Developing the sustainable tourism benchmarking tool. Tour. Econ. **17**(3), 517–531 (2011). https://doi.org/10.5367/te.2011.0073

18. Piñeiro-Chousa, J., López-Cabarcos, M.Á., Romero-Castro, N., Vázquez-Rodríguez, P.: Sustainable tourism entrepreneurship in protected areas: a real options assessment of alternative management options. Entrep. Reg. Dev. **33**(3–4), 249–272 (2021). https://doi.org/10.1080/08985626.2020.1860803

19. Acampa, G., Parisi, C.M.: Management of maintenance costs in cultural heritage. Green Energy Technol., 195–212 (2021). https://doi.org/10.1007/978-3-030-49579-4_14

Inclusive Public Space, Accessibility, and Social Cohesion. A Multi-criteria Monitoring Model for Schuster Park in Rome

Fabrizio Finucci📵, Massimo Mariani📵, and Luca Trulli(✉)📵

Roma Tre University, 00154 Roma, RM, Italy
luca.trulli@uniroma3.it

Abstract. This paper presents the ongoing design research process within the Department of Architecture at the University of Roma Tre. The research focuses on evaluating the impact of excessive tourist influx on certain qualities of inclusive public spaces. It is well established that the accessibility of public places influences tourist destinations and, consequently, economic flow. However, the definition of "public space" is evolving, incorporating elements such as inclusiveness, accessibility, and well-being critical factors for fostering social cohesion, which may be at risk due to excessive tourist flows. The article explores the complexity of managing public spaces in urban environments characterized by high tourist traffic, with particular attention to accessibility and inclusiveness. Using the Schuster Universal Inclusive Park in Rome as a case study, the article examines the park's unique features and outlines the initial steps toward developing a multicriteria monitoring model. This model aims to assess the social impact of the park in the context of Jubilee 2025, considering the interaction between regular use and excessive visitor numbers. The outcome is a preliminary framework for an integrated approach to the evaluation of public spaces. This approach aims to balance sustainable tourism with the strengthening of community cohesion and a sense of belonging.

Keywords: Environmental accessibility · Public spaces · Evaluation and monitoring · Social cohesion

1 Introduction: Public Space, Social Cohesion and Conflict

Defining the rationale for categorizing a space as public is a matter subject to considerable variability. Numerous factors influence whether a space is regarded as public, and several studies have identified this issue as central to the topic on public space [1]. Many contemporary approaches have recognized certain characteristics as essential for the classification of public spaces, such as inclusiveness, accessibility, public ownership, and unrestricted access [2]. However, none of these criteria, whether examined individually or collectively, fully encapsulates the concept of public space. In contemporary debate, additional factors are recognized, including physical spaces that emerge from participatory processes involving collective planning, design, and management [3]. A

O. Gervasi et al. (Eds.): ICCSA 2025 Workshops, LNCS 15899, pp. 318–328, 2026.
https://doi.org/10.1007/978-3-031-97663-6_28

space can be considered public when it acts as a platform for diversity and local identities, allowing for artistic and cultural expression and facilitating collaboration to shape those identities [4]. Furthermore, it is well-established in the literature that high-quality public spaces are instrumental in promoting social cohesion [5, 6]. Definitions of social cohesion often include intangible aspects such as social ties, trust, and solidarity, which are essential for fostering relationships among community members [7, 8]. Numerous studies highlight how well-designed public spaces can enhance social interactions and community ties, which are crucial for cultivating a sense of belonging and collective identity among residents [9, 10]. Public spaces act as vital arenas for cultural expression, significantly contributing to social sustainability. From this perspective, inclusivity and accessibility are key features of public spaces, as they foster inclusive communities, particularly for vulnerable groups. This nurturing of public culture is enriched by cultural diversity while facilitating mobility and economic activity for all [11]. However, major cities increasingly feature areas where high volumes of tourist flows intersect with public and community values. In such cases, many aspects of social cohesion mentioned above may be compromised, undermining the capacity of public spaces to deliver their intended benefits and meet the needs of diverse communities. Overtourism, as a phenomenon, can exacerbate these challenges by exceeding an area's capacity to accommodate tourists, leading to congestion, environmental degradation, and social conflicts. According to Koens et al. [12], overtourism generates uniform impacts on tourism, complicating efforts for local communities to maintain their sense of identity and cohesion. Bertocchi and Visentin [13] note that excessive tourist load, as observed in cities like Venice, has led to tensions between residents and tourists, threatening social cohesion. Rawhani and Middelmann [14] emphasize the importance of managing public spaces in a way that considers the needs of all users residents and tourists alike so as to avoid conflict and foster enduring social cohesion. Without an integrated approach to managing public spaces, especially in areas where tourist flows intersect, a sense of exclusion may arise among residents, resulting in their abandonment of these spaces and a further decline in social cohesion.

This paper aims to propose an evaluation approach that underscores how excessive tourist load can affect the social capacities of public spaces, using the Schuster Park project in Rome as an experimental framework. This project, as research design, comes from a collaboration involving the Department of Architecture at Roma Tre University (under the scientific direction of Prof. Adolfo F.L. Baratta), Fondazione Tetrabondi Onlus, the Department of Human Neuroscience at the Sapienza University of Rome, AITO (Italian Association of Occupational Therapists), and the cultural association AES (Architettura Emergenza Sviluppo). The project envisions the creation of a Universal Inclusive Park within the green area adjacent to the Basilica of St. Paul Outside the Walls, aiming to enhance community engagement and social interaction.

2 The Accessibility of Public Space with High Flows

The complex definition of public space as a social good is inextricably linked to its environmental accessibility for society. This protection is guaranteed by the Fundamental Principles of the Italian Constitution, encompassing both the usage and enjoyment of this good. In this context, Article 3 of the Constitution acknowledges the Republic's responsibility to "remove obstacles of an economic and social order which, by effectively limiting the freedom and equality of citizens, prevent the full development of the human person and the effective participation of all workers in the political, economic, and social organization of the country" [15].

The term "accessibility" denotes "the ability to be easily accessed" [16], safeguarding inviolable human rights such as freedom of movement, self-determination, and personal development following the principles of equality affirmed by the United Nations in the Convention on the Rights of Persons with Disabilities [17]. The conflict generated by anthropogenic actions within space must be mitigated through multidisciplinary and multiscale processes designed to make the space accessible to all. Environmental accessibility, within this context, aims to mitigate conflicts between individuals and their environment. It ensures that spaces, goods, and services are accessible, identifiable, and understandable to all people, enabling full autonomy and safety for individuals with any physical, sensory, or cognitive condition, thus accommodating human variability [18].

Through these processes, public space transcends its material aspects and gains significant value, contributing to individual development while fostering interpersonal, social, and cultural exchanges. This intangible value arises from a process that involves diverse actions and intervention scales, upholding the fixed goal of environmental accessibility in response to evolving needs over time. This diversity of actions is directly linked to the heterogeneity of public spaces, which reflects the unique historical, cultural, and social significance of various contexts, necessitating diverse approaches to interventions.

Simultaneously, distinctions arise between citizens, residents, daily users of public goods, and tourists. These groups differ in behavior and characteristics, particularly in terms of temporality and origin, necessitating interventions designed to ensure accessibility of spaces in scenarios with multiple, simultaneous users. Public spaces characterized by these elements can be understood as complex systems of flows, both tourist and non-tourist [19]. Activities, context, and flows modify the fundamental inputs for designing and implementing strategies to expand the accessibility of public assets, thus promoting universal and social inclusion.

Regarding the Italian national territory, only 0.6% of municipalities have been awarded the "lilac flag," a symbol of accessibility [20]. This statistic, when compared to the number of people with disabilities in Italy and the potential attraction of international visitors, underscores the critical need for accessibility in all its facets. It also highlights the moral and economic losses faced by the Italian state. The actual accessibility of the diverse morphologies of public spaces is closely connected to and influenced by specific tourist flows. This issue has become increasingly relevant, generating significant challenges, especially in areas where tourism continuously creates high user flow, with global interest spurring greater possibilities for inclusion.

In light of the Jubilee 2025, which is expected to attract approximately 35 million pilgrims to Rome over the course of the year, attendance is projected to rise from 54 million to 104 million [21]. This surge will create new needs, requiring routes and supports that must be addressed through appropriate actions, interventions, and performances to ensure the environmental accessibility of public spaces. In this context, Schuster Park an open public space situated near one of the four Jubilee basilicas emerges as a vital subject for interdisciplinary study on accessibility and inclusion. Its flow, coupled with its natural connectivity, make it an important case for examining the intersection of tourism and accessibility.

3   The Design of a Schuster Universal Inclusive Park in Rome

The interaction between people and the built environment evolves through design developments that integrate multiple approaches, enhancing functions with inclusive solutions. Consequently, processes aimed at enhancing environmental accessibility emerge, particularly in public spaces. These processes not only define the bidirectional relationship between the social fabric and the environment but also highlight economic factors linked to tourist flows, which are influenced by place accessibility. These factors establish the necessary conditions to ensure the usability of assets and help define the asset's nature as a public heritage [22].

Within the Italian context, such places, when situated in established urban environments, carry narratives that must be 'listened to and interpreted' before designing any intervention strategy. This approach generates active user participation aimed at formulating integrated solutions to address functional, formal, and social needs. In this context, the quality of public works spanning design to construction reflects performance levels across various areas, particularly in tourism, which often emphasizes consumerism. This highlights an approach focused on fostering awareness and a sense of belonging to the space.

Schuster Park is a large triangular area of over 5 hectares, situated between the Basilica of St. Paul Outside the Walls along Ostiense street and a bend in the Tiber River. Over half of the park consists of permeable surfaces. The current geometric configuration is the result of a project by architect Francesco Cellini and Studio Insula for the Jubilee of 2000. This project transformed the park such that the northern avenue became the main parvis, and the square bordered by the *quadriporticus* incorporated green areas. Additionally, the remains of the Necropolis of St. Paul, located along Ostiense street, were made accessible to the public through a curved, lightweight cover.

The park serves as a public open space used daily and during major events. It is frequented by citizens and tourists, reflecting its strategic location near an important site in Christianity, with nearby amenities such as a metro station, the Roma Tre University, and the Bambino Gesù Children's Hospital. The participatory process involved in developing the design guidelines, which has been renewed in both methodology and activities, addressed the park's environmental accessibility needs. This approach views accessibility not merely as infrastructure but as a fundamental right. An inclusive park should provide a space where children can develop their abilities, accommodating their specific capacities.

The park's play area features two spaces designated for children of different age groups, offering sensory and socialization activities that stimulate multisensory experiences. The rubberized anti-trauma flooring guarantees safety and usability for all. The play equipment features elements with varying levels of challenge, encouraging creativity through the creation of various compositions and shapes. Urban seating in the adjacent area features tub-shaped backrests that accommodate vegetation at varying heights, providing children and all visitors with opportunities for exploration and learning. The design strategically encourages intergenerational social interaction, creating a sensory garden that is accessible to all users.

The park serves as a connector for various functional uses, both within its internal dynamics and those of the surrounding areas. It also facilitates spontaneous activities, encouraging self-organization among users to strengthen social cohesion among regular visitors while integrating occasional users. The play area, located near a senior center (also a subject of intervention), reinforces the park's intergenerational character. The pathway system, designed as a single element with varying service options, is organized as follows: the southern section is designated for inclusive sports activities, the central part is adjacent to existing seating and water points for resting, and the northern section opens into a tranquil, free area enhanced with light and trees [23].

The park is connected to nearby infrastructure through three main axes: to the north, southeast, and southwest. The study of often-overlooked micro-topographies enabled the optimization of the park's layout to maximize accessible walkability in all directions. The park features various facilities, including a skatepark, a bar, spaces for associations, restrooms, and a stage. In compliance with the latest design intervention, the drainage channel running from north to south includes a modular component designed to overcome barriers and connect these facilities (Fig. 1).

Fig. 1. Schuster Universal Inclusive Park project.

The research proposes a series of interventions framed across integrated fields, capable of transforming environments into accessible and inclusive public spaces for all individuals, including those facing various forms of vulnerability. These interventions incorporate ideas and suggestions from users and involve stakeholders with diverse backgrounds. Furthermore, the research facilitators acted as intermediaries, aiming to extend the principles and outcomes of the participatory design process to further levels of design managed by the Jubilee 2025 Society [24].

In this context, in collaboration with non-profit organizations, solutions for orientation and wayfinding were developed, including interactive multilingual totems designed to engage all user categories. During the current Jubilee year, these initiatives positioned Schuster Park as a catalyst for slow and sustainable tourism, which should be protected and promoted in pursuit of universal inclusivity. At the same time, these initiatives can highlight aspects that may compromise the park's capacity to effectively foster social cohesion and deliver its intended benefits.

4   A Multi-criteria Monitoring Process for the Jubilee year

Since construction work on the Park is underway, the paper aims to define the first steps for a monitoring and evaluation system that explores the relationship between the social benefits gained from the Park's presence and the potential effects generated by the flows during the Jubilee year. The coexistence of ordinary, day-to-day functions aimed primarily at the local community and activities related to the event could lead to a reduction in the Park's capacity to provide social benefits. For this reason, Schuster Park serves as a suitable test area for this type of multi-criteria evaluation.

In this context, multi-criteria models are ideal tools for monitoring the effects and impacts of urban dynamics, offering a structured evaluation approach that incorporates various elements of complexity [25] and the multitude of interacting factors in the use of public spaces. These evaluation models facilitate decision-making by integrating various criteria into a cohesive framework that aids in interpreting urban aspects. Multidimensional evaluation allows for the combined examination of the physical and social characteristics of public spaces and an understanding of how this influences user well-being. Several studies demonstrate that the perceived quality of public spaces significantly impacts their ability to generate benefits, indicating that evaluation should also account for subjective factors such as users' perceptions [26]. In some applications related to public space, the Weighted Linear Combination (WLC) approach has been used to integrate several variables into a single assessment, facilitating informed decisions on public space management [27]. Having defined the objective of the evaluation, the proposed method consists of the following operational steps:

1. Division of the park into areas to be assessed, including areal ambits (different park areas or functions), linear ambits (such as paths), and punctual ambits (individual elements like street furniture).
2. Identification of evaluation criteria that incorporate both tangible and intangible aspects into the evaluation.
3. Attribution of specific indicators to each criterion that can synthesize the phenomenon being evaluated; both qualitative and quantitative indicators may be utilized.
4. Data collection will involve direct measurements for quantitative indicators and direct social survey methods for qualitative indicators.
5. Construction of the evaluation matrix, which will consist of the different areas of the Park as rows and the set of criteria/indicators as columns.
6. Assignment of relative weights among the criteria.
7. Development of the matrix with calculation of scores, definition of rankings, and identification of critical elements.

8. Analysis and interpretation of the evaluation results.

A sample scheme of the evaluation matrix is presented in Table 1 below.

To more clearly outline the initial framework of the evaluation system, a preliminary set of indicators can be defined. Concerning quantitative criteria, direct measurements can be utilized. For example, the Saturation Index can be measured as the relative density (number of people) in a specific area (e.g., the play area) within a unit of time (at specific times). Calculated in this manner for each area, this index can be useful as a reliable indicator of potential overcrowding.

For each area, a maximum user threshold can be defined beyond which accessible and enjoyable use is restricted; a second quantitative indicator could be the Load Capacity, which refers to the number of instances within a unit of time when this user limit is exceeded. Repeated use beyond the Load Capacity of certain systems can also lead to deterioration or damage to specific elements. A Deterioration Index expressed as the proportion of degraded areas (for areal or linear zones) and the number of deteriorated elements (for point elements), can help monitor the effects on public spaces and plan recovery and restoration interventions [28]. Similarly, a Noise Index can be established by measuring the sound pressure generated by increased pedestrian traffic.

Finally, with regard to quantitative criteria, various econometric and extra-economic indicators [29] can be employed to quantify the combined effects of the Park and tourist flows, establishing methodologies for measurement before and after the Jubilee events to capture any potential variation. For instance, hedonic price methods can be used to investigate the variability and related market price impacts of the dynamics under study on properties in the vicinity of the Park [30]. Proximity to the inclusive park may positively affect the real estate market, but this potential benefit could be countered by the effects of any excessive tourist influx. According to the qualitative criteria, a set of perceptual elements can be established based on direct surveys, such as questionnaires, interviews, and focus groups composed by the users, who would give perceived scores based on specific characteristics. By capturing the direct expressions of various user categories over time, aspects such as perceived accessibility, space quality, feelings of safety, well-being, emotional qualities, visual attributes, senses of enjoyment, potential dissatisfaction, and perceptions of the Park's symbolic values can be qualitatively investigated and measured for each area. For these measurements, various scales of measurement may be employed. For instance, the Likert scale, with either 5 or 7 points, allows for the expression of the intensity of perception for each criterion. Additionally, perceptual collective maps can be utilized to indicate the intensities of perceptions related to specific criteria [31]. Finally, emotion scales can quantify users' feelings of well-being or discomfort.

The scope of the investigation can encompass all elements that serve as guarantors of the social impacts of an area designed for universal accessibility, also utilizing inclusive crowd-mapping processes to implement additional systems of analysis and evaluation [31]. Once the evaluation matrix is implemented, opportunities arise for further developing the proposed method. The first scenario involves formulating criticality rankings, which can be either partial or aggregated.

To develop these rankings, it is necessary to normalize the input data to ensure comparability and interpretability. Rankings may be partial, referring to individual elements within similar domains, or complete, encompassing all elements regardless of

Table 1. Sample diagram of the evaluation matrix.

Areal Ambits	Quantitative Criteria				Qualitative Criteria			
	C1	C2	...	Cn	C1	C2	...	Cn
Churchyard								
Senior Citizens Center								
Green area of the senior center								
Inclusive playground								
Inclusive skatepark								
Restrooms								
Free green areas								
Basilica Entrance								
Archaeological area								
Stage in the park								
Sensory Garden								
Space for associations								
Bar								
Linear Ambits	**Quantitative Criteria**				**Qualitative Criteria**			
	C1	C2	...	Cn	C1	C2	...	Cn
Access routes to visiting areas								
Pedestrian paths								
Sensory path								
Sports routes								
Punctual Ambits	**Quantitative Criteria**				**Qualitative Criteria**			
	C1	C2	...	Cn	C1	C2	...	Cn
Benches								
Water points								
Wayfinding Totem								
Other sittings								
Lighting								
Trees								
Cable duct crossings								
Hedges								

their domain. This dual interpretation provides various ways of understanding the phenomena that may arise in the park, particularly regarding its ability to correlate specific criticalities with the relevant elements of the park.

The formulation of rankings may also precede the establishment of a priority preference for the criteria. This process, aimed at defining the evaluation perspective, can be conducted through consultations with park users, employing various inclusive methods to determine the weights assigned to each criterion [32]. At the same time, the system can remain an open, unresolved, and non-generative ranking matrix, designed to maintain an active monitoring framework that can be addressed on time through compensatory activities or solutions in response to perceived or identified inconveniences.

5 Conclusion

Accessibility, inclusiveness, and quality of public space are elements that can be compromised for the local community when the space must be shared or managed alongside large flows of tourist use. In this context, this paper aims to highlight the inherent trade-off by proposing an evaluation system for a specific area that, according to the authors, could serve as an ideal case for identifying this dynamic. Indeed, Schuster Park in Rome, where daily use coincides with the Jubilee Year, could illuminate these critical issues and their impact on the local communities. To achieve this, the paper proposes preliminary guidelines for a multi-criteria evaluation of these effects.

The division into distinct categories (reclassified into areal, linear, and punctual) enables a comparison of areas most likely to be affected by overcrowding, and the matrix system will highlight areas experiencing the greatest distortions, both in terms of measuring effects and user perception regarding certain quality profiles. The proposed matrix allows the identification of various elements useful for space management, including:

a) Identifying a hierarchy of the most critical areas where the potential distorting effects of overcrowding are concentrated, as well as determining whether this is more likely to occur in flat, linear, or punctual areas. These indications can help redefine flows, even temporarily, to promote sustainability in terms of environmental accessibility and social quality of the space.

b) The heterogeneity of the criteria enables the correlation of specific issues (overcrowding, noise, etc.) with the areas requiring intervention.

c) The perceived inconveniences reported by the park's local community can guide interventions aimed at reducing critical issues.

d) Continuous monitoring of the state of degradation of the park and specific elements of street furniture can facilitate interventions to mitigate problems.

e) The perceived inconveniences by the park's reference community, relating to the overload experienced in the context, can be enumerated for specific criticalities such as accessibility, livability, access to services, perception of well-being, and various productive opportunities denied due to overlapping flows. This allows for planning potential compensatory measures, even on a temporary basis.

f) A comparison between perceived discomfort and quantified measurements (using quantitative indicators) is useful for understanding possible synergistic and complementary aspects of disturbing elements, or whether the community has an asymmetrical perception of critical elements that does not align with actual surveys.

In conclusion, this provisional system will need to be reviewed and calibrated based on actual implementation, ensuring effectiveness for its intended purposes.

References

1. Zhang, X., He, Y.: What makes public space public? The chaos of public space definitions and a new epistemological approach. Adm. Soc. **52**(5), 749–770 (2020). https://doi.org/10.1177/0095399719852897
2. Carr, S., Francis, M., Rivlin, L.G., Stone, A.M.: Public Space. Cambridge University Press, Cambridge (1992)
3. Mitchell, D.: The Right to the City: Social Justice and the Fight for Public Space. Guilford Press, New York (2003)
4. Zukin, S.: The cultures of cities Blackwell. Cambridge (1995)
5. Aelbrecht, P., Stevens, Q., Kumar, S.: European public space projects with social cohesion in mind: symbolic, programmatic and minimalist approaches. Eur. Plan. Stud. **30**(6), 1093–1123 (2022). https://doi.org/10.1080/09654313.2021.1959902
6. Kim, J., Kaplan, R.: Physical and psychological factors in sense of community: new urbanist Kentlands and nearby orchard village. Environ. Behav. **36**(3), 313–340 (2004). https://doi.org/10.1177/0013916503260236
7. Schiefer, D., Van der Noll, J.: The essentials of social cohesion: a literature review. Soc. Indic. Res. **132**, 579–603 (2017). https://doi.org/10.1007/s11205-016-1314-5
8. Comstock, N., et al.: Neighborhood attachment and its correlates: exploring neighborhood conditions, collective efficacy, and gardening. J. Environ. Psychol. **30**(4), 435–442 (2010). https://doi.org/10.1016/j.jenvp.2010.05.001
9. Jennings, V.: Social cohesion and city green space: revisiting the power of volunteering. Challenges **10**(2), 36 (2019). https://doi.org/10.3390/challe10020036
10. Jennings, V., Bamkole, O.: The relationship between social cohesion and urban green space: an avenue for health promotion. Int. J. Environ. Res. Public Health **16**(3), 452 (2019). https://doi.org/10.3390/ijerph16030452
11. Pineda, V.S.: What is inclusive and accessible public space? J. Public Space **7**(2), 5–8 (2022). https://doi.org/10.32891/jps.v7i2.1500
12. Koens, K., Postma, A., Papp, B.: Is overtourism overused? Understanding the impact of tourism in a city context. Sustainability **10**(12), 4384 (2018). https://doi.org/10.3390/su10124384
13. Bertocchi, D., Visentin, F.: "The overwhelmed city": physical and social over-capacities of global tourism in Venice. Sustainability **11**(24), 6937 (2019). https://doi.org/10.3390/su11246937
14. Rawhani, C., Middelmann, T.: Public space and the cohesion-contestation spectrum. GeoJournal **88**(4), 3535–3548 (2023). https://doi.org/10.1007/s10708-022-10817-y
15. Costituzione della Repubblica Italiana, art. 3 (1948)
16. Conti, C.: Accessibilità ambientale. In: Baratta, A.F.L., Conti, C., Tatano, V. (eds.) Manifesto lessicale per l'accessibilità ambientale. 50 parole per progettare l'inclusione, pp. 39–44. Anteferma edizioni, Conegliano (2023)
17. UN. https://www.ohchr.org/en/instruments-mechanisms/instruments/convention-rights-persons-disabilities. Accessed 18 Mar 2025
18. SITdA. https://www.sitda.net/index.php/cluster-e-ricerca-2/cluster-2/accessibilita-ambientale/. Accessed 18 Mar 2025
19. Romano, I., Marzi, L., Setola, N., Torricelli, M.C.: Analisi dei flussi e dei fattori d'impatto sull'accessibilità e l'identità degli spazi pubblici. Techne **14**, 285–298 (2017). https://doi.org/10.13128/Techne-20783

20. APMARR. https://www.apmarr.it/morfologie/morfologie-n44-in-italia-il-turismo-e-a-mis ura-di-disabilita-si-ma-non-sempre/. Accessed 18 Mar 2025

21. Osservatorio PNRR e Giubilo. https://www.osservatoriopnrrgiubileoroma.it/giubileo-2025-turismo-in-crescita-ma-sfide-da-affrontare/. Accessed 18 Mar 2025

22. Andreotti, J., Mariani, M., Trulli; L.: Gli investimenti per l'accessibilità materiale e immateriale nei luoghi a destinazione culturale nel PNRR. In: De Santis, M., et al. (eds). Convegno Internazionale "Specie di Spazi. Promuovere il benessere psico-fisico attraverso il progetto", pp. 312–319. Anteferma Edizioni, Treviso (2023)

23. Calcagnini, L. (ed.): Uno spazio inclusivo universale a Roma. Parco Schuster, Anteferma Edizioni, Treviso (2024)

24. Magarò, A., Mariani, M., Trulli, L.: Strategia di riprogettazione user-driven per l'inclusività: il Parco Schuster a Roma. Techne 28, 239–300 (2024). https://doi.org/10.36253/techne-15878

25. Baratta, A.F.L., Finucci, F., Magarò, A.: Generative design process: multi-criteria evaluation and multidisciplinary approach. Techne 21, 304–314 (2021). https://doi.org/10.36253/techne-9822

26. Ríos-Rodríguez, M.L., Rosales, C., Alegría, M.L., Trujillo, G.M., Hernández, B.: Influence of perceived environmental quality on the perceived restorativeness of public spaces. Front. Psychol. 12, 644763 (2021). https://doi.org/10.3389/fpsyg.2021.644763

27. Malczewski, J.: Local weighted linear combination. Trans. GIS 15(4), 439–455 (2011). https://doi.org/10.1111/j.1467-9671.2011.01275.x

28. Acampa, G., Grasso, M.: Heritage evaluation: restoration plan through HBIM and MCDA. IOP Conf. Ser. Mater. Sci. Eng. 949(1), 012061 (2020). https://doi.org/10.1088/1757-899X/949/1/012061

29. Acampa, G., Pino, A.: Village repopulation: analysis of extra-economic indicators to evaluate and valorise social generativity in ecovillages. In: International Symposium: New Metropolitan Perspectives, pp. 257–266. Springer, Cham (2024). https://doi.org/10.1007/978-3-031-74679-6_25

30. Bottero, M., Bragolusi, P., Bravi, M., D'Alpaos, C., Dell'Anna, F.: The value of urban parks in the city of Turin: an application of the geographically weighted regression. Valori E Valutazioni 34, 71–87 (2023). https://doi.org/10.48264/vvsiev-20233406

31. Finucci, F., Masanotti, A.G.: Crowdmapping: inclusive cities and evaluation. In: International Conference on Computational Science and its Applications, pp. 80–90. Springer, Cham (2023)

32. Miccoli, S., Finucci, F., Murro, R.: Measuring shared social appreciation of community goods: an experiment for the east elevated expressway of Rome. Sustainability 7(11), 15194–15218 (2015). https://doi.org/10.3390/su71115194

Back to the Roots: A Form of Sustainable Tourism

Giuseppe Sommario[1]([✉]) [iD], Laura Calcagnini[2] [iD], and Giovanni Baratta[3] [iD]

[1] Catholic University of the Sacred Heart, 20123 Milan, Italy
giuseppe.sommario@unicatt.it
[2] Roma Tre University, 00154 Rome, Italy
[3] University of Florence, 50121 Florence, Italy

Abstract. Roots tourism, a phenomenon that involves emigrants and their descendants returning to their lands of origin, is characterized by a high level of emotional involvement and a strong connection to family memory and local culture. Although often defined as "ancestral" or "nostalgic" tourism, roots tourism goes beyond a simple tourist visit: it is an inner journey, where places become symbols of belonging and identity. In Italy, this phenomenon is gaining attention through initiatives that promote the return of emigrants' descendants to their homeland. Italian communities around the world, especially in countries like Brazil, Argentina, and United States, are numerous and highly educated, and the desire to rediscover cultural roots is becoming increasingly widespread.

Roots tourism not only enhances the value of places of origin but also offers opportunities for economic growth in lesser-known regions, providing new avenues for development and revitalizing communities.

This type of tourism stands out for its emotional and cultural potential, as the traveler is not just a tourist but a member of a community seeking to re-establish a deep connection with their past, passed down by grandparents and parents. It is a phenomenon that touches on identity and memory and can therefore be considered a powerful tool for revitalizing marginal areas and fostering a renewed sense of belonging.

Keywords: Emigration · Roots tourism · Sustainable tourism

1 Tourism and Emigration

In 1994, the United Nations World Tourism Organization (UNWTO) defined tourism as "the activities of people traveling to and staying in places outside their usual environment for a total period not exceeding one consecutive year, for leisure, business, or other purposes not related to the exercise of a remunerated activity within the visited environment." Based on this definition, various types of tourism can be distinguished: religious, cultural, ecological, sports, and roots tourism. Therefore, we can say that one of the key factors in tourism is the ability of places to attract travelers who generate tourism.

O. Gervasi et al. (Eds.): ICCSA 2025 Workshops, LNCS 15899, pp. 329–338, 2026.
https://doi.org/10.1007/978-3-031-97663-6_29

It is interesting to note that all forms of tourism involve the movement of a person for a certain period of time to a place different from their usual residence. In fact, what changes from one type of tourism to another are the reasons and activities involved. Consequently, to define roots tourism, it is necessary to consider the reasons and activities that drive the roots traveler and that, as we will see, lead them to visit lesser-known places that are more connected to identity and a sense of belonging than to traditional tourism.

Decision-making processes, although based on reasoning, are influenced by various factors such as context and emotions [1]. It is the context that generates emotions and drives "roots tourists" to reach remote and less attractive places, yet these places provide psychological well-being and a sense of inner peace. Conversely, we can also say that emotions, anticipation, memories, and stories give context and places a special significance. They transform them into sources of emotion and infuse them with a "touristic" appeal that would otherwise be unexpected. The phenomenon of roots tourism is, in fact, than any other deeply tied to the individual and to personal memories. It is a form of tourism that highlights the primacy of the person and the human dimension because it allows travelers to discover something that intimately belongs to them: family memory and roots.

Therefore, roots tourism can be a valuable tool for promoting and enhancing a territory among its communities living abroad. After all, returning to one's homeland has always been a recurring phenomenon in the history of migration. However, only recently it has been recognized as a distinct tourism experience, worthy of being valued and encouraged. In recent times, this phenomenon has been gaining traction in Italy, while some countries, especially Israel but also Ireland, Scotland, and Albania, have long been investing in the promotion of their land and culture among their diasporic communities. They have adopted a targeted strategy by organizing a series of events aimed at their expatriated descendants in the areas most affected by emigration. This is the case, for example, of the project launched by Ireland in 2013, "*The Gathering Ireland*", which established a series of events aimed at promoting Irish culture among potential visitors of Irish descent living abroad. It is estimated that there are 70 million people of Irish origin worldwide, with 40 million residing in the United States.

The objectives of the project included:

1. increasing tourism by attracting more visitors from overseas;
2. creating lasting connections with the Irish diaspora around the world;
3. spreading Irish pride and promoting the country's image and reputation abroad.

The project led to a rise in tourism revenues and contributed to job growth in the sector [2].

Following the strategy adopted by the aforementioned diasporic communities, the Italian Ministry of Foreign Affairs and International Cooperation (MAECI) declared 2024 as the Year of Italian Roots Worldwide [3, 4]. Among the initiatives that embraced this call from MAECI, special mention should be made of the *Piccolo Festival delle Spartenze. Migrazioni e Cultura*, one of the best practices active in the national territory for almost 10 years. Launched in 2016, the Festival began in Calabria, one of the Italian regions most affected by emigration, and in one of the villages most impacted by the phenomenon of abandonment (Paludi). The event aims to serve as a catalyst, capable of revitalizing and promoting a village and its surrounding area; it seeks to attract members of the diaspora back to the land of their ancestors, fostering and strengthening roots tourism. In summary, the event aims to heal the cultural and "sentimental" rift between those who left and those who stayed behind, waiting for the return of their children to their homeland.

Dedicate an itinerant festival to migrations is a strategic and priority choice, as in Italy's history over the past two centuries, there has not been such a persistent, pervasive, and, in some aspects, paradoxical phenomenon as migratory movements. Just consider that, since 1876, more than 30 million Italians have left Italy [5–7] (Fig. 1), and the number of Italian descendants scattered around the world now exceeds 80 million.

Fig. 1. Italians waiting to be admitted to the Ellis Island processing center, New York 1910 [Fonte: Everett Collection/Shutterstock]

In this regard, MAECI states that "Roots Tourism potentially involves an estimated pool of between 60 and 80 million descendants of Italian emigrants worldwide, most of whom reside in the Americas, South Africa, Australia, and European countries" [8]. In addition to recently becoming a "land of immigrants," Italy continues to be a "land of emigrants": since 2020, Italy has seen a decrease of about 652,000 residents; during the same period, however, the number of people choosing to live outside national borders has continued to grow (+11.8%). Today, the community of Italians residing abroad, according to data provided by the Registry of Italians Living Abroad (AIRE) of the MAECI, stands at 6.134 million people, mostly young individuals between the ages of 18 and 34 [9].

Of these, 54.2% are in Europe, 40.6% in the Americas (over 2.4 million, of which 2 million are in Central and South America), 2.7% in Oceania, 1.3% in Asia, and 1.1% in Africa [7] (Fig. 2).

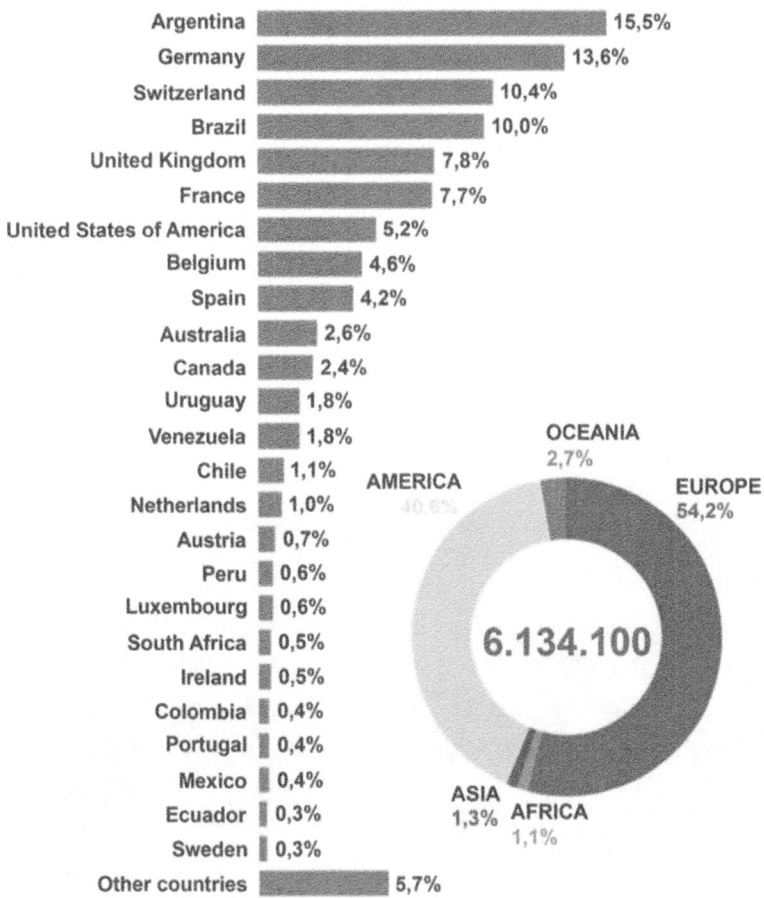

Fig. 2. Destination of residence [Source: Licata, 2024].

In conclusion, the community of Italian citizens officially registered with AIRE has surpassed the population of foreigners regularly residing in the country [10].

2 Roots Tourism

Roots tourism refers to the journey made by migrants or their descendants who return to their land of origin for vacation [11]. However, the phenomenon does not have a single, definitive name. Over the years, it has also been referred to as tourism of origins or return tourism, ancestral or genealogical tourism, diaspora or memory tourism, and nostalgic or sentimental tourism [12]. Definitions that all appear in some way incomplete, "since none manages to encompass all the implications of an experience that is not just about moving through space but is also and above all an inner journey" [13], a movement within oneself.

Among the definitions listed above, the one that most closely defines the phenomenon in question is "roots tourism," a definition that most emphasizes the high emotional involvement that a journey in search of oneself and one's family history entails.

More than tourism, these are characteristics that bring the roots journey closer to a pilgrim's path. And precisely because the emotional involvement is so intense, "the word 'tourism' should be used with caution when referring to the returns of our emigrants and their children to the land of origin." The definitions "roots tourism" and "roots journey," while indicating the same phenomenon, have meanings and semantic fields that only partially overlap: the two terms evoke different imaginations, describe the phenomenon in different ways, and highlight distinct aspects. In this sense, the term "journey" should be preferred over the term "tourism," as the latter only partially addresses the symbolic and emotional value of a journey that changes the life of the one who undertakes it.

Thus, it is a tourism segment with vast potential that, to grow, needs both specific investments and qualified studies and research, capable of providing professionals with the knowledge and data essential to best welcome the roots traveler. This traveler has a double, ambivalent psychological nature, as they are both a tourist, external to the community, and, at the same time, a community member, internal to the community.

3   Root Tourists

The largest communities of Italian descendants are found in Brazil (25 million), Argentina (22–23 million), and the United States (around 20 million); among the regions of origin, Veneto and Calabria rank at the top [14].

Among them, over half hold a degree or a post-graduate qualification: this data not only indicates the spread of academic degrees among the Italian and Italic populations worldwide but also highlights the importance of considering the level of education as a significant element in the process of designing communication and tourism offerings [15].

The knowledge of the Italian language among participants varies, but the majority would be interested in learning the language and therefore attending Italian courses during their roots trip. This data suggests the need to offer language and cultural learning opportunities specifically targeted at this group of tourists. A significant component emerging from the research concerns descendants with Italian citizenship: one-third has never been to Italy, and nearly all express the desire to visit their place of origin [16].

Among the possible activities, the most desired is visiting places connected to family memories and meeting relatives, clearly indicating a desire to reconnect with one's roots.

The profile of the roots traveler/tourist is that of an Italian descendant (mainly third or fourth generation), highly educated, with a strong longing for Italy. The trip is stationary, often for an extended period, and the traveler "is willing to make financial sacrifices to connect with their origins and, in addition to wanting to meet their family and explore the places of their roots, is highly interested in taking Italian language and culture courses, culinary workshops, and activities aimed at learning about ancient crafts" [17].

These are valuable data for developing targeted tourism offerings and promoting authentic and emotional roots tourism, particularly for regions that are currently less popular, such as Calabria, Abruzzo, Basilicata, and Molise.

4 Root Countries

Anthropological places par excellence are villages. They are complex artifacts of architecture, streets, alleys, houses, relationships, experiences and social practices. They are places "where the inhabitants live alongside their patron saints, their deceased, their memories" [18], where the sense of place is still deeply felt. These are the small towns of the interior, those that belong to the very core of Italy (as opposed to the flesh of the plains and cities), according to the famous definition of Rossi Doria [19].

These are the villages of the inland areas, once teeming with life and today largely uninhabited due to the many departures; emigration, which once allowed for the development and rebirth of entire communities, is now one of the symbols of abandonment and escape.

Today, the villages speak to us of uninhibitedness, beauty, new escapes, stays, remnants (objects, houses), returns, and ruins: we are not faced with the ancient monumentlike ruins that so captivated the travelers of the *Grand Tour*.

The rubble, the remnants of the village, speak to us of small stories, small centers, small communities, intimate contexts: this is what roots travelers will find. Their journey will thus be one in which they will immerse themselves among the ruins, the relics of the village, chasing shadows, filling voids, and collecting fragments.

It will be an intimate, minimal journey that will encourage self-discovery and offer the opportunity to grasp the meaning that places hold. Precisely because in the villages, the sense, the feeling of place is still strong, the identity with the place is at its fullest, and the individual is not anonymous to others: everyone knows everything about everyone, for better or for worse (Fig. 3).

This makes departures deeply painful: the entire village, as if it were a funeral procession, would accompany the emigrants to the edge of the settlement, with scenes of tears and embraces that are part of our collective imagery.

But the strong sense of identity also makes the return more emotional and festive: this time, the procession seems like a rite of rebirth. And, in a liquid world where we are losing our connection to places, perhaps roots travel can generate new forms of belonging, serving as a way to refocus attention on places, on their role as containers of stories and bonds, and on their sacredness.

As a result of the migratory hemorrhage, the entire village becomes a place of worship, a pilgrimage destination, for roots travel. And if the village becomes a sacred place of worship, then roots travel becomes a new pilgrimage, acquiring the ritual significance that ancient pilgrimages had in mending fractures and separations. And so, from the *caritas loci* of the Dominicans, we arrive at the cult of the village for emigrants, a place that orients its gaze in the world, even when living far away.

On this love, nostalgia then takes root, a sentiment coined in 1688 by Johannes Hofer to describe a type of illness originating from the poignant desire to return to one's homeland.

In this way, place and nostalgia reach us, passing through Giovanni Pascoli, Cesare Pavese, Mario Merola, Martin Scorsese, Francis Ford Coppola, and other roots travelers.

Fig. 3. In February 2025, Vico del Gargano Mayor Raffaele Sciscio sent out a large number of letters to those who left the Apulian town to seek their fortunes in Argentina, Australia and other European countries: the goal is to rediscover and enhance the cultural, human and social patrimonio of the emigrant families, inviting their descendants to see Vico del Gargano not only as a memory, but as a tourist destination of excellence [Source: www.gazzettah24.it/vico-del-gar gano-lancia-il-turismo-delle-radici-lettera-ai-vichesi-nel-mondo/].

5   The Feeling of Places

It becomes essential to define the sentiment of places. Places are organisms that change in meaning and significance depending on the presence or absence of humans. We all have sacred places that we love because of memories, emotions, personal, family, or collective stories. We are the relationship we have managed and chosen to establish with places. "We are our place, our places: all the real or imaginary places we have lived, accepted, discarded, combined, removed, invented" [20]. We are also the places that have told us their stories, the ones we have dreamed of, left behind, and that, at the moment of farewell, appear more beautiful than ever.

A place is a space that is inhabited, anthropized, humanized, and recognized by the people who feel a part of it. But it is also the product of cultural productions, the images that have shaped it and been inherited. It is a shared experience among those who remain, those who return, and those who have left forever. It is also the sum of the relationships that have been established from it. A place is not only the landscape, but it is also composed of houses, smells, sounds, objects, and social relationships [21]. A place is not just a geographical location, a spatial arrangement, but it is also a "dimension of the mind that requires a symbolic organization woven with time, memory, and oblivion" [22].

An anthropological place is a defined and known space inhabited by a community that defines it in relation to an external space, unknown and therefore threatening, dangerous. The people of the same place are and feel united by gestures, rituals, stories, sensations, perceptions, emotions, memories, festivals, and deities linked to it, to the point that many recent tools aim to present geographies of territories based on this collective experiential and emotional heritage [23]. We inhabit places, but places inhabit us, they possess us, sometimes even if we have never physically lived in them, as in the case of Italian descendants.

Thus, places, the environment, and space profoundly influence the formation of identity, to the point where we speak of "place identity" to indicate a deep feeling we have towards a place.

Place identity is at its highest in those locations that are difficult to reach and inconvenient to live in, which are, in fact, the ones most affected by diasporic exodus. However, despite everything, emigrants and their descendants remain deeply connected to the "remote" places of their origins [24]. According to Environmental Psychology, the discipline that studies the emotional processes characterizing the bonds individuals establish with places, there are many types of attachment (ancestral, functional, symbolic) that we feel towards places, and different categories that lead us to experience deep emotions for them.

Of particular relevance to roots tourism is the emotional-family category, which "concerns attachment to the place [...] that saw the birth and growth of one's ancestors: [...] an attachment not only personal but often familial and traditional, which refers to roots and can even be passed down from generation to generation through oral transmission" [25] (Fig. 4).

Fig. 4. Roots tourism as an emotional journey [https://pixabay.com/it/photos/vecchiaia-gioven tùmano-nonna-360714/].

6 Conclusions

Emigration is a radical experience that profoundly changes those who undertake it and their descendants. All have gone through multilingual disorientations, all have refinished identities, life practices, roots. Roots journeys begin with departure. Leaving, staying and returning stand together, because leaving grounds the need to return: an imperious, violent need arises that never abandons those who leave. A feeling that is nurtured, handed down, until it becomes a journey of roots. These journeys are possible because someone and/or something has remained to wait, guarding the places of ancient roots. Rediscovering one's roots is a spiritual exercise, an ascetic journey, a pilgrimage deep into the soul that changes the mind and heart, both outwardly and inwardly. More than moving through space, one travels within oneself.

To leave, to stay, to return, to get lost, to uproot, to root, to re-root: a continuous challenge, a vertigo, that can generate, invent a new way of being community. That is why root journeys are tourism but, at the same time, they can be a great opportunity for collective rebirth. They are a palingenesis, a way to rewrite the history of the communities that inhabit the villages of Italy's margins that are increasingly at risk of abandonment.

Moreover, such trips are an example of sustainable tourism since they are aimed at recovering the culture of the places of origin constituted by the enjoyment of the places and foods of the local economy and respect for the territory. Such actions benefit the community whose roots tourists originate from.

Ultimately, the journey of roots has something salvific in it, it is a healing journey, the regaining of a space, the search for a new center to give new meaning to places. If emigration is one of the names for abandonment, the journey of roots can be one of the names for the rebirth of villages in Italy's margin, a way to heal the ancient rift and corroborate communities.

References

1. Zammuner, V.L.: Emozioni. In: Girotto, V., Zorzi, M. (eds.) Fondamenti di Psicologia generale, pp. 263–278. Il Mulino, Bologna (2004)
2. Discorev Ireland. http://www.discoverireland.ie/The-Gathering-Ireland. Accessed 19 Mar 2025
3. https://www.esteri.it/it/servizi-consolari-e-visti/italiani-all-estero/turismo-delle-radici/. Accessed 19 Mar 2025
4. https://italea.com. Accessed 19 Mar 2025
5. Bevilacqua, P., De Clementi, A., Franzina, E. (eds.): Storia dell'emigrazione italiana. Partenze. Donzelli, Roma (2001)
6. Bevilacqua, P., De Clementi, A., Franzina, E. (eds.): Storia dell'emigrazione italiana. Arrivi. Donzelli, Roma (2002)
7. Licata, D. (eds.): Il Rapporto Italiani nel Mondo 2024. XIX edizione. TAU Editrice, Todi (2024)
8. Ministero degli Esteri. https://www.esteri.it/mae/it/sala_stampa/archivionotizie/retediplomat ica/2020/07/la-farnesina-a-sostegno-del-turismo-delle-radici.html. Accessed 19 Mar 2025
9. Ministero degli Esteri e della Cooperazione Internazionale. https://www.esteri.it/it/servizico nsolari-e-visti/italiani-all-estero/aire_0/. Accessed 19 Mar 2025

10. Licata, D. (eds.): Il Rapporto Italiani nel Mondo 2022. XVII edizione. TAU Editrice, Todi (2022)
11. De Marchi, D., Mingotto, E.: Turismo delle origini. Quadro preliminare delle potenzialità in Italia. In: CNR-IRISS (eds.) XX Rapporto sul Turismo Italiano, pp. 589–596. Mercury, Firenze (2016)
12. Ferrari, S., Nicotera, T.: Primo rapporto sul turismo delle radici in Italia. Egea, Milano (2021)
13. Sommario, G.: Spartenze, restanze, ritornanze: i viaggi delle Radici come occasione di rifondazione comunitaria, al di qua e al di là dell'Oceano. In: Gabrieli, M., Giumelli, R., Licata, D., Sommario, G. (eds.) Scoprirsi italiani. I viaggi delle radici in Italia, p. 21. Rubettino Editore, Soveria Mannelli (2023)
14. Licata, D.: Il turismo migratorio: viaggiatori speciali nell'Italia di oggi. In: Gabrieli, M., Giumelli, R., Licata, D., Sommario, G. (eds.) Scoprirsi italiani. I viaggi delle radici in Italia, pp. 56–59. Rubettino Editore, Soveria Mannelli (2023)
15. Giumelli, R.: Si va dove si viene. Cosa vuole e cosa cerca il viaggiatore delle radici. Considerazioni sulla ricerca e sul turismo delle radici. In: Gabrieli, M., Giumelli, R., Licata, D., Sommario, G. (eds.) Scoprirsi italiani. I viaggi delle radici in Italia, pp. 97–128. Rubettino Editore, Soveria Mannelli (2023)
16. Giumelli, R.: Si va dove si viene. Cosa vuole e cosa cerca il viaggiatore delle radici. Considerazioni sulla ricerca e sul turismo delle radici. In: Gabrieli, M., Giumelli, R., Licata, D., Sommario, G. (eds.) Scoprirsi italiani. I viaggi delle radici in Italia, p. 111. Rubettino Editore, Soveria Mannelli (2023)
17. Giumelli, R., Sommario, G.: Radici e identità: il Turismo delle Radici, un viaggio di scoperta e rinascita. In: Licata, D. (eds.) Il Rapporto Italiani nel Mondo 2023. XVIII edizione, p. 142. TAU Editrice, Todi (2023)
18. Teti, V.: La restanza. Einaudi editore, Torino, p. 46 (2022)
19. Rossi Doria, M.: La polpa e l'osso. Agricoltura risorse naturali e ambiente. L'Ancora del Mediterraneo, Napoli (2005)
20. Teti, V.: Il senso dei luoghi. Memoria e storia dei paesi abbandonati, p. 4. Donzelli editore, Roma (2004)
21. Miccoli, S., Finucci, F., Murro, R.: Social evaluation approaches in landscape projects. Sustainability 6(11), 7906–7920 (2014)
22. Teti, V.: La restanza, p. 22. Einaudi editore, Torino (2022)
23. Finucci, F., Masanotti, A.G.: Crowdmapping: inclusive cities and evaluation. In: International Conference on Computational Science and its Applications. pp. 80–90. Springer, Cham (2023)
24. Giani Gallino, T.: Luoghi di attaccamento. Identità ambientale, processi affettivi e memoria. Raffaello Cortina Editore, Milano (2007)
25. Giani Gallino, T.: Luoghi di attaccamento. Identità ambientale, processi affettivi e memoria, pp. 19–20. Raffaello Cortina Editore, Milano (2007)

AI-Driven Urban Perception Mapping: Comparing Gemini and LLaVA

Ayse Giz Gulnerman$^{(\boxtimes)}$ (iD)

Ankara Hacı Bayram Veli University, Ankara 06560, Turkey
ayse.gulnerman@hbv.edu.tr

Abstract. This study evaluates the capability of Generative AI (GenAI) tools in determining urban perception through street-level imagery (SLI) in the central part of Ankara. Specifically, Gemini 1.5 Flash and Large Language Vision Assistant (LLaVA) 13B models are utilized to assess predefined perception aspects. While Gemini operates via an application programming interface (API), LLaVA is executed locally using the Ollama platform. The findings indicate that Gemini 1.5 Flash provides consistent results across English, German, and Turkish prompts, whereas LLaVA 13B struggles with non-English queries and occasionally returns NA values for specific perception aspects. Beyond model performance, this study explores the potential contributions of GenAI to urban perception mapping. By integrating auxiliary data such as air quality, noise levels, and temperature, GenAI could enhance urban analytics beyond visual interpretation. However, challenges remain, including limitations in capturing personal experiences, cultural backgrounds, and subjective perception variations. Despite these constraints, GenAI presents a promising approach for large-scale, automated urban perception assessment, supporting sustainable and inclusive urban planning. Future studies should focus on refining multimodal GenAI models, incorporating diverse data sources, and addressing biases to improve the accuracy and applicability of urban perception analysis.

Keywords: Urban Perception Mapping · GenAI · Street-Level Imagery · Mapillary · Gemini · LLaVA

1 Introduction

1.1 Urban Design and Human Perception

Urban area's influence on human well-being has been widely discussed since 1960 [1–3]. Urban designers, architects, psychologists, and sociologists produced theories and empirical studies on how urban space influences human perception and behaviour [4–8] and momentary-emotion and long-term subjective well-being [9, 10].

Urban designers shape cities by arranging and categorizing activity places turning them into functional environment. Lynch [11], emphasizes that urban space cannot be defined solely by its physical arrangement; it must also encompass a meaningful purpose alongside its physical order. In this perspective, when an individual perceives the history,

O. Gervasi et al. (Eds.): ICCSA 2025 Workshops, LNCS 15899, pp. 339–349, 2026.
https://doi.org/10.1007/978-3-031-97663-6_30

customs, nature, and essence of the city in visited locations, a joyful connection with the space emerges.

Montgomery [5] defines the sense of urban space with three elements: activity, form, and image. According to this approach, the design affects its user preference and it is a fact that spaces actively used throughout the day increase the perception of reliability and preference rate. This design, called mixed use, keeps the space alive at all hours of the day. Thus, the space gives the human a sense of trust. Similarly, Jacobs [6] states that human immediately notices the diverse urban spaces where there is mobility, uses and supports that place. The four components must be fulfilled to ensure diversity in the space namely: 1- multifunctionality of the space, 2- low rise and short size buildings blocks, 3- harmonious blend of old and new buildings, 4- sufficient level of population density. Jacobs [6] argues that urban diversity cannot be achieved when even one of these four components is missing.

Lynch [4], Norberg-Schulz [7] define urban perception according to movement experience over the constituent parts of the urban area. Therefore, the urban perception might change based on the motion pattern what is gained from urban experience. Though the individual perception of the urban images formed in the mind in an urban area where these experiences (relations) exist, the presence of common imaginary data has the power to produce social perception. Lynch [4] states that this common imaginary can be analyzed through five elements; paths, nodes, districts, edges, and landmarks which helps to picture mind maps. Jojic [12] visualized Lynch's elements; paths, node, landmark, edge and district by matching them with the real-world examples.

Human urban perception is explained by different perspectives based on urban environment features. Bentley [13] claim that human prefer permeability, diversity, robustness, visual suitability, richness, customization, and readability of urban space. From a different angle, Gestalt theory [8] explains urban perception as focusing on the entire space rather than individual urban elements. According to this theory, the overall image holds a distinct meaning from its components. Humans mentally code entire urban space based on the principles of unity, proximity, continuity, similarity, and simplicity.

Holahan [14] suggests that living environments reflect human personality, as individuals shape urban experiences based on personal needs. Human motion also influences perception. Rapoport [15] classifies it as dynamic (e.g., walking) and static (e.g., sitting), noting that dynamic users prefer narrow, linear spaces, while static users favor open areas. Factors like movement purpose, direction, mode, and speed further affect perception [16]. Argin et al. [17] highlight how smartphones reshape visual attention, altering urban perception in the post-flâneur era.

Urban designers influence experiences through design strategies grounded in nudge theory. Defined by Thaler and Cass [18] and Almaas [19], nudging guides individuals toward better decisions without restricting choices. Examples include a rooftop entry at an opera house and a visually enhanced staircase in a library [19]. While nudging is integrated into architectural design, tracking its effects in complex urban environments shaped by visuals, noise, lighting, smell, and crowding remains a significant challenge [20].

1.2 Mapping Urban Perception and Human Wellbeing

Mapping human-urban interaction is important for re-designing healthy urban environments that can contribute to human well-being, but it remains challenging. Studies show that human emotions (as an indicator of instant human-urban interaction) are volatile and can easily be distorted over time as other emotions interfere with the original experience [21, 22].

Reichert et al. [23] presents the technological developments in the last decade, enabling experiments on the relationship between human mental health and urban upbringing as well as city living in a real-life laboratory. While the impact of urbanization on mental health problems is well-established, determining which of the multiple elements of urban living conveys risk remains elusive [23].

Researches start urban perception studies to unravel these elements in real-life urban context. Mainly studies focus on ambulatory assessment (AA) which means combining ecological momentary assessment with smartphones e-diaries, and physical behaviour data collected by accelerometers, GPS-trackers and hearth rate monitors [24, 25]. AA has important role in psychological assessment by recording urban-live experience. While merging momentary assessment with the urban space, remote sensing data for land-use and weather information, volunteered geographic information (e.g., open street map) for base map, social media data for travel behaviour and connotation of locations etc. are adopted in several studies [23, 24, 26].

Beside AA, there are other approaches focusing on just measuring human emotional states related with urban spaces. Some studies, focus on specifically one functional space (e.g., parks) influence on human sentiment. Kovacs-Györi [27] adopts a lexicon that classifies unigrams (single words) into 8 emotional states (anger, fear, anticipation, trust, surprise, sadness, joy, and disgust) for classifying social media (tweet) content to present human emotional states within or around parks. Another approach to understand environmental influence on human is urban perception. Salesses et al. [28] aims to map which areas of cities are perceived as safer, livelier, wealthier, more active, beautiful and friendly (6 emotional perceptions) over geotagged images from Google Street View imagery under The MIT Media Lab's Place Pulse project. A pioneering study enhanced the former dataset and present Place Pulse 2.0 dataset including near 111K Google Street View images from 56 cities (28 country) with pairwise labelling by over 81K volunteers to tackle limited urban perception studies at global scale [29]. Similarly, Wang et al. [30] assesses street quality over near 126K street view images based on human perception and additionally investigate the perception relationship with the semantics of objects (e.g., sky, road, and plant) in images.

1.3 Large Language Models Use in Mapping

Recent research has increasingly explored the role of Large Language Models (LLMs) in mapping urban perceptions and spatial understanding. For instance, Verma et al. [31] introduced generative agents powered by LLMs that navigate urban environments and simulate human-like perceptions, enabling new ways to assess urban livability and safety. Similarly, Aman and Matisziw [32] combined language and vision models to map urban sentiment, highlighting how transformer-based models can analyze geotagged social media content to understand public emotional responses to urban spaces. In the same direction, Yan et al. [33] proposed UrbanCLIP, a framework that integrates textual and visual data through contrastive pre-training to improve urban region profiling across cities. Complementing these developments, Hochmair et al. [34] benchmarked multiple LLMs including ChatGPT-4, Gemini, Claude-3, and Copilot, on their performance in spatial tasks, demonstrating their potential for geographic reasoning. These studies show that LLMs, especially when integrated with geospatial and visual data, provide a promising foundation for mapping and interpreting urban perception.

1.4 Aim of the Research

The influence of urban environments on human well-being, perception, and mental health has been extensively researched for decades. Various theories, approaches, and techniques have been developed to identify how urban spaces and their elements affect individuals. Generative AI (GenAI), a powerful tool across numerous domains, has the potential to become a key method for understanding and mapping urban influences on human life. This research aims to explore how GenAI tools process urban scene datasets from the perspective of human perception.

2 Methodology

The exploration in this study begins with the selection of the case area (urban space), followed by querying, retrieving, and tidying the open dataset (urban scene images), as well as identifying the GenAI tools and process steps used. This section consists of three subsections: case area, data retrieval and tidying, and data processing.

2.1 Case Area

Three features, urban center, pedestrian-based area, and daily population density are used to determine the case area. Based on these criteria, the Meşrutiyet District, located in the central part of Ankara, the capital city of Türkiye, is selected as the case area (Fig. 1). The Meşrutiyet District features crowded, pedestrian-based streets surrounded by busy roads throughout the day. These streets are lined with old, low to mid-rise buildings that have shops, bookstores, cafes, and bars on the ground floors, while the upper floors primarily contain private offices and workplaces.

2.2 Data Retrieval and Tidying

Mapillary [35] is a pioneering platform that provides street-level imagery (SLI) collected through crowdsourcing. Mapillary offers open SLI data for research via its application programming interface (API). The Mapillary API [36] allows users to query SLIs by defining a bounding box. In the first instance, we queried 532 images (Fig. 2(a)) within the border of Mesrutiyet District. Since Mapillary data is crowdsourced, the content often contains several discrepancies, such as varying camera angles, resolution, thematic content and point of view. The retrieved SLIs include irrelevant data for this research and require filtering.

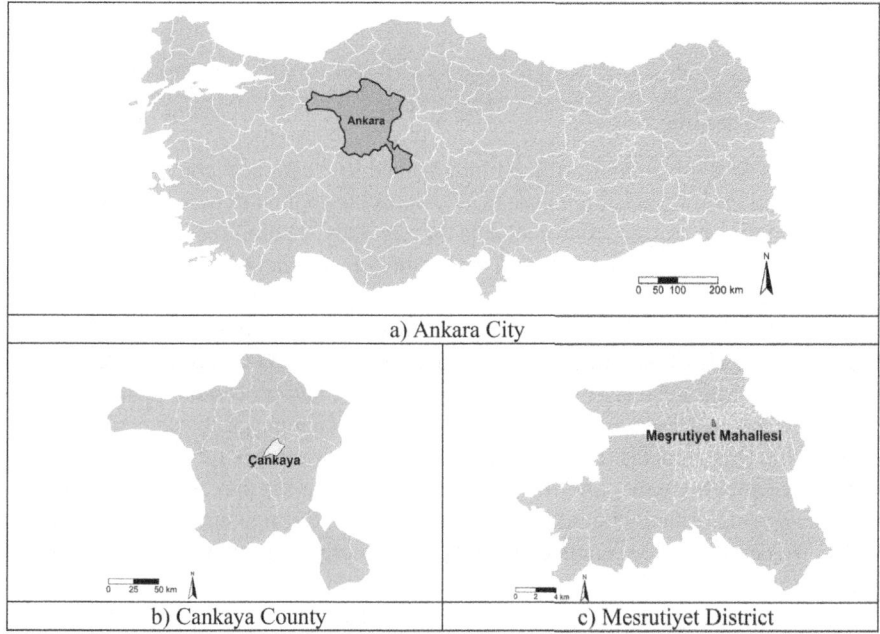

Fig. 1. Location of the case area Mesrutiyet District.

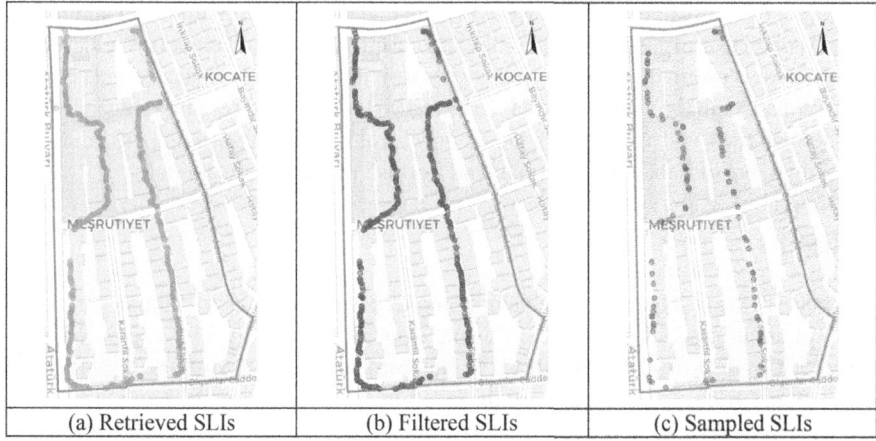

Fig. 2. Retrieved, filtered and sampled SLIs within the bbox of Mesrutiyet District.

After manually filtering the retrieved SLIs, 470 images were retained for further assessment using the techniques explained in Sect. 2.3. During the manual filtering, we considered (1) image clarity, (2) the point of view focusing on covering the street rather than a single object (such as a building, advertising board, or car), and (3) a plausible ground-to-sky ratio. Figure 2(b) displays the filtered 470 SLIs. Although more images are available, we randomly sampled 100 photos for assess in this study, as shown in Fig. 2(c).

2.3 Data Processing

GenAI refers to a sub area of artificial intelligence to create new content based on the given instructions over existing dataset [37]. GenAI is applied to numerous domains to generate text, image, music, code, and data. In this study we used special form of GenAI which combines language models with vision models in order to interpret our SLIs.

Two different GenAI models, Gemini [34] and LLaVA (Large Language Vision Assistant) [37] are used in this study to generate text descriptions for images based on questions asked about the image contents. Gemini is a GenAI tool powered by Google AI operating multimodality actions i.e., understanding and processing different modes of data (text, code, images etc.). In this study we adopt Gemini 1.5. Flash model through Gemini API. This model is recommended excellent performance for diverse and repetitive tasks. LLaVA is another multimodal GenAI model that has the capability of connecting text and visual data. In this study we used Ollama platform to run LLaVA 13B model locally. We designed the sequence of prompt engineering questioning in the following order:

(1) "Which human perception aspects for urban space do you consider? List the aspects."
(2) "Analyze the image and provide a score from 1 to 10 (1 = negative, 5 = neutral, 10 = positive) for each of the following human urban perception aspects.

In order to compare the results, we asked the first question to Gemini and applied the returned perception aspects as input for the second question to both models. We also make the both models return the answers in a csv file format that help to visualize and compare the performance. In the Gemini model we have also tested prompt engineering in English (en), German (de), and Turkish (tr). Due to low local response returning performance of LLaVA 13B, we did not apply German and Turkish prompt in the model.

3 Results

In response to the first question, the Gemini model provides scores for human perception aspects of urban spaces, including: (1) Visual Appeal, (2) Activity, (3) Spaciousness, (4) Order, (5) Comfort, (6) Accessibility, (7) Natural Elements, (8) Cultural Significance, (9) Emotional Tone, and (10) Sensory Stimulation. The Gemini model assigns scores to each aspect prompted in three languages - English (en), German (de), and Turkish (tr). Figure 3 illustrates the scores for each aspect, as queried in English (a), German (b), and Turkish (c) with the Gemini model, corresponding to each sampled image. Based on the prompted query, which specifies a scoring scale from 1 to 10 (1 = negative, 5 = neutral, 10 = positive), pink shades represent negative perceptions, while green shades indicate positive perceptions. The darkest pink corresponds to the most negative perception, whereas the darkest green represents the most positive perception. Similarly, Fig. 3(d) displays the perception scores returned for each sampled image by the LLaVA model. In Fig. 3(d), LLaVA returns 0 values for some processed images, indicating 'Na' (not available) values. These are represented in red.

When comparing the result plots (maps), the Gemini model demonstrates consistency across languages. However, the results prompted in English (en) clearly indicate a more positive perception compared to those prompted in German (de) and Turkish (tr). On the other hand, LLaVA model returns less consistent and capable results after several try,

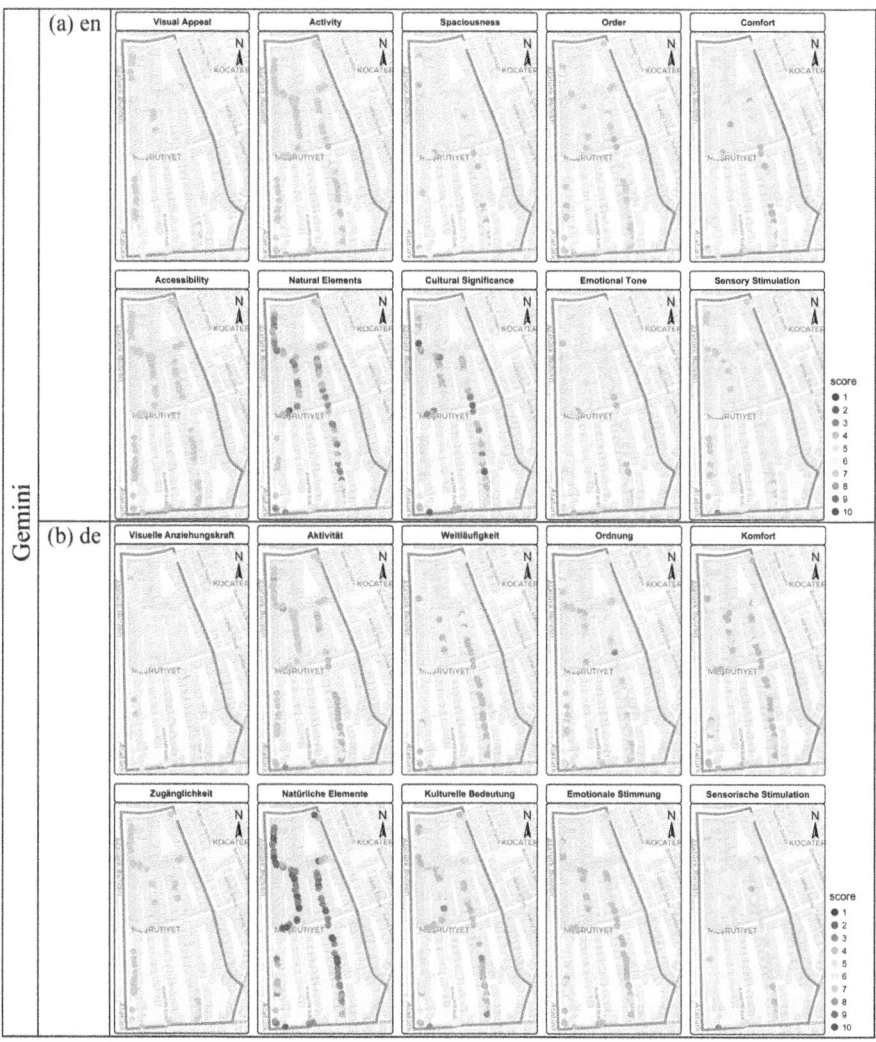

Fig. 3. Human urban perception mapping based on perception aspects using Gemini and LLaVA models.

Fig. 3. (*continued*)

we end up the scoring process with some missing scores for some images. In addition, returned scores also have negative perception tendency compared to Gemini results.

Table 1 summarizes the perception scores generated by Gemini and LLaVA. Gemini (en) prompts yielded the highest scores overall, indicating a more positive perception compared to Gemini (de) and Gemini (tr) prompts. Gemini (de) prompts had slightly lower scores than Gemini (en), but still followed similar trend. The Gemini (tr) prompts had the lowest average scores across most perception aspects particularly for "Spaciousness" and "Natural Elements". LLaVA (en)* which is a refined version the summary, aligning somewhat more closely with Gemini however still presents more negative perception compared to Gemini (en) scores.

Table 1. Average scores of human perception aspect by models.

Model	Language	Perception Aspects									
		1	2	3	4	5	6	7	8	9	10
Gemini	En	6.26	6.69	5.9	6.11	5.51	6.83	4.38	4.42	5.46	6.15
	de	6.03	6.31	5.31	5.77	4.81	6.47	3.22	4.79	4.69	5.63
	tr	5.96	6.06	4.28	5.05	5.61	6.63	3.22	4.16	4.87	5.19
LLaVA	en	3.27	5.29	4	4.99	4.61	4.7	2.64	3.52	4.15	4.1
LLaVA	en*	5.11	5.63	4.35	5.14	4.85	5.05	2.97	3.87	4.61	4.77

* Average score excluding 0/NA values.

4   Conclusion

This study investigates the capability of GenAI tools in determining urban perception in the central part of Ankara. The Gemini 1.5 Flash and LLaVA 13B models are employed for this purpose based on predefined perception aspects. While Gemini is accessed via an API, LLaVA operates locally using the Ollama platform.

The findings indicate that Gemini 1.5 Flash demonstrates consistent performance across different language prompts. In contrast, LLaVA 13B returns NA values for some perception aspects in certain sampled street-level images (SLIs) and exhibits limited accuracy when prompted in German and Turkish.

When comparing the two models, Gemini 1.5 Flash provides more reliable and stable results across all three languages, whereas LLaVA 13B struggles to return perception scores consistently, even in English. However, Gemini 1.5 Flash offers only limited free access, while LLaVA 13B runs locally and is free to use, making it a viable alternative for applications requiring offline processing.

GenAI has the potential to revolutionize urban perception mapping by efficiently analyzing SLI in combination with auxiliary data sources such as air quality, noise levels, and temperature to assess environmental comfort, social media geotagged posts for real-time sentiment analysis, and mobility data for accessibility insights. By integrating multi-source data, GenAI can support data-driven urban planning aimed at enhancing walkability, livability, and well-being in cities.

However, GenAI's interpretative capabilities remain in their early stages, with several challenges in accurately assessing human-centered perception aspects. While GenAI can process and analyze visual data, ambient environmental factors such as sound, air quality, and temperature remain underexplored. Moreover, personal attributes (e.g., personality, gender, and age) significantly influence urban perception, as do individual experiences, familiarity with similar spaces, and cultural backgrounds—all of which GenAI alone cannot fully capture when generating urban scene scores.

Despite these limitations, urban perception assessment remains a complex yet crucial research area with significant implications for human well-being. As GenAI models continue to evolve, future studies should focus on enhancing multimodal AI frameworks that integrate spatiotemporal, sensory, and demographic data to provide a more holistic understanding of urban environments. Additionally, improving language adaptability and cross-cultural interpretation capabilities in GenAI models will be critical for broadening their applicability in global urban studies.

Acknowledgments. This study has not yet received funding from any partners.

Disclosure of Interests. The authors have no competing interests to declare that are relevant to the content of this article.

References

1. Jackson, L.E.: The relationship of urban design to human health and condition. Landsc. Urban Plan. **64**(4), 191–200 (2003)
2. Canter, D.V., Kenneth, H.C.: Environmental psychology. J. Environ. Psychol. **1**(1), 1–11 (1981)
3. Barker, R.G.: Explorations in ecological psychology. Am. Psychol. **20**(1), 1 (1965)
4. Lynch, K.: The image of the environment. The image of the city **11**, 1–13 (1960)
5. Montgomery, J.: Making a city: urbanity, vitality and urban design. J. Urban Des. **3**(1), 93–116 (1998)
6. Jacobs, J.: The death and life of great American. Cities **21**(1), 13–25 (1961)
7. Norberg-Schulz, C.: Intentions in Architecture, no. 74. MIT press, Cambridge (1968)
8. Günay, B.: Gestalt theory and city planning education (2007)
9. Weijs-Perrée, M., Dane, G., van den Berg, P., van Dorst, M.: A multi-level path analysis of the relationships between the momentary experience characteristics, satisfaction with urban public spaces, and momentary-and long-term subjective wellbeing. Int. J. Environ. Res. Public Health **16**(19), 3621 (2019)
10. Dane, G., Aloys, B., Tao, F.: Subjective immediate experiences during large-scale cultural events in cities: a geotagging experiment (2019)
11. Lynch, K.: The city as environment. Sci. Am. **213**(3), 209–221 (1965)
12. Jojic, S.: City branding and the tourist gaze: City branding for tourism development. Eur. J. Soc. Sci. Educ. Res. **5**(3), 150–160 (2018)
13. Bentley, I.: Responsive Environments: A Manual for Designers. Routledge, Abingdon (1985)
14. Holahan, C.J.: Environmental psychology. Annu. Rev. Psychol. **37**(1), 381–407 (1986)
15. Rapoport, A.: The Meaning of the Built Environment: A Nonverbal Communication Approach. University of Arizona Press (1990)
16. Lang, J.T.: Creating Architecture Theory: The Role of the Behavioural Sciences in Environment Design (1987)
17. Argin, G., Pak, B., Turkoglu, H.: Between post-flâneur and smartphone zombie: smartphone users' altering visual attention and walking behavior in public space. ISPRS Int. J. Geo Inf. **9**(12), 700 (2020)
18. Thaler, R.H., Sunstein, C.R.: Nudge: Improving decisions about health, wealth, and happiness. Penguin (2009)
19. Almaas, I.H.: Nudges for a better architecture? An Online Review of Architecture by Arkitektur N (2013). https://www.architecturenorway.no/questions/cities-sustainability/nudge/
20. Gurkaynak, I.: Environmental psychology: nature, history, method. Ankara Univ. J. Fac. Educ. Sci. **21**(1), 1–9 (1988)
21. Levine, L.J.: Reconstructing memory for emotions. J. Exp. Psychol. Gen. **126**(2), 165 (1997)

22. Scherer, K.R.: What are emotions? And how can they be measured? Soc. Sci. Inf. **44**(4), 695–729 (2005)
23. Reichert, M., et al.: Studying the impact of built environments on human mental health in everyday life: methodological developments, state-of-the-art and technological frontiers. Curr. Opin. Psychol. **32**, 158–164 (2020)
24. Reichert, M., et al.: Using ambulatory assessment for experience sampling and the mapping of environmental risk factors in everyday life. Die Psychiatrie **13**(02), 94–102 (2016)
25. Trull, T.J., Ebner-Priemer, U.: The role of ambulatory assessment in psychological science. Curr. Direct. Psychol. Sci. **23**(6), 466–470 (2014)
26. Šćepanović, S., et al.: The healthy states of America: creating a health taxonomy with social media. In: Proceedings of the International AAAI Conference on Web and Social Media, vol. 15 (2021)
27. Kovacs-Györi, A., et al.: Beyond spatial proximity—classifying parks and their visitors in London based on spatiotemporal and sentiment analysis of Twitter data. ISPRS Int. J. Geo-Inf. **7**(9), 378 (2018)
28. Salesses, P., Schechtner, K., Hidalgo, C.A.: The collaborative image of the city: mapping the inequality of urban perception. PloS one **8**(7), e68400 (2013)
29. Dubey, A., et al.: Deep learning the city: quantifying urban perception at a global scale. In: Computer Vision–ECCV 2016: 14th European Conference, Amsterdam, The Netherlands, 11–14 October 2016, Proceedings, Part I 14. Springer, Heidelberg (2016)
30. Wang, L., et al.: Measuring residents' perceptions of city streets to inform better street planning through deep learning and space syntax. ISPRS J. Photogram. Remote Sens. **190**, 215–230 (2022)
31. Verma, D., Mumm, O., Carlow, V.M.: Generative agents in the streets: exploring the use of Large Language Models (LLMs) in collecting urban perceptions. arXiv preprint arXiv:2312.13126 (2023)
32. Aman, J., Matisziw, T.C.: Urban sentiment mapping using language and vision models in spatial analysis. Front. Comput. Sci. **7**, 1504523 (2025)
33. Yan, Y., et al.: Urbanclip: learning text-enhanced urban region profiling with contrastive language-image pretraining from the web. In: Proceedings of the ACM Web Conference, pp. 4006–4017 (2024)
34. Hochmair, H.H., Juhász, L., Kemp, T.: Correctness comparison of ChatGPT-4, Gemini, Claude-3, and Copilot for Spatial Tasks. Trans. GIS **28**(7), 2219–2231 (2024)
35. https://www.mapillary.com/dataset/vistas
36. https://www.mapillary.com/developer/api-documentation?locale=tr_TR
37. Liu, H., Li, C., Wu, Q., Lee, Y.J.: Visual instruction tuning. Adv. Neural. Inf. Process. Syst. **36**, 34892–34916 (2023)

Sustainable and Innovative Approaches for the Enhancement of Cultural Heritage in Fragile Areas. The Case Study of the Sibaritide Cultural Park

Verardi Ferdinando[1][(✉)] and Passarelli Domenico[1,2]

[1] Department of Engineering, Pegaso Telematic University, 80143 Naples, Italy
ferdinando.verardi@unipegaso.it
[2] Mediterranean University, Reggio Calabria, Italy

Abstract. This paper explores how sustainable development, as defined by the Brundtland Report, the 1992 Rio Conference, and the UN 2030 Agenda, requires a multidimensional approach that integrates environmental, economic, and social considerations. It argues that effective sustainability strategies should be tailored to local contexts and embedded in the socio-economic fabric, especially in regions with structural vulnerabilities.

Focusing on the Sibaritide Cultural Park in Southern Italy-a territory rich in natural and cultural heritage but challenged by persistent socio-economic and environmental fragilities. The study presents an innovative cultural planning model. This model combines technological innovation with interdisciplinary, multi-stakeholder governance to address regional disparities and foster internal cohesion.

The Sibaritide initiative emphasizes the importance of inclusive collaboration among all sectors of society to strengthen "social capital" and achieve the UN 2030 Agenda's goal of revitalizing partnerships for sustainable development.

Keywords: Cultural heritage · sustainable development · technological innovation · inclusive collaboration

1 Introduction

The concept of sustainable development, as first introduced by the Brundtland Report and reiterated at the 1992 Rio Conference, emphasized not only environmental concerns but more broadly the responsibility toward future generations. Similarly, the United Nations' 2030 Agenda and its Sustainable Development Goals (SDGs) explicitly criticize the unsustainable nature of current development paradigms, broadening the scope to include economic and social sustainability alongside environmental considerations.

The outcomes of sustainability strategies have demonstrated that rigorous analysis and diagnosis, while necessary, are not sufficient unless interventions are deeply embedded in the socio-economic fabric of the target context. This is particularly pertinent in territories marked by structural vulnerabilities environmental, economic, and social that hinder their development trajectories.

The association of 2030 Agenda SDGs with the sectoral planning policies and their disciplinary instruments that can interpret local specificities and guide the participatory framework, is highly important to guarantee development initiatives that have an impact and are context-sensitive. This integrative approach transcends the reductionist view that sustainability as an environmental issue, rather with a multi-faceted concept of development [1].

The research is founded on the case study of Sibaritide Cultural Park which is an area of great natural and cultural resources, albeit embedded in a context characterised by long-standing social, economic and environmental fragilities, representing the common southern-Italian marginal areas [2]. This study presents a new cultural planning paradigm, which is founded on the integration of technology-led innovation and an interdisciplinary, multi-actor governance structure.

Rather than focusing on global megacities or the dire conditions of the world's least developed regions, the analysis centers on intra-national disparities. It highlights the internal cohesion issues of countries that, despite overall development, continue to struggle with regional imbalances. The Sibaritide initiative aims to address one of the cross-cutting goals of the UN 2030 Agenda: strengthening the means of implementation and revitalizing global partnerships for sustainable development.

This objective underscores the need for inclusive collaboration among all sectors of society from private enterprises and institutions to civil society, academia, cultural entities, and media. Accordingly, the Sibaritide Cultural Park project emphasizes enhancing the collaborative capacity of local stakeholders what development economists often define as "social capital" as a pivotal enabler of sustainable transformation [3].

2 Methodological Aspects. Multi-agent Design Instruments

Some of the design instruments to support integrated policies for plans at different levels are represented by territorial systems, plans and programs capable of providing precise and targeted guidelines, from strategic planning of vast areas to operational plans for land management; from risk reduction to emergency plans and operational plans, they represent just a few of the essential elements for the drafting and implementation of operational plans and programs that are preparatory to land management characterised by suitable resilience qualities. They can also form the database that can be used to achieve an integrated multi-agent and multi-dimensional design, which can absolutely be borrowed from object-oriented programming (OOP). Which, in turn, represents one of the most significant evolutions in the field of software development, a way of conceptualising a program as a set of interacting objects, each of which includes a data structure and a set of operations applicable to them, so as to improve their comprehensibility, reusability and strength. By having a design environment underpinned by ICT procedures, it is possible to conceive and develop projects consisting of a community of components, called agents, that interact with each other and can also be used, retaining their data, in subsequent design interventions. Similar to Agent programming, the type of design just described can be based on the use of objects, since an Agent can be defined as an object or rather an instance of a class that includes the functionalities implemented by the Agent itself, in which methods and properties define the services it makes available to other Agents. Thus, multi-agent and multi-dimensional integrated planning, moreover intended as an opportunity for sustainable development for the territory in terms of governance management and planning, especially for the design of territorial systems, evidently similar, due to their peculiarities, to complex processes over vast areas, such as the case study. The design of new plans and/or programs thus becomes agile and comprehensible to the various actors involved. Working through the different thematic areas of the project, represents an authentic revolution, compared to which there is still much to be explored before operating with less load but with better results in terms of quality over time (even after the realisation of the work). This is perfectly superimposable to object-oriented programming (OOP, Object Oriented Programming), which represents, in turn, a significant evolution in the field of software development, a new way of implementing a project proposal by making use of a set of objects (design elements) that interact with each other, while, each of them, contributes to structuring a complex of operations that can be applied to the realisation of the proposal itself, starting from its design. Objects help the designer to better manage the complexity of procedures, improving their comprehensibility, reusability, identity, classification, inheritance and polymorphism. This new approach leads to the consideration of a new design philosophy for components, to the extent that the development of classes specialised in solving certain problems or implementing certain functionalities has become widely used, especially in the field of programming, where, new languages have been implemented while a new programming philosophy is emerging, thanks to the growing popularity of distributed environments. With a design environment, appropriately supported by ICT procedures, projects can be conceived and developed, formed by a community of components called Agents that not only interact with each other, but can also be used, retaining their data, in subsequent design interventions.

3 Project Objectives Sibaritide Cultural Park

The "Sibaritide Cultural Park" is an integrated development initiative promoted through a formal agreement between the Italian Ministry of Culture (MiBACT) and a consortium of 31 municipalities led by Cassano allo Ionio. The project aspires to systematize and enhance the region's extensive cultural and archaeological assets. Core objectives include: promoting the ancient city of Sibari; fostering a renewed collective identity anchored in the legacy of Magna Graecia; protecting and upgrading cultural heritage through innovative technologies; and facilitating the integration between traditional craftsmanship and emergent creative industries [4]. The broader vision transcends isolated interventions, envisioning cultural heritage as a catalyst for territorial cohesion and socio-economic revitalization [5].

3.1 Setting and Guidelines for the Design of Actions

The collective effort of the 31 municipalities is conceptualized as a comprehensive territorial project, oriented toward sustainable local development grounded in cultural, environmental, and socio-economic values. This effort is not just about stacking up technical projects; it emphasizes strategic cognition that links short and medium range interventions to longer term pathways of development for local people. The final goal is to develop a territorially-integrated system of actions that respects and promotes the three dimensions of sustainability: technical-environmental, economical and social [6]. These dimensions are seen as mutually reinforcing preconditions for successful heritage preservation and development and also for testing new non-extractive models of use of cultural and natural capital [7].

Significantly, social legality and sustainability are necessary though not sufficient conditions for success. The Park must be experienced and internalized by residents as a vital part of their identity, actively engaged with rather than passively accepted. In this sense, emotional investment and shared ownership represent foundational principles for future-oriented development within the region.

3.2 Stakeholder Engagement, Social Capital, Subsidiarity

The area designated as the Sibaritide Cultural Park is not only rich in cultural heritage but also endowed with significant environmental resources. In this context, the principle of subsidiarity the active cooperation between public institutions and private or community actors emerges as a pivotal approach for both heritage and natural resource management. This principle is now widely acknowledged as essential in promoting inclusive and durable development processes.

According to this viewpoint, Article 118(4) of the Constitution, which requires the State, Regions, Metropolitan Cities, Provinces, and Municipalities to support and encourage independent civic initiatives addressing common goods, provides constitutional support for horizontal subsidiarity the collaborative framework that regulates relations between institutional and non-institutional actors [8]. These programs must be founded on the subsidiarity concept and may come from individuals or organizations.

This idea suggests that when private and social initiatives are more effective and efficient in serving the public interest, governmental institutions should work as facilitators rather than as the main executors, encouraging and coordinating them. The Code of Cultural and Landscape Heritage (Legislative Decree 42/2004) offers a strong legal framework to promote public-private partnerships for heritage enhancement in the particular field of cultural heritage, whether it be archeological, historical-artistic, environmental, or anthropological. Article 111 and later in Chapter II describe management practices and acknowledge the crucial role that non-public actors play in processes of valuation.

In a similar vein, global organizations like the International Union for the Conservation of Nature (IUCN) have emphasized the significance of co-management techniques and shared responsibility in the realm of the environment. Through participatory governance models that are frequently influenced by business-oriented approaches, these initiatives encourage creative finance mechanisms and fair benefit-sharing. Additionally, the European Commission has promoted the spread of sustainable tourism best practices for Natura 2000 and other protected areas through its Directorate-General for the Environment. The 2009 recommendations place a strong emphasis on long-term plans that involve all parties involved, growing networks of stakeholders, valuing new tourism trends, and developing alliances with astute players in the industry.

These principles promote a strong interconnection between tourism and local economies, urging the involvement of residents in planning, job creation, and the promotion of conservation-linked tourism.

Consequently, co-management has become a hallmark of the most advanced and sustainable models for managing cultural landscapes and environmental resources. It is also the only viable approach to ensure the continuity and reliability of services essential to park life. Relying solely on public funding exposes the park to risks of operational discontinuity, given the fluctuating and often insufficient flow of government resources.

However, implementing a co-management model requires robust capacity on both the public and private sides. Public authorities must possess technical and administrative competence to manage collaboration frameworks. Private actors, for their part, must cultivate creativity and entrepreneurial vision aligned with the territory's identity and environmental constraints [9].

Creating a virtuous cycle of shared governance also depends on strengthening the community's capacity for cooperation what development theory describes as social capital [10]. This refers to the ensemble of trust-based relationships, shared norms, and behavioral codes that facilitate cooperation within and across institutions. Social capital enhances organizational coherence and is shaped by a community's cultural memory and institutional context.

As economic historians and development economists such as Douglass North have demonstrated, institutional evolution directly influences economic performance by reducing uncertainty, lowering transaction costs, and ensuring the predictability of economic and social interactions. These are all crucial conditions for sustainable development.[11].

Thus, the regeneration of cultural and environmental heritage, the revitalization of the regional economy, and the consolidation of social capital are intertwined goals within the broader Territorial Project for the Sibaritide Cultural Park. The project's success hinges on its ability to articulate a governance system that is not only technically efficient, but socially embedded and forward-looking. Two strategic principles are central to this effort:

Develop a territorially-rooted circular economy, which reinforces local assets and unlocks new opportunities for communities;

Align local development with broader frameworks of tourism and territorial marketing, connecting the region with both domestic and global markets.

These principles translate into operational directives such as strengthening local identity; organizing attractions thematically; promoting plural and inclusive narratives of heritage; constructing a sustainable tourism ecosystem (covering services, mobility, public-private collaboration, and B2B synergies); facilitating new entrepreneurial opportunities; and responding to both current and potential demand.

4   Project Groups for the Sibaritide Cultural Park

Under the terms of the agreement signed between the Municipality of Cassano allo Ionio, acting as lead partner for the 31 municipalities in the Sibaritide area, and the Ministry of Culture (MiBACT), the development strategy was designed in alignment with the foundational principles previously discussed. The guiding vision was to conceive the Sibaritide initiative as a comprehensive territorial project, which places local communities and social capital at its core, operationalizes the principle of subsidiarity, and promotes a circular economy model that is attentive to the regional socio-economic context yet responsive to market dynamics [12].

During the planning process, strategic reference was made to higher-level territorial planning instruments, especially those applicable to the Sibaritide area such as the Regional Landscape Protection Framework and the Provincial Territorial Coordination Plan. These frameworks provided not only normative direction but also key criteria for sustainable development in environmental, economic, and social dimensions.

The resulting strategic concept centers on the reinforcement of collaborative networks and the development of a structured tourism ecosystem. Tourism, by its nature, depends on both localized networks which support the embeddedness of enterprises and communities in the territorial matrix and broader networks that connect local actors with distant publics, potentially generating economic and cultural flows. Hence, the strategy emphasizes connectivity, not only among project components but between local and global scales [13].

The central idea is to build territorial cohesion around a strong and recognizable identity of the Sibaritide, particularly by leveraging the cultural legacy of ancient Sybaris. The objective is to establish a network of public and private services organized around cultural heritage, applying the subsidiarity principle to foster cooperation between institutions, enterprises, and civil society.

This framework supports the creation of a sustainable tourism system that promotes long-term heritage preservation, environmental stewardship, and socio-economic development. The project proposals are grouped into functionally coherent clusters, each supporting the overarching vision.

The first strategic cluster is composed of foundational and enabling projects, essential for supporting both tangible and intangible aspects of the tourism ecosystem. These include:

1. Establishment of the Cultural Park Service Center
2. Implementation of digital marketing and social media strategies
3. Development of interactive applications for geolocation and real-time sharing
4. Creation of a start-up support system and programming of events
5. Development of a creativity hub in the Sibaritide area
6. Design of an integrated system for smart and environmentally friendly mobility within the Park

These initiatives play a pivotal role in building the infrastructure necessary for territorial accessibility, visibility, and stakeholder coordination.

A second cluster focuses on enhancing cultural offerings and improving communication strategies. These actions aim to enrich the quality of the visitor experience while promoting greater awareness of local heritage. They include both physical interventions such as the restoration of cultural sites and digital strategies for content creation and dissemination. The projects in this group are:

1. Promotion of regional goods and resources;
2. Innovation in museums, ICT, and digital tourism tools;
3. Development of educational archaeology formats (Archeo Edutainment);
4. Organization of cultural events and artistic programming;
5. Celebration of the Arbëreshë cultural tradition through dedicated events.

One particularly innovative action is the establishment of artist residencies throughout the territory, which are designed to produce contemporary artworks and itinerant exhibitions, thereby fostering cultural continuity and integration across the Park's spatial dimensions (Figs. 1 and 2).

Fig. 1. Territorial image and spatial location of the projects of the Sibaritide Park – 1

Fig. 2. Territorial image and spatial location of the projects of the Sibaritide Park – 2

5 Recurring Critical Issues and Evaluation Needs

Despite its significant potential, the strategic planning of extensive areas containing exceptional cultural assets is often challenged by a series of structural and procedural limitations that can severely compromise the effectiveness of intended interventions. A comprehensive analysis of the relevant academic and policy literature reveals a set of recurring criticalities, which require careful consideration to ensure the success of large-scale territorial projects such as the Sibaritide Cultural Park.

Among the most frequently observed challenges is the institutional inadequacy of public entities in transitioning from traditional, top-down planning models to more dynamic, inclusive governance paradigms. This is reflected in difficulties related to managing structured and continuous dialogue among stakeholders, often resulting in fragmented institutional action and inefficient decision-making processes.

Another continuing issue relates to the predominance of self-referential planning processes. In many cases, stakeholder participation is merely nominal and key decisions are taken before a real consultation procedure. This threatens both the legality and the adaptive ability of planning initiatives. Moreover, while extensive data collection and analysis may be conducted, these do not always result in a fuzzy understanding of local needs, nor do they necessarily provide accurate understandings of current socio-economic and spatial changes.

An additional problematic lies in the illogicality between strategic goals and operative objectives. There is frequently a separate between the identification of territorial needs, the creation of long-term development visions, and the definition of tangible, actionable priorities. As a result, resource distribution may not align with actual territorial subtleties, thereby diminishing policy effectiveness and implementation capacity.

Furthermore, there is a limited ability to create plans that value territorial identity, balance development and conservation, or establish essential distinctions that can spur innovation. Planning procedures run the risk of perpetuating current stagnation rather than encouraging renewal if such transformational solutions cannot be articulated.

The absence of strong performance indicators that may convert objectives into quantifiable outcomes is another significant flaw. Inadequate monitoring mechanisms, which frequently fall short of producing insightful input for program or policy reform, exacerbate this shortcoming. As a result, there is a considerable chance that tactics will continue to be primarily theoretical, well-written on paper, and rarely put into reality.

An imbalance in stakeholder engagement exacerbates this gap between strategy formulation and execution.

An imbalance in stakeholder engagement exacerbates this gap between strategy design and execution: while the planning phase may attract significant interest and institutional backing, the implementation phase frequently receives less attention and participation. The continuity and robustness of planning initiatives are compromised by this cyclical irregularity.

Integrating evaluation methods into every stage of the planning process, from initial goal-setting to final impact assessment, is crucial to addressing these issues without sacrificing the process's iterative and adaptable nature. The ability to make well-informed judgments, monitor and modify implementation tactics, reevaluate priorities as needed, and understand the wider social and territorial ramifications of the approved policies is improved by the synergy between the policy design and evaluation processes.

Specifically, the introduction of a common organization of ex-ante, in itinere, and ex-post evaluations, supported by evidently clear indicators (implementation, outcome, and impact metrics), can significantly progress governance quality. Such a system enables real-time monitoring, facilitates the identification and correction of deviations, and ensures a comprehensive understanding of program efficiency and effectiveness.

Finally, the transparent dissemination of evaluation findings plays a critical role in reducing asymmetries of information among actors. This not only enhances institutional accountability and public trust but also contributes to the legitimacy of choices made within the broader planning framework, reinforcing democratic participation and adaptive policy learning.

References

1. Gravagnuolo, A., Angrisano, M., Bosone, M., Buglione, F., De Toro, P., Fusco, G.L.: Participatory evaluation of cultural heritage adaptive reuse interventions in the circular economy perspective: a case study of historic buildings in Salerno (Italy). J. Urban Manag. Open Access Volume **13**(1), 107–139 (2024)
2. Passarelli, D.: Le sfide dell'urbanistica oggi, INU edizioni, Roma (2022)
3. Angrisano, M., Nocca, F.: Urban regeneration strategies for implementing the circular city model: the key role of the community engagement. In: Lecture Notes in Computer Science (including subseries Lecture Notes in Artificial Intelligence and Lecture Notes in Bioinformatics), vol. 14108 LNCS, pp. 359–376. Springer, Heidelberg (2023)
4. Verardi, F., Angrisano, M., Fusco Girard, F.: New development policies for the internal areas of Southern Italy. General principles for the valorization of rural areas in Calabria Region. Valori e Valutazioni **2023**(33), 105–116 (2023)

5. Caroli, M.G.: Il marketing territoriale. Franco Angeli, Milano (2001)
6. Trimarchi, M.: Economia e Cultura. Franco Angeli, Milano (2003)
7. D'Angela, F.: La collaborazione nella gestione delle destinazioni turistiche. Giappichelli, Torino (2016)
8. Perulli, G.: Governare il territorio. Giappichelli Editore (2009)
9. Gaeta, L., Rivolin, J., Mazza, L.: Governo del territorio e pianificazione spaziale. Città Studi Editore (2013)
10. Gronroos, C.: Service management and marketing: a customer relationship management approach. In: Trad. Italiana, Management e Marketing dei servizi, De Agostini Scuola, Novara. Wiley, Chichester (2006)
11. Douglas North, C.: Institutions, Institutional Change, Evolution of the Economy. Italian Edition, Il Mulino (1997)
12. Angrisano M.: The canvas model to support the circular urban regeneration projects. In: Lecture Notes in Computer Science (including subseries Lecture Notes in Artificial Intelligence and Lecture Notes in Bioinformatics), vol. 14108 LNCS, pp. 483–497 (2023)
13. Angrisano, M., Nocca, F., Scotto di Santolo, A.: Multidimensional evaluation framework for assessing cultural heritage adaptive reuse projects: the case of the seminary in Sant'Agata de' Goti (Italy). Urban Sci. **8**(50) (2024)

Regenerating the Hidden Cultural Heritage: The Case of the Campo Trincerato in Rome

Laura Ricci⬤, Paola Nicoletta Imbesi(✉) ⬤, and Francesca Perrone⬤

PDTA Department, Sapienza Università di Roma, Rome, Italy
{laura.ricci,francesca.perrone}@uniroma1.it,
paola.imbesi@urniroma1.it

Abstract. The development of contemporary cities is characterized by increasing heterogeneity and dispersion of settlements, activities and services, and public spaces. Urban regeneration can play a key role in the revitalization of marginal or declining urban areas, enhancing the cultural patrimony as a structural component and promoting identity, social inclusion and the local economy. A particular case in point is the nineteenth- and twentieth-century military fortifications of Rome's Campo Trincerato, a system of fifteen forts and three batteries of great historical and documentary value. The forts, today mostly in the process of being decommissioned, can represent, if viewed from a network perspective, an opportunity to configure an offer of spaces for culture capable of activating a process of regeneration of physical and immaterial relations, promoting shared paths of valorization and re-functionalization. Reasoning about the regeneration of this system means not only refunctionalizing structures, but also recomposing contextual, environmental, urban, social, and cultural relationships to restore urban quality and redefine the landscape of the contemporary city's suburbs.

Keywords: Cultural heritage · 20th-century military architecture · Urban regeneration

1 Phenomena and Consequences of Metropolization

Metropolization is the result of a complex set of phenomena and actions concerning the evolutionary process of large urban areas and the territories they cover [1–4]. "*It constitutes a model in which the processes of concentration, commandment, control, coordination, and the creation of codes prevail over other modes of regulation*" [5] (p. 253).

The processes of metropolization that have affected Italian and European cities in recent decades have induced significant transformations in spatial arrangements, as well as changed the meaning of issues related to urban planning, environment and landscape. As a result of these processes, the contemporary city, connoted by a territorially unlimited dimension, is still strongly characterized by the presence of signs of its past (monuments, but also walls, tracks, aqueducts, etc.). Aspects of strong heterogeneity and fragmentation of tissues prevail, as well as a structural lack of public spaces.

© The Author(s), under exclusive license to Springer Nature Switzerland AG 2026
O. Gervasi et al. (Eds.): ICCSA 2025 Workshops, LNCS 15899, pp. 360–372, 2026.
https://doi.org/10.1007/978-3-031-97663-6_32

This creates localised conditions of social, economic, cultural and environmental marginality that affect peripheral urban areas as well as central ones, and that feed a deep sense of insecurity, often making the identity ties between settled communities and the territory fragile [6].On the other hand, the new urban issue proposes a concept of 'periphery,' no longer understood as a physical distance in opposition to central areas, but as a "*transversal condition that includes all those more densely populated areas, where phenomena of degradation, marginality, social discomfort, insecurity and poverty are detectable*" [7] (p. 22). These profound changes are the result of the processes of metropolization [8–10] and lead one to reflect on the significance of issues related to urban planning, landscape and environment and recall the urgency of implementing policies, strategies, procedures and tools that provide integrated solutions to the instances of environmental, social, cultural and economic regeneration of the city [11].

2 Heritage-Led Urban Regeneration Strategies

The notion of "heritage" is subject to debate and may be subject to different interpretations. Cultural heritage is configured as the custodian of the historical-identity memory of the user subjects who have preserved, safeguarded and administered it over time [12–15], representing a manifestation of the dynamic interaction between communities and the contextual place of reference [15, 16]. Cultural heritage is the result of an evolutionary process that has matured through progress and interacting conflicts. It includes not only the tangible evidence of the past, but also contemporary cultural expressions [17], which the community recognizes as the source of its cultural identity [18–21]. In addition, it incorporates values, ideals and traditions, representing a dynamic element capable to adapt to societal transformations and transmit condivised meanings across generations. Cultural heritage can ultimately be considered a cultural practice, intimately linked to the construction and regolation of shared values and meanings. Its very definition is the result of a discursive process that not only interprets cultural heritage but also becomes an integral part of it, influencing and shaping the cultural and social dynamics that constitute it [22].

Cultural heritage can have a significant impact on the revitalization of the contemporary city [23]. Starting from the structuring character of permanences enables the construction of a network of diversified public spaces capable of stitching together the relationships between cities and the permanences themselves, in architectural but also social terms, reconfiguring uneven and fragmented areas to implement a broader regeneration of urban form. It enables the initiation of new unified, integrated and interscalar strategies of public governance that play an effective directing role aimed at initiating processes of urban and territorial rebalancing [24]. Urban regeneration becomes a strategy of reference, not only urban planning, but of social inclusion and local economic development [25], which assumes cultural heritage, as the supporting framework in the definition of a new and more balanced territorial arrangement based on a system of networks, historical and environmental, interactive and integrated; it becomes a framework of coherence of the strategic choices of a process of regeneration of contemporary cities. A process that has as its main objective the priority of the protection and enhancement of cultural heritage, on which to refound the quality of the urban environment, the historical-cultural identity of communities and the very sense of the collective.

In recent years, the new focus on cultural heritage enhancement strategies in the broader context of urban and environmental regeneration has seen the convergence of numerous researches and experiences conducted at national and international level [26]. Researches and experiences that draw the attention of a multiplicity of knowledge, and that have produced new points of view, in any case characterized by the tendency to overcome traditional approaches, linked to the concepts of separation and opposition between protection and transformation, in favor of a dimension connoted in terms of integration, interscalarity, interdisciplinarity, and iterativity, which restores and is well suited to the characteristics proper to regeneration strategies [27].

3   The Campo Trincerato: Rise and Decay of a Modern Fortification

Rome's system of military forts was originated with the issue of defending the capital of the newly formed Italian state in 1870. After the Breach of Porta Pia, with the consequent installation of King Victor Emmanuel in the Quirinal Palace, the former papal seat, from 1871 it became necessary for the new capital of the Kingdom to raf - fortify the city's fortifications, then protected only by the old imperial walls, through the construction of ten or twelve forts, possibly supplemented by second-line batteries. For this purpose, between 1871 and 1876, several plans were submitted, and on August 12, 1877, fearing a coming fresh French attack on Rome from the sea at Civitavecchia, the Royal Decree (No. 4007) was approved, which resolved the defense of the capital by means of an entrenched camp consisting initially of 10 forts and five batteries, possibly supplemented by occasional reinforcing works, along the principal walls. The idea of a permanent entrenched camp, with a circumference of about forty kilometers, prevailed, with forts placed at the main arteries of access to the city, which coincided, in practice, with the ancient Roman consular roads, or on intermediate heights.

Work on the first forts began in October 1877. The direction of these works was entrusted to Luigi Garavaglia, director of the Army Corps of Engineers. The first to be built, fearing a French attack from the sea of Civitavecchia or Anzio, were, to the left of the Tiber, Fort Appia Antica (the first ever), and, to the right of the river, forts Monte Mario, Casal Braschi, Boccea, Aurelia Antica, Bravetta and Portuense, in order to control precisely the territory and connections with the sea of Fiumicino and Civitavecchia. Two years later, with the allocation of additional funds by Parliament, the Ardeatina, Casilina, Prenestina, Tiburtina and Pietralata forts, all on the left side of the Tiber, saw the light of day. After two more years the defensive belt was completed with the forts Ostiense, Monte Antenne and, lastly, Trionfale. The names that were assigned to the forts derived, for the most part, from the areas in which they stood or from the roads, mostly Roman consular, that they presided over.

In 1882, the construction of the connecting roads, even underground, between the various forts was launched and, in July, it was decided to reinforce the 'southern front' with the construction of an additional fort in the Trullo area. At the same time, construction work began on the Appia Pignatelli, Nomentana and Porta Furba batteries (in addition to the Tevere battery near Monte Mario), as well as the Ostiense, Trionfale and Monte Antenne forts. In only five years, the entrenched camp of Rome was completed, at an expense of approximately twenty-three million lire. However, the planned connecting roads were not built (Fig. 1).

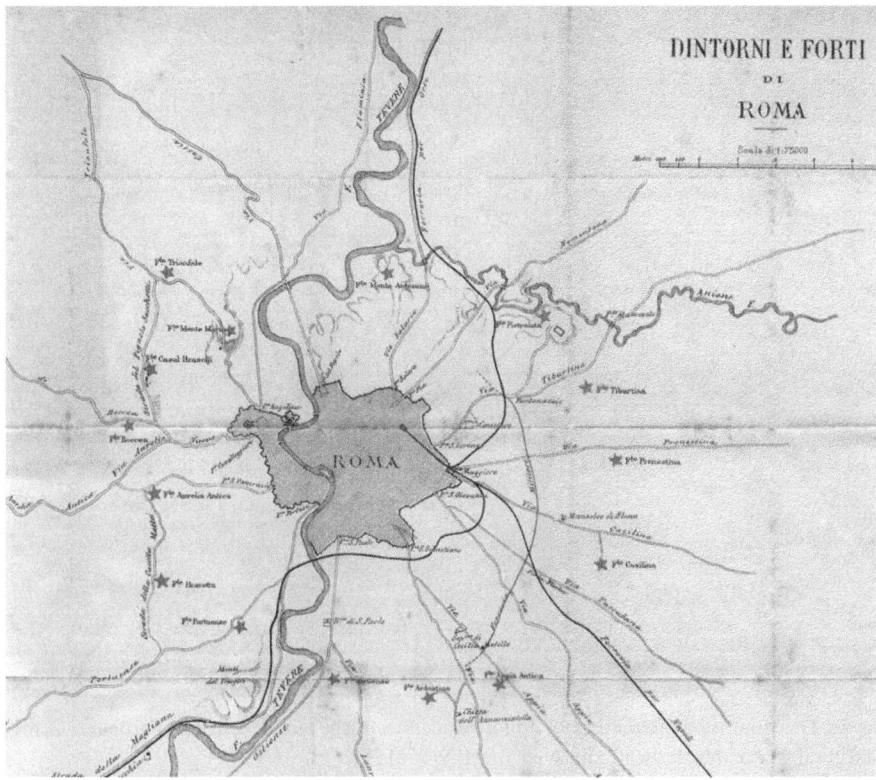

Fig. 1. The forts of Rome in 1883. Source https://www.rerumromanarum.com/2019/02/i-forti-di-roma.html

All the forts had an almost identical, trapezoidal structure, with a "head front" (the side facing outward) one hundred to two hundred meters long and presidated by several gun emplacements, two oblique sides, also manned by artillery batteries, and a "throat front" (the long side of the fort facing the center of the city and in which was the gateway to the fort itself): the center of the head-front, as well as all the corners and the entrance gate, were protected by caponiers (semicircular emplacements in which short-range artillery batteries and machine guns were arranged). The few differences that characterized the various forts were, for the most part, related to the characteristics of the territory on which each was erected: for some the angle of the oblique sides was accentuated or decreased, for others a straight ravine front was preferred, while for still others it was structured with a slightly concave V shape ("tenagliato"), or access was moved to one side of the ravine front rather than to the center of it; some fronts had the ravine front protected by outer embankments, others, where the ground did not allow it, had to be protected by armed caponiers, just as some forts had Carnot-like outer walls manned by riflemen, while others had walls uncovered to possible enemy assaults [28] (Fig. 2).

Fig. 2. The now ruined structure of Monte Antenne in the northern part of Rome's Campo Trincerato. Fonte: https://ilcaffediroma.it/162129/162129-2/

. The Forts of Rome were officially removed from the list of state fortifications by Royal Decree No. 2179 of October 9, 1919, following the recommendation of the then Minister of War [29–31]. This decision marked a significant transformation: the forts ceased to constitute a system of interdependent elements and assumed an isolated configuration. Over time, the spaces between the different structures became progressively denser, extending to encompass the compendium areas, i.e., the buffer zones that originally complemented and supported the fortifications [30].

Since that moment, having become incorporated into the urban fabric, the forts have taken on various functions or have been temporarily abandoned (Table 1):

– among the forts currently or partially abandoned are Monte Mario, Casilina;
– among the forts are Trionfale, Boccea, Bravetta, Portuense, Ardeatina, Monte Antenne;
– among the forts used as barracks are Braschi, Aurelia, Ostiense, Tiburtina, Pietralata;
– among the forts used for Air Force activities are Appia Antica, Casilina;
– among the forts, the only one to have assumed the function of a social cen-tre, as a place of sociability, meeting, entertainment and organization of collective time, and of exchange of ideas, visions, energies and knowledge, is Forte Prenestina.

Table 1. List of the Forts of Rome [32]

Forts of Rome	Years of construction	Surface area (ha)**	Municipality	Current use	Restriction
Monte Mario	1877–1882	8.4	I	Italian Army—8th Infrastructure Department (abandoned)	D.M. *06.08.2008
Trionfale	1882–1888	21.0	XIV	Italian Public Property Agency - Ex-Barracks "Arnaldo Ulivelli" (being delivered to Rome Capital, IT)	D.M. * 23.11-2007
Braschi	1877–1881	8.2	XIV	Italian Army—Barracks "Casal Forte Braschi—Nicola Calipari"	D.M. * 06.08.2008
Boccea	1877–1881	7.3	XIII	Italian Public Property Agency - Ex-Military Prison Forte Boccea (being delivered to Rome Capital, IT)	D.M. * 28.04.2008
Aurelia Antica	1877–1881	5.7	XII	Italian Finance Police - Barracks "Cefalonia Corfu"	D.M. * 11.08.2008
Bravetta	1877–1883	10.6	XII	Italian Public Property Agency (being delivered to Rome Capital, IT)	D.M. * 28.04.2008
Portuense	1877–1881	5.2	XI	Italian Public Property Agency (being delivered to Rome Capital, IT)	D.M. * 13.07.1984
Ostiense	1882–1884	8.8	IX	Italian Police -Barracks "F. Ostiense"	D.M. * 15.11.1975

(*continued*)

Table 1. (*continued*)

Forts of Rome	Years of construction	Surface area (ha)**	Municipality	Current use	Restriction
Ardeatina	1879–1882	11.2	VIII	Italian Public Property Agency (being delivered to Rome Capital, IT)	D.M. * 28.04.2008
Appia Antica	1877–1880	16.5	VIII	Italian Air Force - Re.S.I.A	D.M. * 05.08.2008
Casilina	1881–1882	3.8	V	Italian Air Force - Ex-Air Base Centocelle "Francesco Baracca"	D.M. * 23.02.1984
Prenestina	1880–1884	13.4	V	Italian Public Property Agency -CSOA Forte Prenestino	D.M. * 28.04.2008
Tiburtina	1880–1884	23.8	IV	Italian Army - Barracks "Albanese Ruffo"	D.M. * 29.04.2004
Pietralata	1881–1885	25.4	IV	Italian Army - Barracks "A. Gandin"	D.M. * 23.04.2012
Monte Antenne	1882–1891	2.5	II	Rome Capital, IT	D.M. * 06.8.2008

* Ministerial decree. ** This information was taken from the Wikipedia page Forts of Rome

4   Valorisation of Cultural Heritage for the Care of Territory

The articulation of the museum offer today responds to a change in the forms of use and fruition of the territory - spatial but also cultural - that reflects the evolution of society. The 'museum' institution takes on a dynamic configuration reformulating contents and spatial boundaries and becomes the bearer of an identity proposal: a 'place of memory' that collects, orders and transmits the evidence of a more or less remote past that carries with it messages for the future; a privileged place for maintaining and enhancing a living and active dialogue between what has been, what is and what will be; between cultural values and educational and social inclusion values of a community [33]. This necessary adaptation of the museum institution to the evolution of society and of the forms of enjoyment of cultural heritage has favoured an evolution of its role and its territorialisation, responding to the flexibility and ductility of the museum itself in lending itself *"to be interpreted and thus to change image and frame abruptly"*[34] (p. 10), if not even to allow itself to be conditioned in its 'political' but also social role by the narrative capacity of a society and of a given historical moment [35].

From these premises derives the innovative concept of Ecomuseum, which was born in 1971 from the mind of museologist G.H. Rivière, at the IX conference of the International Council of Museums: *"An exploded, wall-less, interdisciplinary museum, showing man in time and space, in his natural and cultural environment, inviting the entire population to participate in its development by various means of expression, based essentially on the reality of places and buildings that express more than words or images that invade our lives"* The concept of the ecomuseum is proper to the new way of conceiving the territory and the people who dispose and enjoy its assets, where knowledge extends and branches out over time: it embraces all expressions and testimonies of human culture and the concepts of territory and identity [36, 37]. It emerges from the traditional idea of a museum because it is conceived as *"an institution concerned with studying, preserving, enhancing and presenting the collective memory of a community and its host territory, outlining coherent lines for future development"* [38; 2].

The innovative perspective lies in both the functions and objectives of cultural representation and production practices. The fundamental role of local institutions must go hand in hand with the broad involvement of citizens. It is a shared pro-ject with the community, through which one is committed to taking care of one's cultural heritage, not only from the point of view of preserving the material asset, but also from the point of view of enhancing the historical identity (Table 2).

An ecomuseum is composed of a complex layering of environmental, cultural, and social elements that define a specific local cultural heritage. Its components are [39]:

– a reference territory, conceived as a space of valorization, protection, development, identity and innovation;
– heritage as a set of components that communities recognize, protect and promote;
– the communities that recognize, protect and promote the ecomuseum project, because they are moved by a sense of belonging to that particular territory.

Table 2. Museum versus Ecomuseum: a brief summary

Criteria	Museum	Ecomuseum
Reference space	building	territory
Focus	collection of objects	cultural heritage valorization
Organizational priorities	disciplinary	interdisciplinary
Target Audience	visitors	comunity
Political Control	museum institutions	collettivity

The ecomuseum becomes an instrument of knowledge and communication of the cultural heritage and its specific interrelationships with the context, according to a temporal perspective that moves from the past to the present. It is configured as a cultural project capable of transforming and enhancing the 'sense of place', exploiting the local identity and potential of the area. The objective is to foster its economic growth from a tourist and cultural point of view, mobilising the resources present in the area and helping them to form a system (Table 3). *"Making an 'Ecomuseum' means changing the development perspective of a territory, starting from the identification of cultural assets, linking them together in a continuous process of reading and interpretation, which does not aim at the 'museum case', but at the creation of a fluid and diffuse space. An everywhere that can be travelled and used freely, capable of setting in motion unprecedented scenarios of economic development"* [40].

Table 3. Methodological framework for ecomuseum implementation

Dimension	Essential components	Operational tools	Critical issues	Resolution paradigms
Financial	Public/private funds Self-financing	Multi-year planning Partnerships	Financial discontinuity	Source diversification
Governance	Multi-stakeholder representation	Inclusive decision-making processes and agreements	Decision-making asymmetries	Polycentric models
Regulatory	Institutional framework	Operational protocols	Bureaucratic complexity	Procedural standards
Heritage	Systemic mapping	Participatory cataloging	Cultural essentialization	Knowledge integration
Informative	Territorial narrative	Integrated multimedia	Media inadequacy	Strategic coordination
Programmatic	Educational offering	Methodological innovation	Standardization	Co-design
Networking	Collaborative networks	Inter-institutional partnerships	Resource disparities	Experience capitalization
Evaluative	Quali-quantitative indicators	Integrated methodologies	Evaluation complexity	Data systematization

5   Conclusions: For an Ecomuseum of the Campo Trincerato

The redevelopment of fortifications is a complex process to be activated in an inter-institutional form in order to initiate a collaborative management among the actors involved. In the first instance, the transfer of assets to local administrations must be completed (Decree-Law 85/2010, State Federalism; Decree-Law 34/2020, the 'Relaunch' Decree). integrated and participative governance tools must be experimented, which include the possible use of private capital. Among these, Rome's PRG profiles the Integrated Intervention Programme (Rome PRG, 2008, NTA, Art. 14).

If, in general, cultural heritage can be understood as a 'shared resource and common good' for its 'intrinsic value' (aesthetic, spiritual, intellectual) and 'instrumental' (social and economic benefits), the system of modern fortifications presents its own characteristics: a diffuse heritage of 'hidden' structures, multi-scalar architectures placed in the landscape. context. Addressing the theme of the regeneration of fortified places thus becomes a concrete opportunity to refound a new sense of community belonging to history and to experiment with new forms of use; not only by stitching together fragments of the city but by prefiguring new urban identity landscapes. Such structures, especially if systematically read through the concept of historical frame, can constitute the framework for redesigning the form and quality of places and become influential elements in the reconfiguration of the fragmented and discontinuous arrangements of the peripheral areas of the contemporary city.

The theme of the Campo Trincerato, if read at the territorial scale, offers the opportunity for a reflection on the role and possible transformations, from their "functional fall" to their gradual "Patrimonial Growth": the fortifications, having lost their function, remain today in the landscape of the Roman periphery powerful signs in their stylistic identity, but totally dysfunctional in their uses and create voids and urban margins on which today it is possible to make a rethinking in terms of urban and landscape regeneration.

Activating possible regeneration strategies means, from a systemic and multiscalar perspective, contributing to give a new meaning to this heritage and operating according to a new urban paradigm: from closed defensive structures, hidden from view to places of inclusion, knowledge and innovative communication open to the community [31]. In this sense, an innovative territorial museum model could be applied, capable of responding to multiple aspects concerning both the reuse of containers and the definition of new integrated urban landscapes:

– initiating processes of social, functional and landscape recontextualisation of forts, which are all too often inaccessible today
– trigger innovative projects capable of recognising and enhancing historical, cultural and environmental resources and promoting them by developing local economies,
– use technologies of virtual space - 3D digital modelling, interactive and three-dimensional graphic animation, etc. - to restore a memory and a cultural heritage. - to restore a collective memory and identity to the forts and to reconfigure a widespread territorial network that embraces the entire circumference of the Roman periphery.

To make this vast heritage of spaces and meanings usable and accessible again, in addition to the possible forms of reuse, recovering containers and spaces, it will be necessary to overcome the distance between space, time and meaning of these places. If we consider cultural heritage as the historical product of the interaction between community and territory, regeneration processes centered on its enhancement can help design virtuous relationships between settlement, society and heritage itself, reconfiguring the territorial ecosystem in its entirety [41]. All this in an overall network arrangement that links the architectural scale to the urban scale, breaking down and recomposing figures and relations that have often been inaccessible and faded until now, revealing and recontextualising places and architectures as significant and intelligible parts [42]. In other words, rethinking an overall urban project resulting from the redefinition of the relations between *"architectures and open spaces, between architectures and natural elements, between architectures and infra-structures of the territory, between architectures and landscape, principles useful to define the places of contemporaneity"*.

References

1. Ricci, L.: Governare la Città Contemporanea: Riforme e strumenti per la rigenerazione urbana. In: Talia, M. (ed.) Un Futuro Affidabile per la Città, pp. 91–96. Planum, Roma (2007)
2. De Lotto, R.: Assessment of development and regeneration urban projects: cultural and operational implications in metropolization context. Int. J. Energy Environ. **2**, 25–34 (2008)
3. De Alba, F.: Geopolítica metropolitana del Valle de México: Crisis o reconfiguración institucional? In: Borja, J., Wario, H.E., De Alba, F., Iracheta A.X. (eds.) El desafío metropolitan, pp. 121–157. PUEC-UNAM-ALDF, Mexico City (2004)
4. Le Bel, P.M., De Alba, F., Nava, L.F.: La Havane et la Ville de Mexico: Une métropolisation par le patrimoine. Interações **9**, 77–84 (2008)
5. Gaussier, N., Lacour, C., Puissant, S.: Metropolitanization and territorial scales. Cities **20**, 53–263 (2003)
6. Ricci, L.: Governare la città contemporanea. Una nuova questione urbana, in Ravagnan, C.: Rigenerare le città e i territori contemporanei. Prospettive e riferimenti operativi per la sperimentazione. Aracne, Roma, pp. 8–20 (2019)
7. Commissione parlamentare di inchiesta sulle condizioni di sicurezza e sullo stato di degrado delle città e delle loro periferie, Relazione dell'attività svolta, relatore: Onorevole R. Morassut, 5 febbraio 2018, Doc.XXII-bis, n.19 (2018)
8. Indovina, F.: Ordine e disordine della città contemporanea, Franco Angeli, Milano (2017)
9. Oliva, F.: Il Futuro dell'urbanistica: forme e strumenti di governo per la città contemporanea. Urbanistica Informazioni **277**, 4–12 (2018)
10. Oliva, F., Ricci, L.: Promoting urban regeneration and the requalification of built housing stock. In: Antonini, E., Tucci, F. (eds.) Architecture, City and Territory Towards a Green Economy. Edizioni Ambiente, Milano, pp. 205–220 (2017)
11. Poli, I.: Città contemporanea e strategie di rigenerazione: storia, identità e memoria, in Urbanistica Informazioni, INU Edizioni, Roma (2018)
12. D.lgs. 42/2004. Codice dei beni culturali e del paesaggio. https://www.normattiva.it/uri-res/N2Ls?urn:nir:stato:decreto.legislativo:2004-01-22;42. Accessed 28 Mar 2025
13. Baldacci, V.: Tre diverse concezioni del patrimonio culturale. Cahiers d'Études Italiennes **18**, 47–59 (2014)
14. Smith, L.: Heritage, gender and identity. In: Howard, P., Graham, B. (eds.) The Routledge Research Companion to Heritage and Identity, pp. 159–178. Routledge, London (2008)
15. Spennemann, D.H.R.: The shifting baseline syndrome and generational amnesia in heritage studies. Heritage **5**, 2007–2027 (2022)
16. Spennemann, D.H.R.: The nexus between cultural heritage management and the mental health of urban communities. Land **11**, 304 (2022)
17. Pereira Roders, A., Van Oers, R.: Bridging cultural heritage and sustainable development. J. Cult. Herit. Manag. Sustain. Dev. **1**, 5–14 (2011)
18. Bellato, E.: Evoluzioni patrimoniali. Nuovi usi e significati di un concetto ormai storico. In: Zagato, L., Vecco, M., (eds.) Sapere l'Europa, sapere d'Europa, vol. 3, pp. 217–240. Ca' Foscari, Venezia (2015)
19. Lupo, A.: La nozione positiva di patrimonio culturale alla prova del diritto globale. Aedon **2**, 109–120 (2019)

20. Von Truetzschler, W.: The evolution of "cultural heritage" in international law. In: Proceedings of the 15th ICOMOS General Assembly and International Symposium: Monuments and Sites in Their Setting–Conserving Cultural Heritage in Changing Townscapes and Landscapes, Xi'an, China, 17–21 October (2005)

21. Korostelina, K.: Understanding values of cultural heritage within the framework of social identity conflicts. In: Avrami, E., Macdonald, S., Mason, R., Myers, D. (eds.) Values in Heritage Management. Emerging Approaches and Research Directions, pp. 83–96. Getty Publications, Los Angeles (2019)

22. Ricci, L.: Patrimonio Culturale e Rigenerazione Urbana. Luoghi Materiali e Immateriali tra Storia Progetto e Racconto. https://news.uniroma1.it/18102022_1500. Accessed 28 Mar 2025

23. Smith, L.: Uses of Heritage. Routledge, Abingdon (2006)

24. Ricci, L., Ravagnan, C.: Europa mediterranea. Per una strategia di riequilibrio e di riqualificazione della città contemporanea. In: Moccia, F.D., Sepe, M. (eds.) X Giornata Studi INU "Crisi e nascita delle città". Urbanistica Informazioni, vol. 272, pp. 425–430 Inu Edizioni, Roma (2017)

25. Ricci, L., Mariano, C., Iacomoni, A.: Patrimonio culturale e rigenerazione urbana. Per una convergenza intersettoriale e interistituzionale di lungo termine. In: ANANK, Alinea Edizioni, Firenze, no. 96–97, pp. 65–67 (2023)

26. Ricci, L.: Città pubblica e nuovo welfare. Una rete di reti per la rigenerazione urbana in ANANKE, Altralinea, Firenze, no. 92, pp. 93–98 (2021)

27. Mariano, C.: Il ruolo dello spazio pubblico nelle strategie di rigenerazione urbana della città contemporanea, in Urbanistica Informazioni, INU Edizioni: Roma, no. 305, pp. 83–86 (2022)

28. Giannini, G.: I forti di Roma: il sistema di difesa intorno alla città costruito dal Regno d'Italia dopo la Breccia di Porta Pia, Newton, Roma (1998)

29. Gerundino, N.: Forte Prenestino: Il racconto storico-architettonico di un avamposto militare. https://zero.eu/it/roma/. Accessed 28 Mar 2025

30. Ferretti, S.: Le complesse vicende normative dei forti di Roma. In: Proceedings of the Un patrimonio sepolto tra oblio e riscoperta: I forti di Roma, Atti tavola rotonda, Biblioteca del Senato "Giovanni Spadolini", Roma, Italy, 16 April (2012)

31. Spadafora, G., Ferretti, S., Pallottino, E.: I Forti di Roma: Una lettura a scala urbana. In: Bevilacqua, M.G., Ulivieri, D. (eds.) Defensive Architecture of the Mediterranean, vol. XIV, pp. 883–890. Pisa University Press, Pisa (2023)

32. I Forti di Roma. https://progettoforti.wixsite.com/progettoforti. Accessed 28 Mar 2025

33. Di Pietro, I.: La nuova frontiera dei musei: digitalizzazione, comunicazione culturale e coinvolgimento. In: Dottorato di ricerca di Arti Visive, Performative e Mediali, ciclo XXIX, tutor prof.ssa M. Pigozzi. Alma Mater Studiorum, Università di Bologna (2017)

34. Marani, P.C., Pavoni, R.: Musei. Trasformazioni di un'istituzione dall'età moderna al contemporaneo. Marsilio, Venezia (2006)

35. Pinna, G.: Divagazioni sulla storia politica dei musei, 2019–2023. https://giovanni.pinna.info/libro.html. Accessed 28 Mar 2025

36. Cancellotti, C.: "L'écomusée n'est pas musée". Gli ecomusei come laboratori produttori di cultura, territorio e relazione. Altre Modernità 5, 99–114 (2011)

37. Carta di Catania, Atti del Congresso Nazionale Giornate dell'Ecomuseo. Verso una nuova offerta culturale per lo sviluppo sostenibile del territorio, Catania 12–13 ottobre 2007. chrome-extension://efaidnbmnnnibpcajpcglclefindmkaj/. http://www.bda.unict.it/Public/Uploads/article/Carta%20di%20Catania.pdf. Accessed 28 Mar 2025

38. Pilot Project "Ecomuseum of the Landscape," Pr. of Terni, Leader + 2000–2006, 2003. https://www.ecomusei.net/. Accessed 28 Mar 2025

39. L'ecomuseo della Via Latina. https://www.ecomuseodellavialatina.it/ecomuseo/. Accessed 28 Mar 2025

40. Ecomuseo Casilino ad Duas Lauros. Progetto interpretative. https://www.ecomuseocasilino. it/ecomuseo-casilino-i-percorsi/. Accessed 28 Mar 2025
41. Colavitti, A.M., Floris, A., Serra, S.: Nuove prospettive per la rigenerazione urbana e territo- riale. Il riuso del patrimonio militare dismesso tra regimi di tutela e opportunità di sviluppo. In: Camerin, F., Gastaldi, F. (eds.) Rigenerare le aree militari dismesse, Prospettive, dibattiti e riconversioni in Italia, Spagna e in contesti internazionali, pp. 550–562, Maggioli Editore, Sant'Arcangelo di Romagna (2021)
42. Rossi, A., Consolacio, E., Bosshard, M.: La costruzione del territorio. Milano, Clup (1979)

ITINERIS Geophysical Technologies @CNR-IREA: Drone-Based Tests at Altopiano di Verteglia, Avellino (Southern Italy)

Francesco Mercogliano[1,2]([✉]) [ID], Andrea Barone[2] [ID], Giuseppe Esposito[2] [ID],
Filippo Accomando[2] [ID], Andrea Vitale[3] [ID], Gianluca Gennarelli[2] [ID],
Raffaele Castaldo[2] [ID], Pietro Tizzani[2] [ID], and Ilaria Catapano[2] [ID]

[1] University of Naples Parthenope, Naples, Italy
francesco.mercogliano001@studenti.uniparthenope.it
[2] Institute for Electromagnetic Sensing of the Environment, National Research Council of Italy,
(IREA-CNR), Napoli, Italy
{barone.a,esposito.g,accomando.f,gennarelli.g,castaldo.r,
tizzani.p,catapano.i}@irea.cnr.it
[3] Institute for Agriculture and Forestry Systems in the Mediterranean, National Research
Council of Italy (ISAFOM-CNR), Portici, Italy
andrea.vitale@cnr.it

Abstract. Unmanned Aerial Vehicles have become widely adopted platforms for geophysical investigations. In recent years, several geophysical sensors, including magnetometers, ground penetrating radars, hyperspectral cameras and thermal cameras, have been developed for drone-based deployment, thus enhancing the effectiveness of geophysical surveys. This work presents a multi-geophysical survey conducted to test two drone-based geophysical systems, namely, the Mag-Nimbus magnetometer system and the Zond Aereo LF GPR system. The survey was carried out at the Altopiano di Verteglia (Montella, AV - Italy) in the Southern Apennines for investigating near-surface buried metallic pipes. The knowledge of the area makes it an ideal location for our tests, allowing us to compare the results associated with different physical parameters of the target, operating with different drone-based geophysical technologies and configurations, and understand how the collected data can be used to address environmental challenges.

Keywords: UAV · drone geophysics · drone-based GPR · drone-magnetometry

1 Introduction

In the last decade, the rise of Unmanned Aerial Vehicles (UAVs) has revolutionized geophysics. The development of UAV-based geophysics has facilitated data collection expanding it even in inaccessible areas, thereby enhancing spatial coverage and significantly reducing both the physical effort of operators and survey time, compared to ground-based surveys. Consequently, geophysical instruments and sensors have been optimized to be enough compact and light-weight to be mounted as payloads under these vehicles, while still ensuring the acquisition of good-quality datasets.

O. Gervasi et al. (Eds.): ICCSA 2025 Workshops, LNCS 15899, pp. 373–383, 2026.
https://doi.org/10.1007/978-3-031-97663-6_33

Among geophysical methods, Ground Penetrating Radar (GPR) and magnetic surveys are the most widely used for different applications, including geo-environmental, archaeological, geotechnical, and engineering purposes [1]. Their success is attributed to several factors, such as cost-efficiency, versatility, data collection capabilities, and non-invasiveness. Additionally, both methods facilitate the detection of buried targets thanks to their magnetic and electromagnetic sensing capabilities. The application of these methods with UAVs has motivated the design and commercialization of several lightweight and compact sensors. Although an exhaustive list is out the aim of this paper, examples of on the market available magnetometers are the Mag-Arrow by Geometrics (https://geometrics.com/product/magarrow/), the MagDrone by Sensys (https://sensysmagnetometer.com/products/) and MagNimbus by SPH Engineering (shop.sphengineering.com/products/magnimbus-magnetometer). As for GPR, some examples are the Zond Aereo LF, the Zond 500 and 1000 by SPH Engineering and Radar Systems (https://shop.sphengineering.com/collections/gpr-systems), the Cobra CBD and the Cobra-PlugIn by Radar Team (http://www.radarteam.se/index.html). In addition, several GPR prototype systems and ad hoc designed data processing approaches have been proposed in the recent literature (e.g. see [2]).

Aim of this paper is to present a survey conducted to test drone-based GPR and magnetometric technologies, namely the Zond Aereo LF and the MagNimbus, and validate the results obtained from these different instruments operating under various configurations. The testing activity was performed at the Altopiano di Verteglia (Montella, AV – Southern Italy) by the Institute for Electromagnetic Sensing of the Environment of the National Research Council of Italy (IREA-CNR). The instrumentation purchases and the test activity have been financed by the project IR0000032 – ITINERIS, Italian Integrated Environmental Research Infrastructures System (D.D. n. 130/2022 - CUP B53C22002150006) Funded by EU - Next Generation EU PNRR- Mission 4 "Education and Research" - Component 2: "From research to business" - Investment 3.1: "Fund for the realisation of an integrated system of research and innovation infrastructures" in the framework of the WP7 and Activities 7.5, led by IREA-CNR.

2   Materials and Methods

This section describes the drone-based geophysical systems, namely the MagNimbus magnetometer and the Zond Aereo LF GPR system, the investigated area and how the surveys were organized, outlining the data collection strategies and configurations adopted for both the systems. Furthermore, this Section provides some insights into the data processing techniques implemented for each methodology.

2.1   Magnetometric Instrumentation: MagNimbus

The MagNimbus is a magnetometer system for the measurement of the total magnetic field and its vertical variations, produced by SPH Engineering (Riga, Latvia https://www.sphengineering.com/). The system consists of two QuSpin Total-Field Magnetometer (QTFM) Gen-2 atomic sensors, based on rubidium vapor technology, which are assembled into two different split arms (as shown in Fig. 1). The first one is a 1 m long foldable mast, positioned below the UAV approximately 1 m from its base and connected to the onboard computer through a serial port. The second one is instead a fixed mast, mounted above the UAV at a distance of approximately 0.5 m from its top and connected to the onboard computer through a USB port. Considering an approximately 0.2 m vertical length of the UAV body, the distance between the two MaNimbus sensors is fixed to 1.7 m. The total weight of the system is approximately 1.5 kg, making it suitable as a payload for medium sized UAVs such as the Matrice 300 RTK and Matrice 350 RTK quadcopters produced by SZ DJI Technology Co. (Shezen, China store.dji.com/). This allows for easier maneuverability and less battery consumption during the survey flights. The main technical features of the sensors are the very low sensitivity equal to 0.003 nT and the sampling rate up to 500 Hz. Data collection takes place through the use of UgCS SkyHub, and the related software, which also allows power supply for the instrumentation via the UAV batteries. Main features of this instrumentation and further information can be found in the company website [https://shop.sphengineering.com/en-en/products/magnimbus-magnetometer].

2.2   GPR Instrumentation: Zond Aero LF

The radar system Zond Aereo LF (Low Frequency) is a single-channel GPR system, developed by SPH Engineering (Riga, Latvia https://www.sphengineering.com/) and Radar Systems Inc. (Riga, Latvia https://radsys.lv/en), equipped with unshielded dipole antennas. By default, it comes with three center-frequency antennas, 100 MHz, 150 MHz, and 300 MHz (as shown in Fig. 2), operating within bandwidths of 50–150 MHz, 75–300 MHz, and 150–600 MHz, respectively. Being an extra-lightweight GPR system, with a total weight ranging from approximately 0.9 to 1.2 kg, based on the chosen antenna, it is suitable to be mounted as a payload under medium-sized UAVs such as the Matrice 300 RTK and Matrice 350 RTK quadcopters produced by SZ DJI Technology Co. (Shenzen, China store.dji.com/). Power and charging of the Zond Aereo LF GPR system is provided by the connection of the power cable directly to the UAV (or external) batteries. Data collection takes place through the use of UgCS SkyHub (SPH Engineering, Riga, Latvia) on-board computer, which is connected to the radar system by an Ethernet cable. Additional technical specifications and information can be found in [https://shop.sphengineering.com/en-en/products/zond-aero-lf].

Fig. 1. MagNimbus magnetometer in vertical gradiometer configuration mounted on a DJI Matrice 300 RTK drone.

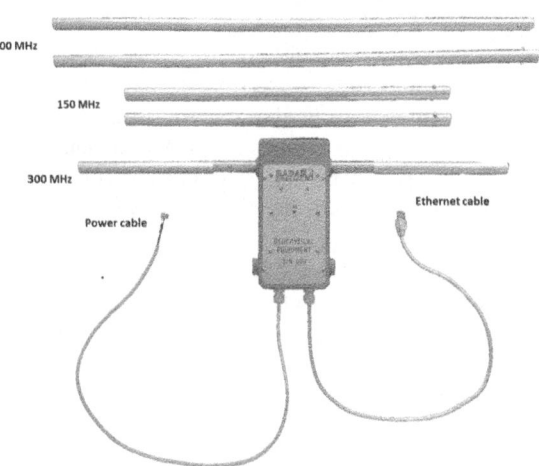

Fig. 2. Photo of the Zond Aereo LF GPR system and its components.

2.3   Test Site: Altopiano di Verteglia (Montella, AV - Southern Italy)

The Altopiano di Verteglia is a small tectonic-karst basin situated in the Northen-Western sector of the Picentini Mountains group (Southern Italy, Fig. 3b). The main massif, the Terminio-Tauro, is characterized by a typical carbonate succession in platform facies, consisting of Jurassic and Cretaceous fissured limestones covered by Quaternary deposits, which are mainly represented by discordant accumulations of pyroclastic products of the Somma-Vesuvius activity and lacustrine sediments [3, 4]. The area has already been partially studied through ground-based geophysical investigations, such as electrical resistivity and seismic methods [5]. Additionally, magnetic measurements have been performed in both ground- and drone-based configurations [6], confirming the presence of three steel pipes systems at variable depth, ranging from approximately 1 to 2 m. These pipe systems (Fig. 3c) and the knowledge of the site made it an ideal location for the testing of the magnetometric and GPR instrumentations, as well as assessing the performance of these different systems in detecting the targets, even when placed at a close distance from each other.

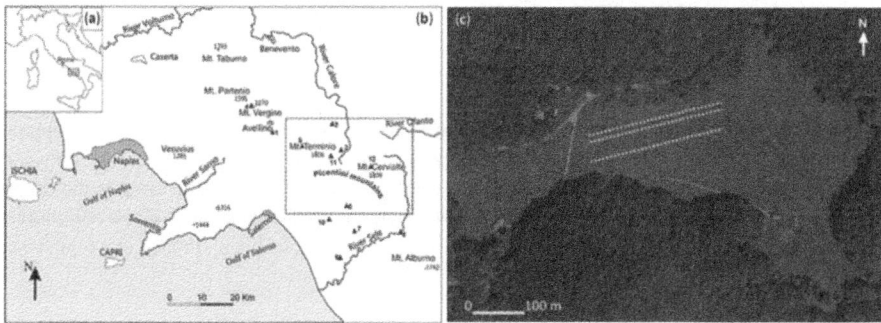

Fig. 3. (**a**) Map of the Italian Country (**b**) Map of the western Campania The dashed box indicates the Picentini mountains system region [modified from [4]) (**c**) Google Earth view (google.it/earth/) of the Altopiano di Verteglia. White dashed lines represent the surface projection of the pipe systems (modified from [6]).

2.4 Magnetometric Survey

The magnetometric survey using the MagNimbus system was performed in the Eastern zone of the proposed test site. In particular, the survey covered an area of approximately $30 \times 120 \text{ m}^2$ (magenta purple in Fig. 4a) with flight lines oriented along a N/NW – S/SE direction and with 2 m spacing (black continuous lines in Fig. 4b). The drone system flew in True Terrain Following (TTF) mode automatically keeping constant the elevation over the surface using real-time data collected by the NRA24 K-band radar altimeter developed by Hunan Nanoradar Science and Technology Co. (Changsha, China http://en.nanoradar.cn/). Specifically, the system was kept at a distance from the ground surface equal to 5 m. Therefore, the two sensors have an elevation of 4 and 5.7 m with respect to the ground surface. The flight speed was set to 2 m/s, while the MagNimbus sampling rate was fixed to 500 Hz.

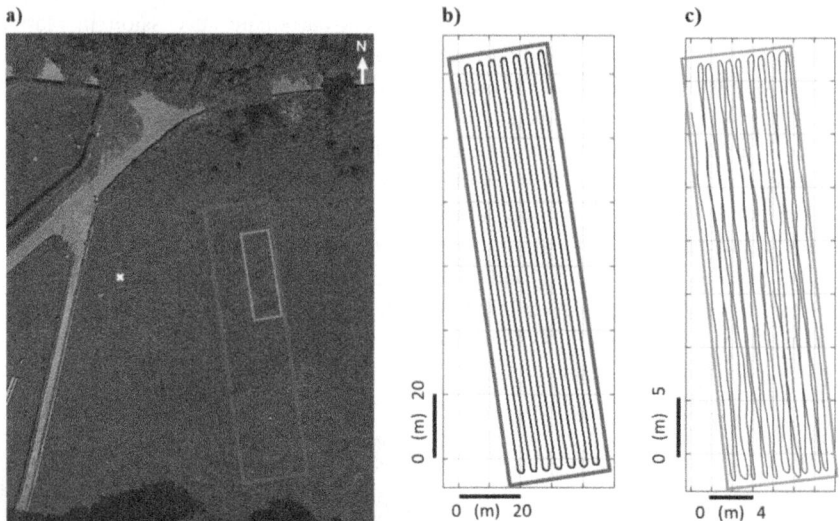

Fig. 4. (**a**) Google Earth view (google.it/earth/) of a zoomed area of the Eastern zone of Altopiano di Verteglia. The purple rectangle represents the area interested by the magnetometric survey, the orange one represents the area interested by the GPR survey, while the white cross is the drone take-off point. (**b**) Distribution of the performed magnetometric flight lines (black continuous lines). (**c**) Distribution of the performed flight lines (blue continuous lines); the red one represents the flight line considered for the processing. (Color figure online)

2.5 GPR Survey

The GPR survey, carried out by means of the Zond Aereo LF GPR system, was also performed in the Eastern zone of the proposed test site. The survey covered a smaller area than the magnetometric survey one and was approximately 10×40 m^2 (orange rectangle in Fig. 4a) with flight lines orientated along an approximately N/NW – S/SE direction and about 40 m long with 0.5 m spacing (blue continuous line in Fig. 4c). The drone system flew in TTF mode, which makes possible to automatically keep constant the elevation over the surface by using real-time data collected by the NRA24 K-band radar altimeter. The drone flew a distance of 1.5 above ground surface. The flight speed was set to 1 m/s, while the Zond Aereo LF, equipped with its 300 MHz center-frequency antenna, operated with a 128 ns time range and 512 samples per scan.

2.6 Data Processing

A first process for magnetic data regards the need to correct the collected data by considering the Earth's magnetic field and its temporal variations; it is done by taking into account the International Geomagnetic Reference Field (IGRF) and by subtracting its values from the measured dataset. However, in the case of vertical gradient configuration this correction is not necessary. Then, heading error correction is performed when the survey is performed by changing the direction of the sensor axis with respect to the direction of the measurement line [i.e., 7]. Among the different strategies to mitigate the heading error effects, we subtract the own median value at each measurement profile. In addition, a low-pass filter is applied to these datasets to suppress both spikes and high-frequency noise from the recorded signal. These operations are performed in the wavenumber-domain based on the properties of the Fast Fourier Transform (FFT) [8].

The first processing step in UAV-based GPR imaging involves standard time-domain procedures [2]. Among them, zero-timing adjusts the time-axis reference. For the system at hand, this task is carried out to ensure that the signal reflection due to air-soil interface occurs at the time instant corresponding to the round trip time that the signal takes to cover the distance of the UAV from the soil surface, as estimated by the radar altimeter [9]. Moreover, when processing UAV-based GPR data, it is crucial to distinguish the signal reflected from the targets of interest from other undesired signal components or environmental clutter. At this regard, the common time gating and background removal procedures are employed to mitigate clutter and reduce noise [10–12]. Time gating consists in selecting a time window containing signals coming from the targets of interest and setting all the signals outside this window to zero. It is worth pointing out that time gating must be carefully used when targets are close to the air-soil interface, as parts of the useful signal may be erased. Background removal is a filtering procedure that consists in replacing the current A-scan with the difference between it and the average of all A-scans composing the radargram. As the time gating, also the background removal must be used with care because it can alter the data. Indeed, if the UAV distance from the soil surface does not change significantly during the flight, the background removal is useful to remove undesired constant signals, i.e. data components occurring at the same time instant for all the measurement points. Examples of these signals are multiple reflections related to the antenna direct coupling and the air-soil interfaces. On the other hand, the background removal also erases information about buried flat interfaces or, in the case of extended (along the measurement direction) targets, it may introduce data artefacts, i.e. signal components that can be erroneously interpreted as localized target reflections.

3 Results

This section presents both the data as collected from the two drone-based geophysical systems (raw data) and the results obtained by after applying the aforementioned processing methods (processed data).

3.1 Vertical Gradient of the Total Magnetic Field

Figure 5 shows the maps of the vertical gradient of the total magnetic field before (Fig. 5a) and after (Fig. 5b) the application of the processing procedures. These maps were computed using a natural neighbors interpolator and a 0.5 m sampling step along both directions. Anomalies of the vertical gradient display the typical alternating magnetic high and low peaks that can be measured over a metallic pipe [13], which generally acquires a permanent magnetization during the manufacturing process.

(a)   **(b)**

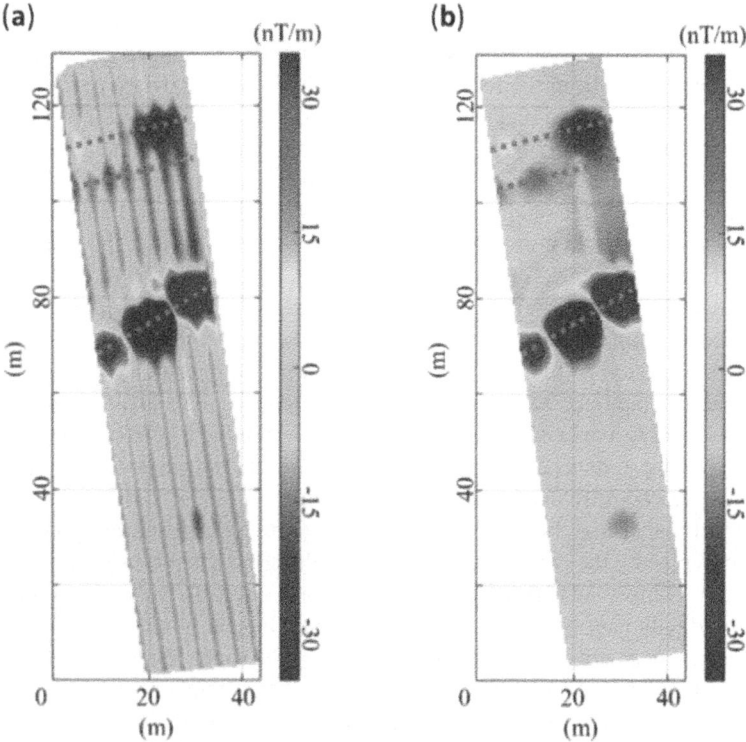

Fig. 5. Maps of the computed vertical gradient before (**a**) and after (**b**) the applied processing procedures. Grey dashed lines represent the surface projection of the pipes.

3.2 Radargrams

The raw radargram acquired during the whole flight of the Zond Aereo LF GPR system is shown in Fig. 6a. From it, the radargram corresponding to a single survey line (depicted by the red continuous line in Fig. 4b) is selected (Fig. 6b) and considered to illustrate the results of the GPR data processing. In the raw radargram, signals coming from the targets of interest are masked due to the strong ringing characteristic of the Zond Aereo LF system and the unshielded nature of the antennas. This represents the first issue encountered, which implies a notable difficulty in determining the zero time. Indeed, the standard procedure for setting the zero time properly requires finding the time instant corresponding to the first positive (or negative) peak of the average A-scan [10–12]. After that, the background removal is applied to reduce the clutter, which represents a not negligible source of disturbance. Finally, the processed radargram (Fig. 7) clearly shows the diffraction hyperbolas associated to the buried targets. Specifically, two close hyperbolas are at the x ranging from about 5 m to 15 m and another one is visible at x ranging from about 30 m to 35 m (see the blue boxes in Fig. 7).

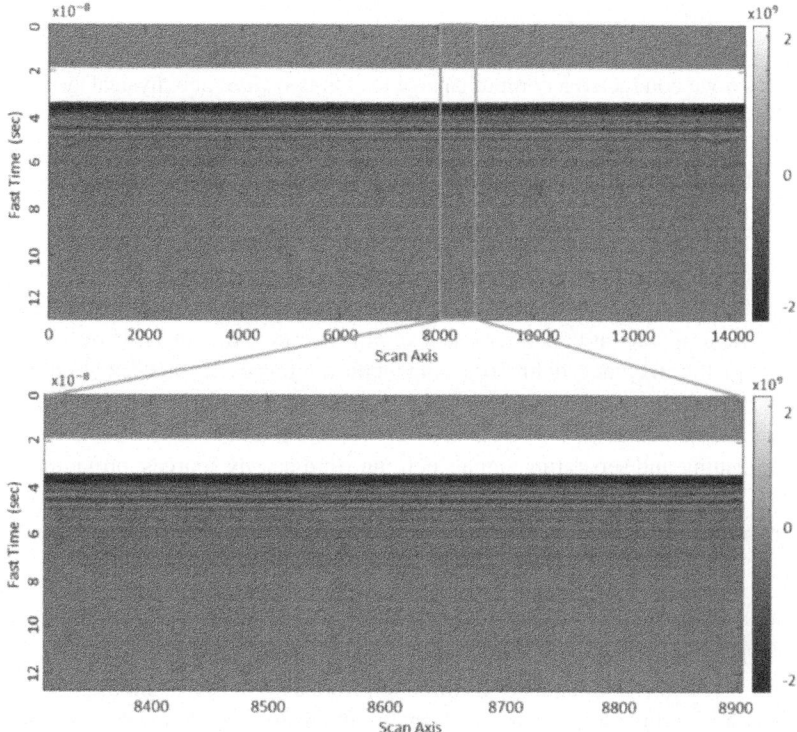

Fig. 6. (**a**) Raw radargram acquired during the whole flight of the Zond Aereo LF GPR system and (**b**) raw radargram corresponding to a single survey line (red continuous line in Fig. 4b).

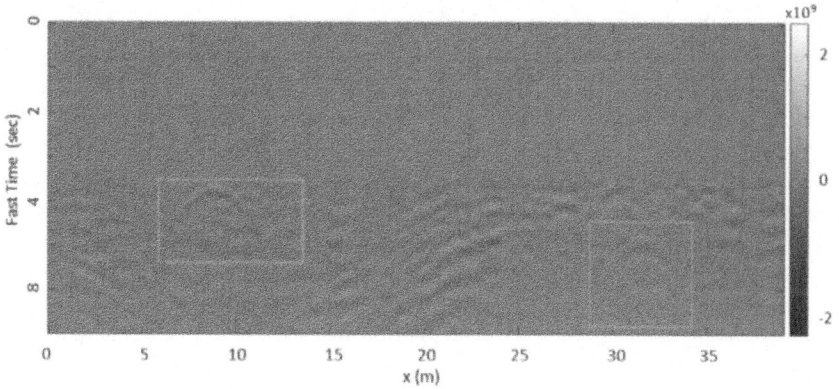

Fig. 7. Analyzed radargram after the time-domain processing procedures (i.e., time zero and background removal); the cyan rectangle highlights the position of the diffraction hyperbolas associated to the buried targets. (Color figure online)

4 Discussions and Conclusions

In our study, we conducted a comprehensive test on two UAV geophysical systems: the MagNimbus magnetometer and the Zond Aereo LF GPR. These evaluations yielded significant insights into their performance and effectiveness across various configurations and operational conditions, highlighting their potential and identifying any limitations to overcome in the future.

The MagNimbus system is a natural gradiometer, consisting of two sensors positioned at different vertical positions. These sensors simultaneously measure the total magnetic field, facilitating the evaluation of the vertical gradient. The vertical gradient is a valuable tool since it benefits from several properties. It is insensitive to temporal variations of the magnetic field, so no magnetic references are needed. Additionally, it is more sensitive to shallow sources since it is less sensitive to magnetic regional fields and deep magnetized bodies. Moreover, vertical gradient has an increased ability in distinguishing and separating signals coming from nearby sources, providing higher resolution. For instance, in the presented test-site, we showed that the vertical gradient made possible the identification of all the three targets (i.e., the three pipe systems), confirming the potential of UAV surveys for high-resolution subsurface investigations [e.g., 14]. However, the adopted flight configuration introduced a significant heading error effect in the collected data. This occurred because, the radar altimeter, necessary for the TTF mode, is mounted on the UAV front to read the correct altitude information. Consequently, as the UAV changes its direction from a flight line to another, the sensors axes also change direction, strongly enhancing the heading error effects. As shown in the filtered maps (Fig. 5b), this effect can be mitigated through a suitable processing.

The Zond Aereo LF GPR system is equipped with very lightweight dipole antennas, which allows the system to be mounted beneath medium-sized drones such as the DJI M300 RTK. This configuration enables the acquisition of data in a very fast and stable way. However, the absence of antenna shielding makes data processing more challenging, since the recorded backscattered echoes result from a broader radiation pattern, leading to increased complexity in data interpretation. Specifically, as shown in the raw radargram (Fig. 6), the antenna coupling, the air-soil interface reflection and the ringing signals mask the signal from targets of interest, whose detection was possible thanks to the data processing. However, it is worth underlining that the exploitation of altimeter data was crucial for the zero time setting. Accordingly, future studies are needed to reduce the uncertainty on the selection of the zero time of the Zond system and to investigate if the encountered uncertainty depends on the considered central frequency. The processed radargram (Fig. 7) shows three diffraction hyperbolas whose spatial location is compliant with that of the magnetic anomalies visible in Fig. 5b, confirming the ability of the Zond Aereo LF GPR system to image the three pipes.

Acknowledgments. These activities were supported by the project IR0000032 – ITINERIS, Italian Integrated Environmental Research Infrastructures System (D.D. n. 130/2022 - CUP B53C22002150006) Funded by EU - Next Generation EU PNRR- Mission 4 "Education and Research" - Component 2: "From research to business" - Investment 3.1: "Fund for the realisation of an integrated system of research and innovation infrastructures" and "Geo Agro Interdisciplinary Analysis interdepartmental LABoratory (GAIA iLAB) – Interdepartmental agreement between CNR-IREA and CNR-ISAFOM".

Disclosure of Interests. The authors have no competing interests to declare that are relevant to the content of this article.

References

1. Reynolds, J.M.: An Introduction to Applied and Environmental Geophysics. Wiley, Hoboken (1997)
2. Catapano, I., Gennarelli, G., Ludeno, G., Noviello, C., Esposito, G., Soldovieri, F.: Contactless ground penetrating radar imaging: state of the art, challenges, and microwave tomography-based data processing. IEEE Geosci. Remote Sens. Mag. **10**(1), 251–273 (2022). https://doi.org/10.1109/MGRS.2021.3082170
3. Calcaterra, D., Ducci, D., Santo, A.: Aspetti geomeccanici ed idrogeologici nel settore sud-orientale del M.te Terminio (Appennino Meridionale). Geologica Romana **30**, 53–66 (1992)
4. Fiorillo, F., Pagnozzi, M., Ventafridda, G.: A model to simulate recharge processes of karst massifs. Hydrol. Process. **29**, 2301–2314 (2015). https://doi.org/10.1002/hyp.10353
5. Scotellaro, C.: Influenza delle argille sulle proprietà elastiche ed elettriche di mezzi eterogenei e porosi ed applicazione del Modello Elettrosismico. Ph.D. thesis (2005)
6. Accomando, F., Vitale, A., Bonfante, A., Buonanno, M., Florio, G.: Performance of two different flight configurations for drone-borne magnetic data. Sensors **21**, 5736 (2021). https://doi.org/10.3390/s21175736
7. Accomando, F., Florio, G.: Drone-borne magnetic gradiometry in archaeological applications. Sensors **24**(13), 4270 (2024)
8. Blakely, J.R.: Potential Theory in Gravity and Magnetic Applications. Revised edn. Cambridge University Press, Cambridge (1996)
9. Esposito, G., et al.: UAV-based GPR systems for infrastructure monitoring. In: Lakhtakia, A., Furse, C.M., Mackay, T.G. (eds.) The Advancing World of Applied Electromagnetics. Springer, Cham (2023). https://doi.org/10.1007/978-3-031-39824-7_15
10. Daniels, D.J.: Ground Penetrating Radar. Wiley, Hoboken (2005)
11. Persico, R.: Introduction to Ground Penetrating Radar: Inverse Scattering and Data Processing. Wiley, Hoboken (2014)
12. Catapano, I., Gennarelli, G., Ludeno, G., Soldovieri, F., Persico, R.: Ground-penetrating radar: Operation principle and data processing. In: Wiley Encyclopedia of Electrical and Electronics Engineering, pp. 1–23. Wiley, Hoboken (2019)
13. Sowerbutts, W.T.C.: The use of geophysical methods to locate joints in underground metal pipelines. Q. J. Eng. Geol. **21**, 273–281 (1988)
14. Accomando, F., Bonfante, A., Buonanno, M., Natale, J., Vitale, S., Florio, G.: The drone-borne magnetic survey as the optimal strategy for high-resolution investigations in presence of extremely rough terrains: the case study of the Taverna San Felice quarry dike. J. Appl. Geophys. **217**, 105186 (2023)

Integrated Mechanical and Electromagnetic Geophysical Imaging of a Complex Aquifer System: The Coastal Plain in Muravera, South-East Sardinia (Italy)

Raffaele Martorana[1] , Luca Piroddi[2(✉)] , Gian Piero Deidda[2] ,
Alessandra Carollo[1] , and Patrizia Capizzi[2]

[1] Department of Earth and Sea Sciences, University of Palermo, Via Archirafi,
22, 90123 Palermo, Italy
[2] Department of Civil, Environmental Engineering and Architecture, University of Cagliari,
Via Marengo 2, 09123 Cagliari, Italy
lucapiroddi@yahoo.it

Abstract. Water management is crucial to lead sustainable development of our societies, and to be effective needs for a detailed characterization of the water resources availability, through the knowledge of their reservoir's main properties in terms of geometries and physical properties. In this way it is mandatory to plan responsible exploitation and use protocols, increasing the system resilience. Usable groundwater scarcity is in fact a major issue to be overcome with smart territorial management. In view of this, the knowledge derived from direct and indirect diagnostic investigations is a key factor to balance the societal pressure over such delicate targets. In the early Twenty-thousands, a geophysical survey using High-Resolution (HR) reflection seismic and time domain electromagnetics (TDEM) was carried out in the south-eastern part of the island of Sardinia, Italy. The main objective of the survey has been to study a very complex coastal aquifer situated in an area where a – still present – huge saltwater intrusion phenomenon had already occurred mainly due to anthropic overexploitation linked to tourism and agriculture. Within this paper, the TDEM results, constrained by seismics, are presented and discussed.

Keywords: TDEM · EM Geophysics · Seismic Reflection · Hydrogeophysics · Sustainable Development · Sea Water Intrusion · Sardinia

1 Introduction

Water scarcity is a major and global issue of contemporary days in large part due to intensive agriculture and industrial use of territories, overpopulation, pollution and Climate Change according to the UN Sustainable Development Goals [1]. Smart territories and communities provide a cultural framework to assess sustainability in natural resources exploitation, protection and renovation thanks to management actions which can be especially effective when taking advantage of the knowledge derived from direct and indirect investigations.

© The Author(s), under exclusive license to Springer Nature Switzerland AG 2026
O. Gervasi et al. (Eds.): ICCSA 2025 Workshops, LNCS 15899, pp. 384–393, 2026.
https://doi.org/10.1007/978-3-031-97663-6_34

In the early Twenty-thousands, a geophysical survey using High-Resolution (HR) reflection seismic and time domain electromagnetics (TDEM) was carried out in the south-eastern part of the island of Sardinia, Italy. The main objective of the survey has been to study a very complex coastal aquifer situated in an area where a – still present – huge saltwater intrusion phenomenon had already occurred, and where important interventions (hotels, various buildings for tourism and agriculture and a dam, just closed to the delta of the river Flumendosa) were planned. The effective management of groundwater is of great importance for tourism and agriculture activities, which is probably the main resource for the economic growth of this area. The deep fresh groundwater must be protected from the progressive salination deriving from prolonged periods of drought, uncontrolled over-exploitation of the groundwater resources for drinking water and irrigation purposes, fish breeding works and decrease of the natural recharge of the coastal aquifers as a result of the Flumendosa upstream damming and of the Climate Change. So, it is vital to distinguish the aquifer sub-systems and their saturation with fresh, brackish or salt water and to know the depth and the morphology of the bedrock. This may be achieved by drilling observation wells and by using surface geophysical surveys in integrated diagnostic protocols capable of providing multi-physical underground information to constrain the geologic reconstruction of the aquifer.

Among various geophysical methods, the TDEM and seismic reflection techniques were chosen to be the most suitable for the indicated purposes. The application of TDEM methods has been widely used for describing the depth and thickness of coastal aquifers [2], defining their physical-chemical properties [3], and assessing marine intrusion and pollution levels [4]. In fact, TDEM has better lateral resolution and is more efficient than Vertical Electrical Soundings when the shallow soils are very conductive, but it is usually unable in delineating the resistive geological conditions [5]. The seismic method, vice versa, is very efficient in solving the structural problem, but it is unable to recognize the different aquifers properties. Shtivelman and Goldman [6] have demonstrated the goodness of the application of integrated TDEM and seismic reflection techniques for a similar purpose.

In the past the area has been studied with several hydrogeological and geophysical methods. G. Barbieri et alii have demonstrated, through resistivity and IP soundings repeated in different times, the connection between saltwater encroachment and the opening of various channels [7]. Other authors have studied the very shallow aquifer [8, 9]. In the area no deep wells are present and therefore no direct information about the deep aquifers and bedrock is available. Preliminary parts of the present investigation have been presented at conferences [10, 11] while the seismic investigation has already been published in the journal Geophysics [12].

1.1 Geological Settings

The Flumendosa is the biggest river in Sardinia, originating from the Gennargentu mountains approximately in the middle of the island and flowing into the Mediterranean Sea on the southern part of the Sardinia East coast. The coastal aquifer here extends from the village of S. Vito to the Mediterranean Sea reaching the width of 7 km westward. Several natural channels flow in the area (Foxi Padrionnas, Foxi Bau Obilu and Flumini

Becciu), probably indicating the old mouths of the ancient delta, but appearing without hydraulic connection to the present river (Fig. 1).

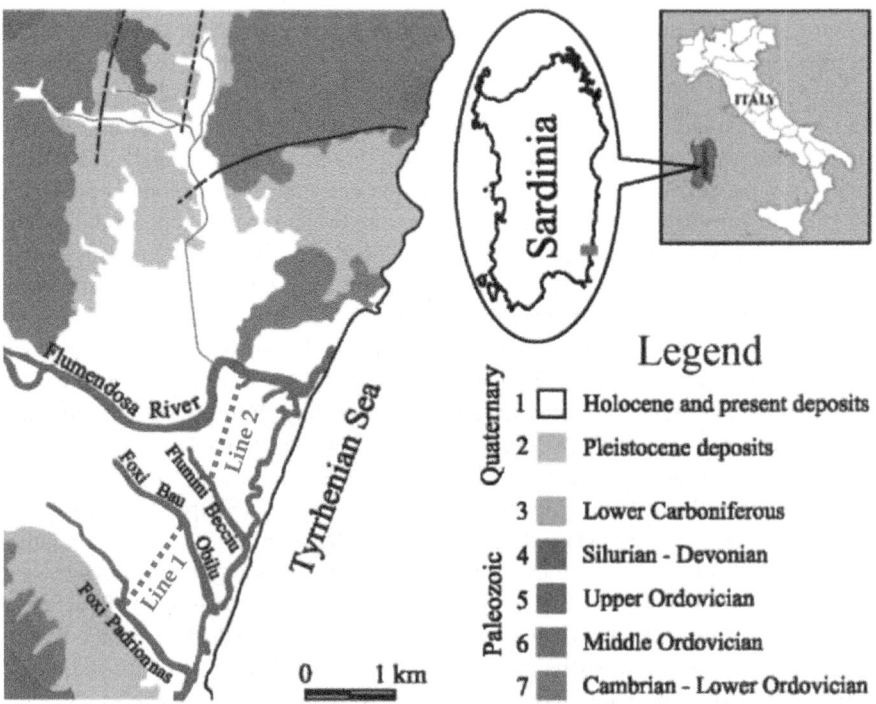

Fig. 1. Simplified geological map of the Muravera plain survey area, showing the location of seismic and geophysical profiles (modified from [12]). Unit 1: Alluvial deposits, including second-order alluvial terraces, colluvial, eolian, and littoral gravels, sands, silts, and clays. Unit 2: Conglomerates and sands forming first-order alluvial terraces connected to the Piedmont alluvial fan. Units 3–6: Metamorphic rocks, mainly metaconglomerates, metasandstones, metasiltstones, metalimestones, and porphyritic metavolcanic rocks, representing the Paleozoic basement. Unit 7: The Arenarie di S. Vito Formation, consisting of irregular sequences of micaceous metasandstones and metaquartzarenites, is the main outcropping unit bordering the Muravera plain. Red dotted lines indicates the geophysical profiles layout: Line 1 indicates the first seismic reflection and the TDEM profile, and Line 2 corresponds to the second seismic reflection and the TEM-FAST profile.

The aquifer consists of a terraced thick deposits of Quaternary alluvium, overlaying a Palaeozoic granite and schist bedrock. An inactive scree-slope joins the alluvial deposits with the surrounding Palaeozoic schist and granite hills. In the plain both ancient and recent deposits are present. The older terraced alluvial deposits are reddened for oxidation and well cemented, while the recent alluvium, also terraced, are poorly cemented and not yet oxidized. Furthermore, the most coastal area is bordered by palustrine deposits and eolian sands and dunes.

Two aquifers are known to be hosted into the alluvial deposits:

- a shallow phreatic aquifer, highly productive, mostly exploited with wells of a considerable diameter. The bottom limit consists of a few meters deep clay layer;
- a deep multilayer confined aquifer, sandwiched between sands and gravel interbedded with clayey-silty strata of varying thickness and extent.

The groundwater replenishment is due to both rain precipitation and irrigation. More than 2000 wells exist in the coastal plain. The presence of salt water has been monitored since the early '70s. At present the sea water encroachment affects half of the coastal plain.

2   Materials and Methods

Two profiles, one parallel to the coast, between the Palaeozoic outcropping and one perpendicular were planned. However, due to the presence of many kinds of tilling, only the parallel one was acquired and it was divided into two lines: about 1000 m of the parallel profile have been exploited (and is presented in the present paper) with both seismic and TDEM measurements along the Line 1 indicated in Fig. 1, while a shorter second inline one had been surveyed with seismics and TEM-FAST for a shallower prospection.

2.1   The Seismic Survey

The seismic data were acquired using single 50-Hz geophones attached to a 48-channel seismograph system with 18-bit recording capability. The sample interval was 0.5 ms and the record length 1 s. Data were recorded using standard common midpoint (CMP) roll-along technique in an end-on configuration with 48 active geophones. Geophone spacing of 5 m and source spacing of 10 m provided 12-fold CMP coverage with a CMP spacing of 2.5 m. Maximum source-receiver offset of 245 m enabled stacking velocities for the relatively deep reflections (e.g., from the bedrock surface) to be determined. Figure 2 shows three shot gathers representative of the entire data set.

Trace number

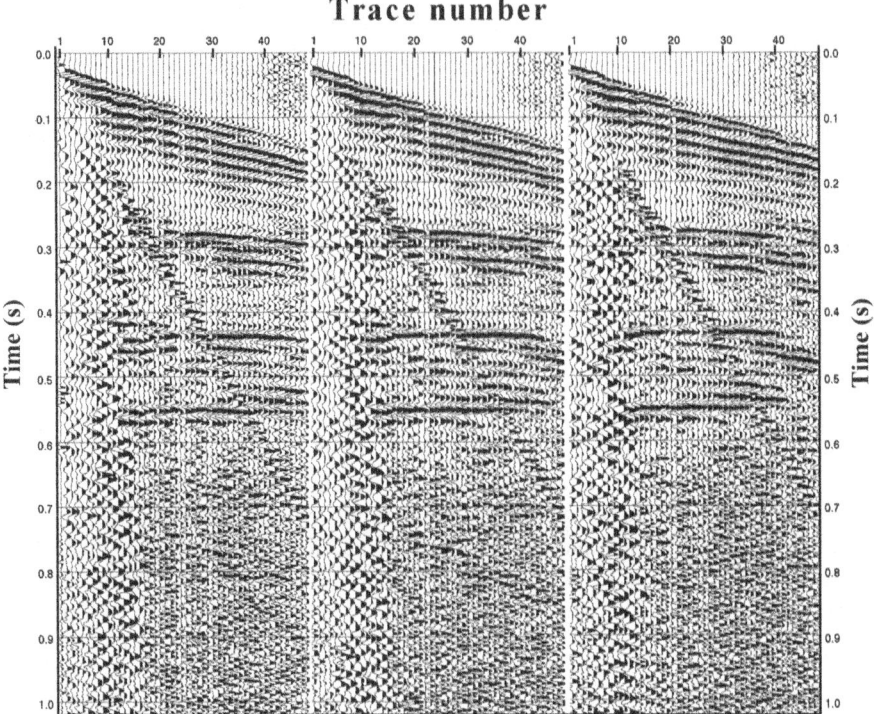

Fig. 2. Three shot gathers representative of the seismic dataset along Line 1, [12].

2.2 The TDEM Survey

The TDEM surveys were carried out along the seismic profile using two different equipment in order to provide a better vertical resolution for the different purposes and very high accuracy in interpretation. The coincident loop configuration was selected using different sizes and multiturn loop in order to increase the penetration depth [13]. In the deep soundings, performed by the Zonge system, a three-turn transmitter loop and two-turn receiver loop, 100 m long, were chosen. In the shallower soundings, an AEMR TEM-48 system, powered by built-in batteries and 12.5 m, 25 m, 50 m and 100 m loop sizes were used. Fifteen TDEM soundings have been carried out in the investigated area, using ZONGE 3 kW Transmitter and GDP32 - six channels - Receiver. Twenty-four frequencies can be selected in binary intervals between 0.0007 Hz and 8 kHz. The experimental data have been collected using a square wave with null phase at five different frequencies, namely 16, 4, 2, 1 and 0.5 Hz. (in six different windows from 0.030ms to 387ms). The transmitting current intensity has been set to 11 A.

Late-time apparent resistivities, after integration and normalization, have been used to interpret by means of mono-dimensional models (Fig. 3). The interpretation has been carried out using ZondTEM1D v.6.1, which is an interactive, graphically oriented, forward and inverse modeling program for interpreting TEM data in terms of a layered earth (1-D) model. The 26 TEM-FAST soundings were interpreted by the 1-D TEM-RES processing and interpretation package.

The TDEM soundings were inverted using one-dimensional initial models with the minimum possible number of layers. The inversions were constrained by incorporating a priori information from the boundaries identified in the seismic section. This approach not only reduced the misfit error from approximately 8% to slightly more than 4% but also improved the lateral continuity of the 2-D geoelectrical sections, allowing for a more geologically plausible interpretation.

TEM Soundings

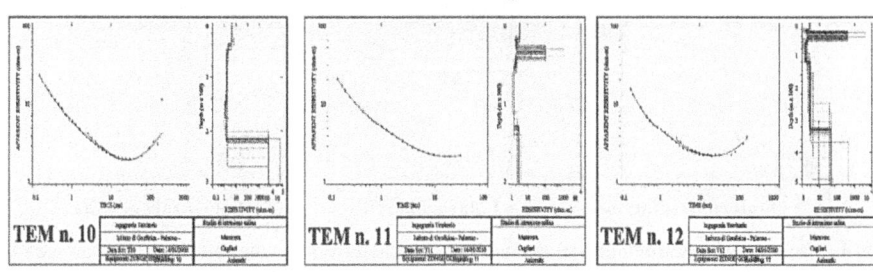

Fig. 3. Three examples of TDEM soundings, showing measured and calculated apparent resistivity curves along with the inverted resistivity model.

3 Results

Seismic data results, already published, are here summarized to allow a holistic portrait of the whole integrated approach. No velocity information from boreholes was available within the area investigated. Therefore, time-to-depth conversion was made based on interval velocities derived from the seismic data. These velocities range from 1700–1900 m/s in the uppermost part of the section to 3400–3600 m/s in the deepest part. The depth section showed several reflectors which reach a maximum depth of about 700 m in the central part. Two strong reflectors dominate the deepest part of the section. The continuity of these events is interrupted in many locations along the entire section. These discontinuities were interpreted as deep faults with vertical displacements up to 100 m. The interpreted units B and C, in Fig. 4, are only supposed on the basis of the geometrical features of the reflectors and on the basis of the seismic-derived interval velocities. Whereas the upper part of the section is dominated by smooth, horizontal reflectors, which are almost undisturbed down to 400 m, even if local amplitude changes of reflectors are present. All reflectors, above about 400 m, were interpreted as boundaries in quaternary alluvium deposits (unit A in Fig. 4). Despite the high quality of the section, seismic data do not allow stratigraphic distinction within the quaternary deposits.

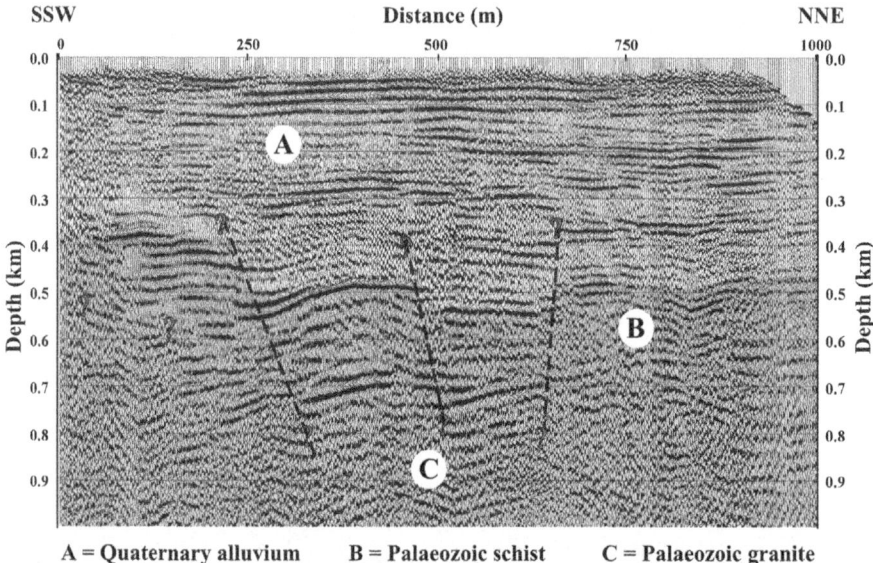

A = Quaternary alluvium   B = Palaeozoic schist   C = Palaeozoic granite

Fig. 4. Preliminary interpretation of the geological structures from the seismic reflection section along Line 1, [12].

The TDEM and the TEM FAST soundings (Fig. 3), have been used to reconstruct 2D section reported in the Figs. 5 and 6 respectively. They show very conductive layers (0.5–10 $\Omega \times$ m) in the shallower part of the section, obviously due to the presence of salt, brackish or fresh water in alluvium or eolian sand deposits. In the central part of the section, lateral resistivity changes are easily visible. High resistivity layers dominate the section below 250 m.

Also in this resistive layer, lateral variations of resistivity can be seen, probably in correspondence of either faults or changes of the Palaeozoic rocks. The TDEM soundings clearly show the connection between the channels and the encroachment areas and distinguish different aquifers.

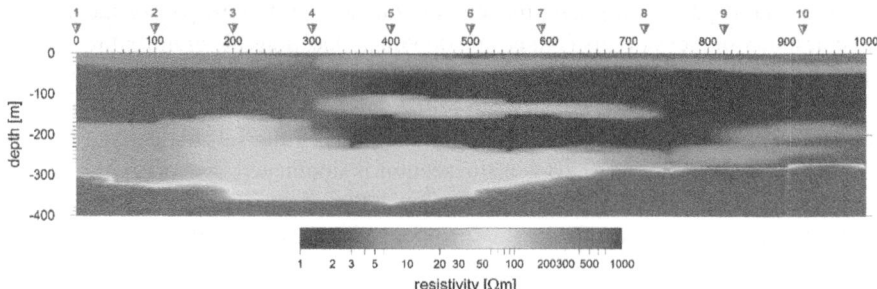

Fig. 5. Electrical resistivity section obtained from the 2D interpolation of inverted TDEM models. Red triangles indicate the locations of the TDEM soundings, black numbers the progressive coordinate in meters along the profile.

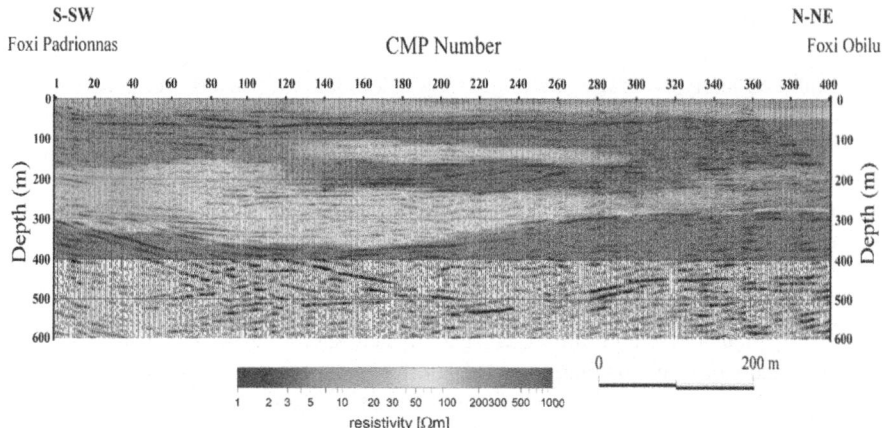

Fig. 6. Overlay of the TDEM section onto the reflection seismic section.

4 Discussion

The integration of seismic and TDEM data provides a comprehensive subsurface characterization of the Muravera plain. The seismic profiles reveal well-defined stratigraphic boundaries and lateral variations in subsurface layers, consistent with previously reported geological interpretations. The presence of discontinuities and velocity contrasts suggests a complex depositional history, with alluvial and colluvial deposits overlaying the Paleozoic basement.

The TDEM data, when overlaid onto the seismic section, confirm the interpreted lithological variations and provide additional constraints on the distribution of conductive layers. The resistivity profiles highlight zones of increased conductivity that correlate with alluvial sediments, while more resistive units correspond to consolidated formations, such as conglomerates and metamorphic rocks. The integration of seismic and TDEM data improves confidence in identifying aquifer-bearing units, as the low-resistivity zones align with potential groundwater-bearing formations. Figure 6 shows some important correspondences: faults, contacts and layering are in many cases exactly positioned. The attribution of low resistivity values to seismic "strata" allows the definition of the geometry and the quality of the aquifers.

A significant aspect of the study is the use of seismic constraints to refine the inversion of TDEM data. The initial unconstrained TDEM inversion exhibited higher misfit errors and lower lateral continuity. However, by incorporating boundaries identified from seismic sections, the inversion process achieved a better fit, reducing misfit error from approximately 8% to slightly above 4%. This methodological improvement enhances the resolution and reliability of the geophysical interpretation.

5   Conclusions

The combined analysis of seismic and TDEM data demonstrates the effectiveness of multi-method geophysical approaches in resolving subsurface heterogeneities in the Muravera plain. Seismic data delineate stratigraphic units with high precision, while TDEM resistivity sections provide complementary information on lithological and hydrogeological properties. The joint interpretation allows for a more robust assessment of potential aquifers and subsurface structures.

By constraining TDEM inversion with seismic boundaries, the study significantly improves the accuracy and lateral continuity of geoelectric sections, leading to a more geologically plausible interpretation. The geophysical survey carried out in the Muravera plain provided valuable information on the aquifers present in the area. In particular, the superimposition of the final TEM sections onto the seismic section—both obtained through independent data processing and interpretation—allows for the transformation of geological information, primarily derived from seismic results, into hydrogeological insights.

These findings emphasize the importance of integrating multiple geophysical methods for groundwater exploration and subsurface characterization in complex geological settings. Future work should consider expanding the survey area and incorporating additional geophysical techniques, such as electromagnetic and gravimetric surveys, to further enhance subsurface models.

References

1. SDG. https://sdgs.un.org/goals. Accessed 30 Mar 2025
2. Francés, A.P., Ramalho, E.C., Monteiro Santos, F., et al.: Contribution of the time domain electromagnetic method to the study of the Kalahari transboundary multilayered aquifer systems in Southern Angola. Hydrogeol. J. **32**(6), 1709–1727 (2024). https://doi.org/10.1007/s10040-024-02822-x
3. Di Napoli, R., et al.: The structure of a hydrothermal system from an integrated geochemical, geophysical and geological approach: the Ischia Island case study. Geochem. Geophys. Geosyst. **12**(7), Q07017 (2011). https://doi.org/10.1029/2010GC003476
4. Martorana, R., Lombardo, L., Messina, N., Luzio, D.: Integrated geophysical survey for 3D modelling of a coastal aquifer polluted by seawater. Near Surface Geophys. **12**(1), 45–59 (2014). https://doi.org/10.3997/1873-0604.2013006
5. Fitterman, D.V., Stewart, M.T.: Transient electromagnetic sounding for groundwater. Geophysics **51**(4), 995–1005 (1986). https://doi.org/10.1190/1.1442158
6. Shtivelman, V., Goldman, M.: Integration of shallow reflection seismics and time domain electromagnetics for detailed study of the coastal aquifer in the Nitzanim area of Israel. J. Appl. Geophys. **44**(2–3), 197–215 (2000). https://doi.org/10.1016/S0926-9851(98)00053-6
7. Barbieri, G., Barrocu, G., Ranieri, G.: Hydrogeological and geophysical investigations for evaluating salt intrusion phenomena in Sardinia. In: Boekelman, R.H., van Dam, C., Evertman, M., ten Hoorn, W.H.C. (eds.) Proceedings of the 9th Salt Water Intrusion Meeting, 12–16 May 1986, Delft, The Netherlands, pp. 659–670 (1986)
8. Ardau, F., Barbieri, G.: Evolution of salt water intrusion phenomena in the coastal plain of Muravera (South-eastern Sardinia). In: Barrocu, G. (ed.) Proceedings of the 13th Salt Water Intrusion Meeting, 5–10 June 1994, Villasimius (Cagliari), Italy, pp. 305–312 (1994)

9. Ardau, F., Barbieri, G., Barrocu, G.: Idrogeologia della piana di Muravera (Sardegna sud-orientale), included in Note illustrative della Carta Geologica d'Italia alla scala 1:50.000 -Foglio 549 Muravera, Servizio Geologico d'Italia, pp. 111–116 (1996)

10. Deidda, G.P., Ranieri, G., Uras, G., Cosentino, P., Martorana, R.: Seismic reflection and TDEM imaging of a complex aquifer system. In: European Geophysical Society, XXV General Assembly, 24–29 April 2000, Nice, France, p. 1 (2000)

11. Deidda, G.P., Ranieri, G., Uras, G., Cosentino, P., Martorana, R.: Joint analysis of seismic reflection and TDEM data to study salt water intrusion phenomena in a coastal area. In: Atti del 19° Convegno Nazionale del GNGTS. 7–9 novembre 2000, Roma, Italy, pp. 1–2 (2000)

12. Deidda, G.P., Ranieri, G., Uras, G., Cosentino, P., Martorana, R.: Geophysical investigations in the Flumendosa River Delta, Sardinia (Italy). Seismic reflection imaging. Gephysics 71(4), B121–B128 (2006). https://doi.org/10.1190/1.2213247

13. Nabighian, M.N., Macnae, J.C.: Chapter 6: Time domain electromagnetic prospecting methods. In: Nabighian, M.N. (ed.) Electromagnetic Methods in Applied Geophysics: Application, Parts A and B. Volume 2. Society of Exploration Geophysicist, Tulsa, Oklahoma (1991)

Outside and Inside the Surface. A Statue of Apollo from Villa Corsini in Castello (Florence)

P. Capizzi[1](✉), A. Di Santi[2], G. Adornato[2], P. Pingue[3], A. Carollo[1],
and R. Martorana[1]

[1] Department of Earth and Marine Science, University of Palermo, Palermo, Italy
patrizia.capizzi@unipa.it
[2] Scuola Normale Superiore, Pisa, Italy
[3] Laboratorio NEST, Scuola Normale Superiore and Istituto Nanoscienze Consiglio Nazionale delle Ricerche (CNR), Pisa, Italy

Abstract. This paper focuses on a marble statue representing the god Apollo as an archer, from the collections of the National Archaeological Museum of Florence (MAF), now exhibited at Villa Corsini in Castello (Florence). The larger-than-life-size statue has been considered a Roman pastiche: a head derived from a 4th century BCE (Before Common Era) prototype was joined to a body inspired by models from the beginning of the 5th century BCE. In this perspective, it would be important to define whether this pastiche is a Roman or a Modern work. Having no information about the provenance of this unique sculpture, this research sheds new light on its biography through the investigation of its materiality. Specifically, 3D Ultrasonic Tomography is employed to examine marble characteristics. The obtained velocity model shows interesting results, highlighting areas of obvious integrations and possible metal pins, to join parts of the statue. The analysis of these results leads to the idea that the statue was probably reassembled in modern times, in a way that is not entirely consistent with its original appearance.

Keywords: Roman marble sculpture · diagnosis · 3D ultrasonic tomography

1 The Statue of Apollo: Roman or Modern *Pastiche*?

A marble statue representing the god Apollo as an archer, from the collections of the National Archaeological Museum of Florence (MAF) is the object of this paper (MAF, inv. n. 13719). The statue has been investigated within the project "BIO-SCULT: Per una 'bio-grafia' delle sculture all'aperto: dalle collezioni fiorentine al Regio Museo di Luigi Adriano Milani, all'alluvione del 1966", carried out by the Scuola Normale Superiore of Pisa (supervisor: Gianfranco Adornato) in partnership with the MAF. The purpose of the project is retracing the history, or rather the "biography", of a selection of pieces belonging to the museum's collection of Classical Sculptures, currently housed at Villa Corsini in Castello, near Florence.

© The Author(s), under exclusive license to Springer Nature Switzerland AG 2026
O. Gervasi et al. (Eds.): ICCSA 2025 Workshops, LNCS 15899, pp. 394–404, 2026.
https://doi.org/10.1007/978-3-031-97663-6_35

The statue is larger-than-life-size (H. 186 cm; H. head, from the top to the chin: c. 25 cm). It is composed of a head derived from a 4th century BCE prototype, joined to a body inspired by models from the beginning of the 5th century BCE (Fig. 1). It would be then important to define whether this pastiche is a Roman or a Modern work. Having no information about the provenance of this unique sculpture, this research sheds new light on its biography through the investigation of its materiality. Specifically, 3D Ultrasonic Tomography is employed to examine marble characteristics.

In order to trace out the "life stages" of the statue of Apollo, the present contribution is structured into two sections: the first is devoted to an essential historical-artistic study of the sculpture, while in the second part the results of 3D Ultrasonic Tomography conducted on the marble are provided.

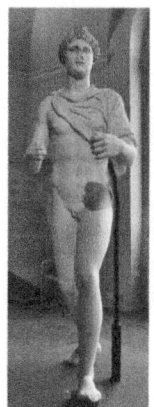  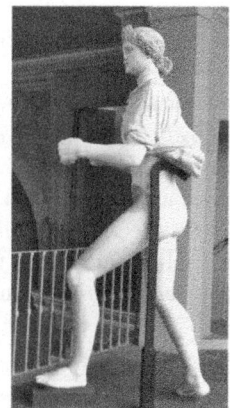 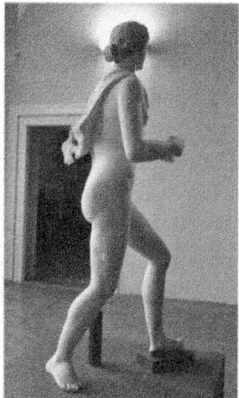

Fig. 1. The statue of Apollo (MAF, 13719). Courtesy of the MAF.

2   History and Art

Today we can admire the Apollo on the Orchestra Balcony of Villa Corsini, an elegant late-Baroque villa in Castello, donated to the Italian State in 1968 and later becoming the new location for the collection of ancient sculptures of the MAF. The statue was in fact moved there from the Archaeological Museum of Florence, located in the heart of the city, during the eighties, along with the other ancient marbles of the MAF, because of the damage done to the museum in the catastrophic 1966 flood [1].

Before the flood, in the early twentieth century the sculpture was placed under the fourth arch of the Archaeological Museum's Garden, according to the project designed by Luigi Adriano Milani, who was the Director of the *Regio Museo Archeologico* of Florence from the beginning of the twentieth century until his death in 1914 and acquired the statue of Apollo along with other ancient marbles in order to form the first museum's collection of Classical sculpture [2].

Unfortunately, as with almost all the other pieces in this collection, Milani did not give any information on the circumstances of the acquisition of the Apollo, and, due to the lack of documentation, the provenance of the statue still remains unknown.

The director provided only a brief description of the sculpture, in which he presented it as an original (Roman) statue depicting Apollo as an archer, without questioning whether the head belonged to the body: "*Statua di Apollo gradiente e saettante, con clamide e faretra. La testa, sua propria, con bocca semiaperta, ha i capelli discriminati annodati all'occipite. Marmo pario. Di restauro il braccio e la mano d. Corrisponde all'Apollo saettante i Niobidi dei sarcofagi romani, tipo del sec. IV a.C.*" [3].

This overall interpretation is still considered pretty valid today, as we can read in the most recent guide of the collection housed at Villa Corsini, edited by Fabrizio Paolucci and Antonella Romualdi, which until now has offered the only published description of the statue [4]. Here Paolucci states that "the head is almost certainly original because, besides being compatible with the rest of the figure in terms of its size and type of marble, it reveals an irregular fracture line at the base of the neck that coincides perfectly with the one on the bust". However, in our opinion, the hypothesis that the head belonged to this statue from its origin is not yet totally convincing, because of some aspects explained here below.

Looking at the sculpture, the first thing we notice is that the head bears evident traces of polychromy, while the body does not preserve any trace of color. Moreover, although one of the last restorations of the sculpture made all the original fractures no longer visible, it is particularly interesting to note that, among these hidden fractures, the one at the base of the neck is clearly recognizable in some historical photographs from the Archives of the MAF (Fig. 2). It is noteworthy that, observing the original fracture, the head is slightly tilted towards the left, even though today we gain a different perception of it.

Fig. 2. Head of the statue of Apollo, MAF 13719. Right: photograph of the statue, early 20th century (MAF Photographic Archive, detail of neg. n. 1350). Courtesy of the MAF.

After these initial observations, we can now take a look at the body of the statue. It represents a walking naked male figure, with the left leg stepping forward, with the foot resting on the ground, and the right leg set back with the heel raised. His arms are bent at the elbows and his forearms are stretched forward, in a gesture interpreted as that of an archer ready to shoot an arrow. The bow would be held with the left hand, while the dart would be shot with the right. The torso, stiffly upright and frontal, does not follow the movement of the arms and it also looks independent from the legs. A short cloak, fastened on the right shoulder, covers part of his chest; it drapes - in a somewhat unnatural way - around the shoulder and the upper part of the left arm, and then it falls backwards, moved by the archer's impetus. A strap is above the cloak: it is visible both on the chest and on the back. So, we would expect to see the quiver of the archer at his back, but surprisingly there is no quiver at all, even if its volume seems to be suggested by a mass of folds. As previously stated by Milani in his description of the statue, the pose of the body is typical of Apollo shooting arrows against the Niobids. This representation, already known from vase paintings of the first half of the 5th century BCE, is also reproduced on some Roman sarcophagi and is the prototype of the famous bronze Apollo from Pompeii (Naples, Museo Archeologico Nazionale, inv. n. 5629).

With reference to this last piece, it should be noted that it is the best comparison for the Apollo of the *MAF*. Moreover, by comparing this Apollo from Pompeii with that of Florence, we can see that this latter has been wrongly positioned in its last arrangement at Villa Corsini: it is clear, in fact, that the left foot is incorrectly raised, altering the original posture of the whole statue. Thanks to the 3D model, we can finally position the statue correctly and discover that the head is actually turned to the left, as previously already noted looking at the historical photographs (Fig. 3a). Apollo, therefore, is turning his gaze in a different direction from the one suggested by the body (and the lost arch); in other words, the head is divergent from the torso.

At this point, what can we say about the chronology of the statue? Unfortunately, we have to admit that the dating of the body is very challenging, also because of its restoration, which made the marble surfaces conspicuously flattened and smooth. Because of this, there are no reliable diagnostic elements indicating an almost certain chronology. Concerning this point, Paolucci has already observed that "no stylistic or formal indication can be inferred from the body, whose original surface, which survives at only a few points, has been reduced by a few millimeters" [4]. However, in our view, some formal inconsistencies, such as the strap without the quiver and the unnatural way in which the cloak drapes around the upper part of the left arm, could make the ancient origin of the body questionable.

Regarding the head, its chronology is simpler to define. Unlike the body, the drill-marks for the rendering of the hair point to the middle of the 2nd century CE. Its typology is also evident: as its hairstyle clearly shows, it derives from the Apollo Lykeios, representing the god with his right arm raised and the hand resting on his head, which is normally turned to the left.

The combination of different models in one sculpture is known for the Roman Age. Accordingly, accepting the idea that the head has belonged to the body since the origin of the Florentine Apollo, it has been assumed that the statue could be "a singular and very interesting *pastiche* from the Roman era which joined an image of the god derived from a 4th-century BCE prototype, to the body of an Apollo as an archer that, because of its frozen movement and the unavoidable lateral view imposed on the onlooker, seems to have been inspired by models and sculptures from the Severan period" [4]. But surprisingly, a further new element could definitively overturn this interpretation. The

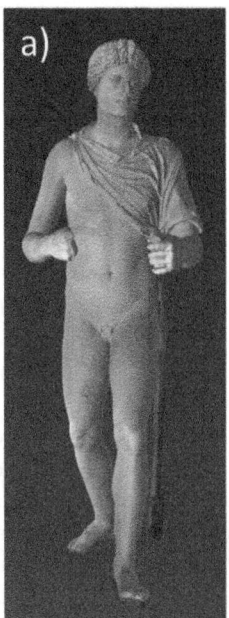 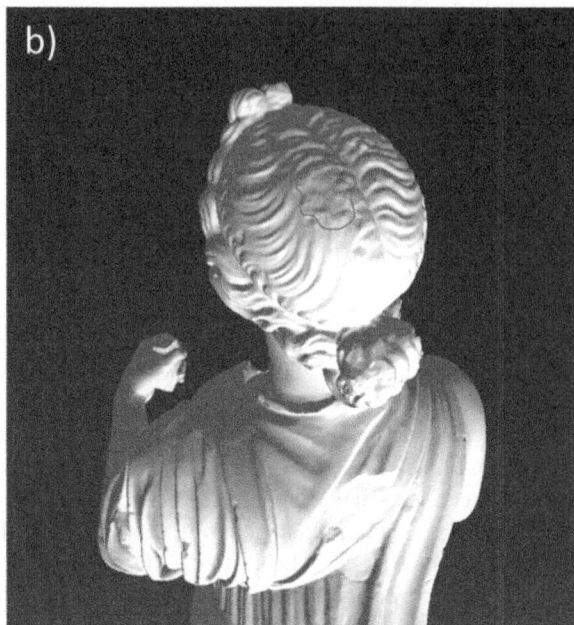

Fig. 3. 3D image of the statue of Apollo (a) and of the statue head (b), MAF 13719 (Elab. Martina Borroni).

3D model actually reveals the presence of an interesting *lacuna* on the top left side of the head that could be the print of the hand originally put on the top of the head (Fig. 3b). An interesting comparison of this trace is offered by the head of an Apollo Lykeios today on display at Palazzo Massimo alle Terme (Rome, Museo Nazionale Romano, inv. n. 55336), which presents the print of the now lost hand on the top of the head [5]. If this were the case, we should think that the head was originally created for a statue depicting the Apollo Lykeios and that only in a later phase of its "life" it was placed on the body of an archer Apollo.

3 Ultrasound Investigations

Ultrasound tomography is a non-invasive technique, increasingly used in cultural heritage applications [6–10]. This technique allows to investigate beyond the surface and to
analyze the mechanical and structural characteristics of the material. The transmission
velocity of ultrasound is measured by a transmitting probe to a receiver, placed at a
known distance. The propagation velocity of ultrasound changes based on the characteristics of the material being investigated, allowing to identify inhomogeneities, linked
to the presence of voids or structural defects.

3D ultrasound tomography was used to investigate the state of conservation of the
statue of Apollo and to evaluate the presence of parts of the statue that may not have
originally belonged to the statue. The data were acquired using the TDAS 16 instrumentation produced by Boviar (with 16 channels). The receiving and transmitting probes
have a central frequency of 55 kHz. For precise measurements, as in this case, the
probes were equipped with special cone-shaped aluminum supports that allowed a more
accurate positioning of the sensor. 400 measurement points were used, distributed homo-
geneously on the surface of the statue, used as transmitting and alternatively receiving
points. In this way it was possible to obtain inversion cells with the dimensions of 5 cm
x 5 cm. The final velocity model was then interpolated and smoothed.

The use of a 3D survey of the statue (Fig. 3) allowed to obtain a 3D tomographic
image of the velocity of the ultrasonic waves (Fig. 4).

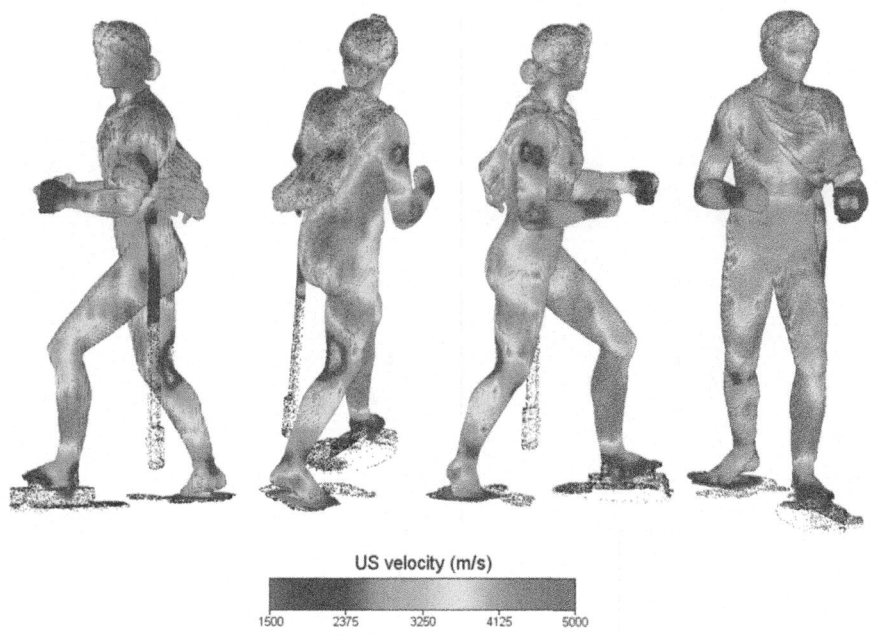

US velocity (m/s)

1500   2375   3250   4125   5000

Fig. 4. 3D ultrasound tomography of the statue.

In order not to damage the surface, the statue was protected by a layer of transparent film that also allowed to position the markers used as transmission and reception points. These points allowed to record the signals that pass through the entire body of the object. The velocity model is obtained through an iterative process, starting from a rectilinear path between source and receiver. The subsequent iterations, instead, provide for the refraction of the rays for each cell, taking into account its velocity. The process stops when the calculated path times are close to the measured ones. The GeoTomCG software version 18.1 [11] was used for data inversion, while 3D rendering was performed using Voxler software version 4.3 [12].

The resulting images of the Apollo tomography show values of the propagation velocities varying from 1500 m/s to 5000 m/s.

The study of these results allowed to identify the position and the extension of the numerous fractures covered by additions of plaster. The lowest velocity corresponds to the area where there is a material with different characteristics, in this case plaster, less compact than marble, and therefore the ultrasound takes longer to pass through it. These areas have been correlated to areas of possible fractures and injuries (Fig. 5). These additions, during one of the last restorations, were camouflaged with a pictorial technique that makes their identification difficult. For example, on the right shoulder there is an evident low-velocity area that corresponds to an integration (Fig. 6). Particular attention should be paid to the left foot which seems to be made entirely of a different material, at least from the point of view of velocity.

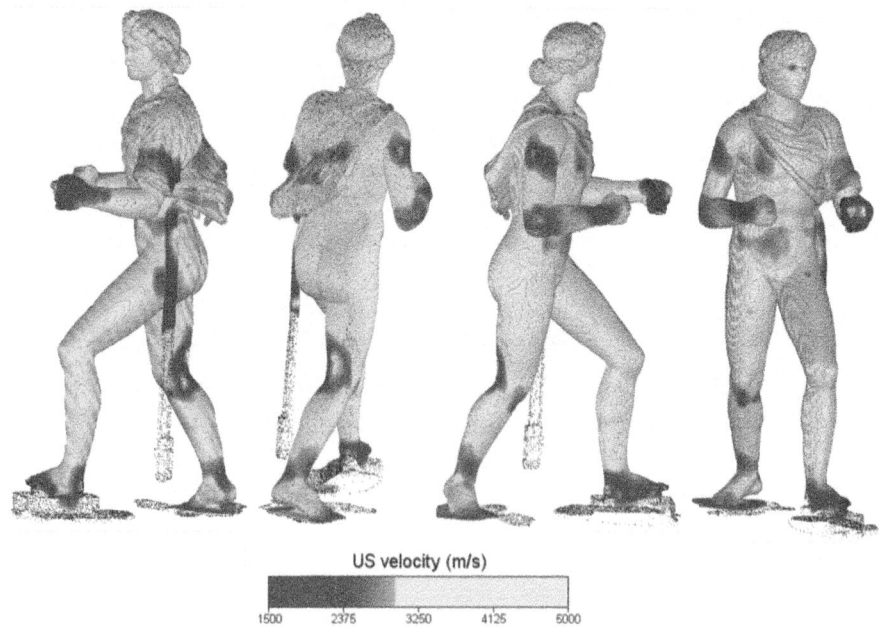

US velocity (m/s)

1500   2375   3250   4125   5000

Fig. 5. 3D ultrasound tomography of the statue: low-velocity areas.

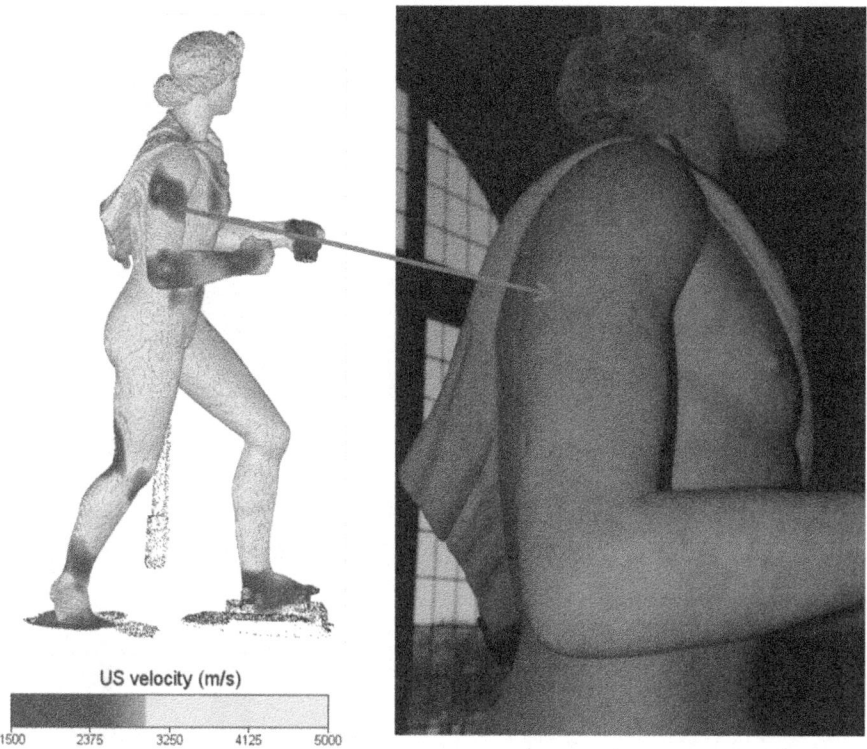

Fig. 6. Low-velocity area in the right shoulder corresponding to an integration.

Inside the statue, the velocity model instead shows some areas with a series of high-velocity zones, with values greater than 4500 m/s (Fig. 7). The hypothesis, also supported by their position, is that these are the areas where there are metal pins for the relocation of the fractured parts. In fact, the metal allows the ultrasound to propagate very quickly. These hypotheses are supported by evidence of body parts that appear to be reattached to each other. Of interest is the shape we see between the head and the neck that seems to correspond to two pins. This would confirm the hypothesis that the head was added to the body at a later stage, most likely in the modern era.

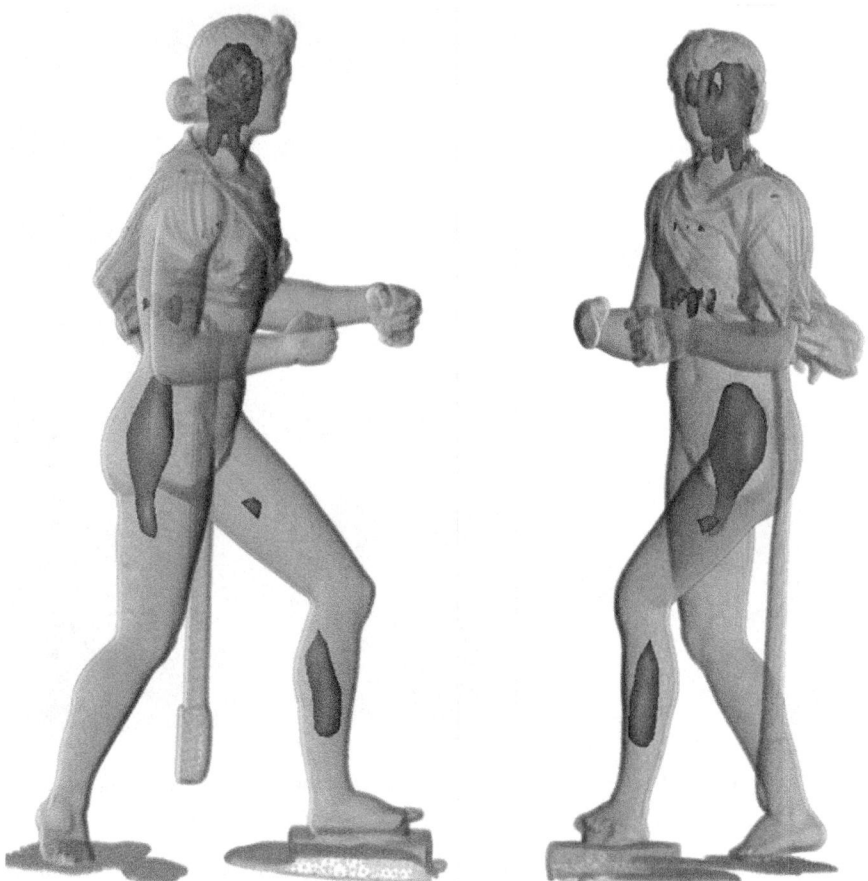

Fig. 7. 3D image of the statue with high-velocity zones in red, probably due to the metal inserts presence.

4 Conclusions

Thanks to the combined historical-artistic and technical-scientific approach, some unexpected results were attained by this preliminary research study on the statue of Apollo.

In spite of the initial opinion, according to which the head could be compatible with the body of the figure because of its size, type of marble and correspondence between the fracture line at the base of the neck and the one on the bust, several elements would now seem to reveal a different biography of this unique piece.

Starting from the analysis of the historical photographs of the statue, we discovered that the fracture at the base of the neck, now hidden because of a more recent restoration of the statue, does not perfectly correspond with the one of the torso, since a visible Modern integration was inserted between these two parts. Moreover, the current positioning of the statue, which is clearly incorrect, as the comparison with the Apollo from Pompeii shows, has altered our perception of the piece and, in particular, it has disguised the original pose of the head, which is actually turned to the left. As a result, it becomes evident that the head and the body are not in harmony from the point of view of the action performed, since the Apollo is turning his gaze in a different direction from the one suggested by the body and the lost arch. Last but not least, as everyone knows, all the evidence shows that the body belongs to an archer figure while the head derives from the Apollo Lykeios. Consequently, if the interpretation of a lacuna discovered by us on the top of the head is correct, the head was certainly not created to be on this body, but on a statue depicting the Apollo Lykeios with the hand resting on the head.

The results of the 3D ultrasound tomography interestingly revealed the probable presence of internal pins, connecting parts of the statue. Near the neck of the statue, two metal pins are probably evident, which could confirm the hypothesis that the head was added to the body in modern times. Some low-velocity areas were also identified that seem to be linked to the presence of modern plaster additions, which were camouflaged with painting techniques. Therefore, the statue we see today, in its last phase of life, could very likely be a modern pastiche, composed of an ancient head of Apollo and a body that is very difficult to date, although the possibility that it could have been made (or heavily reworked) by modern sculptors should not be excluded.

Acknowledgments. We are very grateful to the National Archaeological Museum of Florence (MAF) for its essential collaboration to this research project. We would like to express our gratitude to all the participants of the "BIO-SCULT" project. In particular, we would like to thank Fabio Beltram (Laboratorio NEST, Scuola Normale Superiore) for his support during the scientific analysis. A special thank is also due to the project ARTES4.0 for the 3D scanner purchase.

Paragraphs 1 and 2 are written by Alessia Di Santi; paragraph 3 is written by Patrizia Capizzi; paragraph 4 is written by Alessia Di Santi and Patrizia Capizzi. The preliminary results of our research on the statue of Apollo were presented by Alessia Di Santi and Martina Borroni in the contribution "The Colourful Head of Apollo: Biography through Polychromy. A case-study from Villa Corsini in Castello (MAF)", in the 11th International Round Table on Polychromy in Ancient Sculpture and Architecture: The materiality of Polychromy (Roma, Musei Capitolini - Museo Nazionale Romano, 9-12 novembre 2022), in press.

Disclosure of Interests.   The authors have no competing interests to declare that are relevant to the content of this article.

References

1. Romualdi, A. (ed.): Museo Archeologico Nazionale di Firenze. I marmi antichi conservati nella Villa Corsini a Castello. 1. Le statue, Sillabe, Livorno, pp. 8–17 (2004)
2. Iozzo, M.: Il Museo Archeologico Nazionale di Firenze e il suo ruolo nel quadro degli studi etruscologici. In: Bentini, L., et al. (eds.) Etruschi. Viaggio nelle terre dei Rasna (exhibition catalogue), Electa, (Milano), pp. 453–459 (2019)
3. Milani, L.A.: Il R. Museo Archeologico di Firenze I, Tipografia Enrico Ariani, Firenze, no. 30, p. 311 (1912)

4. Paolucci, F., Romualdi, A. (eds.): L'Antiquarium di Villa Corsini a Castello. Guida alla visita del museo e alla scoperta del territorio, Edizioni Polistampa, Firenze, pp. 139–142, 272–274 (F. Paolucci) (2010)
5. Gasparri, C., Paris, R. (eds.): Palazzo Massimo alle Terme. Le collezioni, Electa, Milano, no. 177, p. 246 (M. Caso) (2013)
6. Sambuelli, L., Bohm, G., Capizzi, P., Cardarelli, E., Cosentino, P.L.: Comparison between GPR measurements and ultrasonic tomography with different inversion algorithms. An application to the base of an ancient Egyptian sculpture. J. Geophys. Eng. **8**, 106–116 (2011)
7. Piroddi, L., et al.: Imaging cultural heritage at different scales: part I, the micro-scale (manufacts). Remote Sens. **15**(10), 2586 (2023)
8. Blitz, J., Simpson, G.: Ultrasonic methods of non-destructive testing. Non-Destructive Eval. Ser. **2**, 280 (1996)
9. Menningen, J., Siegesmund, S., Tweeton, D., Traupmann, M.: Ultrasonic tomography: non-destructive evaluation of the weathering state on a marble obelisk, considering the effects of structural properties. Environ. Earth Sci. **77**, 601 (2018)
10. Capizzi, P., Cosentino, P.L., Schiavone, S.: Some tests of 3D ultrasonic traveltime tomography on the Eleonora d'Aragona statue (F. Laurana, 1468). J. Appl. Geophys. **91**, 14–20 (2013)
11. Tweeton, D.R.: GeoTomCG, Three-dimensional geophysical tomography software (2021)
12. Golden Software, I. Voxler, Quick Start Guide 3D Data Visualization (2018)

Towards Semi-automatic Detection of Illegal Logging: Integrating Optical and SAR Satellite Imagery with StanForD Field-Machine Data

Giandomenico De Luca[1]([✉]) [ID], Lorenzo Arcidiaco[1] [ID], Manuela Corongiu[2] [ID], Tiziana De Filippis[1] [ID], Carla Nati[1] [ID], Martino Rogai[1] [ID], and Gianni Picchi[1,3] [ID]

[1] Institute of BioEconomy (IBE) – National Research Council of Italy (CNR), via Madonna del Piano 10, 50019 Sesto Fiorentino, Italy
giandomenico.deluca@cnr.it

[2] LaMMA Consortium – Regione Toscana, via Madonna del Piano 10, 50019 Sesto Fiorentino, Italy

[3] Forest Science and Technology Centre of Catalonia (CTFC), Crta. de St. Llorenç de Morunys, 25280 Solsona, Spain

Abstract. Illegal logging is a global issue with severe ecological, economic, and social consequences. In Europe, it often occurs as small-scale, selective harvesting, which, despite its limited footprint, significantly contributes to forest degradation, biodiversity loss, and ecosystem disruption. Detecting illegal logging is essential for assessing its impacts and supporting sustainable forest management. However, its fragmented nature poses significant detection challenges, requiring advanced monitoring solutions. This study presents an exploratory data analysis and preliminary results toward a semi-automatic monitoring framework developed within the EU Horizon SINTETIC project (Single Item Identification for Forest Production, Protection, and Management). The framework integrates high-resolution satellite data from Sentinel-1 (SAR) and Sentinel-2 (multispectral) to analyze time-series trends in optical spectral indices and dual-polarized SAR backscatter, identifying distinctive patterns associated with logging events. An unsupervised sliding-window breakpoint detection algorithm was implemented to detect logging-induced disturbances in satellite time series. The method was validated using georeferenced ground data from legal mechanized logging operations, provided in StanForD 2010 standard format. Two logging scenarios were examined: clear-cutting and selective logging. The exploratory analysis provided valuable insights into forest disturbance patterns, while breakpoint analysis successfully identified the timing of logging events in both scenarios. This system offers a promising approach for detecting illegal logging.

Keywords: illegal logging · selective logging · remote sensing · forest disturbance detection · satellite monitoring

1 Introduction

Forest disturbances resulting from human-driven land management practices include extensive wildfires, commercial deforestation, mining operations, infrastructure development, small-scale farming, and timber harvesting. Many of these activities are not only environmentally unsustainable but are also frequently carried out illegally, leading to significant ecological consequences [1]. Selective logging of forests – i.e. selectively removing a limited number of targeted trees, which may not be contiguous, while leaving the remaining trees in the stand –, in particular, has now become a dominant harvesting process in Europe. It ensures ecosystem conservation than a more intensive logging system (e.g. clearcutting – i.e. removal of all trees in the targeted area). However, when unregulated or illegal, it wreaks havoc on ecosystems, altering the forest's light regime, microclimate, and nutrient cycling, with long-term impacts on species composition and biodiversity, up to contributing to increased vulnerability to any other type of natural or human-induced disturbance [2]. Yet, uncertainties remain in fully understanding the impacts of selective logging [3], and detecting illegal logging is critical to assessing its effects and ensuring sustainable forest management [1].

With the introduction of new European legislation addressing deforestation-free products, such as Regulation (EU) No 995/2010 (European Union Timber Regulation – EUTR) and its replacement Regulation (EU) 2023/1115 (Regulation on Deforestation-free Products - EUDR), the European Union has taken steps to curb illegal logging practices. However, in Europe, logging standards are not universally regulated, with practices varying significantly between countries and even within regions (e.g., Italy) due to fragmented national and sub-national governance. These inconsistencies complicate efforts to monitor and manage logging effectively.

On a landscape scale, satellite remote sensing holds great promise for detecting active logging and harvesting [4]. Recent advancements in remote sensing technologies, including high-resolution optical and synthetic aperture radar (SAR) imagery, offer new opportunities to monitor forest degradation and disturbances [5]. SAR, in particular, is less impacted by weather conditions, making it an ideal tool for continuous monitoring. However, although SAR data provides valuable insights into structural changes within the forest canopy, its ability to detect low-intensity selective logging is limited due to the small canopy gaps such harvesting practices produce [2, 3].

However, the main challenge of using remote sensing data to detect low-intensity logging is compounded by the lack of robust field data for comprehensive model training, validation and development. While localized field campaigns have provided valuable insights, a continent-wide standardized approach remains elusive due to the high costs and time demands of such efforts. The integration of detailed, georeferenced ground-based data collected from mechanized logging operations following the StanForD 2010 standard [6] offers a potential breakthrough. A key element of this approach is the integration of detailed ground-based, georeferenced harvesting data, including the number, volume, and location of harvested trees, collected from mechanized legal logging operations. This data might be employed to train and validate advanced classification models, enabling precise correlation between observed forest disturbances and known harvesting activities, leading to more effective monitoring and management of forest ecosystems. In the framework of Horizon EU project SINTETIC (https://sinteticproject.eu/), an intensive and heterogeneous collecting campaign is programmed from project partners across Europe. In this framework, this study aims to assess the sensitivity of Sentinel-1 and Sentinel-2 data in detecting and mapping logging activities, in particular selective logging, utilizing StanForD 2010 machine-field data as geolocation and position reference. By integrating this data with remote sensing tools, we seek to enhance the detection of forest disturbances and improve our understanding of the impacts of selective logging across Europe.

2 Study Areas

Three areas in different parts of Europe were analyzed (Fig. 1): two in Spain (SPAN - 42°06′55″N, 1°27′45″E; SPAN2 - 43°13′34.9″N 3°11′54.1″W), and a third in Scotland (SCOT - 56°43′09″N, 5°46′28″W). These areas were subjected to two distinct types of forest interventions: for SPAN and SPAN2 area, logging was selective, with 168 and 176 trees respectively, removed from an area of approximately 6500 m^2 and 1150 m^2. The trees were randomly distributed, but their selection for felling was predetermined (selective logging). This method preserved full canopy coverage even after logging. In contrast, in SCOT area, all trees within a 13000 m^2 area were felled (clearcutting).

The topography of the two areas differs significantly. The SCOT and SPAN2 areas are located in a flat region, whereas the SPAN area is situated on a hillside watershed with a slight slope oriented toward the south.

Additionally, both areas are characterized by challenging weather conditions, with a high number of cloudy days, which can significantly impact sky clarity and remote sensing observations.

This experimental setup enabled a comparative analysis of the responses of the S1 and S2 signals under two distinct and highly challenging scenarios.

3 Dataset

3.1 StanForD Field-Based Harvesting Data

During the logging process, multiple data points were recorded to track harvesting activities. Specifically, the number of felled trees and the total geometric volume skidded from the forest were systematically documented. Additionally, the geolocation of the logging machine (forest harvester machine) was recorded throughout all phases of the operation, providing precise spatial information about the harvesting process. This information was stored in StanForD 2010 (Standard for Forest Machine Data and Communication) files, a standardized format developed by Skogforsk [6] for communication with forest machine controllers. StanForD 2010 consists of two main components: i) data standard that defines how information is structured and recorded; ii) an XML-based file structure (HPR files) that stores detailed records of the harvesting process. A unique continuous *StemNumber* is assigned to each felled tree (or stem), which is recorded directly by the harvester's onboard computer to the HPR file. Although this data collection is highly detailed, its frequency and completeness still depend on the discretion of the machine operators.

In this study, we utilized geolocation points of logging machinery (StanForD 2010), provided by logging companies, to ensure precise spatial and temporal tracking of harvesting activities. To facilitate data extraction, a custom Python script was developed to efficiently retrieve and restructure information from HPR files into a more accessible format.

3.2 Sentinel-1 SAR Satellite Data

The S1 dataset consisted of a time series of ground range detected (GRD) images, acquired in interferometric wide (IW) mode, for each of the two available polarizations: co-polarized VV and cross-polarized VH. Google Earth Engine (GEE) was exploited for bulk-downloading of the entire dataset. GEE is a cloud computing platform providing calibrated, ortho-corrected Sentinel-1 scenes that have been processed in the following steps using the Sentinel-1 Toolbox [7]: i) thermal noise removal; ii) radiometric calibration; iii) geometric terrain correction (i.e. geocoding) using the Shuttle Radar Topography Mission (SRTM) 30 m digital elevation model (DEM); iv) decibels (dB) backscatter conversion. The pixel spectral resolution was 10 m.

A time series was necessary since Sentinel-1 single image is not enough to differentiate logging activities with reasonable precision [3]. It covered a period of just over two years before and just over one year after the logging event (196 images, SPAN; 269 images, SPAN2; 155 images, SCOT).

3.3 Sentinel-2 Multispectral Satellite Data

The S2 Level-2A (bottom-of-atmosphere) multi-spectral time series was also processed and retrieved from GEE [8]. For this preliminary analysis, two bands were selected: the red band (B3, ~655 nm) and the near-infrared (NIR) band (B8, ~800 nm). These wavelengths were chosen because they are well-established as being highly sensitive to foliar chlorophyll content and are particularly suitable for vegetation monitoring [2]. Additionally, both bands have a fine native pixel spatial resolution of 10 m. The normalized difference vegetation index (NDVI) was then calculated:

$$NDVI = (Red - NIR)/(Red + NIR) \tag{1}$$

The time series (75 images, SPAN; 104 images, SPAN2; 155 images, SCOT), filtered for cloud coverage (with a threshold of 50%), covered the same period as the S1 dataset (Sect. 3.2). Further cloud filtering was conducted using the QA60 cloud mask band [9].

4 Methods

4.1 Processing

The aim of this study was to analyze the responses of optical and SAR satellite signals in order to identify distinctive patterns or biometry characteristics associated with logging events. This involved two separate steps: *ad-hoc* processing for explorative data analysis, and breakpoint identification.

Exploratory Data Analysis. The Harmonic Analysis of Time Series (HANTS) algorithm was employed in this study for robust smoothing and gap-filling of remotely sensed time-series data. HANTS effectively mitigates common remote sensing challenges, such as persistent cloud cover, atmospheric disturbances, and sensor anomalies, which can obscure true seasonal dynamics. The analysis included NDVI time series derived from multispectral Sentinel-2 imagery, as well as VV and VH backscatter from Sentinel-1 data. To ensure a focused analysis, a location mask was generated using georeferenced logging areas from the StanForD 2010 database, allowing targeted evaluation of both affected pixels and their neighboring areas.

Breakpoint Detection. Abrupt changes (breakpoints) in the temporal evolution of the average pixel value within the location mask—calculated at each time step by averaging all pixels in the mask—were detected following selective logging, serving as indicators of forest disturbance. Window-based change point detection, implemented through the *ruptures* library [10], was used for fast time-series segmentation and breakpoint detection. For a comprehensive technical description of the algorithm, please refer to [11]. The model requires only a few parameters to be set: the window length, which is the number of samples used to estimate a change point within the segment, was set to 2; the squared deviations segmentation model (l2) was adopted; the minimum segment length was set to 2 (default); the jump parameter, defining the interval between consecutive points that are used in the analysis, was set to 2; and the expected number of breakpoints was set to 1. Temporal information from StanForD 2010 was used as the reference timeframe for validating breakpoint detection.

5 Results and Discussions

5.1 StanForD 2010 Field-Machine Data

Besides georeferencing and logging timing, several other pieces of information can be retrieved from the StanForD 2010 field-machine database. For example, Fig. 2 presents the volume and diameter-at-breast-height (DBH) distribution of logged stems in the form of boxplots. The total volume exported was 19.44 m^3 10.78 m^3 and 431.49 m^3 for SPAN, SPAN2 and SCOT areas. These data provide key insights into extracted timber volume, influencing canopy gap formation and serving as critical biophysical indicators for remote sensing-based logging detection.

5.2 Satellite Analysis

The temporal distribution of smoothed Sentinel-2 NDVI exhibits a clear decline following logging, with the effect being most pronounced after clearcutting (Fig. 2, left column). In the case of selective logging (Fig. 2, right column), the overall decrease in NDVI is less evident in terms of mean trend but becomes more pronounced during the subsequent dry season. A key indication of this change is provided by the density bins of the curves, where a darker red gradient signifies a higher frequency of pixels within a specific NDVI range. Notably, shortly after selective logging, a greater proportion of pixels exhibit lower NDVI values, as indicated by the brighter red gradient. A

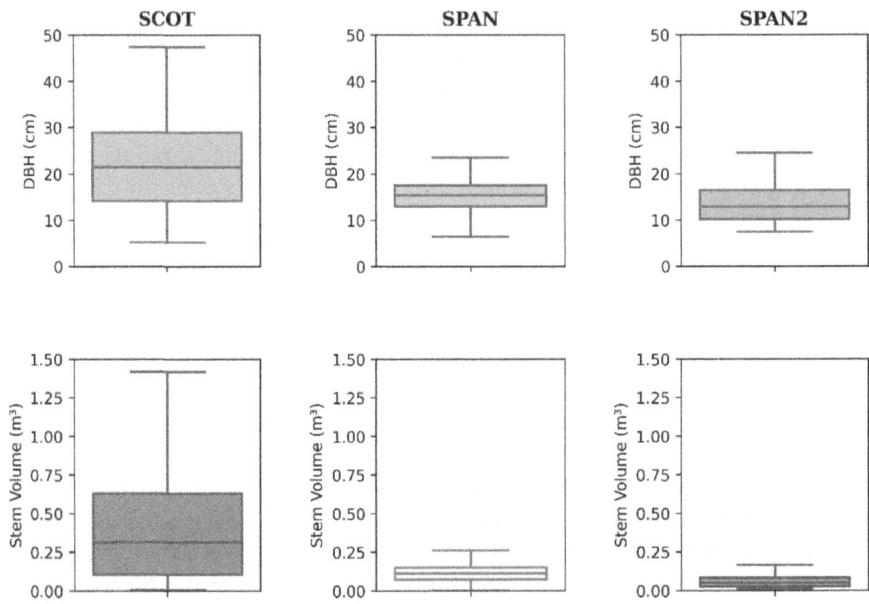

Fig. 1. Boxplot stems volume and diameter at breast height (DBH) distribution.

similar pattern was observed following clearcutting, although weaker. The role of secondary factors potentially influencing NDVI behavior in this specific context—beyond the direct reduction in leaf area due to the removal of targeted trees—should be further investigated. These may include increased shading caused by canopy gaps, the influence of understory vegetation, a more intense dry season affecting vegetation broadly, or a combination of these elements. The preliminary results presented in this study will help guide future analyses in this direction.

The SAR backscatter, on the other hand, seems to not have returned any useful information in this part of the analysis when selective logging was performed (Fig. 2, bottom-right).

5.3 Breakpoint Detection

The algorithm accurately detected breakpoints with high precision and computational efficiency (Fig. 3). The vertical dashed line represents the exact start date of logging, while the blue and red areas in the plots indicate the detected breakpoints. Notably, unlike the previous phase, the SAR backscatter time series used for breakpoint detection was not smoothed. When analyzing the average metric, a discernible shift in the trend cycle is visually apparent. At the time of logging, a distinct—albeit subtle—change in the time series signal is observed. These findings are particularly significant, as SAR data enables continuous monitoring even in regions where persistent cloud cover obstructs optical observations for most of the year.

Both polarizations proved to be potentially useful for logging detection, including selective logging. This supports the notion that the co-polarized channel plays a valuable

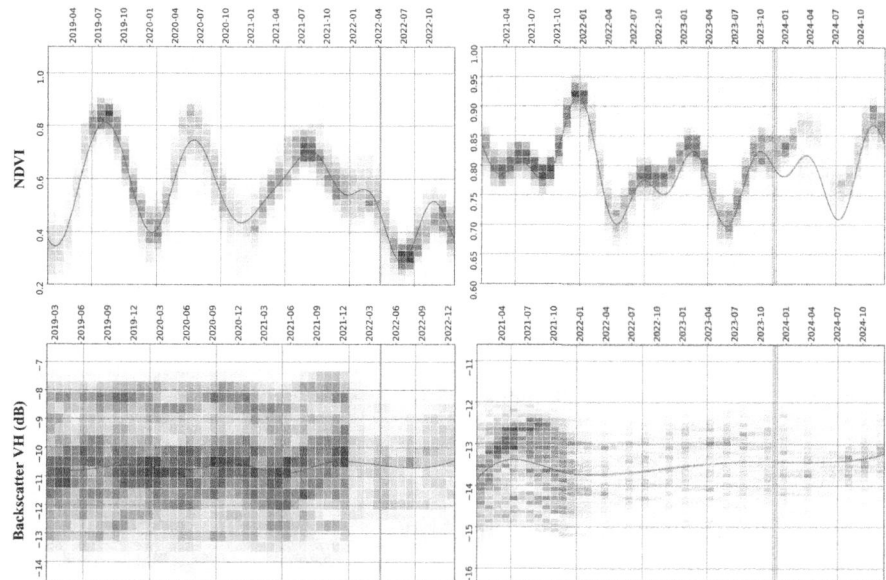

Fig. 2. Temporal distribution of smoothed NDVI (top) and VH (bottom) for SCOT. The blue line represents the mean value while red-gradient bins show the density. The vertical orange and yellow lines indicate the harvesting start and end times respectively.

role and should not be ignored in forest disturbance detection analyses [3], despite cross-polarization being more sensitive to stand volumetric properties and widely recognized in the literature as the most suitable for detecting forest cover changes [12–14]. Hethcoat et al. (2021) [3] observed that VV polarization decreases shortly after selective logging. Additionally, their time-series breakpoint detection approach performed well for logging events exceeding 20 m³/ha. These findings align with the well-documented physical behavior of SAR backscattering in the C-band, where the disruption or removal of volumetric forest components leads to reduced direct surface scattering and/or diminished volume scattering, resulting in lower backscatter values in both co- and cross-polarization channels [1, 11].

In this study, a slight decrease in backscatter values is observable, with a more pronounced reduction in VH polarization. However, it is important to note that the volumetric removal in the selective logging area of Spain (29.9 m³/ha) is only slightly above the minimum threshold observed by Hethcoat et al. (2021).

This suggests that Sentinel-1 time series have significant potential for detecting and monitoring selective logging activities, provided the logging intensity remains at this level. However, the data may not be fully suitable for detecting very low-intensity selective logging (<15 m³/ha) and small felling gaps (<300 m²) [11].

Predictably, the change in the S1 time series signal was more evident in the clear-cutting areas, as anticipated. This is because higher logging intensities enhance the detection of canopy gaps, making them more detectable from satellite [11].

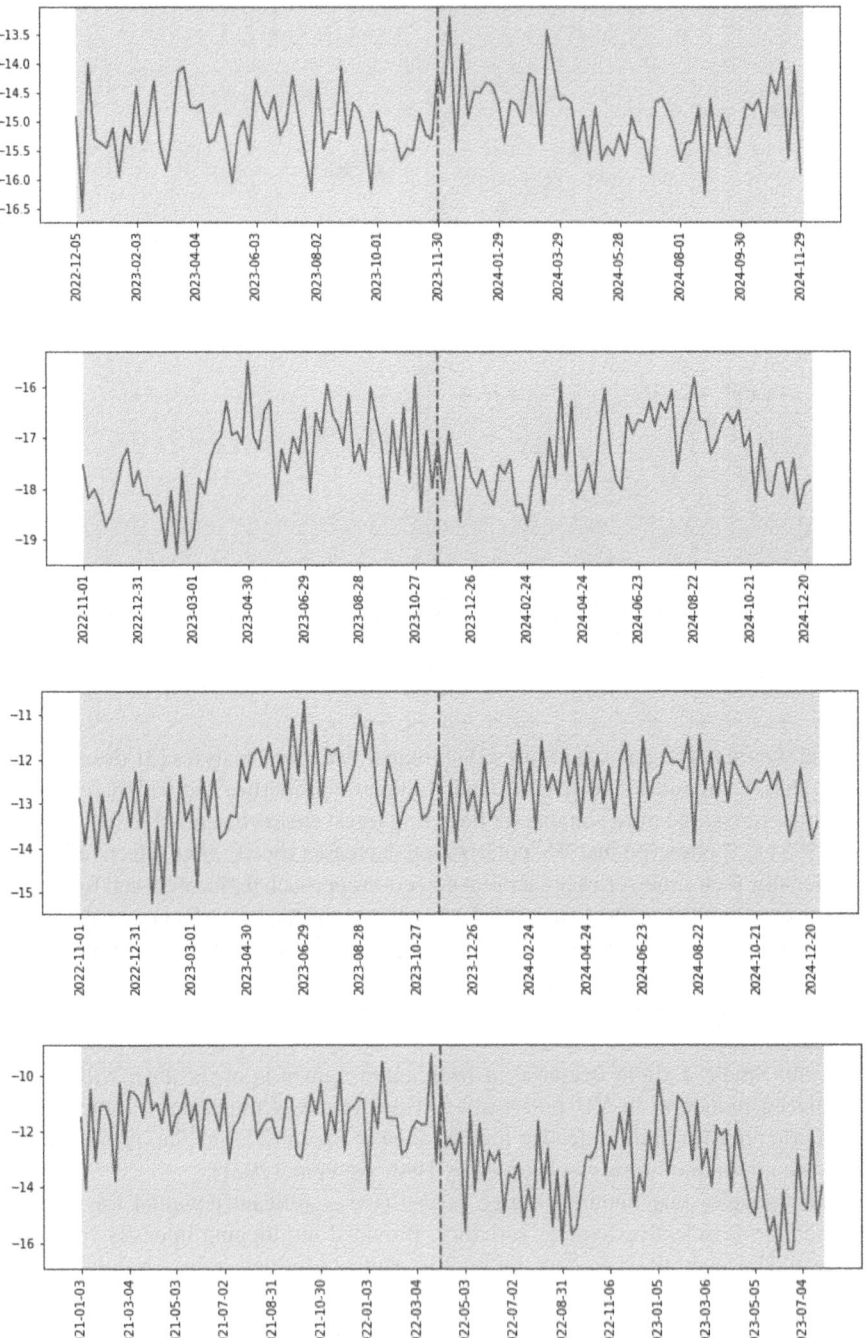

Fig. 3. Breakpoint detection results. The vertical dashed line represents the exact start date of logging, while the blue and red areas in the plots indicate the detected breakpoints. The continuous blue line represent SAR temporal backscatter. From the top: SPAN2 VH; SPAN VH; SPAN VV; SCOT VH.

Selective logging poses a significant challenge, as undetected disturbances due to remaining trees can lead to omission errors [1]. This issue is especially critical for shorter wavelengths, such as X and C-band SAR [12–14]. Investigating these uncertainties, including small-scale disturbances (e.g., roads, wildfires, windstorms) and radar shadows, will be a crucial step for future research, as they can closely resemble logging backscatter responses.

6 Conclusions

The findings of this study demonstrate the potential of integrating SAR and optical data for detecting logging activities across various scenarios, particularly selective logging. SAR data has proven to be sensitive to medium-to-low intensity timber extractions and represent the unique solution in areas where cloud cover obstructs optical observations. This is crucial for the development of semi-automatic detection methodology that generates maps of forest disturbances, including location, timing, and probability, and filters legal operations to focus on unexpected disturbances, such as those from unauthorized harvesting or natural events. For these purposes, StanForD 2010 machine-field data provides standardized, robust ground data in massive quantities, which is essential for effectively training remote sensing models and optimizing detection accuracy.

The objectives defined within the broader timber traceability ongoing framework developed under the EU Horizon SINTETIC project, which attempts to establish a comprehensive end-to-end monitoring system, from standing trees to the final timber product. By integrating freely available satellite imagery, open-source tools, and advanced data analysis with ancillary datasets to identify potential illegal logging activities, the system significantly enhances proactive forest governance and supports sustainable timber markets within the framework of precision forestry.

Acknowledgments. This study was funded by EU Horizon SINTETIC project (grant agreement ID: 101082051).

Disclosure of Interests. The authors have no competing interests to declare that are relevant to the content of this article.

References

1. Balling, J., Herold, M., Reiche, J.: How textural features can improve SAR-based tropical forest disturbance mapping. Int. J. Appl. Earth Obs. Geoinf. **124**, 103492 (2023). https://doi.org/10.1016/j.jag.2023.103492
2. Asner, G.P., Keller, M., Pereira, R., Zweede, J.C.: Remote sensing of selective logging in Amazonia: assessing limitations based on detailed field observations, Landsat ETM+, and textural analysis. Remote Sens. Environ. **80**, 483–496 (2002). https://doi.org/10.1016/S0034-4257(01)00326-1
3. Hethcoat, M.G., Carreiras, J.M.B., Edwards, D.P., Bryant, R.G., Quegan, S.: Detecting tropical selective logging with C-band SAR data may require a time series approach. Remote Sens. Environ. **259**, 112411 (2021). https://doi.org/10.1016/j.rse.2021.112411

4. Verbesselt, J., Zeileis, A., Herold, M.: Near real-time disturbance detection using satellite image time series. Remote Sens. Environ. **123**, 98–108 (2012). https://doi.org/10.1016/j.rse.2012.02.022

5. De Luca, G., Silva, J.M.N., Modica, G.: Short-term temporal and spatial analysis for post-fire vegetation regrowth characterization and mapping in a Mediterranean ecosystem using optical and SAR image time-series. Geocarto Int. **37**(27), 15428–15462 (2022). https://doi.org/10.1080/10106049.2022.2097482

6. Skogforsk: StandForD. https://www.skogforsk.se/english/projects/stanford/

7. Truong, C., Oudre, L., Vayatis, N.: Selective review of offline change point detection methods. Signal Process. **167**, 107299 (2020). https://doi.org/10.1016/j.sigpro.2019.107299

8. De Luca, G., Silva, J.M.N., Modica, G.: A workflow based on Sentinel-1 SAR data and open-source algorithms for unsupervised burned area detection in Mediterranean ecosystems. GIsci Remote Sens. **58**, 516–541 (2021). https://doi.org/10.1080/15481603.2021.1907896

9. De Luca, G., Silva, J.M.N., Modica, G.: Regional-scale burned area mapping in Mediterranean regions based on the multitemporal composite integration of Sentinel-1 and Sentinel-2 data. GIsci Remote Sens. **59**, 1678–1705 (2022). https://doi.org/10.1080/15481603.2022.2128251

10. De Luca, G., Modica, G., Fattore, C., Lasaponara, R.: Unsupervised burned area mapping in a protected natural site. an approach using SAR sentinel-1 data and K-mean algorithm. In: Gervasi, O., et al. (eds.) ICCSA 2020, pp. 63–77. Springer, Cham (2020). https://doi.org/10.1007/978-3-030-58814-4_5

11. Tanase, M.A., Santoro, M., Wegmüller, U., de la Riva, J., Pérez-Cabello, F.: Properties of X-, C- and L-band repeat-pass interferometric SAR coherence in Mediterranean pine forests affected by fires. Remote Sens. Environ. (2010). https://doi.org/10.1016/j.rse.2010.04.021

12. Dupuis, C., Fayolle, A., Bastin, J.-F., Latte, N., Lejeune, P.: Monitoring selective logging intensities in central Africa with sentinel-1: a canopy disturbance experiment. Remote Sens. Environ. **298**, 113828 (2023). https://doi.org/10.1016/j.rse.2023.113828

13. Kuck, T.N., Silva Filho, P.F., Sano, E.E., Bispo, P.D., Shiguemori, E.H., Dalagnol, R.: Change detection of selective logging in the Brazilian Amazon using X-band SAR data and pre-trained convolutional neural network. Remote Sens. **13**, 4944 (2021). https://doi.org/10.3390/rs13234944

14. Villa, P., Stroppiana, D., Fontanelli, G., Azar, R., Brivio, P.A.: In-season mapping of crop type with optical and X-band SAR data: a classification tree approach using synoptic seasonal features. Remote Sens. (Basel). **7**, 12859–12886 (2015). https://doi.org/10.3390/rs71012859

Geospatial Attractiveness Evaluation for Tourism Destination Area Analysis

Rachele Vanessa Gatto[1]([⊠]) [iD], Balázs Cserpes[2], and Jörg Rainer Noennig[2]

[1] School of Engineering, University of Basilicata, Viale dell'ateneo Lucano 10, 85100 Potenza, Italy
rachelevanessa.gatto@unibas.it
[2] Hafen City Universität, Henning-Voscherau-Platz 1, 20457 Hamburg, Germany
{balazs.cserpes,joerg.noennig}@hcu-hamburg.de

Abstract. The European Union's cohesion policy, particularly through initiatives like Smart Specialization, seeks to reduce regional disparities by promoting sustainable tourism development that leverages local resources and cultural heritage. As tourism increasingly drives global economic growth, understanding the factors that enhance destination attractiveness is vital for rural inland areas. This paper aims to contribute to the evaluation of spatial dynamics in tourism by developing a comprehensive attractiveness index. A primary challenge in assessing tourism potential lies in synthesizing georeferenced data and relevant indicators into actionable insights. Using the STESY (Specialized Tourism EcoSYstems) domain framework and the structuration assessment proposed by Gatto, Corrado & Scorza (2025), we construct an attractiveness index that captures the multifaceted nature of cultural tourism value chains. Our methodology integrates both quantitative and qualitative metrics to assess the competitiveness of destination areas. The findings help to highlight regional strengths and weaknesses, aiding policymakers in developing targeted strategies for sustainable tourism development. Furthermore, the study underscores the importance of evaluating carrying capacity and enhancing infrastructure to utilize the maximum tourism potential. In conclusion, this paper presents a robust tool for assessing tourism attractiveness in a given territory, offering valuable insights for policymakers and stakeholders aiming to foster balanced regional development and cultural heritage preservation.

Keywords: Tourism competitiveness · Attractiveness index · Sustainable development

1 Introduction

The European Union's cohesion policy (comprising e.g. the Smart Specialization Strategy) aims to reduce regional disparities by promoting sustainable tourism development that enhances local places and resources [1]. As tourism's economic significance became increasingly evident, the tourism industry emerged as a key driver of economic growth for many countries worldwide. Global trends in tourism markets and consumer behavior indicate that advancements in the tourism sector have substantially boosted the demand

© The Author(s), under exclusive license to Springer Nature Switzerland AG 2026
O. Gervasi et al. (Eds.): ICCSA 2025 Workshops, LNCS 15899, pp. 415–422, 2026.
https://doi.org/10.1007/978-3-031-97663-6_37

for goods and services along the tourism value chain, thereby generating exogenous income [2]. This boosts revenues for local authorities and hospitality-related businesses, particularly in the accommodation and food-service sectors, in high-tourism areas [3]. Furthermore, identifying the attractiveness factors that most decisively determine the competitive position of in-land rural areas is crucial. Analyzing these factors helps to find regional strengths and weaknesses aiding in the creation of visions and strategies for decision making [2]. One of the key factors behind unsuccessful cultural heritage tourism development plans is the insufficient evaluation of a site's tourism potential, particularly in terms of its attractiveness and carrying capacity [4]. Tourism attractiveness of a destination is often considered to be one of the key determinants of its tourism pull. It reflects feelings, opinions, and perceptions of tourists about the destination's perceived ability to satisfy a journey need [5]. Iatu and Bulai (2011) confirm that an adequate service infrastructure in destination areas, alongside the presence of tourism activities, is a key determinant in driving overall success [6]. Existing studies on tourism destination attractiveness underscore the need for a comprehensive inquiry into evolving metrics, the forces driving these measures, and the development of practical indicators for real-world application. In parallel, a vast array of quantitative and qualitative information—often georeferenced—describes the detailed characteristics of sites of interest. However, synthesizing this multitude of variables into appropriate indicators remains a challenge and is rarely addressed. In particular, tourism georeferencing implies an analytical approach to the territory, typically at the municipal level, to effectively consolidate diverse data into actionable insights [5, 7, 8]. This paper aims to contribute to the investigation of spatial dynamics in tourism by proposing an evaluation of destination area attractiveness across a broad territorial context. The objective is to develop a tool capable of comparing and synthesizing the diverse information related to the cultural tourism value chain, thereby enhancing our understanding of a location's capacity to sustain an adequate tourism demand. In the first section, we define the concept of destination area attractiveness and review the current evaluation tools. In the methodology section, we employ the STESY domain framework and integrate Gatto, Corrado & Scorza [9] assessment of the structuration level of destination areas to construct an attractiveness index. The results section presents the application of this index and examines its implications for development strategies. Finally, the paper discusses the limitations of the current approach, outlines future developments, and explores the policy implications of our research.

2 Defining Attractiveness in Tourism Destination

The authors [10] conceptualize attractiveness by three typologies: revealed attractiveness, perceived attractiveness and real attractiveness. First, revealed attractiveness refers to incoming flows of tourisms into a geographical area [10]. Closely linked to this concept, tourism attractions serve as key drivers of visitation. These attractions are characterized by distinct features that capture tourists' interest and motivate them to choose a specific destination. Essentially, tourism attractions shape and respond to tourist flows, influencing both the scale and direction of tourism development [11]. Second, perceived attractiveness captures how individuals or groups view, assess, and value a particular region [10]. Aligned with this statement, attractiveness fundamentally represents the perceived ability of a destination to provide individual benefits as the composite of individuals' feelings, perceptions, and evaluations regarding a destination [12, 13]. Finally, real attractiveness encompasses all the factors—such as infrastructure, services, human capital, innovative capacity, institutions, and government—that enhance a region's appeal and contribute to the overall attractiveness of the host area [10]. Researchers have classified the factors contributing to a destination's attractiveness into primary and secondary features [14]. Primary features include attractor activities, which directly draw tourists to a location, while secondary features encompass tourism infrastructure such as accommodation, transportation, tourist services, and facilities, which describe the tourist supply and capacity of local area to support tourist activity [5]. It is important that destinations that are compared by these measures should provide a similar type of tourism product. [15].

2.1 Evaluation of Existing Methods for Destination Attractiveness Index

Several studies have contributed to defining relevant variables, refining assessment methodologies, and selecting data sources to ensure robust and reliable measurements.

A widely recognized model is the Index of Destination Attractiveness (IDA), proposed by Krešić and Prebežac [15] which integrates multiple interrelated measures into a single composite indicator. In their study on Croatian coastal tourism destinations, variables were identified based on expert assessments of key tourism supply elements, while tourists rated their influence on destination choice using a six-point Likert scale, resulting in a dataset of 4,915 questionnaires. Similarly, Iatu and Bulai [6] applied multivariate analysis and correlations to Romanian territorial-administrative units statistic indicators, ensuring data consistency and relevance across regions. A commonly used methodology involves questionnaire-based assessments that capture perceptions of tourists and experts. Previous studies [16, 17] confirm the validity of perception-based evaluations, integrating them with expert opinions to refine perceived attractiveness assessments [5]. The development of tourism indices and the selection of relevant variables to identify and characterize homogeneous tourist areas are inherently interconnected aspects of a single logical process. This process aims to establish a statistical model designed to measure local tourism attractiveness, ensuring a systematic and data-driven evaluation of tourism dynamics.

3 Methodology

To develop the Destination Attractiveness Index, we refer to STESY domain taxonomy [9], a model that identifies tourism geographies based on territorial elements. This approach enables the detection of specialized tourist destinations within a broad territorial area. This methodology to identify the Destination Area (DAj) is based on the cluster detection of points of interest (POIs) based on their spatial proximity. This spatial approach allows to define the boundaries of each DAj. By considering both the spatial arrangement and the distances between POIs, the algorithm ensures that each DAj represents an area with clear boundaries on the basis of relevant tourism assets, facilitating more effective tourism planning and analysis.

The present paper focuses on the Vulture area in Basilicata (Italy) as a case study, where an attractiveness index was developed by analyzing the number of users' reviews related to tourism services. This analysis moves from a broad regional perspective to a low-dimensional representation DAj using Points of Interest (POIs), including specialized attractors (e.g., cultural tourism) and services (e.g., accommodation, restaurants).

3.1 Data

The data used in this context comes from Google API Places, a service that provides detailed information about places, including user-generated content like **reviews and ratings**. The **DAj** were identified using the STESY model, which categorizes tourism assets into groups. These include **attractors (aj)**, such as castles, churches, and museums, and **services (st)**, like restaurants and accommodations. Table 1 presents a sample of data-set organization.

Table 1. Data-set format

POI ID	Type	DAj	Rating	Number of_review
1	Accomodation (Acc)	23	4,4	146

The dataset includes **78 attractors (aj)**, which consist of cultural and historical landmarks such as castles, churches, museums, and archaeological sites. In addition, there are **442 restaurants (R)**, representing the food and beverage establishments that cater tourists. The **accommodation sector (Acc)** is also well represented, with **417 mapped entities**, including hotels, bed & breakfasts, and other lodging facilities. In total, the **tourism-related services (st),** which combine restaurants and accommodations, amount to **859 entities**, emphasizing the crucial role of hospitality in the region's tourism offer.

3.2 Constructing the Attractiveness DA Index

For each DAj, two averages are calculated:

- Average Number of Reviews (N): This is the average number of reviews for all the POIs within the DAj Services;
- Average Ratings of Reviews (REV): This is the average rating for all the POIs within the services DAj Services.
- Construction of the two-dimensional index: The two-dimensional index is built by combining the two averages calculated above.
- Each DAj will therefore have an attractiveness value that considers both the average number of reviews and the average rating:

$$\textbf{DAj Index} = f(\textbf{N}, \textbf{REV})$$

3.3 Case Study

The case study focuses on Vulture area (ranging from Monticchio Laghi to Alto Bradano) in Basilicata (Italy), a region characterized by low population density (56.3 inhabitants/km^2) and long-standing infrastructural and economic challenges.

The area hosts a regional park, medieval castles, national museums, UNESCO sites, and archaeological landmarks, yet remains undervalued for tourism. This research offers decision making tools for spatial development strategies that leverage local resources, environmental assets, and cultural heritage to foster sustainable and competitive tourism growth.

4 Results and Discussions

We analyzed 19 DAj specialized in cultural tourism within a low-density (rural) area. The comparison between various DAj through the attractiveness index allows us to differentiate and describe the DAj based on their attractiveness characteristics, distinguished by average number of review and average rating of reviews.

Figure 1 and Fig. 2 displays the correlation between the number of reviews and average review scores. DAj with the highest number of reviews (e.g., 35; 38; 33) tend to have above-average ratings, with scores around 3.88–3.98. This suggests that more visited locations maintain a good perceived quality. Indeed, the DAj 35 contain an attraction belonging to the UNESCO category, and the area is recognized as a popular tourist destination with recent infrastructure development.

Some destinations with a moderate number of reviews (e.g., 24; 15) have relatively high ratings (4.42 and 4.29, respectively), indicating that while they may not be among the most visited, they receive very positive feedback from visitors. DAj 24 and 15 are indeed communities with a high dispersion value and are located outside the tourist circuits promoted by local agencies.

The destination with the highest rating (DAj 24, average rating of 4,42) has only 59.7 reviews on average per element, which could indicate a niche of highly satisfied visitors but lower visibility compared to other areas. Some locations with many reviews (e.g., 11 and 14) show ratings around 3.80, indicating a good level of attractiveness but with action-need for improvement in perceived quality.

The destination with the lowest rating 41 (2.85) also has the lowest number of reviews (27.9), suggesting it may be less attractive in terms of both popularity and visitor experience.

The applied index allows for an evaluation of the DAj. The comparison based on the quality of supplied services identifies the DAj that best meet users´ needs and expectations. Within tourism strategy policies, this method can provide a large-scale overview of the attractiveness of DAj, helping to identify where adaptations or investments might be necessary in a comprehensive view of the study area.

Furthermore, this evaluation framework identifies DAj through the analysis of tourism infrastructure and perceived attractiveness. The findings suggest that the applied approach can effectively support decision-making processes allowing the identification of territorial target where to design a coordinated framework for targeted investment

Attractiveness DAj index

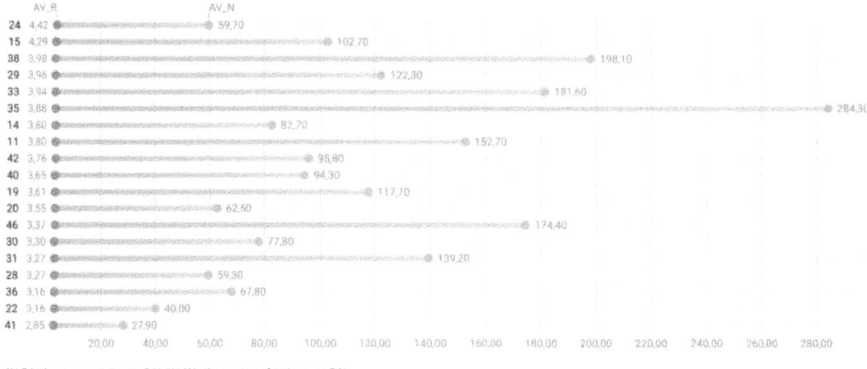

AV_R is the average rating per DAj; AV_N is the average of reviews per DAj

Fonte: Google API places · Creato con Datawrapper

Fig. 1. In the graph, the y-axis represents the average ratings per DAJ, while the x-axis indicates the number of ratings.

Fig. 2. In the figure, the DAj (represented with a color scale) and the points (services) within the Vulture-Melfese study area are shown.

improving the infrastructure of the tourism value chain. The construction of this index integrates both quantitative and qualitative dimensions into a single indicator, enhancing the tourist's perception as final beneficiaries of the territorial tourism ecosystem offering a high level of granularity that improves conventional tourism statistics.

5 Conclusions

This paper proposes to construct a synthetic index of DAj attractiveness applied in a specific context in order to analyze how Vulture area perform in terms of the tourism infrastructures attraction. The proposed index effectively merges quantitative and qualitative components into a single metric, on the basis of high level of territorial granularity that goes beyond traditional statistical units.

As illustrated in Fig. 2, the proposed methodology enables the identification and assessment of the key components of the tourism system, resulting in the creation of a spatial representation of tourism attractiveness in the case study area. This approach is considered highly transferable in other context, as it proves useful meanings in territorial interpretation potentially applicable across various fields of investigation. The simplicity of its structure, combined with the careful selection and evaluation of elements and spatial relationships enables for the transdisciplinary applicability of the results, upon which different sector-specific assessments can be developed.

Potential applications of this approach may include the evaluation of investment scenarios aimed at stimulating local development in Destination Areas (DAj) through both hard and soft measures.

Policy implications derived from this research refer to the opportunity to target territorial marketing actions on those areas with high rating coefficients but only moderate review volumes, in order to boost their visibility and tourist inflow. Additionally, a deeper analysis of the DAj with the highest number of reviews and consistently good ratings may allow to identify local best practices based on effective organization of the tourism local supply chains easily replicated in the weaker DAs of the study area. Moreover, a further scenario could focus on the establishment of a territorial tourism support network that coordinates local stakeholders to ensure a more equitable allocation of public investment, thereby improving a balanced and sustainable overall efficiency of the territorial tourism ecosystem.

However, several limitations need to be considered in the proposed model. First, the index relies on a single source, Google Places, which may introduce bias since the demographics of its users and their representation of potential tourists are not considered. There is no consideration of who is reviewing the locations—such as their age, gender, nationality, or whether the set of reviewers truly reflects the profile of tourists likely to visit the area. Furthermore, while the tourism sector has seen a rise in fake reviews in recent years, the authenticity of the scores used in this index has not been questioned, presenting a significant limitation.

Future research should address these issues by incorporating a broader range of sources, integrating demographic data of reviewers, and evaluating the credibility of the reviews. Additionally, a more comprehensive assessment of DAs attractiveness could include data on tourist flows and the specific features of individual attractions, to provide a more complete picture of the tourism system. The current model only evaluates one dimension of attractiveness, without addressing the appeal of individual tourist attractions—a gap that should be addressed in future research. The next step will primarily integrate data on tourist flows and attraction-specific features to achieve a more comprehensive assessment of DAs attractiveness.

References

1. Świdyńska, N., Witkowska-Dąbrowska, M.: Indicators of the tourist attractiveness of urban–rural communes and sustainability of peripheral areas. Sustainability (Switzerland) **13** (2021). https://doi.org/10.3390/su13126968
2. Kayar, Ç.H., Kozak, N.: Measuring destination competitiveness: an application of the Travel and Tourism competitiveness index (2007). J. Hosp. Market. Manag. **19**, 203–216 (2010). https://doi.org/10.1080/19368621003591319
3. Ziernicka-Wojtaszek, A., Malec, M.: Evaluating local attractiveness for tourism and recreation—a case study of the communes in Brzeski County, Poland. Land (Basel) **11** (2022). https://doi.org/10.3390/land11010039
4. Canale, R.R., De Simone, E., Di Maio, A., Parenti, B.: UNESCO World Heritage sites and tourism attractiveness: the case of Italian provinces. Land Use Policy **85**, 114–120 (2019). https://doi.org/10.1016/j.landusepol.2019.03.037
5. Ul, I., Chaudhary, M.: Index of destination attractiveness: a quantitative approach for measuring tourism attractiveness. Turizam **25**, 31–44 (2021). https://doi.org/10.5937/turizam25-27235
6. Iatu, C., Bulai, M.: New approach in evaluating tourism attractiveness in the region of Moldavia (Romania). Int. J. Energy Environ. **5**, 165–174 (2011)
7. Gismondi, R., Russo, M.A.: Definizione e calcolo di un indice territoriale di turisticità: un approccio statistico multivariato. Statistica (Bologna) **64**, 545–571 (2004)
8. Sarrión-Gavilán, M.D., Benítez-Márquez, M.D., Mora-Rangel, E.O.: Spatial distribution of tourism supply in Andalusia. Tour. Manag. Perspect. **15**, 29–45 (2015). https://doi.org/10.1016/j.tmp.2015.03.008
9. Gatto, R.V., Corrado, S., Scorza, F.: A taxonomy of specialized tourism ecosystems (STESY): toward new geographies for sustainable territorial planning. IJEPR (in press)
10. Musolino, D., Kotosz, B.: A new territorial attractiveness index at the international scale: design, application and patterns in Italy. Ann. Reg. Sci. **72**, 1159–1187 (2024). https://doi.org/10.1007/s00168-023-01239-w
11. Hills, T.L., Lundgren, J.: The impact of tourism in the Caribbean: a methodological study. Ann. Tour. Res. **4**, 248–267 (1977). https://doi.org/10.1016/0160-7383(77)90098-6
12. Hu, Y., Ritchie, J.R.B.: Measuring destination attractiveness: a contextual approach. J. Travel Res. **32**, 25–34 (1993). https://doi.org/10.1177/004728759303200204
13. Mayo, E.J., Jarvis, L.P.: The psychology of leisure travel: effective marketing and selling of travel services. J. Travel Res. **20**, 28–29 (1982). https://doi.org/10.1177/004728758202000313
14. Morachat, C.: A Study of Destination Attractiveness Through Tourists' Perspectives: A Focus on Chiang Mai, Thailand. Edith Cowan University (2003)
15. Krešić, D., Prebežac, D.: Index of destination attractiveness as a tool for destination attractiveness assessment. Tourism **59**, 497–517 (2011)
16. Das, D., Sharma, S.K., Mohapatra, P.K.J., Sarkar, A.: Factors influencing the attractiveness of a tourist destination: a case study. J. Serv. Res. **7** (2007)
17. Sharma, A., Sharma, S.: Heritage tourism in India: a stakeholder's perspective. Tourism Travelling **1**, 20–33 (2017)

Author Index

O. Gervasi et al. (Eds.): ICCSA 2025 Workshops, LNCS 15899, pp. 423–424, 2026.
https://doi.org/10.1007/978-3-031-97663-6

The manufacturer's authorised representative in the EU is Springer
Nature Customer Service Centre GmbH, Europaplatz 3, 69115 Heidelberg,
Germany. If you have any concerns regarding our products, please
contact ProductSafety@springernature.com

Printed and bound by CPI Group (UK) Ltd, Croydon, CR0 4YY
28/04/2026
02098517-0001